ISBN 978-0-266-98630-0
PIBN 10919527

American

UARTERLY REGISTER

AND

MAGAZINE.

Causas rerum videt, earumque progressus. — Cicero.

Conducted by James Stryker.

SEPTEMBER, 1849. . . . Vol. III. No. I.

Philadelphia:

PUBLISHED BY THE PROPRIETOR,

NO. 520 CHESTNUT STREET.

1849.

WM. S. YOUNG, PRINTER.

CONTENTS.

No. 1. Vol. III.

Contents

ERRATA.

On the 16th and 17th pages, for "Pophsin" read "Poussin."

On the 28th page, in the 6th line from the bottom, the word "received" should be struck out.

On pages 47, 49 and 51, in the 1st line at the head of the page, for "September," read "June."

THE AMERICAN

QUARTERLY REGISTER

AND MAGAZINE.

NO. I. VOL. III.

SEPTEMBER, 1849.

HISTORICAL REGISTER.

1849.

UNITED STATES.

It seems, from the official correspondence recently published by the State Department, that the present administration had scarcely been two weeks in power before it was called upon to show its fixed purpose to discharge the duties of neutrality towards the belligerents of Europe with the strictest impartiality. The circumstances of the case were as follows:

The Germanic Confederation, desirous of building up a German navy, applied to the government of the United States, through their minister, Mr. Donelson, in the latter part of the preceding year, to sanction its taking a number of American naval officers into its employment and pay for a stipulated time. Mr. Polk, with the concurrence of his cabinet, naturally gratified by this compliment to the American navy, was disposed to favour the application so far as it could be done with propriety, but deemed it prudent to learn the precise character and duration. of the services expected, with other details, before he decided whether he would ask of Congress authority to grant the permission applied for. With this view, Commodore Parker was despatched to Berlin and Frankfort, and directed there to obtain, under the direction of Mr. Donelson, the desired information. In the month of January he communicated to Mr. Mason, Secretary of the Navy, the result of his inquiries, by which it appeared that "little or nothing" had been done towards the creation of a German navy; that two British mail steamers, recently purchased, and another authorized to be purchased in the United States, constituted the whole naval force they had to oppose to the Danish navy, then consisting of 1,085 guns, and 9,755 men, and comprehending five line of battle ships of eighty-four guns each. He remarks that on the expiration of the armistice between the Confederation and Denmark on the 26th of March, a renewal of hostilities was confidently expected; and, with such disparity of force, he saw no field for an American officer to acquire credit for himself or his country, and further, that the German Confederation itself could not be established without a civil war; he therefore thought, that in the existing state of things, it would be unwise for an American officer to take any part in German affairs, except in the way of advice.

It seemed, from the letter of the German minister of commerce and marine to Commodore Parker, that the American officers wanted were, one commodore, one lieutenant or commander (as the Commodore should choose,) three lieutenants to command three steam sloops, ten lieutenants to command smaller steamboats or gun-boats, and twenty-four passed midshipmen. All of which officers were to be advanced to one grade higher than that which they severally held in the American navy. He also wished for a superintendent of naval construction, and two assistants; and lastly, he requested that an officer should be furnished to aid in arming and manning the steam frigate they had ordered to be purchased in the United States.

Before Commodore Parker's despatches were received by the American government, Baron Roenne, the Envoy from the German government to the United States, applied to Mr. Mason for minute information on the subject of organizing a navy; on the naval school, navy yards, dry docks, naval hospitals; draughts of sailing and steam vessels; guns, and gun-carriages; the police of the navy, and the bureaux for its management, the expense of procuring which information he was ready to pay. Some days afterwards, Baron Roenne asked Mr. Mason to designate an officer to assist in selecting a steam frigate; to take the command of her when purchased, and to superintend her equipment as a vessel of war; and, finally, to take her to Bremerhaven, there to await the further orders of the German government.

The information sought for by the German envoy seems to have been promptly given by Mr. Mason, on the authority of the President, and the proper officers of the Navy yard at New York were required to give such facilities in the equipment of the war steamer, as should be "consistent with the public interests and the business of the yard." An answer to the further requests of Baron Roenne was deferred until Commodore Parker's report was received. Accordingly, on the 1st of

March, Mr. Mason informed Baron Roenne that he had received that report, a copy of which, as well as of the instructions to the Commodore, he transmitted to the Baron. He informs the envoy that the President does not, under existing circumstances, consider it advisable to ask of Congress to permit American officers to enter into foreign service, and that they could not constitutionally enter such service without the sanction of Congress. He farther states that, in case of war between Germany and Denmark, American officers could not be permitted to take part with either. His application, therefore, for an officer to take command of the war steamer must be refused.

Such was the state of things when the present administration came into power. But it was soon perceived that further precautions must be taken to maintain for the United States the character of neutrality in the very probable contingency of renewed hostilities between Denmark and the German government. The order to the officers of the Navy yard to afford facilities for the equipment of the German steam frigate, "the United States," was revoked by the Secretary of the Navy; and, on the 10th of April, Mr. Clayton, the Secretary of State, wrote to Baron Roenne that the president, soon after he came into office, learnt that a large steamer, then fitting out in New York, was to be employed by the German government in its war with Denmark; that the United States, at peace with all nations, wished to preserve those relations of amity which are at once enjoined by their treaties with foreign powers, and by the constitution of the United States. He then refers to the act of Congress of April, 1818, one section of which requires the forcible detention of vessels like the steamer United States, probably intended to commit hostilities against a friendly power; inflicts fine and imprisonment on all persons engaged in such enterprises, and requires the owners of such vessels to give bond that they shall not commit hostilities against any nation at peace with the United States. He states that Denmark, by its minister here, had protested against the fitting out of this steamer, and had received satisfactory assurances from the President that the duties of neutrality should not be thereby violated. He adds, that the President, desirous at the same time to manifest his friendly feelings towards the German nation, and his confidence in their envoy, would make no opposition to the departure of the steamer United States, if the envoy would give his solemn assurance that such steamer would not be employed against any power with which the United States were then at peace.

To this communication, Baron Roenne replies on the 14th, at great length. He refers to the desire of the German people to possess a navy, and the measures they had taken to effectuate their purpose; he says, that having decided on adopting a federal government, they had naturally looked to the United States for aid and advice. They had, therefore, hailed with lively satisfaction the mission of an American envoy to Frankfort, and one of the first requests to him had been to secure the assistance of American officers in building up a German navy. He adverts to the appointment of Commodore Parker, and to his report to the American government, and complains of his advice against the employment of American officers in the German service, as inconsistent with the office he himself had undertaken in Germany, relative to the employment of such officers, and the advice he had given relative to the purchase and equipment of a war steamer in the United States. He notices, also, his own correspondence with Mr. Mason, and he relies on these and other details to show that there was no secresy in this affair, and that when the facilities were granted by the American government for fitting out the steamer, it was known to all that she was intended to be used as a vessel of war. He does not, however, admit that she was designed to be employed against Denmark. The real object, as had been stated to Mr. Mason, was that the vessel was to be taken to Bremerhaven, the German naval station on the North Sea, there to remain until farther orders; that the armistice which existed when the steamer was ordered, had been continued to the 15th inst., and that there was reason to hope that peace had been already concluded. He insists that the purchase of this steamer, as well as of others, had no reference to the war with Denmark, but grew out of the determination of the German government to have a navy. He says, that desirous not to involve the United States in difficulties, or to violate its laws, he had consulted eminent counsel in New York on the act of Congress of April, 1818, according to whose opinion, which he cites, the steamer in question, though "fully furnished, fitted out, and armed," would not come within the provisions of the act, if she were not intended to cruise or commit hostilities against any foreign power then at peace with the United States.

He insists that the "ulterior purpose" of using a vessel of war is not made criminal by the act of Congress, it is only "the proximate and immediate intent" which is looked to; and he gives a solemn assurance that the steamer United States was not purchased or fitted out with intent to commit hostilities against the subjects or property of Denmark, or other powers at peace with the United States, but to go to Bremerhaven, and there receive further orders. These further orders he claims not to know, and says they will depend upon contingencies not now foreseen. He says that although he conceived that the German government might fit out and arm their steamer without violating the act of 1818, yet that their agents, in their anxiety not to compromise the neutrality of the United States, had decided not to fit out the vessel as a war steamer until the consent of the proper authorities was obtained: that consent he hopes will now be granted. He concludes with reiterating the intention of his government, not to violate the laws of the United States, and expresses surprise and mortification at the revocation of the orders to grant facilities for the equipment of the steamer, since like facilities had been granted on many former occasions. Had he received notice that the orders were to be revoked, he would have removed the misconception, to which, judging from the friendly assurances given both by the President and his predecessor, he attributes that revocation.

Mr. Clayton, on the 29th, replied to Baron Roenne, that although it was not the intention of the American government to argue the question that had given rise to the present correspondence, yet the President, from his profound respect for the German government, had thought proper to take the opinion of the Attorney General on the question, a copy of which opinion Mr. Clayton then transmits to the German minister. He then repeats the conditions on which the steamer will be permitted to leave the harbour of New York, and he hopes that the German minister will be prepared to give the required assurance.

According to the opinion of the Attorney General, the steamer which the German government was then fitting out in New York is within the provisions of the act of Congress, of April, 1818. He states the grounds of his opinion, and says that the construction of the law contended for by Baron Roenne, would defeat its purpose.

Baron Roenne, two days afterwards, offers comments on the opinion of the Attorney General. He relies on there being no secrecy in that affair, and on the early sanction of the American government; insists that the present case is not within the act of Congress of 1818; that the assurance he had already given in his note of the 14th ultimo fully met the provisions of that act; that to go further would be inconsistent with his duty to his country, and will not, he is persuaded, be required of him by the President.

Mr. Clayton, on the 5th, says that from the great desire felt to satisfy the German government of the friendly disposition of the United States, he is induced to reply to the argument of Baron Roenne; that secrecy, though a common badge of crime, is not indispensable to it; that the executive branch of the government is not the government, and cannot sanction a criminal violation of law. He shows, from a detailed reference to the facts, that the case is within the law of 1818, and that the minister's construction of his own assurance would render that assurance of no value. He concludes, that as Baron Roenne refuses to give the required assurance, the Collector of New York is instructed to execute the 11th section of the act of Congress, by which the steamer will be detained until her true owner gives satisfactory security that she shall not be employed to commit hostilities against any power now at peace with the United States; and the Baron is at liberty to carry the questions he has raised before the judicial tribunals of the country, by whose decisions the President will cheerfully abide.

Baron Roenne, in a note of the 15th of May, submits to the decision of the President, with a protest, and adds that the bond required will be given by the agents of the German government. The questions on which he has differed from the Secretary of State, will be open for the decision of the courts, should a suit be brought on the bond, which, however, he does not anticipate, a bond was accordingly given by Mr. William Wedding, who was designated as the agent of the "Central Power of Germany."

It seems that Mr. Steen Billé, the Danish Chargé d'Affaires to the United States, on the 2d of April, called the attention of Mr. Clayton to the case of the war steamer "United States," then fitting out in New York, and which, he said, was to retain her American character until she was delivered in a German port. He urges that the case is within the scope of the act of Congress of 1818, and asks for the interposition of the executive. Mr. Clayton states in his reply, that his attention had been drawn to this subject as soon as he took charge of the State Department, and that he had promptly obtained information of the real character and destination of the steamer in question. Mr. Billé was invited to come to Washington from Philadelphia, to receive the necessary explanations. In a subsequent correspondence between him and Mr. Clayton, Mr. Billé expressed himself entirely satisfied with the course pursued by the American government. Mr. Clayton had taken the precaution to require of the American Chargé at Copenhagen, to afford the requisite explanations and assurances to the Danish government. He had given similar instructions to Mr. Donelson, and learned from him that the course adopted by the American government, relative to the steamer United States, was highly approved by the Prussian ministry; and that the members of the German cabinet, at Frankfort, also expressed themselves satisfied with that course. Mr. Duckwitz admitted that as matters then stood, it was fortunate that none of the American officers had accepted the invitation given to them.

It was of importance for the United States to proclaim to the world at this time, when their neutral relations were so likely to be affected by the contests which agitated Europe, that while they are determined on maintaining their rights of neutrality, once so grossly assailed, they were also no less determined strictly to fulfil its duties; and this course was further recommended by the fact, that in their late war with Mexico, those duties had been most scrupulously respected by all other nations, notwithstanding the known sympathies of some of them with our adversaries.

Whilst all interference in the disputes of other nations must be regarded as unfriendly to the peace of the world, and as affording ready pretexts for political ambition, a nation is required to put no restraint on its feelings when they lead only to acts of beneficence,—as in the case of the appeal lately made by the lady of Sir John Franklin to the President of the United States, to aid in the search for her husband, who, having been sent by the British government on an expedition to the Arctic regions, had not been heard of for more than two years.

The President readily and cordially expressed his willingness to use the power he possessed to further her purpose, and orders to the naval department were issued accordingly; but it has been since ascertained that, restricted as is the executive power to the specific objects for which money has been appropriated, the department had no means at their disposal of despatching a vessel at this time in search of the unfortunate explorers.

The United States were this year again visited by the Asiatic cholera, after an interval of sixteen years. It made its first appearance in the spring, and continued to spread and increase in virulence throughout the summer months. In every part of the Union, diarrhœa and other intestinal diseases indicated the presence of that atmospheric poison which is supposed to be the proximate cause of the epidemic; but it was only in the cities and towns that it was aggravated to the specific malady, except in a few rare cases. The western towns suffered much more severely than those on the Atlantic, and none so much as St. Louis and Cincinnati. The disease, in the Atlantic cities, was less fatal than it had been in 1832 and 1833, but this was because it attacked a smaller proportion of the population; for, in general, now as then, not more than one-half of those seized with it recovered. Now as then, too, its ravages were at first principally among those who were exposed to the discomforts of poverty, who were uncleanly in their habits, or who indulged themselves in eating fruit or succulent vegetables. The mortality in some of the western towns was frightful. The smaller comparative number of cases this year, in places where the diminution was observable, may be attributed either to a mitigated form of the disease, except in a few localities, or to increased medical skill in arresting its progress in its incipient stages. A more minute history than has yet been given of this terrible scourge of humanity may contribute to bring it now within the control of medical science. In the Chronicle will be found some further details of its extent and progress.

The new administration soon had another opportunity of exhibiting its determination to respect our treaty obligations towards other countries, as well as its pacific policy. The President, understanding that a secret expedition was in preparation near New Orleans, whose object was the invasion of either Mexico or Cuba, issued a proclamation on the 11th of August, while on a tour through the northern States, for the purpose of warning the citizens of the United States that all such enterprises were in violation of our treaty engagements; that they subjected those persons who were concerned in them to the penalties of the law, and that such persons must, in no extremity, expect the protection or interposition of the government. All officers of the government, civil and military, were further required to aid in arresting the offenders and bringing them to punishment. It has been since understood that Cuba was the object of the expedition, and that the enterprise has been encouraged, and probably set on foot, by persons of weight and influence in that Island, in which there has long been complaints of oppressive exactions on their commerce, and of other acts of misgovernment. Though this timely and decisive course of the Executive has not, it is said, induced all who were engaged in the lawless enterprise to abandon it altogether, it is to be hoped it will so quicken the vigilance of the public officers that they, with the aid of the sober-minded and loyal portion of our citizens, will be able to frustrate the purposes of the expedition. Persons suspected of being engaged in the scheme, to the number of between 400 and 500 men, assembled at Round Island, in Louisiana, where, it was believed, they meant to embark with many others enlisted in other places; but the sloop of war Albany, and some smaller vessels, were ordered to watch their movements, and arrest the expedition, if attempted. Captain Randolph, of the Albany, gave notice to the persons encamped on Round Island that he had proof of the acknowledgments of some of the party that their destination was Cuba; that he should prevent any vessels from furnishing them with arms, or warlike stores; as well as prevent them from embarking on board any of the steamers hovering round the Island; and that, after that day, (28th of August,) he should cut off all supplies of provisions, and "rigidly enforce the blockade." He adds, that he would give them every facility for leaving the Island, except that of embarking in *sea-going vessels*.

The course pursued by President Taylor, in the Cuban affair is similar to that which was adopted by President Jackson when the struggle for Texan independence commenced. On the 4th of November, 1835, Mr. Forsyth, Secretary of State, wrote to the attorney of the district bordering on Texas, in these words:

"It has become necessary for me to call your attention to the probable event of a contest between the different portions of the Mexican empire in the vicinity of the United States. Some of our citizens may, from their connexion with the settlers there, and from their enterprise and love of change, be induced to forget their duty to their own government and its obligations to foreign powers; but it is the fixed determination of the executive faithfully to discharge, so far as its power extends, all the obligations of the government, and more especially that which requires that we shall abstain, under every temptation, from intermeddling with the domestic disputes of other nations.

"You are, therefore, earnestly enjoined, should the contest begin, to be attentive to all the movements of a hostile character which may be contemplated or attempted within your district, and to prosecute, without discrimination, all violations of those laws of the United States which have been enacted for the purpose of preserving peace, and of fulfilling the obligations of treaties with foreign powers."

While the United States were thus disposed to respect the rights of other nations, they were called upon to assert their own. In July, a Spaniard, by the name of Rey *alias* Garcia, was said to have been seized in New Orleans by the order or procurement of the Spanish Consul, put on board of a vessel, and sent to Havana. It was alleged that he had been a jailer in Havana, and had connived at the escape of two prisoners in his custody. A judicial investigation was immediately instituted before a justice of the peace, against the Spanish Consul and other persons supposed to be concerned in the abduction. The magistrate, after a full inquiry, decided that the accused had been guilty of the offence of false imprisonment against Rey. It seems, however, that after this man arrived at Havana, on the 17th of July, and while he continued on board the vessel, then performing quarantine, he declared in a letter to the Captain-General of Cuba; that he had left New Orleans voluntarily, and that he had come to Havana to have a personal interview with the Captain-General. It further appears that Mr. Campbell, the American Consul at Havana, having heard that Rey was forcibly taken from New Orleans, went on board of the vessel to make inquiry of Rey himself, who then declared to Mr. Campbell that he had left New Orleans of his own free will. But notwithstanding these declarations, he, the same day, wrote to Mr. Campbell that he had been taken from New Orleans by force, by order of the Spanish Consul, solicited the protection of the American flag, and permission to return to the United States. He said his name was Juan Garcia Rey, and added that he had not spoken frankly to Mr. Campbell in their former interview on account of the presence of the captain.

On the receipt of this letter, Mr. Campbell wrote to the Captain-General to inform him of the letter he had received from Garcia or Rey, and to ask leave to converse with him before two witnesses who would permit him to answer freely to such questions as should be put to him. This request was at first refused by the Captain-General, the Count de Alcoy, for reasons given at length, but in consequence of a subsequent application and correspondence, which have not been published, Rey was afterwards surrendered to the American Consul, and sent back to New Orleans, where the character of the abduction is to undergo a further judicial examination.[*]

This would seem to be a far more unquestionable case of violated sovereignty than that of Jonathan Robins, which caused so much excitement in 1800, and which John Marshall, afterwards Chief Justice, so signalized by the closest and most conclusive logic perhaps ever uttered in Congress; inasmuch as Robins was delivered to the British Consul in Charleston on the authority of a federal judge; but the gross contradictions, and other inconsistencies of this Garcia or Rey, raise perplexing doubts about the real character of the transaction, and, at all events, incline us to regard him as a much more unworthy object of American protection than Robins.

California has continued to attract adventurers in about equal num-

---

[*] The Spanish Consul de Espano was bound over in the sum of $5,000 to appear at the next Circuit Court to be held in New Orleans.

bers from the United States and from other countries; and their labours have received in general the same liberal reward.   Gold to the amount of nearly two millions of dollars had been coined at the mint of the United States in the month of July, and probably a much larger amount had been exported to England, China, and other countries.   Measures had been taken to form a constitution for upper California, and it can scarcely be doubted that thus provided with a form of government the people of that country will apply to the next Congress to be received as one of the States of the Union.*   On the 1st of July, the immigrant population was estimated at 30,000.

Some of the emigrants from the United States overland to California having, in their march, passed through the Mexican province of Chihuahua, were charged with wantonly destroying the growing crops, and under pretext of having been robbed of some of their horses, they had even fired on the peaceful inhabitants.   Formal complaint of these outrages was made by Don Luis de la Rosa, the Mexican minister, to the Secretary of State, who accordingly applied to Mr. Crawford, the Secretary of War, to interpose the military authority under his control.   He gave the requisite orders, and farther suggested as a more efficient remedy, that permission to pass through the Mexican territory should be refused to all persons who were not provided with passports.

The other portion of our newly acquired territory, New Mexico, has been a source of uncompensated vexation and trouble.   Unprovided with a territorial government by the last Congress, like the Californians, but not like them consoled by new and rich mines for the inconvenience, the inhabitants have been far more discontented than in California.   Nor is this all.   In the absence of all regular government, the neighbouring Indians have made incursions into the territory, and the American citizens found there have been their first victims.   They have even assailed and overpowered small detached parties of United States troops.   It is now found that mounted riflemen are the only species of force competent to keep these marauders in check.   The conflicting claims, moreover, of the State of Texas and the United States to that part of this territory which lies east of the Rio Grande, threaten to prove a theme of troublesome and heated controversy in Congress, whenever the organization of a territorial government there shall be brought up.

In the latter end of July, the people of Florida were alarmed at what they regarded as clear indications of the hostile temper and purposes of the remnant of Seminole Indians still remaining in the southern part of that State.   Murders and other outrages had been committed on citizens of Florida nearly at the same time at two points, on Indian River and Peace Creek, about one hundred miles apart.   Volunteers

* See Quarterly Chronicle for an account of the steps taken by Gen. Riley to effect the election of delegates to a convention and for the organization of a government.

were immediately ordered out by the Governor of Florida, and application was made to the general government for the aid of regular troops. Mr. Crawford, the Secretary of War, wrote to the Governor of Florida that, from the information received at Washington, the outrages at both places were committed by the same party of Indians, not exceeding *five;* that there was no evidence of their receiving the support or countenance of the Indians generally; and that, consequently, there had existed no necessity for the employment of the State troops. He added, that the course taken by the State of Florida was to be regretted, as it would raise a new obstacle to the success of the effort the administration was then making of removing all the remaining Seminoles from Florida. In conformity with these views, two special agents sent by the Governor of Florida to Washington to learn the purposes of the general government, were informed by Mr. Crawford, on the 10th of August, that the administration should rely upon the United States regular troops alone, and should decline the services of the Florida volunteers. That the 7th regiment of infantry, and eight other companies, chiefly of artillery, should be ordered to Florida, under the command of Major General Twiggs. That the operations of the army should be confined to a specific line of posts, in order both to keep the Indians within the limits formerly assigned to them, and to keep the whites from intruding on the neutral ground around those limits. That the government would endeavour to effect the removal of the Indians by contract on liberal terms; but should all pacific methods fail, they would be removed by force.

These purposes of the administration not proving altogether satisfactory to the people of Florida, they held meetings at St. Augustine on the 22d and 25th of August, at which it appeared that the points of disagreement between them and the general government were: that the volunteers were required to be discharged before the regular troops arrived in Florida: that the authors of the late robberies and murders should be brought to punishment: that the Indian agents should be required to reside within the Indian limits, so as to take away all pretexts from the Indians for roaming beyond their bounds: and that the exclusion of Indians as well as whites from the neutral ground was a duty of the general government and not of the State. This last position seems to have been urged in reply to a remark made by Mr. Crawford to the Florida agents; that Florida was not free from blame in this matter, because, having extended her laws over the neutral ground, *"it became her duty rather than that of the general government"* to keep the whites from intruding on that ground; and this intrusion, he doubted not, had been the chief cause of the late disturbance.

According to intelligence from Tampa Bay of the 17th Sept., it appears that Captain Casey of the United States army succeeded in having an interview with some of the Indians; who appointed a future day to have a "talk" with General Twiggs. Billy Bowlegs, it is understood, is willing to deliver up to General Twiggs the Indians who committed the late outrages. The result of the expected interview between General Twiggs and Billy Bowlegs was looked for with the greatest anxiety by the citizens of Florida.

In connexion with the difficulties already enumerated a diplomatic misunderstanding of a serious and unpleasant nature has very recently grown out of a correspondence between the French minister, M. Pouissin, and Mr. Clayton, the Secretary of State.

On the 7th day of February last, one month previous to the expiration of office of the late cabinet, M. Pouissin addressed a note to Mr. Buchanan, then secretary of State, presenting to the consideration of the government of the United States the claim of a Frenchman, M. Port, for indemnification for damages sustained by him in consequence of the acts of officers and agents of the United States in Mexico. It appears from the correspondence published by the government, that during the Mexican war M. Port purchased a quantity of tobacco which had been seized and sold by the agents of the American army. Col. Childs, the commanding officer, having ascertained that the tobacco was private property, caused it to be restored to its proper owner, and the purchase money to be refunded to M. Port. The claim, as presented by M. Pouissin to our government, was for several thousand dollars, being the amount of the difference between the price for which Port had purchased the tobacco and that for which he had sold it. A court of inquiry was immediately convened, which examined into the whole matter, and decided that the claim was unfounded. The evidence before the court rather raised a doubt of the honesty of purpose of M. Port, and went to prove the fact that he was aware when he purchased the tobacco, that it was private property. Gen. Scott confirmed the decision of the court.

Before any action could be had by the government upon the report of the court, Mr. Buchanan went out of office. Soon after the organization of the new cabinet, Mr. Clayton examined into the matter and announced, as the result of his inquiry, that the decision of the court had his entire approbation. This communication of the secretary received an angry response from the French minister, who animadverted with severity on the testimony of Col. Childs before the court, and in a subsequent note to Mr. Clayton, of the 18th of April, remarked, that "the government of the United States must be convinced that it is more honourable to acquit fairly a debt contracted during war under the pressure of necessity, than to evade its payment, by endeavouring to brand the character of an honest man." When the letter containing this offensive language was received, M. Pouissin was not at Washington, and a message was immediately sent requiring his presence. After an interview with the Secretary, he withdrew the letter and expunged the offensive matter. It was believed that the usual friendly understanding between the French embassy and the government was restored, but on the 12th of May, M. Pouissin, commenced another correspondence with the Secretary of State, which has resulted in an open rupture. The facts that led to this unfortunate difference are substantially as follows:

During the Mexican war, Commander Carpender, in command of the sloop-of-war Truxton, forming part of the United States blockading squadron off the harbor of Vera Cruz, was called upon by the captain of the French barque Eugenie, to rescue her from shipwreck, as she had struck upon a reef. After strenuous and laborious exertions, on the part of himself and his crew, he succeeded in doing so, and presented to the captain of the Eugenie his claim for the legal amount of salvage. The captain refused to pay it, and Commander Carpender thereupon restored the vessel, which he had detained from the time of effecting her rescue but thirty hours—abandoning his claim. His conduct in the matter elicited the decided approbation of Mr. Clifford, the American Minister, to whom it was afterwards submitted. It had also been officially approved by Mr. Mason, late Secretary of the Navy. The French captain, however, complained of the treatment to which he and his vessel had been subjected by the detention, and the French Minister addressed a note to the Secretary of State, in which, after narrating the circumstances, he proceeded to say that the Minister of Foreign Affairs of France, requested him to address to the cabinet of Washington the most serious observations on the abuse of authority committed by this officer, in illegally detaining the ship Eugenie. He concluded his note with the following remark: "You will easily comprehend, Mr. Secretary of State, how important it is that such occurrences should not be repeated, and that severe blame, at least, should be laid on those who thus considered themselves empowered to substitute arbitrary measures for justice; and, I doubt not, that you will, without delay, give satisfaction to the just complaints of the French republic." This note, unaccompanied as it was by any testimony to justify the charge against Commander Carpender, was promptly referred to the Navy Department, for the purpose of ascertaining the facts on which his condemnation was demanded.

A detailed statement of the whole case was transmitted from the Secretary of the Navy, in which the conduct of Commander Carpender was justified, and the Secretary of State, in transmitting to M. Pouissin the explanations of that officer, expressed the hope "that they would remove any misapprehension which might exist on the part of the French government, relative to his conduct on the occasion in question."

The explanations were not satisfactory to the French Minister, who, without submitting the case as it then stood to his government, took the matter into his own hands, and passed sentence of condemnation upon the officer and the government of the United States.

He concludes his disrespectful answer, of the 30th May, to Mr. Clayton in these words:—

"I called on the cabinet at Washington, Mr. Secretary of State, in the name of the French government, to address a severe reproof to that officer of the American navy, in order that the error which he has committed, on a point involving the dignity of your national marine, might not be repeated hereafter.

"From your answer, Mr. Secretary of State, I am unfortunately induced to believe that your government subscribes to the strange doctrines professed by Commander Carpenter, of the war steamer Iris; and I have only to protest, in the name of my government, against these doctrines."

On the receipt of this letter, the President directed Mr. Clayton to transmit the whole correspondence to Mr. Rush, the American ambassador at Paris, to be communicated to the French government. The answer of M. Tocqueville, the Minister of Foreign Affairs of France, was entirely unsatisfactory to the government at Washington; and the President thereupon caused M. Pouissin to be notified, by the Secretary of State, that the government of the United States would hold "no further correspondence with him as the Minister of France;" but "that due attention would be cheerfully given to any communication from the government of France, affecting the interests of our respective republics, which may reach the department through any other channel."

Amongst the documents printed in this number will be found so much of the correspondence, published by the government, as will suffice to possess our readers of the whole subject matter in controversy. It is not generally believed that there was any premeditated design on the part of France or its Minister to insult this government; and it is hoped that the friendly intercourse between the two governments will speedily be restored.

Congress, at its last session, for the purpose of having the census (of 1850) more carefully and accurately taken than it has hitherto been, appointed a Census Board, consisting of the Secretary of State, the Attorney General and the Postmaster General, who were required to prepare forms and schedules for the enumeration of the inhabitants, and also for "collecting in statistical tables, under proper heads, such information as to mines, agriculture, commerce, manufactures, education, and other topics," as would exhibit a full view of the pursuits, industry, education, and resources of the country; with a proviso "that the number of inquiries, exclusive of the enumeration, should not *exceed* one hundred."

For the better execution of this duty, so important to the legislator, the statesman, the political economist, and the philosopher, the Board have, by printed circulars, invited the suggestions of individuals relative to the general objects of the Board, and to the particular circumstances of the individual States. With the advantage of this co-operation, and of a more deliberate preparation than was likely to be given to the subject by members of Congress, during the heated and agitating discussions of the session, it is to be hoped that the 7th census will be free from that imputation of error to which its predecessor, in its estimate of the products of the several states, was confessedly exposed; and that the progress of the several states in all the modes that denote civilization, will be placed on evidence beyond cavil or dispute. The numbers within the present limits of the United States, on the 1st of June, 1850, will probably fall little short of twenty-three and a-half millions, showing about a sixfold increase in sixty years.

MEXICO, &c.

An extra session of the Mexican Congress was held on the 1st of July, when President Herrera laid before them the state of public affairs. He presents a favourable view of their finances: the receipts from the 1st of July, 1848, to the 31st of May, 1849—that is, for eleven months—exceed those of the preceding years, $5,239,729; from which he is led to expect that the national income will soon equal its expenditure. He estimates the whole public debt at 100 millions of dollars, when the arrangements now in a train of negotiation with the creditors shall be concluded. Among other legislative measures recommended, are a system of differential duties for the encouragement of Mexican navigation, the consideration of the government monopoly of tobacco, the organization of the National Guards, and a re-organization of the territories of the republic, especially of New or Lower California.

The financial arrangements, to which the President adverted, were with the English creditors. It was agreed between them and the Mexican government that the interest on their debt should be reduced from 5 per cent., as first stipulated, to 3½ per cent., from July 1st, 1846, until 1859, when a new rate shall take place, more or less favourable, according to the condition of the Mexican treasury at that time. Mexico further agrees to pay, on account of interest, $1,500,000 out of each of the three instalments yet due from the United States by the treaty of Guadalupe, and that it will give up to its English creditors the export duties on the precious metals in all the ports of the republic. This convention met with warm opposition in the Senate, and was followed by the resignation of M. Aranguiz, the Minister who negotiated it.

The active politicians are said to be ranged under four parties: ultra democrats, moderates, monarchists, and Santa Annaites, who are said to be as much imbittered against each other as two parties, comprehending a whole community, commonly are.

The State of Chihuahua, annoyed by the unceasing incursions of the neighbouring Indians, seems to have thought any remedy justifiable under the circumstances, and offered a reward of $200 for every Indian killed, or made prisoner. The neighbouring State of Durango was not slow to follow this example of barbarity. It is said that a ranger from Texas, at the head of twenty-five men, Texans and Mexicans, soon entitled himself to between two and three thousand dollars of these wages of blood. As these acts of Chihuahua and Durango were pronounced by the Mexican Congress to be unconstitutional, it is to be hoped that they have been revoked.

Some explanation was given in the Mexican Congress of the charge of selling in Havana the Indians who had been captured in Yucatan. The Governor of Yucatan denies the fact of sale; but he admits that the people of Yucatan, when the alternative was presented to them, of murdering their prisoners, or of transporting them, had chosen the latter. They were, therefore, sent to the government of Cuba, which contracted to support them, and pay them a reasonable price for their labour.

The province of Yucatan seems to be in nearly as wretched a condition as ever. The sum of one hundred and fifty thousand dollars, were furnished them by Mexico without terminating the war, and they are clamorous for further assistance, which, however, the general government of Mexico seems little able to afford.

The insurgents of Sierra Madre are still unsubdued; but according to the official reports, they are more and more closely pressed by the government troops, under Bustamente. The Congress has given a proof of its love of economy in reducing the President's salary from thirty-six thousand to twenty-five thousand dollars.

VENEZUELA. *

The civil contests which have so long distracted Venezuela, seem at length to have terminated; and General Paez, after frequent changes of fortune, or rather of prospect, finds himself in a more hopeless condition, and his rival, Monagas, more firmly established in power than ever. In June last, the odium which General Monagas had excited, having urged some six or eight men to attack the presidential mansion, he made this attack a pretext for assuming the authority of a dictator. His acts drove the people of Coro to insurrection, and, on the 28th of June, they drove the garrison there quartered out of the city. The whole province followed its example, and General Paez, then at Curaçoa, was pressingly invited to put himself at the head of the insurgents. He lost no time in complying with their request, and on the 3d of July he made a triumphal entry into Coro, where he was hailed as "the father of his country." He was soon joined by some of Mo-

* Two celebrated Mexicans have died lately—Mariano Paredes, the former President of the Republic, and General Urrea, the guerilla chieftain. The first died at the city of Mexico of the effects of inebriation, and the other at Durango, of cholera.

nagas' former adherents, and in two days he wrote to his friends in Curaçoa that he had nothing further to desire. "From all quarters," he says, "we see gathering around us those bands of patriots that are about to restore liberty to their country. I have more volunteers than I can arm, and their enthusiasm is beyond description." He issued a proclamation to the people, in which he made a most fervid appeal to their patriotism, their love of liberty, and their resentment against the tyranny they had experienced. Monagas, on the other hand, had the command of neither men nor money—nay, was so destitute that he could not fit out two schooners then lying at Porto Cabello. His overthrow was regarded as a thing settled; yet in a few weeks he managed to place himself at the head of a force, which the various accounts state from 2000 to 5000 men, and Paez soon found himself compelled to yield once more to his fortunate rival. His surrender is thus noticed in the orders of the day of General Silva:

"To-day, at 11 o'clock this morning, the factious Jose Antonio Paez has surrendered at discretion, with all his forces, to the invincible troops of the government. Beaten in two rencontres, and surrounded on all sides in a little valley, he has comprehended his weakness and his temerity; he has, therefore, submitted to the clemency of the government, on conditions which do honour to the principles we profess."

Subsequent accounts say that Paez and his son are in a state of abject poverty and dependence, and Monagas is in the exercise of despotic power.

GUATEMALA.

In Guatemala there has been, in the present year, another revolutionary change; and Carrera, who last year found himself compelled by the popular discontents, especially among the mountaineers, to resign his office of President, has lately returned from his exile in Mexico, and re-established himself in power in the province of Los Altos. His success has induced the administration of Martinez to temporize so far as to revoke the decree of banishment against Carrera, and to ratify the acts of his self-assumed power. It remains to be seen whether he has the means, as he no doubt has the will, of completely superseding Martinez, and of reinstating himself in the presidential authority.

Soon after Martinez became President, the difference between the government of Guatemala and M. de Challaye, the French minister, was amicably adjusted, and he continued in Guatemala as French Consul.

The increased importance of an easy communication between the Atlantic and Pacific oceans, and probably some other considerations of national policy, seem likely to give an interest and consequence to a part of Central America that has been hitherto deemed the most insignificant. Among the several modes of connecting the two oceans, that by Lake Nicaragua has been regarded by many as the most eligible. The State of Nicaragua, a few months since, granted to the New York and New Orleans Steam Navigation Company, through its two agents Clapp and Brown, the right of making a communication between the oceans by Lake Nicaragua and the river St. John. The exclusive right, however, to the navigation of this river is officially denied by Mr. Barclay, the British Consul at New York, to belong to the state of Nicaragua, who affirms that thirty miles of it, below the lake Nicaragua, belongs to the kingdom of Mosquito, and that that kingdom is under the protection of the British government. As the state of Nicaragua will be disposed to sustain her grant, and the government of the United States is bound to protect the interests of its citizens, the right of navigation in question is likely to undergo a close investigation, in which the right of Musquito to separate from the rest of Central America, and its erection into a monarchy, marked, as they are said to have been, by very singular circumstances, may be involved in the discussion.

HAYTI.

In Hayti, the President Soulouque has assumed the state and dignity of emperor. On the 23d of August, an address was circulated in the capital, demanding of the Chamber of Representatives and Senators the title of emperor for Faustin Soulouque. On the 24th, those bodies acted upon the wish of the people thus expressed, and passed a decree conferring on the president the title of Emperor of Hayti. Accordingly, on Sunday, the 26th of August, the imperial crown was placed upon his head by the president of the Senate, and a chain of gold about the neck of the Empress, when the populace shouted *Vive l'Empereur*. He afterwards issued his royal proclamation, and created dukes, barons, &c.; and it is reported that he is preparing another expedition against St. Domingo. Whether his sable majesty will experience, with his new honours, a change of fortune in war, is to be seen.

ARGENTINE REPUBLIC.

In the Argentine Republic, several of the petty States of the confederation seem to be in a state of intestine disorder and revolution. The reconciliation of General Rosas with the French and English governments, seems, from the address of the legislature of Buenos Ayres to him, to be far from cordial as yet. Both governments are complained of for their intervention in favour of Montevideo; and Great Britain, though commended for separating herself from France, is charged with unjustly taking possession of the Falkland Islands, after having relinquished them to Spain, and with having made a settlement on the Straits of Magellan. Even an offensive expression of Lord Palmerston's against the republics of South America, as to their English debts, is indignantly noticed.

FRANCE.

The powers of the Constituent National Assembly expired on the 24th of May, at midnight, and on the following day those of the newly elected. Legislative Assembly commenced. It was understood to be composed of Legitimists, Orleanists, and Bonapartists, altogether amounting to nearly two-thirds of the legislature; of red republicans and socialists, amounting to about 240 members, and of a small number of moderate republicans, not exceeding some sixty or seventy members. On all questions looking to the restoration of the monarchy, the last named party were expected to unite with the monarchists and on the wild theories lately put forth concerning property and the rights of labour, to concur with the socialists.

After the election of the members present was duly verified, the Assembly proceeded to the election of a President, when M. Dupin received 336 votes; M. Ledru Rollin, 182; and M. Lamoriciere, 76. In the composition of the cabinet, of which M. Odillon Barrot was placed at the head, it was thought prudent to comprehend friends to the legitimists, the constitutional monarchists, and the moderates. One more homogeneous in sentiment could not be relied upon to support the measures of the executive.

On the 6th of June, the President, in an official message, made that communication to the Assembly on the affairs of the republic, which the constitution requires. The message was almost as long as that of an American president or governor, and descended to a minuteness of detail without example in similar state papers in Europe. In some general preliminary remarks on the past difficulties and future hopes of the country, he states his own purpose to be "to defend society, so audaciously assailed; to secure a wise, great and honourable republic; to protect family religion and property; to promote all possible improvement and economy; to protect the press against caprice and licentiousness; to lessen the abuses of centralization; to efface the marks of civil discord; and, finally, to adopt a policy in foreign relations, equally free from arrogance and weakness. He then proceeds to detail the condition of France under seven different topics:

1. *Finances.* The public debt, he said, had been increased in 1848, by an annual charge of 56 millions of francs; and the extraordinary expenses in 1848, caused by the revolution of February, amounted to 265 millions. With all the aid afforded by the tax of 45 per cent., and

by loans, the deficit for that year was 72 millions; the deficit for the current year is estimated at 180 millions. He recommends a reduction of expense as well as an increase of revenue.

2. *National Guards,* This comprises nearly 4,000,000 men, of whom 1,200,000 are armed with muskets. The re-organization of the garde mobile has caused a saving of 7,000,000 francs.

3. *Army.* France now has under arms 451,000 men, and 93,754 horses; and 16,495 guns, of which 13,777 are of bronze. The field pieces are 5,139. The navy, in active service, consists of 10 ships of the line, 8 frigates, 18 corvettes, 24 brigs, 12 transports, and 24 light vessels, besides 14 steam frigates, 13 steam corvettes, and 34 despatch steamers. There is also a reserved force of 10 ships of the line, 15 sailing frigates, 10 steam frigates, 6 steam frigates, and 6 mail steamers. These require 950 officers and 28,500.

4. *Agriculture, Industry, and Commerce.* Since February last, twenty-one farming schools have been added to the twenty-five previously in existence. 122 Agricultural Societies, and more than 300 minor institutions have aided in distributing the funds voted for the encouragement of agriculture. The organization of the national studs for the breeding of horses has been greatly modified and improved. The supply of food is sufficient for the wants of the people. The foreign commerce of the country had greatly declined in 1848; the consumption of iron, coal, wool, and silk, especially, had decreased: but they have progressively advanced in the present year.

The administration is disposed to apply the labour of convicts to agriculture. In 400 county prisons there are 26,653 convicts; in twenty-one central depots, 17,789 convicts; and in twelve houses of correction, 3,600 juvenile offenders.

There are distributed by the charitable institutions of France, for the relief of the sick, the aged, the blind, deaf, and dumb, 116 millions annually; yet this immense sum is small, compared with the amount wanted. The government is resolved to supply the deficiency.

5. *Public Works.* The progress of the new canals, decreed by the Constituent Assembly, has been suspended for want of funds. On the rail-roads undertaken by the State, 800 millions had been expended on them to the end of 1847. The engineers required 130 millions to complete them, but sixteen millions only have actually been contributed. The several lines are particularly noticed. The mining business has made some progress, as has also the number of smelting-houses.

6. *Public Instruction.* France has 68 establishments of higher instruction, with 6,269 students; and 1,226 secondary establishments, with 108,065 pupils. There are also 56 lyceums, 309 commercial colleges, and 955 private establishments. The primary schools received 2,176,679 boys, and 1,354,056 girls. The revolution has given a new impetus to the subject of juvenile instruction.

7. *Foreign Affairs.* "It is the destiny of France," he says, "to

shake the world whenever she moves, and to calm it when she becomes quiet." He commends the pacific policy of his predecessors. He adverts to the troubled state of Europe after the revolution in February, from the Baltic to the Mediterranean, and to its condition when he came into power. France, unwilling to go to war, endeavoured by uniting her friendly mediation with that of England, to bring about peace between Sicily and the king of Naples, but without success. A similar interposition in the war between Piedmont and Austria, had no other effect than to lessen the exorbitant demands of the latter for indemnity. In the case of the Pope, who was compelled by a conspiracy to fly from Rome, where he had recently been so popular, he said the French government had one of three courses to pursue: which were, either to oppose by force the threatened intervention of Austria and Naples, and thus involve France in a war with all catholic Europe; or to allow the powers in coalition to re-establish the authority of the Pope on their own terms; or, lastly, to exercise an independent action, and to take Rome under the protection of France. The expedition to Civita Vecchia had the sanction of the National Assembly; and it was confidently expected that it would have been cordially welcomed by a large majority of the Roman people. The opposition it encountered, he attributes to Garibaldi, at the head of a band of refugees from all parts of Italy. This unexpected contest has frustrated the negotiations of France in favour of Denmark in her contest with the central government of Germany. The opposition to the Assembly at Frankfort, as well as the war between Austria and Hungary, are then noticed; but while he forbears to commit himself in favour of either of the belligerents, he thinks proper to state that Russia has recognised the French republic. He concludes this exposition of the affairs of the republic with some general declarations of his course of action, and with the recommendation of some special laws to the legislature for the amelioration of the condition of the people; professing, however, that he would not "cradle the people in illusions and utopias, which only exalt the imagination to end in deception and misery," and that whenever he sees "an idea which contains the germ of practical result," he will cause it to be studied, and if it be applicable, he will propose to the Assembly to apply it.

The royal tone of that part of the message which related to the President's views and purposes was little calculated to win the confidence of any class of the republican party; and his open denunciations of the socialists, his opposition to the republican party in Rome, and his guarded and forbearing language towards the enemies of Hungary, hastened, if it did not suggest, a conspiracy on the part of the red republicans to bring about a new revolution. On the 13th of June, the party, of which Ledru Rollin was considered to be the head, endeavoured to effect one of those popular movements by which power has so often been made to change hands in Paris first, and eventually throughout

France. But the military, faithful to the executive, crushed the conspiracy at once. Ledru Rollin succeeded either in making his escape from Paris, or in concealing himself, and finally found his way to London. Popular insurrections in the other principal cities of France seem to have been planned by the conspirators, but it was only at Lyons that there was any serious demonstration. There too the *emeute* was effectually quelled by the military, amounting to 50,000 men, and as many as 1200 persons were arrested on suspicion of being concerned in these insurrections.

The policy of the executive towards Rome was persevered in, and encountered a fainter opposition in France, from the general desire of the people, and of the military portion especially, to wipe out the tarnish the French arms had received at the gates of Rome. In the paramount love of national glory, the cause of republicanism seemed to be forgotten. General Oudinot had fallen into discredit, and orders were sent on to supersede him in the chief command of the forces before Rome, but when intelligence was received that he had obtained possession of the city, they were revoked By a telegraphic despatch. The final assault was made on the 29th of June, but the whole army did not enter the city until the 3d of July. Garibaldi, with five or six thousand men, left the city, when its further defence was found impracticable.

In a letter from the Pope to General Oudinot, dated the 5th of July, he makes his acknowledgments for the triumph of order over anarchy, and for liberty restored to honourable and Christian individuals, who, he says, will no longer be considered culpable for enjoying the blessings which God has bestowed on them, and for worshipping him with religious pomp, without the risk of life or liberty. He sends him some copies of the history of his pontificate, which, he says, will show that the triumph of the French arms has been over the enemies of human society, and which must call forth the gratitude of all honest men in Europe and in the world.

The city was placed under the government of General Rostolan, who issued a proclamation to the inhabitants, enjoining the strict observance of order—suppressing political associations or clubs—and forbidding all violence or insult to the French soldiers, or persons in friendly conversation with them. Three cardinals, commissioned by the Pope to take charge of the government, arrived at Rome on the last of July, and their authority and functions were announced the next day in a general order issued by General Oudinot. He states that thenceforth the Holy Father or his representatives would resume the entire administration of the country, but adds that the public security would not the less be under the special guarantee of the French army; that the Roman troops in the provinces occupied by the French would be under the command of the general-in-chief; and that the military authority would be preserved to fulfil the high mission that France had intrusted to it, for the interest of the Roman people, and the temporal authority of the pontiff.

In the mean time, the re-instatement of the Pope in his temporal sovereignty was very unpalatable to the liberal party in the French National Assembly, and the subject gave rise to an animated debate on the 6th and 7th of August, in which the course of the administration was assailed by M. Arnaud and M. Jules Favre, and defended by M. De Tocqueville and M. De Falloux, members of the cabinet. The opposition maintained that the expedition to Rome had been subservient to the policy of Austria, and faithless to the cause of civil freedom—the administration insisted that interested as France was in the safety of Italy, it had no alternative but war or intervention; and that the restoration of the Pope's temporal power afforded the only security for his independence. They added, that they wished all liberal guarantees accorded to the Roman States, and that, without such concessions, the temporal power could not be sustained. The ministerial party prevailed by a decisive majority.

Saving the discussions on the Roman expedition, little of interest or importance was said or done in the legislature from its meeting in May to the latest dates in August. The parties of which the assembly is composed, distrustful of each other, could co-operate in no course of public policy, and no one of them had sufficient confidence in its own strength to attempt any favourite measure. All appears to be in a state, if not of transition, at least of suspense, doubt, and uncertainty. It is clear that the wishes and expectations of every party from the revolution have been disappointed, and it is almost equally clear that the present hopes of each are balanced by its fears.

The law for restraining the liberty of the press, which the ministers introduced in the latter part of July, may be considered an exception to this course of forbearance. The first provision of the law, which assigns to the ministry the duty of prosecuting the offences of the press against the chief magistrate, constituted the chief theme of debate in the discussion of this law. The word *offence*, as explained by the reporters of the bill, reaches to every shade of attack, so as not to affect the right of criticism and of free discussion. But what, said the opponents of the bill, is the limit between the legal offence and the right of free discussion? where shall the attack be arrested, or the offence begin? The President of the republic is made responsible by the constitution, and can he elude this responsibility by sheltering himself under this species of inviolability? The debate continued for six days, with great eloquence and skill on both sides, when the several amendments to this provision were rejected, and it was adopted by a vote of 395 against 153. The other clauses of the bill passed after little or no discussion.

Early in August, M. Passy, the Minister of Finance, laid before the assembly his budget for 1850, as well as a general exposition of the national finances.   He shows that, notwithstanding the additions which were made to the public debt in 1848, the deficit for the present year will be one hundred and eighty-four millions.   The expenses for 1850, together with the sinking fund, will amount to 1,591,000,000 francs; and the receipts, including the impost on liquors, will produce but 1,271,000,000 francs; so that the deficit will be not less than 320,-000,000 francs.

To meet this exigency, the Minister proposes a loan of 200,000,000; the laying of new imposts; the suspension of the operation of the sinking fund, which would disengage sixty-five millions; and lastly, some special means applicable only to the expenses of public works.   This scheme of revenue was threatened with serious opposition in the assembly.

From those who are dissatisfied with the present state of things which now exists in France, rumours and suspicions of meditated political changes naturally arise, and one of the most prevalent of late has been that it was the purpose of the President or of a party to elect him Emperor.   The imputation has found its way into the journals, and has derived a support from the fact that the principal discussions in the legislature seemed to be at bottom contests between monarchists and republicans.   The little confidence, therefore, with which the republican party had first viewed him has gradually grown less, and all his acts and movements have been most narrowly watched.   His late tour to Rouen, Havre and other towns, was supposed to be made for the purpose of feeling the popular pulse, and no small exultation is manifested that he met with little to encourage the ambitious schemes imputed to him.   At Rouen, indeed, he was treated with the ceremonious respect due to the chief magistrate of the nation; but at Havre there was more frankness in his reception.   The Mayor of that city in his address reminded the President of the pledges he had formerly given at Tours in support of the republic—remarked that France had reached her political majority; and concluded with these words: "Be the first regular founder of the French republic: let the love of France be your crown, and your glory will be immortal.   Washington had no other, and his memory will live for ever."   To this address, he returned a short, polite answer, which was by no means an echo to the counsels of the mayor.   Brief as it was, he twice told the citizens of Havre that there could be no prosperity for their commerce without "stability and order."   On a subsequent visit to the interior he was received with more enthusiasm by the people.   At Epernay, the bishop of Chalons, with the clergy and local authorities, received, went out to meet him, and the populace shouted "Vive Napoleon"—"Vive l'Empereur!" His popularity in the provinces and with the army is said to be on the increase.

No one seems to think that the political structure, which has been lately reared in France with so much labour and ingenuity, will last until its cement is hardened by time; but the time and character of the change, we believe, no human foresight can scan. The frightful excesses in Paris in June last, and the delirious theories which caused them, has so weakened the cause of republicanism in France, or more properly speaking, has so checked its progress, that the chances at present seem to be greatly in favour of monarchy; which, however, while it is distasteful to so many of the most intelligent and efficient of the population, who no longer believe it to be a necessity of civil society, gives no better assurance of permanency or peace than a republic. The prospect is clouded with uncertainty, whichever way we look.

On the 13th of August the national assembly adjourned to the 1st of October, and its last sitting exhibited one of those scenes which had too often disgraced legislative bodies, and which is thus stated in the journals. On the evening before the adjournment, one of the Mountain party, M. Gastier, had used some disrespectful expression towards the chief magistrate, when M. Pierre Bonaparte, who sat near Gastier, and who is as remarkable for his attachment to his cousin as for his devotion to republicanism, observed, "If you knew the President, you would not thus speak of him;" to which the other replied, "Hold your tongue, you are an imbecile." "You called me an imbecile," he said, and at the same moment he gave Gastier a blow on the cheek. The tumult that ensued induced the president of the assembly to suspend its proceedings; but as soon as order was restored, M. Bonaparte asked pardon of the assembly for the act to which he had been suddenly provoked. The assembly, after some angry discussion, decided to leave M. Gastier at liberty, and to hold M. Bonaparte bound to appear before the tribunal of police. This affair, as some of the journalists remark, made but a sorry close to the labours of the session, and they add, with a sarcasm, that this species of rencounter seems to be the only thing that the democrats of France have borrowed of the Americans in general, and of the congress at Washington in particular.

M. Bonaparte's offence was the greater, as M. Gastier is an old man of seventy. He was, three days afterwards, made to expiate the wrong, by a fine of two hundred francs,—the highest pecuniary penalty allowed in such cases, without, however, the addition of imprisonment.

In the mean time, General Oudinot had been suspended in the command at Rome, and ordered to Paris. After his recall, the command devolved for a while on Gen. Rostolan, who has also been displaced, and Gen. Randon, a cavalry officer who served in Algeria, sent to occupy that difficult and important position. His instructions, it is said, are to carry out the line of conduct prescribed in a letter transmitted on the 18th of August, by the President of the Republic to Col. Edgar Ney, his orderly officer at Rome. This letter has excited much attention—is generally admitted to be the official expression of the sentiment of the cabinet, and therefore has produced a profound sensation both in Europe and America. President Bonaparte writes as follows to Col. Ney:

" The French Republic has not sent an army to Rome to put down Italian liberty, but, on the contrary, to regulate it by preserving it against its own excesses, and to give it a solid basis, by replacing on the pontifical throne the prince who (the first,) had boldly taken the lead in all useful reforms.   I learn with pain that the benevolent intentions of the Holy Father, as well as our own action, remain sterile in the presence of hostile passions and influences.   The desire of certain persons appears to be to make proscription and tyranny the bases of the Pope's return.   Say to General Rostolan from me, that he is not to permit that, under the shadow of the tri-coloured flag, any act be committed that can lower the character of our intervention.

" I thus sum up the restoration of the Pope's temporal power :—a general amnesty, the secularization of the administration, the code Napoleon, and a liberal government."

The President then complains that the cardinals, in their proclamation, had made no mention of the sacrifices of the French soldiers, nor even adverted to France, which silence he regards as an insult.   He declares that France will be respected, and thus continues:

"When our armies made the round of Europe, they left every where, as the mark of their passage, the destruction of the abuses of feudality, and the germs of liberty.   It shall not be said that in 1849 a French army can have acted in a different sense, and brought about different results."

He directs that the army be thanked in his name " for its noble conduct," and that every thing be suitably provided for its accommodation.

It is stated in the London Chronicle that when this letter, which was published at Rome, was received at Gaeta, and laid before the Pope by Cardinal Antonelli, " His Holiness merely folded his arms, raised his eyes to heaven for a few moments, then handed back the letter to the cardinal without uttering a word."   It is also reported that on consultation with the cardinals, he ordered that no notice whatever should be taken of the letter, and that his ministers should act as if unconscious of its existence.   On the other hand, the French troops at Rome are said to have received the letter with strong expressions of satisfaction and joy—the Romans fraternized warmly with the inhabitants and hoped that their day of deliverance was at hand.   Gen. Rostolan, it is understood, was recalled because he refused to communicate the letter formally to the army.

The cardinals at first granted permission to have the letter published in the official journal, but subsequently withdrew it, and threatened to leave the city.   They, however, remained, notwithstanding the French officers, in obedience to the last instructions from Paris, were interfering to prevent the re-actionary and despotic measures of the cardinal-government.

Thus the extraordinary relation of the French and Roman people still continues, and the former have learned that it is a difficult task to meddle with the internal quarrels of a foreign state. By this seizure and possession of Rome, France stands, too, in a delicate and anxious position before the world, and presents the anomalous case of a republic having been made, seemingly against its will, to uphold a despotic government, and having forced the people of Rome to receive assistance which they did not ask or desire. What will be the ultimate effect of this recent demonstration on the part of the French president and his cabinet, we will not venture to predict. It may be approved by England and Russia, and cause the speedy return of the Pope to Rome.

GREAT BRITAIN.

THE new Navigation law, abrogating a policy of two hundred years' standing, having passed both houses of Parliament, and received the royal assent, the subject next in national importance which engaged the attention of the British legislature was that of the affairs of Canada. It soon appeared, as might have been expected, that the ministry decided on supporting the course of Lord Elgin, the Governor General; and on this question, as well as every other in which ministers were opposed, they had a majority in both houses of Parliament. The act of the Canadian legislature, for the indemnity of the sufferers in the insurrection, therefore, received the royal sanction. In fact the disorderly and rebellious spirit exhibited by the opponents of that law in Canada cooled and alienated many of those members of the British Parliament whom their former loyalty would have most recommended.

Finding their opposition to be as fruitless in England as it had been in Canada, the malcontents became the open advocates for separation from the mother country—some proposing annexation to the United States, but the greater number, an independent government. In this state of things, the former colonial parties seemed to be transposed—the people of Lower Canada, who had been the most disaffected portion of the colony, were now the cordial supporters of the British government, while those who had been previously deemed the most loyal subjects of the British dominions, were in almost open revolt.* These

---

* There has recently been another riot at Bytown with loss of life on both sides. In consequence of the confused and excited condition of the public mind, nothing very satisfactory can be gathered respecting the real state of parties in Canada, and their respective influence upon the destiny of the Province.

The French Canadians, a vast majority of whom support the present executive government, are divided into those who follow the leadership of Lafontaine and those who follow Papineau; the latter are ultra-republicans, almost of the "red" school; the former include almost all the French members of the house of Assembly.

The great body of the British population take ground against the present executive, and are denominated tories, conservatives, &c. At page 165 will be found an article on Canada, containing the views on both sides of this really important question.

discontents have not yet subsided; and a home league, the avowed purpose of whose principal movers was, at first, separation from Great Britain, has been organized, and is industriously seeking support. Originating, however, as it did, in a single act, whose consequences are neither serious nor permanent, its influence is likely to lose strength rather than to gain it by time; and thus the loss to Great Britain of her North American provinces, which must one day certainly take place, is likely to be postponed to some future conflict of local interests or feelings.

In the latter part of July, a convention of the malcontents, styling themselves "the British American league," assembled at Kingston, in Canada West, and, after a deliberation of three days, issued an address to the inhabitants of Canada, dated the 21st July.   They complain of the free trade principles adopted by Great Britain, by which the interests of her Colonies, which are such large consumers of her manufactures, and whose products are now virtually excluded from her markets, have been sacrificed. _ They further complain that the Colonial legislature has recently been ruled by a faction, whereby those concerned in the late rebellion have been rewarded, and the public debt increased.   After setting forth these grievances in detail, three subjects are recommended to their earnest attention,—1st. A union of all the British American provinces, for the furtherance of which, a conference with the other provinces, by delegates, is proposed.   2d. Retrenchment and economy in the public expenditure. 3d. Protection to home industry. Urging the Canadians to the steady and warm support of these three objects, they add, "So shall you elevate this your country into a great nation of freemen, fostered by and in amity and connexion with Great Britain, preserving her time-hallowed institutions, adopting her old trade principles, under which she has flourished for centuries, and under which her people have grown to be the richest on the face of the globe —those great trade principles which, in the neighbouring Union, have also been adopted, and have established that mighty and prosperous nation."   Annexation to the United States, though occasionally mentioned by some of the speakers in terms of favour, is never once hinted at in the address.

The bill for removal of the disabilities of Jews from sitting in the British parliament, after passing the House of Commons, was rejected in the House of Peers by a majority of twenty-five.   As the ministry seem to have had this bill much at heart, it may be regarded as one of the few questions in which they were defeated during the late session of parliament.   It will probably be renewed at the next session, by the re-election of Baron Rothschilds in London.

Though the British government did not interpose in behalf of the Hungarians, and although Lord Palmerston, in a public speech on the 21st of July concerning continental affairs, declared that he considered the union of Hungary with Austria essential to the peace and safety of

Europe, yet the favourable terms in which he spoke of the Hungarians, and the strong hopes he expressed for the preservation of their national rights, are not likely to be without their effect on the political destinies of that brave and gallant people, in their final adjustment with Austria.

The Queen of Great Britain, accompanied by Prince Albert, their children, and a retinue of lords and ladies, during the month of August, paid a visit to Ireland. As this visit was intended, no doubt, to have a political effect—to reconcile the differences between the English and the Irish, we note its progress and result. The Queen embarked in the Victoria and Albert yatch, commanded by Lord Adolphus Fitzclarence, attended by a fleet of smaller vesssls. The reception in Ireland was exceedingly gratifying—the hearty and affectionate manner of the Irish—the entiré unanimity of all classes in giving to the royal party a joyous and triumphant welcome produced a strong effect upon the mind of the Queen; and the visit seems to have terminated with the same enthusiasm with which it commenced. At Dublin, Cork and Belfast, the multitudes who poured out to receive her manifested, up to the hour of departure, the same joyous delight which marked her arrival. This memorable visit, it is believed, has removed a world of prejudice and dissatisfaction, and has proved that the Irish people are as sincerely attached to royalty and to the present sovereign as the English are. To express the unmixed gratification of the Queen at the exhibitions of Irish loyalty, the young Prince of Wales has been created Earl of Dublin.

After leaving Ireland, the Queen proceeded to her residence at Balmoral in the Highlands of Scotland, where she was to remain until the 20th of September. It seems that the Scotch show almost as much enthusiasm as the Irish on the occasions of the Queen's visit; and it is very apparent that, whatever changes the future may have in reserve, at the present time, this royal lady has a deeper hold upon the affections of her people, than any other monarch in Europe. To add to the joy which such an assurance must create, the harvest throughout the whole of Britain has been abundant, and even Ireland is beginning to revive under the prospect of a better supply of the aliment of life.

But as a check upon the exuberant feelings which we have described, the cholera has committed, during the months of August and September, fearful ravages in England and Scotland. In London, four or five hundred died in a single day; and elsewhere the mortality has been very great, so that the devastations of the pestilence have shrouded the metropolis and other cities in gloom.

Peace once more reigns throughout the whole British domain in India, and the only annoyance which the government now meets in all Asia is the refusal which China is said to make to the admission of English subjects into Canton, as it had agreed to do by treaty.

The mediation of Great Britain between Prussia and Denmark has at length succeeded in effecting a pacification between these powers, and in adjusting the Schleswig Holstein affair. The interposition of the British government in any great question of European politics must always have more or less weight on the parties; yet though the present ministry are known to have also interposed between Austria and Sardinia, between the King of Naples and the Sicilians, and were believed to have interposed to prevent the Russian invasion of Hungary, and the French invasion of Rome, yet of all these cases of interventions, which to their credit were invariably in behalf of the weaker party, that of Denmark was the only one in which there was any open manifestation that their interposition had been effective.

GERMANY..

THE prospect of German unity and confederation, for some time obscured, seems to have almost totally disappeared. As the German sovereigns, especially the Emperor of Austria and the King of Prussia, began to regain their former authority, the weight of the Frankfort assembly or parliament visibly declined. Their numbers gradually diminished, notwithstanding the protests which some of the delegations made against their own recall by the princes they represented. On the 19th of May, the Archduke John was deposed from the Regency, by a vote of one hundred and twenty-six to one hundred and sixteen, and overtures were said to have been made to the King of Wurtemburg offering him the Regency. A like offer was made to the King of Bavaria without success. The assembly soon after adjourned to Stutgard, where there was often not a quorum, which they tried to reduce, before they left Frankfort, to one hundred members; and thus gradually declining, they may be now considered as having only a nominal existence. Thus has passed away the fondly cherished project which was to exalt the German name, by endowing it with power, wealth, and civil freedom. The sentiment of nationality, though disapproved for the present, still exists, however, ready to manifest itself under more favourable circumstances.*

THE King of Prussia sought to avail himself of the sentiment, just mentioned, so as to offer a constitution, for the greater states of Germany, of which he would be the head. In a proclamation, dated at

* The question of German confederation is still unsettled, according to the latest accounts. For the present it is stated that a directory of seven members is to sit at Frankfort as an executive commission for the common interests of Germany. A congress of Princes is expected to be held at Laybach at which, as rumour goes, the King of Naples and the Pope will be present or represented. All, however, is still in doubt at the time that we are writing.

Charlottenburg, May 15th, 1849, he announced this purpose, after having given his reasons for not accepting the crown tendered to him by the Frankfort assembly, and uttering strong denunciations against that body. He stated that the constitution about to be formed, would be submitted to a Diet of all the states composing the confederation, for its approval and sanction. The following day he put forth an address to the army, in which he adverts to the insurrections which had been quelled at Dresden, Breslau, and Dusseldorf, and to others then breaking out in the western districts of Prussia, and other parts of Germany, under the pretext of German unity.

The new German constitution which issued from Berlin soon afterwards, and was the joint work of the Kings of Prussia, Saxony, and Hanover, in its principal features closely resembles the constitution of the United States. The legislature consists of two houses. The Senate is chosen for six years, and its members must be thirty years of age. The members of the popular branch are distributed somewhat according to numbers. The whole number of members is one hundred and sixty-seven, of whom Prussia elects forty, Bavaria twenty, Saxony, Hanover and Wurtemburg, twelve each, Baden ten, and the smaller states (thirty-two in number) sixty-one.

The powers of the federal government are nearly the same as in the United States. They extend the regulations of commerce, which must be uniform, to the post-office, the mint, weights and measures, patents for inventions and literary property, imposts, the army and navy, and diplomatic intercourse. But it differs from the American constitution in the following particulars: half the Senate is renewed every three years: the people choose electors who choose the representatives of the people, and are, moreover, chosen for four years: the King of Prussia is the head of the federal government, and in case of his disability, the King of Bavaria. Whether Austria is to be admitted to the confederation, and on what terms, are questions to be hereafter determined. The insurrections in Baden, and other parts of Germany, having been previously quelled, by the 1st of August, all the German states, except Austria, Bavaria and Wurtemburg, had acceded to this constitution of the three kings. The enactments of the central power at Frankfort have since been entirely disregarded by Prussia, as in the occupation of the Duchy of Baden, during the insurrection there, without the authority required by the constitution of Frankfort, in the elections in Prussia, and in its foreign relations.

In the election, the democratic or republican party determined not to vote for the primary electors, so that three-fourths are said to have kept aloof. The republicans have decided on a new organization, and to meet not at Berlin, but at Magdeburg or Habberstadt. They propose to change their name from the *democratic* to the *popular* party. These indications of the prevalence of republican sentiments, has had its influence in the Prussian parliament, where, although in the recent elections there was a large majority of moderates or conservatives, the body is considered to be, on the whole, rather liberal; and, in truth, a certain portion of civil freedom is now deemed, in every part of Germany, an indispensable moral want—a political necessity—to which the most arbitrary of their governments must pay some respect.

Prussia, no longer disposed to conciliate the Frankfort Parliament, has adjusted the Schleswig Holstein question by an armistice and treaty with Denmark, on the 17th of July. By the terms of the treaty, Schleswig is to be governed for the present by two commissioners chosen by Prussia and Denmark, and with whom a third commissioner, nominated by the British sovereign, is to be associated as umpire.

A congress of those who did not take part in the elections, assembled at Cothen, in August, and, according to the report of a committee, it appeared that of 468,405 primary electors, only 115,116, less than one-fourth voted. The congress is composed chiefly of deputies from the eastern provinces of Prussia. At a banquet they toasted "Victorious Hungary," and made a collection for the wounded of Baden. Their next meeting is also to be at Cothen, but the time was not fixed. From these signs of the state of public feeling, one would infer that monarchy in Prussia must rely for its continuance on military force, conducted by unceasing vigilance and prudence. It will, no doubt, however, be greatly strengthened by the successes of Austria and Russia against the Hungarians.

AUSTRIA.

The Emperor Francis Joseph, having, by his manifesto of May 12, announced that the Emperor of Russia would co-operate with him to reduce the Hungarians to subjection, the cause of that brave people was defended in a paper which, though addressed by the Hungarian minister, Count Teleki, to the French minister of Foreign Affairs, seems to have been intended as an answer to the imperial manifesto. He first aims to prove the right of the Hungarians to an independent government; then the gross injustice of the house of Austria towards them; and, lastly, that the cause of Hungary is that of civilization against barbarism. He states that the Hungarian army amounts to nearly 200,000 men.

To this powerful force, the allied emperors were prepared to oppose, it was said, 250,000 men; but it was hoped that the rare military talents which Bem, Gorgey, and Dembinski had recently exhibited, and the resistless force with which the cause of freedom commonly inspires its champions, would more than compensate for the disparity of numbers. It was forgotten that the inferiority of the Hungarians in resources, especially in money, that is so important an element in modern

warfare, made a yet greater difference than that of numbers, and, in
· fact, rendered the contest a most unequal one.   Trusting, however, to
the goodness of their cause, as well as their own indomitable spirit,
and flushed with their late successes, they firmly prepared for the fearful struggle.   The scenes of their operations have been so distant, the
localities so imperfectly known here, and the accounts coming through
interested channels, have been so partial or defective, that it is but a
very imperfect sketch which can at this early day be given of them.
    The plan of the allies appears to have been to press on the Hunga-
rians, by the Austrians from the west, and the Russians from the east,
until the Hungarian armies, hemmed in on all sides, would be compelled to yield to the overpowering force of their enemies.   In May
and June, however, before the vast power of the allies were fully brought
to bear on them, the vigour, skill, and enterprise of the Hungarian
chiefs obtained frequent successes, and the hopes as well as admiration
of their numerous friends, both in Europe and the United States, were
raised very high.   But, even there, they themselves seemed to be but
too well aware of the difficulties of their situation.   In a public address
to the people of Hungary by Kossuth, as Governor, and his ministry,
on the 29th of June, which was intended to rouse the nation to one
united effort for their independence, the extent of their danger was
thus frankly laid before them:
    "We will neither flatter nor discourage, but we declare openly that
unless the whole nation rise up to defend itself to the last drop of its
blood, all the noble blood already shed is in vain, and our country will
fall—the Russian knout then ruling over an enslaved people, on the
ground where the ashes of our ancestors repose."
    In this address, the Hungarian force is stated to be 200,000 men.
But when examined in detail, it appeared that more than one-third of
this number consisted of irregular forces, of little avail against compact, disciplined, and well-appointed armies, unless they have been
routed: so that Georgey, Bem, and Dembinski, had each an army of
not more than from 40,000 to 50,000 men.
    In July, when more than 150,000 Russians had penetrated by diffe-
rent routes into Hungary and Transylvania, the tide of success began
to turn.   Pesth, the metropolis, in which a few weeks before Kossuth
had entered amid the acclamations of the people, was taken possession
of by the Russians under Paskiewitch; the town of Debrinski surrendered to the Russian General Theodyiff; and Georgey, placed between
two Russian armies which he was utterly unable to oppose, made a fortunate escape by a masterly retreat, and united his force with that of
Dembinski, but not until the latter had been compelled to give way
to a superior force under the walls of Waitzen.
    In the south, however, the Hungarian arms were more successful.
Jellachich was defeated by Bem, and Peterwardien was for the time
relieved.   The city of Raab was also taken by the Hungarians, which

conquest, the sanguine thought, threatened the safety of Presburg, and even of Vienna. But this seems to have been the last important success of the Hungarians. Bem's army was defeated by the Russians under Luders; and Georgey was compelled to surrender unconditionally to Paskiewitch.[*] Further resistance was hopeless, and Kossuth, with the force under Dembinski, retreated to the mountainous part of Hungary, in the north-east. Probably the forces were soon disbanded, and Kossuth, after winning the applause and admiration of the world for his self-devotion to his country, his eloquence, and his talents as a statesman, is now compelled to seek personal safety in a foreign land.

The fate of this gallant people, whom the friends of civil liberty and of rational independence in both hemispheres have so admired and so neglected, cannot be contemplated without the liveliest anxiety. Will they be reinstated in their former political condition? or will all vestiges of their ancient rights be effaced, and the arbitrary government to which they are now subjected, aim to amalgamate them with the rest of its dominions? or will Russia, profiting by the hatred of the Magyars for the Austrians, interfere in their behalf, and hope one day to make them dependents, by the influence of panslavism? These and similar questions present a wide field for conjecture.

DENMARK.

The pretensions of her subjects in the Duchies of Schleswig and Holstein, no longer receiving the cordial support of the king of Prussia, after his open breach with the Frankfort Parliament, was soon adjusted, favoured as that adjustment was by the mediation of Great Britain, and by the good wishes of most of the other European powers.

At first, Denmark seemed overmatched on land by the Prussian forces sent against her, aided, as they were, by her rebellious subjects; and she put in active requisition her superior naval strength, which all Germany was made to feel by her blockade of all the northern ports through which the Germans received foreign merchandise; and, finally, she redeemed her former failures at the battle of Fredericia, in which her army of 20,000 men obtained a victory over 14,000 Germans.

The armistice with Prussia took place on the 17th of July, and the protocol of the treaty consists of the five following articles:

---

[*] The forces of Georgey were, in fact, surrendered to Gen. Rudijer, whom Paskiewitch had sent to Grosswarden. They consisted of 30,000 infantry, 5,000 cavalry, and 144 cannon. The remaining corps that submitted to Gen. Luders, in Transylvania, consisted of twelve battalions of infantry, eight squadrons of cavalry, and seventy-four cannon. A cloud of suspicion hangs over Georgey, probably without cause; who is at large, and has retired to his patrimonial estate in Styria. The fortress of Comorn, at the last accounts, still held out; it was said to be well provisioned, and the garrison to consist of 20,000 men. The Esterhazys are there, and are opposed to a surrender, except on conditions which the Austrians will not grant.

1. Schleswig is to have a separate constitution, and is not to be joined with Holstein.

2. A definitive organization of the Duchy of Schleswig shall be arranged by the contracting parties.

3. This article concerns the Duchies of Holstein and Lunenburg.

4. The question of succession is reserved for future regulation.

5. The guarantee of the great powers of Europe is claimed for the exact execution of the definitive articles of peace.

This armistice or treaty was as unsatisfactory to the people of Schleswig, as it was to the Germans generally, and those who represented the central power of Germany entered a formal protest against it.

ITALY.

The political condition of this country now seems likely to be restored to what it was two years ago. The revolt of the Sicilians has wrought no change in their favour, and the whole island is again subjected to the arbitrary power of the king of Naples.

Since our last Historical Register was prepared for the press, events of great importance have occurred at Rome. That city, after the expulsion of the Pope, was governed by a triumvirate who refused admission to the French forces under Gen. Oudinot, sent, as alleged, to free Rome from the double evil of absolutism and anarchy. Garibaldi, a patriot leader of great courage and address, who commanded a band of Lombard and Roman soldiers, directed the military defences, and resisted to the last; but nothing could withstand the superior discipline and resources of the French army. After much severe fighting, with considerable loss of life, all further resistance seemed useless. At one bastion, carried by assault, the slaughter with the bayonet was very great: nearly an Italian regiment was destroyed. The French troops, *en masse*, entered the city on the 3d of July, and on the 5th took possession of the Castle of St. Angelo. The triumvirs, Mazzini, Armellini, and Saffi, fled to the coast, and took refuge on board a British vessel of war, which conveyed them to the island of Malta. Garibaldi, with his band of adventurers amounting to several thousands, left the city as the French entered it, and made his way through the papal dominions. He subsequently fell in with an Austrian force, and being worsted in the engagement, his followers were dispersed, and he with his wife and a few friends, after many hair-breadth escapes, reached Dalmatia. When last heard from, he had, by a series of adventures, succeeded in obtaining a temporary refuge in the city of Genoa, until he should find an opportunity to quit Italy.

After his entry into Rome, Gen. Oudinot, on the 15th of July, had the restoration of the papal government proclaimed, and the Pope's banner displayed at the castle of St. Angelo, with the discharge of one hundred cannon. The General himself was met on the steps of the grand entrance to the cathedral by Monsignore Marino Marini, who delivered a congratulatory and fulsome address, and to whom he replied that France had confided to its soldiers a great and holy mission, which had been accomplished in the re-establishment of the temporal power of the Pope. He then reviewed the troops, which consisted of about 20,000 Frenchmen and 3,000 Romans. The reception of the general-in-chief by the populace was cold and formal, and in some instances the soldiery were insulted.' No sooner, therefore, had the French assumed authority within the city, than the difficulty of their position was manifest,—obliged to struggle on the one hand against the powerful influence acting on the mind of the Pope, and on the other against the evil passions generated during the siege and conquest of the city. Oudinot, as we have stated in the history of France, issued a proclamation, in which he declared that all power was provisionally in the hands of the military authorities—that the assembly was dissolved —that the clubs were closed—that persons not belonging to the military, were prohibited wearing arms—that all publications by the press, not authorized by the military council, were for the present prohibited; and Gen. Rostolan was named Governor of Rome.

The keys of the captured gate were sent by the general-in-chief to Pius IX., who presented in return his best thanks and a papal decoration. Instead of returning himself to Rome, and carrying out the liberal policy which he initiated in Italy, he remained at Gaeta under the protection of the king of Naples, and deputed a commission of cardinals to rule the city. The first act of this new government was to institute a tribunal for the prosecution and trial of the authors and abettors of the revolution for the outrages alleged to have been committed against religion, its ministers, and the pontiff. Savelli, the Pope's former minister of the interior, was installed at the head of the police, under the control of the French authorities. He issued a decree declaring the value of paper money, and imposing fines and imprisonment on all refusing it. The system of lotteries too was restored at Rome; and the dividends on the public debt due in June were refused to be made, on the plea that the government was at that time republican.

We have already stated in another place that General Oudinot was recalled, and that Count Rostolan, who succeeded to the command of the forces, was himself displaced to make room for Gen. Randon,* who had been commissioned with full instructions, in accordance with the letter of the President of the Republic to Col. Ney. The present indications at Rome are an opposition of the people to the cardinals, and a reaction in favour of the French. The stand of France on the question of a liberal government for the papal states, seems to have been taken, from which she cannot retrace her steps without a loss of honour. What course the Pope will take, remains yet to be developed. He will, doubtless, in this new state of things, take counsel of the Catholic princes, and be guided by their advice.

---

* By the latest accounts, it would seem that Gen. Randon, from some cause, does
   ⌐ to Rome. See Chronicle.

VENICE.

Venice, after its obdurate and gallant resistance to the Austrians, has, at length, been compelled to surrender.   The capitulation was agreed to on the 22d of August, and was in accordance with the conditions prescribed by Marshal Radetzky in his proclamation of the 14th, viz.: A full and unconditional surrender of the city, forts, arsenals, arms, &c., a general pardon to soldiers and non-commissioned officers, and a permission to all persons to leave the city.

This once noble emporium of commerce has been doomed to a degradation that was not anticipated.   Her privilege, as a free port, is withdrawn, or what is the same thing, it is confined to the little island of San Giorgio Maggiore.   Thus the main prop of her greatness is taken away,—a fatal blow is struck at her commerce, and the advantages once enjoyed by Venice are to be transferred to her more loyal rival Trieste.

The conduct of the conquerors is represented to have been generally calm, and, as far as political offences are concerned, moderate.   The occupation of the city took place without disturbance, the Austrians met with a cold and silent reception from a people who, for seventeen months, had resolutely resisted them, and who only yielded when resistance was hopeless.   The president of the subverted republic, Manin, with Gen. Pepe, and other leaders in the revolution, were generously sent to Corfu by the commander of the French squadron, before the Austrians entered the city.   Such is the termination of the noble struggle maintained by the Venitians for so many months, and thus the Lombardo-Venitian kingdom is secured to the house of Austria.   The valour, and persevering efforts of the Venitians seemed to have deserved a better fate; of their conduct throughout the trying scenes of the contest it may be said that it was stained by none of those crimes which add to the evils of civil war.

THE IONIAN ISLANDS.—Cephalonia, the largest of these islands, has been the scene of a serious disturbance.   Partly from political motives and partly from motives of plunder, an outbreak of the people took place, and they drove the police out of Scala.   Troops were sent from Corfu to Argostoli, where the chief excesses took place.   One of the most respected citizens was burned alive in his own house, with two of his servants, and other outrages were committed.   To suppress the revolt, vigorous measures were employed by the Lord High Commissioner Ward, who communicated the details of the affair to his Highness Sp. Focca Stefano, the President of the Senate of the island. Subsequently the commissioner had a narrow escape with his life from the fury of the insurgents.   Martial law was proclaimed, and a portion of the English squadron sent from Malta to overpower the insurgents and restore tranquillity.

The Ionian Islands once belonged to Venice, but were organized into a separate state and placed under the protection of Great Britain by the Congress of Vienna. A constitution was drawn up in 1817, and ratified by the British government, under which is appointed a superintendent or governor in the person of the Lord High Commissioner.

RUSSIA. ·

THE sole attention of the Emperor Nicholas, for the last half year, seems to have been turned to the commotions and sanguinary conflicts in Germany; in which he became an active participant, upon the pretext of maintaining the inviolability of his own, as well as of the Austrian dominions. The history, therefore, of Russia for that period is so intimately connected with the operations, political and military, in Germany, that it is mostly embraced in what we have already written.

Perhaps the power of this colossal empire is more distinctly felt and acknowledged at this time, than it has ever been at any preceding period. Called in by Austria to assist in reducing the insurgents of Hungary to subjection, the Emperor of Russia at once brought to bear against the valiant and refractory Magyars an overwhelming force. As we have seen, resistance was unavailing, and the combatants for constitutional rights succumbed to the allied powers.

The motives which induced the northern autocrat to take part in the Hungarian war, are avowed in a circular addressed by Count Nesselrode, his Minister for Foreign Affairs, to his envoys at foreign courts. The words of the circular are: "The dangers which threatened the security of our frontier have been removed. Hungary has returned to the rule of her legitimate sovereign. The integrity of the Austrian territory, as guarantied by the treaty of Vienna, is secured. Such are the results that the co-operation of the Emperor has afforded to his imperial, royal and apostolic majesty. It is also the only remuneration he ever had in view, when he associated his banner with that of his august ally. Our co-operation, granted in good faith, has been accepted with confidence. These sentiments have formed the basis of the relations between the two sovereigns. They will be equally present in the alliance of their empires. The task of the emperor is performed. His troops have received an order to evacuate the Hungarian territory."

Such is the avowal, by this conqueror of Hungary, of the inducements which prompted him to aid the house of Hapsburg. In accordance also with the spirit of the declaration he has made, that "he will suppress revolution wherever it may show itself," he has concentrated immense armies, gathered from the extreme limits of his empire, and has established on the frontiers of Poland a more vigorous police than ever, so that a stranger is scarcely allowed to enter the country. The boldness and energy of his movements correspond with the extent of his means.

It is a little remarkable that neither Turkey, nor France, nor England, offered any efficient remonstrance, or hinderance against these demonstrations on the part of Russia, especially in the case of Hungary, before it was prostrated by the combined power of Russia and Austria. Now that its heroic defenders are driven from their country, there has been an effort made to save some of them from the vindictive pursuit of the conquerors. Kossuth, Dembinski, Perczel, and others who fled into Turkey, have been demanded of the Sultan, who declined to deliver them up, and they are said to have been furnished with passports by the British Ambassador. The Sultan has, in this particular, shown a becoming spirit, and it may be that the powerful interposition of the British government will save Turkey from the vengeance of the two Emperors.

Judging from the reception that was given by Nicholas to the French Ambassador, General Lamoriciere, it would seem that he desires to conciliate France; and it has been supposed, until the recent independent ground taken by the French President in relation to the Pope, that the French cabinet was inclined to become the ally of Russia, and a party to the suppression of the spirit of revolution and of free governments in Europe.

That we are on the eve of some important events, for good or ill, is certain. Two millions of men are under arms in Europe, and amidst the hostile array of principles and doctrines there is reason to apprehend some new and serious agitation. It is only by the interposition of an overruling Providence that the threatening storm can be repressed, and a wise and pacific course adopted by the great powers, that will lead to the establishment of peace and good government.

(We refer to the Quarterly Chronicle of events, which we place immediately after the History, for many interesting and valuable historical items, that could not be incorporated in the preceding pages.)

QUARTERLY CHRONICLE.

—

June, 1849.

1. Some interesting accounts were received at this date from the coast of Africa. The United States brig, Bainbridge, was lying at Porto Praya, a harbour in St. Iago, one of the Cape de Verde islands. The other vessels of the squadron were cruising on the coast. It is stated in a letter from an American officer, that the republic of Liberia had been successful in the New Cessters war, which was undertaken for the purpose of destroying the slave factories from Cape Mount to Cape Palmas. The Spaniards headed the natives, and offered a vigorous resistance; but the factories were burned and the slaves released. The English also had destroyed the factories at Gallinas. President Roberts believes that, with two or three armed vessels, he could keep the whole of that coast free of slavers. The letter of the naval officer alluded to thus continues:

"The principal factories on this part of the coast are now broken up, but there are many by-places where slavers can easily obtain a cargo, and it is almost impossible to prevent them; for such is their despatch, that, in three or four hours, they will take in six hundred slaves, and by daylight be out of sight of land. Should a man-of-war, be cruising in the neighbourhood, the slaves are put in canoes, in irons, and sent up or down the coast, to some convenient place for shipment. Not long since, a canoe-load of them was capsized on their way from Cape Mount to New Cess, and the whole of them drowned; and a few days afterwards their bodies were washed up on the beach, in irons.

"St. George del Mina (or El Mina) is one of the principal places on the gold coast. It is a very strong Dutch possession, very prettily situated, and kept in nice order and repair. The Dutch officers were very kind and polite to us during our stay. This castle was built by the Portuguese for the purpose of carrying on the slave trade, and was captured from them during the thirty years' war by the Dutch, who have held it ever since. El Mina is celebrated for its gold, as large quantities are found in the neighbourhood; and, after a rain, every one in the villages begins to wash for gold. The negroes are very skilful in washing for it; the work is done almost entirely by the women.

"About eight miles to the eastward of El Mina is Cape Coast Castle, an English possession, which is a very pretty place, and very strongly located. It has but a small garrison, and, like El Mina, the principal trade is in gold dust. The natives are exactly the same in appearance,

except that those of Cape Coast seem to be more lively—whether from
an extra allowance of government or grog, I could not find out. We
were all very much pleased with the English officers there, who were
very polite and kind. This castle is the spot where L. E. LAN-
DON died, and who was so much regretted by every one. A neat
stone, with an inscription to her memory, is placed in the parade ground.
Cape Coast is represented as a very unhealthy place.''

Notwithstanding these partial successes in the attempts made to
suppress the slave trade, the committee in the British house of Commons on that subject recently reported that, after a careful investigation, they had come to the conclusion that no system of force can effect the suppression of the slave trade; and that their main reliance is
"on the improvement and civilization of Africa." See Documents.

1st. Amongst the news recently received from Senegal, the *Courier
de la Gironde* notices an event which cannot fail to have the happiest
effect on commerce. An expedition attempted by Capt. Bouet, on the
Grand Bassam river, has produced results which would appear fabu-
lous, had they not acquired a great degree of authenticity from the
very source whence they emanated. On the 4th of March last, M.
Bouet, then commanding the Serpent, succeeded in crossing the bar of
the river, which has acquired such an evil reputation, and his entrance
was hailed by salvos of artillery from the fort and the ships in the harbour. The dangers of the exploring expedition were terrible. Of
four officers Capt. Auguste Bouet lost three; the fourth, with the sur- ,
geon, and a few white seamen, whom he succeeded in saving, returned
to France in a condition truly deplorable. M. Bouet himself was attacked by illness no less than three times; but his energy was not in
the slightest degree subdued by sickness. "Thanks to Heaven," says
the letter which apprises us of these details, "he has succeeded, and
the happiest results have crowned his enterprise. He has discovered
two magnificent lakes, where palm-oil is so abundant that the ship had
not vessels enough to hold it. Now, according to the dealers themselves, palm-oil gives a profit of eighty per cent., whilst gold only yields
fifty or sixty."

The adjoining villages are said to overflow with produce of all sorts.
Capt. Bouet has, however, visited unknown regions, established relations, and asserted the power of France in the midst of a country the
very centre of the gold trade, the only commerce hitherto carried on
at Grand Bassam. He has discovered, what all skilful geographers
already suspected, that the Grand Bassam is a confluent of the Niger.
It being the dry season, the want of water prevented its exploration;
but in the rainy season there are six feet of water, and the river may
be ascended as far as the cataracts of Abouesson, fifty leagues distant.
At that place the traveller is within sixty leagues of Sego, and the
course of the Niger is still continued. Thus the anticipations of Capt.
Bouet are confirmed, and every day adduces fresh proofs of their cor-

rectness. When the steamer Guettander proceeds to Grand Bassam, that vessel, which only draws two feet of water, will entirely solve the problem. Thus, a well armed and well supplied vessel will penetrate to the interior of the country, a district of which Capt. Bouet has seen a part himself, and which is the *entrepot* and the passage for the caravans of the gold and silk merchants, and where the gallant captain discovered, and inhabited for two days, a city more ancient and more important than Timbuctoo.

We have also accounts, at this date, from the Sandwich Islands. If the statements received by the N. Y. Journal of Commerce be correct, the prospects of the kingdom of Kamehameha III. are gloomy indeed. It is stated that the native population is diminishing so rapidly that, by the end of the next ten or fifteen years, scarcely a native will be found on the islands. Indeed, one of the oldest resident physicians there has expressed the opinion that this result will be realized within the next *five* years. Four-fifths of the population have disappeared since the first visit of Capt. Cook, a period of seventy years, and about one-sixth of the remnant have died within the last year. The missionaries estimate the number of deaths during the past year at about ten thousand, or more than one-tenth of the whole population. A majority of the infants born were among the victims. The present population of the islands is about eighty thousand.

2*d.* The following information from the far West was received at this date at St. Louis.

A considerable portion of Col. Fremont's property, abandoned in the mountains, has been recovered, some of it being in the possession of Mexicans, who have been arrested, charged with a participation in the murder by the Indians of Dr. Kearn and Bill Williams, who went in search of it.

Col. Washington, in command of the Department of New Mexico, had issued his proclamation in pursuance of the provisions of the treaty of peace with Mexico, advising the inhabitants of the territory ceded to the United States to decide by the 30th of May (last,) whether they will become American citizens, or retain the character of Mexicans.

Captain Chapman, of the Santa Fe Guards, having received information of Indian depredations, set out to chastise them. He came suddenly upon a large force of Apache Indians, whom he defeated in a fight, and killed two hundred of them. The Indian chief was killed by Lieut. Kendrick.

Stations have been established on the Atlantic, by virtue of the Act of March 3, 1849, for the prevention of wrecks, and for the saving of the crews and passengers of wrecked vessels. The method adopted in saving lives is the same as is used in England, viz.: to throw lines on board the vessels either by means of rockets or by attaching them to balls fired from carronades. When this is accomplished, the persons in danger can be brought on shore by means of the life cars, which are furnished with rings so that they can be hauled along the line to and from the wreck. They are made sufficiently large to contain two or three persons, with openings in the decks for the purpose of ventilation. The surf boats and life boats are both to be constructed of galvanized iron, and will be furnished with floats of India rubber, so that they cannot be capsized, no matter how heavy the surf may be.

4th. The news is received of a battle in Java, between the Javanese and Dutch, some time during the last spring, in which the former lost 5000, and the latter 250.

Also an account of a battle, about the same time, on the island of Borneo, between the Rajah, Sir J. Brooke, and the hostile Dyaks. He had succeeded in burning their towns, and had sent to the admiral on that station for an additional force.

The London Times contains a letter from Admiral Charles Napier, late at the head of the channel fleet, to Lord John Russell, in which is repeated the apprehension, some time since expressed by the Duke of Wellington, of danger to England from the increase of the French navy. He states that France has twenty war steamers capable of carrying two thousand men each, in which they transported, in less than thirty hours, an army to Civita Vecchia. Referring to the remonstrance on the part of England against the invasion of the Roman States, he inquires if England is in a condition to remonstrate. He thus continues:—"When Rome is taken—which I fear it will be—if we offer any threat, if we say one offensive word, what is to hinder the French collecting the very steam vessels that transported the French army to the capital of the catholic world, at Cherbourg, and transporting an army to the capital of protestant England? It may be argued that the French have their hands full already—that they are quarrelling among themselves. What, my lord, would unite them so soon as a war cry? It appears the government have got the better of the red republicans. The president, in his speech, tells France that they have an army of 450,000 men; they have a sailing navy nearly equal to our own, and a steam navy far superior."

5th. The Western Indians have been very troublesome, especially the Camanches, attacking emigrants and committing outrages of various kinds. Some of the Seminole Indians and others, who were removed to the West, were suspected of a disposition to unite with the more savage tribes. The following graphic account, published in June, is from the Little Rock (Ark.) Banner:

"The Indians begin to assume a savage appearance about here, they all paint and wear scalp locks, we met two the other day almost entirely naked, with the exception of a blanket and a small piece of cloth about their loins: they were armed with bows and arrows, rode without saddles, and in lieu of a bridle had a piece of rope about the lower jaw of the horse; they belonged to the Wachita tribe. About two miles beyond Little river, we met the celebrated Seminole chief, Wild Cat, with twelve warriors, all painted, and in their war dress: they had plenty of whiskey, which sold for twenty cents per pint, and were of course very drunk. Old Wild Cat is a fine-looking Indian, but he has a countenance that would do honour to an imp of Satan. His neck, wrists, arms and waist, were encircled with silver plates given him at Washington, and engraved with his name. The current report here is, that he is in league with the Camanches, and appearances seem to favour it. A few weeks ago he was at Fort Smith with some of his people: and there bought a quantity of gunpowder and whiskey; with these he returned, and is now on his way to the Grand Prairies: what his real intentions are, is not known, but I think that he intends nothing good. One thing is certain, as all the reports confirm, that the Camanches and other tribes are on the offensive."

6th. The New Albany Bulletin contained an interesting account of an operation performed by Dr. Sloan, of New Albany, upon the eyes of Rev. N. Hoskins, of Crawford county, Ia., who had been blind from birth. The Bulletin states:

"Mr. Hoskins was taken home to Crawford county before the bandages were removed, and when this was done, we are informed by a gentleman residing in that neighbourhood, the operation was found to have been eminently successful. He describes the emotions of the patient when suddenly possessed of a sense so novel to him, to be of the most enthusiastic description. Things which he had long been acquainted with, through the medium of the other senses, became possessed of a new and surpassing beauty, and roads which he had been used to travel fearlessly when blind, had to be again learned. His wife and children, *whom he had never seen*, his friends, his parishioners, his home, every thing endeared to him, became an unending source of delight and new-born gratification. He had the same confused notions of distance, which we see the smallest children manifest, and took the liveliest pleasure in beholding the great variety of colours. In short, he was compelled to *learn* to see, in precisely the same manner that the smallest child does, and to him it was an occupation of the most gratifying nature."

10th. *The fossil remains of an elephant* were found a short time since, in the construction of the Rutland and Burlington rail-road, upon the slope of Mt. Holly, one of the highest mountains in Vermont. Professor Agassiz states that this is the first true elephant found in a fossil condition in the Northern States. He says it is certainly not the same kind of elephant which had been found in the Kentucky cave, and that it is a question whether it is identical with the fossil European elephants or not.

At this date a terrible *steamboat explosion* occurred on the Ohio river, by which thirteen persons were killed. A number of the crew and deck passengers were killed and blown overboard by the violence of the concussion. Twenty-eight others were severely scalded, some

of them so severely that but slight hopes are entertained of their recovery.   The killed and wounded were chiefly deck passengers; none of
the cabin passengers were injured.   The cook was drowned, and the
second engineer badly scalded, who has since died.   The boat was
much shattered, and shortly after the lamentable disaster, was towed
to Evansville.   The scene on board was of the most heart-rending description.   The "Embassy" was from Pittsburgh, and bound to St.
Louis.

11*th. Prince Albert*, of England, attended the anniversary festival
of the merchant-tailors of London, in company with the Duke of Wellington, Prince George of Cumberland, Viscount Hardinge, Marquis of
Exeter, and others of the nobility, and was admitted a member of the
fraternity.   Among the toasts drank, was "The health of His Royal
Highness Prince Albert, citizen and 'merchant-tailor.'"   He responded in a very appropriate speech.   This cultivation of the commons seems to be regarded by the royal pair in England, as the true
safeguard of the monarchy.   The Queen's visit to Ireland was marked
throughout by the condescensions of royalty.   Prince Albert is about
getting up for the public an exhibition of works of art on a grand scale,
to be held in one of the great parks of London.

A battle was fought in Yucatan between the Indians and the whites,
in which the latter were defeated with considerable loss.   The Yuca-
teco garrison of Titul, consisting of 535 men, had evacuated the
place for want of provisions, and were intercepted by an overwhelming force of Indians, who attacked them with great fury.   The
Yucatecos, after standing their ground until a large number of them
were slain, gave way and fled, leaving their ammunition, baggage, &c.,
in the hands of their foes.   Of the detachment, 187 reached Sabau
with their colonel, bringing with them two officers and fifteen soldiers
wounded.   Two days afterwards, however, 100 more of the fugitives,
with two subalterns, reached Sabau.   Seventy-eight head of cattle
were captured by the Indians.   Subsequently, it will be seen, that on
the 9th September, the Yucatecos defeated the Indians at Valladolid.

12*th.* Meetings were held in California, in relation to a general convention, and the organization of a territorial government.   On the 3d
and 4th of June, General Riley, Governor of California, had issued
two proclamations.   In the first of which, he declares himself "the
executive of the existing civil government," and appointed the 1st of
August for holding a special election of delegates to a general convention, and for filling the offices of judges, prefects, alcaldes, &c.,
who were to hold their offices until others should be chosen at a general election in November next.   He also summoned a convention for
framing a state constitution, or a plan for a territorial government, to
meet on the 1st of September, at Monterey, and to be composed of
thirty-seven delegates.   In the second proclamation, he warned the

settlers not to countenance the legislative assembly of the district of San Francisco. This last mentioned body published a counter address, and recommended a convention to be held at San Jose, on the 3d Monday of August, for the purpose of organizing the territorial government.

On the 12th of June, a meeting was held at San Francisco, which was addressed by Hon. T. Butler King, at which the importance of organization was urged, and a committee appointed, who reported on the subject, and, without recognising any power in General Riley to appoint the time and place of a convention, still, for the sake of unanimity, recommended the same time and place. A meeting was also held at San Jose, which approved of the course and recommendations of Gen. Riley. Harmony of action was subsequently restored, and the election held on the 1st August,—for an account of which, see the Chronicle for August.

13*th.* The mountain party in Paris, consisting of 25,000 men, headed by Etienne Arago, Jr., and Ledru Rollin, attempted an insurrection for the purpose of overthrowing the existing government. It entirely failed. The troops were faithful to the government, and the president is said to have exhibited much firmness and presence of mind on the occasion. On the 15th, there was a similar movement in Lyons, and fighting in the streets. The insurgents were routed, and order restored. Twelve hundred arrests were made. The president has released two hundred and twenty-five of them, the rest are to be tried. Ledru Rollin, once a distinguished member of the provisional government, and leader of the socialists, fled from France.

A curious instance of the instability of human affairs is afforded by the fact, that about twelve months previous a prefect of one of the French departments received the following telegraphic despatch :

"Monsieur Le Prefet: Arrest by all possible means, the citizen Louis Napoleon Bonaparte, should he present himself in your department.   Ledru Rollin."

A year later, the same prefect received another despatch in the following terms :

" Arrest by all possible means, the citizen Ledru Rollin, if he present himself in your department.
                Signed by   Dufaure."
                The minister of Louis Napoleon.

The following programme of the proposed government of the mountain party, was published as having been found among the documents at the Conservatoire des Acts et Metiers, after the suppression of the revolt:

Ledru Rollin, dictator of the democratic and social republic, with the right of life and death over every French citizen.

BOICHOT, sergeant-major of the 7th light infantry, minister of war.

DEVILLE, ex-notary, minister of expeditive justice.

NADAUD, journeyman mason, minister of the public works.

FELIX PYAT, minister of the interior.

GREPPE, minister of agriculture and commerce.

PIERRE LEROUX, minister of public instruction.

GENT, minister of foreign affairs.

BOURZAT, minister of marine.

Sergeant RATTIER, general commandant-in-chief of the armed force, with dictatorial right of election.

M. ANTONY THOURET, minister of the police.

After the *manifestation* at Paris on the 13th, the French Assembly voted the interdiction of the clubs, and the regulation of public meeting. Without debate, the following articles were adopted:

Art. 1. Government is authorized, during the year which shall follow the promulgation of the present law, to interdict clubs and other political meetings which would be of a nature to compromise the public security.

Art. 2. Before the expiration of the year, there shall be presented to the Assembly a bill, which, interdicting clubs, shall regulate the exercise of the right of meeting.

A member of the Left moved to insert *"assure and,"* before the word "regulate," in Art. 2. The amendment was not even seconded.

Art. 3. At the close of the year, an account shall be rendered to the National Assembly of the manner in which this law shall have been executed.

Six of the democratic papers in Paris, *La Reforme, La Peuple, La Democratic Pacific, La Revolution, Democratique et Sociale, La Republique*, were suppressed at the same time, by order of the government.

14th. We give the following remarkable instances of longevity of persons now living in this country, as they are stated in our exchange papers of this date. The first is from the Ashville (N. C.,) Messenger:—

"There are living on Spring Creek, in this county, perhaps two of the 'oldest inhabitants' in our country. Mr. Wm. Woody, 111 years old, and can now '*wade and split water* like a coon,' wading every branch and creek that happens to cross his path; is in good health, and of a sound mind.

"Mr. M. Davis, his close neighbour, is 103 years old, and, we understand, is also in good health and spirits. The former is 30 years beyond the scriptural allotment, namely, 'four-score years;' the latter, 23 years. Unite their progeny, and they could nearly people a new county."

"*George Buckhart,* living in Harlan county, Ky., is one of the most extraordinary men of the age, and perhaps is the oldest man now known to be living. He is one hundred and fourteen years old; was born in Germantown, Pa., and has lived for several years in a hollow sycamore tree."

14*th.* In Frankfort, Ky., the case which had been pending for some time in the U. S. Circuit Court, between Messrs. Morse and O'Rielly, and which originated in an injunction laid by Morse against the use of the Columbia Telegraphic Instrument by O'Rielly, on the line extending by Louisville to Nashville, was decided yesterday. The decision was made in favour of O'Rielly—which restores to him the use of the Frankfort line. The Court decided that the invention and use of Bain's instrument would be no infringement of the injunction obtained by Morse last fall on the use of the Columbian instrument. This decision enables O'Rielly to complete his telegraphic communication to New Orleans.

Opposite Louisville, Ky., on the Indiana shore, a duel was fought between John T. Gray, Esq., and Captain Henry C. Pope, of that city, which resulted in the death of the latter gentleman. The weapons used were shot-guns, loaded with bullets—distance, twenty paces. At the first fire, Captain Pope fell mortally wounded, and died in a very short time. Immediately after his fall, he requested permission to see Mr. Gray, and a most affecting reconciliation took place, in which they both expressed their deep regret at the unfortunate occurrence.

15*th.* A wild boy (coloured,) was found in the woods in the island of Jamaica, in the cane-fields of a plantation. He was incapable of uttering words, or understanding what was said to him. He was ten years old—in a state of nudity—and no one knew how long he had been in that condition, or where he came from.

16*th.* A tornado swept over a portion of New York and Massachusetts. As an instance of its violence, on a farm in Oneida, N. Y., the trees of a large orchard were uprooted—a barn was driven from its foundation—fences prostrated—the mansion-house unroofed, and chimneys blown down. At Freetown, Mass., the trees on an acre of woodland, including some of the heaviest timber in the vicinity, were entirely prostrated.

18*th.* At a meeting of the National Institute, a brief memoir was read by Mr. Schoolcraft on the Oneida stone—a curious and unique monument of the nationality of the Oneida tribe, in western New York. This stone, of which Mr. S. presented a specimen, has imparted a name to the tribe, who call themselves the *People of the Stone.* Mr. S. describes it as a boulder of sienite of the drift stratum, and traces its origin to the primary beds in the north-eastern mountain ranges of that State. But its chief interest arises from the ancient and intimate connexion which this extraneous mass of rock has with the tribal origin, liberties, and security of this celebrated member of the Iroquois confederacy. Its palladic value furnishes, indeed, a curious coincidence of thought with a well-known fact in Grecian history.

20th. JARED SPARKS, Esq., was inaugurated as president of Harvard University, and the ceremonies were of a very interesting character. Among them was the planting of what is known as the " President's Tree." The students bore a fine spruce tree in great state to the College yard, where, after it had been properly placed in a hole dug for the purpose, President Sparks, assisted by the Marshal and six of the senior class, placed the earth properly around it. The address of the president, after the ceremony of inauguration had been completed, was devoted to an exposition of the course, extent, and effects of education in this country. In the course of it, he said that for a century and a half after the settlement of this country there were but five colleges, and now there are over one hundred and twenty. He also expressed his belief that there was more money expended in the United States for collegiate education than in any country in the world. They are, in truth, too, American Colleges, where all are on an equality—the poor and the rich,—talent and merit only giving pre-eminence.

21st. Several vessels arrived at Sante St. Marie, with copper and iron from Lake Superior: about 150 tons of the former, and more than 200 of the latter.

A sad catastrophe occurred at Niagara Falls. A daughter of Mr. De Forrest and a son of Mr. Samuel Addington, of Buffalo, fell into the stream together at " Hog's Back," and were instantly precipitated over the falls.

22d. A public meeting was held at Kingston, Jamaica, on the subject of the violation of the slave trade treaties by the Spanish and Brazilian governments. Among other statements, it was asserted that during the past year the slave trade was as great as it had been for seven years prior to the abolishing it.

The following facts, some time ago brought before the Imperial Parliament, were reproduced, to show the effect of emancipating negroes: That since the passing of the British Emancipation Act, of 153 sugar estates then in cultivation on the island, 140, containing 168,032 acres, have been abandoned, and the works broken up.

These plantations employed at that time 22,533 labourers, and since the same period 455 coffee plantations, occupying 188,000 acres, and employing in 1832, 2083 labourers, had also been abandoned and the works broken up.

The coloured people are making some progress in the island of Jamaica. Ten of them are members of the colonial legislature.

In relation to the slave trade in the Spanish Islands, the La Verdad, a Spanish paper, remarks:

"During the last four months, 2400 negroes have been introduced into Cuba, and other shipments are expected daily, as it is known that 10,000 negroes have been purchased at the price of $8,50 each, on the coast of Africa. Representations, it seems, have been made to the Governor-general, that it would be expedient to permit the importation of negroes from Brazil, and the Attorney Olaneta, on being consulted by the Count of Alcoy, gave it as his opinion that such importation would not be in violation of existing treaties."

25th. Mr. Clayton, the Secretary of State of the United States, addressed a note to L. H. Breisach, Esq., dated at New York, who had sent to the President a letter enclosing the proceedings of a meeting of Hungarians and others; the Secretary holds the following language:—

"The government and the people of this country are profoundly interested in the events which are now passing in Hungary, and all information calculated to throw light on the present struggle between that country and Austria and Russia, cannot fail to be welcome.

"It is the policy and practice of the United States to recognise all governments which exhibit to the world convincing proofs of their power to maintain themselves.

"If Hungary sustains herself in this unequal contest, there is no reason why we should not recognise her independence. Congress, it is believed, would sanction such a measure, and this government would be most happy in that event to enter into commercial as well as diplomatic relations with independent Hungary."

26th. An industrial Congress, so-called, recently assembled at Cincinnati. The grand object was the discussion of all subjects bearing upon the prominent reforms of the age; the establishment of principles by which reformers are to be guided in the furtherance of such questions as Anti-Slavery, Temperance, Land-Reform—the Rights of Labour, the Abuses of Capital, Abolition of Capital Punishment, &c.

There were representatives in attendance from five or six States in the Union, and the discussions were quite able. Among the speakers were several females—Mrs. Townsend, of Providence, R. I.; Mrs. Burns, of Cincinnati; and one or two others. The world is full of reformers.

27th. One of the most terrible and melancholy disasters that has ever been recorded occurred this day at sea. *The barque Charles Bartlett*, of Plymouth, Mass., was run down, about seven hundred miles to the westward of Cape Clear, by the steamer Europa, in a dense fog, and sunk in three minutes. She had one hundred and sixty-two passengers on board, and only forty-three were saved. The following are the particulars from the Liverpool Times:

"The steamship Europa, Captain Lott, arrived here on Sunday morning last, after an extraordinary passage of ten days and eighteen hours from Boston to this port. On board the Europa we were grieved to find that she had forty-three persons, the survivors of the passengers and crew of the American barque Charles Bartlett, which vessel the Europa ran down at sea on the 27th ult., about seven hundred miles to the westward of Cape Clear, causing the loss of *one hundred and thirty-four lives.* The Charles Bartlett, Captain Bartlett, was an American ship of four hundred tons burden, chiefly loaded with lead and chalk, and having one hundred and sixty-two steerage passengers, one cabin passenger, and a crew of fourteen men, outward bound for New York, and at the time of the collision was going at the rate of about five knots an hour, close-hauled on the wind. The Europa was sailing at the rate of eleven and a-half or twelve knots per hour. At the time of the collision both vessels were enveloped in a dense fog, which prevented those on board of either vessel seeing beyond a few yards. At about half-past three o'clock, the look-out of the Europa suddenly perceived the ship through the mist, and had just time to announce the fact, when a dreadful collision took place, the Europa striking the Charles Bartlett amidships and cutting an awful chasm in her side, killing several persons on board. The barque began immediately to settle down, and in a few minutes sunk. The scene during those few minutes was appalling in the extreme. A crowd of suffering passengers, maimed and broken by the collision, lay dead or dying at the spot where the bows of the Europa had entered. Some of the individuals who crowded the decks appeared panic-stricken, others ran shrieking to and fro in despair, while some rushed forward and eagerly seized upon the opportunities which were presented for giving them a chance of safety.

"The most strenuous exertions were made on the instant, by all on board the Europa, for rescuing from the imminent peril which pressed upon them as many individuals as possible. Hand-buoys and ropes were thrown over, boats were lowered, and every man was busied in those few fearful minutes in rescuing the struggling sufferers from the waves. Yet, with all the exertions that could be used, only forty-three individuals were saved out of one hundred and seventy-seven, who had recently been alive on board the unfortunate ship. Amongst those preserved was the captain of the Charles Bartlett, the second mate, and seven seamen. Of forty women who were on board only one was saved. It is a remarkable circumstance that the second mate of the Charles Bartlett, and all the men of his watch, who were below at the time of the collision, were saved, whilst the whole of the watch on deck, with two exceptions, perished. The boats of the Europa, which had been lowered immediately on the collision taking place, and which had been actively engaged in picking up the unfortunate sufferers, were near being engulfed in the vortex which the sinking of the barque

created. No blame whatever can be imputed to those in charge of the
Europa. The collision was purely accidental; no human foresight
or prudence could have prevented it; and on the unfortunate circumstance taking place, every exertion was made to save the crew and
passengers of the sunken vessel. The damage sustained by the Europa
was very trifling.

"Immediately after the accident, a committee was formed, electing
Mr. Bates as its chairman, and Mr. Peabody secretary, for the purpose
of giving a tangible form to the benevolence of the gentlemen and
ladies on board. Subscriptions to the amount of £352 5s. were collected on the instant.

"We may here observe that, at one of the committee meetings on
board the Europa, the following resolution passed unanimously:

"That we have witnessed, with feelings of intense interest, the bold
and rapid movements of Capt. R. B. Forbes, of Boston; that his self-
sacrificing and daring leap into the sea to save the passengers of the
Charles Bartlett, commands our admiration, and we rejoice that these
deeds were performed by the missionary of the Jamestown."

29th. A desperate battle was fought on the 29th, between the Prus-
sians and the insurgents, in the neighbourhood of the villages of Calas-
che and Muglennsteine, between Carlsruhe and Radstadt. The insurgents were entirely defeated. Peneker has taken possession of Baden.
The head-quarters of the Prince of Prussia were at Oos.

29th. The French troops, under Gen. Oudinot, made the last and successful assault on Rome. The fighting was very severe, and one regiment of Italians was almost cut to pieces. The next day, the Constituent Assembly, finding that further resistance to the French arms
would be in vain, ceased hostilities, and virtually surrendered the city
to the besiegers.

29th. The spirit-stirring proclamation of Kossuth, the Hungarian, to
his countrymen was published.
After telling the people that "their Fatherland was in danger," he
proceeds:

"Fired by our sense of duty, we tell you, people of Hungary, that
the Austrian Emperor sends hordes of Russian barbarians for your destruction. We tell you that a Russian army of 40,000 men have invaded our Fatherland, from Galicia through Arva, Zips, Saros, and
Zemplin, and are constantly pressing forward ready for battle. We
tell you, beside, that in Suebenbergen, Russian troops have entered from
Bukowena and Moldau, with whom our army has already had bloody
conflict. We tell you that, relying on Russian troops, the Wallachian
rebellion has again broke out in Suebenbergen, and that the Austrian
emperor has collected his last forces to uproot the Hungarian nation.
We tell you once more, fellow-countrymen, although it is as certain as

God in heaven, that if the Russians succeed in conquering our Hungarian Fatherland, the subjugation of every nation in Europe will be the consequence. We can expect no foreign aid; the rulers, who look on our righteous struggle with coldness and silence, will chain up the sympathies of their people. We can hope in nothing but a just God and our own strength."

He thus concludes his forcible and eloquent address:

" This strife is not a strife between two hostile camps, but a war of tyranny against freedom, of barbarians against the collective might of a free nation. Therefore must the whole people arise with the army; if these millions sustain our army, we have gained freedom and victory for universal Europe, as well as for ourselves. Therefore, oh strong, gigantic people, unite with the army and rush to the conflict. Ho! every freeman! To arms! To arms! Thus is victory certain— but only thus. And therefore do we command a general gathering for freedom, in the name of God and the Fatherland."

Accounts from Circassia were received which mention that the Russians had sustained a severe defeat from the Circassians. The fortress of Totcha was captured by the Circassians, and of the garrison of 3,600 Russians one-third were put to the sword.

The Danes obtained a victory over the Holsteiners, who lost forty-seven pieces of artillery, and 3,000 men killed, wounded and prisoners.

30th. News from Chagres, up to this date, were received by the steamer Panama. The accounts from the Pacific are important. Upwards of $1,500,000 in gold had arrived at Valparaiso, and after being run into bars, assayed and marked, had been forwarded to England. The emigration from Chili to California continued. Merchandise was at low prices at San Francisco. All the better classes of the population had been frightened from Panama by the cholera.

JULY, 1849.

1st. The *Journal de Constantinople* has a letter from Trebisond, containing the latest intelligence from Persia. The Salar (one of the insurgent chiefs) was still blockaded in Mached, and dangerously ill. His brother-in-law Jaffer Kooli Khan, who beheaded the Koords and Turkomans, had made his submission, and had gone to Teheran, where the Persian government had received him with high honours. The surrender of Mached was daily expected. Sultan Moorad Mirza, uncle to the Schah, had assumed the command-in-chief of the Persian army; he had carried by storm, after a siege of fifty-five days, the fortress of Sebzewar, where the sons of the Salar, Emir Islam Khan and Hadji Mehemet Khan had retired. The former had succeeded in making his escape.

We learn from the Toronto Globe that a most frightful accident occurred on board the steamer Passport, on Thursday evening, on her passage from Montreal to Kingston. It is represented by passengers that the engineer was absent, the assistant in his berth, and the boat left in charge of an incompetent person. When off Lancaster (sixteen miles below Cornwall, about nine o'clock in the evening,) the boat struck the ground. The under deck was loaded with steerage passengers. The order to stop the engine and back out was promptly given, but the ignorance of the person in charge of the engine led to a most sad catastrophe. Instead of backing, he opened a cock which let the hot steam in among the steerage passengers. A shriek instantly broke forth, which was heard for several miles. The nature of the accident being for some time unknown, the steam continued to be discharged upon the poor creatures, adding to their insufferable agony. Four persons jumped overboard, two of whom were drowned. The nature of the terrible mistake being ascertained, the steam was at once shut off. Medical assistance was soon procured, when it was found that *forty-four* persons were severely scalded. The scene during the night is represented to have been horrible in the extreme—men, women, and children, in dreadful agony, continued their shrieks throughout the night. When the boat reached Cornwall, nine persons had died. About twenty were left at that place, and the remainder taken to Kingston, where four more had died, and many others were in a critical state. They were all immigrants.

The St. Joseph (Mo.) Gazette gives the following estimate of the number of emigrants and wagons that have crossed the plains *en route* for California:

"In making this estimate we give the number of wagons, and from this make our calculations as to the number of persons now on the plains. The wagons that crossed the river at this place, by ferry and steamboats, number 1,508; at Duncan's ferry, four miles above St. Joseph, 685; at Bontown, Savannah, and the ferries as far up as the bluffs, say 2,000. This makes the number of wagons 4,193. A fair average would be about four men and eight mules or oxen to each wagon. From this statement it would appear that there are 16,772 persons on plains, besides 33,544 mules and oxen. A number of emigrants, anticipating some difficulty in getting through with wagons, went with pack mules, which would probably increase the emigration to at least 17,000, and the number of cattle and mules to at least 34,000. From the best information we can get, about 10,000 persons have left Independence, which will increase the number of persons to about 27,000."

2d. Governor Fish, of New York, communicated to Major General Winfield Scott the resolution of the legislature thanking him for his gallant and meritorious conduct during the late campaign in Mexico. To which the veteran general-in-chief responded:

"This is the second time, within a third of a century between, that

I have been distinguished by the emphatic approbation of the legislative and executive of this great and patriotic state.

. "The reward far surpasses my merits or expectations; but, as a good citizen, I bow in humble thankfulness to the partial judgment of my countrymen."

3d. The following handsome compliment to the courage and benevolence of American seamen was communicated by the British chargé, Mr. Crampton, in a letter to Hon. J. M. Clayton:

"It is with peculiar pleasure that I fulfil the instructions of Her Majesty's government, in transmitting to you herewith a gold medal, bearing the portrait of Her Majesty the Queen, which Her Majesty's government desire to present to Capt. Oliver Gorham, of the United States brig 'Adelphi,' in acknowledgment of the services rendered by him in rescuing the master and crew of the British barque 'Jane Blain,' of Sligo, in very severe weather, when that vessel was in a sinking condition.

"I have also the honour of transmitting to you two silver medals, which Her Majesty's government wish to present to Mr. Lovell and to Mr. Hussey, the two mates of the 'Adelphi,' in acknowledgment of their services on that occasion.

"I would request, Sir, that you will be so obliging as to cause these medals to be forwarded to the persons for whom they are destined."

4th. The Winchester Republican, of a recent date, contains a description of a Virginia farm owned by *Wm. A. Carter*, of Newtown. We register the account, that our Northern farmers may see what is done in the South, and as an instance of the agricultural enterprise of the country.

After describing the mansion house, which is large and finely situated, the capacious barns, the milch cows, one hundred head of beeves, and one hundred hogs, the writer proceeds:

"His tract of land contains one thousand two hundred acres, laid off into convenient fields, about three hundred of which are covered with good timber, more than sufficient for fuel and fencing. Mr. C., however, is not neglectful of more enduring materials. He is increasing yearly his stone fencing—a mode of enclosure which we are glad to see coming into general use.

"Even a townsman can readily see the evidences of good farming on Mr. Carter's estate. He superintends it himself, and therefore has every thing well done. He has three hundred acres in wheat, of three varieties: the Mediterranean, Zimmerman, and Blue Stem. This will yield not less than twenty bushels to the acre—six thousand in all; a cheering product, and enough to feed a thousand people a whole year.

"Mr. Carter has one hundred acres in corn, with a fair prospect for eight barrels to the acre at least, and eighty acres in oats, the finest we have seen any where, which will average fifty bushels to the acre. He raises annually one hundred bushels of clover-seed.

"We find that Mr. C. uses vast amounts of stable manure, and depends much upon clover and plaster for maintaining the vigour of his land. Of the fertilizing qualities of these he has had ample and certain proofs in a succession of large crops. His land, we believe, cost him but little more than $20 an acre, and he is gathering from it a product equal to the average of the best Jefferson farm."

5th. The *ten hour law* in Pennsylvania went into effect. It applies to cotton, woollen, silk, paper, bagging, and flax factories,—in which, a period of ten hours' labour on any secular day is considered "a legal day's labour." The law also prohibits the employment in such factories, of any minor under thirteen, under the penalty of fifty dollars.

Anti-rent Decision.—The Albany Freeholder states:—The case of Stephen Van Rensselaer *vs.* Thomas Shaver, which was argued before Judges Watson, Harris, and Parker, in February last, has been decided. The opinion of the court was unanimous, that no power is conferred upon the judges to stay the proceedings in the collection of rent. Judge Wright, who was not upon the bench when the case was argued, reviewed with the other judges the evidence and arguments presented to the court, upon whom, by an arrangement between them, we understand devolves the duty of writing out the opinion of the court.

Since this decision—very recently—Robert Murphy, of Westerlo, a deputy sheriff, was shot at Rensselaerville, N. Y., by two men, disguised as Indians, whilst he was engaged in serving processes. After he was wounded, he was refused admittance into a house, by some females, because he was a sheriff. The anti-rent hostility to legal proceedings does not seem to be subdued.

The female American doctor, *Elizabeth Blackwell,* whom we have noticed as having obtained a degree at Geneva College, N. Y., and as having contributed a creditable article on ship fever, has gone to Paris, and was lately admitted a pupil, by the directors of the Hospital of Maternity. Her appearance in that city created a considerable sensation, especially among the fairer sex, one of whom remarked, "Oh! it is too horrid! Only to think, that those long fingers of hers have been cutting up people!" A gentleman writing from Paris, describes her thus:—"I have seen the doctor in question, and must say, in fairness, her appearance is quite prepossessing. She is young and rather good-looking; her manner indicates great energy of character; and she seems to have entered upon her singular career from motives of duty."

It is stated in the English papers, that the Czar of Russia has published a *ukase* for the regulation of the Universities. These institutions have become so many hot-beds of conspiracy,—the secret societies among the students are imbued with liberal ideas. To prevent the spread of the contagion, the Czar has prescribed that the number of the students at each University shall not exceed three hundred, and has forbidden the reception of applicants until the number has been reduced to that figure.

NIAGARA SUSPENSION BRIDGE.—The extensive circus and equestrian troupe of Col. Mann crossed the suspension bridge en route to Canada. The company occupied 22 horse teams, headed by the large four-horse band wagon, together with their baggage and paraphernalia. As little delay occurred as at any ordinary bridge, and the men and horses appeared quite at home.

The whole flooring of the bridge (800 feet long) appeared occupied at one time, and presented, from the water's edge, (320 feet below,) a scene of unequalled beauty and grandeur—the wires resembling more a spider's web woven across this otherwise impassable chasm, than the firm and solid carriage way.

The fare on teams has been reduced, and several hundred head of cattle, within the last few days, have availed themselves of the bridge as a crossing place.—*Buffalo Commercial.*

8*th.* The Rev. Theobald Mathew, or 'Father Mathew,' the celelebrated Irish philanthropist, who arrived some days previously in the packet ship Ashburton—was received with great courtesy and distinction by the authorities of New York, and this day celebrated mass in St. Peter's church. After mass he delivered a feeling discourse in which he contrasted the wide-spread blessings of Providence in this land with the miseries of his native country. On a subsequent day he visited Brooklyn, and administered the pledge to seven thousand persons.

He then proceeded to Boston, and was received with due formality on the common by the governor of the state,—twenty thousand people having gathered to witness the reception. He has since administered the temperance pledge to immense numbers of his countrymen, and presented them with medals, which, it is said, many wear as amulets.

Three Egyptian youths have arrived at Glasgow, Scotland, for the purpose of learning how to build marine steam engines. One of them will be sent to Mr. Napier's works in Glasgow, and the other two sent to a foundry at Greenock. They will have an excellent opportunity in that country, famed for regard to the Sabbath, and religious observances, to learn that Christianity constitutes the basis of European civilization, intelligence, superiority, and whatever tends to their comfort and elevation above the nations of the East.

A TRADING PRINCESS.—The *Journal du Havre* of July, says:— "For some days, every one has been able to perceive, in the roadstead in front of the bathing establishment of Frascati, a large steamer. This vessel, named the William, belongs to the Princess of Orange, who is at present at Dieppe, for the benefit of bathing. Thence she is about, it is said, to proceed to Palestine. This Princess is an intrepid tourist, and proceeds where she pleases in her yacht. Independently of this steamer, she possesses, we are informed, eleven steamers, which trade for her with England, Russia, and the Netherlands. Her revenue is estimated at three millions of francs."

TAHITI.—The English missions have been re-established or rather re-enforced at the Society Islands. The Rev. Messrs. Thomson and Howe are at Tahiti. Mr. Thomson has been on the ground for the last ten years. These two missionaries maintain Divine worship in four different chapels in the country, scattered over an extent of twenty miles of coast, besides other services every Lord's day in the town, for the native population. In addition to these duties, they preach regularly in English to a congregation composed of seamen and the mission families, they superintend schools in the town and country, and have in charge a press for printing in the native language.

The Turkish Government has established an agricultural school and model farm near Constantinople.

A discovery has been made by chemical process to make available the vast peat bogs of Ireland, and a gentleman named Owen, assisted by Lord Ashley, is working the adventure to a considerable extent. By a detailed statement, it appears that 100 tons of peat, which cost £8, and the labour of converting it, a further £8, yield carbon of ammonia, soda, vinegar, naphtha, candles, camphine oil, common oil, gas and ashes, to the value of £91 16s. 8d. Mr. Owen, it is stated by Lord Ashley, has experimented upon thousands of tons of peat during the last twelve months, with similar results.

AMERICAN TRACT SOCIETY.—"The *manufacturing* department of this Society," says the Am. Messenger, "is regarded as one of the most complete, if not one of the most extensive, in the world. The most improved machinery is so disposed as to secure the greatest regularity and efficiency in each branch of the printer's, binder's, and engraver's art. Twelve power presses—double medium—propelled by steam, with smaller proof and hand presses, besides the composing-room, occupy the fifth story of the front building. Steam embossing-presses, hydraulic and binder's presses, with about 100 folders, stitchers, forwarders, and finishers, are found on the fourth floor; while the fourth and fifth stories of the adjacent building, recently procured, are filled with case-makers, gilders, and folders. Besides warming the entire premises in winter, steam is made to heat the glue of each case-maker, boil the paste, hoist the paper, and do the drudgery of many men.

By these combined operations, between 2,000 and 3,000 books, and about 30,000 smaller publications are manufactured each day—all filled with divine knowledge."

12th. This day being the anniversary of the battle of Aughrim, a very serious collision took place between a party of armed Orangemen and Catholics, near Castle William, in county Down, Ireland. The Orange party having celebrated the day at Ballymore, and being on their march home, whilst passing a defile called Dolly's Brae, found their party waylaid. All the pass and surrounding hill were occupied by an immense number of Roman Catholics, provided with pikes and fire-arms, and plainly contemplating a general massacre. The Protestants, aided by a small party of police and military, stood upon their defence, and succeeded in forcing their way through the pass, after a short struggle, in which forty or fifty persons are said to have been killed or wounded, on both sides, much the greater portion being of the Roman Catholic party. Thirty-eight Ribbonmen have been taken prisoners.

On the same day a similar riot occurred at St. John's, Nova Scotia. Fire arms were used on both sides, and lives lost.

The immense extent of *the coal trade of the United States* appears from the fact that thirty-one brigs and schooners laden with coal recently arrived in one day at Boston from Philadelphia, and it may be added that in all probability a much greater quantity of coal than all these vessels carried arrives in New York every day, by the canals and railroads or in schooners and barges, from the Pennsylvania, Maryland, and Virginia mines.

Two fatal encounters recently occurred during the canvass in Kentucky for members of the Convention to revise the constitution. The first was between Cassius M. Clay, and Cyrus Turner, a member of the Legislature. Mr. Clay was making an emancipation speech when the difficulty happened—a bloody encounter ensued;—he ripped open the bowels of Turner with a bowie knife, and killed him. Clay, himself, was desperately wounded by some person in the crowd, but has recovered.

The second affray was between Judge Campbell and Benedict Austin, at Paducah. The latter used insulting language, and struck the Judge several blows in the face, when he drew a pistol and shot Austin dead on the spot.

In neither case have the survivors been subjected to a judicial trial.

At about the same date, there were *five executions for murder* in one day.—Three negroes named Nicholas, George and John, were hung in Charleston, S. C.; in Baltimore, Conrad Vender was hung for the murder of Mrs. Cooper; and in New York, Matthew Wood for the murder of his wife.

15th. California Gold.—We have been furnished, from the Mint, with the following statement:

The deposits of California Gold, during the six months ending 30th of June, were—

At the Philadelphia Mint, ...	$1,000,818
At the New Orleans Mint, ...	174,185
	$1,175,003
Add the amount deposited at the Philadelphia Mint, to the 15th inst., ...	87,392
Deposits of 1848, ...	44,177
Total deposits as far as ascertained, . . .	$1,306,572

16*th.* The ceremonies, in honour of the memory of Ex-President Polk, took place in Philadelphia.

The eulogium was pronounced by the Hon. George M. Dallas.

Subsequently, at Boston, on the 25th, funeral solemnities were celebrated, and Judge Woodbury delivered the eulogium.

The ship Louis Philippe sailed from Baltimore for San Francisco, with the frames of sixty-four houses ready to be put up, and merchandise valued at $100,000.

She had also on board the observatories and instruments of the astronomical expedition to the southern hemisphere, under charge of assistants—

Passed Midshipman Archibald MacRae;
Passed Midshipman H. C. Hunter.

A fire occurred in Allegheny city, and in consequence of the bad conduct of the firemen, who refused to act and would not suffer other persons to check the progress of the flames, thirty houses and a church were burnt.

At the same time there was a fire at Mauch Chunk, which is said to have destroyed property valued at $150,000.

20*th.* The Boston papers of this date contain the following interesting statement concerning a green-house curiosity, in the possession of Mr. Allen, of Salem:

"Mr. Allen has a *fig tree* that is a curiosity. It fills the entire back wall of one of his houses, and is trained in the same way as the peach, the branches stretching right and left from the trunk some thirty or forty feet, and is very vigorous. The variety is the black fig of St. Michael. It is now in fruit with the third crop for the season. Upwards of 3,000 figs, by count, have been gathered the present season, and it is still yielding its delicious fruit in abundance. When fully ripe, this fig bursts with its own richness. The fruit is fine, and a good variety for forcing. There are several other varieties of figs growing in the houses, but none so prolific as the St. Michael.

"The growing of fruit under glass is quite extensive in Massachusetts, and a vast amount of wealth is invested in this delightful branch of industry. There is probably more fruit grown in this way in Massachusetts than in all the other States of the Union, and there is a ready demand for all that is grown."

20th. About this date some Indians in Florida committed numerous depredations on Indian river—making attacks on the settlements, plundering houses and firing on the inhabitants. The outrage produced great excitement in Florida; and, as we have heretofore noticed in the Register, a body of United States troops have been sent to Florida, under the command of General Twiggs, to repress further outrages and bring the offenders to punishment.

General Twiggs has had an interview with Bowlegs, the Seminole chief, who promised to deliver up the guilty persons, and to preserve peace with the United States.

25th. Several conflicts, with various success, occurred at this period between the Hungarians and their invaders, which we have recorded in another place. Processions in Hungary were formed by the ecclesiastics that greatly excited the people. They carried before them a colossal sword, and a flag on which was inscribed, "Death to the Austrians and Russians." The seat of the Magyar government was on a steamboat which passed up and down the river, and was defended by cannon.

At Pesth the Austrian General Haynau, who is noted for his severity, issued a proclamation that exhibits a cruel and vindictive spirit, odious in these enlightened days.

He tells the Hungarians,—

"We have again planted the imperial standard on your steeples. But our feelings are far different from what they were when we left you a short time ago. Doomed to death is every person, no matter of what rank or sex,—doomed to instant death on the spot of the crime, is every one who dares to assist the cause of the rebels by words, or by deeds, or by revolutionary dress; doomed to instant death is every one who dares to insult any of my soldiers, or of those of our allies; doomed to instant death is every one who enters into traitorous communication with the enemies of the crown, or who maliciously presumes by rumours to assist the rebellion, or to conceal weapons.

"If you heed not my warnings—if even a part of you should venture, with audacious insolence, to transgress my orders, then annihilation will be your lot. Then, making *all pay for one, and one for all,* will I regard *your lives and properties as forfeit,* in atonement for your crimes. Your *fair city,* inhabitants of Pesth, which is now partially touched with the traces of just punishment, will then be *reduced to a heap of ashes*—a monument of your treason and of its castigation. Believe me that I am a man of my word, whether to punish transgression or to reward merit.—*Pesth, July 24.*"

30th. The Christian Times makes the following statement:

"Dr. Giacinto Achilli has been arrested in Rome, and thrown into the inquisition. At eleven o'clock, P. M., on Monday, 30th July, three men in plain clothes took him into custody in the house where he was staying. They stated that they did so by order of the French prefect. They had no paper of authorization whatever. In other words, Dr. Achilli has been imprisoned, without any warrant, in the name of the French republic. The government of the city of Rome was, in point of fact, at that time in the hands of the authorities appointed by Gen. Oudinot.

"Dr. Achilli has been cast into one of the secret dungeons of the Holy Office. Our readers are aware that in these same dungeons the bones and other remains of former victims were brought to light in the beginning of 1849.

"Dr. Giacinto Achilli is a protestant of above five years' standing. Formerly 'Vicar of the Master of the Holy Palace,' under Gregory XVI., professor of theology and professor of moral philosophy at the college of the Minerea, he subsequently became a protestant, and is well known, both in England and many other parts of Europe, as one who, from conscientious motives, had quitted the Roman Catholic church. He exercised the right which the *de facto* constitution of Rome gave him to take up his residence there, and to labour in the dissemination of the Holy Scriptures, and in the propagation of his principles among those who were disposed to hear him."

The news at this date is interesting from the far West. From the *Salt Lake*, the settlement of the Mormons, we have a statement from A. W. Bubbit, who arrived at Council Bluffs, which we condense:

"The agricultural prospects of the country were very promising, and the settlers were in the enjoyment of excellent health.

"We learn that 15,000 emigrants had passed through the valley during the season, and that about 3,000 would winter there.

"Many of the emigrants had embraced the Mormon faith, and would settle in that section of the country.

"The surrounding tribes of Indians were very friendly, and had not offered to molest the whites.

"Merchandise was remarkably cheap, caused by many of the emigrants abandoning their wagons, goods, &c., so that they could travel with greater facility and reach their destination before the cold weather set in. Most of the articles thus left sell at one-fourth their value.

"Perkins & Tyler's trains, which were this side of Fort Laramie, had *stampeded* one hundred and fifty teams.

"These trains had picked up along the plains several persons who had been badly hurt.

"Mrs. Hawks was accidentally killed during the journey.

"General Wilson would winter in the valley.

"Major Simondson had established a government post at Smith's Works, on the Bear river.

The citizens of Great Basin had held a meeting and agreed to estab-

lish a provisional government.* They call their abode the State of
Deseret.

"Intelligence from the Upper Missouri states that the Omaha and
Pouci Indians had a battle on the 4th of August. The Poucis were
the aggressors. It appears, while hunting the day before, they killed
three of the Omaha tribe—which led to the battle. The Poucis were
defeated—losing 20 warriors, including their chief, 42 horses and much
other property. The Omahas lost 4 killed, 9 wounded.

"The Sacs and Foxes were about making war on the Pawnees."

From California we have the following items :—

The Boston Journal says that, several of the early shipments from
that city to California proved to be exceedingly profitable. For instance, a lot of wooden pails (twenty dozen) sold out there for $36 a
dozen—$720 for the lot. A frame house, which cost $62, sold for
$1,500. One-half of an invoice of wooden-ware, the whole of which
cost in Boston about $80, has sold for $720, and it is calculated that
the other half will sell for enough to make the whole invoice nett $1,500.

Mr. Albert Macy, who was one of the passengers in the Aurora,
from Nantucket, writes:—Time is worth, in San Francisco, from one
to two dollars an hour. I have taken thirty dollars for two days'
work, and thirty dollars for two and a half days' work this week. I
have still two *adobe* chimneys to build this week.

" We have sold off nearly all our things, and the following are some
of the prices that we got :—

"For our house, which cost at home, $100, we got $1,300 ; for the
tent, which cost $50, we got $250 ; our wagon cost $100, and sold
for $312 ; a cook stove, which cost $15, sold for $125 ; for 50 lbs. of
saleratus we got $150 ; (three dollars per lb. ;) for 1,500 lbs. of bread,
$165 ; for 100 lbs. of butter, $100 ; six bbls. of flour, $48 ; two bbls.
of pork, $30. We have sold nearly all our small stores, our whole
sales amounting to about $2,500. For one thousand poor sawed cedar
shingles we got $30.

" If any of my townsmen are coming to California, tell them to bring
only two suits of clothes, and those thick ones. I wish I had only
what I have got on. I can get fine white shirts for $5 per dozen.
Mechanics should bring their tools."

" Dry goods and clothing are very low, as most of the emigrants
bring clothes of their own. It costs fifty cents to have a shirt washed,
when you can buy as good a one as I ever wore, at auction, for 25
cents. You can purchase calico at from three to six cents per yard,
while it costs $25 to make a dress. So you see that labour is much the
highest commodity in the market, and, wherever it attaches, it makes
an exorbitant price. The best of beef can be bought for twelve cents

* See Chronicle for August for form of government.

per pound, but a dinner of roast beef costs about $1 50. An ordinary cook gets $12 per day and found; and a man gets $500 per month for driving a team."

August, 1849.

1st. In conformity with the proclamation of Gen. Riley to that effect, the election in California for settling the affairs of the government, was held to-day.* The Alta California describes the contest and the result in San Francisco. We give all the names and figures—they may be interesting to refer to hereafter.

"The election ordered by Gen. Riley took place yesterday. It was one of the most animated and spirited contests which San Francisco ever witnessed. Between the hours of 11, A. M., and sunset, 1,519 votes were taken. There were a great many tickets in the field, and the canvassing by the friends of each was ardent, yet proper and orderly. The whole day passed without disturbance of any character. Below will be found the figures from the official canvass, as furnished us by the judges and inspectors of election. Those candidates to whose names a star (*) is prefixed were elected:

Judge of the Superior Court—*Peter H. Burnett, 1,298; Kimball H. Dimmick, 212.

Prefect—*Horace Hawes, 913; William A. Buffum, 444: Clarence Livingston, 118.

Alcalde—*John W. Geary, 1,516.

Second Alcaldes—*Frank Turk, 1,005; *John T. Vioget, 936; J. Mead Huxley, 459; Wm. Landers, 457; B. Simmons, 51.

Sub-Prefect—*Francisco Guerrero, 1,503; J. R. Curtis, 1,399; William H. Davis, 97.

For Town Council—*Talbot H. Green, 1,510; *Henry A. Harrison, 1,491; *Alfred J. Ellis, 1,354; *Stephen Harris, 1,323; *Thos. B. Winston, 1,052; *John Townsend, 1,052; *Rodman M. Price, 840; *William H. Davis, 835; *Bezer Simmons, 825; *Samuel Brannan, 823; *William M. Stewart, 815: *G. B. Post, 691; John H. Merrill, 616; Wm. C. Parker, 528; Thomas J. Agnew, 526; M. L. Mott, 481; F. D. Kohler, 472; T. W. Perkins, 439; J. P. Haven, 405; Moses G. Leonard, 384; H. H. Booker, 303; J. H. Peoples, 124; J. V. Plume, 170; R. Haley, 144; A. J. Grayson, 108; S. A. Wright, 84.

Delegates to the Convention—*Edward Gilbert, 1,512; *Myron Norton, 1,436; *Wm. M. Gwin, 1,073; *Joseph Hobson, 839; *Wm. M. Stewart, 833; John A. Patterson, 520; Jonathan D. Stevenson, 495; E. Gould Buffum, 451; A. H. Sibley, 184; William Burgoyne, 54; A. C. Peachy, 35.

Supernumerary Delegates—*Wm. D. M. Howard, 876; *Francis J. Lippitt, 874; *A. J. Ellis, 872; *Francisco Sanchez, 872; *Rod-

---

* See afterwards a more recent account of the convention.

man M. Price, 871; S. W. Haight, 489 ; Wm. M. Smith, 430 ; J. B. Bidleman, 431 ; A. C. Peachy, 40; Scattering, 31.

As we have yet to hear from the district of San Jose, it is not certain that Judge Burnett is elected. Judge Dimmick will receive the undivided support of his district, undoubtedly; but we do not think the vote, in its varied precincts, will overcome Burnett's majority, which is now 1,086.

These officers, elected as above, will continue in office until the first of January, 1850, when their places will be supplied by the officers elected at the regular election to be held next November. The salaries are fixed by the governor, but cannot exceed, for Superior Judges, $4,000 per annum; for Prefects, $2,500; and for other Judges, $1,500. The salaries will be paid out of the civil fund accruing from customs, unless otherwise ordered from Washington.

MONTEREY, (CALIFORNIA,) August 1, 1849.

The measures for settling the affairs of our government proposed in Gen. Riley's proclamation, have met with approbation throughout the country, and to-day has been the day of election for delegates to a Convention, to meet on the 1st of September in this town, to form a State constitution, and also for local magistrates in the different districts.

The delegates chosen in this town yesterday were: Messrs. Thomas O. Larken, H. W. Halleck, C. S. Botts, Lewis Dent, and Parifiew Ord."

We have another important entry to make, at this date, in relation to the proposed new *State of Deseret*, embracing the Mormon country about Salt Lake. We copy from the Bulletin:

"The Mormons residing in the valley of the Great Salt Lake have framed a constitution for a state government, which is to be submitted to Congress at its next session, and which is to govern them until Congress shall authorize some other form of government. The document is the result of the labours of a convention, held in their city in March last, of inhabitants residing in that portion of California lying east of the Sierra Nevada. They have chosen as the title of their state, the 'State of Deseret,' a *Mormon* epithet for the '*Honey Bee*,' significant of industry and its kindred virtues.

"The constitution is in the usual form of such documents among our new States. The three departments of government, legislative, judicial and executive, are established. The legislative is to consist of two houses, the members of which are to be 'free white male citizens of the United States,' and bound by oath to a support of the constitution of the same. A governor and lieutenant governor, with the customary officers, compose the executive, and the judiciary consists of a supreme court, with such other tribunals as the legislature shall establish.

"The Declaration of rights guaranties a perfect freedom to worship

God according to the dictates of conscience, and the legislature cannot establish any one religion, or interfere with any man's mode of worship, provided 'he does not disturb the public peace, nor disturb others in their religious worship.' Not a word is said about slavery, and as the Mormons are all, or nearly all, from free states, the probability is that the idea of introducing slaves into their territory has not been entertained at all.

"These are the main features of this interesting document, and their liberal, enlightened character must please all American citizens. The general assembly adopted the instrument in July, and elected Almon W. Babbitt as their delegate and representative to Congress, to urge upon that body the admission of the new state into the Union."

By the late California papers we learn that a census has recently been taken of the inhabitants of Oregon, which shows that the population of that Territory is 8,902. This number includes the foreign population, which amounts to less than 300 souls. Gov. Lane has issued a proclamation, fixing the number of members of Council and House of Representatives to which each county is entitled, and ordering their election on the first Monday of June. The election for a delegate to Congress is to be held on the same day. By the census there are 2,500 voters in the territory; but, in consequence of the absence of many of them in California, and by reason of there being some six candidates, it is supposed that the successful aspirant for the office of delegate will not receive more than two hundred votes. The rage among the people of Oregon for gold-hunting is greater than ever, and both the newspapers have suspended operations in consequence thereof.

1st. The Regents or "establishment" of the Smithsonian Institution held a meeting at the Smithsonian edifice.

PRESENT.

Zachary Taylor, President of the United States, and *ex officio* President of the Institution.
John M. Clayton, Secretary of State.
W. M. Meredith, Secretary of the Treasury.
Jacob Collamer, Postmaster General.
Thomas Ewbank, Commissioner of Patents.
W. W. Seaton, Mayor of Washington.
Joseph Henry, LL.D., Secretary of the Smithsonian Institution.
The President took the Chair.
This being the first meeting of the establishment, the Secretary gave an account of the Institution, of the plan of organization adopted by the Board of Regents, and of the progress made in carrying the several parts into operation.
The chairman of the executive committee, Mr. Seaton, gave to the meeting an account of the disbursements of the Institution, and the state of its funds.

The following gentlemen having been recommended by the Regents and officers of the Institution, and being duly considered by this meeting, were, on motion of Mr. Meredith, unanimously elected honorary members of the Smithsonian Institution, viz.:

Dr. Robert Hare, of Pennsylvania.
Albert Gallatin, of New York.
Dr. Benjamin Silliman, of Connecticut.
Washington Irving, of New York.

On motion of Mr. Clayton, it was

Resolved, That a committee of three be appointed to draught and report by-laws and regulations for the future meetings of the establishment.

Whereupon the President appointed Mr. Clayton, Mr. Meredith, and Mr. Seaton, the committee.

On motion of Mr. Collamer, the Secretary of the Institution was added to the said committee.

On motion, the meeting then adjourned to meet again on the call of the President.

(See Statistics for an account of this Institution.)

1st. The Queen of England prorogued Parliament, and immediately afterwards departed for Ireland, accompanied by Prince Albert and her children. The royal yachts reached Cork harbour on the 2d August. We have elsewhere noticed the manner of her reception. It was loyal and enthusiastic throughout.

The visits of the monarchs of England to Ireland have not been frequent. The first was by Henry II. in 1171—with a fleet of four hundred ships, and marching to Dublin with his army, he entertained the Irish chieftains with great state and magnificence. The second was by John in 1210, who robbed the Jews to pay the expenses of his visit. He was twelve days on the passage.

The third was the visit of Richard II. in 1394, with a large army. He subsequently made another visit. In 1689, James II. arrived there from France to make a stand for his kingdom. He held a parliament in Dublin. In June, 1690, William III. advanced to meet him, and in the battle of the Boyne defeated him and took the kingdom.

Cromwell's invasion can hardly be termed a royal visit. The next who came was George IV. in 1821.

Twenty-eight years afterwards, Queen Victoria with her whole family pays her Irish subjects a visit.

It is stated by those who have been curious to examine the fact, that during the greater number of the royal visits, the weather has been unusually boisterous and unpropitious.

A FINANCIAL OPERATION IN RUSSIA.—Five millions of rubles were lately transported from the fortress of St. Petersburg to the depot of the bank, to replenish its resources. The sum was taken from the vaults of the fortress in the presence of the assistants of the comptroller

of the empire, the members of the Committee of Revision, the delegates
from the Bourse, and the foreign commercial chargé d'affaires, and escorted to the bank by infantry and cavalry. The council of the bank,
in full sitting, and in the presence of the above gentlemen, assured
themselves that the sum was the same as that taken from the fortress.
The act relative to the removal was then signed by all present, and
among other things, establishes the fact that there remained in the
vaults of the fortress of Peter and Paul, after the removal of the five
million of rubles, 101,528,595 rubles.

2*d.* The Emperor of Russia, on a recent occasion, addressed to the
Russian and Polish catholic bishops the following speech:

"I do not wish for a new religion; a new sort of Catholic creed has
been invented abroad, and I desire that it may not be introduced into
my empire, because these innovators are the worst agitators, and without faith it is impossible that any thing can subsist. The west at this
moment offers a fair specimen of what men come to if they have no
faith—how great are the follies and absurdities which they commit.
Look at Rome; I predicted all that would happen there. Faith has
entirely disappeared in the west. The manner in which the Pope has
been treated is a plain proof the true faith exists in Russia alone, and
I hope (making the sign of the cross) that this holy faith may be maintained here. I told the late Pope Gregory XVI. things which he had
never heard from any body else. The present Pope is a good man,
his intentions are excellent, but his principles savour too much of the
spirit of the age. The King of Naples is a good catholic; he had been
calumniated to the Pope, and now the Pope is compelled to have recourse to him."

Bishop Holowinski replied—"Your majesty, the Holy Father was
obliged to yield to circumstances and the spirit of the age."

The Emperor—"Very possibly; but all these disorders arise from
want of faith. I am not a fanatic, but I have firm faith. In the
west they have run to two extremes—fanaticism and impiety."

The following are the *ecclesiastical grants for Australia* as lately
apportioned:

"The sum of 30,000*l.* per annum in New South Wales had been
appropriated by parliament for the maintenance of religious ordinances,
and distributed between the churches of England, of Scotland, and of
Rome, and the Wesleyan Society. These appropriations the bill proposes to make perpetual, and in amount unalterable, save on the side
of increase. Of the 30,000*l.* devoted to public worship in New South
Wales, the Church of England, claiming 95,733 members, will have
an appropriation, by this measure, of 15,715*l.*—the Church of Rome,
numbering 56,262 members, will have 9,333*l.*—of Scotland, 21,909,
will get 3,634*l.*—Wesleyans, 7,935 members, and 1,316*l.*"

Two WILL CASES, which, in respect of the amount of property

involved, and peculiarity of the bequests, are very remarkable ones, have lately been before the Courts of Massachusetts and Pennsylvania for adjudication.

The first is a suit brought by the heirs at law of Edward B. Phillips, contesting the validity of his will, by which, among other legacies, $100,000 was left to Harvard University, to be applied to the support of the observatory attached to that institution. This suit originated from the following circumstances:

"Mr. Phillips, in 1837, became a resident of Lynn, living at Nahant, and in June, 1848, committed suicide at the Brattleboro' water cure establishment. The will bequeathed in usual form $100,000 to Charles Emory and Charles G. Loring, in trust, the interest of the same to be paid in quarterly instalments to Charles Beck and wife during their lives, and after their decease to Abby S. Beck and Theresa Phillips, his sisters; $100,000 to Harvard University, as a fund for one or more astronomical observers, or for the purchase of astronomical instruments, as may be thought desirable by the college corporation; $60,000 to Charles Emory and John H. Gray, or the survivor; the remainder of his property and all his personal effects to his cousin, William Phillips.

"The will was contested by the heirs at law upon the following grounds: 1st, that the will was made on the Lord's day, October 10, 1847; 2d, because E. B. Phillips was not of a sound mind at the time of making his will; 3d, that he was unduly influenced in the making and signing of said will; 4th, because said will is not attested by three competent witnesses, nor any competent witnesses; 5th, because the persons whose names are attested to said will are interested in the probate of the same; 6th, because the Court of Probate of Essex has not proper jurisdiction; 7th, because said will is not attested by the testator in the presence of three or more competent witnesses."

The other is the case of Hilyard et als. *vs.* Peter Miller, on a writ of error to the Common Pleas of Northampton county, before the Supreme Court of Pennsylvania, on a judgment obtained against the plaintiffs, in an action of ejectment brought by Peter Miller, defendant in error, in the court below, to test the will of the late Peter Miller, of Easton, the defendant's uncle.

Peter Miller, deceased, by his will gave all the residue of his estate, after some small legacies to trustees, with directions that it should be leased, loaned and invested, so that the income of his estate might form a fund for the purpose mentioned in his will. His purpose was to assist with loans of money on bond and mortgage, at interest, farmers and mechanics who want to purchase farms, or having purchased, want to pay for them, or make improvements in the borough of Easton, or townships adjacent. The estate is to accumulate so long as applications to borrow money continue. By this will it is further directed that if it should so happen, in the lapse of time, that the income of the estate fund should accumulate beyond the applications for such loans, and should be likely to remain so, and the amount thus unemployed would safely justify the undertaking, and when mechanics and others may be in want of employment, then an asylum shall be built out of the avails of the income fund, for the benefit of poor widows and single women, and the same be supported and maintained out of the means from said fund.

The heir at law contends that the will is void in law, because it creates a perpetuity, and if suffered to stand, would be injurious to the public welfare. That nothing is given in charity, or if any thing was intended, it is uncertain, both as to the amount of the fund devoted, and the time when it shall be applied. That the intention of the testator, which must govern, is at war with every rule of law on the subject of charitable uses. The plaintiffs in error contend that it is a charity, and must stand or fall upon the point, what was the intention of the testator? The estate is worth over three hundred thousand dollars, the whole of which is tied up by this very strange devise.

3*d*. This day was observed as a day of fasting, humiliation and prayer, throughout the United States, on the recommendation of the President, who had previously issued a proclamation to that effect. The following is a copy of that document:

"At a season when the Providence of God has manifested itself, in the visitation of a fearful pestilence, which is spreading its ravages throughout the land, it is fitting that a people, whose reliance has ever been on His protection, should humble themselves before His throne, and, while acknowledging past transgressions, ask a continuance of Divine mercy.

"It is, therefore, earnestly recommended that the first Friday in August, be observed throughout the United States, as a day of fasting, humiliation and prayer. All business will be suspended in the various branches of the public service on that day; and it is recommended to persons of all religious denominations to abstain, as far as practicable, from secular occupations, and to assemble in their respective places of public worship, to acknowledge the infinite goodness which has watched over our existence as a nation, and so long crowned us with manifold blessings; and to implore the Almighty, in His own good time, to stay the destroying hand which is now lifted up against us.

"Z. Taylor."

Under this date we deem it appropriate to record some interesting facts and incidents connected with "the visitation" to which the President has referred, and which will serve to mark its fatal progress and ravages; reserving for the Statistics, the tabular statements of mortality.

During the preceding summer months, the cholera raged throughout the United States to a fearful extent. In the Atlantic towns it was not so devastating as in 1832, but on the western rivers its sweep has been appalling. In the cities of St. Louis and Cincinnati the deaths sometimes amounted to 150 and 200 per day. At the beginning of July, a gentleman, writing from St. Louis, thus described the horrors of the pestilence:

"Calamities are all around us. Death is every where. Cholera is dealing its blows to the right and left, and thousands of our people have been hurried to their graves. A well man now, may be, an hour hence, a corpse. The sextons, the undertakers, and even the horses of the city, are worn out with the dreadful work of burial. Carts and furniture wagons have to supply the places of hearses, which, though numerous, are insufficient to carry out the coffins, though piled one upon another.

"Many dead bodies lie, without a friend to execute the rites of interment, until a public officer or a sister of charity comes to put them in the ground. Some persons, to save expenses which they are not able to bear, bury their friends in the woods or on the sand-bars of the river. Many is the house, lately full of inhabitants, that now has scarcely one left to tell the story of the departed. Husband and wife will take their tea together at evening, and before the next morning, one or both is ready for the grave.

"Some of the sextons, overtasked, bury the dead at half the usual depth. The city government have abdicated their powers before an indignant populace, and the duties of the board of health are devolved upon a committee of citizens. The public school-houses are turned into hospitals, and the chief business of the living is to take care of the sick and dying, and to bury the dead. Many members of the city government, and probably not less than 10,000 of the citizens, have fled. The stillness of the Sabbath reigns, while death is doing its work. The newspapers do not, it is said, report half the cases, because all the forms of law are paralyzed, and officers do not discharge their duties. A dullness, nervousness and lack of energy are manifested by every one. The atmosphere is hot and humid. Flies swarm in myriads. Vegetation grows with the rankest luxuriance, and animal life sinks proportionably."

If more be wanting to complete the sad picture, we have the following description by the correspondent at St. Louis of the Buffalo Express:

"You can have no proper idea of the ravages of the fell disease or its effects. The city, from a population of near 70,000 is now reduced to not over 30,000. Every body has fled but those too poor to leave, or whose business compelled them to remain. The streets are deserted, except by the hearse and the mournful procession moving to the gloated cemeteries. The blackened ruins, instead of having been removed and giving way to new places of business, as they would but for the pestilence, now present a sad spectacle of desolation. Few steamboats are running, and those go away loaded with the affrighted population, and bring back no passengers. The deaths, as reported for several weeks, have been from 100 to 160 per day; while it is conceded by all who know, that from one-quarter to one-third are not reported, so that the actual number of deaths, for some time past, has not been much less than 200 per day—or say 1,200 a week—and that too in a population of from 30,000 to 35,000.   Of course, hearses are constantly to be seen in the streets, and the entire night is spent in burying the dead.

From *Cincinnati* the details received were of the most mournful kind.   One paper stated:

"The alarming augmentation of interments that are daily occurring, the flight of families from the city, the consternation that is depicted upon every countenance, and the united testimony of all our physicians, admonish us that far more systematic and efficient measures must be taken, both by the people and the city authorities, before we can look for any amelioration of the epidemic.

"Our reporter, on returning from St. Joseph's cemetery, on Friday evening, met nine funerals, the last one unattended by any train, but consisted simply of a rude wagon, in which the rough coffin of an adult was placed at length.   An aged woman was leaning upon the coffin on one side and weeping, and an aged man sat upon the other side, the tears also coursing down his cheeks.   He was driving the horse.   This was all of that mournful attendance upon the grave—a father and mother forced by poverty to perform the funeral rites of a beloved son."

Another paper refers to numerous rumours it has heard of persons supposed to have died of cholera recovering while preparations were being made for their interment; and mentions, as one of them, that one of the pall-bearers at a funeral declared, while walking by the hearse, that he heard a noise in the coffin.   The hearse was stopped, the coffin opened, and the person who was about to be interred found breathing. He was conveyed home, and, it was stated, would probably recover.

For a period of eight weeks, the mortality in the city was 4,628. Another account says 4,114.   At one time there were 2,500 houses vacant.

From *Dayton*, Ohio, a flourishing place, connected with Cincinnati by canal, the accounts were truly deplorable:

"On account of the fatality attending families in which it made its appearance, the idea that the disease is contagious has become prevalent.   Physicians themselves are panic-stricken—patients suffering from disease are left to die alone and neglected; husbands desert wives in this fearful extremity, and daughters forget what they owe to their mothers."

Sandusky city, another place in Ohio, suffered terribly from the cholera. The account from that place stated that the epidemic had reached a crisis which threatened to produce most disastrous consequences:

"Of a population of 3,000, there are not more than 700 remaining. The deaths for the last two days amount to above one hundred, and it is still on the increase.   Most of the inhabitants who have escaped the dreadful malady have left the city in dismay. Business of every description is entirely suspended, and the various hotels, together with the post-office and public stores are all closed. Many of our physicians had fallen victims to the disease, and those who have escaped its ravages have precipitately fled from the region of death. The sick are suffering in a dreadful manner for the want of medical aid and assistance. The living are not only unable to attend to the wants of the sick, but cannot bury their dead. There are none to be found to dig graves or make coffins. The markets are entirely deserted, and the few inhabitants remaining are under the necessity of sending to Cleveland and other ports on the Lake for provisions and medical assistance."

Birmingham, a flourishing town in the vicinity of Pittsburgh, was desolated by the scourge. The Pittsburgh Gazette says:

"The disease in this ill-fated town is rapidly on the increase, and is now spreading through all parts of it. The greatest consternation prevails, and few who can leave their houses remain in them. The stores are closed, and the streets blocked up by the furniture wagons and carts, removing families into the country, while the manufactories are, with very few exceptions, shut up."

The following affecting incident is recorded in the western papers:

"A family near Charleston, Miami county, Ohio, were last week attacked with cholera. First the father died—then three of the children and the mother were taken—a boy of thirteen being the only one remaining in health. The sick children all died on Thursday; and during that night, with the three dead bodies lying in the room, the boy, alone and unaided, faithfully watched and nursed his mother! On the next day, some neighbours came in, gave a decent burial to the deceased, and were compelled, so noxious and offensive was the room in which the woman lay, to remove her, for the time, out of doors to the shade of a tree near by. The boy was taken to Tippecanoe by some friends, and remained there for a few days, was seized with cholera, and died after a short illness! The mother is recovering; but the noble-hearted boy, who so faithfully watched with her during that fearful night, has gone to his reward."

The New York Courier and Enquirer contains another touching instance of the desolation that has fallen on families:

"A gentleman extensively engaged in manufacturing, told us yesterday, that a fine little fellow, twelve or fourteen years old, recently came to him and asked for work. He told him he had none to give him—but was prompted, by the tears which started to his eyes, as he was turning away, to inquire into his circumstances. The boy told him where he had lived, in the Tenth avenue—and that within a few days his father, mother, two brothers, two sisters, and an apprentice boy, who lived with them, had died of the cholera, and that he was the sole survivor of them all! Such an appeal was not to be resisted; the little fellow soon found a place, and is now at work."

We add another orphan story equally affecting; this scene was in the same city:

"A clergyman attending the funeral of a woman, who died in Wall street, on the 11th inst., says:—'I found the two children sitting by the side of the coffin, and as no other individual was present, the desolate room was as silent as the tomb. I offered a short prayer, and at the close of each sentence, the children repeated that prayer, word for word. They had been accustomed in that manner to repeat their mother's prayers. They then waited for the privilege of riding on the hearse, to accompany the remains of their mother to the place of burial.'"

Sometimes a parent was left alone, his whole family being swept away by the pestilence.

"A few days since, a child belonging to a young mechanic residing in the upper part of the city, was attacked with the cholera, and died in a few hours. On the succeeding day the second child was attacked with the malady, and on the following day she also died. The third child, the youngest and the only one remaining, was taken down the same day, and while the mother was attending upon her, she also was attacked by the same disease, brought on by care and anxiety, and another day had scarcely elapsed, before she, too, was numbered with the dead. The remaining child lingered for a day or two longer, when it followed its mother to the world of spirits. Thus, in the short space of a week, was a husband and father deprived of wife and children."

We have said, that in some instances whole families were swept away; we copy from the Cairo Delta, (Ill.) one of those instances:

"We are informed that a week or two since, in a little settlement between Ohio city and Charleston, Mo., every member of three families, numbering thirteen persons in all, died of the cholera. Their names were Hill, Welch and Brecken. A doctor named Myers, who had been attending them, was also taken with the disease, and died alone. The bodies were found in the houses, and in too decomposed a state to be placed in the coffins provided for them. They were buried as they were found. The three or four inhabitants not taken with the disease fled. In all the instances of great fatality of which we have read, resulting from the cholera, this appears comparatively the greatest."

Had we room, we might increase the mournful account—we might add to the list of the sufferers many more instances of the fatal progress of the pestilence. It was not confined to any class or age. The poor and the rich alike were its subjects. It respected not persons—the temperate and the intemperate fell before it. It struck down some of the finest intellects and noblest spirits in the land—Gaines, Duncan and Henrie, Ogden, Lawrence, Woolley, Lord, Scovel, Lyon, Hamilton, Griswold, and many others,—the brave, the learned, and the pious.

And of the devoted and fearless physicians who attended the sick, and the dying, throughout all the scenes of this gloomy period, numbers lost their lives from the effects of incessant watchings. Such were Brainerd, Lane, Barbour, Hadduck, Harrison, Lathrop, and many besides them, who regarded not fatigue, labour, health, or life itself, under the promptings of a stern sense of duty, and a self-sacrificing spirit.

The ravages of the pestilence were not confined to our own country. The angel of death, who seemed to have come across the Atlantic to us, re-visited the eastern world during the past summer with more fatal effect in some places than at the first visitation. Especially was this observable in England and France. In the cities of Paris and London nearly one thousand have died in a day. The ravages of the disease were felt throughout Europe—Berlin in Prussia, and Birmingham in England, are said to have been the only large cities exempted. Every where, too, as in this country, it struck down its victims from all ranks and descriptions of persons without discrimination. In France, as in the United States, the President of the republic was attacked by it. A distinguished Marshal of France, and Catalini, who had been the most brilliant star in the musical world, were its victims.

We have recorded thus much in this place concerning this fearful pestilence, which, with its attendant scourge, war, has made the year 1849 emphatically a year of death and mourning. In this notice we have intended to do no more than to chronicle its advent, and by the instances we have given of its fatal visits, to exhibit the virulence of its attacks. It is perhaps true that it was not so violent in some places, especially on the Atlantic coast, as in 1832; but on the western rivers it was equally if not more so. Under the statistical head we shall give some figures and tables showing the extent of the mortality, and from which can be collected the data for determining comparative results.

9*th.* The President of the United States, Gen. Zachary Taylor, left the seat of government on a northern tour. He was accompanied by Dr. Wood of the army, a member of his family, and several other gentlemen. At the rail-road depot, near Baltimore, he was received with acclamation by a large concourse of people, and was greeted with much enthusiasm on his arrival in the city. On the 10th he left Baltimore, and proceeded to York and Lancaster, Pa. On his way he was met by Governor Johnston, with a committee of citizens, who welcomed him to the State. When he arrived at Lancaster, in answer to the address made to him, he said:

"I have come to Pennsylvania with no political purposes in view, but that I might witness in person her agricultural, manufacturing, and mining operations, and I am gratified to know that thus far the people have welcomed me, without distinction of party, to this renowned commonwealth. I have come among you, too, in a plain and unostentatious manner, feeling that I should nevertheless receive kindness and hospitality wherever I visit or sojourn. In this spirit the people met me at my first entrance into the State, and in this spirit they have escorted me from place to place."

At Harrisburgh he was received with much courtesy by all classes of citizens. At Carlisle he became indisposed, but rallied sufficiently to go on to Chambersburgh, and to Bedford Springs, where he seemed to fully recover his health. At Pittsburgh he arrived on the 18th, and met with a very flattering reception from the citizens, headed by Hon. Walter Forward. After leaving Pittsburgh, en route to Erie, the same gratifying expression of good feeling on the part of his fellow-citizens was tendered to him at all places through which he passed. When he came near to Erie he was found to be very ill, his disorder having returned, and it became necessary to convey him rapidly into the town to private lodgings. Here he became seriously ill, so that fears were entertained for his life. The Vice President left Buffalo and went on to Erie to be with him.

The crowd who had assembled to see him were disappointed, and indeed the termination of his journey was destined to be entirely different from that which was expected when he left home. It was his intention to have passed through the State of New York, and to have attended the great agricultural fair which was to be held at Syracuse on the 12th September; but his extreme debility, and the precarious state of his health, forbade the accomplishment of this purpose. He therefore hastened to Niagara Falls, passed rapidly through Buffalo, Albany, New York city, Philadelphia, and Baltimore, and arrived at Washington after an absence of four weeks. It was matter of surprise to many that the President should have hazarded a tour during a season so especially unpropitious, whilst the air, every where, was tainted with the epidemic poison, and the excitement consequent upon receptions rendered him more than usually liable to an attack.

Since his return we are gratified to learn that he has regained his wonted health.

9th. A very serious rail-road accident occurred on the New York and Philadelphia road. As the morning train of cars from Philadelphia was approaching Princeton, the locomotive, tender, and the truck of the baggage-car, were precipitated into the canal, by the switch near the bank having been maliciously turned for the special purpose of causing an accident. Fortunately the passenger cars maintained their position upon the track, but the sudden check to a speed of about twenty miles an hour, caused the way car to be crushed into the body of the forward deck car, carrying death and dismay to those unfortunate passengers in that portion of the train. Two persons were crushed to death, and eighteen others more or less injured.

11th. The President of the United States issued his proclamation warning all citizens against connecting themselves with an armed expedition which it was supposed was about to be fitted out from the United States to invade the island of Cuba. (See History and Documents.)

13th. The Hungarian General, Georgey, surrendered his whole army, between 30,000 and 40,000 men, to the Russian General, Rudiger. The surrender was made near Grosswardein, at the village of Saellosz, and was without conditions—Georgey only claiming, as a favour, the intervention of Field Marshal Paskiewitch, the Russian general-in-chief.

Previous to this surrender of Georgey, it appears that Kossuth and his ministers, sensible of the desperate condition of affairs, had resigned all power, civil and military, into the hands of Arthur Georgey. Upon this transfer being made, Georgey issued a proclamation to the Hungarians, in which he says:

"The provisional government has ceased to exist. The governor and the ministers have voluntarily resigned office, and government is broken up. Under these circumstances a military dictatorship is a necessity, which I assume provisionally, together with the civil power. Citizens! whatever can be done for the country, in our position of extremity, I shall endeavour to accomplish, either peaceably or by force of arms, whichever necessity requires; but, at any rate, so that the enormous sacrifices already made shall be lightened."

To the commander of the strong fortress of Comorn, General Klapka, he addressed a letter requiring him to surrender that strong hold of the Hungarians into the hands of the Austrians. We give his reasons for this order in his own language:

"General, the die is cast—our hopes are crushed! Our power has been broken by the House of Hapsburg-Lorraine, aided by the armies of Russia. The struggles and the sacrifices of our great nation were fruitless, and it were madness to persevere. General, you will think my actions at Vilagosh mysterious and even incredible. I will explain my motives to you and to the world. I am a Hungarian. I love my country above all things, and I followed the dictates of my heart, which urged me to restore peace to my poor and ruined country, and thus save it from perdition.

"General, this is my motive for what I did at Vilagosh. Posterity will judge me.

"General, by virtue of the dignity of Dictator, which the nation conferred on me by the (dissolved) parliament, I summon you to follow my example, and by an immediate surrender of the fortress of Comorn, to end a war of which the protraction would for ever crush the greatness and the glory of the Hungarian nation."

Comorn had a garrison of 20,000 men, and one year's provision. The garrison refused to surrender, and at the latest accounts was resolved to hold out, and "laugh a siege to scorn." But if the whole country submits, they too must in the end yield.

Kossuth with Dembinski, Perczel and others, succeeded in escaping, and reached the Turkish dominions, where they were protected by the Sultan. The English minister at Constantinople is said to have interfered in their behalf. A story has found its way into the papers, and seems to be credited, that Kossuth carried off with him the Hungarian crown and the State jewels. Of this crown, a curious account is related, from which it would appear that it was originally presented by the Pope 800 years ago to the sovereign of Hungary—that it was once packed away in a cask—then stolen by a maid—pawned by a Queen to the Emperor of Germany—was stolen again and fell into the hands of the Turks—was returned by Solyman—was given to the Emperor Ferdinand, and at last restored to the Hungarians.

The statements concerning the submission of the Hungarians, and the flight of Kossuth and his compatriots, are still confused and involved in much uncertainty at the time we are writing. In our next number we shall be able to give a more satisfactory and definite narrative of these interesting events.

14th. A very singular optical illusion was observed on the Catskill mountains. The following account is written by an eye-witness:

"The afternoon was a memorable one for the mountain. The optical illusion of last Monday week was reproduced, but more transcendently beautiful than it had ever appeared before. It is the third time in twenty years that this extraordinary phenomenon has been perceived. Mrs. A. and myself were sitting on the rock in front of the piazza, when she suddenly exclaimed, "Look, look!" I did so, and the whole hotel was surrounded in the cloud before us. The whole house was assembled immediately, and we ran out to the point of rock from which the phenomenon of last Monday had been perceived. We were scarcely there a minute when a beautifully arched rainbow was formed in the cloud, exactly in the centre of which was seen the entire group, precisely as they stood on the ledge of the rock. It was not merely their shadows, but the entire form of each person in the group was distinctly visible; each person saw the whole group, not merely the reflection of his own image. This lasted about five minutes, when the rainbow disappeared, and the phenomenon of Monday last succeeded; each person saw his own shadow, of huge dimensions, reflected on the cloud and surrounded by a halo of light, but was unable to see that of his neighbour. I shall never in my life see any thing of the kind again, and if I had not seen it, I could have formed no conception of its effect; it was perfectly thrilling. The poems of Ossian, the Children of the Mist, the Death Fetch of the Germans, the spectral phantoms that were fearful visions to less enlightened ages, were all realized distinctly and palpably before us. This visit to the Catskills has revealed to me more of the wonders of nature than all else that I have seen put together."

15th. The convention for the union of the two sections of the democratic party, (Hunkers and Barnburners,) met at Rome, New York. The leaders on both sides were present, and though there was no formal settlement of differences, yet they progressed so far towards it, as afterwards, in subsequent conventions, to agree upon union tickets to be supported at the next election. The consequence will probably be, that in the coming conflicts the two great parties, (Whig and Democrat,) will battle with undivided strength for the supremacy. A united front in the one will oblige harmony and increased energy in the other. The strife of party can never cease in our country as long as the press is free,—the right of private opinion unrestricted,—the people sovereign, and the desire of office prompts men to struggle for power.

16*th*. The following are the details of a sad disaster in the harbour of Mazatlan:

"The French ship Roland, Captain Bajoux, was wrecked upon the Creston rocks, in our harbour. She was lying at anchor, bound for San Francisco, when a severe tempest sprang up in the night of the 10th, which resulted as above. Out of forty-five passengers, consisting of Americans, French, Mexicans, Spaniards, and the others who had already gone on board, twenty-five have perished, having most of them drowned—some, however, being severely bruised and wounded. Five of the sailors managed to get off into a boat, but suddenly the Roland went to pieces, and carried them down with her. The English frigate Champion rendered prompt and energetic aid to the sufferers. Eight of the passengers were picked up and saved by the British officers, whose conduct deserves the highest praise. Two of those officers are reported to have jumped overboard into the sea to rescue some drowning persons from the ill-fated ship. A man named Paul Adams was one out of eight saved by the officers of the Champion."

16*th*. A company of United States troops, commanded by Captain H. B. Budd, had a fight with the Apache Indians at Los Vegas. It was represented as a hand to hand conflict. Lieut. Burnside and two others of the troop were wounded. A considerable number of the Indians were sabred—six prisoners and thirteen horses were brought in.

Several riots recently occurred at Montreal, one especially on the night of the 14th inst., when about thirty persons went into La Fontain's house, broke open the gates and entered the garden. A number of shots were fired by the persons in the house, said to be a body of disguised mounted police.

A man named Mason was shot, ten slugs entering his body, killing him almost instantly. A number of others are said to have been wounded.

There is a growing feeling in favour of the independence of Canada, or its annexation to the Union. A plan is suggested for the partition of the country into three States. The Montreal Gazette propounds this scheme; and the following are stated to be the division and boundaries proposed:

1. The State of Canada West, to include the whole of Upper Canada

down to the foot of Lake Ontario. The population of this would be exclusively English, with the exception of some fifty or sixty thousand French, scattered over it or settled near Detroit.

2. The State of Canada East, to include the districts of Quebec and Three Rivers, with the exception of some of the southern townships. The population of this would be almost exclusively French, with the exception of Quebec, where the Irish labouring classes are pretty numerous, but go with the French—the mercantile classes having no political influence, and indeed being quite apathetic.

3. The State of Central Canada, to consist of the Ottawa district, and of that portion of Upper Canada which lies between the Ottawa and the St. Lawrence, of the district of Montreal and of that of St. Francis, leaving to Canada East the bordering parishes of purely French character, and taking on the south the townships of British law and settlement.

21st. The American Association for the promotion of Science, opened their meeting at Cambridge, Mass., Professor Henry presiding. A paper on the Aurora Borealis was read by Prof. Secchi, of Georgetown College; one on the polar plant, or Rosin Wood, whose leaves stand with their edges north and south, by Prof. Gray; a communication by the president on the Altona Observatory; a lecture on the structure of coral animals, by Prof. Agassiz; a paper on the prime meridian, by Lieutenant Davis. Many other interesting subjects were brought before the association, and it was agreed that the next meeting shall be held at New-Haven.

22d. The meeting of the Peace Congress was held in Paris this day. About 1,500 persons were present. The celebrated M. Victor Hugo in the chair. The flags of all nations adorned the hall. The stars and stripes of the United States occupied a conspicuous position, floating side by side with the tri-colour of France and the English union-jack. Mr. Cobden and his party were received with applause, and the American gentlemen were saluted with enthusiastic cheers. The names of parties who gave in their adhesion to the principles of the Congress were read, and then M. Victor Hugo's speech, amidst intense applause. It is described as an exquisite piece of composition and replete with the most benevolent sentiments.

Among the gentlemen present from England were Messrs. Cobden, Villiers, Hindley, Sturge, &c. Some of the French members were Victor Hugo, Horace Say, Joseph Garnier, Michel Chevalier, M. L. Archevêque, &c.

Among the American names were Elihu Burritt, Hon. C. Durkie, Rev. A. Mahon, President of Oberlin Institute, Rev. Dr. Allen, formerly President of Bowdoin College, Professor Walker, Rev. P. Berry, &c. From Belgium, M. Vischers.

Mr. Cobden proposed to restrain war by cutting off supplies—by appealing to the consciences of all men who have money to lend to withhold the sinews of war. Among the speakers was a coloured man of the name of Brown, who described himself as an escaped slave from the United States.

The French Minister of Public Works invited the members to visit the palace of Versailles, which was accepted by 1,000; and the great fountains played, hitherto exhibited only to crowned heads. They had also an interview with the President of France.

The Congress adjourned on the 25th. Victor Hugo, the president, delivered a farewell address, before quitting the chair, which was received with tremendous acclamations. It happened to be the anniversary of the massacre of St. Bartholomew, of which the eloquent chairman was reminded only a short time before he spoke, and of which coincidence he availed himself in a masterly manner. A correspondent of the Times, speaking of the incident, says:—

"He reminded his auditory that in the same city where streams of blood once flowed, and the tocsin of destruction was heard from the tower still standing near them, and where unheard of atrocities were committed in the name of religion, men were assembled on a mission of peace and love—men from distant countries, and members of various creeds. The Catholic and Protestant, the Quaker and the Presbyterian, grasped each other's hands in brotherly love, and the ministers of different forms of Christian worship led the way in that holy work. I never saw enthusiasm excited to such a pitch as at that moment. The acclamations died away only to be renewed again and again, and at length the Americans and English stood up and gave seven rounds of hurrahs."

26th. President Faustin Soulouque was crowned Emperor of Hayti. (See History.)

He is said to have sent $38,000 to England to purchase a crown. Heretofore he has been represented as a man of a blood-thirsty and cruel nature, who has put his enemies to death without mercy. He promises now to rule according to law. These are his words:

"Full of confidence in the Supreme Will, which on two solemn occasions has evinced for me its benign solicitude, I preserve the happy hope of being able worthily to respond to your expectations, by maintaining all the institutions which guaranty the rights of citizens; by causing order and peace to reign in the Empire; by assuring the triumph of the principles of liberty and equality; and by maintaining, at the price of all sacrifices, the independence of the country, and the integrity and indivisibility of its territory.

"Haytiens! The Legislative body will at once be called on to engage in the revision of the constitutional compact, in order to put it in harmony with the new order of things; I will observe its prescriptions and cause them to be observed; I swear it before God and man."

Accounts were received from the Dominican Republic:

The National Congress has decreed to Santana the title of Liberator and General-in-chief of the Dominican forces, in return for his efficient services.

Buenaventura Baez, member of the Senate, has been elected President of the Republic by the electoral college, and proclaimed by Congress on the 18th August; he would no doubt accept.

Perfect tranquillity prevailed. Much impatience was felt for the installation of the new President, as great changes in the progress of affairs were expected under the new administration.

Nothing was positively known in relation to the question of the "French Protectorate," but, under all the circumstances, it was difficult to believe that France would interfere in the affairs of the country.

27th. A steamboat disaster happened off the Coast of Florida, west of Egmont Bay: A large steam vessel, the *Mary Kingsman*, chartered by the government to carry thither 110 mules and 20 horses, having on board about 33 persons, teamsters and hands, exploded one of her boilers, by which nineteen men were killed and eight wounded —the latter brought in, of whom two have died since. All the horses and mules were so badly scalded or injured that they were thrown overboard.

31st. Further interesting news from California up to this date were received by the Empire City steamer, which arrived at New York, and brought *nearly half a million in specie.*

The number of gold washers on the streams had increased. The Peruvians and Chilians had been pretty thoroughly driven out from the middle and north forks, and there seems to be a disposition to drive them altogether from the mining country. Some of the old miners are doing better than they did last year—and all have been successful, but there has been considerable suffering. It is hard work to mine, but it is said to give a good appetite and sound sleep. The miners average about an ounce a day.

The number of emigrants who arrived by sea at San Francisco in the month of August, were 3806 males, and 87 females—of these, 3385 were Americans. On the 30th August, there were 61,385 tons of shipping in the harbour.

The convention for framing a State constitution for California assembles at Monterey 31st August. The composition of the body, as far as known, is as follows:

DISTRICT OF SAN FRANCISCO.—*Regular.*—Edward Gilbert, Myron Norton, Wm. M. Gwin, Joseph Hobson, William M. Stewart.

Supernumeraries.—W. D. M. Howard, Francis J. Lippitt, A. J. Ellis, Francisco Sanchez, Rodman M. Price.

DISTRICT OF SAN JOSE.—*Regular.*—Joseph Aram, K. H. Dimmick, J. D. Hoppe, Antonio M. Pico, Elam Brown.

Supernumeraries.—Pedro Sansevain, Julian Hanks, A. M. Pico.

DISTRICT OF MONTEREY.—*Regular.*—H. Wager Halleck, Thomas O. Larkin, Lewis S. Dent, Chas. T. Botts, Passificus Ord.

DISTRICT OF SONOMA.—*Regular.*—Joel P. Walker, Robert Semple, L. W. Boggs, M. G. Tallejo.

DISTRICT OF SAN DIEGO.—*Regular.*—Miguel de Pedrorena, Henry Hill.

Supernumeraries.—Cave S. Couts, John Forster, Wm. Richardson.

The convention was said to be composed of men of intelligence and integrity.

A letter from San Francisco says that Giving and King will go to the United States Senate, and that a constitution will be formed and a legislature elected by the 1st of November.

Gen. Smith had gone on an expedition to the mountains of the Sierra Nevada.   Colonel Fremont was at Monterey.

Lieutenant Beale, bearer of despatches, had arrived at San Francisco and proceeded to Gen. Smith's head-quarters.   The Hon. Thos. Butler King had been dangerously ill of bilious fever, but had so far recovered as to be considered out of danger.   Gen. Riley had also been sick.

The following is the religious intelligence from San Francisco.

The following churches have been organized in the city:

1. Roman Catholic—Service administered every Sabbath at their church on Vallejo street.

2. First Baptist, Rev. O. C. Wheeler, pastor—Service every Sabbath at their new church on Washington street, near the corner of Stockton.

3. First Presbyterian, Rev. Albert Williams, pastor—Service every Sabbath at their large tent on Dupont street, near Pacific.

4. Protestant Episcopal, Rev. F. Mines, rector—Service every Sunday, for the present, at the house of J. H. Merrill, Esq.

5. Methodist.—We understand that this denomination has commenced the erection of a church at the head of Washington street.

6. Congregational.—The Rev. T. D. Hunt has consented to officiate occasionally for this church until the first of November next.

In connexion with the above, it is proper we should state that Sabbath schools are established in the Baptist, Presbyterian, and Episcopal churches, and there is also one attached to the chaplaincy.

31st.   Further particulars from the far west.   In addition to what we have already selected from the California letters, we insert the following:

"Upon the San Joaquin and its tributaries there are some twenty thousand men now at work, who will earn, by January next, some $20,000,000.   According to this calculation, this country will yield not less than $40,000,000 annually—an income unprecedented in the annals of the world.   A word to those about starting for this region.

Stout, hard-working men are those who acquire the most gold. Boarding-tents are plenty all over the mineral country, and board varies from $3 to $5 per day. Parties, of from three to five, are the most successful. All large parties break up from a want of unity of feeling, after reaching here; in fact, they are unprofitable. Machinery is of no use, and does not sell for the freight it costs. The flourishing cities of Sacramento, Stockton, Benecia, and others, are the best evidence of the immense value of this wealth, in populating a land that only needs labourers to make it one of the finest grazing and agricultural countries in the world.".

The Expedition to the Salt Lake.—By letters very recently received, says the Intelligencer, news is brought that the exploring party, under command of Captain Stansbury, of the Topographical Engineers, now *en route* for the great Salt Lake in Upper California, entered Fremont's South Pass in the Rocky Mountains on the 5th of August. The party were all in good health and fine spirits, having accomplished two-thirds of the journey towards their destined field of exploration. They pursue the ordinary Oregon route as far as Fort Hall, where they leave it, and, turning short to the south, enter the valley of the great Salt Lake and its tributaries.

Letters from Gen. Collier's party, bound for California, dated Santa Fe, August 16th, have been received. They expected to leave on the 18th, and to be at San Diego in forty days or less. They go by the Southern route, direct to the mouth of Salt river and the Gila. The writers speak of the pilgrimage across the plains as one of excessive toil. Life on the prairies is any thing but a trip of pleasure. One letter, published in the Cincinnati Gazette, says:

"Thousands will now testify that *the truth has been suppressed,* and point with sorrowing hearts to the numerous graves along the line of their march as evidence that toil, privation, sickness, and death, go with the train of the poor, deceived, and starving emigrants. Even at this point, where comparatively but few have congregated, I witness the destitute and broken in spirit, far from home or friends, and without the means of going forward, or of returning. Many have found to their cost that it would have been far better to have staid at home, letting 'well enough alone.' I have conversed with hundreds 'going to California,' but I am yet to see the first man who had any settled plan for the future, or any fixed idea of what he is to do, should he reach there. The heart-ache has been cast broadcast on the way, and there is yet to be much more of it in the future."

He describes the country between the Arkansas and Santa Fe as utterly wretched, and dear at a gift. The picture of vice and profligacy given is truly deplorable. Crowds were assembled around the gaming-tables in every public house, and numerous groups were seen seated on the ground in every street, engaged in the same vice.

From Venezuela we have the judgment passed upon the unfortunate Gen. Paez, in these words:

" President Monagas, considering that the war which was begun on the 21st June last has ended, as the principal chiefs and all the soldiers of the Paez faction, who wished to upset the present government of the republic, have surrendered—this glorious triumph over, and the punishment of a great part of the insurgents who have lost their lives on the battle-field, having given the government power to use towards those who have surrendered, the clemency which they have demanded, and which has always been its policy—it is decreed:

"Art. 1. The chief of the faction, Jose Antonio Paez, will be expelled for ever out of the territory of the republic, and will remain in Europe. However, his departure from the country will only take place when the tranquillity and security of Venezuela will allow it.

"Art. 2. Those who have surrendered with the said Paez, will be expelled out of the country, or detained prisoners for a certain time, according to their degree of culpability, as it will be decided by the executive power.

"Art. 3. The executive power retains for some time the power to detain, as security, those it will be thought convenient, to discharge from exile or prison, and either to modify or change one penalty into another."

31*st.* Late files of the *Correo del Isthmo,* announce the arrival at his place of destination, of the Hon. E. G. Squier, U. S. Chargé to the republic of Nicaragua. His arrival seems to have been regarded as an event of remarkable importance. It is heralded in all the journals as a new era for Nicaragua, and he entered the city amid discharge of cannon, martial music, and the most tumultuous and enthusiastic rejoicings. On being presented to the President, Mr. Squier made a long address, tendering his thanks for the warmth of his reception, and assuring him that these sentiments are fully reciprocated, and that it is the earnest desire of the government of the United States to cultivate, in every way, the most cordial relations with the republic of Nicaragua. He assures him, further, that it shall be his aim to confirm the present harmony between the two republics—and " to this end, and to secure the permanent welfare of both, it is essential that they should pursue a system of policy exclusively American." He proceeded as follows:

" A cardinal principle in this policy is a total exclusion of foreign influence from the domestic and international affairs of the American republics. And while we would cultivate friendly intercourse, and promote trade and commerce with all the world, and invite to our shores and to the enjoyment of our institutions the people of all nations, we should proclaim in language firm and distinct, that *the American Continent belongs to Americans,* and is sacred to American freedom.

We should also let it be understood, that if foreign powers encroach upon the territories, or invade the rights of any of the American States, they inflict an injury upon all, which it is the duty and determination of all to see redressed."

The President, in his answer to Mr. Squier, remarked, that "Nicaragua had long felt the necessity of sheltering itself under the bright banner of the North American confederacy."

It is easy to perceive that the position taken by Great Britain in regard to the *Mosquito* question, and the anticipated action of our government upon it, have excited the deepest interest among the people of Nicaragua. The papers discuss the question at length, and protest in most earnest tones against the course pursued by the English government.

The occupation of the port of San Juan by the English, under the pretext of protecting the Mosquito nation, is denounced as an outrage upon the rights of the State of Nicaragua.

The papers contain a correspondence between the authorities of Nicaragua and the British Consul-General, Frederick Chatfield, in which the former states, that having read in the *Correo del Isthmo* a copy of the contract between the government and Dr. Brown, of New York, for making a canal through the river San Juan, he deems it prudent to inform the government that his own government will object to any arrangement which does not provide for the discharge of the debts which the State of Nicaragua, in common with the other States of Central America, have assumed. The Nicaraguan Minister, in reply to this, as well as other notes, charges the British government with the most wanton and unprovoked assault upon the sovereignty and independence of the State, and enumerates various acts by which this hostility has been manifested.

Foremost among them, of course, is the declaration that the Queen of Great Britain has decided to sustain the pretensions of the Mosquito King, and that she would consequently visit with severe punishment any act of the State of Nicaragua in violation of them. The threat to chastise any nation for maintaining its sovereignty, is denounced as an unexampled violation of justice and international rights.

The accounts from the *Cape of Good Hope*, state that the excitement in relation to the reception of convicts of that place was at its height. The anti-convict association had placed beyond the pale of social intercourse all persons who favoured the convict measure. The official members of council had been obliged to resign, and on leaving the council chamber they were jostled and kicked by the mob. Other outrages had been committed, manifesting a determined spirit in the inhabitants to resist the action of the government.

APPENDIX

QUARTERLY CHRONICLE.

SEPTEMBER, 1849.

3d. The first legislative assembly of MINESOTA convened at St. Paul. Governor Ramsay, accompanied by the executive and judicial officers of the Territory, met both branches of the legislature in joint meeting, and delivered his message. He recommends the adoption of a code of laws suitable to the position and wants of the territory; the providing a system of taxation whereby a territorial treasury may be established; the adoption of an efficient school system; the organization of the militia, as a safeguard against the lawlessness of the Indians, of whom twenty-five thousand are estimated to be located within the limits of the territory, and the restraining or suppression of the traffic in ardent spirits by Indian traders.

The Governor remarks:

"No portion of the earth's surface, perhaps, combines so many favourable features for the settler as this territory. Watered by the two greatest rivers of our continent—the Missouri sweeping its entire western border; the Mississippi and Lake Superior marking its eastern frontier; and whilst the States of Wisconsin and Iowa limit us on the South, the possessions of the Hudson's Bay Company present the only barrier to our dominion on the extreme north—in all embracing an area of one hundred and fifty thousand square miles; a country sufficiently extensive to admit of the erection of four States of the largest class, each enjoying in abundance most of the elements of future greatness. Its soil is of the most productive character, yet our northern latitude saves us from the malaria and death which in other climes are so often attendant upon a liberal soil."

The governor seems to have had some difficulty with the Winnebago Indians, who had left the possessions set apart for them in the west, with the intention of returning to their old hunting grounds in Wisconsin and Iowa. He sent out a detachment of thirty United States troops to intercept and drive them back, but the Indians secreted themselves in the swamps and tamarac bushes. The soldiers returned much fatigued without having seen any traces of the Winnebagoes.

Intelligence from the plains and the burning of Bent's fort has been received at Independence.

Messrs. Paladay and Riley, who accompanied one of the government trains, under charge of Capt. Keits, as far as the little Arkansas, arrived by way of Bent's fort. Mr. Paladay had been in the employ of Wm. Bent, at the fort. On the 16th August, he was sent over in the direction of Kit Carson's settlement, on the Moro. In returning, he fell in company with the train of Capt. Keits. While they were encamped at the Hole in the Rock, they heard distinctly a loud report resembling that of cannon. They journeyed on—crossed the Arkansas river on the 22d August, and came up to the site of the Fort, and saw that the rubbish of the buildings was all that was left. It had been burnt down by the Indians, and was still smoking and burning on the 24th, when they left it. They now were able to account for the report, as the magazine belonging to Bent had been fired. The guns and traps were consumed, and it is supposed all the goods, books, &c., of Bent's concern, had shared the same fate. The pack saddles and riding apparatus were not destroyed, as they were still in the bastions. What had become of Mr. Bent, or any one connected with the concern, they could not tell; there was no trace of them or their whereabouts.

3d. One of the most remarkable aërial voyages on record took place in France.

M. Arban, a French aëronaut, ascended in his balloon from the Chateau des Fleurs (the Vauxhall of Marseilles) at half-past six in the evening of the 2d inst., and alighted at the village of Pion Forte, near Turin, in Italy, the following morning; at half-past two, having accomplished the distance, about 400 miles, in eight hours.

He passed the Alps by moonlight—he says:

"I was occasionally obliged to ascend, in order to pass over the peaks. I reached the summit of the Alps at eleven o'clock, and as the horizon became clear, and my course regular, I began to think of supping. I was now at an elevation of 4600 metres. It was indispensably necessary for me to pursue my journey, and reach Piedmont. Chaos only was under me, and to alight in these regions was impossible. After supper, I threw my empty bottle into the snow beneath."

His course was on a level with the top of Mont Blanc, far above the clouds, and the mountain "resembled an immense block of crystal, sparkling with a thousand fires."

He alighted in a large farm yard near Turin, without any accident having occurred.

The paper money in the south of Europe is producing much embarrassment and distress. During the bloody scenes of the past year, specie has disappeared, and all sorts of devices were adopted to supply its place.

The Austrians and Hungarians have each, for months past, been manufacturing continually vast quantities of bank notes, which are forced into circulation. The report of the bank of Vienna, lately published, gives a specie deposit of twenty-seven millions to a paper circulation of almost two hundred and sixty millions, and this probably is far short of the mark! Kossuth, who had a mania for financiering, was by no means behind-hand with Austria in putting forth paper money; presses were kept at work day and night manufacturing it. The Austrian notes were declared worthless, and vast quantities of the Hungarian came into circulation, and passed readily. One of the first acts of the Austrian government, since the submission of Georgey, is to declare these worthless. The Russians, however, take them freely at par, and it is thought that some arrangement will be made less fatal to the Hungarians on the part of Austria.

11th. At Pittsfield, Mass., the *American Board of Commissioners for Foreign Missions,* held its fortieth annual meeting. Hon. Theodore Frelinghuysen, the President, in the chair.

The corporate members of this great religious association are amongst the most prominent men in the union. Twelve hundred persons were in attendance from a distance, and the concourse of people altogether was very great.

Addresses were to be delivered by Gov. Briggs, Chancellor Frelinghuysen, and others.

Ex-Chancellor Walworth, Chief Justice Hornblower, Drs. De Witt, Cox, Woods, Williams, Williston, Beecher, Dana, Hawes, Cummings, Hon. W. J. Hubbard, Samuel T. Armstrong, and many other distinguished gentlemen were present.

11th. The GREAT AGRICULTURAL FAIR at Syracuse, New York, was opened this day. It was supposed that between fifty and one hundred thousand people assembled on the grounds to witness the exhibition. The President of the United States had appointed to be present, but was prevented by sickness. Mr. Clay, Vice-President Fillmore, Governor Fish, General Wool, and many other distinguished gentlemen were there. The Albany Evening Journal remarks:

"This Fair was more than successful—it was triumphant, and has demonstrated, renewedly, that the spirit of progress is working wonders for the cause of agricultural mechanism, domestic economy, agriculture, horticulture, &c. The great feature of this Fair was its show of horses, cattle and sheep. In these respects the improvement in blood, condition and management, was marked and gratifying. The display of agricultural implements, household industry and general mechanism, was in the highest degree creditable to the industry and genius of the sons, and to the diligence and taste of the daughters of our State.

"The show ground was well chosen and admirably fitted up. The arrangements were such as to give every facility to visiters. Excellent order was preserved throughout.   There was literally a stream of vehicles carrying visiters to and from the grounds from 8 A. M. till 6 P. M.   And yet there was but little confusion and no accidents."

The N. Y. Express describing the stock on exhibition says the quantity was made up of fat, working and matched cattle, cows, young cattle, bulls and calves, and embracing Devonshire, Durham, Herefords, and many others.   One yoke of pure, bright red, three years old steers, part Durham, owned by G. W. Sheldon, Sennet, Cayuga, which weighed 3,800 lbs., also a yoke of large working cattle owned by G. Sheldon, of the same place, were much admired.   Clement Leach, of Madison county, had a yoke of heavy, six years old, fat cattle, which were worked until December last, since which they have been fed; they weighed 5,400 lbs.   He also had another yoke of fat cattle, fed in the same way, which weighed 4,622 lbs., and a remarkably fine heifer, three years old, of Durham grade, which weighed 2,066 lbs.

17th. A Council of the Catholic Hierarchy of France.—The Archbishop of Paris has convoked a provisional council, which met in the chapel of St. Sulpicias in Paris, on the 17th Sept.   Besides the Archbishop of Paris, there were present the Archbishop of Meaux, the Bishops of Versailles, Blois, and Orleans, and a host of the most distinguished theologians of the French church, among whom were MM. Cousson and Icard of the Sulpicians, and Jesuit Ravignan, and other writers of scarcely less reputation.   This body very rarely meets, and only in great emergencies, and a thousand reports are circulated as to what can have brought it together.   Its ceremonial is peculiar, as the members sit in conclave, worship together, and go through the formulary of the church with the greatest severity.   All the proceedings of the council are secret, and a portion only of its acts are ever made public.   It is maintained by many that the *concordat* of the Emperor Napoleon prohibits the re-union of this body, and the President has therefore issued a decree legalizing it.

20th. The *Grand Lodge of the independent order of Odd Fellows* in the United States concluded a six days' session at Baltimore.   They established a new grand lodge in New York.   A committee was appointed to prepare a block of marble to be placed in the national monument to the memory of Washington.

21st. A New York paper of this date remarks:

" The commencement of the Jewish year has been celebrated for several days past by our Jewish citizens, who will, on next Monday, observe the great day of atonement, fasting for twenty-four hours.   The Jewish year begins at the new moon, which varies from the 5th of September to the 5th of October, and this year it began on the 16th instant.   The first month of the Jewish year is called Tisri, and corresponds to part of September and part of October.   The reason given for making the year commence at this season is a tradition that the world was created in September."

26th. The annual convention of the Protestant Episcopal Church for the diocese of New York, assembled in the city of New York. The Rev. Dr. Creighton presided. It is well known that this diocese has been deprived for a long time of regular episcopal services, by the indefinite suspension of the bishop, and this session of the convention was made especially important by the decisive action of that body in the matter. After an animated and prolonged discussion a resolution was adopted by which it is made the duty of the standing committee to present an address to the house of bishops praying for relief, and for a declaration, according to the canon of 1847, upon what terms or at what time the sentence shall expire.

The trial and suspension of Bishop Onderdonk produced, at the time, an unusual sensation; it was the subject of remark every where— amongst all classes, religious and irreligious. Many, both ministers and laymen, expressed their entire approbation of the propriety of the sentence. So strong was this sentiment that no efforts were made, for a long time, either to procure his restoration or to modify the sentence. And even now when the first definite movement for the relief of the diocese was made, a large party in the convention, headed by the Hon. Luther Bradish and Judge Jay, were so strongly opposed to even the possibility of restoration that they offered a protest in writing against the proceedings of the majority. Objections being made by Hon. J. C. Spencer to the reception of the protest, the convention refused to receive it.

26th. We have recorded the desolation and gloom which pervaded the city of St. Louis a few weeks since,—we now give an extract from a letter recently published, by which it will be seen how soon health succeeds to sickness, and activity to depression; and how soon the heart, relieved from the dread of impending judgments, can fly back again to enjoy the light things of life. The letter we refer to is of this date, and runs on after this manner:

"Our city is again as healthy and as full of business as ever. Indeed, a greater amount of business is being done, probably, than for many years past. A steady tide of eastern population is flowing in, more than sufficient to supply all the vacancies made by the king of terrors during the summer. The burnt district again begins to look like a city. Large three and four story fire-proof buildings are supplying the places of the comparative shanties that were destroyed, and in the rise of property and increase of rents, the property holders, upon whom the loss in the great fire chiefly fell, already feel more than indemnified.

"The prospect now is, that the coming winter will *be as gay and bustling* as any that have preceded it. The only theatre our city affords is crowded nightly. By the way, St. Louis would be a fine opening for some eastern manager; as it is at present, we have no theatre during the winter, when most we need one."

The eminent and universally admired authoress, Miss Frederika Bremer, has arrived in this country. Her coming creates something of a sensation in literary circles. Already, says a New York letter, ere she has been in the new world half an hour, she is overrun with visiters welcoming her to our shores.

The *annual Fair of the American Institute* is being held in the city of New York, and is probably the most extensive and remarkable exhibition of the results of national industry given in any part of our country. It is held in Castle Garden, which is the best place that could have been selected for the display, it having an immense amphitheatre, so constructed that a full view of the entire interior may be had at any point. The number of new inventions is astonishing, and the displays of fabrics and fancy articles, works of art, &c., command admiration.

In the front of the gallery are a series of arches composed of box and other green material, containing in the centre the words Flora, Pomona, Ceres. Behind these are arrayed a fine display of dahlias. The collection of fruits is as yet small, but select, and the other department comprises giant pumpkins, squashes, ears of corn three feet long, beets, carrots, onions, &c., in proportion. The amphitheatre is filled with the most splendid specimens of every thing—it would be useless to enumerate here—and the stage is occupied by a production of the ladies' fair hands, bouquets of flowers comprised of shells, zephyr worsted work, wax-work, &c.; the "tout ensemble" of the whole being very pleasing.

A floral design for a conservatory called forth the admiration of all who saw it. The design and the execution reflected equal honour upon the fair hands which put it together. It was a sort of delightful bower consisting of a series of circles of evergreens and creepers, and flowers of every variety and hue, interwoven with artistic skill. Beneath was water, in which gold fish disported, and on the summit was a beautiful little cage containing two rice birds.

The rarest exotics and the choicest domestic flowers were disposed in such harmony as to produce a magic effect. There were five bouquets so arranged as to form a high arch; and at the base in the centre was a larger one, which contained the greatest variety, and the most gorgeous of those glorious creations which Cowley so happily describes when he calls them "stars of the earth." Every eye hung with delight on this picture.

Among the other articles deserving of attention, was a rare plant called "Feather Grass," which was exactly like the plumage of the bird of Paradise. Another curiosity is the Aristolochia Braziliensis, which is a perfect nondescript. Last, not least, a stalk of Indian corn, thirty feet high, which grew in New York.

The opening address was delivered by Hon. Henry Meigs. We have only room for a portion of it:

"He referred to the invention of Whitney, by which more cotton could be picked from the seeds in one day, than a human being could pick in many weeks; so that now there is as much cotton cloth made here every year as would nearly give a garment to the whole human race.   Fulton, an American, first took the wind out of the sails of the ships of mankind, and made them go against wind and tide, leaving the sail vessels behind as if they were at anchor.   An American, following in the wake of Franklin, has invented a plan by which intelligence of what is passing a thousand miles off, can be communicated in a few minutes.   Junius Smith, another American, first confidently asserted the practicability of ocean steam navigation, when almost every seaman had decided against it; and now he is cultivating the tea plant in America, so successfully, that Americans will have, of their own growth, more tea than they can drink.   The Russian emperor has employed an American to make one of the most magnificent roads in the world—that from St. Petersburg to Moscow.   He next adverted to the mechanical skill of Americans, their omnibusses to ride in for sixpence, for which Cleopatra would have given a province; and carts and wagons for the most common purposes, that were never equalled by the triumphal cars of the Roman conquerors for beauty of workmanship, strength and utility.   The lesson Americans have now to learn, is to fortify the independence they have won.   *   *   *

"Agriculture alone produces in this country what is worth more in gold than can be expected from the placers of California for a hundred years.   The little island of Great Britain, in 1844, raised by agriculture three thousand millions of dollars. - Our grass is worth one hundred millions of dollars.   Washington, in his day, was the greatest farmer in the world.   He possessed in one body 10,060 acres of land, kept twenty-four ploughs going at all times, sowed 600 bushels of oats in the year, 700 acres of wheat, and as much more in corn, barley, potatoes and beans; 500 also laid down in grass; 150 acres of turnips, 140 horses, 112 cows, 235 working oxen, 500 sheep.   In one fall he killed 150 hogs, weighing 18,560 pounds, for his own use, exclusive of provisions for the negroes."

DISASTROUS WRECK AND LOSS OF LIFE.   The Boston papers give the following account of a dreadful shipwreck on the Massachusetts coast, during the recent severe gale:

"The British brig, St. John, Captain Oliver, from Galway, Ireland, 5th ult., for this port, with one hundred and twenty immigrant passengers, came to anchor wide off Minot's Ledge, Cohasset, about six o'clock yesterday morning.   She soon, however, dragged her anchor; the masts were then cut away, but continuing to drag, she struck upon the rocks and became a total wreck.   The captain, officers and crew, with the exception of the first mate, took to the boat and landed safe at the Glades, a short distance off; but, as last reported, *ninety-nine* of the passengers were drowned.   There were fourteen cabin passengers, chiefly women and children, who are among the lost.   Those who were saved, numbering but twenty-one, got on pieces of the wreck and landed near White Head, at the north end of the Cohasset rocks.   Twenty-five bodies were washed ashore this morning.

"The names of the drowned are probably unknown to the captain. He reports one hundred and twenty-six souls on board, twenty-one of whom were saved, leaving ninety-nine lost.   The brig was in ballast.

"The scene was witnessed from the Glade House, and is represented to have been terrible,   The sea ran mountain high, and as soon as she touched, the waves swept the unfortunate human beings upon her crowded decks by dozens into the sea.   The spectators of this awful sight imagined that they could hear the cries of the victims as they were swept away, but as no boat, save the life-boat, could have lived in the gale, it was found impossible to render aid.

"When the St. John struck, her small boat was got ready, but was swamped at the side by a large number jumping into her.   Shortly after the long boat broke her fastening, and floated off from the vessel. The captain and several others swam to, got on board of her, and landed in safety near the Glade House.   The second mate, two men and two boys of the crew were drowned.

"After the ship struck the rocks, she thumped awhile, but shortly went to pieces, holding together not more than fifty or sixty minutes. Seven women and three men came ashore on parts of the wreck, alive, but some very much exhausted.   Two dead bodies were also taken from pieces of the wreck.

"Great difficulty was experienced in saving those who came ashore, on account of the surf, which would throw them upon the rocks and then carry them to sea again.   The poor creatures would cling with a death grasp to the clothes of those who came to rescue them, and were with difficulty made to release their hold, even after having reached a place of safety."

On the 27th September, a most destructive fire occurred at Owego, New York.   The entire business portion of the place was laid in ruins.   The loss of property was at first estimated at $500,000.   It has since been ascertained to have been $325,000, of which $110,000 was insured.

STATISTICS.

SMITHSONIAN INSTITUTION.

IN a former number of this Journal we inserted an abstract of the second annual report of the learned Secretary of the Institution, Dr. Joseph Henry. It is due to the cause of science that we should present more full statements respecting the nature and operations of this Institution, which the Secretary says "is designed to endure as long as our government shall exist," and the grand purpose of which is certainly one of the noblest within the reach of human effort—"the increase and diffusion of knowledge among men."

"JAMES SMITHSON, Esq., of England, left his property in trust to the United States of America, to found at Washington an institution which should bear his own name, and have for its objects "the *increase* and *diffusion* of knowledge among men." This trust was accepted by the government of the United States, and an act of Congress was passed August 10, 1846, constituting the President and the other principal executive officers of the general government, the Chief Justice of the Supreme Court, the Mayor of Washington, and such other persons as they might elect honorary members, an establishment under the name of the "SMITHSONIAN INSTITUTION, FOR THE INCREASE AND DIFFUSION OF KNOWLEDGE AMONG MEN." The members and honorary members of this establishment are to hold stated and special meetings for the supervision of the affairs of the Institution, and for the advice and instruction of a Board of Regents, to whom the financial and other affairs are intrusted.

The Board of Regents consists of three members ex-officio of the establishment, namely, the Vice President of the United States, the Chief Justice of the Supreme Court, and the Mayor of Washington, together with twelve other members, three of whom are appointed by the Senate from its own body, three by the House of Representatives from its members, and six citizens appointed by a joint resolution of both houses. To this board is given the power of electing a Secretary and other officers, for conducting the active operations of the Institution.

The Act of Congress establishing the Institution, directs, as a part of the plan of organization, the formation of a Library, a Museum, and a Gallery of Art, together with provisions for physical research and popular lectures, while it leaves to the Regents the power of adopting such other parts of an organization as they may deem best suited to promote the objects of the bequest.

After much deliberation, the Regents resolved to divide the annual income into two equal parts—one part to be devoted to the increase and diffusion of knowledge by means of original research and publications—the other half of the income to be applied, in accordance with the requirements of the Act of Congress, to the gradual formation of a Library, a Museum, and a Gallery of Art."

The following is the PROGRAMME OF ORGANIZATION, as presented by the Secretary, Professor Henry, to the Board of Regents, and adopted December 13, 1847.

GENERAL CONSIDERATIONS WHICH SHOULD SERVE AS A GUIDE IN ADOPTING A
PLAN OF ORGANIZATION.

1. WILL OF SMITHSON. The property is bequeathed to the United States of America, "to found at Washington, under the name of the Smithsonian Institution, an establishment for the increase and diffusion of knowledge among men."

2. The bequest is for the benefit of mankind. The government of the United States is merely a trustee to carry out the design of the testator.

3. The Institution is not a national establishment, as is frequently supposed, but the establishment of an individual, and is to bear and perpetuate his name.

4. The objects of the Institution are—1st, to increase, and 2d, to diffuse knowledge among men.

5. These two objects should not be confounded with one another. The first is to increase the existing stock of knowledge by the addition of new truths; and the second to disseminate knowledge, thus increased, among men.

6. The will makes no restriction in favour of any particular kind of knowledge; hence all branches are entitled to a share of attention.

7. Knowledge can be increased by different methods of facilitating and promoting the discovery of new truths, and can be most efficiently diffused among men by means of the press.

8. To effect the greatest amount of good, the organization should be such as to enable the Institution to produce results in the way of increasing and diffusing knowledge, which cannot be produced by the existing institutions in our country.

9. The organization should also be such as can be adopted provisionally, can be easily reduced to practice, receive modifications, or be abandoned, in whole or in part, without a sacrifice of the funds.

10. In order to make up for the loss of time occasioned by the delay of eight years in establishing the Institution, a considerable portion of the interest which has accrued should be added to the principal.

11. In proportion to the wide field of knowledge to be cultivated, the funds are small. Economy should therefore be consulted in the construction of the building; and not only should the first cost of the edifice be considered, but also the continual expense of keeping it in repair, and of the support of the establishment necessarily connected with it. There should also be but few individuals permanently supported by the Institution.

12. The plan and dimensions of the building should be determined by the plan of organization, and not the converse.

13. It should be recollected that mankind in general are to be benefited by the bequest, and that, therefore, all unnecessary expenditure on local objects would be a perversion of the trust.

14. Besides the foregoing considerations, deduced immediately from the will of Smithson, regard must be had to certain requirements of the act of Congress establishing the Institution. These are a library, a museum, and a gallery of art, with a building on a liberal scale to contain them.

SECTION I.

Plan of organization of the Institution, in accordance with the foregoing deductions from the will of Smithson.

To INCREASE KNOWLEDGE, It is proposed—

1. To stimulate men of talent to make original researches, by offering suitable rewards for memoirs containing new truths; and,

2. To appropriate annually a portion of the income for particular researches, under the direction of suitable persons.

To-Diffuse Knowledge. It is proposed—

1. To publish a series of periodical reports on the progress of the different branches of knowledge; and,

2. To publish occasionally separate treatises on subjects of general interest.

DETAILS OF THE PLAN TO INCREASE KNOWLEDGE.

I. *By stimulating researches.*

1. Rewards offered for original memoirs on all branches of knowledge.

2. The memoirs thus obtained to be published in a series of volumes, in a quarto form, and entitled "Smithsonian Contributions to Knowledge."

3. No memoir, on subjects of physical science, to be accepted for publication, which does not furnish a positive addition to human knowledge resting on original research; and all unverified speculations to be rejected.

4. Each memoir presented to the Institution to be submitted for examination to a commission of persons of reputation for learning in the branch to which the memoir pertains, and to be accepted for publication only in case the report of this commission is favourable.

5. The commission to be chosen by the officers of the institution, and the icable, concealed, unless a favourable deci-

to be exchanged for the transactions of lite-
nd
be
of

be
of the Regents to Congress.

1. The objects, and the amount appropriated, to be recommended by counsellors of the institution.

2. Appropriations in different years to different objects; so that, in course of time, each branch of knowledge may receive a share.

3. The results obtained from these appropriations to be published, with the memoirs before-mentioned, in the volumes of the Smithsonian contributions to knowledge.

4. Examples of objects for which appropriations may be made.

(1.) System of extended meteorological observations, particularly with reference to the phenomena of American storms.

(2.) Explorations in descriptive natural history, and geological, magnetical, and topographical surveys, to collect materials for the formation of a Physical Atlas of the United States.

(3.) Solution of experimental problems, such as a new determination of the weight of the earth, of the velocity of electricity, and of light; chemical analyses of soils and plants; collection and publication of articles of science, accumulated in the offices of government.

(4.) Institution of statistical inquiries with reference to physical, moral, and political subjects.

(5.) Historical researches, and accurate surveys of places celebrated in American history.

(6.) Ethnological researches, particularly with reference to the different races of men in North America; also, explorations and accurate surveys of the mounds and other remains of the ancient people of our country.

DETAILS OF THE PLAN FOR DIFFUSING KNOWLEDGE.

I. *By the publication of a series of reports, giving an account of the new discoveries in science, and of the changes made from year to year in all branches of knowledge not strictly professional.*

1. These reports will diffuse a kind of knowledge generally interesting, but which, at present, is inaccessible to the public. Some of the reports may be published annually, others at longer intervals, as the income of the Institution, or the changes in the branches of knowledge may indicate.

2. The reports are to be prepared by collaborators, eminent in the different branches of knowledge.

3. Each collaborator to be furnished with the journals and publications, domestic and foreign, necessary to the compilation of his report, to be paid a certain sum for his labours, and to be named on the title-page of the report.

(4.) The reports to be published in separate parts, so that persons interested in a particular branch can procure the parts relating to it, without purchasing the whole.

(5.) These reports may be presented to Congress, for partial distribution; the remaining copies to be given to literary and scientific institutions, and sold to individuals for a moderate price.

The following are some of the subjects that may be embraced in the reports:

I. PHYSICAL CLASS.

1. Physics, including astronomy, natural philosophy, chemistry, and meteorology.

2. Natural history, including botany, zoology, geology, &c.

3. Agriculture.

4. Application of science to arts.

II. MORAL AND POLITICAL CLASS.

5. Ethnology, including particular history, comparative philology, antiquities, &c.

6. Statistics and political economy.

7. Mental and moral philosophy.

8. A survey of the political events of the world, penal reform, &c.

9. Modern literature.

10. The fine arts, and their application to the useful arts.

11. Bibliography.

12. Obituary notices of distinguished individuals.

II. *By the publication of separate treatises on subjects of general interest.*

1. These treatises may occasionally consist of valuable memoirs, translated from foreign languages, or of articles prepared under the direction of the Institution, or procured by offering premiums for the best exposition of a given subject.

2. The treatises should in all cases be submitted to a commission of competent judges previous to their publication.

3. As examples of these treatises, expositions may be obtained of the present state of the several branches of knowledge mentioned in the table of reports. Also of the following subjects, suggested by the Committee on Organization, namely, the statistics of labour, the productive arts of life, public instruction, &c.

SECTION II.

Plan of organization, in accordance with the terms of the resolutions of the Board of Regents, providing for the two modes of increasing and diffusing knowledge.

1. The act of Congress, establishing the institution, contemplated the formation of a library and a museum; and the Board of Regents, including

these objects in the plan of organization, resolved to divide the income into two equal parts.

2. One part to be appropriated to increase and diffuse knowledge by means of publications and researches, agreeably to the scheme before given. The other part to be appropriated to the formation of a library and a collection of objects of nature and of art.

3. These two plans are not incompatible with one another.

4. To carry out the plan before described, a library will be required, consisting, 1st, of a complete collection of the transactions and proceedings of all the learned societies in the world; 2d, of the more important current periodical publications, and other works necessary in preparing the periodical reports.

5. The institution should make special collections, particularly of objects to verify its own publications.

6. Also a collection of instruments of research in all branches of experimental science.

7. With reference to the collection of books, other than those mentioned above, catalogues of all the different libraries in the United States should be procured, in order that the valuable books first purchased may be such as are not to be found in the United States.

8. Also catalogues of memoirs, and of books in foreign libraries, and other materials, should be collected for rendering the institution a centre of bibliographical knowledge, whence the student may be directed to any work which he may require.

9. It is believed that the collections in natural history will increase by donation as rapidly as the income of the institution can make provision for their reception, and therefore it will seldom be necessary to purchase any articles of this kind.

10. Attempts should be made to procure for the gallery of arts casts of the most celebrated articles of ancient and modern sculpture.

11. The arts may be encouraged by providing a room free of expense, for the exhibition of the objects of the Art Union and other similar societies.

12. A small appropriation should annually be made for models of antiquities, such as those of the remains of ancient temples, &c.

13. For the present, or until the building is fully completed, besides the Secretary, no permanent assistant will be required, except one to act as librarian.

14. The duty of the Secretary will be the general superintendence, with the advice of the Chancellor and other members of the establishment, of the literary and scientific operations of the institution.; to give to the Regents annually an account of all the transactions; of the memoirs which have been received for publication; of the researches which have been made; and to edit, with the assistance of the librarian, the publications of the institution.

15. The duty of the assistant secretary, acting as librarian, will be, for the present, to assist in taking charge of the collections, to select and purchase, under the direction of the secretary and a committee of the board, books and catalogues, and to procure the information before mentioned; to give information on plans of libraries, and to assist the Secretary in editing the publications of the institution, and in the other duties of his office.

16. The Secretary and his assistants, during the session of Congress, will be required to illustrate new discoveries in science, and to exhibit new objects of art; also, distinguished individuals should be invited to give lectures on subjects of general interest.

17. When the building is completed, and when, in accordance with the Act of Congress, the charge of the national museum is given to the Smithsonian Institution, other assistants will be required.

The explanations and illustrations of the preceding programme by Doctor Henry are very full and ably drawn. Our limits will only allow us to insert the following general remarks:

"The programme embraces the general propositions adopted by the Board of Regents at their last meeting, as the basis of future operations. It is intended to harmonize the two modes of increasing and diffusing knowledge, and to give to the institution the widest influence compatible with its limited income. That all the propositions will meet with general approval cannot be expected; and that this organization is the best that could be devised, is neither asserted nor believed. To produce *a priori* a plan of organization which shall be found to succeed perfectly in practice, and require no amendment, would be difficult under the most favourable circumstances, and becomes almost impossible where conflicting opinions are to be harmonized, and the definite requirements of the act establishing the institution are to be observed. It is not intended that the details of the organization, as given in the programme, should be permanently adopted without careful trial; they are rather presented as suggestions to be adopted provisionally, and to be carried into operation gradually and cautiously, with such changes, from time to time, as experience may dictate.

"That the institution is not a national establishment, in the sense in which institutions dependent on the government for support are so, must be evident when it is recollected that the money was not absolutely given to the United States, but intrusted to it for a special object, namely: the establishment of an institution for the benefit of men, to bear the name of the donor, and, consequently, to reflect upon his memory the honour of all the good which may be accomplished by means of the bequest. The operations of the Smithsonian Institution ought, therefore, to be mingled as little as possible with those of the government, and its funds should be applied exclusively and faithfully to the increase and diffusion of knowledge among men.

"That the bequest is intended for the benefit of men in general, and that its influence ought not to be restricted to a single district, or even nation, may be inferred not only from the words of the will, but also from the character of Smithson himself; and I beg leave to quote from a scrap of paper in his own hand, the following sentiment bearing on this point: 'The man of science has no country; the world is his country—all men, his countrymen.' The origin of the funds, the bequest of a foreigner, should also preclude the adoption of a plan which does not, in the words of Mr. Adams, 'spread the benefits to be derived from the institution not only over the whole surface of this Union, but throughout the civilized world.' 'Mr. Smithson's reason for fixing the seat of his institution at Washington obviously was, that *there* is the seat of government of the United States, and *there* the Congress by whose legislation, and the Executive through whose agency, the trust committed to the honour, intelligence, and good faith of the nation, is to be fulfilled.' The centre of operations being permanently fixed at Washington, the character of this city for literature and science will be the more highly exalted in proportion as the influence of the institution is more widely diffused.

"That the terms *increase* and *diffusion* of knowledge are logically distinct, and should be literally interpreted with reference to the will, must be evident when we reflect that they are used in a definite sense, and not as mere synonymes, by all who are engaged in the pursuits to which Smithson devoted his life. In England there are two classes of institutions, founded on the two ideas conveyed by these terms. The Royal Society, the Astronomical, the Geological, the Statistical, the Antiquarian Societies, all have for their object the increase of knowledge; while the London Institution, the Mechanics' Institution, the Surry Institution, the Society for the Diffusion of Religious

Knowledge, the Society for the Diffusion of Useful Knowledge, are all intended to diffuse or disseminate knowledge among men. In our own country, also, the same distinction is observed in the use of the terms by men of science. Our colleges, academies, and common schools, are recognised as institutions partially intended for the diffusion of knowledge, while the express object of some of our scientific societies is the promotion of the discovery of new truths."

Connected with the last annual report to which we have before referred, is the report of Professor Jewett, the assistant secretary, on the subject of a library. It is one of the most able and interesting papers of the kind that we have seen. We condense his comparative statistics of the public libraries in Europe and the United States:

"Of Great Britain, France, Italy, the United States, Belgium, Holland, Germany, and the Scandinavian kingdoms, it appears that the smallest of the last, Denmark, is, in the proportion of its population, the richest in books, while Spain and Russia are beyond all the rest of Europe.

"The following table exhibits the number of books in each country, as ascertained by recent examinations:

	No. of Libraries.	Aggregate vols.	Libraries having over 10,000 vols.
Germany,	103	5,578,000	68
France,	241	4,771,000	121
Great Britain,	31	2,001,000	23
Russia,	120	1,321,000	16
United States,	182	1,294,000	43
Denmark,	13	660,000	5
Belgium,	31	614,000	16
Sweden,	16	258,000	7
Spain,	21	354,000	5
Norway,	14	157,000	2

The average size of libraries possessing more than 10,000 volumes is represented in the following table, which also contains the number of volumes in the largest library of each country, and the number of volumes to each million of inhabitants:

	Average size of Libraries above 10,000 volumes.	No. of volumes in the largest Libraries.	No. of vols. to each million of people.
Germany,	80,000	600,000	136,000
France,	35,000	800,000	145,000
Great Britain,	85,000	420,000	83,000
Russia,	69,000	464,000	28,000
United States,	17,000	70,000	64,000
Denmark,	123,000	400,000	330,000
Belgium,	35,000	100,000	153,000
Sweden,	43,000	150,000	120,000
Spain,	57,000	200,000	30,000
Norway,	74,000	126,000	150,000 "

To this statement may be added some facts in relation to particular libraries in Europe and the United States.

The Royal Library of Copenhagen contains 463,000 volumes, and 22,000 manuscripts, while that at Stockholm, founded by Gustaf Vasa, contains 70,000 volumes. There are also in other parts of Denmark, and Norway, and Sweden immense collections, of which no computation has been made. The *Bibliotheque du Roi*, at Paris, contains 800,000 printed books, and 100,000 manuscripts, not counting duplicates, and receives an increase of 15,000 volumes annually. This library is open to the public, male and female, without any limitation other than a strict surveillance of a special police.

In the United States the improvement of libraries during the last twenty years has been immense. When Washington Irving wrote his History of the Life and Voyages of Columbus, the material could not be had in America. There are now several libraries containing all he would desire. There is yet much imperfectness in our collections, so much so that it is probable that even now the citations of Gibbon's great history could not be verified on this continent. The library of Harvard now contains 70,000 volumes, and is well selected, and the foundations for immense collections have been laid by more than one of the Universities of the United States, and especially by those under the control of the Roman Catholic church.

In relation to the inadequacy of our collections, notwithstanding the vast additions that have been made within a few years, Professor Jewett remarks:

"In Mr. Wheaton's History of International Law—a production which reflects great credit upon American talent and scholarship, and which procured for its lamented author the honour of election to the French Institute—139 works are referred to in the notes. A much larger number were, of course, consulted, many of which are mentioned in the body of the work. Thirty-nine among the most important and expensive of those which are formally cited, are not to be found in the largest law libraries in the United States. More than one-half of the remainder are common books, to be found in any well selected general library of 5,000 volumes. This work was written in Europe. It could not have been written in this country from the materials contained in our public libraries.

"If we take a book of a different kind, demanding for its composition a thorough knowledge of the history of one of the physical sciences, and, consequently, requiring the assistance of authorities less accessible and of less general importance, the result will be all the more striking.

"In the first volume of Hoefer's History of Chemistry, 251 works are referred to. Of these, about fifty are common books, to be found in almost any library of 5,000 volumes. Of the remaining 191, I cannot find 75 in all our public libraries.

"Mr. J. R. Bartlett informs me that of 204 works which he refers to in his report on the progress of ethnology, 129 are not to be found in the public libraries of New York, nor in any others probably in the United States. The cost of the books which, in order to prepare his work, he had to procure at his own expense, was $1,000. And yet this report is only a pamphlet of 151 pages.

"From these facts it is manifest that there is no exaggeration in the language of one of the members of our Board of Regents, from South Carolina, who, in a report to the Senate, in 1836, stated that "our whole body of literature, if collected in one place, would not afford the means of investigating one point of science or literature through all, or even a considerable portion of what has been written on it." Here, he adds, "where the foundations of government repose on the aggregate intelligence of the citizens, the assistance afforded by public institutions to the exertions of intellect is but one-tenth of that within the reach of the mind of civilized Europe."

Upon the subject of the accumulation and use of enormous libraries, the Professor further remarks:

It has been supposed by some not acquainted with researches requiring many books, that very large libraries are superfluous. They calculate, perhaps, how many books a man can read in a long life, and ask what can be the use of more. Indeed, many men fond of reading feel like an English writer of some note, who describes his pain as amounting to "midsummer madness" when he entered a large library and reflected how small a number of all the books it contained he could read through.

"In my youthful days," says De Quincy, "I never entered a great library, say of 100,000 volumes, but my predominant feeling was one of pain and disturbance of mind, not much unlike that which drew tears from Xerxes, on reviewing his immense army, and reflecting that in one hundred years no one soul would remain alive. To me, with respect to the books, the same effect would be brought about by my death. Here, said I, are 100,000 books, the worst of them capable of giving me some pleasure and instruction, and before I can have had time to extract the honey from one-twentieth of this hive, in all likelihood I shall be summoned away.

"Now I have been told by an eminent English author, that with respect to one single work, namely: the History of Thuanus, a calculation has been made by a Portuguese monk, which showed that barely to read over the words, and allowing no time for reflection, would require three years' labour at the rate of, I think, three hours a day. Further, I had myself ascertained that to read a duodecimo volume in prose of four hundred pages, all skipping being barred, and the rapid reading which belongs to the vulgar interest of a novel, was a very sufficient work for one day. Consequently, three hundred and sixty-five per annum, that is with a very small allowance for the claims of life on one's own account and on that of one's friends, one thousand for every triennium, that is ten thousand in thirty years, will be as much as a man who lives for that only can hope to accomplish. From the age of twenty to eighty, the utmost he could hope to travel through would be twenty thousand volumes, a number not, perhaps, above five per cent. of what the mere current literature of Europe would accumulate in that period of years."

Now, supposing for a moment that there were no other use to be made of books but the reading of them through at so many pages the hour, one would think it might have occurred to this writer that there are among the frequenters of a large library a great variety of men, with a wide diversity of interests, tastes and pursuits; that though each might not be able to read through more than two thousand books—one-tenth part of the supposed number—still fifty men, whose reading was in different directions, might call for a hundred thousand.

Of *the financial condition* of the Smithsonian Institution, the following report was made by the executive committee, Messrs. W. W. Seaton, J. A. Pearce, and A. D. Bache, up to the 1st of January, 1849.

The whole amount of Smithson's property received into the treasury of the United States on the 1st September, 1838, was $515,169. The interest which had accrued on the same up to 1st July, 1846, when, by the act of Congress, the funds were placed under the direction of the Board of Regents, was $242,129. This sum, together with the accruing interest, the Board of Regents were authorized to expend in the erection of a building and in defraying the current expenses of the Institution.

During the last two years and four months, in which the Institution has been under the charge of the Regents, there has been expended towards attendance of the Regents, and incidental and miscellaneous expenses, the erection of the building, improvement of grounds, salaries of officers, the sum of	.	.	.	.	.	.	.	.	.	.	$106,520 19

During the same time, there has been received
from interest and the sale of treasury notes,
the sum of $115,964 60
From the Secretary's lectures at Princeton, . 1,000 00
                                                          ——————
                                                          116,964 60

Leaving a balance on hand of   10,444 41

Funds of the Institution.

Amount of Smithson's bequest, . . . $515,169 00
Interest due thereon to 1st July, 1846, . . 242,129 00
                                                          ——————
                                                          $757,298 00
Balance on hand 1st January, 1849, . . 10,444 21
Treasury notes on hand, ... 226,000 00
Permanent fund, ... 515,169 00
                                                          ——————
                                                          751,613 21
If to this we add the premium of 8 per cent., which treasury
notes now bear, say 18,000 00

The funds of the Institution will be . . . $769,613 21
    Thus showing, that after an expenditure of $106,520 19, the cash on hand
and the value of the cash investments, exceed the amount on hand, on the
organization of the Institution, in September, 1846, by about $12,000, subject,
however, to a few outstanding accounts not yet presented, estimated at
$7,500.

STATISTICS OF IMMIGRATION.

FROM THE NEW YORK COMMERCIAL ADVERTISER.

    THE number of immigrants who arrived at New York *by sea,* during the month
of June, 1849, was 29,078; being an increase of 6,031 over the number arriving
in June, 1848. The number who arrived in July was 30,698; being an increase
over July, 1848, of 5,476.
    Thus the number who arrived in June and July of the present year was 59,176,
against 47,669 last year; an increase of 11,507 in two months.
    The increase in the present year is 32,818 over the number arriving in the same
time of last year. And the number arriving in seven months of the present year
is more than fourfold the number who arrived in an equal time of 1844.
    The following table will show the places of birth of immigrants who arrived
in the year 1849, and the reader will be enabled to ascertain therefrom whence
the vast increase in the number of immigrants arriving in this country is principally derived.

*Table showing the countries in which the immigrants were born, who arrived at
    New York in the first seven months of* 1849.

1849.	Jan. to May.	June.	July.	Total in 7 mos.
England	9,248	4,345	3,072	16,665.
Ireland	50,820	12,691	13,765	77,276.
Scotland	2,869	1,557	1,573	5,899.
Wales	601	367	312	1,280.
Germany	18,366	8,088	7,688	31,142.
France	594	247	555	1,396.
Holland	581	431	730	1,742.
Italy	85	224	132	441.
Switzerland	383	356	126	865.
Spain	102	25	15	142.

1849.	Jan. to May.	June.	July.	Total in 7 mos.
Poland	35	1	20	56.
Russia	10.		7	17.
Belgium	5	2	10	17.
Sweden	43	24	241	308.
Portugal	10	4	182	196.
West Indies	96	80	122	298.
Denmark	86		22	108.
Norway	2	578	1,395	1,975.
East Indies	4		1	5.
Mexico	6	1	5	12.
Canada	40	8		48.
Africa	8			8.
Nova Scotia	33	30	20	83.
South America	11	3	3	17.
China	1	1		2.
Sicily	3	3		6.
Sardinia	1		90	91.
Turkey	3	12		15.
Greece			4	4.
Sandwich Islands			8	8.
	84,046	29,078	30,098	143,222.

Of the 143,222 immigrants who arrived in the first seven months of the present year, 101,220 were born in Great Britain and Ireland, or nearly 71 per cent., being an increase in the proportion over the previous year of 4 per cent.; and of the remaining 42,002 there were 34,142 who were born in Germany, or nearly 24 per cent., being a decrease in the proportion since last year of 4½ per cent. In brief, the comparison shows thus:

Seven months of 1848, from Great Britain   67 per cent.
    do.   1849,   do.   71   do.
    do.   1848, from Germany   28½   do.
    do.   1849,   do.   24   do.

There are not the same means of making a comparison as to the place of birth of immigrants arriving in previous years, as the particularity with which the Commissioners of immigration cause a register to be kept of the birth-place of each immigrant was not then practised, but a good approximation may be made by taking the ports whence the vessels arrived with passengers at New York. In the first seven months of 1846 there were 60,220 immigrants who arrived at this port, as follows:

From British ports	38,488	From Sweden and Norway	640
French ports	10,593	Spain	5
Hanse Towns	6,322	Italy and Sicily	178
Belgium	2,637	All other ports	194
Holland	1,110		
			60,220

It is quite impracticable to separate the nationalities of the passengers who arrived from these ports; but it may be assumed (with hopes of tolerable accuracy) that the number of passengers from British ports represents the number of immigrants from that country, and this gives a proportion of sixty-three per cent. arriving thence in the first seven months of 1846, and the progress since then is as follows:

Seven months 1846.   Proportion of immigrants arriving at New York, born
              in Great Britain   63 per cent.
Do.   1848   do.   67   do.
Do.   1849   do.   71   do.

There is one fact of considerable interest presented to view in regard to the progress of the business of transporting passengers to this country; and that is the great increase in the numbers who make the passage in the winter. In the months of January, February, and March, 1844, there were but 2,101 passengers arriving at New York by sea; though in the same months in this year there were no less than 26,706, an increase of *thirteen fold*, while the total increase of immigration in the seven months is only *fourfold*. In 1844 only about *one-seventeenth* of the number of immigrants arriving in the first seven months arrived in January, February, and March; while in the present year nearly *one-fifth* of the whole arrived in the first three months.

The inference to be drawn from this state of facts may be that the condition of the people in Great Britain during the winter is deteriorating, and that they are compelled to emigrate in the depth of the cold season, and incur its severities and dangers on the ocean, from the fear that if they wait until a more genial time they will be left without the means of emigrating at all. And this view is strengthened apparently by observing the large numbers who arrive here in a state of complete destitution. The proportions arriving in the first three months out of the seven are as follows:

	Total arrived in seven months.	Arrived in the first 3 months.	Proportion arriving in first 3 months.
1844	34,655	2,101	6 per cent.
1845	48,560	4,435	9 do.
1846	60,220	5,360	9 do.
1847	102,118	9,882	9¾ do.
1848	110,404	15,327	13¾ do.
1849	143,922	26,703	18¾ do.

It is true, however, that an inference just to the contrary may be drawn; that the increased numbers of those who embark in the winter may result from the more general possession of means to encounter the greater length and privations of a winter voyage; as also from the expediency of remaining in their own country so long as the time of year affords employment and the means of subsistence. It may be supposed that those who come in the summer are under a pressing necessity to come, which leaves no choice of time; others, better off in the world, can afford to stay until the harvesting is done, &c., and make their voyage in the comparatively idle season.

In answer to an inquiry as to the proportion between the Foreign and Native population, in New York, the Journal of Commerce thus replies:

In 1845, the number of foreigners in the city of New York was 128,495, or a fraction more than one-third of the whole population, which was 374,223, including 12,913 coloured. The whole number of voters was 63,937. Of the 128,495 foreigners, 60,946 were aliens; i. e., as we understand it, foreigners not naturalized.

The increase of our population from 1840 to 1845, was 58,591. A proportionate increase since taking the population of 1845 (371,223) as a new basis would give us at present about 425,000; of whom 150,000 or 160,000 may be foreigners, and the rest natives. As nearly half the foreign population in 1845 were aliens, it may be presumed (taking into view the immense influx of foreigners since, and the fact that no foreigner can be naturalized until he has been in the country at least five years) that half of the present foreign inhabitants are aliens. On the other hand, it should be noted that a larger proportion of foreigners than of natives are adults, and consequently that other things being equal, a larger proportion of them would be voters. If the proportion of voters among foreigners, aliens included, were as great as among the natives, the number of foreign voters in the city in 1845 would have been over 20,000, and would now be about 25,000. But in point of fact, we are inclined to think it is now about 18,000 out of a total of 73,000. That is to say, about one-quarter of the whole.

It may be that we have not made a sufficient allowance (not in the increase of voters but of population) on account of the extraordinary influx of immigrants within a few years past; but our view of the matter is, that comparatively few of them take up their residence here, while the vast majority pour into the West, or seek a home in other cities and villages, or among the farmers of this and the neighbouring states.

As to the proportion of Irish, Germans, &c., composing the foreign population of this city, an approximation to the truth may be obtained by referring to the results of the last census, (1845,) when, of the 128,495 foreigners, 96,584 were natives of Great Britain and Ireland, 24,416 of Germany, 3,710 of France, 508 of Mexico and South American States, and the remaining 3,277 of other European countries than those above mentioned. Of the immigration since 1845 a much larger proportion than before consists of Germans; but still the Irish predominate. Next year a new census will be taken, which will give us the information sought for exactly.

THE COMMERCE OF THE LAKES.

We are indebted to the Hon. E. G. Spaulding, of Buffalo, for the report of the Committee of the Board of Trade of that city, to the United States Agent, appointed by the government to procure statistical information in relation to the Commerce of the Lakes.

The extent and importance of our internal commerce must be our apology for making copious extracts from this able and interesting document.

The vast and increasing commerce of the West having attracted the attention of the General Government, an agent has been appointed whose duty it is to procure all necessary information in regard to its growth and progress. All information in regard to the tonnage employed on the western lakes, and the value of property annually conveyed to and fro, has heretofore been furnished the government by Col. J. J. Abert, the head of the Topographical Bureau. This gentleman has been indefatigable in his exertions to place before Congress the extent of the trade of the West, the facilities for doing business at the several shipping points, and the necessity for increasing those facilities by furnishing adequate harbour room and erecting suitable works for the protection of life and property. The very loose manner in which the official returns from many of the collection districts have been made, has rendered the obtaining of accurate information a work of immense labour. To obviate this an agent has been appointed, whose duty it is to visit the several ports of entry and obtain the information desired. At the request of Mr. Milford, the agent referred to, the Board of Trade of Buffalo, took measures to furnish information in regard to this point, by the appointment for that purpose of a proper committee.—It is due to Mr. James L. Barton, one of the committee, to say that the great bulk of the labour has devolved upon him, and the very creditable manner in which the report has been prepared, is an evidence that much time and attention have been bestowed on the subject.

BUFFALO, N. Y., August, 1849.

William Milford, Esq., U. States Agent for procuring statistical information in relation to the Commerce of the Lakes.

SIR—Your communication addressed to the Board of Trade of this city, requesting their assistance in procuring, for the use of the Home Department at Washington, information on the following subjects having reference to the commercial transactions at the port of Buffalo, during the year 1848, viz.:

1. Imports, coastwise, quantity and value;
2. Do.   foreign,   do.   do.
3. Exports, coastwise, do.   do.
4. Do.   foreign,   do.   do.

5. Number of steamers, steam propellers and vessels, registered and licensed in the district, their tonnage and value;

6. Number of steamers and vessels, and their aggregate amount of tonnage;

7. Population of the city, January 1, 1849;

8. Works of internal improvement constructed or being constructed for the benefit of commerce, has been referred to a committee consisting of the undersigned, who, having devoted much time and careful attention to the subject, present the following report as the result of their labours:

1st. *Imports, coastwise, quantity and value.*

From the well known fact of the shortness of the trips, particularly across Lake Erie, and the rapidity with which the business is transacted during the season of navigation and the very little real necessity there is for doing it, the manifests of cargoes do not contain a full and precise statement of the kind and quantity on board, consequently a full and perfect account of the entire imports cannot be obtained. In addition to this, vessels running from port to port within the same district are not required by law to report their cargoes. The business done in this way is very large, but the details of it, it is impossible to arrive at. It embraces large quantities of lumber in all its varieties, corn, oats, barley, pork, beef, cheese, butter, ashes, potatoes, and numerous other agricultural products.

From a careful abstract made from manifests of vessels in the Custom House and records kept by the Board of Trade, the committee were enabled to obtain the following imports. This list is longer and more in detail than is usually made in reporting imports, the great and leading articles more commonly only being given. It has not been elaborated for the purpose of show merely, but principally with a view to exhibit the varied kind of articles which enter into and form the lake commerce.

Article	Unit	Quantity	Article	Unit	Quantity
Flour	barrels	1,347,406	Wool	bales	40,024
Corn meal		3,016	Hops		24
Buckwheat meal		155	Cotton		445
Rye flour		382	Hides, slan'd	No.	70,750
Pork and bacon		108,112	Hogs, live		32,516
Beef		53,812	Hogs, dressed		8,551
Wheat	bushels	4,520,117	Beef cattle		675
Corn		2,341,291	Horses		811
Oats		560,000	Sheep		74
Barley		28,505	Iron, pig	tons	4,132
Rye		17,800	Iron, bar		184
Potatoes		28,309	Iron, bars of	No.	6,009
Peas and beans		5,364	Iron, bundles of		786
Butter	pounds	7,301,861	Nails and spikes	kegs	6,488
Lard		6,253,735	Lead	pigs	27,953
Cheese		9,530,568	Sugar, La.	hogsheads	350
Dried and other fruit	packages	2,453	Do. do.	barrels	940
Fish (lake)	barrels	6,620	Tallow		4,490
Whiskey and high-			Lard and other oil		3,323
wines	casks	38,850	Soap grease		1,337
Clover and grass seed		22,020	Coal	tons	12,950
Ashes		13,690	Lumber	feet	43,121,302
Flaxseed		11,847	Shingles	M	4,060
Tobacco	hogsheads	385	Staves	ps.	8,091,000
Leather	rls.	3,313	Hemp	bales	865
Furs and pelts	pks.	2,808	Sandpaper	reams	1,660
Shot	kegs	231	Shoe pegs	bushels	365
Cranberries	barrels	322	Starch	barrels	214
Eggs		2,513	Do.	boxes	3,376
Copper ore	tons	1,163	Candles, stearines		1,103

Copper, pigs	number	160	Soap			223
Corn brooms	dozens	1,268	Beeswax	pkgs.		380
Sheep pelts	number	77,960	Black walnut logs			
Feathers	sacks	2,096	and crotches	No.		733
Rags		1,330	Saleratus casks and			
Hogs' hair & bristles		1,032	barrels			666
Grindstones	tons	1,658	Beer bottles	No.		16,872
Fire brick	No.	31,111	Cane poles			10,000
Fire clay	barrels	821	Broom corn	bundles		2,519
Hay rakes	dozen	174	Oil meal	sacks		824
Hay forks		78	Do.	casks		230
Scythes		82	Do.	tons		458
Axes		246	Railroad ties	No.		65,000
Shovels and spades		360	Cedar posts and logs			3,000
Hoes		51.	Do. do.	cords		320
Sad irons	barrels	24	Oars	No.		11,047
Hoops, flour barrel	M.	250	Oars	feet		22,814
Ale and beer	barrels	375	Handspikes	No.		1,582
Mineral paint		350	Liverpool salt	bushels		2,500
Castor oil		42	Cannon, (U. S.)	No.		75
Popped corn		19	Muskets, do.	boxes		515

SUNDRIES.—Household furniture, merchandise, plaster, ginseng, mint oil, various kinds of roots, barrels of hickory nuts and chestnuts, glue, horns, bones, cider, vinegar, maple sugar, bundles of flax, veneering, boxes of glass and glass ware, mineral specimens, &c., &c., &c.   packages 22,217

ALSO—Large quantities of ship timber and plank, ships' knees, spars, pine saw logs, building and docking timber.

Forming an estimated value of $22,743,404.

This property is the growth and product of the States of Pennsylvania, Ohio, Kentucky, Indiana, Illinois, Iowa, Wisconsin, Michigan, Tennessee, Louisiana, Missouri, Canada, and that portion of New York bordering on the Lakes. In arriving at a valuation, the utmost care has been taken to obtain the actual worth of the different articles in the market. Flour is valued at $4 72 per bbl., wheat at 92 cents, corn 43¾ cents, and oats at 30 cents per bushel; pork and bacon, including smoked hams, at $10 65 per bbl., which was the average price of mess pork; butter at 12 cents per pound, lard $6 63½; cheese $5 88½; and for the various other articles, the books of dealers and others conversant with the market have been consulted. The committee are satisfied the gross valuation might easily, without doing injustice to the trade, have been much increased.

2d. Imports, foreign, quantity and value.

In abstracting the various manifests, it was not discovered, until the work was nearly finished, that the distinction between coastwise and foreign imports, had not been made. The great labour of going over the work for that purpose was not deemed of sufficient consequence to undertake it, and the preceding table of imports coastwise, includes the foreign. The kind and description of the foreign imports are, pine lumber and shingles, saw logs, railroad ties, sheep pelts, grass seed, plaster, horses, furs, some wheat and flour, Liverpool salt, wool and numerous small articles which enter into our retail trade. The value of the imports, as made up at the Custom House, was $129,004, viz.:

Foreign goods imported in American vessels					28,910
Do. do. foreign do.					100,094

$129,004

3d. Exports, Coastwise, quantity and value.

It is utterly impossible to specify the articles under this head : they include almost every thing that can be enumerated. The property landed at Buffalo from the Erie Canal, the Albany and Buffalo Railroad, the manufactures and productions of this city, and the merchandise sold in this city to the Western trade, constitute the exports.

The States using the Lake route in 1848 for transporting their merchandise and other supplies, were Ohio, Pennsylvania, Michigan, Illinois, Indiana, Wisconsin, Iowa, Missouri, Kentucky, Tennessee, New York bordering on lake Erie, and Canada West.

(Condensed tables are here given from the statements of the canal office, of the various quantities and valuation of canal imports, for the year 1848, and also, of the different kinds of property, quantities and value, which cleared by the Albany and Buffalo Railroad.

These tables, or similar ones, we have given in a former number. The report thus proceeds:)

From the foregoing statements the value of the Export Commerce (including Foreign, which amount will be given under its proper head) of Buffalo during the year 1848, may with considerable certainty be arrived at.

Property landed here from the Erie canal, originally destined for the Western States   29,486,393

do.   do.   do.   Canada West   46,382

do. for Buffalo and that portion of New York on and near Lake Erie   8,072,345

Received by the Albany and Buffalo Railroad   3,212,832

    11,285,177

To determine what amount of this sum of 11,285,177 dollars, enters into the Lake Commerce, the committee think, that by adding to it the value of manufactured articles of iron-mongery, cabinet ware, leather, white lead, upholstery, and the production of numerous other manufactures in this city; a large portion of dry goods of light weight but valuable, brought on by railroad originally started for the Western States; the export of the largest portion of the salt brought up the canal; the large amount of merchandise sold wholesale and retail to the Western traders;—it will not be exaggerating to place the value at three-fourths of the canal and railroad importation, which will give an amount of   8,463,883

Forming a total of   37,996,658

These statements show that the importations from the Eastward into this city, in 1848, were equal to the sum of $40,817,952; of which amount $37,996,658 entered into and formed the export commerce of this Port that year, to the Western States. The value of the imports from the Lakes so far as they can be arrived at, is $22,143,404, making the total of the Lake Commerce, of imports and exports from this port in 1848, $60,140,062.

4th. Exports, Foreign, quantity and value.

The Committee are unable to specify in detail the articles which make up our Foreign export trade, and can only refer to them by name. They consist of merchandise received by the Erie Canal originally destined for Canada, various articles of merchandise purchased in this city, as well as considerable wheat, flour, pork and whiskey used on the public works in Canada, and for the trade of the St. Lawrence. The amount of exports as given at the Custom House is $254,254, as follows:—

Exports, Foreign goods in American vessels   6,089

"   "   "   Foreign   "   52,906

"   Domestic produce in American vessels   51,938

"   "   "   Foreign   "   143,321

    254,254

5th. Number of Steam Boats, Steam Propellers and Vessels Registered and Licensed in the District of Buffalo, their tonnage and value.

By referring to the Custom House records, we find the following named Boats, Propellers and Vessels, their tonnage and the number of persons employed thereon, registered and licensed in this District in 1848.

(Here follows a table containing the names in full and the tonnage of all the lake vessels, which is thus summed up by the Committee:)

Forming a total as follows:—

Class.	Number.	Tonnage.	Valuation.
Steamers	28	16,741.31	$884,000
Propellers	14	4,925.40	206,000
Brigs	32	7,430.75	225,000
Schooners	86	13,531.39	401,300
Sloops and Scows	4	106.54	6,100
Total	164	44,744.49	$1,722,400

To arrive at the value of this property was a most difficult matter. It would not answer to put it down at the original cost, nor yet so low, as to satisfy those owning it that we had placed a value upon it far below its real market as well as intrinsic worth. To obviate these objections, the committee not only appraised the several vessels, but they referred the matter to an experienced ship-carpenter, and to others well conversant with the property. The several parties made separate estimates without consultation with each other, and the amount arrived at, as stated in this report, is the result of the mode adopted.

6th. Number of persons employed.

By reference to the books at the Custom House, we ascertain the number of persons employed on the various vessels licensed and registered in this District in 1848, were—

Employed on Board Steamers		803
Do.	Propellers	275
Do.	Brigs	330
Do.	Schooners	714
Do.	Sloops and Scows	14
Total number employed		2,136

7th. Number of Arrivals and Departures during the season, of Steamers and Vessels, and their aggregate tonnage.

From the Custom House books, the number of arrivals and departures reported (which do not include all) and gross amount of tonnage was—

For quarter ending March 31, 1848.	No.	Tons.	Hands.
Arrivals from Foreign ports, American ves.	728	45,391.27	1,456
Do. do. Foreign			
Cleared to do. American ves.	728	45,391.27	1,456
Do. do. Foreign ves.			
Arrivals, coastwise	6	2,185.23	133
Cleared, do.	8	3,329.52	187
For the quarter ending June 30.			
Arrivals from Foreign ports, American ves.	845	53,301.19	1,708
Do. do. Foreign ves.	263	55,417.79	3,304
Cleared to do. American ves.	866	54,831.41	1,816
Do. do. Foreign ves.	264	53,906.77	3,242
Arrivals, coastwise	1,202	330,540.23	16,175
Cleared, do.	1,235	356,330.35	16,953

For the quarter ending September 30.

			No.	Tons.	Hands.
Arrivals from Foreign ports, American ves.			740	46,643.19	1,495
Do.	do.	Foreign ves.	239	49,365.79	2,891
Cleared to	do.	American ves.	758	49,990.41	1,588
Do.	do.	Foreign ves.	231	47,168.77	2,837
Arrivals, coastwise			1,052	289,223.23	14,153
Cleared,	do.		1,081	311,787.35	14,834

For the quarter ending December 31.

Arrivals from Foreign ports, American ves.			837	52,832.70	1,732
Do.	do.	Foreign ves.	114	30,663.78	1,634
Cleared to	do.	American ves.	846	53,631.24	1,782
Do.	do.	Foreign ves.	116	29,702.13	1,642
Arrivals, coastwise			832	230,559.37	11,135
Cleared,	do.		742	208,101.05	10,095

The entrance and clearance of American vessels from and to Foreign ports in this statement appear very large; the reason of it is this—a steam ferryboat runs regularly across the Niagara river from Black Rock, which is included in the other arrivals and departures. To arrive at the number that justly and properly belongs to commerce, the committee exclude all the American arrivals and clearances from and to Foreign ports in the quarter ending March 31, and seven-eighths of the same during the remainder of the season. This, we are informed by the officials at the Custom House, would give a very near account of the number of American vessels engaged in commercial business with Foreign ports.

A statement of the entire number of arrivals and clearances we have given, and making therefrom the deductions above stated, shows that as near as the accounts can be made up, the arrivals and departures were 8084, with an aggregate tonnage of 2,045,175 tons.

8th. The population of the city, January 1, 1849.

Much diversity of opinion exists as to the real number of our population—many judicious persons putting it as high or higher than 45,000. The last official census was the State census of 1845, which gave the number 29,837. Estimating from the number of votes polled, and from the number of children at our public schools, which is the only guide we have, the committee prefer placing the number at 40,000, to going beyond it. In 1850, only one year from this time, the United States census will be taken, when the true number will be ascertained. In estimating as we have to do now, the committee prefer erring by putting the number under, than over the real amount.

The answer to the ninth inquiry, viz.: The works of internal improvements constructed for the benefit of commerce, is deferred to a subsequent number.

GROWTH AND COMMERCE OF MILWAUKIE.

Among the Lake ports which have sprung up as if by magic in the west, none have perhaps had a more rapid growth than Milwaukie, situated upon the Wisconsin shore of Lake Michigan. From the statistics of the place recently collected for the agent of the government, and published, it appears that in May, 1834, Mr. Solomon Juneau was the only white settler within the limits of what is now the city of Milwaukie. The following table of census returns, taken since that period, exhibits the rate of increase in the population.

1838,	700
1840,	1,700
1842,	2,700

1846,—June 1,	·	·	·	·	·	9,655
1847,—Dec. 15,	·	·	·	·	·	14,661
1849,—Aug. (estimated)	·	·	·	·	18,000

Equally rapid has been the augmentation in the exports of produce, &c. It was in 1845, that the first shipments of wheat and flour, to any extent, were made from Milwaukie. The following table shows how this business grows.

EXPORTS FROM MILWAUKIE.

							Wheat bushels.	Flour bbls.
1845,	·	·	·	·	·	·	95,510	7,550
1846,	·	·	·	·	·	·	213,448	15,756
1847,	·	·	·	·	·	·	508,011	35,840
1848,	·	·	·	·	·	·	612,574	92,732
1849,	·	·	·	·	·	·	1,148,807	201,942

It is proper to remark that the exports for 1849, in the above table, embrace those from July 1, 1848, to July 1, 1849, while those for the four previous years are for the season of navigation in each year respectively.

The value of exports from Milwaukie in 1848 were of manufactured articles $1,714,200, and of agricultural products $2,098,469, making a total of exports of $3,812,669. The value of imports of merchandise, &c., for the same period was $3,828,650. There are in Milwaukie five flouring mills, propelled by water power, and one by steam, containing seventeen run of stone, each run capable of turning out 80 to 100 bbls. flour per day, and consuming in all 7000 bushels wheat daily.

There are thirty-nine sail vessels owned in, and sailing out of that port, of which the total tonnage is 5,542; also, stock in steamers and propellers of 3000 tons; making the total tonnage owned in the port 8,542.

Sixteen sail vessels are engaged exclusively in the lumber trade, and the remainder in freighting produce and merchandise.

ARRIVALS DURING THE SEASON OF 1848.

Steamers,	·	·	·	·	·	·	498
Propellers,	·	·	·	·	·	·	248
Barques and brigs,	·	·	·	·	·	119
Schooners,	·	·	·	·	·	·	511
Total,	·	·	·	·	·	·	1,376

MICHIGAN.

The growth of this youthful member of the confederacy has been wonderfully rapid. In 1830 her settlement had hardly commenced; now her population is not less than 400,000. Her soil bears every species of grain which thrives in the State of New York. In 1847, she exported over one million of barrels of flour, an amount ten times greater than all the wheat and flour that passed through the Erie canal from west of Buffalo in 1835. Her total tonnage in 1847 was over 35,000, and its value is estimated at $1,757,250. The aggregate commerce for the same year was over thirteen millions. Her fisheries yield $200,000 a year; her wool product is over $400,000. Iron, copper, salt, and plaster, are indigenous and abundant.

COMMERCE OF CINCINNATI.

From an interesting article in the Cincinnati Gazette, in reference to the commerce of that flourishing city, we gather the following statistics of some of the principal articles of trade. The commercial year opens on the 1st of September, and closes on the 31st of August.

IMPORTS.				1846-7.	1847-8.	1848-9.
Cotton, bales,	.	.	.	12,528	13,476	9,058
Coffee, bags,	.	.	.	59,337	89,242	74,961
Molasses, barrels,	.	.	.	27,216	51,001	52,591
Rice, tierces,	.	.	.	1,145	2,494	3,365
Sugar, hogsheads,	.	.	.	16,649	27,153	22,685
Do. barrels,	.	.	.	7,196	11,175	7,575
Do. boxes,	.	.	.	5,177	2,928	1,847
Total packages,	.	.	.	129,248	188,469	172,582
EXPORTS.				1846-7.	1847-8.	1848-9.
Cotton, bales,	.	.	.	5,077	6,123	4,009
Coffee, bags,	.	.	.	13,037	18,587	18,907
Molasses, barrels,	.	.	.	9,046	18,832	17,750
Sugar, hogsheads,	.	.	.	4,908	5,559	8,443

PORK AND BEEF.

The following is a comparative statement of the stock of Pork and Beef exported from Cincinnati, and in the Inspection Warehouse, at New Orleans, on the first of the last three months.

PORK.				July 1.	August 1.	Sept. 1.
Clear, barrels,	.	.	.	53	102	151
Prime Mess,	.	.	.	116	57	27
Mess,	.	.	.	22,224	22,187	18,816
Mess, Ordinary,	.	.	.	4,988	5,078	4,500
Soft Mess,	.	.	.	648	132	90
Prime,	.	.	.	6,172	5,093	3,124
Prime Ordinary,	.	.	.	....	....	....
Soft Prime,	.	.	.	522	478	502
Rumps and Chines,	.	.	.	2,348	2,721	2,647
Inferior and Damaged,	.	.	.	618	916	567
Not Inspected,	.	.	.	3,252	2,319	1,880
Total, barrels,	.	.	.	40,941	39,084	32,604
BEEF.				July 1.	August 1.	Sept. 1.
Prime Mess, tierces,	.	.	.	30	...	...
Do. barrels,	.	.	.	650	276	...
Mess, barrels,	.	.	.	1,114	662	346
Mess, Ordinary,	.	.	.	162	196	132
Prime,	.	.	.	462	541	492
B. Beef,	.	.	.	27	49	59
Inferior and Damaged,	.	.	.	..	202	219
Rumps,	.	.	.	39	...	...
Mess and Prime, half barrels,				1,288	1,203	107
Total,	.	.	.	3,772	3,129	2,323
Total tierces,	.	.		30	....	....
Total barrels,	.	.		2,451	1,926	1,248
Total half barrels,	.			1,288	1,203	1,075
				3,772	3,129	2,323

The stock of Lard, as near as can be ascertained, is 13,500 tierces and barrels, and 43,000 kegs. Last year, 2,000 barrels and 3,660 kegs.

COMMERCE OF NEW ORLEANS.

We extract from the New Orleans Price Current the following tables, showing the trade of that port for a number of years past. The amount of tonnage entered during the year 1848–49 was 898,920 tons, against 900,448 last year. The value of the exports for the year ending 30th June last was $65,392,571, against $67,182,323 the previous year. The value of the receipts from the interior, during the past four years, was as follows:

1848–9 . . $81,989,692	1846–7 . . $99,633,256
1847–8 . . 79,779,151	1845–6 . . 77,193,464

COMPARATIVE RECEIPTS AT NEW ORLEANS FOR FOUR YEARS.

ARTICLES.	1848–9.	1847–8.	1846–7.	1845–6.
Apples, barrels,	54,987	39,518	30,612	26,775
Bacon, asst. casks, &c.,	32,056	45,119	36,932	25,213
Bacon, barrels and boxes,	32,156	. . . . .	. . . . .	. . . . .
Bacon Hams, hogsheads,	19,831	18,539	14,518	12,092
Bacon in Bulk, pounds,	217,900	381,140	425,163	492,700
Bagging, pieces,	72,941	77,682	60,982	96,601
Butter, kegs,	57,972	45,213	51,384	44,170
Butter, barrels,	2,144	1,156	872	1,492
Bees'-wax, barrels,	481	698	1,109	1,204
Beef, barrels and tierces,	80,590	50,260	53,968	62,231
Beef, Dried, pounds,	20,300	56,100	49,000	98,200
Buffalo Robes, packs,	23	14	55	1,031
COTTON.				
La. and Mi., bales,	811,205	883,144	453,842	765,315
Lake, bales,	15,781	13,734	4,356	14,276
N. Alabama and Ten., bales,	217,078	227,561	211,502	222,677
Arkansas, bales,	46,733	64,294	35,279	34,876
Mobile, bales,	35,164	19,857	16,379	6,356
Florida, bales,	5,065	4,268	16,966	5,884
Texas, do.,	11,356	10,007	2,345	4,249
Corn Meal, barrels,	12,097	47,543	88,159	3,905
Corn in Ears, barrels,	295,711	509,583	619,756	358,573
Corn, Shelled, sacks,	1,706,312	1,083,465	2,386,510	1,166,120
Cheese, boxes,	54,287	52,362	57,429	57,392
Coal, Western, barrels,	315,000	320,000	356,500	262,800
Dried Peaches, barrels,	469	385	3,009	127
Dried Apples, barrels,	2,495	1,173	5,761	930
Flaxseed, tierces,	1,188	4,393	962	823
Flour, barrels,	1,013,177	706,958	1,617,675	837,985
Feathers, bags,	3,939	2,594	3,498	4,607
Hemp, bales,	19,856	21,584	60,238	30,980
Hides,	30,570	47,662	98,342	112,913
Iron, Pig, tons,	413	701	1,151	1,083
Lard, hogsheads,	790	459	143	45
Lard, tierces and barrels,	214,362	216,031	117,077	107,639
Lard, kegs,	275,485	303,661	275,076	334,969
Lead, pigs,	508,557	606,966	650,129	785,394

	1848–9.	1847–8.	1846–7.	1845–6.
Lead, Bar, kegs, . .	949	787	1,291	1,431
Lead, White, kegs, . .	7,795	9,203	11,686	7,853
Molasses, barrels, . .	155,807	159,460	61,710	132,363
Oil, Linseed, barrels, .	1,409	2,327	3,637	1,136
Oil, Castor, barrels, .	2,628	1,199	1,439	2,379
Oil, Lard, barrels, . .	8,842	5,401	2,573	2,606
Potatoes, barrels, . .	146,116	151,860	142,888	107,058
Pork, tierces and barrels, .	530,643	356,480	302,170	369,601
Pork, boxes, . . .	18,279	. . . .	. . . .	. . . .
Pork, hogsheads, . .	18,499	14,201	9,452	9,988
Pork, in bulk, pounds,	10,273,680	13,564,430	8,456,700	9,740,752
Packing Yarn, reels, .	2,211	3,333	2,193	1,193
Skins, Deer, packs, . .	1,301	1,361	1,784	4,364
Shot, kegs, . . .	4,377	5,258	3,992	8,103
Sugar, hogsheads, . .	125,592	128,112	82,011	93,109
Sugar, barrels, . .	5,873	. . . .	. . . .	. . . .
Tallow, barrels, . .	10,622	4,357	6,658	8,255
Tobacco, leaf, hogsheads,	52,335	55,882	55,598	72,890
Tobacco, chew, kegs, .	2,315	6,390	3,930	3,040
Tobacco, bales, . .	33	118	1,001	1,105
Whiskey, barrels, . .	125,029	135,333	126,553	117,104
Window Glass, boxes, .	575	4,260	3,805	2,831
Wheat, barrels and sacks, .	238,911	149,181	833,649	403,786

COTTON FACTORIES IN ALABAMA.

The Montgomery Journal notices two new factories under headway in Autoga county. One with a capital of $100,000, to work 3,500 spindles and 100 looms, to manufacture cotton goods alone, and will go into operation next January. The other has a capital of $75,000, and will be for cotton and woollen goods. Both are near the Alabama river, have fine water power, and are situated in a healthy and abundant provision region.

It affords us sincere pleasure to chronicle such enterprises, which are sources of individual as well as public benefit. With the staple commodity at the doors of her factories, and possessing operative labour of the cheapest character, we see no reason why the South should not compete with the North in the manufacture of cotton fabrics. The establishment of a cotton factory and of other nurseries of productive industry, will accomplish more for the independence of the South, than any resolves on paper can possibly do. The people of Georgia have long since made this important discovery, and it affords us pleasure to observe that Alabama is becoming fully alive to the wisdom of the policy pursued by Georgia.

PUBLIC MONEYS—TREASURY OF UNITED STATES.

U. S. TREASURER'S STATEMENT,

Showing the amount at his credit in the Treasury, July 23d, 1849.

In what place.	Amount subject to draft.
Assistant Treasurer, Boston, Mass.	$209,882 58
Assistant Treasurer, New York, N. Y.	815,057 29

Assistant Treasurer, Philadelphia, Pa.	92,723	91
Treasury United States, Washington, D. C.	164,212	35
Assistant Treasurer, Charleston, S. C.	85,335	92
Assistant Treasurer, New Orleans, La.	632,633	77
Assistant Treasurer, St. Louis, Mo,	79,630	17
Depository at Buffalo, N. Y.	4,867	80
Depository at Baltimore, Md.	23,667	02
Depository at Richmond, Va.		
Depository at Wilmington, N. C.	1,306	95
Depository at Savannah, Ga.	4,176	47
Depository at Mobile, Ala.	46,446	83
Depository at Nashville, Tenn.	7,790	92
Depository at Cincinnati, Ohio,	79,022	41
Depository at Pittsburgh, Pa.		
Depository at Norfolk, Va.		
Depository at Little Rock, Ark. (late receiver,)	18,351	78
Depository at Jeffersonville, Ind.	281,450	86
Depository at Chicago, Ill.	14,926	43
Depository at Detroit, Mich.	12,082	96
Depository at Little Rock,	2,551	96
Suspense account,	$2,304 71	
Mint of the United States, Philadelphia, Pa.	710,000	00
Branch Mint of the United States, Charlotte, N. C.	32,000	00
Branch Mint of the United States, Dahlonega, Ga.	26,850	00
Branch Mint of the United States, New Orleans, La.	79,421	95

	$3,424,391	13
Deduct suspense account,	2,304	71
Net amount subject to draft,	$3,422,086	42

Treasury Department, July 31, 1849.

The receipts into the Treasury during the quarter ending the 30th of June, 1849, as nearly as can now be ascertained, were, namely:

From customs,	$5,794,256 50
" lands,	279,685 26
" miscellaneous sources,	63,500 00
" loan of 1847, (Treasury notes funded,)	2,986,600 00
" loan of 1848,	2,017,450 00
	$11,141,491 76

Expenditures of the United States from 1st April to 30th June, 1849:

Civil list, miscellaneous, and foreign intercourse, (including $3,500,000 under the treaty with Mexico,)		$3,909,143 12
On account of the army, &c.	$2,268,203 69	
" Indian Department,	441,717 41	
" fortifications,	129,127 52	
" pensions,	162,380 17	
		3,001,428 79

On account of the navy,	2,041,912 94
Interest on public debt and treasury notes,	1,765,223 58
Reimbursement of treasury notes,	2,998,850 00
Redemption of public debt,	641,175 00
Premiums and commissions on purchase of public debt,	60,443 81
Redemption of treasury notes purloined, &c.	54 05
	$14,418,231 29

W. M. Meredith, Sec. of Treasury.

NEW YORK SUB-TREASURY.

The following statement of the movements of the Sub-Treasury at New York, for July and August, may not be uninteresting at this time:

Balance on hand, 1st July,		$1,086,581 90
Receipts during July and August, 1849:		
On account customs,	$5,557,862 37	
" Patent Office,	3,040 50	
" of loans,	6,000 00	
" Post Office department,	62,780 28	
" miscellaneous,	41,375 65	5,671,048 80
		$6,757,630 79
Payments during July and August, 1849:		
Treasury Drafts,	$3,660,598 61	
Post office do.	99,342 22	3,759,490 83
Balance, August 31st, 1849,		$2,997,689 96
Funds set apart to pay interest on Stock, &c.		$1,037,487 50
Payments of interest during July and August:		
Instalments due July, 1848,	306 25	
" " January, 1849,	4,173 03	
" " July, 1849,	760,903 03	
Coupons,	172,855 00	
Interest on Treasury notes funded,	11,424 93	
" " " outstanding,	12,160 50	961,822 74
Balance on hand,		$75,664 76

SPECIE.

The following is the export of specie from New York for the week ending 8th Sept.

Ship Republic, Maranham, Mexican dollars,	$3,000
Ship St. Dennis, Havre, Mexican dollars,	15,000
Ship Prince Albert, London, Mexican dollars,	55,000
Steamer Canada, Liverpool, British silver,	1,015
" " " gold dust,	2,160
Total,	$76,175
Previously reported,	$1,837,034
Total from January 1st to September 8,	$1,913,109

CALIFORNIA GOLD.

We have been furnished from the mint with the following statement:
The deposits of California gold, to the 31st of August, were,

At the Philadelphia Mint,	$1,740,620 07
At the New Orleans Mint,	175,918 73
	$1,916,538 80
Add the deposits of 1848,	44,177 00
Total deposits from California,	$1,960,715 80

The coinage of gold dollars at the mint in Philadelphia, to

the 31st ult. was	$462,539 00
At the Branch Mints, to July 31st,	133,227 00
Total coinage of gold dollars,	$595,766 00

STATISTICS OF CHOLERA.

In Philadelphia, the first official bulletin was issued on May 30th, and the last on August 19th, the board of health having declared at the latter date that cholera was no longer epidemic. The whole period of its duration was 82 days, during which time there were reported 2,131 cases, and 744 deaths, or one death in 2.86 cases. On the 14th July the greatest number of deaths occurred, viz., 32; cases 84; and on the 29th of July the greatest number of cases, viz., 90; deaths 24. The increase on the last date was owing to the violent breaking out of the disease in the Alms House.

During the months of May and June there were reported 278 cases and 97 deaths, or one death in 2.86 cases. In July 1566 cases, and 578 deaths, or 1 in 2.70. In August 277 cases, and 69 deaths, or 1 in 4.01 cases.

The whole population of Philadelphia, city and county included, amounts to about 350,000. This will give a ratio of cases to population of 1 to 164.24. The ratio of deaths to cases during the whole epidemic was 1 to 2.86 cases, and the ratio of deaths to population was 1 to 470.4 inhabitants.

1849.

Locality.	Population.	Cases.	Deaths.	Ratio of cases to population.	Ratio of deaths to cases.	Ratio of deaths to population.
Philada.,	350,000.	2,131.	744.	1 in 164.24	1 in 2.86	1 in 470.4

1832.

Locality.	Population.	Cases.	Deaths.	Ratio of cases to population.	Ratio of deaths to cases.	Ratio of deaths to population.
"	160,000.	2,314.	754.	1 in 69.1	1 in 3.06	1 in 212.2

By a comparison of the above tables it will be seen, that while the whole number of cases and deaths was more than half less in 1849 than in 1832, the mortality was much the same in the two epidemics.

The above statement of the number of deaths (744) reported during the prevalence of the epidemic, is from the daily bulletins of the Board of Health. But the reports of *interments* from cholera, from May 30th to August 19th, make the number of deaths 962, and up to September 8th, 1,012.

The discrepancy is owing to the fact that daily reports were not made by many physicians—that several cases were reported by the coroner, &c. Although the daily bulletins ceased on the 19th of August, there were cases reported up to the 8th of September, and in the last week in August there were 15 deaths in one block.

In NEW YORK the board of health commenced daily reports May 11th, and discontinued them about the 1st of September.

The following table shows the number of deaths by cholera at New York and Philadelphia during the summer of 1849.

Periods.		New York.	Philadelphia.
Week ending May 18th,		1	
" " 26th		13	
" June 2d		29	3
" " 9th		121	3
" " 16th		145	5
" " 23d		148	14
" " 30th		286	80
" July 7th		317	170
" " 14th		484	179
" " 21st		714	195
" " 28th		692	136
" Aug. 4th		678	95
" " 11th		423	40
" " 18th		387	42
" " 25th		233	16
" Sep. 1st		171	18
" " 8th		94	16
		4,936	1,012

In CINCINNATI the deaths from cholera for four months preceding the 30th of August were 4,114.—

The mortality was, proportionally, still larger in St. Louis. We have not the official statement, but the deaths within the same period were reported to be as high as 5,000.

At Buffalo, it is stated, that within three months 1,000 died, or one-fourth of the whole population. The disease prevailed in this place mostly among the emigrant and transient population.

In England and France the cases have been very large. In Paris in one day there were 900 cases and 600 deaths—another account says, the deaths in three days exceeded 1,600. As late as the 8th of September the deaths from cholera and diarrhœa in London, were for the week 1,663—and there have been as many as 475 in one day within the London districts.

It is our intention to collect together the facts for an accurate and succinct statement of the amount of mortality during the year 1849, at the places both in the old and new world most severely visited by the cholera—until then what we have given in this number must suffice.

Several theories have recently been started in relation to the origin or cause of the disease. A French physician, Dr. Andraud, in a communication to the Academy of Sciences, at Paris, stated the result of sundry experiments to prove that the absence of electricity in the atmosphere was the cause of cholera. This theory was combated by many, and especially by Professor Olmstead of Yale College, who denied that there was any unusual connexion between the condition of atmospheric electricity and the prevailing epidemic. Another theory makes the origin of the cholera to depend upon the action of an atmospherical element or condition, termed Ozone, the nature of which however seems to be but little understood, and about which scientific men do not seem to be entirely agreed. A later, and at present more favoured theory is founded on a discovery recently made by Dr. Brittan and Mr. Swayne of Bristol, England, of the existence of "certain peculiar bodies or organisms," hitherto undescribed, as constituents of cholera evacuations, and as also found in the atmosphere and water of the districts infected by cholera. It is stated that these organisms are of the fungous kind; that they are developed in the human intestines and are the cause of the peculiar flux which is the characteristic of malignant cholera. The evidence of these singular discoveries is before the College of Physicians in London, and an elaborate article is expected from Dr. Brittan on the subject.

We close with the following extract on the *law of epidemics.*

"The average visitations of new fatal exotics, have been calculated as recurring at each revolution of 300 years, and there is none on record which has been less fatal than Asiatic cholera. After the first appearance of an exotic epidemic failing of naturalization, it has a tendency to repeat its visits once in each revolution of sixteen years. Thus the sweating sickness, according to Dr. Collier's statement, which was said to have been brought into England along with the army of Richmond, afterwards Henry VII., first appeared at Milford Haven, in the year 1486, when, meeting with no epidemical condition, it soon disappeared. It repeated its visitations under epidemic influence in 1503; and it reappeared altogether five times, with an average interspace of sixteen years; not until its fourth visitation reaching the Court, and proving fatal to many of the courtiers in six hours—Henry VIII. owing his restoration from a severe attack to the well known vigour of his constitution. At its fifth and last return, or sixth visit in 1551, it carried off 120 in a day within the precincts of Westminster alone, where the two sons of Charles Brandon, both Dukes of Suffolk, died of it. From 1486 to 1551 is a space of sixty-six years, which, divided by four, leaves an aggregate of sixteen and a half years, which agrees with the interspace between the two visits of Asiatic cholera. Arguing from these facts, we may expect a return of the present scourge in 1865, and from the curious laws which have governed former epidemics, also in 1882, 1899, and lastly, in 1916, allowing an interspace of a little over sixteen years between each visit. A space of some three centuries may then be expected, during which time the earth will be free from any awful scourge, and then a new and terrible pestilence will start forth on its voyage of death, sweeping millions from existence by its fearful presence."

ECCLESIASTICAL STATISTICS.

The estimates of some of the religious denominations in the United States are given as follows:

From one source we have this table,—

DENOMINATIONAL STATISTICS.

The Methodists in the United States, including the church North and South, and those denominated protestant, number in their body 1,178,626 members.

The Protestant portion number but 83,600 of this large aggregate. The number of Methodist churches is not reported in the tables from which these statistics are compiled. The number of ministers in the Episcopal portion of this body is 5,080.

The Baptists, including the Regular, Anti-Mission, Free-will, and others, have 11,266 churches, 6,598 ministers, and 813,921 members.

The Presbyterians, Old School and New, have 1,027 churches, and 3,264 ministers, and 335,453 members.

The Congregationalists have 1,866 churches, 1,912 ministers, and 193,093 members.

The Episcopalians have 1,092 churches, 1,404 ministers, and 67,550 members. Here are 212 more ministers than churches.

The Lutherans have 1,425 churches, 299 ministers, and 149,626 members.

The Associate, Reformed, Cumberland, and other Presbyterians, together with Reformed Dutch and German Reformed churches, have 2,052 churches, 2,091 ministers, and 241,840 members.

The Roman Catholics have 967 churches, 917 ministers, and 1,199,700 members.

The Unitarians have 244 churches. The number of ministers and members not reported, but the number of ministers is doubtless as large as the number of churches, if not larger. If the churches contain, on an average, as many as the Orthodox Congregational Churches, the aggregate number would be 27,532.

The number of churches of these several denominations, exclusive of Methodists, which are not reported, is 21,981. Allowing the Methodists 10,000 churches, the whole number would be about 33,000.

The whole number of ministers in these denominations is 22,808, and the whole number of members of churches 4,197,141.

The Baptists have the largest number of churches and ministers. The Catholics have the largest number of members. The Methodists have the largest number among the Protestant denominations. The Old School Presbyterians have 725 more churches than the New School, 162 more ministers, and 23,953 more members. The Old and New School Presbyterians together have 2,160 more churches than the Congregationalists, 1,625 more ministers, and 141,360 more members.

According to another estimate—

The regular Baptists are put at 667,750, and churches at 8,295; more than 250,000 likewise are embraced in Anti-Mission, Campbellites, Free-will, &c. Methodist Episcopal, 629,660; South, 465,533; Protestant and others, 81,000. Presbyterian, Old School, 192,033; New School, 155,000; Congregational, 127,196; other Presbyterian sects, 140,000. Dutch Reformed, 32,840; German Reformed, 69,750; Protestant Episcopal, 67,550; Lutheran, 163,000; Roman Catholic, 1,231,300; Christian Connexion, 325,000. Romanists include every body belonging to them, men, women and children; and most of the others include only communicants.

THE CHURCH IN CANADA.

The diocess of Toronto (Canada West) covers an extent of country twice as large as all the diocesses of England put together, containing upwards of 100,000 square miles with a population of 700,000 souls.

There are ninety-seven missionaries in the diocess in connexion with the Propagation Society, as well as many others who are maintained out of various resources. The Bishop of Montreal, who administers also the diocess of Quebec, has earnestly urged upon the society the need of a division of his diocess, which comprises 200,000 square miles and a population of 800,000 souls. A census of the Lower Province was taken in 1831, and the following is the general result. Church of Rome, 403,472; Church of England, 34,620; Church of Scotland, 15,099; Methodists, 7,019; Presbyterians, 7,811; Baptists, 2,461; Jews, 107; other denominations, 5,577. The numbers at the last census, in 1847, was 782,677. The total number of the clergy at this period, in the same division of the province, was thirty-six, of whom twenty-two were paid wholly, and six in part, by the Society for the Propagation of the Gospel. The clergy at the present time amount to eighty-seven, and the proportion of the clergy to the Church of England population, which, eighteen years ago, was rather more than one to a 1000, is now as one to 500.

THE NEXT HOUSE OF REPRESENTATIVES.

The gain of a democratic member of Congress in Maryland leaves it entirely uncertain which of the two parties will have a majority in the House of

Representatives. If the eleven members yet to be elected should be of the same politics as those representing the same districts in the last Congress, there would be, in a full House, a whig majority of *one*. Thus:

	New Congress.		Old Congress.	
	Whig.	*Dem.*	*Whig.*	*Dem.*
Illinois,	1	6	1	6
Missouri,	0	5	0	5
Arkansas,	0	1	0	1
Iowa,	0	2	0	2
Vermont,	3	1	3	1
Maine,	2	5	1	6
Georgia,	4	4	4	4
Pennsylvania,	15	8	17	7
Florida,	1	0	1	0
South Carolina,	0	7	0	7
Ohio,*	10	10	11	9
New York,	32	2	24	10
New Jersey,	4	1	4	1
Massachusetts,†	9	0	9	0
Michigan,	1	2	0	3
Delaware,	1	0	1	0
Wisconsin,‡	2	1	0	2
New Hampshire,	2	3	2	2
Connecticut,	1	3	4	0
Rhode Island,	2	0	1	1
Virginia,§	1	13	6	8
North Carolina,	6	3	6	2
Tennessee,	4	7	5	6
Kentucky,	6	4	6	4
Indiana,	1	9	4	6
Alabama,	2	5	2	5
Texas,	0	2	0	2
Maryland,	3	3	4	2
	113	107	116	103

YET TO BE ELECTED.

	Whole Number.	Last Congress.	
		W.	*D.*
Mississippi,	4	1	3
Louisiana,	4	1	3
Vacancy in Ohio,	1	0	1
" Massachusetts,	1	1	0
" Virginia,	1	0	1
	11	3	8

* One vacancy by the death of Rudolphus Dickinson, Dem.
† One vacancy.
‡ The act of Congress admitting Wisconsin into the Union authorizes her to send three members from and after the 4th of March, 1849, until the next apportionment.
§ One vacancy by the death of Mr. Newman, Dem.

Brought forward,	11	3	8
Elected as before stated,	220	113	107
Total,	231	116	115
	115		
Whig majority,	1		

Such will be the political complexion of the House, if the remaining eleven members should be politically the same as before.

The elections in Louisiana and Mississippi take place on the 5th of next month. The vacancies in Ohio and Virginia will be filled before the next meeting of Congress. Also the vacancy in Massachusetts, if a choice can be effected, which is very doubtful. Three or four trials have already been made without success.—*N. Y. Jour. Com.*

COLLEGE STATISTICS.

During the past quarter many of the Colleges throughout the country have held their annual commencement. We state the occurrence of such as have come under our notice, with the honorary degrees conferred.

YALE COLLEGE COMMENCEMENT.—The graduating class consisted of 95, of whom 33 had parts in the performances. The degree of A. M. was conferred on 47 persons, of whom two were from other institutions. That of LL. B. was conferred on six graduates of the Law School; and that of LL. D. on his Excellency Joseph Trumbull, governor of the state.

CAMBRIDGE UNIVERSITY.—At the annual commencement of this institution the graduating class numbered seventy-seven. Forty medical students received the degree of M. B., and forty-two law students the degree of laws.

The degree of doctor of laws was conferred upon the Hon. Judge Eustice, of Louisiana, Hon. Richard Fletcher, associate justice of the S. J. court of Massachusetts, Hon. Horace Mann, and Hon. Theophilus Parsons, Dane Professor of Law at Cambridge university.

The degree of doctor of divinity was conferred upon Rev. G. W. Burnap, of Baltimore; Rev. Levi W. Leonard, of Dublin, N. H., and Rev. Charles Kittredge True, of Charlestown.

UNION COLLEGE, Schenectady, N. Y. July 25.—Degree of A. B., in course, conferred on one hundred and eleven members of the senior class. Honorary degree of D. D. on Rev. George W. Blagden, Rev. Alfred E. Campbell, and Rev. David Murdock; LL. D. on Hon. Greene C. Bronson, and Hon. John C. Spencer, both of Albany. Four individuals received the honorary degree of A. B., and five of A. M.

MIDDLEBURY COLLEGE, (Congregational,) Middlebury, Vt., July 25.—Graduates seven. Degree of A. M., in course, on five of the alumni. Honorary degree of D. D. on Rev. Samuel C. Jackson, of Andover, Mass., an alumnus of the class of 1821; LL.D. on Hon. Carlos Coolidge, of Woodstock, Vermont, governor of the state.

AMHERST COLLEGE, (Congregational,) Amherst. Mass., August 8.—Graduates 29. Honorary degree of A. M. conferred on Rev. Wm. A Benedict, of the presbytery of Columbia, under appointment as a missionary of the American Board to India.

COLLEGE OF NEW JERSEY.—The 102d anniversary of this venerable institution was held. A large class graduated. The college, it is understood, was never in a more prosperous condition. The degree of D. D. was conferred on the Rev. John G. Lorimer of Glasgow, Scotland, and the Rev. Edward D. Smith of New York; and that of LL. D., on William P. Finley, President of the College of Charleston, South Carolina, and on the Hon. Judge Wayne, of Savannah, of the U. S. supreme court.

UNIVERSITY OF PENNSYLVANIA.—Commencement celebrated in the Chinese Museum, Philadelphia. The degree of A. B. was conferred on nineteen graduates; of A. M. on thirty, and of M. D. on nine.

RUTGER'S COLLEGE, (Reformed Dutch,) New Brunswick, N. J., July 25.—Graduates thirteen. Degree of A. M. conferred on ten alumni. Honorary degree of D. D. on Rev. David Landsborough, of the free presbytery of Irvine, Scotland. Honorary degree of LL. D. on the Hon. Jas. Buchanan, Lancaster, Pa.

UNIVERSITY OF MICHIGAN, Marshall, Mich., July 18.—Graduates, twenty-three. No honorary degrees. Address before the Society of Inquiry by Rev. Prof. Thomas Stone, of the Baptist theological seminary at Kalamazoo; and before the literary societies, by Hon. Lewis Cass.

COLLEGE OF ST. JAMES, (P. Episcopal,) near Hagerstown, Md, July 26.—Degree of A. B. conferred on four graduates, and of A. M. on two members of the class of 1846.

WILLIAMS COLLEGE.—At the annual commencement the class of graduates consisted of fifty-two. The degree of D. D. upon Rev. Parsons Cooke, of Lynn, Mass., and Rev. Asa D. Smith, of the city of New York.

COLUMBIA COLLEGE.—The annual commencement of this institution was celebrated on the 2d inst., in the Church of the Crucifixion, Dr. Moore, the president, in the chair. Gen. Winfield Scott, and quite a number of distinguished literary and professional gentlemen were among those present. The degree of LL. D. was conferred on the Rev. R. W. Harris. Fifteen gentlemen received the degree of A. M. Gen. Dix delivered the address before the Peithologian and Philolexian Societies.

GENEVA COLLEGE, (Episcopal,) Geneva, N. Y., August 1.—Hon. degree of D. D. conferred on Rev. William D. Wilson, and Rev. J. F. McLaren. Hon. degree of LL. D. on Henry R. Schoolcraft and Hiram Denio.

JEFFERSON COLLEGE, (Presbyterian,) Canonsburgh, Pa., August 1.—The degree of A. B. was conferred on fifty-four graduates. Hon. degree of D. D. on Rev. Joseph T. Cooper, of Philadelphia; Rev. George A. Lyon, Erie, Pa.; and Rev. J. T. Pressley, of Erskine College, S. C. Honorary degree of LL. D. on Hon. Thomas Bradford, Philadelphia, and Hon. Thaddeus Stevens, Lancaster, Pa.

DARTMOUTH COLLEGE, (Congregational,) Hanover, N. H., July 26.—Graduates thirty-nine. Degree of A. M. on ten of the alumni; and of M. D. on thirteen. Honorary degree of D. D. on Rev. Zedekiah Barstow, and Rev. Clement Long. Honorary degree of LL. D. on Edward Everett, LL. D., late president of Harvard University, Hon. Samuel S. Wilde, of Boston, and Hon. Amos Kendall, of New Hampshire. Honorary degree of A. M. on Hon. John Sullivan, attorney general of New Hampshire, and on Col. Bliss, son-in-law of the President of the United States.

UNIVERSITY OF VERMONT, (Congregational,) Burlington, Vt., Aug. 1.—Graduates seventeen. Honorary degree of LL. D. was conferred on Hon. Jacob Collamer, postmaster general.

COLUMBIAN COLLEGE, (Baptist,) Washington city, July 18.—Degree of A. B., in course, conferred on fifteen graduates, and the degree of A. M. on six of the alumni. Honorary degree of D. D. was conferred on the Rev. J. B. Jeter.

WESTERN RESERVE COLLEGE, (Presbyterian and Congregationalist,) Hudson,

Ohio, July 12.—The degree of A. B. was conferred on thirteen individuals; and of A. M. on nine of the alumni. Honorary degree of LL. D. on Hon. Peter Hitchcock, of the supreme court of Ohio.

MADISON UNIVERSITY, (Baptist,) Hamilton, N.Y., August 15.—Degree of A. B. conferred on twenty-one graduates, and of A. M. on eleven. Hon. degree of D. D. on Rev. Silas Bailey, president of Granville college, (Bap.,) Ohio; and of LL. D. on Robert Lush, Esq., London, England.

KENYON COLLEGE, (Episcopal,) Gambier, O., August 8th.—Graduates, ten. Hon. degree of D. D. on Rev. Joseph Muenscher, Ohio; of LL. D. on George P. Williams, professor of mathematics in Michigan university, and on Edward C. Ross, professor of mathematics in the free academy of the city of New York.

HAMILTON COLLEGE.—The commencement exercises were on Wednesday the 25th of July. The degree of A. B. was conferred on forty-seven young gentlemen of the graduating class, and the degree of A.M. on fifteen. The degree of D. D. was conferred upon Rev. M. L. P. Thompson, of Buffalo, N. Y.; Rev. M. N. McLaren, of Brooklyn, N. Y.; and Rev. Geo. Rees, of Fishguard, South Wales. The degree of LL. D. was conferred on Hon. Samuel Beardsley, of Utica, N. Y. Rev. Dr. Sprague, of Albany, delivered an address to the literary societies.

WATERVILLE COLLEGE, (Baptist,) Waterville, Me., Aug. 8.—More than twenty graduates. The literary fraternity was addressed by the Rev. Dr. Caruthers, of Portland, Me., and the Enosophian Society by the Rev. Theodore Parker, of Boston. G. Saxe, Esq., of Vermont, also delivered a poem. Honorary degree of D. D. conferred on Rev. S. Peck, of Boston, and Prof. E. B. Smith, of the New Hampton seminary, N. H.

BROWN UNIVERSITY.—On Wednesday last this college celebrated its *eightieth* anniversary commencement. On Tuesday morning the Phi Beta Kappa society held its annual meeting. The oration before the Philomenian and United Brothers society was delivered by the Rev. E. H. Chapin, of New York.

TRINITY COLLEGE, (Episcopal,) Hartford, Conn., August 2.—Honorary degree of A. M. conferred on Rev. W. S. Bartlett, Chelsea, Mass., Rev. Ralph Hoyt, New York, and H. S. Sandford, Esq., of the American legation, Prussia. Hon. degree of LL. D. on Hon. Isaac F. Redfield, judge of the supreme court of Vermont.

WESLEYAN UNIVERSITY, (Methodist,) Middletown, Conn., August 1.—Graduates thirty-one. Honorary degree of D. D. on Rev. Simeon North, LL. D., president of Hamilton college.

DICKINSON COLLEGE, (Methodist,) Carlisle, Pa., July 12.—Oration before the Belles Lettres Society, by Job R. Tyson, Esq., of Philadelphia. The degree of A. B. was conferred on twenty-one individuals, one of whom belonged to the class of 1848.

GRANVILLE COLLEGE, (Baptist,) Granville, O., July 18.—Honorary degree of D. D. on Rev. R. W. Cushman, Washington city, LL. D. on Thomas Corwin.

WABASH COLLEGE, (Presbyterian,) Crawfordsville, Ind., July 19.—Graduates eight. Honorary degree of D. D. on Rev. John Blackburn, pastor of Maberly Chapel, Pentonville, London.

· MARIETTA COLLEGE, (Presbyterian and Congregational,) Marietta, Ohio, July 26.—Graduates fourteen. Degree of A.M. was conferred on seven of the alumni.

CENTENARY COLLEGE, (Methodist,) Jackson, La., July 20.—Graduates three.

EXTENT OF THE BRITISH COLONIES.

(From a Lecture by Rev. Edward Bickersteth.)

"The colonial empire which God has given to this country is unparalleled in the history of all nations. The four chief empires that have prevailed over the earth, in connexion with the church of God—Chaldean, Persian, Grecian, and Roman—had an exceedingly contracted dominion in comparison with that which Britain now possesses.

"The Spanish, Portuguese, French, Dutch, Danish, and other nations have established colonies; but no other nation has now an extent of colonial empire to be compared with that of Great Britain.

"The British colonies, in the remarkable providence of God, have been acquired since the Reformation, during the period from the reign of Elizabeth to the present day.

"In Europe, besides the British and Channel Isles, we have Heligoland, Gibraltar, Malta, and the Ionian Islands. In Africa, we have Sierra Leone, Cape Coast, the Ascension, St. Helena, the Cape of Good Hope, the Mauritius, the Seehelles, and Aden; in Asia, the vast continent of Hindoostan, with mighty annexed possessions. We have also Penang, Malacca, and Singapore, and Borneo. In Australia and New Zealand, new empires are rising up under the sway of the British crown. In North and South America, in the western hemisphere, we have a widely separated dominion, extending from our remote possession of the Falkland Isles, by British Guayana and the West India islands, to our wide-spread territories in North America. No other kingdom has such a dominion influencing every part of the world. It embraces a population of above 130,000,000 subjects, while probably 50,000,000 more are under our influence.

"The population of our colonies, apart from Hindoostan, is as follows, by returns to Parliament in 1842 :—

North America, ...	1,621,152
West Indies, ...	901,082
Other Colonies, ...	2,152,101
Total, ...	4,674,335

"This population probably now exceeds 5,000,000.

That of our eastern empire is reckoned at . . .	100,000,000
That of the British Islands, ...	27,000,000
Of the other colonies, ...	5,000,000
Total, ... :	132,000,000

Thus, taking the population of the earth at 1,000,000,000, nearly one-seventh of its population are our fellow-subjects, besides the vast numbers more or less under our influence.

"The Roman colonies under that fourth empire were the germs of the civilization of northern and western Europe. May the British colonies be the germs, not only of the civilization, but of the Christianizing of all heathen countries."

(From another source we have obtained the amount of expenditure incurred in the maintenance of these vast possessions :—

On the average of the last fifteen years, the direct cost of the colonies to Great Britain, under the four heads of civil, naval, military, and extraordinary expenditure, had amounted to at least £4,000,000 a year, exclusive of the sum paid for emancipating slaves. Last year the military force in the colonies consisted, in all, of 45,000 men of all ranks. These troops were scattered about in various stations over 37 colonies. The storehouses of these stations contained stores of the estimated value of £2,500,000, a sufficient amount of stores, if they did not perish of themselves, for about 20 years' consumption during peace. In most of these stations considerable sums have been annually expended in fortifications and other ordnance works, and the total sum expended upon them in the course of the nineteen years from 1829 to 1847 had amounted to £3,500,000. For instance, during that period, the government had expended in North American ordnance works in all about £1,300,000.

EDUCATION IN IRELAND.—An appendix to the fifteenth report of the Irish commissioners of national education has just been published, showing the state of the schools in connexion with the board for the year 1848. It appears from this document that there has been a steady annual increase in the number of scholars from the institution of the schools in 1833 till now: the numbers in the first year being 107,042 in 789 schools; in 1847, 402,632 scholars in 3825 schools; while last year there were 507,469 scholars in 4109. This shows an increase in 1848 over 1847 of 104,837 scholars and 312 schools; but in point of fact the new schools taken into connexion with the board amount to 426; the difference being caused by the fact that 114 old schools were struck off the rolls in the course of the year. Of these 426 new schools, 146 are situated in Ulster, 114 in Munster, 104 in Leinster, and 62 in Connaught. Of the 114 schools struck off the roll, it appears that in comparatively few cases was the removal caused by the violation of the commissioners' rules. In most of them the schools appear to have been permanently closed, and in several the reason assigned is the inefficiency of the teacher. There are 50 agricultural schools in connexion with the board, of which eight model agricultural schools are in operation, and 21 in course of building, while 21 ordinary agricultural schools are in operation.

POPULATION OF LONDON.—The number of deaths registered in London during a week in September last was 3,183; that is equal to 454 every day, 19 every hour, and one person every three minutes. This may appear very alarming to some readers, but they must bear in mind that the vast extent and population of the metropolis, London and its surrounding districts, contains nearly 3,000,000 persons. If this immense number of persons were placed in a line, at a distance of 14 yards apart, they would reach to the extent of 25,000 miles, or more than the circumference of the globe; so that if persons died at the above rate, viz., one every three minutes, and allowing 1000 births every week, it would then be 26 years before all the people in London were extinct.

SHOE BUSINESS IN LYNN.—The shoe business is the life of Lynn. Only women's, misses' and children's shoes are made here. Engaged in this business there are of manufacturers, or men who "carry on" the business, 78; of cutters, or men who "cut out" the shoes, 175; of men and boys employed in making shoes, 2458; of men and boys so employed, but living out of town, 900; of women and girls employed in binding shoes, 4925; of the same so employed and living out of town, 1600; making of employees an aggregate of 10,058. The number of men and boys employed in making shoes is more than seventy per cent. larger now than it was in 1842. The increase of the number of women and girls employed in binding shoes has, we presume, been correspondingly great. But it should be stated that the shoe business in 1842 was unusually depressed; that much less of it was done during the last than will probably be done during the present year. The number of pairs of shoes made during the last year was 3,190,000; the number purchased from other towns was 350,000; making in all 3,540,000 pairs. The cost of the materials of these $1,435,545; that of making them $957,030; making the cost of the 3,540,000 pairs of shoes to have been $2,392,575. The cost of making shoes now is about one-sixth less than it was a dozen years ago.—*Lynn Pioneer.*

(ORIGINAL COMMUNICATIONS.)

LEGAL REFORM IN THE STATE OF NEW YORK.

(BY A MEMBER OF THE NEW YORK BAR.)

THE late movements in the state of New York to effect a reform in the practice and pleadings, and a codification of the law, have excited general attention and interest, and produced a desire for information on the subject in other states. The object of these remarks is, to gratify that desire as far as may be practicable, by a general account of the matter.

The state of New York was the first among the states of this Union, to attempt the reduction into a systematic form of the various statutes which had passed her legislature, to simplify their language, to supply omissions, and conform them to the expositions of the courts, or to correct those expositions, when they departed from the intent of the statutes. In 1825, the legislature committed this work to John Duer, Benjamin F. Butler, and Henry Wheaton. The latter being appointed Chargé des affaires to Denmark, in the spring of 1827, resigned his place, and John C. Spencer was appointed. This Board continued in the commission until the work was completed. But in consequence of the engagements of Mr. Duer, the third and fourth parts were prepared by the other members, aided by his occasional advice. These facts are stated in the preface to the first edition. Two special sessions of the legislature were held in 1827 and 1828, to consider the reports and bills presented by the legislature, and the whole was completed by the 1st of January, 1829. The work consisted of four parts, arranged substantially according to Blackstone's divisions, which, indeed, were formed like those in the Institutes of Justinian. Each of these parts were divided into chapters, titles, articles, and sections, so that all the statutory law on a given subject was collected in its appropriate place. Technical phraseology was rejected, except in the names of process, provisos were discarded, sections were broken up so as to express a single idea; and a plain, simple, yet flowing language was employed, calculated to render clear and explicit the enactments upon the most abstruse subject.

The completion of this great work was hailed with the highest satisfaction by the liberal and enlightened in this country and in England. It is said that Lord Brougham and other lawyers of the first eminence in Great Britain expressed great admiration of the boldness of the undertaking, and of its complete success, and it is known that the English parliament has condescended to copy verbatim from it, very freely in their enactments upon the most important and intricate subjects, while many of the states of this Union have engrafted large portions of the work into their statute-books, and others have adopted it as a model for the revision of their own laws.

Codification, strictly speaking, was not the aim of the work. It was a codification of the statute law, and occasionally of portions only of the common law. The value of the latter was so evident, and the whole work gained so much in public estimation, that many enlightened and sanguine citizens began to entertain the belief that the whole common law could be reduced to a written code, like the Roman and other institutes of the civil law. This belief grew and strengthened so much, that the convention which in 1846 formed a new constitution, inserted in it a mandate to the legislature, to appoint a commission for that purpose. They also inserted a direction to organize another commission "to revise, reform, simplify, and abridge the rules and practice, pleadings, forms, and proceedings of the courts of record of the State."

Commissioners, under both of these injunctions, were organized at the session of the legislature in 1847, one called the code commission; the other, the commission on practice and pleadings. Mr. Walworth, the late Chancellor, John A. Collier, and Alexander Worden, were appointed the code commissioners, their term of office limited to two years, with salaries of $2000 each, and provision for clerk hire. Mr. Walworth declined the appointment, and Anthony L. Robertson, of New York, was substituted. John A. Collier accepted and remained in the commission about a year, when he resigned, without any report of his proceedings. Seth C. Hawley, of Buffalo, was, in 1848, appointed in his place, and during that year the commission consisted of Messrs. Worden, Robertson, and Hawley. Mr. Robertson appears not to have acted with his colleagues, and the latter, in 1849, reported a revisal of four chapters of the Revised Statutes, but made no progress in codifying. The term of office of Mr. Robertson having expired in 1849, John C. Spencer was appointed in his place, but refused to accept under the circumstances. Mr. Worden, therefore, announced his own resignation to take effect on the 1st of November, 1849. The experiment of codifying does not seem to have been even commenced.

The commission on practice and pleadings was organized in 1847, by the appointment of Nicholas Hill, Jun., David Graham, and A. Loomis. Mr. Hill soon resigned, on the ground of entire disagreement with his associates upon the plan and extent of the proposed reform. David Dudley Field was appointed in his place. The commission thus formed, reported to the legislature Parts I. and II. of a Code of Procedure, as it was termed. The title to the name of code might be questioned, as the proposed enactments were confined to distinct subjects of practice and special rules of pleading, leaving the large mass of common law principles and general usages untouched. Yet they were very sweeping and very radical. They were expressed in terms so brief and general, as to be incomprehensible to any one who was not previously well acquainted with the existing practice and system of pleading.

The first part of the report related to the courts of justice and their jurisdiction,—a subject scarcely within the commission. Even this was not complete, but left much, even of previous statutory law unaffected. But as this part can possess little interest for the general reader, it will not now be further remarked upon. The second part related to civil actions. It is impossible to state in detail the various new propositions which it contained. Within the limits to which this article ought to be confined, a selection of the most prominent and important can only be presented.

The part last mentioned commences with the following provision:—

The distinction between actions at law and suits in equity, and the forms of all such actions and suits, heretofore existing, are abolished: and there shall be in the state hereafter, but one form of action for the enforcement or protection of private rights, and the redress of private wrongs, which shall be denominated a civil action.

It will be for professional men to expound this clause, and understand what is meant by there being but one form of action,—and that to be called a civil action.

Other sections contain the following provisions:—Every action must be prosecuted by the real party in interest, except that an executor, administrator, or trustee of an express trust, or person expressly authorized by statute, may sue without joining with him the person for whose benefit the suit was instituted. This, it will be seen, sweeps away the whole doctrine respecting assignments of rights in action, and gives a fixed legal interest to the assignee. The exception as to an executor seems quite unnecessary, as he is the only person who has any vested interest in the assets of the estate. A married woman is allowed to sue alone, and in her own name, when the action concerns her separate property, and to sue and be sued alone when the action is between herself and her husband. All persons having an interest in the subject of the action, and in obtaining the relief demanded, are to be joined as plaintiffs, and any person may be made defendant who has an interest in the controversy adverse to the plaintiff. No action is to be abated by the disability of any party, or the transfer of any interest therein, if the cause of action survive; and the assignee may be substituted for the original party.

Actions are to be commenced by a summons signed by the party or his attorney, which may be served by any one on the defendant personally, and in certain cases by publication.

All the forms of pleading heretofore existing are abolished, and hereafter those forms and the rules by which the sufficiency of the pleadings is to be determined, shall be those provided by the act. The pleadings are, a complaint, a demurrer, an answer, and a reply. The complaint is to contain the names of parties, &c., and "a statement of the facts constituting the cause of action, in ordinary and.concise language, without repetition, and in such a manner as to enable a person of common understanding to know what is intended"! and a demand of the relief claimed. Six grounds of demurrer are specified, some of which include what have usually been the subjects of pleas in abatement,—which are abolished. The answer is to contain a denial of each allegation in the complaint, or of a sufficient knowledge to form a belief, and a new matter of defence. The reply is to contain a similar denial of the new matter in the answer, or of knowledge sufficient to form a belief. All material allegations in the complaint not controverted in the answer, and all such allegations in the answer not controverted in the reply, are to be taken as true; but new matter in the reply may be controverted on the trial. No demurrer was allowed to any pleading but the complaint; but this was stricken out in the amendatory act of 1849, hereafter mentioned, and it may be interposed to any pleading. A power of amendment, almost without limit, is given.

Defendants can be arrested only on an order of a judge, founded on affidavit. Writs of injunction are abolished, and orders substituted. Indeed, process under seal is universally dispensed with, and the mere direction of the attorney substituted. Issues of law arise upon demurrer, or where the fact is not controverted. All actions are issues of fact, and are to be tried by jury, or by referees, or by the court; and a jury trial may be waived.

Judgment may be given for or against one or more of several plaintiffs, or defendants. Any relief, where there is an answer, may be given, consistent with the complaint and embraced in the issue. Judgment records are abolished, and an entry is to be made of every judgment in a book, by the clerk, and a copy thereof, with the papers on each side, constitutes the judgment roll.

The proceedings heretofore had under a creditor's bill, to reach effects of the defendant after an execution returned unsatisfied, are continued under an application to a judge and an order by him. Any person indebted to a defendant against whom an execution has been issued, may pay the amount thereof to the sheriff, which is to discharge him.

Instead of a fee bill for costs, specific sums are allowed in different stages of an action; and a per centage may be allowed on the amount recovered in the discretion of the court. Appeals and reviews are allowed, in certain cases from the decision of a single judge, to the court in term, and finally to the Court of Appeals; but security for costs must in all cases be given; and where a judgment is rendered for the recovery of money on the assignment or delivery of property or documents, the execution can be stayed only by giving security for the payment of the amount recovered or the fulfillment of the judgment, in case of affirmance.

Provision is made for the stating of a case by the parties, and submitting it to a court for decision. Actions to obtain a recovery in aid of the prosecution or defence of a suit, are abolished. Parties to suits may be examined by their adversaries, in the same manner as witnesses before or at the trial; and their testimony may be rebutted by other evidence. When thus examined, they may testify in their own behalf in respect to any matter pertinent to the issue; but if any new matter be introduced not responsive to the inquiries of the adverse party, the latter may be examined as to such matters. Persons immediately benefited in the result of the action, may be examined in the same manner as parties. Excepting such persons and parties, all others are competent witnesses whether interested or not.

In the preceding enumeration of provisions, those have been omitted which have been subsequently altered by the legislature, and also such as were in force at the time.

This first part was adopted by the legislature of 1848, with few alterations in substance. A very cursory examination seems to have been bestowed upon its contents by the committee of the Senate, and it has been stated in debate in the House of Assembly, that this part passed that body without having been once read. The act took effect on the 1st of July, 1848.

At the session of 1849, the commissioners on practice and pleadings made three further reports. One of them, called their second report, is confined to amendments and additions, or rather, alterations of the act previously passed, consisting of forty-seven sections. As they introduce no new principles, a specification of them is unnecessary.

The third report also contained additions and amendments to the first report, and provisions respecting special proceedings and jurors. It contained a bill for establishing tribunals of conciliation, by which the county judge of each county, and a special judge in New York city, are to hear the complaints, allegations, and explanations of parties, inform them of their respective rights, and endeavour to reconcile their differences. Any person may serve a written notice on his adversary, requiring him to appear before the judge. If a reconciliation is effected, a memorandum is to be entered in a book of records, and signed by the parties, which is to be a final determination of the controversy. The plaintiff in any action is not to recover costs, unless he show that he has notified the defendant to appear before the judge, and the defendant is not to recover costs when he failed to appear, pursuant to a notice. In actions between partners, or between principal and agent, neither party shall recover costs unless he has offered to submit the controversy to arbitration. No fees are to be allowed the judge of the tribunals. These propositions were not adopted by the legislature. Writs of scire facias, quo warranto, of prohibition of nuisance, and of waste, are proposed to be abolished, and actions substituted. Instead of certiorari, writs of review; instead of mandamus, the writ of mandate; instead of *ad quod dammum*, the writ of assessment, are provided, and the writ of habeas corpus ad subjiciendum, is to be called the writ of deliverance. The substance of the former proceedings was re-enacted. Numerous provisions were also reported respecting the drawing, summons and impannelling of jurors, the only material new one being that which required permanent jury lists for the courts of Justices of the Peace.

These propositions, however, were not all adopted by the legislature; but selections were made of such as seemed connected with the portion of the code already in force.

The fourth report of the commissioners relates to criminal law and practice, and is so full of novelties that it is wholly impossible to specify them within the limits of this article. The mode of examining persons accused before magistrates is very minute and cumbrous. Grand juries are to find indictments only against persons already held to answer by a magistrate, in other cases they are to *present* the offender, who is to be examined in the same manner as on complaint before a magistrate. Forms of indictments are given, of which the following is a specimen. For rape,—"Forcibly ravished E. F., a woman of the age of ten years or upwards:" for grand larceny,—"Feloniously took and carried away a gold watch, the personal property of C. D., of the value of more than twenty-five dollars:" for an assault and battery,—"Assaulted and beat C. D." On the trial, the defendant's counsel is always to close the argument. Sundry changes in the nature and description of offences are introduced, as if they belonged to practice. But as this report has not been adopted, and is to come before the next session of the legislature, it is needless to speak of it more in detail.

In 1849, a revision of the act of 1848 was made by the legislature, and radical and important changes were made. These were chiefly in matters not noticed in the foregoing abstract. The provisions contained in the second and third reports of the commissioners which were deemed useful, were incorporated with the original act, and although strong remonstrances were made by the commissioners, the new and revised act was passed. A law was also passed continuing the commissioners until the 1st day of December, 1849, to enable them to suggest further amendments of their code. It is understood that they are occupied in preparing a code of the law of *evidence* in civil and criminal cases, supposing the subject to be within their province.

In these statements the writer has endeavoured to repress the expression of his own opinions, however strongly tempted, and has limited himself to a general survey of the work, or rather of its most important points. Incomplete, and constantly referring either to existing statutes or to the common law, and to pre-existing practice, the code is far from being systematic, and was incapable of general analysis.

The general sentiment of judges and lawyers in the state of New York, seems to be quite adverse to the projects of the commissioners. A report of the judiciary committee of the assembly of 1849, reviewed their labours up to that period, with great severity, and pointed out errors of haste, carelessness or ignorance, calculated to shake public confidence in the commissioners, if not in their system. And it is quite doubtful whether the main part of their work will stand the ordeal of one or two more sessions of the legislature. In the mean time, great confusion prevails in the practice, and a large portion of the time of the courts is consumed in settling the construction of the new enactments. And what is peculiarly unfortunate, is that a construction in one judicial district is sometimes, if not often, directly at variance with the construction given in another district. The difficulty is increased by the circumstance that, in matters of practice, they have no common superior to settle their differences,—the court of Appeals having no jurisdiction over such subjects.   HISTORICUS.

SKETCHES OF THE LIVES OF SAMUEL STANHOPE SMITH, AND TIMOTHY DWIGHT.

(In some of the preceding numbers we have given to our readers memoirs of distinguished men, whose connexion with the prominent historical events of their times imparted an interest to their lives.

We now present, from the pen of a highly esteemed and erudite contributor, notices of men, eminent for learning and piety, who presided over venerable and distinguished literary institutions at an early period of our national history, and one of whom especially, was an active sharer in the struggle for independence.)

PRESIDENT SMITH.

SAMUEL STANHOPE SMITH was born March 16th, 1750, at Pequea, Lancaster county, Pennsylvania. His father was the Rev. Robert Smith, a distinguished clergyman of the Presbyterian Church, who emigrated from Ireland, and established, and for many years superintended an academy which supplied many able and excellent ministers to the denomination with which he was connected. His mother was Elizabeth Blair, daughter of the Rev. Samuel Blair, and sister to

Samuel and John Blair, both of whom were among the most promi- nent clergymen of their day. She was a lady of high intellectual en- dowments as well as excellent moral qualities, and fitted to grace the most exalted station in society. The son, at a very early period, gave indications of possessing a mind of no common order, and the parents quickly determined to give him the best advantages within their reach for cultivating it. When he was only six or seven years old, he com- menced the study of the languages in his father's school; and as his fa- ther had employed some most accomplished teachers from abroad as his assistants, perhaps scarcely any school in the country, at that day, furnished better advantages for becoming thoroughly grounded, es- pecially in the classics. The only language allowed to be spoken in the school was Latin; and whoever uttered a word in the mother tongue was marked as a culprit. Young Smith made the best of his oppor- tunities, and was distinguished for his improvement in every branch to which he directed his attention.

From his earliest childhood he seems to have evinced a serious turn of mind, and to have taken little interest in the sports in which his school-fellows indulged. He was accustomed to listen to sermons from the pulpit with great attention, and often at the close of the service could repeat a considerable portion of what he had heard.

When he was in his sixteenth year, he was sent to college at Prince- ton. It was during the period that intervened between the death of President Finley and Dr. Witherspoon's accession to the presidency, while the college was under the charge of several eminent professors, and among them his maternal uncle, the Rev. Dr. John Blair. Not- withstanding his youth, he entered the junior class, and immediately took rank among the very best scholars. Dr. Witherspoon arrived from Scotland, and entered on the duties of his office, while he was an under- graduate; and before he had completed his eighteenth year, he had re- ceived the degree of Bachelor of Arts under circumstances the most honourable to his talents and acquirements, and the most gratifying to his ambition.

After his graduation, he returned to his father's house, and spent some time, partly in assisting him in conducting his school, and partly in vigorous efforts for the higher cultivation of his own mind. He read the finest models in polite literature on the one hand, and in in- tellectual and moral philosophy on the other. He also occasionally tried his hand at writing poetry, but he was not much flattered by the result of his efforts, and he seems to have abandoned his devotion to the muses on the ground that "poeta nascitur, non fit."

He had not been long in this new sphere of labour, before he was invited to return to Princeton, as a tutor in the college, especially in the departments of the classics and Belles Lettres. Here he remained for two years, discharging his duties with great acceptance, and at the same time pursuing a course of theological study in reference to the ministry. At the end of this period, he resigned his office in the college, and was licensed to preach by the Presbytery of Newcastle.

As his health had suffered not a little from severe application, he determined to spend some time as a missionary in the western counties of Virginia. When he reached that part of the country, he received a most cordial welcome from many Irish Presbyterians who had settled there, and at the same time found a state of things that seemed to promise well to an earnest and faithful minister.

On the appearance of a preacher of cultivated mind, exemplary deportment and captivating oratory, it was not strange that there should be an intense and general interest awakened by his ministrations. Accordingly, he soon became an almost universal favourite. So powerful an impression did he make, that some of the most wealthy and influential persons soon set on foot a project for detaining him there as the head of a literary institution; and within a short time, the funds requisite for establishing such an institution were subscribed. The necessary buildings were forthwith erected, and the seminary was subsequently chartered by the legislature, under the name of Hampden Sydney College.

While these preparations were going forward, Mr. Smith was laboriously occupied in performing the missionary tour which had been the original object of his visit to Virginia. The new college being now nearly ready to commence its operations, he returned to the north and formed a matrimonial alliance with the eldest daughter of Dr. Witherspoon. He then went back to Virginia, and took upon himself the double office of principal of the seminary and pastor of the church; and the duties of each he discharged in such a manner as to fulfil the highest expectations that had been formed concerning him.

But after three or four years his constitution, which was never vigorous, was found to be giving way under the vast amount of care and responsibility to which his situation subjected him. A slight bleeding at the lungs commenced, which admonished him to take at least a temporary respite from labour; and by the advice of his friends he resorted to a watering-place among the western mountains, which was then acquiring considerable celebrity under the name of the "Sweet Springs." A residence there of a few weeks caused his unfavourable symptoms in a great measure to disappear, so that he returned to his family with his health in a great degree renovated.

At this period (1779) he was invited to the chair of Moral Philosophy in the College of New Jersey, and, notwithstanding his strong attachment to the infant seminary in Virginia, of which he might be said to be the founder, the prospect of a more extended sphere of usefulness in connexion with his alma mater, induced him to accept the appointment. Upon his arrival at Princeton, however, a most unpromising state of things presented itself. The college was then in ruins, in consequence of the uses and abuses to which it had been subjected by both the British and American soldiers, during the previous years of the revolutionary war. The students were dispersed, and all its operations had ceased. Mainly by the energy, wisdom and generous self-devotion of Mr. Smith, the college was speedily re-organized, and all its usual exercises resumed. For several years, Dr. Witherspoon, though retaining the office of president, was engaged, as a member of Congress, in the higher affairs of the nation; after this, he spent some time in Great Britain in endeavours to collect money to replenish the exhausted funds of the institution; and not long after his return, he was afflicted with total blindness and many bodily infirmities, which, in a great measure, incapacitated him for the duties of his office as president. It is not too much to say, therefore, that during this whole period, notwithstanding Dr. Witherspoon's name could not fail to shed glory over the institution, and he was always intent on the promotion of its interests, whether present or absent, yet it was indebted for no small degree of its prosperity to the unceasing vigilance, the earnest efforts, the distinguished ability of Mr. Smith.

Some time after he had become established in his professorship at Princeton, there was a recurrence of his former malady in a greatly aggravated form, which, for a time, clouded the bright hopes which the commencement of his career had inspired. In November, 1782, he was suddenly overtaken with a violent hemorrhage from the breast, which was checked only by a copious bleeding in the arm and feet. The same thing occurred at a little later hour the next day, and so regularly for several successive days, the blood being restrained in each case only by the use of the lancet. Mr. Smith having remarked that the flux returned at stated intervals, proposed to anticipate its approach by opening a vein, a little before the time when he had reason to expect it. His physician objected to this, on the ground that his strength was so far gone that it would be preposterous to hazard the letting of blood beyond the absolute necessity of the case. He, however, remained steadfast in his own opinion, and at length obtained a lancet from his physician, with a view to his using it upon himself, when he felt that his case demanded it; and continued to use it till he finally succeeded in subduing the disease. For a considerable time he was so far reduced as to be unable to help himself or to speak above a whisper; but his strength gradually returned, so that he was able, at no distant period, to resume his duties in the college. For several years, however, he never ventured an effort in the pulpit, unless on some rare occasion, and then with the utmost caution and restraint.

In the year 1785, Mr. Smith was elected an honorary member of the American Philosophical Society, in Philadelphia; an institution distinguished not only for being the first of its kind in the order of time in the country, but for numbering among its members many of the most brilliant and profound and erudite minds of which the country could boast. The same year he was appointed to deliver their anniversary address; and he met the occasion in a manner which would, of itself, have conferred lasting honour upon his name.   The object of the address was to explain the causes of the variety in the figure and complexion of the human species, and to establish the identity of the race. It was published in the " Transactions of the Society," and was subsequently published in an enlarged and improved form, in a separate volume.   With this work, his reputation as a philosopher, both at home and abroad, is chiefly identified.

In 1783, he was honoured with the degree of Doctor of Divinity from Yale College; and in 1810, with the degree of Doctor of Laws from Harvard University.

Dr. Witherspoon died in 1794, and the same year Dr. Smith succeeded him as President of the college.   Besides being highly popular as the head of the institution, he had now acquired a reputation as a pulpit orator which rendered it an object for many, even in remote parts of the country, to listen to his preaching.   His Baccalaureate discourses particularly, which were addressed to the senior class on the Sabbath immediately preceding their graduation, were among his finest efforts; and it was not uncommon for persons to go even from New York and Philadelphia, a distance of some forty miles, to listen to them.   He published a volume of sermons, not far from the beginning of this century, which were regarded as an important contribution to that part of our national literature.

In the spring of 1802, when the institution was at the full tide of its prosperity, the college edifice, through some instrumentality that was never fully ascertained, was consumed by fire, together with the libraries, furniture, and fixtures of every description.   After the first stunning effect of the calamity had passed away, but one sentiment pervaded all ranks of the people, and that was a determination to contribute the necessary funds to rebuild the house, and sustain the institution.   Accordingly, Dr. Smith made a tour through the southern states for the purpose of soliciting aid, and returned in the following spring with about one hundred thousand dollars, which, with liberal collections made in other parts of the Union, enabled him to accomplish vastly more than he had ventured to anticipate.   This was his crowning achievement.   The college was popular and prosperous, and numbered two hundred students.

From this period nothing occurred in Dr. Smith's life worthy of special remark until the year 1812, when, by reason of repeated strokes of palsy, he became too much enfeebled to discharge any longer the duties of his office.   He, therefore, at the next commencement, tendered his resignation as president, and retired to a place which the Board of Trustees provided for him, and there spent the residue of his life.   For several years he occupied himself in revising and preparing for the press some of his works; but at length disease had made such havoc with his constitution that he was scarcely capable of any mental labour, though he was still visited by many of his friends, and to the last was the pride and joy of the domestic circle. After a long course of gradual and almost imperceptible decline, he died with the utmost tranquillity on the 21st of August, 1819, in the seventieth year of his age. A sermon was preached on the occasion of his death by the Rev. Dr. Woodhull of Freehold. His remains repose by the side of his illustrious predecessors.

Dr. Smith is known chiefly as a pulpit orator and a philosopher, though his influence was widely felt in almost every department of society. His personal appearance was dignified and imposing, and his manners, in every respect, fitted for the most polished society. He was one of the men of mark in his generation,—one of the men whose names can never die.

PRESIDENT DWIGHT.

Timothy Dwight was born at Northampton, Mass., May 14th, 1752. He was the son of Timothy and Mary Dwight. His fatu. was a graduate of Yale College, a merchant in Northampton, a person of excellent understanding and exemplary piety. His mother was the third daughter of the great Jonathan Edwards, and inherited, in no small degree, his remarkable intellectual and moral qualities. She conducted the education of this son entirely during his earliest years; and under her skilful training, he quickly gave indications not only of a thirst for knowledge but of a facility at acquiring it, which shadowed forth, in no faint degree, the eminence to which he was destined. As an evidence of his great precocity he is said to have mastered the alphabet at a single lesson; and at the age of four, he could read the Bible correctly and fluently.

When he was six years old, he was sent to the grammar school and though his father objected to his studying Latin at so early an age, yet so intense was his desire to study it, that he contrived to avail himself of a grammar owned by one of his fellow pupils, and thus stealthily undertook the accomplishment of his purpose. The consent of his father having at length been obtained, through the intercession of his instructor, that he should prosecute the study of the languages, he made such rapid progress that, but for the discontinuance of the school, he would have been fitted at the age of eight years to enter college.

In consequence of the interruption which now occurred in his classical studies, he was brought again under the instruction of his mother, who seems to have drilled him most thoroughly in the elementary branches, and especially in geography and history. It was a great advantage to him, that he enjoyed, not only a daily intercourse with his parents of the most improving and elevating kind, but that his father's house was the resort of many persons of high intelligence, whose conversation, especially on the political topics of the day, was fitted as well to enkindle in his bosom the fire of patriotism, as to quicken his intellectual aspirations.

In his twelfth year, he was sent to Middletown to pursue his studies, under the direction of the Rev. Enoch Huntingdon. Here his application was most intense and successful. In September, 1765, when he had just passed his thirteenth year, he was admitted a member of the Freshman class of Yale College; having read not only the classical authors which were required for admission, but no inconsiderable part of those which were included in the college course.

The first two years of his college life hardly fulfilled the promise of either intellectual or moral development which his earlier years had seemed to give. Various circumstances contributed to this untoward result; but happily the slight delinquencies with which he was chargeable drew towards him the considerate and monitory regards of one of the officers of college, (the late Hon. Stephen Mix Mitchell of Connecticut,) through whose influence he was reclaimed and restored when his feet had only begun to slide. This timely and benevolent in'. ,rence he often afterwards acknowledged with the warmest gratitude, as having been the means, under Providence, of giving a better direction to his life.

At the commencement of his junior year, he set himself in good earnest to repair the loss of preceding years. And from this time to the close of his college course, his industry as a student was almost unparalleled. Not at all satisfied with doing in the best manner whatever was included in the prescribed course, he became a proficient in various other branches, and especially devoted himself with no inconsiderable ardour to poetry and music. It is hardly necessary to say that he attained to the highest rank in scholarship, and was equally distinguished for the variety and thoroughness of his acquisitions. He . graduated in 1769, when he was a little past seventeen; and though h. ;nd his class-mate Strong (afterwards Rev. Dr. Strong of Hartford,) were regarded as equally deserving of the first honour at commencement, yet it was actually conferred upon Strong in consideration of his being the elder, with an understanding that the case should be reversed when they should receive the degree of Master of Arts.

Shortly after he left college, he took charge of a grammar school at New Haven, where he remained for two years. During this period, beside fulfilling his duties as a teacher with the utmost diligence, he devoted no less than eight hours each day to intense study.

In September, 1771, he was chosen a tutor in Yale College; and notwithstanding his extreme youth, being at that time only in his twentieth year, he showed himself fully adequate to the responsibility of the station. Here he continued for six years, devoting himself with the utmost assiduity to the culture of his own mind on the one hand, and to the improvement of his pupils and the general interests of the college on the other. So intense and incessant was his application to study during this period, that his health became seriously impaired, and there was much reason, for a time, to believe that his constitution was effectually undermined; though he succeeded, chiefly by means of regular and vigorous exercise, in restoring his bodily system to its accustomed soundness. His eyes, however, which had been weakened first, from reading too much by candle-light, and afterwards from too early and severe application after recovering from the small-pox, never regained their wonted strength, but were a source of serious embarrassment to him, through his whole subsequent life.

In March, 1777, he was married to Miss Mary Woolsey, daughter of Benjamin Woolsey, Esq., of Long Island. They became the parents of eight sons, who have been distinguished in the various walks of public and private usefulness. Mrs. Dwight, who was an eminent example of the domestic and social virtues, survived her husband many years, and died recently at New Haven at an advanced age.

In consequence of the tumult at first occasioned by the revolutionary war, the students of college dispersed in May of this year, accompanied by their tutors to various places, where they might pursue their studies in greater safety and quietude. Mr. Dwight went with his class to Weathersfield, and remained with them till the ensuing autumn; and in the mean time he was licensed to preach by a committee of the Northern Association of the county of Hampshire, Massachusetts. So great was his popularity among the students of college, that when it was ascertained by them that the office of President was likely to be vacated by the resignation of Mr. Daggett, they made out a formal petition of the corporation that Mr. Dwight might be chosen as his successor; and but for Mr. Dwight's own interference, the petition would have been presented.

As Mr. Dwight had been a watchful and deeply interested spectator of those great public events which brought on the revolution, and as he never doubted that the cause of the colonies was a righteous cause, so he was ever ready to help it forward by any service that he was able to render. Accordingly, within a few months after he was licensed to preach, we find him accepting the appointment of chaplain in General Parson's brigade, which belonged to the division of General Putnam. He joined the army at West Point in October, 1777, and remained with it somewhat more than a year. The duties of this highly responsible station, as of every other which he had previously occupied, he discharged with the most scrupulous fidelity. While he laboured to the utmost for the promotion of the spiritual interests of those among whom he was thrown, he contributed not only by the patriotic discourses which he delivered, but by the patriotic songs which he composed, to put new vigour into the aspirations and efforts of his countrymen for national liberty. Here he made an acquaintance with many of the leading officers of the army, and especially with Washington, who formed a high estimate of his talents and virtues, and ever afterwards honoured him with his friendship.

Mr. Dwight resigned his chaplaincy in obedience to the dictates of filial duty. His father had died at Natchez, where he had gone to provide a settlement for two of his sons, leaving a widow and thirteen children, of whom Mr. Dwight was the eldest. As the family were left without any adequate means of support, this generous and devoted son and brother immediately quitted the army and removed with his own family to Northampton, where, for a series of years, he lived with the responsibility of this double charge upon him. His labours during this time would seem almost incredible. With his own hands he worked upon the farm during the week, and on the Sabbath supplied some vacant congregation in the neighbourhood. He established a school also for both sexes which acquired great celebrity, and which marked an epoch in the history of education, at least in that part of the country. He rendered important services in a civil capacity, representing the town not only in the county conventions, but during two years in the state legislature; and his influence in these important places, was not only always for good, but was most efficient, and often decisive of important measures. So conspicuous had he become, about the close of the revolution, on the arena of political life, that some excellent men, who were by no means unmindful of the interests of the church, gave it as their decided opinion that his services ought to be retained for the welfare of the state; and there was an incipient movement to ensure his election to the continental Congress, which was abandoned only because he would not consent to be considered as a candidate. He had sacredly devoted himself to the Christian ministry, and he was inflexible in the purpose to spend his life in what he regarded the noblest of all causes.

While Mr. Dwight was a member of the legislature of Massachusetts, he occasionally preached in Boston and its vicinity; and attracted so much attention by his services in the pulpit, that he received invitations to settle in the ministry from two highly respectable congregations. Both these invitations, however, he declined; but in July of the same year, 1783, he accepted a call from the church and congregation in Greenfield, Connecticut, and on the 5th of November following, was regularly constituted their pastor.

As the stipulated salary of Mr. Dwight was found entirely inadequate to the support of his family, his expenses being not a little increased by the great amount of company which his eminent character and attainments drew to him from almost every part of the country, he found it necessary to resort to some employment not immediately connected with his profession. Accordingly, he established an academy, which very soon became extensively known, and as long as it continued, enjoyed the patronage of distinguished men from most of the different states.   To this institution he devoted six hours of each day, while at the same time he discharged the appropriate duties of the ministry with great fidelity and acceptance.   Though he preached regularly twice on the Sabbath, it was generally from short notes; and it was his own opinion that his preaching then was more effective than when in subsequent life, and upon change of circumstances, he wrote out his sermons and read them as they were written.

In 1787, he was honoured with the degree of Doctor of Divinity from the college of New Jersey; and in 1810, the degree of Doctor of Laws was conferred upon him by Harvard University.

In 1794, he was invited to the pastoral charge of the Reformed Dutch Church in Albany; a circumstance that was rendered remarkable by the fact that he belonged to another denomination, and one with which the Dutch church, at that time, had but little intercourse.   He declined the call, partly on the ground that there were some minor things in the constitution of the church to which he could not conscientiously give his consent.

Upon the death, in 1795, of Dr. Stiles, President of Yale College, the public eye was very generally turned towards Dr. Dwight as his successor; and in accordance with this general expectation, he was chosen shortly after to the office of President, and was inaugurated in September of that year.   He had resided at Greenville for twelve years, where he had been going on in an increasingly useful and honourable course; and it is no matter of surprise that the loss of such a man should have occasioned some regret, not only to his own immediate flock, but to the whole surrounding community.

In this office Dr. Dwight continued to the close of life, associating with it, however, to all intents and purposes, the duties of three professorships, viz., belles lettres, oratory and theology, besides being the pastor of the college church, and preaching to the students regularly twice on the Sabbath.   In addition to this, he took upon himself a vast amount of occasional labour, besides being constantly exposed to interruption from the numberless visiters who thronged to his house from every part of the country and the world.

Dr. Dwight was accustomed to devote the full vacation to travelling in various parts of New England and New York.   In 1815, he made his last journey; and his preaching and conversation at various places left the impression that he was never capable of finer intellectual efforts than at that time.   At the opening of the next term, he appeared in his full vigour, but in February following he was attacked with a most distressing malady, from which he never entirely recovered.   The physicians supposed at one time that they had gained the mastery over it, and he recovered so far that he resumed his labours in the college chapel, at the commencement of the summer term.   It became soon apparent, however, that there was little reason to expect any radical or permanent recovery; but he kept on labouring, even beyond his ability, until he was arrested by the near approach of death. In the prospect of his departure, he evinced great Christian dignity and composure and trust, and was attentive even to the minutest courtesies of life, to his very last hour. He died on the 11th of January, 1817, and his funeral was attended, three days after, with every demonstration of public and private respect.

Dr. Dwight's printed works are among the most valuable which his generation has produced. His System of Theology has, for many years, been more widely extended both in this country and in Great Britain, than any other system, either ancient or modern. The style of its orthodoxy is Calvinistic, but not in the extreme form. The work containing the record of his observations on the successive journeys he took in New England and New York, is full of instructive and amusing incident, though he has shown himself perhaps sometimes rather credulous in respect of facts. The two volumes of his posthumous sermons, together with the occasional discourses which he published during his life, are fine specimens of that kind of composition. Though his chief merit was by no means that of a poet, he wrote considerable poetry during his life, and some of it has received high commendation on both sides of the Atlantic. His principal poetical works are the "Conquest of Canaan," and "Greenfield Hill."

It is now universally conceded that Dr. Dwight was among the most gifted and splendid minds that have adorned the American pulpit. He had a fine commanding person, a voice of great compass and melody, a countenance radiant with intelligence, and a manner absolutely majestic. There was not much variety in his tones in the pulpit, and yet he sometimes held his audience as by a spell. His sermons, in his latter years, when we knew him, were always written, and somewhat closely read, and accompanied with little or no gesture; but he contrived to make himself powerfully felt by his hearers, notwithstanding. His prayers ordinarily were a repetition of the same thoughts in nearly the same language; but on extraordinary occasions, not a vestige of any thing like form could be detected. As the president of a college, he is acknowledged to have accomplished more than almost any other man who has occupied a similar station. The witnesses to his ability and fidelity, his dignified independence and conscientious adherence to right in every thing, are found every where, and in every profession and occupation. New England will always reckon him among the most illustrious of her sons.

(For the Register.)

THE PHONETIC REFORM.*

In adapting an alphabet to any language, the theory of the proceeding is very simple. First, we must analyze the language, to determine the elementary sounds by which its various words are made up; next, we must assign to each of these elements an arbitrary mark, called a letter, which we agree shall always stand as the representative of the sound to which it is assigned. The table of these elements forms the only consistent alphabet; by the aid of which, the reduction of the language to writing, and the consequent power of reading, are readily accomplished. For, great as is the number of words in a language, the number of its elementary sounds is but few, scarcely ever exceeding forty. The labour of learning to associate the forty marks with the forty sounds, and *vice versa*, is very trifling, and when we have succeeded in this, *spelling* is but the arrangement of these letters in the order in which the sounds they represent occur in any word; *reading* but the utterance of the sounds in the order of their representative letters.

We may illustrate this theory, of the formation and office of an alphabet, in the following manner. If we pronounce the words *say, nay, ode,* we perceive in the beginning of each elementary sounds, which are represented in the received alphabet by the marks *s, n, o.* For reasons to be presently manifest, let us replace these marks by others; and let †, §, ¶, represent the sounds in question. Of course, then, all words, English or foreign, containing no other elementary sounds than these, may be spelled by the marks at our command. For example, the words *oh, own, no, known, sew, snow, sown,* will be symbolized, if we have respect to their *sounds* alone, by ¶, ¶ §, § ¶, § ¶ §, † ¶, † § ¶, † ¶ §.

We have mentioned that the elementary sounds with which we have been dealing, are represented in the received alphabet by *s, n, o.* In theory, therefore, the above words should be spelled, *o, on, no, non, so, sno, son;* but the actual spelling is, save in one instance, widely different. We have the sound *o* represented by the four signs *oh, ow, ew,*

---

* In nothing, perhaps, is the progressive spirit of the age more distinctly marked, than in the new and ingenious phonetic system, which boldly proposes to abandon the present alphabet and modes of writing and printing the English language.

We are indebted for the present article on the subject, to a literary friend of this city, who is a zealous advocate of the proposed "reform," and which he has clearly and forcibly exhibited.

Without expressing any opinion of our own on the propriety of the whole change as contemplated, we have no doubt our readers will see with us much in the system that is capable of useful application, and will peruse with pleasure the interesting and spirited sketch and vindication of the new art by our correspondent.—ED.

o; while the sign *o* represents its own sound and three others besides, in the words *no, on, non, son.*

The reader will now be prepared for the statement that the alphabet in use for representing the English language is thoroughly unphilosophical, since it provides no signs for recognised elementary sounds, and different signs for the same elementary sounds. Our language contains thirty-four elements, and requires, therefore, so many letters in its alphabet. In fact, there are provided for the purpose only twenty-six, two of which (c, q,) are superfluous, and four (j, x, i, u,) are compounds, leaving but twenty elementary letters. For the representation of the fourteen sounds thus unprovided for, all sorts of expedients have been adopted, except the manifest one of selecting new letters. Thus the simple vowel element heard in the word *do,* (for which *o* is a very false representative,) is expressed in twenty-nine different ways; as in R*eu*ben, gall*eo*n, Buccl*eu*gh, br*ew*, br*ewe*d, r*heu*m, r*hu*barb, d*o*, sh*oe*, m*o*ve, man*oeu*vre, t*oo*, m*o*ved, s*ou*p, b*ou*se, thr*ou*gh, Br*ou*gh*a*m, rendezv*ou*s, surt*ou*t, billetd*ou*x, C*ow*per, r*u*ling, tr*ue*, r*u*le, br*ui*sing, br*ui*se, H*u*lme, t*wo*, *who*. Again, the simple consonant element heard in the beginning of the word *s*ure is expressed in twelve different ways, in the words *ch*aise, spe*ci*al, p*sh*aw, *s*ugar, *sch*edule, con*sci*ous, *sh*all, wi*sh*ed, A*ssh*eton, ce*ssi*on, mo*ti*on, fu*chs*ia.

To render still more clear the unphilosophical manner in which the English language is represented, we shall give a table, the first column of which contains all the separate sounds which are heard as elements in our speech, and also certain compound sounds, (the dipthongs, and j, ch,) which it is found convenient to classify with the simple elements. The sounds thus enumerated (which are heard in the Italic letters of the words cited,) are the true English alphabet, and each should have its separate sign always to be used for, and always representing, the sound to which it is adapted. In the second column, as a contrast to this simple principle, "one sound, one sign," we record the number of ways by which, in practical spelling, the sound is represented.

Sounds.	Number of representatives.	Sounds.	Number of representatives.	Sounds.	Number of representatives.	Sounds.	Number of representatives.
e*e*l	40	*u*p	24	*ba*y	7	*th*y	2
*a*le	34	w*oo*d	8	*ti*e	12	*s*own	19
h*ea*rt	12	b*uy*	26	*di*e	8	*z*one	18
*aw*e	21	*bo*y	11	*ch*eer	7	ru*sh*	12
*ow*e	34	*bou*gh	10	*j*eer	9	rou*ge*	7
woo	29	*f*ew	30	*c*ap	19	*r*ay	10
*i*ll	37	*y*ea	4	*g*ap	7	*l*ay	12
*e*ll	36	*w*ay	4	*f*ie	12	*m*ay	13
*a*m	16	*h*ay	4	*v*ie	8	*n*ay	19
*o*dd	13	*p*ay	6	*th*igh	7	ha*ng*	7

We have here, then, to represent forty elements, as many as six hundred and fourteen symbolizations, or fifteen and a third, on the average, to each element! But this is not all. The combinations selected to express simple sounds are no more stable in the performance of this function than the single letters themselves. If the digraph *sh* were always to express the elementary sound which it does in *shun*, we might accept this as a satisfactory, though a singular, arrangement; but four other meanings have been assigned to it, as in dis*h*onor, mis*hap*, thres*h*old, Mas*h*am (Masam.) Again, *ea* has not always the sound it has in *heart*, but various others, as in *heal*, *great*, *head*, *react*, *create*, while in *beau*, *beauty*, Beaucham (Beecham,) and *beaufin* (biffin,) it is impossible to say what office the digraph performs. A table showing the various effects of combinations of this kind cannot be readily inserted here. Were there space to do so, we should discover that there are two-hundred and twenty-nine combinations having, in the whole, six hundred and four different meanings, or an average of two and two-thirds to each.

The mathematical inference from these numerical statistics is startling, but fully borne out by experience; namely, *that no set of rules can be framed for determining the pronunciation of an English word from its present spelling, or the present spelling of an English word from its pronunciation.* No word is so simple as not to foil us. Suppose us to hear the word *say* for the first time, and to be called upon to spell it by the aid of the alphabet, or the so-called analogies of spelling. The alphabet would point out *sa* as proper, but the dictionaries would not allow of it. The *analogies* will leave us to select between nineteen ways of representation for the consonant sound, and thirty-four for the vowel, (see the above table,) giving nineteen times thirty-four or six hundred and forty-six spellings, for this simple word of two sounds. When, at last, we turn to the dictionary for authority, we should as soon expect to find the spelling *sseeighe* (from the analogy of his*s*ed and weig*h*ed,) as that of *say*. But reverse the question. Given the spelling, required the pronunciation. Referring to analogies, we should find that the letter *s* has given to it five different values; *a*, 8; *y*, 5; *ay*, 4; giving $5 \times 8 \times 5 \times 4$, or eight hundred possible pronunciations!

This poverty and instability of the received alphabet; this lawlessness in spelling, this uncertainty of pronunciation, have long been submitted to as an evil, to be condemned by the reflecting, and sported with by the witty, but not to be remedied. We have been content to acquire the ability to read and spell, by treasuring in the memory the symbolization of each separate word in the language for itself;—a stupendous effort, which few ever wholly accomplish,—in which the educated, after years of labour, are only partially successful, and which the great body of our race renounce in despair. On this last point, the statistics of ignorance leave us no room to doubt. "England and

Wales," says the British Quarterly Review, "with their sixteen millions of people, contain nearly eight millions unable to write their name, and not less than five millions unable to read their mother tongue." If we deduct two millions for persons disqualified from learning by tender age, or imbecility, the numbers are reduced, respectively, to six and three millions. The British Registrar General's report for 1846, shows that, of those who signed the marriage register in that year, one woman in two, and one man in three signed with their marks. In the U. S. it appears by the Census of 1840, that one person in thirteen of the adult *white* population, above twenty, is unable to read or write. Nor is the probability to be passed without notice that these statistics greatly understate the real amount of ignorance. Shame would lead many to prevaricate rather than confess themselves "illiterate;" while others, and a large number, would be shown, by a more strict examination than the census-taker is able to make, to have claimed a knowledge altogether useless for any practical purpose; their reading, perhaps, averaging a word a minute, their writing being illegible.

For evils so serious, there is a simple remedy. Give to the English language a rational alphabet, containing a letter for every elementary sound; give, in other words, a phonetic alphabet, and the highways of knowledge, reading and writing, are opened to all, in from twenty to eighty hours of application, and the education of the poor becomes possible and certain. Nor is this all. The English language, from the simplicity of its grammatical structure, and from its strength, copiousness and variety, is the admiration of the scholar, and the pride of those to whom it is the mother tongue. That it should be more widely diffused, so as to become the acknowledged medium of international communication, as it were the universal language, is surely no unpatriotic desire. Considering the wide-spread commerce of the Anglo-Saxon race, such a desire might readily be consummated, were their language rationally represented; but, never, while the present repelling system of orthography is retained.

But the phonetic reform, the necessity of which we have so faintly pictured, has already been commenced. About ten years since, Mr. Isaac Pitman, an Englishman, published a method of shorthand, founded on a Phonetic alphabet. A more perfect system of writing than this can hardly be conceived. Based on the truest philosophy, and elaborated by a mind of extraordinary inventive power, Phonography (for such it is named,) is an art by which we are enabled, after a moderate amount of application, to write with the rapidity of speech what may be read with the ease of print; thus adapting itself, not merely to the wants of reporters, as a class, but to the great body of the intelligent community. The system has found great favour with the public. The sale of the elementary phonographic works has gone on steadily increasing, since the art was promulgated, and has now reached to sixty thousand copies per annum in Great Britain and America. Four monthly magazines, of wide circulation, are published in England, and two in this country, altogether in the mystic characters of phonography; while for purposes of correspondence, note-taking, and all other objects to which writing is applicable, the art is spreading in a manner truly surprising to those who have made no examination of its claims upon the public attention.

This extensive use of phonetic *writing* could not fail to make more apparent the necessity of phonetic *printing*. In effecting this result, the phonographers, now grown to a large and an organized body, all cordially co-operated; but prominently active was Mr. A. J. Ellis, a philologist of distinguished ability. His course of procedure was eminently practical, and had for its object not so much to construct a *new* as to re-construct the old alphabet. All the old letters (except q, x, and k,) were retained, to represent in the phonetic alphabet those elementary sounds which they most frequently have in the present spelling; thus e, u, c, are phonotypes for the sounds italicised in end, *up*, can. The completion of the alphabet, of forty letters, required seventeen new signs, and these were invented to harmonize as completely as possible with the familiar Roman letters.* At last, after many experiments and much expense, the scheme was finally perfected in 1846, when the publication of phonetic literature with the new types was commenced, and has since been untiringly prosecuted; the demand of the public exceeding the supply. Of the works published, we may enumerate the New Testament (two sizes,) Book of Common Prayer, Gay's Fables, Rasselas, Vicar of Wakefield, the Essentials of Phonetics (a scientific work of two hundred and fifty pages,) Shakspeare's Tempest, Bible Histories, Phonetic Reader, and a very large number of books for elementary instruction, to which should be added three monthly magazines in England and one in this country.

Though we think no argument can weigh against the fact, apparent to reason, and confirmed by numerous experiments, that phonetic printing would practically annihilate the labour of learning to read, we must in candour state the objections usually made to any attempt towards its substitution for the received method, presenting such answers to these objections as our space will permit.

I. "Phonetic spelling would obscure etymologies." Our reply is given in the words of Dr. Franklin. "Etymologies are at present very uncertain, but such as they are the old books would still preserve them, and etymologists would there find them. Words, in the course of time, change their meanings as well as their spellings and pronunciations, and we do not look to etymology for their present meaning. If I should call a man a knave and a villain, he would hardly be satisfied with my telling him, that one of the words originally signified only a

---

* The addition of fifteen characters to the English phonetic alphabet of forty, completes what is called the Ethnical Alphabet, by means of which we are enabled to write all known languages.

lad or a servant, and the other an under ploughman or the inhabitant of a village." We may add, that those who most strenuously urge this objection cull their examples from the Latin, of which they have a smattering, utterly heedless of the fact that four-fifths of our language is derived from the Anglo-Saxon, of which they are quite ignorant. The true answer is, however, that the sole office of spelling is to record speech, and not to trace the histories of words. To adopt the illustration of Klopstock, we should as properly require the artist of a flower-piece to paint the *odours* as well as the colours.

II. "The distinction between words of different meaning and similar sound (as *see, sea,*) would be destroyed." Dr. Franklin replies, that "this distinction is already destroyed in pronouncing them, and we rely on the sense alone of the sentence to ascertain which of the several words, similar in sound, we intend." We may add that the phonetic spelling really compensates the loss by providing different forms for words now spelt alike but differently sounded,—as *bow, eat,* &c.

III. "All the books written would be useless." This objection has no weight when applied to the phonotypy of Pitman and Ellis, since its resemblance to the spelling under the old system is so striking that we pass from one to the other without the slightest real difficulty. So much is this the case, that it is found, by experience, the greatest saving of time and labour to teach those learning to read by the phonetic method, in the first instance: when this is accomplished, the scholar, turning to a book in the present printing, though confused at first, soon learns, by the aid of a little guessing, to thread his way among its mazes.

IV. "The printing proposed will be so strange in its appearance as effectually to bar its general acceptance." We reply, that this strangeness of appearance is altogether a supposition; and could we have an opportunity of showing the reader a specimen he would rather be surprised at the familiarity of its aspect.

V. "It would impair the English language." To this objection the answer is, that it mistakes entirely the purpose in view, which is simply to provide an improved means of *recording* the language, not of altering it.

VI. "It is a desecration to change the characters used by our forefathers." To this, in an age of rail-roads and magnetic telegraphs, we need make no reply. The desecration has already taken place several times. We have discarded the Runic characters of the bards, and the letters of the Anglo-Saxons; while the spelling of Shakspeare's day would be a riddle to these conservative objectors far harder to solve than any which phonetic printing proposes to them.

We cannot more fitly conclude this article than by the following quotation from the Westminster Review of April last:

"The disciples of the Phonetic Reform movement now amount to some thousands; and the cause has all the executive elements of success:—the energy and enthusiasm of a self-raised son of the people, working to promote a system invented by himself and for the people's use; the aged wisdom and practical knowledge of the venerable father* of a great and successful practical reformer; the learning, countenance, and purse of a man of education, position and wealth. If, then, it has also, as we believe it has, internal elements of success; if, like Christianity, (we say it reverently,) it be born among, necessary to, and demanded by the people, like Christianity we think it must succeed. It destroys it not that it should have as enemies those who would admire it as an elegant pastime while confined to the scholar and *dilletanti*, but who, with the geometer of old, think it degrading to pander to the vile and material necessities of the herd. It wants not the assistance of the *faineant*, who thinks it 'perhaps not a bad thing in itself, but too difficult to carry out.' It leaves the contemptuous mockeries of its 'snubbishness' to the flunkey-quelling Thackerayian pen. To the derisive fun of *Punch* we 'would not an we could' reply in phrase jocose. Punch, it is no joke. Your mirthful company of wearers of motley have done more than aught else to strip the motley from society and from the man—they have shown us ourselves undressed; they must help us tear the bizarre and motley garb from our language, and make it decent. . . . But should they oppose it, the million-tongued voice of uneducated labour will still be strong enough to doom our present cacography and shout, 'Away with it! why cumbereth it us.'"

(For the Register.)

NOTES ON MEXICO.

BY AN OFFICER OF THE AMERICAN ARMY.

I WRITE of Mexico as I saw it—of its institutions and people—of their manner of living and customs—of the soil and climate, the mountains and valleys. The subject is extensive, and embraces much that is deeply interesting; but within the limits of an article I can do no more than glance at the various objects that present themselves to notice.

Mexico, until very recently, was almost a fabled land. The tales that were told of its marvellous wealth, of the mild serenity of its clear blue sky,—the grandeur of its mountain scenery, and the beauties of its fertile valleys,—the grace of the dark-eyed Señoritas, and the proud bearing of the gay caballeros, partook more of the romance of Eastern story, than the sober lessons of historic truth. The web of fiction had been so artfully woven around every thing that was said and written about that country, that it was deemed almost an earthly paradise. In

* Rowland Hill, Sen.

fact, accurate notions of Mexico were not entertained by the citizens of the United States, until their victorious legions had traversed the land "from Palo Alto to Chapultepec." The practical observations of our own people filled up the unwritten void in Mexican history, and they brought home with them, what could not be acquired from books, a current knowledge of the country and people.

The first conquest of Cortez seems hardly real, and yet it comes down to us so well authenticated there is no room for doubt. If we take up the history of that romantic story as written by Prescott, and carefully trace the march of Cortez from his first landing upon the coast, till he was master of the kingly city, the events pass before us in such quick succession that we are almost bewildered by the changing scenes. We behold a small band of strangers, numbering only a few hundred, who have set out to conquer a powerful people; the leader of this band burns his ships to infuse the bravery of despair in his troops. With an energy that never falters, and a patience that never wearies, he keeps his eyes fixed on the goal of all his hopes, the "halls of Montezuma's king," and, relying upon his own resources, prepares to break down every barrier that may oppose him. He pierces the mountain passes, and treads upon the broad savannahs of Mexico. The Cholulans, a people mighty in numbers and in strength, are conquered, and their city razed to the ground; the Tlascalans he defeats, and compels to become his allies; then, with giant strides, he passes the Cordilleras mountains into the valley of Mexico, and invests the imperial city. The history of its capture—the "noche triste," that terrible night when Cortez and his men were driven from the city—his retreat—the fierce conflict upon the plains of Otumba—his return and final capture and destruction of the city—form altogether a series of marvellous events, almost too incredible for belief, but yet too well authenticated to be disputed.

It is a source of deep regret that so much of the political history of that interesting country has been lost to the world. The traditionary stories that we have, fail to remove the gloom and uncertainty that hang over the history of Montezuma and his people, and a correct history of the colonial times of Mexico has never been given, but lies buried in the unrevealed recesses of Spanish archives.

There seems no bright and happy future for Mexico and her people, —no cheerful morn comes down upon "the dark and troubled night" of the past.

.   .   .   .

The political history of Mexico, since the gaining of her independence, is made up of revolutions and counter-revolutions. The principles of right and justice were lost sight of in the great struggle for power, and every change forged another link in the chain which was to bind the people down in slavery. Under the most favourable circumstances in which Mexico can be viewed, there is nothing to raise up hope for the future. There are so many conflicting interests—so many enmities to punish, and friendships to reward—so much bitterness of feeling on the one side, and want of love for the country on the other, that it will be found impossible to harmonize these discordant materials, and bring order out of this chaos.

Spain wrote the history of her vice-royal government in Mexico with the point of the sword dipped in blood. She recorded it in all the valleys, and upon every hill top, and all the people read it. Revolution came. The people of Mexico, who for years, and even centuries, had submitted to the rod that smote them, now rose up in the pride and strength of manhood, and hurled down those who had been their task-masters. Spain, with all her grinding tyranny, was driven from the land, and they built up new altars and new institutions. They had a long and severe struggle. The accumulated miseries of war, pestilence and famine, visited them, and they only reached national independence through much suffering and waste of life.

As men always will, who are fixed and determined in their purposes, they conquered; but to them success seemed worse than defeat. They conquered the Spaniards, but had not gained a victory over themselves. Though they were free from the unjust government of the viceroys, they were still under the sway of the worst passions of our nature. The Mexicans had their eyes directed singly to a change of rulers, and never imagined they could make their condition worse. With no future course marked out, upon which the contending elements might harmonize, they very naturally fell into the other extreme of anarchy and confusion. The establishment of their independence seemed to be a stepping-stone to disorder and misrule, and ere they had wiped the dust and blood of battle from their brows, were made but too sensible that they had not bettered their condition. They had only exchanged foreign for domestic despotism.

The mutations in the government of Mexico, for the first few years after her independence was declared, are curious in their way, and may not be uninteresting to the reader. These changes I will briefly note.

Upon the close of the revolution, Iturbide, who had been of much service during the struggle for independence, was called to the throne as Emperor, and assumed the reins of government in the winter of 1821. His reign was short and troubled; the people disapproved of his administration, and, without force or violence, stripped him of his power, and sent him into exile to a foreign land. Now that Iturbide was dethroned, and the country in fact without a government, they contemplated forming a regular system which should ensure public security. A question arose as to the kind of government they should form, and, following our example, agreed upon a federal union and a republic. But the people of Mexico were not ready to receive democratic institutions. The leaders were not aware that a republican form of government could not exist unless based upon the virtue and intelligence of the people. With a population, ignorant and debased, they hastened from a despotism to the opposite extreme. Twenty-five years of revolution and misrule tell to the world how much the leaders erred. The people were ready for a change, but not so great a change; the grand results should have been produced gradually, as they were fitted to enjoy them.

The constitution was proclaimed on the 4th day of October, 1824, and the states of Mexico were declared to be united into a Federal Republic. Victoria, who had devoted himself to the cause of freedom, and made more sacrifices than any of the leading men, was installed as first President in January, 1825. But so active was the spirit of evil, that the new President was hardly seated in the chair of state, before "pronunciamentoes" were proclaimed against his government. The early troubles, however, were not serious, and for about three years the country enjoyed comparative tranquillity and quiet. It was at this time that the two political parties of the country were organized, which have contributed largely to bring ruin and misrule upon the country. They were not influenced by pure and patriotic motives, but by the selfish consideration of personal aggrandizement. These parties took the names of the Escoceres and the Yorkinos, or the Scotch and York lodges. The former advocated a strong national government with central power, and the latter a confederated republic, after the example of the United States.

Victoria's administration did not close without the bursting of the storm which had been long brewing. In December, 1827, General Bravo raised the standard of rebellion against Victoria, and although this revolt was soon put down, the seeds had been widely sown. Gomez Pedraza was the successor of Victoria. He was elected over Guerraro, who was his competitor. The new administration was soon involved in difficulties. The Yorkinos, who pretended to be the republican party, were not willing to abide by the decision of the people in the late election, and, in consequence, "pronounced" against the new President. Santa Anna now appeared upon the stage, and headed this movement. It soon became popular, and resulted in Pedraza being driven from the country, and Guerraro placed in the Presidential chair, who was declared to be duly elected. Bustamente was made vice-president.

Guerraro, like his predecessor, was doomed to misfortune and short-lived power. Bustamente soon "pronounced" against him, overthrew him, and seated himself in the chair of state. The country enjoyed comparative quiet and peace for three years, until 1832, when Santa Anna raised his voice in opposition to the government, deposed Bustamente, and re-called Pedraza to serve out the unexpired three months of the term for which he was originally elected.

In 1833, Santa Anna made himself President, and from that time to the period of his late exile was the master spirit of the country, and nearly all the time he was in it held the reins of government, as president, dictator, or absolute tyrant. He was not, however, exempt from the troubles which marked the course of his predecessors. His enemies were numerous and powerful, and stirred up revolution against him. "Pronunciamentoes" followed each other in quick succession, and it required all his energy and address to keep his seat. To make himself secure, he usurped power. In 1836, he overthrew the federal constitution, by establishing in its stead a strong central government. This new declaration was known as the "plan of Toluca." All state governments were abolished, and the whole power of the country was given to the central government at the city of Mexico. In 1841, the "plan of Toluca" was followed by another "pronunciamento," which resulted in the "plan of Tacubaya," by the 7th article of which Santa Anna is declared dictator. In accordance with the last "plan," a congress assembled which formed a kind of government instead of that guarantied by the federal constitution, and which it declared void. The instrument which this congress proclaimed, was styled "Basis of political organization for the Mexican republic." Mexico was, in fact, no longer a republic, but had sunk back into a worse state than she was before she threw off the Spanish yoke. After this new organization of the government, the same troubles continued to exist; and down to the time of the war between that country and the United States, revolutions were constantly taking place.

And what has Mexico gained by her revolutions? What has she gained by all her years of toil and suffering, by the blood she shed, and the misery of her people? She has gained absolutely nothing. In exchange for the shackles of old Spain she parted with whatever of security to person and property she knew under the Spanish viceroys. It is true, Mexico is nominally free, and on paper passes as a republic; her statesmen style their people the "magnanimous Mexican nation," and talk about "God and liberty." The people nominally enjoy the elective franchise, but the privilege of voting is a farce to them, and they know no more what it means than they know of our constitution. Their boasted freedom exists only in name, and when the parade and show of their pretended free institutions are looked into, the truth will soon appear. It will be found to be the worst possible form of despotism. The great body of the people have no more to do with the government than have the Laplanders with theirs, and they are as debased, ignorant and superstitious.

I can say with safety that the name of freedom has rather been a curse than a blessing to this people, as they neither knew how to enjoy liberty, nor prepared themselves for its enjoyment. They are now, and ever have been since the revolution, in a most deplorable state. Anarchy is sown broad-cast over the land. Murders are an every-day occurrence, and robbery, which is followed as a gentlemanly calling, is carried to almost as great extent, as it is by the banditti and highway-men of Europe. The "Give me your money or your life" associations exist in every part of the country, and their members infest all the highways. They despoil their victims at the city gates, and laugh at the police, most of whom are in their pay. There is neither security to person nor property, unless protected by iron bars and thick walls. No gentleman in Mexico thinks of moving from his own threshold without being armed to the teeth, and were you to meet a Mexican gentleman and his family travelling from his country-house into town, you would think, from the number of his escort, that a prince of the royal blood was passing along.

Since the Spaniards were driven from the country, every thing like enterprise has been going backward, and a stranger at once perceives an entire want of energy. Every thing seems going to ruin—there is no life—no improvement. Decay is written every where. It is seen in the public buildings, which are tumbling down in ruins, and at which the people gape and stare, without making any exertion to rebuild them. It is seen in the sinking bridges, once fine noble structures laid in ce-ment, and in the once elegant paved country roads, now almost im-passible for want of repairs. In some parts of the country they have allowed whole towns and villages to fall into ruins, and they quietly content themselves in mud huts built in the shadows of their former homes. In every part of the country one notices fine structures half finished, which were begun during the time of the "viceroys." In this half-finished state they are likely to remain.

.   .   .   .

When the Spaniards took possession of Mexico they found a beau-tiful world, and it is not strange that this new clime was so inviting, and held such an important place in the consideration of the Spanish government. No wonder it was an El Dorado to them, since in all the beauties and riches of nature it so far excelled the old world. Na-ture seems to have been lavish of her rich and choice gifts, which have literally descended in showers upon the land. In geographical position, it is not surpassed by any country on this continent. Washed by two seas, it has a gradual slope towards the shore of each from an eleva-tion of more than twelve thousand feet. On each declivity, upon the same parallel of latitude, it has all the climates of the world, from the burning sun of the tropics on the coast, to the eternal snows of the mountains which overlook the valley of Mexico. The productions of every clime grow here in great abundance, the delicious fruits of the tropics uniting upon the same hill-side with the productions of the more temperate regions.

In point of climate, Mexico cannot be excelled. An eternal spring bends its blue and cloudless sky over this earthly paradise the live-long year, and flowers, rich, beautiful and rare, are blooming around you, loading the air with their sweet fragrance from summer until sum-

mer comes again.   For many weeks together there will hardly be a
cloud to obscure the brilliancy of the sky, and upon the high table-lands
the air is so. pure that the stars shine almost as brightly at midsummer, as they do in this latitude in mid-winter.   In these elevated
regions I noticed that there is no twilight which deserves the' name.
As soon as the sun has bathed its bright face in the western sea, the
shades of night draw around without the presence of that lovely season which the poets call eventide.   It is dark almost as soon as the
sun has gone down; no lingering of day—no gradual drawing of the
robes of night.   There is only one step from daylight to darkness.

But nature has not alone given to this country a cloudless sky and
spring-like climate, but she has stored the earth with riches, which
not even the wildest 'speculators can calculate.   Deeply veined in her
almost inaccessible mountains lie buried, gold, silver, and precious stones.
The soil of Mexico is rich and productive, and requires only an active
and enterprising population to bring forth in greater abundance than any
other country upon this continent.   Agriculture has made no advances,
it is not known as a science.   The whole routine of farming is rude
and thriftless in the extreme, and if it was not for the natural richness
of the soil, would not support the population.   The wealthiest landholders are very deficient in all the implements of husbandry.   They
use the same kind of plough that was used in the time of Moses, to
which are fastened two or four poor lazy oxen..   Besides the ploughman, there is one man with the team armed with a long pole shod with
iron, whose duty it is to stir up the animals.   I have seen as many as
thirty of these teams in one field, and sometimes almost doubted in
my own mind whether they moved.   One modern plough, drawn by two
good horses, would do more work in one day, than ten of these ancient
implements.   Their hoes, spades, shovels, and, in truth, all instruments
used in farming, are made of wood, and sharpened with iron to prevent
their wearing out.

The face of the country is different in appearance from most other
parts of North America.   From the waters of the Gulf of Mexico on
the east, there is a gradual slope until you rise to the summit of the
great Cordillera ridge of mountains which bounds the valley of Mexico,
and on the western side there is the same slope to the shore of the Pacific ocean.   The country is properly divided, both by its climate and
by its geographical position, into three great divisions, viz., the Tierra
Calliente, or the hot country,—the Tierra Templada, or the temperate
region,—and the Tierra Frizada, or the frozen region.   The first, or
the Tierra Calliente, extends from each sea upward until you reach the
height of about three thousand feet.   This is the region where tropical
fruits and other productions of warm climates are grown in greatest
abundance, and where the weather is hot the whole year round.   The
Tierra Templada, or temperate region, extends from the Tierra Calliente upwards, and embraces all the elevated table-lands which abound

in Mexico. The Tierra, Frizada embraces the region of perpetual snow. As you go north, these table-lands increase in width until they are finally merged into the vast sandy deserts of New Mexico and California. In the Tierra Templada, the extremes of heat and cold are never felt, the thermometer ranging from 60° to 80° all the year. Here all the fruits and grains of the temperate zone are raised; crops follow crops in quick succession, and the labours of the husbandman are never ended. Upon these high table-lands, the air is very rare and respiration difficult. All strangers find great difficulty in breathing when first they go into these elevated regions.

In Mexico there is not the same change of seasons that we have in the United States. The variations of spring, summer, autumn and winter, are unknown, and the year is divided into two seasons only, the rainy and the dry season. The rainy season usually begins in April or May, and some years rain will fall every day for three or four months. The remainder of the year no rain descends, and the weather is dry and clear. During the rainy season, the rain does not fall all day, but begins about mid-day and rains very hard for two or three hours, when the sun will again appear, and the clouds break away. I have been told by the inhabitants that they have known periods of nearly two years when not enough rain would fall to wet the ground to the depth of two inches. A perpetual spring reigns in the valley of Mexico. There, there is no sear and yellow leaf—no perceptible change in the foliage; the new leaf pushes the old one off with a gentle force, and comes so gradually that you are hardly aware of its approach.

Mexico is deficient in rivers and creeks, and water is scarce all over the country. The want of regular rains during the year will always be a great draw-back upon its agricultural interests. The ground for cultivation is watered almost wholly by irrigation from the mountain streams, or raised from the rivers. Good timber does not abound until you reach the elevation of four or five thousand feet, when fine pine timber is found, and all the mountain sides are covered with it nearly up to the region of perpetual snow. From Vera Cruz to Jalapa, about seventy miles, and which is the Tierra Calliente, on the east slope very few large trees are found. The country is either covered with bushes, known here as chapparel, or spread into prairie land. The foliage in this region is very thick and luxuriant, much more so than can be found any where out of the tropics. Northern Mexico differs in appearance from both central and southern Mexico. From the Rio Grande, the country, for nearly two hundred miles, is almost a perfect level until you reach the Sierra Madre mountains. This is a bold chain of rugged mountains which forms an admirable western barrier to the valley of the Rio Grande.

The population of Mexico is truly a mixed and motley people. When the Spaniards conquered the country, they found a distinct race, whose origin will perhaps always remain a mystery. I was surprised to see how the people have retained their separate distinct individuality. All the exertions of the Spaniards have not been able to destroy the distinctive characteristics of this race, and to mould their manners, habits and customs, to the standard of European life. Their religion alone has been changed, and, in most, if not in all other respects, they remain as Cortez found them. In visiting them in their little villages, and seeing their habits of life, I was induced to believe that they are the very same people Montezuma left, so much do all the manners and customs of their life correspond to those of the Aztec race. At the present time, the population of Mexico is something more than seven millions of people, of whom not more than one million have white blood in their veins; these are the Spaniards, their descendants, or the offspring of their intermarriage with the natives of the country. Of this population nearly five millions are Mexican Indians, the descendants of the ancient rulers of the country. The latter class, who form the great body of the population, and are emphatically the people of Mexico, are a wretched race of beings, poor, ignorant and servile. In many parts of the country they still retain the language of their ancestors, and when addressed in Spanish, they understand no more what is said to them than if they had been spoken to in Chinese. I found them a distinct people. They principally congregate in villages called Pueblos, containing from one hundred to one thousand inhabitants. Their costume, mode of life, and habitations, all indicate extreme poverty. The men dress in a very coarse cloth, which they make from the fibres of the American aloe, or in the skins of different animals. The women wear no other dress, for the most part, than a chemise and a skirt tied at the waist. Both sexes very generally go bare-headed, and some wear sandals upon their feet. These poor beings are the hewers of wood, and the drawers of water for their more lordly masters. They till the soil, fill up the ranks of the army, and pour riches into the coffers of the church. Their huts are very rude indeed, being built of mud, or poles covered with leaves or reeds, and very seldom containing more than one room, in which are seen, very frequently, the donkeys and dogs with the family. Their beds are a few mats upon the hard ground. They are filthy in their persons and lazy. Though indolent in their habits, they do much hard work. A large proportion of the produce of the country, which is taken to the town to be sold, is carried upon the backs of these poor creatures, and the loads which they carry are really astonishing. I have seen them carry, strapped to their backs, as much timber, charcoal or earthenware, as a mule could well carry.

When these people are travelling to market they seldom walk, but always move along on a trot in Indian file, and this, too, with heavy loads upon their backs, and the burden sometimes increased by the addition of one or two children.

Though nominally free, they are in fact and practically speaking, slaves, and in a state of bondage much worse than negro slavery. There is a system of servitude in Mexico called peonism, and the subjects of it are called peons. There is a sort of implied contract between the master and his servant, by which the latter is to receive five dollars a month for his labour. These wages are to support the labourer and his family, and the master is under no obligation to take care of them in sickness or old age. The servant is compelled to purchase every thing he needs from the master's store, and cannot leave him while in his debt. The latter is always the case, and the practical working of the system is to reduce these people to abject slavery under a more charming name. When they once become attached to an estate they never leave it, since they are always in debt, and generally pass with it, if conveyed away. I knew one man in the state of Nuevo Leon whose estates numbered upon them seventy thousand of these poor people. They comprise more than three-fourths of the Mexican nation.

The food of the common people is very simple and nutritious, and which strangers soon learn to like. They have two standard articles of food that are used by all classes, and which may be called national dishes. They are called Tortillas and Frigoles, the former being made of pounded corn, and baked in thin cakes; the latter is a black bean stewed in lard and water. No Mexican table is complete without these two national dishes upon it.

W. W. H. D.

[To be continued.]

CANADA.

In our last Quarterly Chronicle we mentioned that we had received "from an English gentleman, of high character, a communication on the subject of the Canadian troubles;" and which we promised to insert in a future number. The writer takes strong ground against "the rebellion losses bill," and the policy of the present whig administration in Great Britain. Being in correspondence with the leading loyalists of Canada, his views will help to explain the origin of the excitement, and the cause of the unpopularity of Lord Elgin.

We shall, therefore, by its publication, be in the line of our prescribed duty, which is to enlighten the public mind in matters of general interest, and especially in those which belong to the political history of the times. As well, however, to do justice to the subject as to justify the strong language of the writer, who attributes the origin of the difficulty to the "ignorance of the British people" in regard to the colonies, we precede his article with an extract from the London Sun, of May 16th, for the purpose of showing the sentiment and feelings on both sides.   The reader will be able to see, too, how deep-seated is the animosity of the rival parties on this question, and that though the agitators may be repressed, as they undoubtedly will be by the arm of power, and by some alterations in the machinery of the colonial government, still the pent-up dissatisfaction of the ultra-royalists, fed by the rivalry of the two races, must, ere long, again show itself in hostile attitude to the home government, or in a separation from it.

A peculiar feature of the recent disturbance is, that the malcontents are Anglo-Saxons, composed of that part of the population who, in 1837, sustained the government against the then insurgents, who were principally French.   Now the action is reversed, and the latter are the abettors of the government, and formed the special police to preserve the peace.   In our June number will be found the particulars of the great riot which occurred on the 26th of April, at Montreal, and resulted in the destruction of the parliament house, and the assault upon the Governor-General, Lord Elgin, who, from that period, until very recently, has been shut up in a barricaded house through fear of the populace.   In the mean time, Sir Allen M'Nab has been to England to procure, if possible, the disallowance of the obnoxious bill, and the recall of Lord Elgin.

It is understood that he has been unsuccessful.   Before he went he is reported to have said, that if the bill were forced upon the country, "it would be a question for the people of Upper Canada to consider, whether it would not be better for them to be governed by the people on the other side of the river than by a French Canadian majority." And the Montreal Courier held the following language:—"Let parliament pass the bill, let the governor sanction it if he pleases, but while there is an axe and rifle on the frontier, and Saxon hands to wield them, their losses will not be paid."

Such bold language, connected with the violent and seditious conduct of the malcontents in Canada, on the occasion referred to, doubtless aroused the indignation of the supporters of the administration at home, and may account for the severity of the London Sun, which treats the subject in the following manner:—

"Nothing can justify a precipitate condemnation of the course pursued by the government towards the Canadas, previous to the examination of those official despatches which will be laid, on Friday evening, before both houses of the Imperial Parliament. Whatever may be the nature of the provisions made in that Bill of Indemnity which has originated the insurrection at Montreal, the perfectly constitutional manner in which that measure has been carried through the Canadian Legislature leaves us, however, no reason to doubt that the recent outbreak is the infamous result of a conspiracy on the part of a lawless and unprincipled minority. We may each of us entertain a different opinion as to the advisability or non-advisability of indemnifying indiscriminately all those who may have happened to suffer pecuniary losses during the last deplorable rebellion. One may, another may not, conceive that some definite distinction ought to have been made between those individuals who were injured in their property through their sympathy for the government, and those who sustained losses from their complicity with the insurgents. Such is strictly a question of morality, of expediency, or of convenience, upon the merits of which the views of the multitude might remain divided until the day of judgment. But upon this point there neither does, nor can there exist, any hesitation whatever—namely, that the Indemnity Bill (good or bad, expedient or inexpedient, convenient or inconvenient as it may be to individuals,) has been passed into a law calmly, honestly, dispassionately, legally, constitutionally. No one can assert to the contrary. The fact is also notorious in both hemispheres. The bill itself is exclusively a Canadian measure. The mother country has not interfered in the matter to the extent of one tittle. The home government has dictated no policy, it has not even gone to the length of hinting a suggestion. The Indemnity Bill is, we repeat, an exclusively Canadian measure. It has emanated from Canadian intelligence; it has been sanctioned in principle and accepted in form by Canadian statesmen; it has received the countenance of two successive administrations—a conservative administration and a liberal administration. It has been passed with large majorities through the upper and lower chamber of the Imperial Parliament. Those majorities were not only majorities of the whole houses, but majorities of the members of British blood. Those majorities were not the packed majorities of a cabinet, they were the free and honourable majorities of Canadian representatives. Such was this Bill of Indemnity, which, on its receiving the royal assent through the lips of his Excellency the Governor-General, was made the pretext for an insurrectionary movement, more dastardly and infamous than any recorded in the annals of our colonial possessions.

"Finding that their prejudices went for nothing against the force of public opinion, finding that they had been outnumbered by the members of their own legislature—the rebel conspirators rose at a preconcerted signal. Mind—these rebels are the tory gang! They are that Orange faction whose virulence and insolence are unfortunately not restricted to Canada. True to their audacious principles, they rose. Availing themselves of their accidental local superiority in point of numbers, they domineered over their loyal fellow-citizens.   Montreal became a prey to their wanton brutality, and some of its noblest adornments have irreparably fallen under their licentiousness.   The Parliament House was burned by incendiaries; the public records and state papers were consumed in the conflagration.

"One course, and one course alone, remains open to the government. The nature of that course is perfectly obvious.   The robbers, the pillagers, and incendiaries, who have recently desolated the streets of Montreal, must be put down with the strong hand of the law, whose majesty they have violated.   They must be compelled to make a bitter expiation.   Their most prominent leaders must be subjected to summary and condign punishment.   And as to the recall of Lord Elgin, justice requires that the policy of his administration should, first of all, be proved to have been harsh, peremptory, or in any respect unconstitutional.   Hitherto, the fault of his government (if such, indeed, can be called a fault,) has been its excessive leniency.   That leniency has, with the Orange minority of conspirators, produced its own evil fruits. This must henceforth be followed by a rigorous suppression of those rebellious passions, which are only fostered into maturity by the generosity of a genial administration.   This we maintain to be the only rational course open to the government, as a beginning.   First of all, the infliction of a tremendous penalty on the insurgents; then the resumption of a regenerative policy for the Canadas.   Before that policy, however, is again taken up, the cabinet must act upon the following principle,—In the presence of rioters, not one shadow of a concession."

We may now introduce the communication of our correspondent, for the purpose, as we have before stated, of informing the public mind. Although his language is, at times, as strong and caustic as that in which the preceding extract is couched, there is no doubt of his sincerity, nor that he speaks the sentiments of a large party in Canada.

His communication is therefore given as we have received it; without intending, on our part, to express an opinion either on the policy of the British government, on the question of the independence of Canada, or of its annexation to the United States.   It is due, however, both to ourselves and our readers to remark, that no British subject, residing in this country, stands higher in the esteem of our citizens than does the writer of the following article:—

To the Editor of the Register:—

The conquest of Quebec, by Wolfe, in 1759, was one of the causes which led to the independence of the thirteen United States. Braddock's defeat took place but a few years before, and this event occurred within one hundred and fifty miles of Baltimore. At that time, the French and Indians drew a complete cordon around the thirteen provinces from Quebec to Florida, and were supplied by their settlements in the west. The English colonies existed on the margin of the Atlantic, and, without the protection of Great Britain, could have been utterly destroyed by the French and Indian allies, all of whom were catholics, and influenced by the Jesuits, burning with pious zeal for the destruction of protestants. The fall of Quebec extinguished the power of this vast confederacy, and left the British colonies comparatively free. This consideration doubtless had its weight, with the signers of the Declaration of Independence.

After the revolution, England did all in her power to secure the affections of her remaining North American colonies. To the French of Lower Canada she granted a parliament and other English institutions, but she omitted to make the government of the colony English in toto. The French there retained their language and peculiar laws, and having always a majority in their legislature, they were able to embarrass the Governor, oppress the English party, and stop all progress or advancement in the settlement, and civilization of the country. Hence, the present backward state of the lower province, which, notwithstanding its many advantages, barely raises sufficient food to supply its scattered inhabitants. Mr. Papineau gained the ascendency in the French Canadian Parliament some twenty or thirty years ago, and retained it until the rebellion of 1837, when the constitution was suspended for a year or two, and restored when the act of the union of the two provinces was effected. During Mr. Papineau's rule of about fifteen years, the English part of the inhabitants suffered every injustice,—the taxes were chiefly paid by them, but they received nothing back from the provincial exchequer. Every office and grant which the parliament could make were given to Frenchmen. In granting money for public schools, it was always given to Frenchmen, for Mr. Papineau took care that none but his countrymen should be nominated as trustees; and it is a fact that, as trustees could not always be found in the remoter districts who were capable of reading and writing, there are instances upon record where these illiterate trustees have given certificates of competency to a teacher signing them with a cross †! and this, too, whilst an English gentleman was residing, as magistrate, in the same village. So, too, with all grants for roads, bridges and the like. Frenchmen had all, Englishmen nothing. Is it surprising, then, that discord arose, and that a war of races ensued? No public improvements could be made, and the progress of society was at a dead lock. Mr. Papineau and his countrymén, in the meantime, indulged in schemes for establishing a French nationality, and becoming independent of England. The British government was constantly making concessions, sending Governor after Governor, and each receiving the treatment of his predecessor. At last, in the winter of 1837, when the military force was unusually small in the country, Mr. Papineau and his friends took up arms. They were speedily put down, however, and the next winter they tried it again, with the same sort of success.

The disaffection in Upper Canada arose from different causes. Settled originally by refugee loyalists from the United States, who found it a beautiful and fertile country, they were followed by other settlers from the United States, who were not loyalists. These latter, joined by some English and Scotch radicals, who had forced their way there, formed the nucleus of disaffection, which going on and increasing in strength, and stimulated by Mr. Bidwell, an American, and by Mackenzie a Scotchman, the malcontents at length took up arms in imitation of the French in Lower Canada. This act of aggression roused all the latent loyalty of the country, and Mackenzie was defeated and expelled from the province in the winter of 1837-8.

Then the British ministry formed the notable scheme of uniting the two provinces, and bringing them into one legislature, because as Upper Canada was English, and Lower Canada French, it was supposed one would neutralize the other. The mixture, however, as may be supposed, proved a bad one, and, like mixing the *acid* and *alkaline* portions of a soda powder, the effervescence was increased. As soon as the members from the two Canadas met in the same legislature, the radicals of the English portion united with the French portion, (all of the latter, or nearly so, being opposed to English rule,) and put the English government in a minority. The folly of the measure was seen too late. The government had gained nothing with the French, and lost all with the English. In 1839, all this was predicted in the Albion, and the absurdity of the contemplated union shown, as follows:

"Suppose in your united legislature you have one hundred members, how will they vote? Of the fifty French, forty, at least, will vote against the government; of the English fifty, fifteen at least will be radicals, and on a vote the members will be—

French, disaffected,	. . . . .	40
English radicals,	. . . . .	15—55
English loyalists,	. . . .	35
Loyalists from Lower Canada,	. . . .	10—45

Leaving a majority against the government." This actually came to pass in the second session of the united parliament! The government then formed the further notable scheme of introducing "a responsible government;" the meaning of which is, that the legislature shall be regarded as speaking the sentiments of the people, and that the votes of the legislature shall govern all things, even the acts of the Governor. This has been adopted and carried out, and has ended in driving the loyal party into rebellion! Nothing, indeed, could ensue from such a plan, with a legislature constituted of such elements as I have mentioned, but discord and confusion. The dead weight of forty French votes out of the hundred was worse than Mr. O'Connell and his tail in the English parliament at home, because it was relatively more numerous. The real number of members in the united parliament is forty-two from each province, making eighty-four in all, and not one hundred; but the practical result is the same, as the relative numbers are the same in reference to political sentiment. It is easy to see that, with an English population alone, there would be a loyal majority.; but the French dead weight overpowers every thing, and hence the folly of uniting these provinces.

Flushed with victory, the dominant party have carried on a system of revenge and persecution against their old enemies, which is a disgrace to legislation; and, at last, after turning every loyal man out of office and putting rebels in their places, they have passed the bill for indemnifying the rebels of 1837–8, and for calling upon the loyal party to pay the money; for, be it remembered, that it is the English who contribute nine-tenths of all the taxes and duties which go into the provincial treasury. The French dress in their home-spun, and drink maple sugar and water; the English dress in silks and broad-cloths, and drink rum, gin, brandy and wine, on all of which they pay duties.

The atrocities committed, and the acts of injustice perpetrated against loyal men, are calculated to surprise any one; indeed, for some time past, it was dangerous to be known as a loyal person, if the vengeance of the government could reach him,—the Governor-General sanctioning every thing. No wonder, then, that he has been expelled from the St. Andrew's and Thistle society of Montreal, and has been obliged to seek refuge in a barricaded house. He is not wealthy, and the radicals have worked his income up to £7,500 a-year, a much larger sum than your Presidents receive, of which he spends about one-third, and lays by the rest. As the government at home have sanctioned all these acts, and participated in this persecuting system against the loyalists, the latter are becoming weaned from the mother country, and casting about for a new state of political existence, and annexation to the United States is the favourite remedy.*

So, then, the very party, nay, the very men, who, in 1837, were the firmest in their attachment to the mother country, now seek to cast her off. Many of my own personal friends, who turned out as volunteers, and bore all the rigours of a Canadian winter to expel Mackenzie from Navy Island, are loudly calling for a union with the stripes

* In England the prevailing opinion seems to be, that if Canada is separated from the mother country, the people will form an Independent Republic.

and stars! And this is their argument:—"It was our wish and pride to live under the British government, but that government has put us under the French domination. We will not live under the French, and would rather join the Americans." The consummation of this resolution will depend, I think, on the issue of the Rebellion Losses Bill. If it be stopped by the government and Lord Elgin recalled, matters will assume a new and more peaceable aspect; if not, the future must be pregnant with trouble. I should add, that the free trade system introduced into the colony by the home government, and the withdrawal of protection from the colonial produce in the home market, have added to the bad feeling. It would seem as if the free traders at home were determined to cast the colonies off, and this I believe to be really the case; and the object will sooner or later be effected if the whig government remain triumphant in England. The whig ministry insult the loyal colonists in two ways,—first, they invade their pockets by free trade, and, next, insult their feelings by rewarding traitors and rebels. The folly of such a system is most palpable.

The recent outbreak at Montreal and the destruction of the Parliament House was the work of the loyalists, and a friend writes to me from Montreal, that there was not one man among them who would not have laid down his life for the queen! The animosity is to the French rebels, not to the royal family of England.

If a good tory ministry could be made up in England, the whigs would certainly be ousted on this Canada business; but, alas, our best men have passed away, and the party was broken up by the treason of Peel when he turned free trader in 1846.

The tory government of George the Third lost the thirteen provinces by a system too stringent; and the whig government under Victoria seem destined to lose Canada by a system too lax. A century or nearly so elapses between the two events, and every thing in the civilized world would seem to have been improving but British colonial wisdom. What, then, is the cause? I answer, the ignorance of the British people in regard to the true nature and feeling of the colonies and colonists.   B.

That the reader may have as satisfactory a view as possible of the present position of this perplexing question, we subjoin an extract from the Inquirer, containing a summary of the opinions entertained in England:

"A London correspondent of the National Intelligencer says, that 'a great change has taken place in England with regard to its colonial policy,' and quotes the London Examiner thus:—'Are not the British North American colonies, one can hardly help asking, in connexion with these facts, beginning reasonably to think that they are too old and mature to walk any longer in leading-strings; the cords held, too, by parties far too distant and uninformed to handle them with any adroitness?'

"The correspondent continues:—

" 'This question is very pertinently put at this juncture, and, we think, can only be answered affirmatively. The British North American colonies contain nearly three million of people—considerably more than were in the 'thirteen United States' at the Declaration of Independence. Each of the seven present British North American colonies contains a population sufficient to constitute an independent federal State, and equal to many of those of the United States at the last census of the republic. Lower Canada is as populous as Massachusetts, Upper Canada is equal to Indiana, and New Brunswick and Nova Scotia are each on a par with Michigan. The total number of men on the rolls of the militia for the seven colonies is very nearly 400,000; which would imply a total population of 2,800,000. These colonies have lately, so far as respects the mother country, been more in a state of management than government; but the means by which we have hitherto managed them have all nearly disappeared. We once managed them through the means of a faction among themselves, and this has most properly vanished. The monopolies of our markets which they once enjoyed, and which bound them to us, have also perished, or are perishing, to the advantage, we think, of both parent country and colonies.

" 'All the advantages which we can now possibly derive from these remote and cumbrous colonies, they would yield, we think, to a much greater extent, were they independent of us to-morrow. Mercantile profit was the chief object of their establishment, but our commerce with the old colonies which have become independent of us is immeasurably superior to any thing which it could have been had they remained in their colonial dependence; and there is nothing in the condition of Canada or Nova Scotia, or New Brunswick, which would prevent our predicting the same results for them under similar circumstances.

" 'About a quarter of a million of emigrants leave the shores of the United Kingdom annually, but the greater majority of them find their final abode, not in our colonies, but in the United States. As regards our military strength, these colonies, so far from increasing it, tend to weaken it, by scattering our force and wasting our means. Late parliamentary returns show that, in 1846, we had a military force stationed in Canada alone, amounting to 6,485, at a cost, for pay and rations only, of £268,681. But this is a great reduction from 1843, when the military amounted to 11,951, and their pay and rations were £473,328. Even now, the army for the protection of about a million and a half of people is very nearly three-fourths of what you require in the United States for a population at least four times as large. Probably the cost of the forces serving in the British North American colonies, for the five years ending with 1847, including barracks, fortifications, &c., has not been less than £6,000,000: what this would swell to, in case of a war, we will not venture to conjecture.'

"These expressions of opinion possess no little interest, in connexion with the intelligence by the 'last steamers.' It seems that in the British House of Commons, on a recent occasion, Mr. Gladstone took the strongest ground against the "rebellion losses bill." He contended that the passage of the bill 'involved imperial as well as local considerations;' that 'its provisions were at variance with the honour and dignity of the crown,' and he 'denied that the sense of the Canadian people had been pronounced in favour of the measure.' Lord John Russell complained of the *tendency* of Mr. Gladstone's remarks; said that 'it would imbitter the feelings of hostile parties,' and affirmed that 'it would be the duty of the government to leave the act in operation.' The whole subject was discussed with great warmth; when, finally, the matter was postponed until the 15th, when the subject was resumed, and with the following results, as we gather from the European Times:

"'A long debate took place, in which all the circumstances of the dispute in Canada were recapitulated, but the main argument prevailed that a line cannot now be drawn with reference to Lower Canada which was not prescribed in the case of Upper Canada, when the previous indemnity bill was passed. It was felt in the House of Commons that the people of Canada, in the exercise of their legislative rights, are the fittest judges of what is best to be done. All parties, including Lord Elgin, Lord John Russell, Sir Robert Peel, Mr. Herries, Mr. Gladstone, Mr. Herbert and Mr. Roebuck, all organs of great sections of politicians, disavow the intention of compensating rebels. The rules and the exceptions have been discussed in the Canadian Parliament upon which the title of the claimants is to be decided. A responsible colonial government has constitutionally sanctioned the measure. It would indeed be a most unwise step for the imperial Parliament to interfere almost on the first occasion when an appeal has been made to them by the unsuccessful minority in the colony. Such an interference would aim a blow at the very root of representative government. Such is the prevailing impression, coupled, however, with the strongest repugnance that any of the money should directly or indirectly flow into the pockets of notorious convicted rebels. Upon a division on the second evening, a majority of 291 over 150 rejected the amendment of Mr. Herries.

The question was again mooted in the upper House of Parliament on Tuesday evening. Lord Brougham, in a very elaborate speech, went over all the arguments which had previously been adduced unsuccessfully in the Commons, whereby it was aimed to reverse the system of representative government, and to prove that the minority in the legislature of Canada ought to be supported, and their views carried into effect in spite of a 'tyrant majority.' The efforts of Lord Brougham might have been disregarded, but that, to the general surprise of the house, Lord Lyndhurst re-appeared on this occasion on the scene of politics. His lordship, in the support of Lord Brougham's views, with undiminished vigour, delivered an able, argumentative, and effective speech, which, we fear, will create as much sensation in Canada as it did in the House of Peers, and which will not tend to pour oil on the troubled waters of the colony.

" 'The effect of this speech was to marshal a formidable opposition to the ministers, who, upon a division, only carried their point by a majority of three, the numbers, including proxies, being ninety-nine to ninety-six. It is, however, decisive of the question; and without seeking to dwell upon a subject, which necessarily must give pain to many parties whose feelings we respect, we think they must perceive, from the tone of the debate in both houses, that *all parties* on this side cherish the connexion which now so happily subsists between the mother country and the colony; and that no one entertains the idle belief that the sanction of the crown to the rebellion losses act, or, to speak more properly, its refusal to disallow it, can bring about any permanent differences between those whose interests are as identical with our own, as we are identical 'in race, in language, and in blood.' '

"In conclusion, we may remark, that the imperial government—consisting of Queen Victoria, Lord John Russell, and the other ministers—together with majorities in both houses of Parliament—have sustained Lord Elgin and the French Canadians. The determination of the British in Canada, who protest against the obnoxious bill, is yet to transpire."

RUSSIA.

(The following spirited sketch from Blackwood will be especially interesting and valuable at this time, when Russia has acquired, by recent events, so commanding an influence in the affairs of the continent of Europe. We have added to it a notice of the present political position of the Czar.)

"Russia is the most extraordinary country on the globe, in the four most important particulars of empire—its history, its extent, its population, and its power.

"It has for Europe another interest—the interest of alarm, the evidence of an ambition which has existed for upwards of a hundred and fifty years, and has never paused; an increase of territory which has never suffered the slightest casualty of fortune; the most complete security against the retaliation of European war, and a government at once despotic and popular—exhibiting the most boundless authority in the sovereign, and the most boundless submission in the people—a mixture of habitual obedience and divine homage—the reverence to a monarch, with almost the prostration to a divinity.

"Its history has another superb anomaly: Russia gives the most memorable instance in human annals of the powers which lie within the mind of individual man. Peter the Great was not the restorer or the reformer of Russia: he was its moral creator. He found it, not as Augustus found Rome, according to the famous adage, 'brick, and left it marble:' he found it a living swamp, and left it covered with the fertility of laws, energy, and knowledge; he found it Asiatic, and left it European; he removed it as far from Scythia as if he had placed the diameter of the globe between; he found it not brick, but mire, and he transformed a region of huts into the magnificence of empire.

"Russia first appears in European history in the middle of the ninth century. Its climate and its soil had till then retained it in primeval barbarism. The sullenness of its winter had prevented invasion by civilized nations, and the nature of its soil, one immense plain, had given full scope to the roving habits of its half-famished tribes. The great invasions which broke down the Roman empire had drained away the population of the north, and left nothing but remnants of clans behind. Russia had no sea by which she might send her bold savages to plunder or to trade with southern and western Europe; and while the man of Scandinavia was subduing kingdoms, or carrying back spoils to his northern crags and lakes, the Russian remained, like the bears of his forest, in his cavern during the long winter of his country; and even when the summer came, was still but a melancholy savage, living like the bear upon the roots and fruits of his ungenial soil.

"It was to one of those Normans, who, instead of steering his bark towards the opulence of the south, turned his dreary adventure to the north, that Russia owed her first connexion with mankind. The people of Novgorod, a people of traders, finding themselves overpowered by their barbarian neighbours, solicited the aid of Ruric, a Baltic chieftain, and of course a pirate and robber. The name of the Norman had earned old renown in the north. Ruric came, rescued the city, but paid himself by the seizure of the surrounding territory, and founded a kingdom, which he transmitted to his descendants, and which lasted until the middle of the sixteenth century.

"In the subsequent reign we see the effect of the northern pupilage; and an expedition, in the style of the Baltic exploits, was sent to plunder Constantinople. This expedition consisted of two thousand canoes, with eighty thousand men on board. The expedition was defeated, for the Greeks had not yet sunk into the degeneracy of later times. They fought stoutly for their capital, and roasted the pirates in their own canoes, by showers of the famous 'Greek fire.'

"These invasions, however, were tempting to the idleness and poverty, or to the avarice and ambition of the Russians; and Constantinople continued to be the great object of cupidity and assault. But the city of Constantine was destined to fall to a mightier conqueror.

"Still, the northern barbarian had learned the road to Greece, and the intercourse was mutually beneficial. Greece found daring allies in her old plunderers, and in the eleventh century she gave the Grand duke Vladimer a wife, in the person of Anna, sister to the emperor Basil II.—a gift made more important by its being accompanied by his conversion to Christianity.

"A settled succession is the great secret of royal peace; but among those bold riders of the desert, nothing was ever settled, save by the sword; and the first act of all the sons, on the decease of their father, was to slaughter each other, until the contest was settled in their graves, and the last survivor quietly ascended the throne.

"But war, on a mightier scale than the Russian Steppes had ever witnessed, was now rolling over Central Asia. The cavalry of Ghengis Khan, which came, not in squadrons, but in nations, and charged, not like troops, but like thunder-clouds, began to pour down upon the valley of the Volga. Yet the conquest of Russia was not to be added to the triumphs of the great Tartar chieftain; a mightier conqueror stopped him on his way, and the Tartar died.

"His son Toushi, in the beginning of the thirteenth century, burst over the frontier at the head of half a million of horsemen. The Russian princes, hastily making up their quarrels, advanced to meet the invader; but their army was instantly trampled down, and, before the middle of the century, all the provinces and all the cities of Russia were the prey of the men of the wilderness. Novgorod only escaped.

"The history of this great city would be highly interesting, if it were possible now to recover its details. It was the chief depot of the northern Asiatic commerce with Europe, and it had a government, laws, and privileges of its own, with which it suffered not even the Khan of the Tartars to interfere. Its population amounted to four hundred thousand—then nearly equal to the population of a kingdom. In the thirteenth century it connected itself still more effectively with European commerce, by becoming a member of the Hanseatic League; and the wonder and pride of the Russians was expressed in the well known half profane proverb, 'Who can resist God, and the great Novgorod?'

"There is always something almost approaching to picturesque grandeur in the triumphs of barbarism. The Turk, until he was fool enough to throw away the turban, was the most showy personage in the world. The Arabs, under Mahomet, were the most stately of warriors, and the Spanish Moors threw all the pomp, and even all the romance, of Europe into the shade. Even the chiefs of the 'Golden Horde' seemed to have as picturesque a conception of supremacy as the Saracen. Their only city was a vast camp, in the plains between the Caspian and the Volga; and while they left the provinces in the hands of the native princes, and enjoyed themselves in the manlier sports of hunting through the plains and mountains, they commanded that every vassal prince should attend at the imperial tent to receive permission to reign, or perhaps to live; and that, even when they sent their Tartar collectors to receive the tribute, the Russian princes should lead the Tartar's horse by the bridle, and give him a feed of oats out of their *cap of state.*

"But another of those sweeping devastators, one of those gigantic executioners, who seem to have been sent from time to time to punish the horrible profligacies of Asia, now rose upon the north. Timour Khan, the Tamerlane of European story, the Invincible, the Lord of the Tartar World, rushed with his countless troops upon the sovereignties of Western Asia. This universal conqueror crushed the Tartar dynasty of Russia, and then burst away, like an inundation, to overwhelm other lands. But the native Russians again made head against their Tartar masters, and a century and a half of sanguinary warfare followed, with various fortunes, and without any other result than blood.

"In the fifteenth century Russia began to assume a form. Ivan III. broke off the vassalage of Russia to the 'Golden Horde.' He had married Sophia, the niece of the Greek emperor, to which we may attribute his civilization; and he received the embassies of Germany, Venice, and Rome, at Moscow. His son, Ivan IV., took Novgorod, which he ruined, and continued to fight the Poles and Tartars until he died. His son Ivan, in the middle of the sixteenth century, was crowned by the title of Czar, formed the first standing army of Russia, named the Strelitzes, and established a code of laws. In 1598, by the death of the Czar Feodor without children, the male line of Ruric, which had held the throne for seven hundred and thirty-six years, and under fifty-six sovereigns, became extinct.

"Another dynasty of remarkable distinction ascended the throne in the beginning of the seventeenth century. Michael Romanoff, descended from the line of Ruric by the female side, was declared Czar. His son Alexis was the father of Peter the Great, who, with his brother Ivan, was placed on the throne at the decease of their father, but both under the guardianship of the princess Sophia. But the princess, who was the daughter of Alexis, exhibiting an intention to seize the crown for herself, a revolution took place in 1689, in which the princess was sent to a convent. Ivan, who was imbecile in mind and body, surrendered the throne, and Peter became sole sovereign of Russia.

"The accession of Peter began the last and greatest period of Russian history. Though a man of fierce passions and barbarian habits, he had formed a high conception of the value of European arts, chiefly through an intelligent Genevese, Lefort, who had been his tutor.

"The first object of the young emperor was to form an army; his next was to construct a fleet. But both operations were too slow for his rapidity of conception; and, in 1697, he travelled to Holland and England for the purpose of learning the art of ship-building. He was forced to return to Russia after an absence of two years, by the revolt of the Strelitzes in favour of the princess Sophia. The Strelitzes were disbanded and slaughtered, and Peter felt himself a monarch for the first time.

"The cession of Azof by the Turks, at the peace of Carowitz in 1699, gave him a port on the Black Sea. But the Baltic acted on him like a spell; and, to obtain an influence on its shores, he hazarded the ruin of his throne.

"Sweden, governed by Charles XII., was then the first military power of the north. The fame of Gustavus Adolphus in the German wars, had given the Swedes the example and the renown of their great king; and Charles, bold, reckless, and half lunatic, despising the feebleness of Russia, had turned his arms against Denmark and Poland. But the junction of Russia with the "Northern League" only gave him a new triumph. He fell upon the Russian army, and broke it on the memorable field of Narva, in 1700.

"Peter still proceeded with his original vigour. St. Petersburg was founded in 1703. The war was prosecuted for six years, until the Russian troops obtained a degree of discipline which enabled them to meet the Swedes on equal terms. In 1708, Charles was defeated in the memorable battle of Pultowa. His army was utterly ruined, and himself forced to take refuge in Turkey. Peter was now at the head of the northern power. Frederick Augustus was placed on the throne of Poland by the arms of Russia, and from this period Poland was under Russian influence.

"Peter now took the title of 'Emperor and Autocrat of all the Russias.' In 1716 he again travelled in Europe. In 1723 he obtained the provinces on the Caspian, by an attack on Persia. But his vigorous, ambitious, and singularly successful career was now come to a close. The death of a Russian prince is seldom attributed to the course of nature; and Peter died at the age of fifty-two, a time when the bodily powers are still undecayed, and the mental are in the highest degree of activity. The day, still recorded by the Russians with the interest due to his extraordinary career, was the 28th of January, 1725. In thirty-six years he had raised Russia from obscurity to a rank with the oldest powers of Europe.

"We hasten to the close of this sketch, and pass by the complicated successions from the death of Peter to the reign of the empress Catherine.

"The Russian army had made their first appearance in Germany, in consequence of a treaty with Maria Theresa; and their bravery in the "Seven Years' War," in the middle of the last century, established their distinction for soldiership.

"Peter III. withdrew from the Austrian alliance, and concluded peace with Prussia; but his reign was not destined to be long. At once weak in intellect, and profligate in habits, he offended and alarmed his empress, by personal neglect, and by threats of sending her to a convent. Catherine, a German, and not accustomed to the submissiveness of Russian wives, formed a party against him. The people were on her side; and, what was of more importance, the guards declared for her. An insurrection took place; the foolish Czar, after a six months' reign, was dethroned, July, 1762, was sent to a prison, and within a week was no more. The Russians assigned his death to poison, to strangulation, or to some other species of atrocity. Europe talked for awhile of the "Russian tragedy!" but the emperor left no regrets behind him; and "Catherina, Princess of Anhalt Zerbst," handsome, young, accomplished, and splendid, ascended a throne of which her subjects were proud; which collected round it the élite of Germany, its philosophers and soldiers; which the empress connected with the *beaux esprits* of France, and the orators and statesmen of England; and which, during her long, prosperous, and ambitious reign, united the pomp of Asia with the brilliancy and power of Europe. The shroud of the czar was speedily forgotten, in the embroidered robe which Catherine threw over the empire.

"But the greatest crime of European annals was committed in this bold and triumphant reign. Russia, Prussia, and Austria, tempted by the helplessness of Poland, formed a league to seize upon portions of its territory; and the partition of 1772 took place, to the utter astonishment of Europe, but with scarcely a remonstrance from its leading powers.

"Poland had so long been contented to receive its sovereign from Russia, its religious disputes had so utterly weakened the people, its nobility were so profligate, and its peasantry were so poor, that it had lost all the sinews of national defence. It therefore fell an easy prey; and only waited, like a slave in the market, till the bargain for its sale was complete.

"In 1793, a second partition was effected. In the next year, the Polish troops took up arms under the celebrated Kosciusko; but the Russians advanced on Warsaw with a force which defied all resistance. Warsaw was stormed, twenty thousand gallant men were slain in its defence, Suwarroff was master of the unfortunate capital; and, in 1795, the third and last partition extinguished the kingdom.

"Having performed this terrible exploit, which was to be terribly avenged, the career of Catherine was closed. She died suddenly in 1796.

"Paul, her son, ascended the throne, which he held for five years— a mixture of the imbecility of his father, and the daring spirit of his mother. Zealous for the honour of Russia, yet capricious as the winds, he first made war upon the French Republic, and then formed a naval league to destroy the maritime supremacy of England. This measure was his ruin. England was the old ally of Russia—France was the new enemy. The nation hated the arrogance and the atheism of France, and resolved on the overthrow of the Czar. In Russia the monarch is so far removed from his people, that he has no refuge among them in case of disaster. Paul was believed to be mad, and madness, on a despotic throne, justly startles a nation. A band of conspirators broke into his palace at midnight, strangled the master of fifty millions of men, and the nation, at morning, was in a tumult of joy.

"His son, Alexander, ascended the throne amid universal acclamation. His first act was peace with England. In 1805, his troops joined the Austrian army, and bore their share in the sufferings of the campaign of Austerlitz. The French invasion of Poland, in two years after, the desperate drawn battle of Eylau, and the disaster of Friedland, led to the peace of Tilsit. Alexander then joined the continental system of Napoleon; but this system was soon found to be so ruinous to Russian commerce, as to be intolerable. Napoleon, already marked for downfall, rejoiced to take advantage of the Russian reluctance, and instantly marched across the Polish frontier, at the head of a French and allied army amounting to the astonishing number of five hundred thousand men.

"Infatuation was now visible in every step of his career. Instead of organizing Poland into a kingdom, which would have been a place of retreat in case of disaster or victory, and would have been a vast national fortification against the advance of Russia, he left it behind him; and, instead of waiting for the return of spring, commenced his campaign on the verge of winter, in the land of winter itself, and madly ran all the hazards of invading a boundless empire of which he knew nothing, of which the people were brave, united, and attached to their sovereign, and of which, if the armies had fled like deer, the elements would have fought the battle. His army perished by brigades and divisions. On the returning spring, three hundred thousand men were found buried in the snow; all his spoil was lost, his veteran troops were utterly destroyed, his fame was tarnished, and his throne was shaken.

"He was followed into France by the troops of Russia and Germany. In 1814, the British army under Wellington crossed the Pyrenees, and liberated the southern provinces of France. In the same year, the Austrian, Prussian, and Russian armies marched to Paris, captured the capital, and expelled Napoleon. The battle of Waterloo, in the year after, destroyed the remnant of his legions in the field, threw him into the hands of the British government, and exiled him to St. Helena, where he remained a British prisoner until he died.

"Alexander died in 1825, at the age of forty-eight, and, leaving no sons, was succeeded by his brother Nicholas, the third son of Paul—Constantine having resigned his claims to the throne."

(The Emperor Nicholas has exhibited great energy of character and steadily increased the resources and power of his Empire. Poland, he has completely denationalized and incorporated within the Russian territory.   During his reign the Ural mountains have produced immense quantities of gold, and filled the coffers of the government.

The Czar has evinced a persevering and determined opposition to the revolutionary spirit, which has within the two past years convulsed the greater portion of Europe.   The steps taken by him to suppress it, have been of so decided a character that even during the late struggle in Hungary, there has been no disturbance within his own dominions, and by the powerful aid which he afforded to Austria, the surrender of the gallant Majjars has been compelled.   In Italy the agitation and conflict have ceased in the occupation of Rome by the French troops, the capitulation of Venice to Austria, and the submission of Sardinia to the terms of Radetsky.   In Prussia, the storm of revolution is quelled, whilst the legions of the Muscovite have brought the refractory subjects of the Emperor of Austria to his feet.

In the mean time, to the astonishment of all lookers-on, the ambassador of the French Republic has been received at the Court of Russia with the highest honours; and the President of that Republic, Louis Napoleon, is about forming a matrimonial alliance with the daughter of the King of Sweden.   Thus the great powers seem to be harmonizing and shaping their measures for the restoration and establishment, if possible, of monarchical rule throughout all continental Europe, and the master spirit of the movement is Nicholas, the Czar and Autocrat of Russia.)

(For the Register.)

HUNGARY.

Of all the great and startling political events of the past two years, not one, probably, has excited a deeper interest throughout Christendom than the recent struggle between Hungary and Austria.

The brave and patriotic Majjars, who had baffled the arts of Austria and routed her armies, were not daunted by the invasion of the Muscovite, and even for a time successfully resisted the combined power of two great empires; but when a belief in their success was strongest, and meetings were held in this country and England to offer to them the public expressions of sympathy and encouragement, they were hemmed in and overwhelmed by numbers, and surrendered unconditionally to the general of the Czar.   Russian intervention proved fatal to their independence; and Kossuth, Bem, Dembinski and others, their late distinguished and gallant leaders, are now, like Garibaldi the Italian patriot, fugitives in search of an asylum where they may escape the "rebel's fate."

Although the revolutionary storm has subsided, yet the interest in the people who have fought at such desperate odds for national rights and free institutions has not abated; and we believe our readers will thank us for placing before them, a brief sketch of their resources, their political history, and the impelling motives to the contest in which thay have been engaged.

We cannot better commence this summary than with a copious extract from the Edinburgh Review, in which are exhibited the resources, character, and internal improvements of the Hungarians in a very striking light.

"The efforts of Hungary in the (late) war are a measure of her internal resources. Those efforts have excited the more surprise, because the nature and extent of her resources are, in general, so imperfectly understood. In December last, at a time when civil war was raging in the south of Hungary and in Transylvania, 130,000 Austrians, moving concentrically from nine different quarters, passed the frontiers. Prince Windischgrätz left Schönbrunn, confident of returning with victory, and with the title of "Debellator Hungariæ." The game was supposed to be driven by his rangers into the toils, and to be there waiting unconditional surrender or destruction. But neither the generals nor the statesmen of Hungary bated a jot of heart or hope. They knew the courage, the endurance, and the patriotic fervour of their people. Within a narrow circle, between Theiss, the Maros, and the Transylvania frontier, they speedily organized an army of nearly 200,000 men. Powder-mills, cannon foundries, manufactories of muskets, percussion caps, and saltpetre, sprung up on the instant; and as the Croatian sulphur-mines were in the enemy's hands, their sulphur was prepared from *mundic*, or sulphurate of iron. Within four months, the Austrians were driven from Hungary; so diminished in number and disorganized by cold, hunger, and defeat, that, but for Russian intervention, the war would already be at an end.

"The defensive strength of a country depends upon its physical conformation, its artificial means of communication and resistance, and the number, the temper, and organization of its inhabitants. A glance at the map shows that Hungary, by the arrangement of its mountains, plains, and rivers, is adapted to every species of warfare, from the guerilla to the battalion. Its northern bulwark, the Carpathian mountains, extends from Presburg and the Danube to Transylvania, a space of four hundred English miles, broken by only three considerable passes; Nádas, Jablonka, and Dukla, while the continuation of this lofty barrier is crossed by only four narrow defiles to the east and south—the approaches to Bukovina, Moldavia, Wallachia. On the south the Carnian Alps, and the rivers Saave and Danube, afford a frontier almost equally impracticable to an invader. The plains and hills on the west towards the Styrian mountains are less capable of defence, being more adapted to the action of large masses. Between Presburg and Pesth, the rivers sometimes hurry in rapid torrents, and sometimes stagnate in lakes and morasses. The internal communication by roads is very irregular. Some Hungarian counties have highways which rival English turnpikes, while others are advanced little beyond driftways and tracks, bad in all seasons, and nearly impervious in autumn and winter. An invading army, unacquainted with the country, and incumbered with baggage and artillery, will meet, therefore, with no ordinary difficulties. Even Austrian officers, whom previous command of Hungarian regiments had in some degree familiarized with the line of march, were baffled, in the late spring campaign, by the natural or accidental impediments they encountered.

"Hungary contains an area of 110,000 English square miles, and a population of at least fourteen millions. This extensive area is not more remarkable for the productiveness of its soil, its favourable climate, and mineral wealth, than for the various, and generally promising character of its inhabitants. All the races of Hungary have, indeed, their several capabilities. The Slovacks are intelligent, for the most part, and inclined to commerce; the Croats good soldiers, and in the upper classes able *employés;* the Servian officers, in the military frontier, are, many of them, expert mathematicians; while the ordinary characteristics of the Wallach are, an aptitude for growth and cultivation; and of the Germans, steadiness and industry. But the Majjar—or Hungarian Proper—who has given his name to the country, is also the most prominent feature in the group of races. The genuine Majjar, like the Roman patrician, is an agriculturist, a fearless, we had almost said a born rider, fond of field sports and pastoral occupations. His figure is tall and well proportioned; his demeanour grave, and almost melancholy; his attachment to his home and to his municipal rights ardent; his disposition peaceful, and even indolent, until he is wronged or oppressed—and then indomitably firm, patient, and enterprising. Since our attention has been turned by recent events to Hungary, we have been impressed by the resemblance between the Hungarian country gentleman and yeoman of the present day, and the English gentleman and yeoman of Clarendon and Lucy Hutchinson, of Walker and Vandyke. But the character of the Hungarian, like the resources of his native land, is not yet fully developed. His occasional indolence or haughtiness have to be purged away by the fiery baptism of war; and his warm affections, his firm principles, his active intellect, and native energy will come out the purer from this ordeal.

The customary avocations of the Hungarians in time of peace have tended to organize and discipline them for a crisis like the present. Their law proceedings—for like all free people they are habitually litigious—their magisterial duties, and their municipal and county elections have given them habits of business, and taught them to act in concert. Their powers of adaptation, decision and arrangement, have not been palsied by bureaucratic maxims and official routine. Hence, while the Austrian cabinet vacillates between violence and concession, and is at a loss when it cannot be formal, Hungary has already produced in the various departments of war, internal administration and finance, such men as Kossuth, and Görgey, Csanyi, Szemere, and Duschek. During the last twenty years, indeed, the kingdom generally has made great progress in internal improvement. Without the aid or even the countenance of government, the Hungarians have constructed roads, and called into a new existence the Danube by means of steamboats, built a suspension-bridge,—the wonder of Europe, —from Buda over to Pesth; have opened railways, and, by the embankment of the Theiss and by regulating the streams of the Maros and the Sarviz, acquired millions of acres for pasture or tillage. Within the same

period the productions of agriculture have been greatly multiplied, the culture of tobacco and oleaginous crops (rape, linseed, &c.,) encouraged, the
breed of sheep and the quality of wool improved; while the settlements accorded to German and English artisans have introduced into the towns a
fresh class of thriving and ingenious citizens. And all these improvements
have been accomplished under the discouragements and drawbacks of the
Austrian rule, by a people possessing rather the substance than the symbol
of wealth. For although raw materials of every kind abound in Hungary,
there is a great scarcity of money. An inlet into the commercial world,
by a railroad from the Danube to Fiume, would relieve Hungary of its
teeming and superfluous produce, supply capital for public works or private
enterprise, and open new and eager markets for English manufactures."

It must be admitted that the foregoing extract presents very favourably the people and resources of Hungary, and had their late efforts
been successful, it is more than probable that such a people, with such
means at command, would have risen high in the scale of nations.
Their political history is full of remarkable incidents, from which we
only select such particulars as are necessary to carry out the design of
this article.

The Magyars, or Majjars, were originally from the Northern part
of Asia. They passed the Ural mountains in the seventh century—
in the eighth, they penetrated towards the coast of the Black Sea, and
thence migrating westerly, they occupied Pannonia, and permanently
settled in Europe, about the year 887. They were called by the Byzantians, Hunigures or Unigures. From them, the country that had
been successively inhabited by Gepidi, Bulgarians, Huns, Goths and
Lombards, was called Hungary, and the people Hungarians. Their
leader, Duke Almus, was the founder of the Arpad dynasty, which governed the nation until the beginning of the fourteenth century.

This prince divided the land among his followers, according to the
heads of the tribes, to all who distinguished themselves in battle. They
were repeatedly defeated by King Henry I. and Otto, Emperors of Germany, and in 955 were induced to confine themselves within fixed limits
and to cultivate their land. Towards the end of the tenth century,
Christianity was introduced among them and ten bishopricks established.

The pope sent to the then reigning Duke a crown, and this prince
acting in unison with the magnates of the land, gave to the people a
constitution which is still regarded by the Hungarians as a principal
source of law and right. The Magna Charta of the country, however, was not obtained until the year 1222, and was extended by the
Congregatio generalis regni (the Assembly of the States General) under
King Andrew III., about the year 1300. After the death of this sovereign another race of princes succeeded, some of whom were distinguished for military prowess in their fierce contests with the Turks
and Germans, and others, for their efforts in promoting commerce and
industry, in establishing seats of learning, and in ameliorating the condition of the peasantry.

A great battle, called the battle of Mohacs or Mohatsch, in 1526 extinguished the royal line of Jagellon, and Ferdinand of Austria was the first of his family to whom the Hungarian sceptre was confided. Notwithstanding the political necessity which made a prince of the house of Hapsburg the ruler of the country, the Hungarians have always contended for their legal rights as an independent people. A note addressed by Count Teleki,* in behalf of the provincial government of Hungary to the French Republic, will show the grounds upon which they put their national independence. The language of Teleki is as follows:

"Hungary has ever been independent of Austria. Ferdinand I., the first Prince of the House of Austria that ever reigned in Hungary, received the crown in 1526, in accordance with an election by the Diet. He swore to maintain the Constitution and independence of Hungary. All his successors took the same oath. The crown of Hungary first became hereditary in the House of Hapsburg, in virtue of the Pragmatic Sanction, passed by the estates of Hungary, in 1687. In 1723, this settlement was extended by the Hungarian Diet to the female line of the House of Hapsburg (second Pragmatic Sanction.) But the independence of Hungary was maintained and guarantied not less by these very acts than by the oaths of all of the kings of the House of Hapsburg-Lorraine, even down to our own days. By article 10, of the year 1790, the Emperor King Leopold II. recognised Hungary as a free and independent State in its whole Legislative and Administrative system. Hence the article 3, of the year 1848, by which a parliamentary government was settled in Hungary, introduced no change in its relations to Austria. This law was no more than a development of all the foregoing laws. It was passed by a unanimous vote of the two Houses in the Hungarian Diet, and was formally sanctioned by the king, Ferdinand V. All that we demanded of the House of Austria, was that our charter should henceforward be a truth; our demands did not go one step beyond what had been guarantied to us in succession by all our kings."

By the 10th article of the compact between Leopold and the people, thus referred to by Teleki, it is expressly declared that "Hungary was a country free and independent in her entire system of legislation and government; that she was not subject to any other people, or any other state, but that she should have her own separate existence, and her own constitution, and should consequently be governed by kings crowned according to her national laws and customs."

This article was confirmed by the late Emperor Ferdinand as king of Hungary, on the 11th of April, 1848, and thus the constitutional independence of Hungary was made as clear as any fact in history, having been repeatedly and solemnly recognised and renewed by the Emperors of Austria. The devotion of the people to their free insti-

---

* For the note of Teleki to the French Republic, see documents.

tutions has always manifested itself in a decided opposition to any infringement of their constitutional rights.—A late able writer remarks: "Five times in the course of a single century (1606—1711) did the Hungarian people rise in defence of their constitution and of what was still dearer to them, their liberty of conscience."

The concessions of Ferdinand in 1848 to the demands of the members of the Hungarian Diet who came to Vienna for the purpose of obtaining a confirmation of charter rights, of civil and religious freedom, of a parliamentary government and a union of classes, were especially obnoxious to his imperial advisers. They alleged that the concessions were extorted at a time when the Emperor's freedom of action was suspended by revolutionary violence.

For an explanation of this part of the subject, viz., the demands on the part of the Hungarians, and the events which immediately led to the recent conflict between the Majjars and the Austrians, we refer the reader to our Historical Register of 1848, at pages 40, 41, &c., of the 2d volume. An account of the contest itself will be found in subsequent pages of the history and chronicle.

In relation to the impression, which has prevailed to some extent, that the recent war was a war of races—that it originated in the hostility of the Majjars to the other people who inhabit Hungary, it may be proper to state some facts for the purpose of correcting any errors that may exist on this point. That there have been disputes and rivalries between the races, and that Austria fomented these difficulties, there can be no doubt, but the Hungarian insurrection was not confined to the Majjars; for Wallachs, Germans, Slovacks, Ruthenes and Jews united in the common cause. They were contending for the ancient independence of their kingdom, and in the late provincial government, two of the most important posts were filled by Vukovich and Duschek, the former a Servian, the latter of Sclavonic blood.

The following statement taken from the table of Haüffler, exhibits the several tribes or races existing in Hungary, and the names of those who united with the Majjars,—.

Wallachs.	in Hungary,	930,000	
	" Transylvania,	1,287,340	2,317,340.
	" Military Frontier,	100.000	
Germans.	in Hungary,	986,000	
	" Transylvania,	250,668	1,422,168.
	" Military Frontier,	185,500	
Slovacks—in Hungary,		2,220,000	2,220,000.
Ruthenes—in Hungary,		350,000	350,000.
Wends—in Hungary,		50,000	50,000.
Croats.	in Croatia,	660,000	
	" Military Frontier,	692,966	1,352,966.
Servians.	in Hungary,	740,000	
	" Military Frontier,	203,000	943,000.
· Total			8,655,474.

Of these, there sided with the Majjars—

Wallachs.	{ in Hungary,	930,000 }	1,030,000.
	{ " Military Frontier,	100,000 }	
Germans.	{ in Hungary,	986,000 }	1,171,000.
	{ " Military Frontier,	185,000 }	
Slovacks—all,		2,220,000	2,220,000.
Ruthenes—all,		350,000	350,000.

	4,771,000.
The Majjars themselves amount to	4,855,670.
The Jews who were enthusiastic on their side	250,000.

Total   9,876,670.

S.

NEW YORK IN OLDEN TIMES. *

EARLY STATE OF THE CITY—COURTS—MEDICAL SCIENCE. *

"After the Dutch had got permission of the natives to build a fort on the island of New York, in the year 1623, they made it in the form of a regular square, with four bastions, on a point of land at the entrance of the North and East rivers, where the government house was afterwards built. At different periods this fort was strengthened by making the stone wall thicker, and then another wall outside the first. The Dutch director-general and the commandant, besides the other officers, had houses within the fort; and in 1642, a church was built in the south-east corner. The church and houses were burnt down in 1741.

"In 1765, Governor Colden, who resided in the fort, intending to receive into it and protect the stamp papers expected hourly from England, took into the fort Major James, and, by his directions, had the rampart of the fort prepared for defence or offence against the inhabitants, by forming embrasures of cord-wood and dirt, and mounting cannon.

"When the house in the fort was burned down, and the troops were removed, the inhabitants dismantled the fort, and pulled down to the ground the north curtain which faced Broadway; and in 1790–91, the fort was entirely demolished, and the stones sold or made use of to build the Government House. The ground was all levelled, so that no trace remains of the old fort, or where it stood. When they were removing the ruins of the old church or chapel, several vaults were dis-

* Selected from Valentine's Manual for 1849. The narrative is in homely style, and may not interest all our readers. The facts, however, are important, as exhibiting the infancy of the great commercial metropolis of the Union, and the administration of justice in those early times.

covered. In one of them was found the remains of the lady of Lord Bellamont, in a leaden coffin.

"After this fort was built by the Dutch, the persons who came over from Holland to settle in America, for the purpose of trading with the natives for furs, &c., and who could not reside in the fort, built houses under the walls of the fort, and formed the first street, which they called Pearl Street. From time to time, as they grew in numbers, and found friendly intercourse with the natives, they increased the extent of the city, which must have contained, in 1686, a number of houses and streets.

"The Dutch, in imitation of what was done in Holland, built dykes in Broad Street, as far up as the city hall, as posts were found standing about ten or twelve feet from the houses, on each side of the way, not long ago, when the street was new paved. The city was first enclosed with a wall or pallisades, from Trinity Church across Wall Street to the East river.

"In 1744, it had pallisades, with block houses, surrounding it from river to river, from near the air furnace to the ship-yard, at the edge of what was called the meadows, on the west side.

"Not long before this, the water out of the fresh water pond or kollock, ran down to both rivers; to the North by a ditch, and to the East by a small rivulet, which became so wide as to require a log to be laid across it to walk on. On the hill, near the river, was a windmill. Some years before this, there was a wind-mill between what was called Crown street and Cortland street. Here it was, that, not forty years ago, the Indians still residing in the lower part of the State, at particular seasons of the year, came to the city and took up their residence, until they had disposed of their poultry, brooms, shovels, trays, baskets, &c.

"In 1746, there was wheat growing where now St. Paul's Church is built, and then there were not twenty houses from Division street to fresh water. In 1744, several Indian canoes, one after another, came down the East and North rivers, landed their cargoes in the basins near the Long bridge, and took up their residence in the yard and store-house of Adolphus Phillips, where they generally made up their baskets and brooms, as they could better bring the rough materials with them than ready-made baskets and brooms. They brought with them, if they came from Long Island, a quantity of dried clams, strung on sea-weed and straw, which they sold or kept for their own provisions, besides the flesh of the animals they killed.

"Clams, oysters and fish-meat, formed the principal food, together with squashes and pumpkins, of the natives of the lower part of the State. Those in the upper part, besides the fish of the rivers, wild water-fowl, and animals of different kinds, Indian corn, squashes and pumpkins, at particular times in the spring were visited with such amazing flights of wild pigeons, that the sun was hid by their flocks from shining on the earth for a considerable time; then it was that the natives laid in a great store of them against the day of need.

From the proceedings of the Burgomasters and Schepens, as recorded in the Manual of the Common Council, we make some extracts. The first describes a meeting of the Court to nominate officers, at which the celebrated Peter Stuyvesant was present.

TUESDAY, 1st February, 1661,
In the City Hall.

Present,

The *Heeren*,

PIETER TONNEMAN,	JACOB STRYCKER,
ALLARD ANTHONY,	GOVERT LOCKERMANS,
MARTIN CREGIER,	TIMOTHEUS GABRY,
CORNELIS STEENWYCK,	JACOBUS BACKER.

" At the court of the Schout, Burgomasters and Schepens, appeared the Honble. Valiant Heer General Petrus Stuyvesant, to assist at the nomination of the succeeding Burgomasters and Schepens.

" The Heer-officer rising, asks, if any of the magistrates had any objection that he should co-operate with the magistrates in the nomination of succeeding Burgomasters and Schepens. Question being put, it was decided that he could not, inasmuch as it manifestly conflicted with the jurisdiction of the Heer Schout, and the laws and customs of the city Amsterdam, in Europe.

" The Heer Director General decides that the Heer Schout shall have vote and co-nomination, assuring them that it shall be so concluded by the Director General and Council of New Netherland. Burgomasters and Schepens declare that if the Director General and Council should so decide, so it must be with them.

" Whereupon the Heer Director General proposed that the nomination be postponed until the *acte* thereof be given to the Burgomasters and Schepens.

" After some further debate over and hither, the meeting adjourned until four o'clock in the afternoon, which being again complete,

" The Heer Schout, Pieter Tonneman, exhibited to the court a certain *acte* from the Honble. Director General and Council of N. Netherland, which reads as follows:—

" The Director General and Council of N. Netherland comparing the previous with the present instruction of the Schout of this city, decide for cause that the Schout must preside in the court of Burgomasters and Schepens, and consequently have opinion and vote in the annual nomination of the subaltern magistrates of this city, and all other matters wherein he is not a party. Thus done at the assembly of the Honble. Lords Director General and Council, holden in Fort Amsterdam in New Netherland, the first of February, Anno 1661.

P. STUYVESANT.

" By order of the Honble. Lords Director General and Council of New Netherland, was signed,

C. V. Ruyven, *Secty.*

" Which being read in court, Burgomasters and Schepens say that it is contrary to the instruction, he not bringing with him his instructions, and that Burgomasters are thereby deprived of their authority.

" The Heer Director General reading the instruction of the Heer Schout says, that by the first rank remaining to the Schout he understands the presidency.

"Whereupon, the Heer president states that the college concludes that the Heer Schout shall co-operate in the nomination for the present time, and desist from any further, unless it be otherwise decided by the Honble. Lords Majores.

" The Honble. Director General and the Heer officer are satisfied therewith; whereupon, the Schout, Burgomasters, and Schepens, proceeded to nominate Burgomasters and Schepens for the ensuing year."

The following account of a trial held before the court of Burgomasters establishes the fact that *the Courts of New Amsterdam used torture to enforce confession.*

Tuesday, 25th April, 1662. }
" *Present,*   In the City Hall,   }

The Heeren.

Pieter Tonneman,   Jacob Strycker,
Paulus Sundertzen Vander Grist,   Jacobus Backer,
Olof Stevenson Van Cortlandt,   Isaack Greveraat.
Johannes de Peyster,

" The prisoner, Reyer Cornelissen, heard on interrogatories, hath answered thereon, as appears by said interrogatories; declaring besides, that he bought from a negro, by the new bridge, the sack of grain which he had thrown into the water by the cripple bush; but says, he does not know the negro; and gave for the corn five and a half guilders, and that he had the same corn at Andries Joghemsen's house, where he lodged; declaring that he purchased a mackerel and took a white loaf from the house with him, and then to have carried the sack along, intending to bring the grain to the mill.

" Seletje, the wife of Andries Joghemsen, sent for to court, appears ; who was asked, if Reyer Cornelissen, the prisoner, lodged at her house? —Answers, Yes.

"Further asked, how he behaved himself there?—Answers, Has no complaint against him, except that he owes her nine guilders.

"Asked if he had a sack of corn at her house?—Answers, Saw no sack of corn at her house.

"Whereupon, Reyer Cornelissen says he had the same under his bed.

"Again asked, if she also saw him take a sack of corn with him?—Answers, Hath not seen.

"And, whereas, Reyer Cornelissen denies what has been laid to his charge by declaration, the Heer officer demands that he shall be further heard *after having been subjected to torture!*

"*The worshipful court grant the request.*

FRIDAY, the 28th April, 1661. ⟩
In the City Hall. ⟩

Present,

The same Court.

"The prisoner, Reyer Cornelissen, was again questioned anew on the four interrogatories respecting his theft, and *if such were true?—Answers, Yes.*

"After which, the demand and conclusion on and against Reyer Cornelissen was delivered to the worshipful court by the Heer officer.

The worshipful court of the city having considered the demand and conclusion of the Heer officer, and heard the confession of the prisoner, Reyer Cornelissen, condemn the aforesaid Reyer Cornelissen Van Soestberger, to be taken to the place where criminal justice is usually executed, *and there to be tied to a stake, severely scourged,* and *banished, out of the city's jurisdiction for the term of ten years;* and further mulcted in the costs and charges of justice."

EARLY MEDICAL SCIENCE IN NEW YORK.

We copy from the eloquent and elaborate discourse of the late President of the New York Academy, *Professor John W. Francis,* the following account of the early state of medical science in that city. The details are interesting, and no less novel than instructive and curious. The discourse abounds in facts of singular value to the medical and philosophical historian.

"New York has been signally blessed in her physicians. Imperfect as are the records concerning our early Dutch doctors, I find many prominent individuals among them, who, to medical erudition and scientific knowledge, added experience in political councils, and rendered services of no small consideration to the public weal. Several came direct from Holland, the land of their birth and the place of their education. Their public trusts were for the most part assigned to them by the authorities of the Dutch West India Company. Johannes Megaolensis and his son Samuel, were recognised as the most conspicuous of these public worthies; they were men of learning and character; the son Samuel was a physician, and received his earlier education at Harvard University, and graduated M.D. at Leyden. He practised medicine at New Amsterdam for some time; but was subsequently elected by the people as one of the commissioners to negotiate with the British the articles for the capitulation of the Province. About the same time Johannes La Montagne, who was also one of the council, was pronounced a skilful doctor of medicine. A post mortem examination is recorded in 1691, and Johannes Kerfbyl and five others of the faculty, testified to the accuracy of the statement set forth. The subject was the body of Governor Slaughter, who died suddenly, under suspicious circumstances. The details are sufficiently minute, and evince an acquaintance with autopsic investigations creditable to the pathological knowledge of the times. There was a sufficient variety in the nativities of these doctors. Kerfbyl appears to have been the most eminent among them; he was a graduate of the University of Leyden, a member of the Colonial Legislature under the Earl of Bellamont, and a friend of Leisler, he came from Holland, and died about 1699. John Lockhart was a Scotchman; Thomas Thornhill and Robert Brett were Englishmen. Lucal Van Effinchoane seems to have been from Germany. Gilles Gandineau, who signs himself Chirurgo-Physician, was a Frenchman. He was a liberal contributor of money to church affairs. The prevailing language of the place was the low Dutch; some, however, used the German, some the English, and others the French, while the Portuguese was used by the Jews. The population of New York, at that period, was 4,202, including 575 slaves. Among the records on the subject of the pathological examinations, we find that the council ordered that, eight pounds, eight shillings, be paid by Mr. Collector, to the Chirurgeons for opening and inspecting said body. This, I believe, may be pronounced the first or earliest example of a post mortem examination in the annals of our science in this country. John Bard and Peter Middleton, sixty years after, 1750, dissected, in this city, the human body, for the purpose of imparting medical instruction.

"At the commencement of 1700, there arrived in this city an individual, whose name has, in his descendants, become familiar in our ears, and historical in the political annals of the Union. John Van Beuren, of Van Beuren, near Amsterdam, in Holland, a pupil of Boerhaave, and a graduate of Leyden, at the age of twenty-two years, was, upon the recommendation of his great teacher, appointed surgeon of a Dutch fleet, which sailed for New York, after touching at the coast of Africa. Soon after his arrival in this city, he, at the instigation of the Governor, was chosen physician and surgeon to the then Alms House; he enjoyed a large practice At the age of twenty-five he was married, and had five sons and three daughters, and from him issued the whole family of the Van Beurens.

The distinguished Cadwallader Colden, eminent as a philosopher, naturalist and writer, gave us the first particular account of our climate in 1720. He also wrote on the Sore Throat Distemper in 1735, and

on the Malignant Fever, which prevailed in New York in 1741—2.
His " Principles of Action in Matter," evinced great acumen, and was
a production of high repute.   His History of the Five Nations is universally known,   Colden was remarkably skilled in botanical knowledge; and· from the Linnæan correspondence, recently published by
Sir James Edward Smith, we find that it was Colden himself, and not
his distinguished daughter, who received the high compliment of having
a plant of the tetandrous class, named Coldentia.   Colden was the first
American expositor of the Linnæan system in the New World.   This
classification he taught on the banks of the Hudson, almost immediately after its announcement by the illustrious Swede.   Kalm, the traveller, the Professor at Abo, a pupil of Linnæus, with whom Colden
became personally acquainted, might have given him the first intima-
tions of the artificial system, as it is known that its principles were
expounded in America before they were recognised in Great Britain.
Indeed, Hudson first naturalized the sexual system by adapting it to
English plants, in 1762.

"About a century ago, Dr. Johnson, of Perth Amboy, in New Jersey, was sedulously devoted to *Flora*, and maintained a correspondence on subjects of natural history with the philosophers of Europe.   In one of his letters, he says, he thinks the information he imparts will be found profitable to an inquirer of like facts, one Mr. Linnæus.   I have not yet satisfied myself whether Johnson was not a.
practitioner in New York at that early date.   In 1740, Isaac Dubois
took his degree of Doctor of Medicine at Leyden, at which time he
published a dissertation on the use and abuse of blood-letting.   He,
doubtless, had listened to the instructions of Boerhaave.   He exercised
the art in New York.   Contemporary with Dubois, was a physician
of note, of the name of John Nicoll, he was imprisoned by Leisler, and
subsequently presided as judge on the trial of the accused Governor.
Dr. John Bard, long a distinguished clinical practitioner in New York,
published several papers on the yellow fever, and an essay on the nature
and cause of the malignant pleurisy, which proved so fatal to the inhabitants of Long Island in the winter of 1749.   He further added to
the usefulness of a life of great toil, by private instruction in practical
medicine.   I at present remember but one of his immediate pupils, Dr.
Henry Mott, who exercised for many years the art, both on Long Island, where he was born, and also in this metropolis, and where he, in
1840, died at the advanced age of eighty-three years.   Dr. Mott was
a promoter of the mercurial practice in the sore throat distemper, and
other diseases, and was much associated during his professional career
with Dr. Ogden and Dr. Muirson; but he will be long remembered in
our annals as the father of Valentine Mott, the great chirurgeon of our
times, the improver of the art, and the introductor of surgical anatomy
and pathology in our schools of medical science.   Dr. Peter Middleton's Historical Inquiry, on the ancient and present state of medicine,

delivered twenty years after, 1769, was a most effective essay. Middleton was learned, acute, and practical; in manner singularly refined, and of a generous nature. He arrived in this country with Dr. Wm. Hunter, of Scotland, who came to Rhode Island in 1752, and who was rendered famous by his anatomical lectures there. Middleton also wrote an excellent paper on croup, and was the first professor of the practice of physic in the newly-organized medical school connected with Columbia College. Middleton died in New York, in 1781. He was a man of rare excellence, widely known, and admired by all.

"Dr. John Jones, ever to be remembered as a physician to Washington, and the surgeon to Franklin, was a native of Long Island: he completed his education abroad, at London, Leyden, and Paris. As surgeon, he held the first rank among practitioners of the art in that day. In 1768, he was chosen an associate in the same school with Middleton. His volume on wounds and fractures, published in 1776, and subsequently reprinted, attests his great qualifications. Percival Pott and William Hunter are to be enumerated among his scientific friends. Dr. Samuel Bard, the associate of Middleton, Clossy, Smith, Tennant and Jones, as the founder of our first medical school, was conspicuous for his classical and general knowledge and his great practical skill in medicine. He was first professor of natural philosophy, and subsequently of clinical medicine, and was long Dean of the Faculty in Columbia College. In his later years, he was the President of the College of Physicians and Surgeons of the University of the State of New York, upon its re-organization in 1811. His acquirements while at Edinburg secured him the Hope medal for Botany, and Haller commended his thesis for the doctorate, "De Viribus Opii." To Dr. Bard, clinical medicine and humanity at large are greatly indebted for his successful efforts in laying the foundation of that important institution, the New York Hospital. Few surpassed Bard in all the best and noble qualities which constitute intellectual and moral excellence. His memory is still cherished with the most grateful associations by the few of our venerable citizens who still abide with us.

"In 1781, Dr. Richard Bayley, of this city, published his letters addressed to Dr. William Hunter, of London, on Angina Trachealis, a tract of singular merit, and from which we are justified in giving to him the merit of being the first writer who understood the nature and treatment of croup. He wrote a volume, of deep interest, on the yellow fever of New York, as it prevailed in 1795: and in which work he attempted to give distinctiveness to the terms contagion and infection. As Health Physician to the Port of New York, he addressed a series of letters to the New York Common Council on that subject, which more than any other for a long time engrossed his attention, the origin of the yellow fever, and the nature and expediency of quarantine laws. Too much cannot be said in behalf of the exertions he made to establish our Lazaretto, and the state regulations which originally existed, to lessen the evils of pestilential miasmas.

"The first medical degree conferred in this city, was that of Bachelor of Medicine, in 1769, upon two candidates, Samuel Kissam and Robert Tucker; and in 1770, that of Doctor of Medicine, upon Samuel Kissam, the first named of these gentlemen. I must trespass a moment concerning this Kissam. The first graduated Doctor of Medicine in the Western Hemisphere calls for a word or two. The family of Kissams, early left England and embarked for America. A part of them emigrated to Long Island, where Samuel was born, at Madnan, now Great Neck, about the year 1745. His father, John, had five sons, of whom the most eminent was Benjamin Kissam, eminently distinguished as a lawyer at our bar, and the preceptor of the late venerable statesman, John Jay. He was also the father of the late prominent surgeon, Dr. Richard S. Kissam.

EARLY LAW BOOKS.

It is very curious to remark that we have no distinct data of the precise period at which any ancient Law Treatise was written. If we may credit the sanguine testimony of some old chronologers,* about 441 years B. C. Mulumnius Dunvallo, or M. Dovebant, wrote two books upon the laws of the Britons,—1. "Municipalia;" 2. "Leges Judiciariæ." 356 years B. C., Mercia Proba, Queen and wife of King Gwintelim, composed a treatise upon the laws of England, in the British tongue, termed "Mercherleg." 872 years A. D., Alfred, King of the West Saxons, compiled a work called, "Breviarium quoddam, quod composuit ex diversis legibus Trojanorum Græcorum, Britannorum, Saxonum, et Dacorum." 635 years A. D., Sigabert or Sigesbert, Orientalium Angloram Rex, wrote, termed "Legum Instituta;" and King Edward the Confessor (who begun his reign A. D. 1051,) composed a work entitled, "Ex immensa legum congerie, quos Britanni, Romani-Angli, et Daci condiderunt, optima quæque selegit, ac in unam coëgit, quam vocari voluit legem communem."

After the Conquest, Henry II. compiled a treatise† on the common law, and "Statutes" of England, divided into two *tomes*, and entitled, 1. "Pro Republicâ Leges;" 2. "Statuta Regalia." The next works that we have are in the reign of Henry III. 1. Bracton's Tractate. 2. Glanville de Legibus. And we have a few other treatises before the Year Books, which commence in the reign of Edward III., some of

----

* Gildas-Gervasius, Tilburiensis, Galf of Monmouth, William of Malmesbury, Polidore Vergil, Harding, Caxton, Fabian, Balæus, Sir Edward Coke, Preface, Rep. tarmed, κατ' ἰξοχην, The Reports.
† In the Red Book in the Exchequer.

which, though broken, yet of the best kind are in the library of Lincoln's Inn.

The first law book was Littleton's Tenures,* probably published by the learned judge himself, at the press of J. Letton and W. Machlinia, Anno 1481,† regno Edw. IV. *This* edition has no title, numerals or catch-words. The type is barbarous and broken; and the text is crowded with abbreviations. Of *this* edition there are supposed to be *five* copies; 1. In the public library at Cambridge; 2. In the library of the Inner Temple; 3. In Earl Spencer's library; 4. In the possession of Mr. Johnes; 5. In the library of the Right Honourable Thomas Greenville. There is a fine copy in the King's library at the British Museum, and which was undoubtedly printed at London by Letton and Machlinia, as will be seen upon a reference to a note subscribed at the end.

The next edition was probably that of Machlinia, who was then living at Fleet Bridge, according to a note at the end. The letter in *this* edition is less rude, and more like the modern English black-letter than the letter used in the former edition. The different chapters of sections commence with a blank space for the illumination of the capital letter, which is printed in a small character at one corner. It has no numerals or catch-words.

The editions of Pynson are five in number,—1st. folio, 1516; 2d. duodecimo, 1525; 3d. sextodecimo; 4th and 5th, folio and without dates.

Sir Edward Coke, Dugdale,‡ and Bishop Nicolson, conjecture that the first edition was printed "at Rouen in Normandy, by William de Tollier ad instantiam Ricardi Pinson, the printer of Henry VIII.;" and that it was first printed about the twenty-fourth year of Henry VIII., Anno 1533. But the fact of the former edition being printed by Letton and Machlinia, who were printers in the reign of Edward IV., fully shows the precedence, in point of time, to be due to their joint impression.

It is important to remark, that there are, at the public library, two ancient manuscripts of the Tenures extant in the University of Cambridge. The first is imperfect at the beginning, and in the chapter on warranty. It is written on vellum. The second is on paper, and only the second leaf is torn. This M. S. has the following passage:—*Iste liber emptus fuit, in cœmeteriæ S'ti Pauli, London, 27th die Julii, anno regis E. 4ti, 20mo.*, 10s. 6d., *i. e.*, temp. Littleton, July 20, Edward IV., Anno, 1481. The year before his death.

* "The origin of Printing," 39—40. Ame's Hist. Typography.
† Dr. Middleton's Account of Printing in England.
‡ Original. Judiciales.

THE CLERGY OF THE NINETEENTH CENTURY.

BY BISHOP POTTER.*

THE onward flow of time has brought us to a position, unlike any occupied by our predecessors in the sacred office. We live when, with the many, there is more of intelligence and thoughtfulness; but not perhaps when, with the few, there is more of high sagacity, or far-reaching faith. We live when industry has vindicated for itself a new and more commanding place, among the powers that direct the legislation and opinion of the world; but not when the toiling millions it employs are always admitted to a corresponding elevation. We live when there is great activity, and in some sense great and almost universal earnestness; but not when that activity is always tempered by forecast, nor that earnestness duly subdued by religious feeling. We live when there is more of Christian faith than there was in the eighteenth century, and more of Christian toleration than there was in the sixteenth; but alas! it does not become us to boast that even now a practical and life-transforming faith or sincere toleration in the heart is very abundant. We live when despotism of every kind, civil and religious, has much to fear; but not when legitimate authority, be it the authority of law, or the moral sway that belongs to age, wisdom, or parental power has every thing to hope. Practical and all-embracing charity is more active than it once was; but it is not always more wise, or more patient. Institutions, usages, opinions, all are arraigned with a free and bold hand, and to all is applied the salutary test "by their fruits ye shall know them;" but the trial is not always conducted with caution or discrimination; and there is too little care to conserve the good, while we eradicate the ill.

Such, I conceive, are some of the features of the age in which we live. Besides those which affect all classes of men, there are some that bear, with peculiar effect, upon our own profession. The clergy are no longer the peculiar guardians and dispensers of knowledge. They are no longer clothed with the exclusive privilege of legislating for the Church, nor even of teaching it. They are no longer an independent corporation, sovereign over the law, or exempt in good part from its jurisdiction. There was a time, when they owned hardly any but an eccle-

---

* These remarks, characterized by an elevated tone and by the true spirit of Christian philanthropy, are extracted from a late charge of the learned and eloquent divine, whose name is affixed.

They will command the respectful attention and consideration of the enlightened and sincere of every religious sect.

siastical superior—when they could successfully claim a control over the property and persons even of laymen—when they could, almost at will, summon all the powers of the state to do their bidding—when the absent husband could hardly correspond with his wife, except through the clerk in orders—when all laws were drawn up, all treaties reduced to form, all deliberations of cabinets, and even of parliaments aided and guided by ecclesiastics—and when they held possession not only of cathedrals, churches, convents, and monasteries, but of all colleges and schools of learning also. How different is it now, when they are merged, by law, into the one class of citizens,—amenable to the same laws, mere sharers in the same intellectual and social privileges, and left to contend on less than equal terms for the direction of public opinion! ; I say less than equal, not so much because of the political disabilities under which they sometimes labour, as because I fear, that the growing and almost morbid jealousy of interference, on the part of the clergy, in things secular, excludes them too much from that promiscuous commerce with men, and from that free conflict with the difficulties of life, which seems almost essential to the utmost force of character, as well as to the highest degree of culture.

And what is the duty of the ministers of Christ in such an age? Is it to denounce it? Is it to shut out from our hearts all respect for it— all sympathy with it? Is it to dwell exclusively on its defects, and bring these into exaggerated contrast with the fancied glories of some age that has gone by? Is it to war only against the outward *forms* which have been assumed by the social intellectual or religious spirit of the time, while we overlook or take perhaps into our very heart, the worst elements in that very *spirit*?—Or, is it our part, on the other hand, to idolize the age, to seize upon some of its grosser achievements, and to set these in array against all the past? Is it to regard the spirit of the age as a Divine Inspiration, which has only to move on unobstructed and unopposed, to accomplish, for man, the most beneficent results?—Or, in fine, is it our province to regard the characteristics of our age as inevitable effects from causes that have been at work heretofore, and to conceive that the vicissitudes of the future, like those of the past, must be governed by a blind and uncontrollable destiny?

Neither of these courses, I should suppose, was the dictate of true wisdom. We are placed here as teachers and guides of our time. To fulfil that mission as we ought, we must, in the first place, understand our age; we must, in the second place, sympathize to a certain extent with it; and we must, in the third place, be resolved that we will, God being our helper, do something to improve it. We must understand our age, in order to be understood by it. We must so far sympathize with its great movements, that they who are borne along by them will not be disinclined to listen to us; and improvement we must believe to be possible, or we shall not be induced to attempt it. But how can one understand his age, unless he be willing to see and to admit both its

merits and its defects;—or, how can he have due sympathy with this
or with any period of history, unless he remember that, in all periods,
the same corrupt heart of man holds sway; and that hence the same
essential evils, however differing in shape or in degree, must prevail in
all. And he who, with a right good will, would labour to exalt and
bless mankind, must surely have faith in the efficacy of right efforts
rightly applied; and he must go forth hopefully, in the strength of God
and of a good cause, to his work. He must be neither a fatalist nor an
optimist. Both the form and the spirit, the body and the pressure of
the time, he is to accept as *facts*—facts which he cannot set aside,
though he may leave them out of view; and he is to consider that it is
through these facts, and in the light that they cast upon his path, that
he is to labour for the service of the Church of God. These facts he
would study and analyze by the aid of a high scriptural philosophy;
and he would study them, not for purposes of speculation, but that he
may the better help to guard whatever of blessing we inherit from the
past, and to compass whatever of blessing is possible in the future.
Could we but station such minds, vigilant, large-hearted, forecasting,
hopeful, at the great reservoirs of human opinion and influence, what a
benign change might be wrought even in a single generation on the
moral habits of mankind! The faithful and enlightened student of
history finds, since the flood, no age or civilization that he would willingly reproduce, even if he could; and he knows full well that there
is none, though ever so much desired, which could be reproduced; since
the forces that now mould societies and nations are not the forces that
they once were. He turns therefore to the Present, as an inevitable
yet ever changing, and ever to be modified fact; and he would so work
that this great fact shall be the harbinger of one brighter and more
blessed soon to succeed it. The blessings that the world has gained,
he would remember and own that he may be contented and thankful;
the blessings that the world has still, through God's help, to achieve,
he would never forget, lest he be tempted to indolence or to self-com-
placency.

THE THORN-CROWN.

FROM SELECTIONS OF SACRED LATIN POETRY, BY PROFESSOR
R. C. TRENCH, OF LONDON.

(The Hymnologies of the church in the middle ages contain a
genuine religious poetry—a rythmical expression of the deepest feelings of man. The majesty of the Latin language, which its admirers
so much boast of, no where appears more conspicuously than in its

religious uses; and the rhymes resulting, as they commonly do, from the construction, seem to set a stamp upon the completeness of the expressions.)

ENGLISH VERSION.

Si vis verè gloriari,
Et a Deo coronari
  Honorē et gloriâ,
Hanc coronam contemplari
Studeas, atquē sectari.
  Portantis vestigia.

Man! in glory would'st thou shine!
Would'st thou of a crown divine
  Be the eternal wearer!
See this crown of sharpest thorn,
Mark it well—by whom 'twas borne—
  Follow him the bearer.

Hanc cœlorum Rex portavit,
Honoravit et sacravit
  Sacro suo capite;
In hac galeâ pugnavit
Cum antiquum hostem stravit,
  Triumphans in stipite.

This, the King Eternal wore it;
This he hallow'd when he bore it
  On his brow so glorious;
This, the helm that graced his forehead,
When that ancient foe abhorred
  Down he smote victorious.

Hæc pugnantis galea
Triumphantis laurea
  Tyara Pontificis:
Primum fuit spinea,
Postmodum fit aurea
  Tactu sancti verticis.

Helm on Soldier's forehead shining,
Laurel Conqueror's brow entwining,
  High Priest's mitre dread!
'Twas of thorns! but now, behold,
'Tis become of purest gold,
  Touched by that blest head!

Spinarum aculeos
Virtus fecit aureos
  Christi passionis;
Quæ peccatis spineos
Mortis æternæ reos
  Adimplevit bonis.

All the thorns so rough and base
Turn'd to gold by wond'rous grace
  In that precious blood:
All our human thorns and briers,
All our fierce and foul desires,
  Turn'd by him to good.

De malis colligitur
Et de spinis plectitur
  Spinea perversis:
Sed in aurum vertitur,
Quando culpa tollitur,
  Ejusdem conversia.

That thorn-crown of sins was wound
Oblique, twisted round and round,
  Every touch a smart;
And that crown is turn'd to golden
When, by sin no longer holden,
  He renews the heart.

A VISIT TO THE SULTAN.

BY LIEUTENANT LYNCH, U. S. NAVY.

WE were led to the entrance of the southern wing (of the palace of Cherighan on the Bosphorus) and again throwing off our overshoes, entered a lofty and spacious hall, matted throughout, with two broad flights of stairs ascending from the far extreme to an elevated platform or landing, whence, uniting in one, they issued upon the floor above. On the right and left of the hall were doors opening into various apartments, and there were a number of officers and attendants on either side, and stationed at intervals along the stairway, all preserving a silence the most profound. The Secretary, who had gone before, now approached, and beckoned to us to follow. But here an unexpected difficulty was presented. The chamberlain in waiting objected to my sword, and required that I should lay it aside. I replied, that the audience was given to me as an officer of the United States, and that the sword was part of my uniform, and that I could not dispense with it. My refusal was met with the assurance that the etiquette of the court peremptorily required it. I asked if the custom had been invariably complied with, and inquired of the dragoman whether Mr. Carr, our Minister, had, in conformity with it, ever attended an audience without his sword, but even as I spoke, my mind, without regard to precedent, had come to the alternative, no sword, no audience.

Whether the Secretary had, during the discussion, referred the matter to a higher quarter, I could not tell, for my attention had been so engrossed for some minutes, that I had not noticed him. He now came forward, however, and decided that I should retain the sword. At this I truly rejoiced, for it would have been unpleasant to retire after having gone so far. It is due to Mr. Brown, the dragoman, to say that he sustained me.

The discussion at an end, we ascended the stairway, which was covered with a good and comfortable, but not a costly carpet, and passed into a room more handsomely furnished and more lofty, but in every other respect of the same dimensions as the one immediately below it. A rich carpet was on the floor, a magnificent chandelier, all crystal and gold, was suspended from the ceiling, and costly divans and tables, with other articles of furniture, were interspersed about the room, but I had not time to note them, for on the left hung a gorgeous crimson velvet curtain, embroidered and fringed with gold, and towards it the Secretary led the way. His countenance and his manner exhibited more awe than I had ever seen depicted in the human countenance. He seemed to hold his breath, and his step was so soft and stealthy, that once or twice I stopped, under the impression that I had left him behind, but found him ever beside me.

There were three of us in close proximity, and the stairway was lined with officers and attendants, but such was the death-like stillness that I could distinctly hear my own foot fall, which, unaccustomed to palace regulations, fell with untutored republican firmness upon the royal floor. If it had been a wild beast slumbering in his lair that we were about to visit, there could not have been a silence more deeply hushed.

Fretted at such abject servility, I quickened my pace towards the curtain, when Sheffie Bey, rather gliding than stepping before me, cautiously and slowly raised a corner for me to pass. Wondering at his subdued and terror-stricken attitude, I stepped across the threshold, and felt, without yet perceiving it, that I was in the presence of the Sultan.

The heavy folds of the window curtains so obscured the light, that it seemed as if the day were drawing to a close, instead of being at its high meridian.

As with the expanding pupil the eye took in surrounding objects, the apartment, its furniture, and its royal tenant, presented a different scene from what, if left to itself, the imagination would have drawn.

The room less spacious, but as lofty as the adjoining one, was furnished in the modern European style, and, like a familiar thing, a stove stood nearly in the centre. On a sofa by a window, through which he might have looked upon us as we crossed the court, with a crimson tarbouch, its gold button and blue silk tassel on its head, a black silk 'kerchief around his neck, attired in a military blue frock and pantaloons, and polished French boots upon his feet, sat the monarch, without any of the attributes of sovereignty about him.

A man, young in years, but evidently of delicate and impaired constitution, his wearied and spiritless air was unrelieved by any indication of intellectual energy. He eyed me fixedly as I advanced, and on him my attention was no less riveted. As he smiled I stopped, expecting that he was about to speak, but he motioned gently with his hand for me to approach yet nearer. Through the interpreter he then bade me welcome, for which I expressed my acknowledgments.

The interview was not a protracted one. In the course of it, as requested by Mr. Carr, I presented him, in the name of the President of the United States, with some biographies and prints, illustrative of the character and habits of our North American Indians, the work of American artists. He looked at some of them, which were placed before him by my attendant, and said that he considered them as evidences of the advancement of the United States in civilization, and would treasure them as a souvenir of the good feeling of its government towards him. At the word civilization pronounced in French I started; for it seemed singular, coming from the lips of a Turk, and applied to our country. I have since learned that he is but a student in French, and presume that by the word "civilization" he meant the arts and sciences.

When about to take my leave, he renewed the welcome, and said that I had his full authority to see any thing in Stamboul I might desire.

While in his presence, I could not refrain from drawing comparisons and moralizing on fate. There was the Sultan, an Eastern despot, the ruler of mighty kingdoms, and the arbiter of the fate of millions of his fellow creatures; and, face to face, a few feet distant, one, in rank and condition, among the humblest servants of a far-distant republic, and yet, little as life has to cheer, I would not change position with him, unless I could carry with me my faith, my friendships, and my aspirations.

My feelings saddened as I looked upon the monarch, and I thought of Montezuma. Evidently like a northern clime, his year of life had

known two seasons only, and he had leaped from youth to imbecility.
His smile was one of the sweetest I ever looked upon; his voice almost
the most melodious that I had ever heard; his manner gentleness itself,
and every thing about him bespoke a kind and amiable disposition.   He
is said to be very affectionate, to his mother especially, and is generous
to the extreme of prodigality.   But there is that indescribably sad expression in his countenance, which is thought to indicate an early
death.   A presentiment of the kind mingled perhaps with a boding fear
of the overthrow of his country, seems to pervade and depress his spirits.
In truth, like Damocles, this descendant of the Caliphs sits beneath a
suspended fate.   Through him the souls of the mighty monarchs who
have gone before, seem to brood over the impending fate of an empire
which once extended from the Atlantic to the Ganges, from the Cau-
casus to the Indian Ocean.

AARON BURR AND HIS DAUGHTER. •

THE history of every nation is fraught with romantic incidents.
England has the story of her Alfred; Scotland of her Wallace, her
Bruce, her Mary, and her Charles Stuart; Ireland her Fitzgerald;
France her Man with the Iron Mask and Marie Antoinette; Poland
her Thaddeus, and Russia her Siberian Exiles.   But we very much
doubt whether any exceeds in interest the singularly touching story of
Aaron Burr and his highly accomplished, his beautiful and devoted
daughter Theodosia.   The rise and fall of Burr in the affections of his
countrymen, are subjects of deep historical interest.   At one time we
see him carried on the wave of popular favour to such giddy heights
that the Presidency itself seemed almost within his grasp, which he
only missed to become the second officer in the new republic.   He became
Vice-President of the United States.   How rapid his rise! and then
his fall, how sudden, how complete!   In consequence of his duel with
Gen. Hamilton, he became a fugitive from justice, is indicted for murder
by the Grand Jury of New Jersey, flies to the South, lives a few months
in obscurity, until the meeting of Congress, when he comes forth and
again takes the chair as President of the Senate.   After the term ex-
pires, he goes to the West, becomes the leading spirit in a scheme of
ambition to invade Mexico, (very few will now believe that he sought
a dismemberment of the Union,) is brought back a prisoner of state to
Richmond, charged with high treason, is tried and acquitted, is forced
to leave his native land, and go to Europe.   In England he is suspected, and retires to France, where he lives in reduced circumstances,
at times not being able to procure a meal of victuals.
   After an absence of several years, he finds means to return home.

He lands in Boston without a cent in his pocket, an object of distrust to all.   Burr had heard no tidings of his daughter since his departure from home.   He was anxious to hear from her, her husband, and her boy, an only child, in whom his whole soul seemed bound up.   The first news he heard was that his grandchild died while he was an outcast in foreign lands, which stroke of Providence he felt keenly, for he dearly loved the boy.   Theodosia, the daughter of Burr, was the wife of Governor Allston, of South Carolina.   She was married young, and while her father was near the zenith of his fame.   She was beautiful and accomplished, a lady of the finest feelings, an elegant writer, a devoted wife, a fond mother, and a most dutiful and loving daughter, who clung with redoubled affection to the fortunes of her father, as the clouds of adversity gathered around him, and he was deserted by the friends whom he formerly cherished.   The first duty Burr performed after his arrival here, was to acquaint Mrs. Allston of his return.   She immediately wrote back to him that she was coming to see him, and would meet him in a few weeks in New York.   This letter was couched in the most affectionate terms, and is another evidence of the purity and power of woman's love.

In the expectation of seeing his daughter in a few days, Burr received much pleasure.   She had become his all on earth.   Wife, grandchild, friends, all were gone; his daughter alone remained to cheer and solace the evening of his life, and welcome him back from his exile.   Days passed on—then weeks—and weeks were lengthened into months—yet naught was heard from Mrs. Allston.   Burr grew impatient, and began to think that she too had left him, so apt is misfortune to doubt the sincerity of friendship.   At length he received a letter from Mr. Allston, inquiring if his wife had arrived safe, and stating that she had sailed from Charleston some weeks previous, in a vessel chartered by him on purpose to convey her to New York.   Not receiving any tidings of her arrival, he was anxious to learn the cause of her silence.

What had occurred to delay the vessel?—why had it not arrived?—these were questions which Burr could ask himself, but no one could answer.

The sequel is soon told.   The vessel NEVER arrived.   It undoubtedly foundered at sea, and all on board perished.   No tidings have ever been heard respecting the vessel, the crew, or the daughter of Aaron Burr—all were lost.   This last sad bereavement was only required to fill Burr's cup of sorrow.   "The last link was broken" which bound him to life.   The uncertainty of her fate but added to the poignancy of his grief.   Hope, the last refuge of the afflicted, became extinct when years had rolled on, and yet no tidings of the loved and lost one were gleaned.

Burr lived in New York until the year 1836, we believe, when he died.   The last years of his life were passed in comparative obscurity. Some few old friends, who had never deserted him, were his companions; they closed his eyes in death, and followed his body to the grave, where it will rest till the trump of the Almighty shall call it into judgment.

Such is a brief sketch of the latter part of the strange and eventful history of Aaron Burr. None of the family now live—it has become extinct—and his name but lives in the history of his country and in the remembrance of those who knew him.

GREEN TEA—HOW COLOURED.

During a visit I paid to a tea manufactory, in the city of Shanghae, I happened to meet some merchants who came from the celebrated green tea district of Wheychou. Thinking this a good opportunity for obtaining some information regarding the mode of colouring green teas, and as I was accompanied by Mr. M'Donald, an excellent Chinese scholar, I had some questions put to them on this subject. They would not acknowledge that any colouring matter was used in the manufacture of their teas, and pretended to laugh at the idea of such a thing. They said, moreover, that they were aware the practice of colouring was a common one about Canton, where inferior teas were made,—but that they never coloured their teas in Wheychou. They then skilfully enough tried to change the subject by telling us that we should not give credence to all we heard. "If *we* did so," said they, "we would make some strange mistakes with regard to the productions and manufactures of your country. For example," they continued, "it is commonly reported that you buy our teas in order to convert them into opium and re-sell them in that form to us. Now, we do not believe that you do that;—and neither should you believe all you hear about the colouring of our green teas." After giving us this sage advice, they asked us very gravely how we used this tea in England,—and if it was true that we had the leaves boiled and beat up with sugar and milk?

It is, however, a difficult thing to get the truth out of a Chinaman; and from information which I had received I knew quite well that our Wheychou friends were deceiving us in the present instance. Shortly afterwards I had an opportunity of seeing the whole process; and as it is one of considerable interest, I noted it down at the time with great care, and now send you a copy of my observations.

The superintendent of the tea makers managed the colouring part of the business himself. In the first place, he procured a portion of indigo which he threw into a porcelain bowl, not unlike a chemist's mortar, and crushed it into a fine powder. He then burned a quantity of gypsum in the charcoal fires which were roasting the tea. The object of this was to soften the gypsum in order that it might easily be pounded into a fine powder in the same manner as the indigo had been. When taken from the fire, it readily crumbled down, and was reduced to powder in the mortar. These two substances having been thus prepared, were then mixed up in the proportion of four parts gypsum to three of indigo, and together formed a light blue powder which in this state was ready for use. This colouring matter was applied to the tea during the last process of roasting. The Chinese manufacturer having no watch to guide him, uses a joss stick* to regulate his movements with regard to time. He knows exactly how long the joss stick burns, and it of course answers the purpose of a watch. About five minutes before the tea was taken out of the pans, the superintendent took a small porcelain spoon and lifted out a portion of the colouring matter from the basin and scattered it over the tea in the first pan; he did the same to the whole, and the workmen turned the leaves rapidly round with their hands in order that the colour might be well diffused.

During this part of the operation the hands of the men at the pans were quite blue. I could not help thinking that if any drinker of *green* tea had been present during this part of the process his taste would have been corrected—and, I hope I may be allowed to add, improved. It seemed perfectly ridiculous that a civilized people should prefer these dyed teas to those of a natural green. No wonder that the Chinese consider the nations of the West as "barbarians." One day Mr. Shaw, a merchant in Shanghae, asked the Wheychou Chinamen their reasons for dyeing their teas:—they quietly replied, that as foreigners always paid a higher price for such teas, they of course preferred them—and that such being the case, the Chinese manufacturer could have no objection to supply them!

I took some trouble to ascertain precisely the quantity of colouring matter used in the process of dyeing green teas; certainly not with the view of assisting others, either at home or abroad, in the art of colouring, but simply to show green tea drinkers in England—and more particularly in the United States of America—what quantity of gypsum and indigo they eat or drink in the course of the year. To $14\frac{1}{2}$ pounds of tea were applied rather more than an ounce of colouring matter. For every hundred pounds of green tea which are consumed in England or America, the consumer really eats more than half a pound of gypsum and indigo: —and I have little doubt that in many instances Prussian blue is substituted for indigo. And yet, tell these green tea drinkers that the Chinese eat dogs, cats and rats, and they will hold up their hands in amazement and pity the taste of the poor Celestials.

In five minutes from the time of the colour being thrown into the pan the desired effect was produced. Before the tea was removed the superintendent took a tray and placed a handful from each pan upon it.

* A small reed, covered with odoriferous dust, which the Chinese use to burn before idols.

These he examined at the window to see if they were uniform in colour; and if the examination was satisfactory he gave the order to remove the tea from the pans—and the process was complete. It sometimes happened that there was a slight difference amongst the samples: and in that case it was necessary to add more colour, and consequently keep the tea a little longer in the pan.—*Foreign Correspon. Athenæum.*

THE TOMATO.

This plant or vegetable, sometimes called Love-Apple or Jerusalem Apple, which belongs to the same genus with the potato, was first found in South America. The use of this fruit as food, is said to have been derived from the Spaniards. It has been long used also by the French and Italians. The date of its introduction to this country is unknown. It is said that the tomato has been used in some parts of Illinois for more than fifty years. Its introduction on our tables, as a culinary vegetable, is of recent date. Thirty years ago in this vicinity, it was scarcely known, except as an ornament to the flower garden, and for pickling. It is now cultivated in all parts of the country, and found either in a cooked or raw state on most tables. In warm climates it is said, that the tomato is more used than in the northern, and has a more agreeable taste. It is now much used in various parts of the country, in soups and sauces, to which it imparts an agreeable acid flavour; and is also stewed and dressed in various ways, very much admired, and many people consider it a great luxury.

We often hear it said that a relish for this vegetable is an acquired one; scarcely any person at first liking it, but eventually becoming very fond of it. It has, indeed, within a few years, come into very general use, and is considered a particularly healthy article. A learned medical professor in the West pronounces the tomato to be a very wholesome food in various ways, and advises the daily use of it. He says that it is very salutary in dyspepsia, and indigestion, and is a good antidote to bilious disorders, to which persons are liable in going from a northern to a warmer climate. He recommends the use of it also in diarrhœa, and thinks it preferable to calomel.

The tomato is a tender, herbaceous plant of rank growth, but weak, fetid and glutinous. The leaves resemble those of the potato, but the flowers are yellow and arranged in large divided branches. The fruit is of light yellow, and a bright red colour, pendulous, and formed like the large squash-shaped pepper. There are smaller varieties, one pear-shaped variety, also red and yellow. These are eaten and relished by many from the hand. The red are best for cooking—the yellow for slicing like cucumbers, seasoned with pepper, salt and vinegar, and eaten raw.

The seed should be sown in the early part of March, in a slight hot bed, and the plants set out in the open ground early in May. In private grounds it will be necessary to plant them near a fence, or to provide trellises for them to be trained to, in the same manner as for nasturtians; they will, however, do very well if planted out four feet distant from each other every way. But a nice way to keep the plant erect, and the fruit from the ground is to drive down four stakes, so as to make a square, say two feet each way, around the stakes. These will keep the vines from falling, and expose the fruit nicely to the sun for ripening. They will bear till frost.—*Journal of Agriculture.*

ANTIQUITY OF TREES .

An interesting item from the justly celebrated Lindley, his Vegetable Kingdom.—London, 1846.

"THE distinguished botanist Martins states that in Brazil are found a kind of locust trees, which fifteen Indians with outstretched arms could just embrace at the bottom—they measured *eighty-four feet in circumference,* and sixty feet where their boles (bodies) became cylindrical.

"By counting the concentric rings—Martins arrived at the conclusion that they were of the *Age of Homer,* and three hundred and thirty-two years old in the days of Pythagoras. Another was counted, and carried up to *four thousand one hundred and four* years, far beyond the time of our Saviour."

When we reflect upon the brevity of animal and vegetable life—in the presence of such a tree, how can we fail to behold such a life as it had without feelings of awe! What causes such a difference in behalf of this tree? For after all it is true living—it drinks the dews and the rains—moves in all the breezes and storms, breathes the air and feels the electric spark—and has done so since the earth was young!

Forty times the age of the most venerable of the race—four or five times older than Methuselah! As old as some of our phenomenic changes—beginning where a different phenomena of vegetation had recently ceased.—*Judge Meigs.*

In connexion with the interesting fact stated on the preceding page, for which we are indebted to the Recording Secretary of the American Institute, we add some further instances, which seem to be well established, and are truly astonishing.

We may remark, that within a few years, both in America and France, the age and size of trees have been discussed in a very philosophical manner; especially by M. Decandolle, a great botanist who investigated fully the physiology of plants, and published an elaborate and profound paper entitled "the Antiquity of Trees."

"A certain *Baobab tree* of Africa is considered by Humboldt as the oldest organic monument of our planet; and Adanson, a distinguished botanist, by ingenious calculations, has ascertained its age to be 5150 years. The method adopted by Adanson for finding its age, was by making a deep cut in the side of the trunk, and counting the concentric rings, by which he ascertained how much the tree had grown, in three centuries; and having already learned the growth of young trees, he established his general law through the average growth. The enormous dimensions of the trunk of this tree bear a striking disproportion to the other parts. Examples of the species have been seen, which, with a trunk ninety feet in circumference, were only twelve feet in height. A still larger one was seen by Mr. Golberry in the valley of the two Gagnacks in Africa; it was thirty-four feet in diameter. The flower is of the same gigantic proportions as the tree. Such colossal masses of timber might be hollowed out into by no means straitened dwelling-houses.

"One of the most celebrated trees described by travellers of recent times, is the *Great Dragon tree* of the island of Teneriffe. It derives its name of *dragon's blood*, by which it is popularly known, from the circumstance of a liquor of a deep red colour like blood flowing from its hoary trunk during the dog-days. This exudation soon becomes dry and brittle by the action of the atmosphere, and is the true dragon's-blood of the apothecaries, and other venders. The wonderful size and appearance of this tree excited the admiration of Humboldt, who thus describes it:

—"We were told that the trunk of this tree, which is mentioned in some very ancient documents as marking the boundaries of a field, was as gigantic in the fifteenth century as it is at the present moment. Its height appeared to us to be about fifty or sixty feet; its circumference near the root is forty-five feet. . . . The trunk is divided into a great number of branches, which rise in the form of a candelabrum, and are terminated by tufts of leaves, like the yucca which adorns the valley of Mexico. It still bears every year, both leaves and fruit. Its aspect feelingly recalls to mind 'that eternal youth of nature' which is an inexhaustible source of motion and of life." This giant plant was laid prostrate by a tempest in 1822.

"The fact here noticed by the learned traveller, that the tree annually bore leaves and fruit, affords indubitable proof of a very remarkable circumstance connected with the vegetable kingdom. In man and all other animals, we find an organization and a process of life going on which is destined to cease at a certain period. Mortality is written in irrevocable characters on every thing which treads the earth, or wings the air, or cleaves the flood. Life in these, is like sand in the hour-glass; its very motion, so to speak, involves the necessity of its becoming exhausted at last, and ceasing to move. But it is otherwise with trees. They appear to possess the power of growing on for ever without exhibiting any symptoms of decay, unless from accidental or extraneous causes.

"Cypresses of gigantic dimensions are met with in Mexico. At Atlexo there is one seventy-six feet in girth; and another at St. Maria del Tuli, in the province of Oaxaca, which is one hundred and eighteen feet in circumference! This is larger than the dragon tree of the Canaries, and all the baobabs of Africa. 'But,' says Humboldt, 'on examining it narrowly, M. Anza observes, that what excites the admiration of travellers is not a single individual, but that three united trunks form the famous *Sabino of Santa Maria del Tuli.*' The fact of the threefold nature of the stem, seems to have escaped the notice of some writers; it is of importance in determining which is really the largest organic monument of our planet. There is another cypress at Chapultepec in the same region, which is said to be one hundred and seventeen feet ten inches round, and the younger Decandolle considers it even older than the baobab of Adanson.

"One of the most curious and beautiful of nature's productions, is the Banian or Burr tree, the *Ficus Indica* of botanists. Each tree forms in itself a grove, composed of numerous stems connected together, some of which are of the size of a large tree. On the island of Nerbuddah, near Baroach, in Hindostan, there is still standing a celebrated banian called the *Cubbeer Burr.* The tradition of the natives is, that it is three thousand years old. It is supposed by some to be the same tree that was visited by Nearchus, one of Alexander the Great's officers. The large trunks of this tree amount in number to 350, the smaller ones exceed 3000, and each of these is constantly sending forth branches and hanging roots to form other trunks. The circumference of this remarkable plant is nearly 2000 feet. Milton, in his "Paradise Lost," has described one of these trees as that of whose leaves our first parents 'made themselves aprons' after the fall.

> ——————— 'Soon they chose
> The fig-tree, not that kind for fruit renowned,
> But such as at this day, to Indians known,
> In Malabar or Decan, spreads her arms,
> Branching so broad and long, that in the ground
> The bended twigs take root, and daughters grow
> About the mother tree, a pillar'd shade
> High over-arched, and echoing walks between.'

The following remarks are very apposite to the subject:—

"Trees have figured in literature, and struck their roots deep in the poetry of all ages. Although a taste for the picturesque does not characterize the ancients, and there is little description of natural scenery in their prose works, yet we find exceptions in regard to trees. One remarkable instance will promptly occur to all classical scholars: it is the famous platanus, in the shade of which Socrates kept his place while he discoursed, constantly moving from the sun; it is mentioned both by Plato and Cicero. The choral allusions to groves, in Greek Tragedy, are also familiar. The Latin word *lucus*, carried religious associations which belonged to no other term, and was shadowy with such imaginations as hover over Virgil's line,

> Et caligantem nigra formidine lucum.

"These superstitions were founded on natural sentiment; as he may understand who will recall some twilight hour, when he found himself musing and gazing into the recesses of a dark ancient tree till overtaken by night. The poet is one who can unfold the Herculanean papyrus of such thoughts, and decipher the hieroglyphic of imagination, and translate the vagueness of these inklings into the idiom of common life. Perhaps it has never been more completely done than by Wordsworth, in the YEW TREES:

> 'A pillar'd shade,
> Upon whose grassless floor of red-brown hue,
> By sheddings from the pining umbrage tinged
> Perennially—beneath whose sable roof
> Of boughs, as if for festal purpose decked
> With unrejoicing berries, ghostly shapes
> May meet at noontide—Fear and trembling Hope,
> Silence and foresight—Death the skeleton,
> And Time the shadow,'—etc.

"I wish attention were more frequently drawn, by parents and other educators, to the individuality of great trees, which have each their physiognomy, as much as so many men. And could we read the character, in these lineaments of trunk and boughs and 'shadowing shroud,' we should read the impressions of spring tides, of droughts, and of tempests. An old tree is an old friend, and we do well to take pains that our sons may hereafter love its very wrinkles. The tree of the park, and the tree of the forest, are as different as the old knotty, gnarled, unmovable baron, and the alert, smooth, thriving, average dweller in cities. The same reasons operate in both cases. Character becomes more inspissated, juicy, full of tannin and fibrin, where there has been elbow-room for the mighty branches to wrestle with the winds. Look at an 'old field' of the South, in which a thousand young pines have sprung up spontaneously, side by side, and you are instantly reminded of a boarding-school of sweet young ladies; the same name would do for all. On the other hand, I do know a solitary tree, fit for Druids, and predominating over a waste meadow, which is so reverend in its eloquence that it preaches a sermon to me whenever I pass or contemplate it. 'Those mossed trees, that have outlived the eagles,' should covenant with us to leave something of their kind for our descendants.''

POETRY.

THE world is full of Poetry—the air
Is living with its spirit; and the waves
Dance to the music of its melodies,
And sparkle in its brightness. Earth is veil'd
And mantled with its beauty; and the walls,
That close the universe with crystal in,
Are eloquent with voices, that proclaim
The unseen glories of immensity,
In harmonies, too perfect, and too high,
For aught but beings of celestial mould,
And speak to man in one eternal hymn
Unfading beauty, and unyielding power.

The year leads round the seasons, in a choir
For ever charming and for ever new;
Blending the grand, the beautiful, the gay,
The mournful, and the tender, in one strain,
Which steals into the heart, like sounds, that rise
Far off, in moonlight evenings, on the shore
Of the wide ocean resting after storms;
Or tones, that wind around the vaulted roof,
And pointed arches, and retiring aisles
Of some old, lonely minster, where the hand
Skilful, and moved with passionate love of art,
Plays o'er the higher keys, and bears aloft
The peal of bursting thunder, and then calls
By mellow touches, from the softer tubes,
Voices of melting tenderness, that blend
With pure and gentle musings, till the soul
Commingling with the melody is borne,
Rapt, and dissolved in ecstasy, to Heaven.

'Tis not the chime and flow of words, that move
In measured file, and metrical array;
'Tis not the union of returning sounds,
Nor all the pleasing artifice of rhyme,

And quantity, and accent, that can give
This all-pervading spirit to the ear,
Or blend it with the movings of the soul.
'Tis a mysterious feeling, which combines
Man with the world around him, in a chain
Woven of flowers, and dipp'd in sweetness, till
He tastes the high communion of his thoughts,
With all existences in earth and heaven,
That meet him in the charm of grace and power.
'Tis not the noisy babbler, who displays,
In studied phrase, and ornate epithet,
And rounded period, poor and vapid thoughts,
Which peep from out the cumbrous ornaments
That overload their littleness. Its words
Are few, but deep and solemn; and they break
Fresh from the fount of feeling, and are full
Of all that passion, which, on Carmel, fired
The holy prophet, when his lips were coals,
His language wing'd with terror, as when bolts
Leap from the brooding tempest, armed with wrath,
Commission'd to affright us, and destroy.

THE WEAVER'S SONG.

Weave, brothers, weave!—Swiftly throw
    The shuttle athwart the loom,
And show us how brightly your flowers grow,
    That have beauty, but no perfume!
Come, show us the rose, with a hundred dyes,
    The lily that hath no spot;
The violet, deep as your true loves' eyes,
    And the little forget-me-not!
        Sing, brothers, sing! weave and sing!
            'Tis good both to sing and to weave:
        'Tis better to work than live idle;
            'Tis better to sing than to grieve.

Weave, brothers, weave!—Weave and bid
    The colours of sun-set glow!
Let grace in each gliding thread be hid,
    Let beauty about you blow!
Let your skein be long, and your silk be fine,
    And your hands both firm and sure,
And time nor chance shall your work untwine,
    But all—like a truth—endure!
        So—sing, &c.

Weave, brothers, weave!—Toil is ours;
  But toil is the lot of men:
One gathers the fruit, one gathers the flowers,
  One soweth the seed again!
There's not a creature, from the thron'd king
  To the peasant that delves the soil,
That knows half the pleasure the seasons bring,
  If he have not his share of toil!
          So—sing, &c.

VOICE OF THE PESTILENCE.

Breathless the course of the Pale White Horse,
  Bearing the ghastly form—
Rapid and dark as the spectre bark
  When it sweeps before the storm!
Balefully bright through the torrid night
  Ensanguined meteors glare—
Fiercely the spires of volcanic fires
  Stream on the sulphurous air!

Shades of the slain through the murderer's brain
  Flit terrible and drear—
Shadowy and swift the black storm drift
  Doth tremble the atmosphere!
But swifter than all, with a darker pall
  Of terror around my path,
I have arisen from my lampless prison—
  Slave of the High God's wrath!

A deep voice went from the firmament,
  And it pierced the caves of earth—
Therefore I came on my wings of flame
  From the dark place of my birth!
And it said, "Go forth from the south to the north,
  Over yon wandering ball—
Sin is the King of the doomed thing,
  And the sin-beguiled must fall!"

Forth from the gate of the Uncreate,
  From the portals of the abyss—
From the caverns dim where vague forms swim,
  And shapeless chaos is!
From Hades' womb—from the joyless tomb

Of Erebus and Old Night—
From the unseen deep where Death and Sleep
  Brood in their mystic might—
I come—I come—before me are dumb
  The nations aghast for dread—
Lo! I have past as the desert blast,
  And the millions of earth lie dead.

A voice of fear from the hemisphere
  Tracketh me where I fly—
Earth weeping aloud for her widowhood—
  A wild and desolate cry!
Thrones and dominions beneath my pinions
  Cower like meanest things—
Melt from my presence the pride and the pleasance
  Of pallor-stricken kings!
Sorrow and mourning supremely scorning,
  My throne in the boundless air—
My chosen shroud is the dark-plumed cloud—
  Which the whirling breezes bear!

Was I not borne on the wings of the morn
  From the jungles of Jessore,
Over the plain of the purple main
  To the far Mountain shore?
To the isles which sleep on the sunbright deep
  Of a coral-paved sea;
Where the blue waves welter beneath the shelter
  Of Heaven's serenity?
From the womb of the waters, athirst for slaughters,
  I rose that thirst to sate—
These green isles are graves in the waste of the waves—
  This beauty is desolate!
From the wide Erythrean the noise of my pæan
  Rolled on the southern blast—
Eternal Taurus made answering chorus
  From the glaciers lone and vast!
Did I not pass his granite mass;
  And the rigid Caucasian hill—
Over burning sands—over frost-chained lands,
  Borne at my own wild will?

Then hark to the beat of my hastening feet,
  Thou shrined in the sea;
Where are the dreams that the ocean streams
  Would be safety unto thee?
Awaken! awaken! my wings are shaken,
  Athwart the troubled sky
Streams the red glance of meteor lance
  And the glare of my eager eye.

Hearken, oh hearken! my coming shall darken
The light of thy festal cheer;
In thy storm-rocked home on the northern foam,
Nursling of Ocean—hear!*

THE MAN OF ROSS.

"Rise, honest muse, and sing the Man of Ross."

THE true history and character of the individual, to whom the muse
of Pope, thus invoked, arose and gave immortality in song, are but
little known to the world at large, although almost every reader of the
poet's lines must have felt an interest in a being so noble as the Man
of Ross was there represented to be.   John Kyrle was the proper ap-
pellation of the person whom local circumstances caused to bear the
title of the Man of Ross.   He was a native of the parish of Dymock,
in the county of Gloucester, and was born on the 22d of May, 1637.

At the decease of his father, John Kyrle, who was the elder of two
sons, found himself inheritor of little more than the family dwelling-
house in the town of Ross in Herefordshire, together with a few
patches of land in the neighbourhood.   But these possessions seem to
have been quite sufficient to maintain him respectably, as he did not
follow up the profession of the law, but permanently took up his residence in the district of his nativity.   In truth, his frugal way of life,
as well as his economical and judicious mode of managing his property,
soon placed him in the most easy circumstances, and enabled him to
make repeated accessions, by purchase, to the patrimony which had
descended to him.   But, though frugal in his habits, the subject of our
notice was far, very far indeed, from exhibiting at any period of his
career a spirit of avarice or money-hoarding.   On the contrary, he was
endowed with one of the most generous and noble hearts that ever fell
to the lot of man, and hence, in reality, his celebrity, hence the immortality of his name as the Man of Ross.   It was as a most extensive
and unostentatious benefactor of his species that Pope enshrined John
Kyrle in undying verse, and gave his name to all coming time.

The portraits of the Man of Ross display a regular, well-formed
countenance, rather square in general outline, and strikingly expressive

* The most recent accounts state that the mortality from cholera in London is frightful, and
the skill of the best physicians is exercised in vain.   In one week more than 2000 have died
in that city alone.   The disease is raging in different parts of the kingdom, among the poor
and the rich.

of mild cheerfulness and benevolence. The brow is open and expansive. In person, he was tall, thin, and well-shaped, and during his whole life his usual attire was a suit of brown, after the fashion of the day. He maintained his health by regular exercise from his youth upwards, turning his own hands to service in his favourite pursuits of horticulture and planting. A spade and a watering-pot were usually seen in his grasp, as he passed backwards and forwards between his dwelling and his fields. Having speedily increased his means, as we have said, and made his income respectable, he lived well, and enjoyed himself frequently with his friends, though much company was not agreeable to him. It was his practice, as his habits became fixed, to entertain a party of his acquaintances on every market-day, and on every fair-day, in the town of Ross. Nine, eleven, or thirteen (he seemed partial to odd numbers,) were the usual sum of the guests at the invitation dinners. His dishes were plain and good, and the only beverages which appeared on his table were malt liquor and cider. At ordinary times, moreover, he loved dearly to see his neighbours dropping in upon him in the evening, was cheerful always with them, enjoyed a pleasant tale, and was uniformly discomposed and sad when time brought round the parting hour. His character is truthfully depicted in the following lines of Pope. Throughout his long life of eighty-seven years, his benevolence did not tire—his care of the poor was incessant, he settled their disputes and ministered to their relief.

> " But all our praises why should lords engross?
> Rise, honest muse! and sing the man of Ross:
> Pleased Vaga echoes through her winding bounds,
> And rapid Severn hoarse applause resounds.
> Who hung with woods yon mountain's sultry brow?
> From the dry rock who bade the water flow?
> Not to the skies in useless columns tost,
> Or in proud falls magnificently lost,
> But clear and artless, pouring through the plain
> Health to the sick, and solace to the swain.
> Whose causeway parts the vale with shady rows?
> Whose seats the weary traveller repose?
> Who taught that heaven-directed spire to rise?
> 'The Man of Ross,' each lisping babe replies!
> Behold the market-place with poor o'erspread—
> The Man of Ross divides the weekly bread.
> He feeds yon almshouse, neat, but void of state,
> Where Age and Want sit smiling at the gate.
> Him portioned maids, apprenticed orphans bless'd,
> The young who labour, and the old who rest.
> Is any sick? the Man of Ross relieves,
> Prescribes, attends, the med'cine makes, and gives.
> Is there a variance? enter but his door,
> Balked are the courts, and contest is no more."

The town which Mr. Kyrle so long adorned was justly proud of him during his life and deeply reverenced his memory when he was laid in his tomb. The name of the Man of Ross was not bestowed in the first instance by Pope, but was previously the common and popular designation of Mr. Kyrle in the country around Ross. He never married. The poor of the district were his children and his family. From them he was removed at a venerable age, and the whole population followed the remains of the good man to the grave. He died on the 20th Nov., 1724.

FIRST IMPRESSIONS OF FATHER MATHEW. •

(From his address to the Mayor of New York, a few weeks after his arrival in America.)

FROM the moment I caught the first glimpse of American land every incident has awakened renewed pleasure and delight. I have gazed with rapture on the bold outline of your coast, and have admired the beautiful scenery of your noble bay, unrivalled for its maritime capabilities, and designed by nature as the entrepot of trade and of commerce for the Western world. I have seen your majestic rivers dotted with richly freighted vessels, bearing the teeming produce of your luxuriant soil to far distant nations; and, oh, sir, I could not look on these winged messengers of peace and plenty without associating with them the magnanimous bounty of a brave people to our afflicted nation. I have visited your busy warehouses, your thronged streets, and bustling thoroughfares, and have been forcibly struck with those exterior evidences of mercantile greatness and prosperity which shadow forth the high commercial destiny that yet awaits your already glorious republic.

I have seen in the comfort and abundance enjoyed by all, in the total absence of squalid poverty, and in the liberal remuneration which awaits honest toil, proofs of prosperity which contrast strikingly with scenes that have often harrowed my soul, in that poor old country which, trodden down and oppressed as she is, is still the land of my birth and my affections. I have visited your God-like institutions, upheld with a munificence worthy of your mighty republic, by which you imitate, at an humble distance, the mercy of the Redeemer, making "the blind to see and the dumb to speak." I have minutely inspected their internal arrangements, and witnessed, with intense satisfaction, the philanthropic system, and the absence of all religious exclusion, on which those asylums, sacred to humanity, are based and conducted.

I have also inspected with admiration that stupendous structure, the high bridge; the reservoirs sufficiently capacious to supply an abundance of the purest water to your multitudinous citizens. Magnificent works, far, far surpassing the boasted aqueducts of ancient Rome. Nor, in my intercourse amongst your people, could I overlook that manly independence of character, that decorum and self-respect, so worthy of freemen, which characterize American citizens; and which may be observed as well in the joyous celebration of their national fetes, as in their commingling with each other in the active duties of social life.

Oh, sir, what a powerful influence must the example of such a people necessarily exercise on the distresses of mankind! After years of toil and anxiety, I am cheered and consoled to find my humble efforts worthy of such high approval; and I feel inspired with a new energy to commence, with the Divine assistance, my exertions in the States under such glorious auspices.

Joining in the aspirations of one of your most distinguished Presidents, I fervently pray that "he who holds in his hands the destinies of nations may make yours worthy of the favours he has bestowed; and with pure hearts, pure hands, and sleepless vigilance, that you may guard and defend to the end of time the great charge he has committed to your keeping."

PROGRESS OF TEMPERANCE IN AMERICA.

It may be interesting to our readers to possess, in connexion with the foregoing remarks by the "Apostle of Temperance," the following statement of the beginning and progress of the Temperance reform in the United States.

"The first periodical devoted exclusively to temperance was published at Albany in New York, and was called 'the Temperance Recorder.' Of this paper twenty thousand copies of the first number were gratuitously distributed at the expense of one of our most wealthy and benevolent citizens (the Honourable Stephen Van Rensselaer, of Albany,) who, in addition, subsequently contributed large sums to advance the cause. In the course of a few years, the circulation of this paper had increased to two hundred and twenty thousand copies monthly. For two years, a Quarterly Temperance Magazine was also published, for which some of the most able men of our country were writers, it being intended chiefly to influence the educated classes. Another very important effort was the getting up of a Temperance Almanac. Of this useful publication one press alone in one year, printed seven hundred and fifty thousand copies, which were sold at about two pounds sterling the thousand. A powerful argumentative paper, entitled "the Ox Discourse," aimed particularly at the traffic, was also printed and circulated to the number of two millions and two hundred thousand—a copy for every family in our nation. While this amount of printing was going on in the state of New York, under the auspices of the Temperance Society, the Religious Tract Society issued millions of pages on the subject. The Seaman's Friend Society, also made great efforts to benefit seamen, and enlighten them as to the effect of strong drink.

"Gentlemen of wealth, who did not become members of the society, contributed largely to our funds, hoping in that way to be the means of benefiting their country. On one occasion, when a great object was to be attained, fifteen gentlemen of influence and wealth each gave one thousand dollars. The New York State Society alone has expended nearly one hundred and fifty thousand dollars, and circulated nearly fifteen millions of periodicals, tracts, almanacs, &c.

"At a very early period one of our most prominent objects was to organize the whole country into societies—the American society at the head, then the state, county, town, and school-district societies, the smallest being auxiliary to the next above it, and so on, up to the parent society, in order that once in every year the total results of the general efforts might be brought to one point. In the state of New York alone, we had about two thousand societies, numbering from four to five hundred thousand members, and in all the Union, nearly ten thousand societies, and about two millions of members. The opinion at length became very general, that to make, vend, or drink ardent spirits as a beverage, was immoral, and should cease. National and State, county and town, temperance conventions, had declared this to be their opinion; religious bodies had also expressed the same sentiment. Spirits were excluded from the sideboard and table, and few but such as disregarded public opinion were found to continue their use. Such an effect was produced on their manufacture, that out of 1200 distilleries which had existed in the state of New York at the commencement of the temperance reformation in 1826, less than 200 now remain, the consumption of ardent spirits throughout the whole Union being reduced from five-eighths to three-fourths. In consequence of facts collected with great care, and placed before the underwriters of New York, which proved beyond question, that by far the greater part of all the disasters at sea were occasioned by the use of spirit, they unanimously resolved to take off five per cent. on the premium of insurance of all vessels sailing on the temperance principle, and also voted fifteen hundred dollars to place temperance papers on board ships sailing from the various ports of the United States. This was not done as a temperance movement, but from motives of self-interest, on the same principle as they would have voted money to save any property in jeopardy. Our cause was also much benefited by the government of the United States voting to do away with the spirit rations in the army."—(*Delavan.*)

BIOGRAPHY.

—

MEHEMET ALI.

THIS celebrated man, who died recently at Alexandria, had risen from an obscure origin to a station of such distinction as few men attain to. The history of his life forms one of the most striking portions of the history of the East for a long series of years.

Mehemet Ali was born at the town of Cavalla, in Roumelia, the ancient Macedonia. In Mahommedan countries, the natives keep no reckoning of their age, and the pasha could not tell precisely what his own age was: but he was easily flattered into the belief that he was born in the same year that gave birth to the two most illustrious heroes of the present era—Napoleon Bonaparte and the Duke of Wellington —1769, thus making him at his death of the age of eighty years, which may be considered correct within a year or two. He commenced life as a tobacconist in his native town, but he afterwards volunteered into the army, to which his taste was more congenial. In his new career, he soon obtained high favour with the Governor of Cavalla, by his efficient assistance in quelling a rebellion and dispersing a band of pirates; and on the death of his commanding officer he was appointed to succeed him, and married his widow.

Mehemet Ali was installed in the pashalic of Egypt in 1806, on condition that he should send to the Sultan 4,000 purses, which represented at that time the sum of about £24,000 sterling. The pashalic of Egypt was then commonly called the pashalic of Cairo, and it extended only to Middle Egypt and the Delta; Upper Egypt being divided into several districts and administered by the Mameluke Beys, and Alexandria with a part of the western province, by a pasha independent of the pasha of Cairo. A few months after the installation of Mehemet Ali in the pashalic of Egypt, the Porte consented to give him also the pashalic of Alexandria, as a reward for the services he had rendered to the Ottoman Empire in 1807, on the occasion of the evacuation of Lower Egypt and the city of Alexandria by the English.

After the destruction of the Mamelukes, he made himself master of Upper Egypt; he obtained from the Sublime Porte the government of that part of the country, and at the same time considerably increased the land tax and the duties of customs on the internal trade.

He received orders from the Porte to attack and disperse the Wahabees, a fanatical sect of the Mahommedan religion, who had pillaged the holy cities of Mecca and Medina, and in the year 1811 he sent his army in Arabia against the Wahabees. This war lasted six years, cost the viceroy immense sums of money, and a great number of men, and was finally brought to a close by Ibrahim Pasha. In 1813, Mehemet Ali himself went to the Hedjaz for a time, to hasten the result of the expedition. During his absence, the Porte, jealous of his power, secretly appointed Lateef Pasha, viceroy of Egypt, but Mohammed Bey, Mehemet Ali's Minister of war, pretending to enter into the views of Lateef Pasha, engaged him to declare himself publicly viceroy of Egypt, and then decapitated him.

In 1815, Mehemet Ali, convinced of the great advantages of discipline and military tactics in the art of warfare, resolved upon having his army properly drilled; but his soldiers were very averse to this measure, and threatened an insurrection. He therefore sent his mutinous troops into Ethiopia, under his third son, Ismael Pasha, who on that occasion conquered the provinces of Dongola, Berber, Shendy, Sennaar, and Cordofan, whilst he raised a new army, which was drilled by French and Italian officers. He then offered the Sultan to assist in quelling the Greek insurrection against the Porte, and, on the 16th of July, 1824, Mehemet Ali's fleet, consisting of one hundred and sixty-three vessels, sailed for the Morea, under the command of Ibrahim Pasha, who, for three years, kept the country in subjection, but was obliged to retreat after the battle of Navarino on the 26th of October, 1827.

In 1830, the Porte conferred upon him the administration of the island of Candia. He then turned his thoughts to the possession of Syria, and 6,000 Egyptians having emigrated to that country he demanded the restitution of them from Abdallah Pasha, the governor of Acre. The reply he obtained was, that the emigrants were subjects of the Sublime Porte, and that they were in the Sultan's dominions as well in Syria as in Egypt. The viceroy, enraged at this answer, sent him word that he himself would come and take his 6,000 subjects, and "one man more." Accordingly, on the 2d of November, 1831, Mehemet Ali sent into Syria a powerful army, under command of his son, Ibrahim Pasha, who, in a few months, reduced the whole country to submission. On this the Porte declared Mehemet Ali a rebel, and sent a strong army into Syria, but Ibrahim Pasha's troops invariably overcame the Sultan's, and several important battles were fought, which insured to the Egyptians the possession of the country. The European powers interfered, and, under their guarantee, peace was signed on the 14th of May, 1833. Syria and the district Adana were ceded to Mehemet Ali, in conjunction with the pashalic of Egypt, on his acknowledging himself a vassal of the Sultan, and engaging to remit to the Porte the same tribute as the former pashas of Syria. According to this arrangement Mehemet Ali paid for Egypt 12,000 purses; Syria and Adana, 18,000 purses; and Candia, 2,000 purses; making together 32,000 purses, or £160,000 sterling per annum.

Mehemet Ali continued in the quiet possession of Syria until 1839, but the Porte disliked very much the occupation of that country by the Viceroy of Egypt, so that after organizing an army and a strong fleet in the beginning of 1839, the Sultan Mahmoud sent his troops into Syria under the command of Hafiz Pasha, to expel the Egyptians, but Ibrahim Pasha proved too powerful for him, and the Turkish army had to retreat. England, Austria, Russia, and Prussia, then, in conjunction with the Porte, signed a treaty on the 15th of July, 1840, and informed Mehemet Ali that he was no longer to remain in Syria; but the viceroy, confiding in the promised assistance of the French, seemed determined to keep the country.

The allied powers, finding that the viceroy would not evacuate Syria, by fair means, determined upon driving him out by force. The first engagement took place on the 10th of October, 1840, near Beyrout, when the Egyptian army was completely routed, and the town taken. Caiffa and Saida were bombarded in the same month, Tripoli and Tarsous soon followed, and on the 3d of November, of the same year, the bombardment and taking of Acre, in the short space of four hours, ought to have convinced Mehemet Ali that any further resistance was useless. The town of Alexandria was blockaded by an English squadron; still Mehemet Ali was not inclined to submit, as he entertained hopes that France would come to his aid, but in the end he found he could no longer temporize, and acceded to the terms proposed, the hereditary pashalic of Egypt in his own family being secured to him.

The withdrawal of the Egyptian troops from Syria commenced in December, 1840, when 54,000 men and 6,000 women and children took the road of the Desert to Suez; but what with sickness, desertion, privation, and the opposition they encountered on their march, not 25,000 reached Egypt. Ibrahim Pasha proceeded by sea from Gaza, with the sick and wounded, and landed at Damietta, on the 21st of February, 1841, whilst the remainder of the troops marched by El Arish. Before the evacuation of Syria, the Egyptian army consisted of 85,000 men; of these only 33,000 returned to their country.

The firman sent by the Sultan to Mehemet Ali, was dated from Constantinople, the 13th of February, 1841, and, after some modifications, was finally accepted by Mehemet Ali, on the 10th of June, 1841. The following are the conditions on which Mehemet Ali was granted the hereditary pashalic of Egypt:—

1. The succession to the government of Egypt within its ancient boundaries to descend in a direct line to Mehemet Ali's male posterity, from the elder to the elder, among the sons and grandsons—the nomination to be made by the Sublime Porte.

2. The pasha of Egypt to rank as a vizier of the Ottoman Empire, without having in his character, with the exception of hereditary right, any other prerogatives than those enjoyed by other viziers.

3. All treaties entered into between the Sublime Porte and the Euro-

pean powers are to apply to Egypt as well as to any other part of the
Ottoman Empire.

4. The pasha has authority to coin his own money in Egypt, but
the coins are to bear the name of the Sultan.

5. The standing army of Egypt is to be composed of 18,000 men,
and 400 men are to be sent yearly to Constantinople.

6. The Viceroy of Egypt has the right to appoint officers of the
land and sea forces up to the rank of colonel and below that of general
of brigade, but a general of brigade being a pasha, the Porte alone can
name pashas.

7. The Viceroy of Egypt cannot build vessels of war without authority from the Sublime Porte.

8. The yearly tribute payable by the pasha of Egypt to the Sublime Porte, fixed at $2,000,000, has since been reduced to a million
and a third of Spanish pillared dollars, about £270,000 sterling.

9. The hereditary title is liable to revocation, should any of Mehemet Ali's successors infringe any of the aforesaid conditions.

The Sublime Porte also granted to Mehemet Ali, without the hereditary succession, the government of the provinces of Nubia, Darfour,
Sennaar, and Cordofan, and all the territories annexed thereto, situate
out of Egypt.

The pasha of Egypt differs from the other pashas of the Ottoman
Empire, in that the former collects the revenues himself, whilst the law
of the empire is that pashas are not to collect the revenues.

Until last year Mehemet Ali enjoyed a very strong constitution; his
stature was short, and his features formed an agreeable and animated
physiognomy, with a searching look, expressive of cunning, nobleness,
and amiability. He always stood very upright, and it was remarkable,
from its being unusual among Turks, that he was in the habit of walking up and down in his apartments. He was most simple in his dress,
and cleanly in his person. He received strong impressions easily, and
was very frank and open, and could not easily conceal his mind. He
loved his children with great tenderness, and lived in the interior of his
family with great simplicity and freedom from restraint. He was very
fond of playing at billiards, chess, draughts, and cards. In his latter
years he became very merciful and humane, and generally forgave the
greatest faults. The European papers were translated to him, and
he was sensibly affected by any attacks directed against him. His
activity was very great. He slept little in the night, and invariably
rose before sunrise. He received daily the reports of his ministers, dictated answers, and frequently visited any improvements or changes
going on in the public works. He learned to read only at the age of
forty-five. He principally studied history, and was particularly interested with the lives of Napoleon and Alexander the Great.

The only language he spoke was Turkish; he understood Arabic,
but did not like to speak it. The late Viceroy did not observe the

tenets of the Mohammedan religion with any rigour, and never cared about fasting in the month of Ramazan.   He was the first Mohammedan ruler who granted real protection to Christians, raised them to the highest ranks, and made some of them his most intimate friends. His freedom from superstition was as remarkable as his toleration in religion, and in many instances he shook off the yoke of those absurd prejudices to which all those of his faith humbly bow their heads.

He was buried at Cairo, in a new alabaster mosque built by himself in the citadel. The procession from the palace was composed of a vast concourse of the people; of the European consuls in uniform, with many of the European residents, and a great number of troops with arms reversed.   On emerging from the palace the coffin was laid at the foot of the grand marble staircase, the attendants gathered round, and the chief mufti, a venerable old man, advanced, raised his hands, and, amidst profound silence, repeated three times, with a pause for mental reflection between each, "*Allah 'hoo akbar*," (God is great;) after which, he twice repeated, "*Salam aleykoun*," (Peace be with you;) and then the procession started, the principal officers and grandees emulating each other for the honour of carrying the coffin on their shoulders.   On passing the harem, a separate building a little to the north of the palace, the shrieks and lamentations of the women were most piercing.   Twenty-six buffaloes were killed and distributed among the poor, with twenty-six camel loads of bread and dates, and a considerable sum of money.

Mehemet Ali's first severe illness occurred in January, 1848, when he proceeded to Malta and Naples, where, having rallied a little, he returned to Egypt in April, improved in bodily health, but with his constitution shattered, and his mental faculties totally prostrated.   His appearance had undergone a complete change; his eyes had lost that searching and intelligent look for which his highness was so remarkable; his cheeks were shrunk and his voice was quite feeble.   His medical men having then declared his total unfitness to attend to the affairs of the country, the late Ibrahim Pasha assumed the reins of government, and at his death was succeeded by Abbas Pasha.   From that time until within a few weeks of his death, Mehemet Ali took his daily drive in his carriage, and lived in his palace in the same style he was wont to do, but none except his immediate attendants were permitted to approach him.

He had many children, but only five sons and three daughters are now living, viz., Said Pasha, Admiral of the Egyptian fleet, born in 1818; Haleem Bey, born in 1826; Mehemet Ali Bey, born in 1833; Nazleh Hanum, born in 1837, widow of the Defterdar Mohammed Bey; Zeinab Hanum, born in 1824, and married in 1845 to Kamil Pasha. Haleem Bey was four years in Paris, where he received a liberal education.   Mehemet Ali's second son, after the late Ibrahim Pasha, was Toussoon Pasha, born at Cavalla, who left an only son, Abbas Pasha, born in 1813, at present Viceroy of Egypt. Toussoon Pasha died of the plague at the camp of Damanhour in 1816. Mehemet Ali had also at Cavalla, by the same wife, a third son, Ismael Pasha, who died in the war in Sennaar. Another son of Mehemet Ali, Houssein Bey, born in 1825, died in 1847 at Paris, where he had been sent for his education. Mehemet Ali had twelve brothers and two sisters, all of whom are dead.

ALBERT GALLATIN. •

THE name of this eminent statesman and scholar has been honoured in this country and Europe for more than half a century. Born in a foreign land, he came early in life to America, bore arms as a volunteer during our struggle for independence, and subsequently became one of the foremost of our citizens, whether we regard his talents, his services, or his devotion to the great interests of the republic. The following sketch presents the most prominent incidents of his life, but we regret that we have not room for a more extended notice; for we believe it highly advantageous to trace the steps and to mark the progress by which great men have arrived at eminence. Great talents and splendid achievements, it is true, are necessarily confined to a few; but it is the duty of every individual to aim at excellence in his own sphere, however humble. Many of the same qualities are requisite to make a good tradesman or skilful mechanic, which are needed to form a great statesman or general. We shall find that such a man was early distinguished from the frivolous or dissolute around him by devotedness to his object; that he made it his study, his pleasure. We shall find that he was not discouraged by difficulties, but rather stimulated by them to more vigorous efforts; that he never consulted his own ease or gratification, when they stood in the way of his grand design; that he was characterized by a disregard to trifles of all sorts, and by a steady aim at the most important ends. Now as these, among other good qualities, insured to him success and distinction, so we may be assured that the same causes will produce the same effects, in whatever situations they may be applied. We select from the New York Evening Post:

"Albert Gallatin was born at Geneva, in Switzerland, on the 29th day of January, 1761. He was left an orphan in his infancy, and was educated under the maternal care of a distant relation and very dear friend of his mother. He pursued his studies in Geneva, and graduated at the University of that city in 1779. Among his teachers at that period was Müller, the celebrated historian, and among his classmates was Dumont, the friend of Mirabeau and the interpreter of Bentham.

Contrary to the wishes, but without the opposition of his relatives, Mr. Gallatin emigrated to the United States in the nineteenth year of his age. He arrived at Boston on the 14th July, 1780. A letter followed him to this country from La Rochefoucauld to Dr. Franklin, requesting him to take a little interest in Gallatin and his companion who embarked with him. Soon after his arrival in this country, the young adventurer proceeded to Maine, and resided at Machias and Passamaquoddy, where he served as a volunteer under Col. John Allen, commander of the fort of Machias; and also made some advances to support the garrison.

"In the spring of 1782, through the interest of Dr. Cooper, he was chosen instructor of the French language in Harvard University, which place, however, he soon left for the South. In the winter of 1783—4, he was engaged at Richmond, in prosecuting the claim of a foreign house, for advances made to the State of Virginia, which brought him into contact with the public men of that State, and procured for him the acquaintance and personal friendship of Patrick Henry. In 1784—5, he acquired some large tracts of land in Western Virginia, on which, with the moderate patrimony which he had then received, he determined to take up his permanent residence. Disturbances among the Indians, and other circumstances, compelled him to abandon the project, and in 1786 he purchased a place and settled in Fayette county, Pennsylvania. He was elected in the fall of 1789 a member of the Convention to amend the Constitution of Pennsylvania, in which Convention he united himself with the Democratic party. He there opposed the system of immediate electors for President, and favoured universal suffrage without distinction of colour.

"In 1790 he was elected a member of the House of Representatives of the State, to which post he continued to be re-elected till he took a seat in Congress, about two years after. He was chosen United States Senator in 1793, but was declared not entitled to a seat, because not a *citizen* under the Constitution. He was in the Senate, therefore, but two months, during which period the deliberations of that body were for the first time open to the public. Mr. Gallatin returned to Fayette county in 1794, after an absence of eighteen months, during which period, or immediately after, he married a daughter of Commodore Nicholson, a distinguished officer of the revolutionary war.

"Shortly after his return, broke forth the famous 'whiskey insurrection,' which originated in Allegheny county, about fifty miles from his residence, out of the forcible resistance to the serving of writs against distillers who had not paid the excise. Forty such writs had been issued, of which thirty-four were against distillers in Fayette county, and had been served without opposition. The distillers then met and determined to resist. In the rebellion which followed, Mr. Gallatin was active in resisting the adoption of warlike and treasonable resolutions, and gradually procuring for the United States commissioners a favourable reception.

"On the 14th of October, 1795, he was again elected, by the concurring vote of all parties, member of the Legislature, and the same day, and without his knowledge, a member of Congress for the adjacent district of Washington and Allegheny counties. He took his seat in Congress in December, 1795, and was elected by the same district three successive terms, and would have been the fourth, but for the accession of Thomas Jefferson to the Presidency, by whom he was appointed Secretary of the Treasury, in 1801.

"Mr. Gallatin addressed himself at once to the extinguishment of the public debt, which amounted to over $100,000,000. Between the 1st of April, 1801, and the 1st of January, 1812, the disbursement on account of the public debt was $52,400,000.

"In 1813, he was appointed one of the commissioners to Ghent, and during his absence negotiated at London the commercial convention between this country and England which succeeded the war. The rest of his public life was passed in the diplomatic service. He was a minister to France from 1816 to 1823, within which period he was deputed in 1817 to the Netherlands, and in 1818 to England, to which country he was appointed Minister Plenipotentiary in 1826. He returned to this country in 1827, and took up his residence in the city of New York. During this period he has constantly kept his eye upon public affairs, though not taking any public responsibilities.

"In 1840 he published an essay on the North-eastern Boundary question, and more recently an historical dissertation upon the map of Mr. Jay, which was read before the New York Historical Society. He has also, since his retirement, published two elaborate and ingenious pamphlets on the currency. To Mr. Gallatin, as much as any one, the public owes the resumption of specie payments by the banks of New York, in May, 1838.

"During his retirement, Mr. Gallatin made several valuable contributions to the New York Historical and Ethnological Societies, besides those we have referred to."

He died at Astoria, near New York, on the 12th of August, 1849. Our limits will not permit us to descant upon his merits as a statesman, a scholar, and a citizen. His career has been an eventful one, and he died full of years and honour.

In the obituary for May last will be found a notice of the death of Mrs. Gallatin, a lady of great worth, whom in the short space of three months Mr. Gallatin has followed to the grave. His funeral obsequies were performed at Trinity Church, New York, on the 14th of August, and the following gentlemen were the pall bearers: Cornelius W. Lawrence, Dr. J. A. Smith, Judge S. Jones, Judge Ulshœffer, William B. Astor, Beverly Robinson, Robert Hyslop, and Dr. Watson.

OBITUARY NOTICES.

*JUNE, 1849.

Died, at Goshen, New Hampshire, MRS. ELIZABETH GRINDELL, at the advanced age of 104 years. She leaves a descendant of the fifth generation.

At Ogechee, some weeks previous, MRS. LOURANIA THROWER, who was at least *one hundred and thirty-three* years of age.

At a census taken in 1825, her age was put down at 110, and some accounts made her 137 at the time of her death. She had seven children before the revolution; her youngest living child is between 70 and 80; she has great-grand-children 30 years old, and a number of great-great-great-grand children living in Florida. Her sight failed her for a while, but returned about 20 years ago, so that she could thread a needle, or read the finest print. Her faculties remained almost unimpaired till her death. She had been a member of the Baptist Church for more than a hundred years.

In England, GEN. CHARLTON, of the British army, at the advanced age of ninety-four years, seventy-seven of which he spent in the military service of his country, which he entered as a cadet, saw much active service, hard fighting included, and had the good fortune to be "gazetted," as they say in England, in every grade.

At Rush, Monroe County, New York, CAPTAIN ELNATHAN PERRY, ninety years old. He was a venerable relict of the revolutionary era —having entered the army at fifteen, and fought at Bennington, Saratoga, Monmouth, Eutaw, Yorktown, and many other fields of the war for independence.

At Dublin, Ireland, CLARENCE MAGNAN, a somewhat distinguished writer. He died in abject penury. He was well known by his poetical translations from German literature, being the author of "Anthologia Germanica," "Leaflets from the German Oak," and a variety of essays in the "University Magazine." The misery in which he lived for many years was very great, as his wretched health prevented him from labour. Within the last ten days he was an inmate of one of the temporary hospitals provided for cholera patients.

15th. In England, SIR CHARLES R. VAUGHAN, formerly ambassador to the United States. He was the fourth son of Dr. Vaughan, a physician of considerable reputation at Leicester, whose care in the educa-

---

* A part of the Obituary of June, 1849, will be found in the June number.

tion of his sons is testified in the success achieved by several of them in their respective professions. Besides the subject of this notice, one of these was the late Sir John Vaughan, one of the justices of the Court of Common Pleas. Sir Charles Vaughan was originally designed for the medical profession, and took the degree of M. B. at Oxford. He obtained a travelling fellowship on the Ratcliffe foundation, and was thus led in the earlier period of his life to visit many countries in Europe and Asia. In 1809 he acted as private secretary in the Foreign-office, having been appointed by Earl Bathurst. In the following year he became, under the administration of the Marquis of Wellesley, Secretary of Legation and Embassy in Spain, and was Minister Plenipotentiary to the Confederated States of Switzerland, and in 1825 Envoy Extraordinary to the United States of America, having been sworn a member of the Privy Council.

Hon. CALVIN BLYTHE of Philadelphia, an eminent lawyer. At a meeting of the members of the Philadelphia bar, held on the 20th June, his public services and private worth were noticed after the following manner:

"Calvin Blythe, whose death, we in common with our fellow citizens deplore, was born in the county of Adams, where he also died. In this county, the career of his usefulness as a citizen, and his greatness as a man commenced. In 1813 he marched as a private soldier in a company of Adams county volunteers to the North-Western frontier. He was at the battle of Chippewa, Lundy's Lane, Buffalo, and at the storming of Fort Erie. He was by the side of the gallant Adjutant Poe, who fell at Chippewa, and was appointed his successor. At the close of the war he returned to his native county and completed his law studies. He commenced the practice of law at Mifflintown, (then) Mifflin county, and was successful. The people showed their appreciation of him by electing him to the House of Representatives, and afterwards to the Senate. He was appointed Secretary of the Commonwealth by Gov. Shultz; and he was twice appointed President Judge of the Judicial district composed of Dauphin, Lebanon, and Schuylkill counties. He was twice appointed Collector of the Port of Philadelphia.

"After the expiration of the term of his office as Collector under President Tyler, he devoted the remainder of his life to the practice of the law at the Philadelphia Bar, where his kindness of heart as well as his professional worth, caused him to be most highly cherished.

"The death of such a man is not only a loss to be lamented by the Bar, of which he was a most esteemed member, but by the community at large, of which he was one of the most useful members as well as purest ornaments."

20th. At Paris, of cholera, MADAME CAVAIGNAC, the mother of the celebrated Gen. Cavaignac.

At the city of Paris, GEN. DONADIEU, who took a prominent part in politics under Louis XVIII. and Charles X.

Also, recently, at the same place, LADY BLESSINGTON, an English lady, and MADAME RECAMIER, a French lady; both were celebrated for their personal charms and accomplishments, and received the homage of many distinguished personages in Europe. The latter was frequently visited by kings and princes.

22*d*. In Greenville Co., Virginia, MRS. E. MASON, the mother of John Y. Mason, late Secretary of the Navy, aged seventy-six years. About a month before, her husband died at the age of eighty. They were distinguished by all the virtues which grace private life, and had been married fifty-seven years.

At Lexington, Ky., ELISHA J. WINTER, ESQ., formerly President of the Lexington and Ohio Rail-Road Company.

The Louisville Courier says that a wayward son of Mr. Winter's, who had long been estranged from his father, upon hearing of the illness of his parent, hurried from Cincinnati to Lexington to nurse him. He performed his filial duties with fidelity, was attacked with cholera at the funeral, and died. And thus, of a large family of the most promising boys in Lexington, but two survive Mr. Winter—and one of them has long been an inmate of the Lunatic Asylum.

At Albany, N. Y., HON. HARMANUS BLEECKER, formerly Minister of the United States to the Hague; a gentleman of fine acquirements, and excellent sense, who deservedly stood high in the estimation of his fellow citizens.

In Russia, MAJOR WHISTLER, a celebrated American Engineer, who was in the employ of the Emperor; and under whose direction the great rail-roads of Russia have been constructed.

JULY, 1849.

In Gallatin, Ky., CAPTAIN JACOB WATTS, one of the very earliest settlers of the Miami Valley, in the ninety-third year of his age. While a boy he left New Jersey, with his father's family, for the Redstone settlement, on the western frontier of Pennsylvania, and was at that place when the Declaration of Independence was adopted and published. He mingled freely in the frontier conflicts of the revolutionary war, and the Cincinnati Chronicle says of his subsequent career:

"He was one of the small party that planted themselves at the mouth of the Little Miami, and commenced the village of Columbia in the fall of 1788, which was the first settlement made within the limits of Judge Symmes's purchase. Being a bold, fearless adventurer, he left the settlement, erected a block-house on his land, seven or eight miles in the wilderness, to which he removed his family, and began an improvement soon after the commencement of the Indian war which was terminated by the treaty of Greenville in 1795. During the war his block-house was attacked by a strong party of Indians, who were repulsed and compelled to retreat."

In Rahway, New Jersey, of cholera, MARY KNIGHT, sister of the brave Gen. Worrall, at the age of ninety. She was one of those devoted women that helped to relieve the horrible sufferings of Washington's army at Valley Forge—cooking and carrying provisions to them, alone through the depth of winter, even passing through the outposts of the British army in the disguise of a market woman. And when Washington was compelled to retreat before a superior force, she had the tact and courage to conceal her brother, Gen. Worrall, (when the British set a price on his head for his bravery,) in a cider hogshead in the cellar for three days, and fed him through the bung-hole; the house in the mean time being ransacked four different times at Frankfort, Pennsylvania, by the British troops in search of him, without success.

3d. At Sandystown, New Jersey, REV. JAMES G. FORCE, at the age of eighty-four—and fifty-seventh of his ministry. He was a graduate of Princeton College, and at the time of the Revolutionary war, although a youth, he took up arms in defence of his country, and participated in the battle of Springfield, New Jersey.

4th. In Boston, HON. JOHN R. ADAN. He graduated at Harvard University in 1813, and read law in the office of the late Judge William Prescott, in that city. He presided over the City Council several years, represented Suffolk County in the Senate, and was several times a Counsellor of the Government. Distinguished by his sound judgment, unerring prudence, and honourable fidelity, he passes away most sincerely respected and deeply lamented.

At Hanover, Indiana, of cholera, REV. SYLVESTER SCOVEL, D. D., President of Hanover College. He was born March 3d, 1796. He graduated at Williams College in 1822, pursued his theological studies at Princeton, was licensed by the Presbytery of Albany, and preached between four and five years in New Jersey and Pennsylvania. In 1820 he went to the West as a missionary of the Board of Missions; and after labouring about seven years as a missionary and a pastor, he was appointed an agent of the Board, in the service of which he spent eleven years. He became President of Hanover College in 1846, a little less than three years ago.

5th. At Cincinnati, of cholera, MRS. DR. REDINGTON. She was the wife of a physician, and herself a practitioner. The disease which carried her off was occasioned by fatigue in constant attention to a sick patient. She is spoken of as a most exemplary woman in all the walks of life. As a physician, she promised well, and though not presented to the world with the same eclat as Miss Blackwell, she was considered one of the pioneers in that branch of medical reform.

At Mobile, Ala., COLONEL JAMES DUNCAN, Inspector General of the army of the United States. He was born in the vicinity of Newburgh, New York, and was, at the time of his death, about thirty-eight years of age. He graduated at the Military Academy at West Point in 1835. After graduating, he entered the army as lieutenant of the 4th regiment of artillery, in which capacity he served in the Seminole war. He was with Gen. Gaines at Withlacoochee, in Florida, and was there slightly wounded. In command of a portion of the light artillery, he joined the army of General Taylor at Corpus Christi.

He highly distinguished himself at Palo Alto, with Ringgold and Ridgely. At Resaca de la Palma, after May, with his dragoons, had taken the battery of Gen. La Vega, we find Duncan, with his light artillery, advancing upon and routing the dense bodies of the Mexican cavalry and their serried ranks of infantry.

Ringgold, Duncan and Ridgely, in those two battles, did much to illustrate the efficiency of an arm of warfare which was before but little appreciated in our country. Those splendid achievements, to which Colonel Duncan largely contributed, established the prestige of our arms, and laid the foundation of our future success.

For his services there, Lieut. Duncan was promoted to a captaincy, and afterwards was raised to the brevet rank of Lieut. Colonel. Again he was found at Monterey, in the midst of the foremost in that glorious victory. Again was he rewarded by a promotion to the rank of Colonel.

It were impossible in this brief notice to do justice to the merits of Colonel Duncan, or to illustrate his gallantry and his services by any elaborate detail of his achievements. After he joined the forces under General Scott, he and his already famous wing of the artillery were found at Vera Cruz, at Cerro Gordo, at Churubusco, at Molino Del Rey, and at the gates of Mexico. Wherever the services of that arm of warfare could be called into action, and opportunity presented, it was availed of by the gallant Duncan. The services he rendered to his country in all those brilliant battles won for him an enviable distinction and an enduring fame.

On his return to the United States, after the closing of the campaign, he was received, honoured and feasted, as his brilliant achievements merited. Further honours from his grateful country awaited him. The death of Col. Croghan, Inspector General of the army, gave to the President the opportunity to do signal honour to the gallant Duncan, and confer upon him a substantial reward. He was appointed to fill the vacancy occasioned by the death of Col. Croghan. In the performance of the duties of this office the messenger of death found him.

8th. At Quebec, JOHN WILSON, the vocalist. He introduced many new pieces of music into the United States.

9th. At St. Louis, Missouri, Pierre Choteau, Esq., in his ninety-first year. He was one of the founders of St. Louis, and the last survivor of the La Clede party.

At Washington, D. C., Mrs. D. P. Madison, widow of James Madison, fourth President of the United States. She was born on the 20th May, 1767, and was eighty-three years old at the time of her death.
The maiden name of this venerated lady was Paine. She was born in Virginia, but her parents, who were members of the Society of Friends, removed, while she was yet very young, to Philadelphia.
Before she had attained the age of twenty she married a gentleman by the name of Todd, who died within three years after, leaving her the mother of an only son. We have heard that Mr. Madison formed the acquaintance of the young Mrs. Todd, while he was a boarder at the house of her mother. He married her in 1794, he being at the time a member of Congress. During the Presidency of her husband, Mrs. Madison presided as the female head of the family, and sustained that position in the executive residence with grace and dignity.
Upon the expiration of Mr. Madison's presidential service, she retired with him to Montpelier, in Orange county, Virginia, where she administered, with a warmth and a grace of manner never surpassed, all the rights of hospitality, in the house of her distinguished husband. Visited by crowds of American citizens, and by strangers from Europe who were desirous of seeing so noble a statesman, no one ever left his house without carrying away with him the strongest sense of the courtesies and accomplishments of his lady. After his death, she continued to reside at Montpelier, and finally came to Washington, in 1843, to reside at her house on President's Square, where she breathed her last.
No distinguished stranger ever visited Washington who did not consider it his duty as well as his pleasure to wait upon her and pay his respects to her. Blessed almost to the last with good spirits and the kindest social feelings, she mixed in the society of all her old friends in Washington with a kindness and warmth of manner which attracted every heart and eye around her.
She was the most considerate and polite person we have ever known. Instead of pushing herself forward on any occasion, and even claiming what was due to her, she would, on the contrary, disclaim all pretensions and distinctions. She seemed determined to sacrifice all idle etiquette, and all selfish discrimination, to the ease and happiness of others. With that exquisite tact which arose from her sagacious mind, and with that delicate sympathy which was the fruit of her good and generous feelings, she was ever willing to give up her own place and her own comfort for those around her. Her circumstances were in perfect accordance with her disposition, and the liberal gifts of fortune were liberally participated with all around her. The happiness she herself enjoyed, she bestowed on others; and the sunshine of her own bosom

gladdened with its warmth and brightness the little world of which she was the centre—her family and friends.

11th. At Louisville, Ky., F. F. Chew, Esq., of the State of Mississippi. He was on his way with his wife and five children to Washington, where he was to fill a situation under the government, when he was attacked by cholera.

12th. At 'Tunbridge Wells, Eng., Horace Smith, the poet and novelist, in his seventieth year. His brother James, who shared with him the authorship of the "Rejected Addresses," died some years ago. Horace was also the author of Brambletye House and some other novels which had a certain degree of success in their day. He is described as "a man of correct taste and the most generous sympathies, a delightful writer both in verse and prose, a cheerful and wise companion, and a fast friend. No man had a wider range of admirable and genial qualities; and far beyond that private circle of which he was the great charm and ornament, his loss will be deeply felt. To those who had the advantage of his friendship, it is irreparable."

At New Orleans, Thomas Tobey, Esq. He was one of the oldest and most respectable merchants of that city. He was a native of Philadelphia.

14th. At St. Louis, Lieut. Col. Samuel MacRee, of the United States army, in his forty-ninth year. Col. MacRee was long attached to the army, and had seen much active service. He was in the Florida war, and during the Mexican war was a most efficient officer in his department. So well was his conduct appreciated by the government, that the brevet of lieutenant colonel was conferred on him for his services on the Rio Grande.

At Lexington, Ky., Daniel Bradford, Esq., of cholera. He was for a long time connected with the press of Kentucky, and was much respected by his fellow-citizens. Daniel Bradford was the son of John Bradford, the pioneer of printing in the West. The elder Bradford established the Kentucky Gazette in Lexington, when a large part of Kentucky was a wilderness, and the North-western Territory was the home of savages. Upon the retirement of John Bradford from the editorship of the paper, Daniel Bradford assumed it, and conducted the paper in an able, judicious, and gentlemanly manner. Mr. Bradford was a magistrate of Fayette county for many years, and was an upright and faithful citizen.

14th. At Pensacola, Samuel C. Lawrason, M. D., Surgeon U. S. Navy, and Surgeon of the Germantown sloop of war.

The death of this good and most estimable man—the valuable officer, the firm and sincere friend, has been greatly regretted by those who have known him long and well. His great devotion to his duties, his long and most efficient and arduous sea service, brought him to an early tomb.

16th. At New York, of cholera, DAVID B. OGDEN, ESQ., one of the oldest and ablest lawyers in the United States. He had been likened to the late distinguished Jeremiah Mason, of Boston, on account of his tall physical form, and his intellectual powers, and more particularly for his style and manner of pleading, which are said to have much resembled Mr. Mason's. Mr. Ogden bore a high character for integrity as well as talents, so much so that it was remarked by one who had known him for years, that *" incorrupta fides "* ought to be inscribed on his tomb.

At a meeting of the bar at which the Hon. Samuel Jones presided, Hiram Ketchum, Esq., said that:—"his earliest recollections ran not back to the time when Mr. Ogden stood not at the head of his profession in the State, and regretted that so few of the glorious associates of his day remain among us.—Mr. Ogden early stood before this bar as no unworthy competitor with Emmet, of Hamilton, of Harison, of Henry, of Wells and of Williams. But where are they? There remains nothing of them but the recollection of their burning eloquence and their personal virtues.—We cannot say that our much esteemed friend was prematurely taken from among us, for we had enjoyed the honour and example of his society for several years; but he has now gone down to the grave full of years and full of honours. He was a man of truth; of plain exterior—ostentation dare not approach him—his intellect, like his person, was majestic—to his professional brethren his heart was always open and fair."

He more than once represented the city of New York, in the Legislature of the State, but he never sought political preferment. He desired rather the distinctions of his profession. Mr. Ogden was a sincere Christian, and the qualities of his heart as well as of his head were of the highest order.

19th. At Thompson, Connecticut, the REV. DANIEL DOW, D. D., in the seventy-seventh year of his age, and the fifty-third of his pastoral relation to the First Congregational Church in that town. During his long life Dr. Dow was distinguished among the clergy of Connecticut for his abilities, his uprightness, his interest in all the concerns of education, public improvement, and philanthropy, and for many years was one of the trustees of Yale College, while he was among the original founders and ever an efficient friend of the Theological Seminary at East Windsor.

22d. At Red Sulphur Springs, Tenn., MAJOR JAMES M. SCANTLAND. He was a volunteer in the Mexican war, and fought at Monterey and Cerro Gordo. At the latter place he received a severe wound in the head, to which his death is ascribed.

23d. At New York, of cholera, JOHN L. LAWRENCE, ESQ, a very prominent and influential citizen and at the time of his death, City Comptroller. He was one of the Secretaries of the Commissioners—

Messrs. Adams, Gallatin, Clay, and Russell—who negotiated the Treaty of Peace with Great Britain at Ghent. He was chosen a member of the Legislature from New York, and took a distinguished part in the formation of the State constitution in 1822. He was frequently elected to the Legislature, and for the last two years he has been in the Senate of this State. He was a lawyer of high standing, but seldom appeared at the bar. His pursuits were more confined to the settlement of large estates. For many years he has had confided to his care large and important trusts, all of which he has managed with great fidelity.

25th. At St. Louis, MR. SYLVESTER LABADIE, in his seventy-first year. Like all of that class who never, by contact with other and later generations, lost their character for simplicity and real worth, Mr. Labadie, though living much retired from the world, yet enjoyed the respect of all who knew him.

29th. At Port Chester, West Chester Co., N. Y., HON. JOHN I. MORGAN, the father-in-law of Gen. John A. Dix, in his eighty-first year. He was well known as an eminent democratic politician, and had filled the posts of Alderman, member of Congress, and Collector of the port of New York, and possessed great kindness of heart and urbanity of manner.

At Philadelphia, DANIEL J. DESMOND, ESQ., for many years consul for several Italian States.

At Cambridge, Mass., WILLIAM MANNING, in his eighty-fourth year. He was the oldest printer in the State, having been a member of the old firm of *Manning & Loring*, publishers in Spring Lane, Boston. He was afterwards Messenger to the Governor and Council at the State House; and in every capacity acquitted himself with fidelity and ability.

29th. At Lisbon, Portugal, CHARLES ALBERT, Ex-King of Sardinia, after intense suffering. His body was embalmed, and placed in the cathedral, to await the arrival of a steamer appointed to take his remains to Genoa. On his death being known, the church-bells of Oporto were tolled, minute guns were fired, and the public offices were ordered to be closed for three days. A general mourning was likewise directed, to last for eight days, as an additional mark of respect to the deceased.

AUGUST, 1849.

1st. Near Frederick, Maryland, JAMES LARNED, Esq., Chief Clerk in the office of the First Comptroller of the Treasury. He was the type of courtesy, manliness, and integrity. Confided in by all, he was pre-eminently the friend of the orphan and the widow, for whom he had ever an attentive ear and a helping hand.

At St. Louis, Mo., of the prevailing epidemic, Rev. WHITING GRIS-

WOLD, rector of St. John's church in that city. He nobly fell at his post, a faithful, exemplary, and universally beloved clergyman; who for several weeks had zealously devoted himself, day and night, to the unremitting discharge of duty, in visiting the couches of the sick and dying.

At New York, Dr. A. T. HUNTER, a distinguished physician; also, PHILIP I. ARCULARIUS, one of the oldest citizens, a man of unaffected simplicity and great kindness of heart.

At Germantown, Pa., JOSEPH N. TAGERT, Esq., at the advanced age of 92.   The deceased was for forty years President of the Farmers' and Mechanics' Bank of Philadelphia.

At Kingston, U. C., THE COUNTESS OF ERROL, aged 21, the daughter of the Honourable Charles Gore, the Major-General commanding in Upper Canada, and was married only a short time since to the Earl of Errol, an officer in the Rifle Brigade; on which occasion, it is said, the Queen, and others of the royal family, sent her magnificent presents.

3d. At Lexington, Ky., of cholera, Hon. AARON K. WOOLLEY, aged 50, formerly Judge of the Circuit Court; State Senator for many years from the Fayette district; and, at the time of his decease, was Law Professor in Transylvania University, and one of the candidates for the Convention in his district.

4th. At Rutherfordton, N. C., JOSHUA FORMAN, at the age of 72. This venerable man was the original founder of Syracuse, and, as early as the year 1807, introduced the first resolution in the New York Legislature for an inquiry into the expediency of connecting Lake Erie with the Hudson by a canal.

At Lansingburgh, N. Y., ALEXANDER WALSH, Esq., in his 61st year, for many years one of the most active and energetic merchants in the county of Rensselaer, and an early and devoted friend to agriculture.

In London, Rev. C. B. ST. GEORGE, Chaplain of the Tower. He was seized with cholera whilst preaching.

In New York, WM. H. IRELAND, a prominent citizen and active politician for many years.

In Beaver County, Pa., General JOHN MITCHELL. He was twice Sheriff of Centre County, and twice elected to Congress.   He was the first Engineer on the Erie Extension Canal, and superintended the construction of the French Creek Feeder; repeatedly represented his fellow-citizens in the State Legislature, and under Gov. Wolf was appointed Canal Commissioner, and served in that capacity until Gov. Ritner's election.

At Chestnut Park, Herts, Eng., Mrs. CROMWELL RUSSELL, only

daughter and heiress of Oliver Cromwell, Esq., who was the grandson of Henry Cromwell, Lord Deputy of Ireland, and third son of the Lord Protector Oliver Cromwell. After the death of Oliver Cromwell, in 1658, Richard, his eldest son, succeeded to the sovereign power, but his rule lasted only seven months and twenty-eight days. He preferred the tranquillity of private life, and survived, in retirement, to the advanced age of eighty-seven. Pennant, the quaint historian, mentions that his father had told him that he used often to see, at the Don Saltero Coffee-house at Chelsea, poor Richard Cromwell, "a little and very neat old man, with a most placid countenance, the effect of his innocent and unambitious course." Richard left no male issue; consequently, the representation of the Lord Protector's family was carried on by the descendants of his (Richard's) next brother, Henry, of whom, as we have already stated, Mrs. Cromwell Russell was the heir and representative.

At Philadelphia, Charles Chauncey, Esq., a highly respected gentleman, distinguished for his abilities as a lawyer, and for his courtesy and kindness in all the relations of life.

At New York, Signor De Begnis, the celebrated musician.

At Bangor, Maine, William Abbott, Esq., the Mayor of that city, aged 73 years.

At Astoria, near New York, Hon. Albert Gallatin, aged 89. (See Biographical notice.)

14*th*. At New Haven, Conn., Thomas G. Woodward, Esq., one of the editors of the New Haven Daily Courier, aged 61.

17*th*. At Baltimore, Rev. Daniel E. Reese, a much respected clergyman of the Methodist Episcopal Church, and one of the oldest in Baltimore.

In England, Rev. Henry Coleman, an American well known for his devotion to the study of agriculture. He was about to return home, and had actually engaged his passage, but died before the day of his departure. With him, agriculture was an absorbing passion, aside from the more important duties of his vocation, and he gave to its study a power of mind which enabled him to gather the richest and most valuable results. He has left much behind him that the agriculturist has reason to be grateful for; but the seal of death is on more that would have led to greater and more beneficent results. Few persons have enjoyed such opportunities as he of studying European agriculture; and, had his life been continued a few years longer, the harvest of knowledge he reaped by observation and close investigation, would have been put forth for the general benefit. It has passed away with him, and there is, therefore, the double regret for an accomplished and pious man departed, and the loss of what would have been of incalculable value to agriculturists.

At St. Louis, at the hospital of the Sisters of Charity, Captain DAN DRAKE HENRIE. He is noted for his hair-breadth escapes from the Mexicans, when taken prisoner with Cassius M. Clay, and others. When the war broke out between Texas and Mexico, he entered the army at the age of sixteen—was taken prisoner at Mier—subsequently joined the Rangers under Col. Jack Hays, and with M'Culloch, Walker, and other indomitable spirits who composed that band, will long be remembered for their daring achievements.

19*th*. At Brooklyn, L. I., Rev. JOHN CROES, aged 63. He was the son of the late Bishop Croes, of New Jersey.

At Indianapolis, Rev. JOHN M'ARTHUR, D. D., formerly Professor in the Miami University, Ohio.

At York, Pa., Rev. LEWIS MAYER, D. D., Professor in the Theological Seminary of the German Reformed Church.

In Frederick, Md., COL. JOHN THOMAS, aged 85, the father of ex-governor Francis Thomas.

At Utica, N. Y., THOMAS ROCKWELL, Esq., in his 74th year, Cashier of the Branch Bank at Utica. In alluding to Mr. Rockwell, the Utica Observer says: "He was always as regular as time itself, at the bank, and finally sank down as he was standing at his desk, and literally died at his post."

20*th*. At Avon Springs, N. Y., COL. EDMUND KIRBY, Paymaster of the United States army. Colonel Kirby joined the army as an Ensign of the 4th Infantry, in July, 1812, and served with distinction during that war as aid to Major General Brown. He joined the army under General (now President) Taylor soon after the battles of Palo Alto and Resaca de la Palma, and acted as a volunteer aid to General Taylor at the battle of Monterey. When the regular troops of General Taylor's army were ordered to join the army under General Scott, Colonel Kirby was attached to General Scott's command, and served under that distinguished officer, as chief of the pay department, while the army remained in Mexico, Just two years prior to the day of his death he was in the sanguinary conflict at Churubusco. And throughout the whole war he was eminently distinguished for energy, activity, and zeal. His wife was a daughter of General Jacob Brown.

At Washington, D. C., LUND WASHINGTON, Jr., Esq., aged 56. Mr. Washington was favourably known in connexion with the public press of that city some years ago, and lately as a clerk in the State Department.

At Providence, R. I., CYRUS BUTLER, Esq., aged 82. Mr. Butler was the wealthiest man in the State, probably the wealthiest in New England. He was the chief benefactor of the Hospital for the Insane, which bears his name, and to which he contributed $40,000.

22d. At Brooklyn, N. Y., REV. THOMAS BURCH, aged 81. He was connected with the ministry of the Methodist Episcopal Church for nearly half a century, and was highly esteemed by all who knew him.

24th. In Orange County, N. Y., S. S. SEWARD, Esq., the venerable father of Ex-Governor Seward of New York, he bequeathed to a school called the Seward Institute $20,000 besides their house and lot.

At South Hingham, Mass., COL. WASHINGTON CUSHING, in his 75th year. He was an officer in the war of 1812.

At Brookline, Mass., REV. JOHN PIERCE, aged 76· He was a strenuous and early advocate of total abstinence, and a famous pedestrian.

In New York, REV. AUSTIN DICKINSON, an editor of some celebrity. Besides other publications, he conducted the *National Preacher* for many years with much success.

25th. At Cleveland, Ohio, Hon. AUSTIN E. WING, of Michigan. He was for many years a Delegate in Congress from the Territory of Michigan, and since the admission of that State into the Union, he has held various offices there. Until recently he was U. S. Marshal. He was about 58 years of age, and was a man much esteemed.

At Schenectady, N. Y., REV. JOHN AUSTIN SALES, D. D., of cholera. He was a professor in Union College.

27th. At Morristown, N. J., Hon. GABRIEL H. FORD, at the advanced age of 85 years. Though his life had been thus protracted beyond the period of active usefulness, the intelligence of his death was received through a wide circle of friends with emotions of sorrow and regret. He was, we believe, the oldest surviving member of the New Jersey bar, having been more than half a century one of its conspicuous ornaments. After a long and successful practice, he was appointed Presiding Judge of the Court of Common Pleas for the eastern district of the State, and in November, 1820, was elevated to the bench of the Supreme Court as one of the Associate Justices, which place he continued to occupy with honour and ability for twenty-one years: after which long public service he retired with the confidence and respect of all parties to the enjoyment of private life.

At Paris, of old age, M. RAY, one of the distinguished members of the court of Charles X.

At Cincinnati, of the cholera, J. P. HARRISON, M. D., Professor in the Ohio Medical College—an able physician and a pious man.

At Utica N. Y., Dr. Amariah Brigham, Superintendent of the Lunatic Asylum. He was formerly a physician of high popularity in Hartford, and when called to the Utica Asylum, was Superintendent of the Connecticut Retreat for the Insane. He was a man of great benevolence and purity of character.

DOCUMENTS

AND

STATE PAPERS.

THE two following papers, which we have inserted under this title may be regarded as not strictly belonging to it. We shall therefore be excused for offering an explanation.

Having heretofore given extracts from one of them, a strong desire was expressed by many of our readers to have both papers entire; and we promised that when a fitting opportunity offered we would publish them under the head of documents and state papers, as their great length forbid the insertion elsewhere.

It will be seen that they are the productions of Judge Upshur, formerly secretary of state of the United States, and of the Hon. John C. Spencer, also a late and distinguished member of the cabinet. The first paper embraces the views of Mr. Upshur on the Constitution of the United States, as furnished by him to Mr. Macgregor of London, who obtained also the examination of those views by Mr. Spencer, and embodied them all in his great work or report, on the progress and resources of America, prepared by order of the committee of the Privy Council, and presented to both houses of parliament. They thus became in one sense state papers and *documentary* explanations of the American constitution.

Neither of these papers have been published in this country, and indeed very few copies of the large and elaborate book in which they are contained have ever found their way to our private or public libraries, and through no other medium have they been presented to the public eye. But having been published in Europe by authority as the received constructions by the northern and southern sections of the Union, of the Constitution of the United States, they may justly be classed among the important and remarkable productions of the day, and should be regarded with deep interest by every intelligent and inquiring citizen, however much he may differ from some of the opinions advanced.

We trust, too, that they may beget an anxiety to understand more thoroughly the true exposition of our constitution, to abide by its spirit, and maintain it in its integrity as the true bond of the Federal Union.

We insert with the articles the preliminary remarks of Mr. Macgregor on the constitution of the United States, and his introductory notices of the distinguished authors.—(ED. OF REG.)

From Macgregor's Report to Parliament, on the Regulations, Resources, &c. of the United States of North America.

In comparing the government of the United States of America with those of other nations, we must remember that when the Anglo-American colonies declared their independence, their moral and physical condition was very different from that of all republics which had previously existed, or that have since arisen. The people were generally intelligent, their habits frugal and industrious; and, unlike the Europeans of South America, their ideas were free from the thraldom of religious intolerance.

The abilities of the great men who conducted their assemblies were solid rather than brilliant; practical rather than theoretical. They had the good sense and discrimination, notwithstanding their separation from the government of the mother country, to adopt the constitution and laws of the then most free government on earth as the ground-work of theirs : making a royal hereditary chief magistrate, a titled privileged nobility, and a national church establishment, the only remarkable exceptions.

Their immense territory, with soils yielding every production under heaven, and abounding in numerous navigable rivers, lakes, and harbours,— fisheries, woods, and minerals, placed all natural advantages in their immediate possession.

Their language and education enabled them to enjoy all the benefits of English knowledge and literature, without the labour or expense of translation, or paying for copyrights. They had also the earliest advantages of discoveries in the arts and sciences, without restrictions as to the rights of patents.

With the peculiar good fortune of being governed at that critical period by honest men, they had the knowledge of all ages and countries to guide them.

Possessing, therefore, such extraordinary advantages, the Anglo-Americans were enabled to avoid most of the blunders committed by the Spanish-American republics. It was the misfortune of the latter to have been, previously to their independence, ruled, or rather awed into passive obedience, by the most darkening monarchical and ecclesiastical government; a government and hierarchy that grew up, and acquired strength, during centuries of ignorance, tyranny, bigotry and intolerance ; under a government and a church that profited not by the march of modern civilization and religious liberty, but that enchained the liberty of written and spoken language, and the expansion of the intellectual faculties. Neither had the history of the Spanish colonies, in their first settlement and progress, any example of that persevering, laborious, and enduring character, which was animated, and cherished, and supported by the spirit and the love of civil and religious liberty; and which so eminently distinguished the Pilgrim Fathers, the Quakers, and even the Roman Catholics, who first encountered and overcame all the privations, difficulties, and dangers of the American wilderness.

The character and conduct of the conquerors and colonists of Spanish America, and of their civil and ecclesiastical government ever-afterwards, present a contrast which, on becoming independent of Spanish authority, rendered the moral, intellectual, and even physical character of the people, and of those who were called upon to rule, incompatible with intelligent, tolerant government, with impartial justice, and with civil and religious liberty.

The democratic form of the United States government arose as much from necessity, as from any predilection which the leading men of the time cherished for it. No person could claim sovereign right. The wealth of the country was too equally divided to give any one individual the means, if it were possible, either of corruption, or of an overwhelming share of power.

The constitution and laws were, otherwise, as nearly as possible accommodated to the ideas of the people, and to the former order of government.

The different states retained their representative governments, much the same as before the revolution, with the power of making laws for their internal administration; but all the states were united under one general government.

This head, or supreme government, was formed of three branches, or states—the President, the Senate, and the House of Representatives.

The problem for time to resolve was, whether this form of government possessed within itself the power of carrying into execution the laws which are necessary for the security of persons and property, and for the orderly maintenance of civil and religious liberty.

The constitution was not inconsiderately, nor quickly adopted. On the 17th of September, 1787, thirteen years after the meeting of the first continental congress, nine after the declaration of independence, and four after the acknowledgment of that independence by England, the constitution was agreed to.

The views taken by the federalists and the democrats, of the constitution of the United States, have frequently been greatly opposed to each other. Of the several jurists who have written on the constitution of the United States, the authors of the Federalist, and Judge Story and Chief Justice Kent are the most eminent. The late Judge Upshur appears to us to have analyzed that celebrated act with very great ability, even if his conclusions should be considered not strictly in accordance with the originally intended and real principles of the constitution.

A short time before his lamentable death, he sent me his views on the constitution of the United States. They are so remarkable that I have extracted the leading parts, and also those of the Honourable Mr. Spencer, as absolutely necessary to a just understanding of the constitution of the United States, as a confederative government, and as elucidating the several constitutions of the several states. Mr. Upshur was one of the highest legal authorities in the United States. His predecessor in the office of secretary of state, Mr. Legaré, was also a profound lawyer, and my personal friend. He was carried off suddenly while on a visit to Boston, in 1842; and Mr. Upshur, who succeeded him, was destroyed, with several others, in 1843, by the bursting of a monstrous cannon on board a steam frigate. A more pure-minded states-man, and more virtuous man than Mr. Upshur, I believe there did not exist. His views, however, on Nullification, and on many constitutional principles, have been disputed by some of the most learned jurists in America.

JUDGE UPSHUR'S STRICTURES.

"A work," says Mr. Upshur, "presenting a proper analysis and correct views of the constitution of the United States, has long been a desideratum with the public. It is true that the last fifteen years have not been unfruit-ful in commentaries upon that instrument: *such* commentaries, however, have, for the most part, met a deserved fate in immediate and total oblivion. A few have appeared, however, of a much higher order, and bearing the stamp of talent, learning, and research. Among these, the work of Judge Story and the 'Commentaries' of Chief Justice Kent hold the first rank. Both these works are, as it is natural they should be, strongly tinctured with the political opinions of their respective authors; and as there is a perfect concurrence between them in this respect, their joint authority can scarcely fail to exert a strong influence upon public opinion.

"The authority of great names is of such imposing weight, that mere rea-son and argument can rarely counterpoise it in the public mind; and its preponderance is not easily overcome, except by adding like authority to the weight of reason and argument in the opposing scale. I hope it is not yet too late for this suggestion to have its effect upon those to whom it is ad-dressed.

"The first commentary upon the constitution, the 'Federalist,' is decidedly the best which has yet appeared. The writers of that book were actors in all the interesting scenes of the period, and two of them were members of the convention which formed the constitution. Added to this, their exten-sive information, their commanding talents, and their experience in great public affairs, qualified them, in a peculiar degree, for the task which they undertook. Nevertheless, their great object was to *recommend* the constitu-tion to the people at a time when it was very uncertain whether they would adopt it or not; and hence their work, although it contains a very full and philosophical analysis of the subject, comes to us as a mere argument in support of a favourite measure, and, for that reason, does not always com-mand our entire confidence. Besides, the constitution was then untried, and its true character, which is to be learned only from its practical operation, could only be conjectured. Much has been developed in the actual practice of the government, which no politician of that day could either have foreseen or imagined. New questions have arisen not then anticipated, and difficul-ties and embarrassments, wholly unforeseen, have sprung from new events in the relation of the states to one another, and to the general government. Hence the 'Federalist' cannot be relied on as full and safe authority in all cases. It is, indeed, matter of just surprise, and affording the strongest proof of the profound wisdom and far-seeing sagacity of the authors of that work, that their views of the constitution have been so often justified in the course of its practical operation. Still, however, it must be admitted that the 'Federalist' is defective in some important particulars, and deficient in many more. The constitution is much better understood at this day than it was at the time of its adoption. This is not true of the great principles of civil and political liberty which lie at the foundation of that instrument, but it is emphatically true of some of its provisions, which were considered at the time as comparatively unimportant, or so plain as not to be misunderstood, but which have been shown by subsequent events to be pregnant with the greatest difficulties, and to exert the most important influence upon the whole character of the government. Contemporary expositions of the constitution, therefore, although they should be received as authority in *some* cases, and may enlighten our judgments in most others, cannot be regarded as safe guides by the expounder of that instrument at this day. The subject demands our attention now as strongly as it did before the 'Federalist' was written.

"Judge Story fills a high station in the judiciary of the United States, and has acquired a character for talents and learning which ensures respect to whatever he may publish under his own name. His duty, as a judge of the supreme court, has demanded of him frequent investigations of the nicest questions of constitutional law; and his long service in that capacity has probably brought under his review every provision of that instrument, in regard to which any difference of opinion has prevailed. Assisted, as he has been, by the arguments of the ablest counsel, and by the joint deliberations of the other judges of the court, it would be indeed wonderful if he should hazard his well-earned reputation as a jurist, upon any hasty or unweighed opinion, upon subjects so grave and important. He has also been an attentive observer of political events, and, although by no means obtrusive in politics, has yet a political character scarcely less distinguished than his character as a jurist. To all these claims to public attention and respect, may be added a reputation for laborious research, and for calm and temperate thinking.

"The first part of Judge Story's work relates to a subject of the greatest interest to every American, and well worthy the study of philosophical inquirers all over the world. There is not within the whole range of history an event more important, with reference to its effects upon the world at large, than the settlement of the American colonies. It did not fall within the plan of our author to inquire very extensively, or very minutely, into the mere history of the events which distinguished that extraordinary enterprise. So far as the first settlers may be regarded as actuated by avarice, by ambition, or by any other of the usual motives of the adventurer, their deeds belong to the province of the historian alone. We, however, must contemplate them in another and a higher character. A deep and solemn feeling of religion, and an attachment to, and an understanding of, the principles of civil liberty, far in advance of the age in which they lived, suggested to most of them the idea of seeking a new home, and founding new institutions in the western world. To this spirit we are indebted for all that is free and liberal in our present political systems. It would be a work of very great interest, and altogether worthy of the political historian, to trace the great principles of our institutions back to their sources. Their origin would probably be discovered at a period much more remote than is generally supposed. We should derive from such a review much light in the interpretation of those parts of our systems, as to which we have no precise rules in the language of our constitutions of government. It is to be regretted that Judge Story did not take this view of the subject. Although not strictly required by the plan of his work, it was, nevertheless, altogether consistent with it; and would have added much to its interest with the general reader.

His sources of historical information were ample, and his habits and the character of his mind fitted him well for such an investigation, and for presenting the result in an analytic and philosophical form. He has chosen, however, to confine himself within much narrower limits. Yet, even within those limits, he has brought together a variety of historical facts of great interest; and has presented them, in a condensed form, well calculated to make a lasting impression upon the memory. The brief sketch which he has given of the settlement of the several colonies, and the charters from which they derived their rights and powers as separate governments, contains much to enable us to understand fully the relation which they bore to one another, and to the mother country. This is the true starting point in the investigation of those vexed questions of constitutional law, which have so long divided political parties in the United States. It would seem almost impossible that any two opinions could exist upon the subject; and yet the historical facts upon which alone all parties must rely, although well authenticated, and comparatively recent, have not been understood by all men alike. Our author was well aware of the importance of settling this question at the threshold of his work. Many of the powers which have been claimed for the federal government, by the political party to which he belongs, depend upon a denial of that separate existence, and separate sovereignty and independence, which the opposing party has uniformly claimed for the states.

"It appears to be a favourite object with the author, to impress upon the mind of the reader, at the very commencement of his work, the idea, that the people of the several colonies were, as to some objects, which he has not explained, and to some extent, which he has not defined, '*one people.*' But although the colonies were independent of each other in respect to their domestic concerns, they were not wholly alien to each other. On the contrary, they were fellow-subjects, and for many purposes one people. Every colonist had a right to inhabit, if he pleased, in any other colony; and, as a British subject, he was capable of inheriting lands by descent in every other colony. The commercial intercourse of the colonies, too, was regulated by the general laws of the British empire, and could not be restrained or obstructed by colonial legislation. The remarks of Mr. Chief Justice Jay are equally just and striking :—' All the people of this country were then subjects of the King of Great Britain, and owed allegiance to him, and all the civil authority then existing or exercised here, flowed from the head of the British empire. They were, in a strict sense, fellow-subjects, and, in a variety of respects, one people. When the revolution commenced, the patriots did not assert that only the same affinity and social connexion subsisted between the people of the colonies which subsisted between the people of Gaul, Britain, and Spain, while Roman provinces, to wit, only that affinity and social connexion which results from the mere circumstance of being governed by the same prince.'

"The historical facts stated by both of these gentlemen are truly stated, but it is surprising that it did not occur to such cool reasoners, that every one of them is the *result of the relation between the colonies and the mother country, and not the result of the relation between the colonies themselves.* Every British subject, whether born in England proper or in a colony, has a right to reside any where within the British realm, and this *by the force of British laws.* Such is the right of every Englishman wherever he may be found. As to the right of the colonist to inherit lands by descent in any other colony than his own, our author himself informs us, that it belonged to him 'as a British subject.' That right, indeed, is a consequence of his allegiance. By the policy of the British constitution and laws, it is not permitted that the soil of her territory should belong to any, from whom she cannot demand all the duties of allegiance. This allegiance is the same in all the colonies as it is in England proper; and, wherever it exists, the correspondent right to own and inherit the soil attaches. The right to regulate commercial intercourse among her colonies belongs, of course, to the parent country, unless she relinquishes it by some act of her own; and no such act is shown in the present case. On the contrary, although that right was resisted for a time by some of the American colonies, it was finally yielded, as our author himself informs us, by all those of New England; and I am not informed that it was denied by any other. Indeed, the supremacy of Parliament, in most matters of legislation which concerned the colonies, was generally—nay, *universally* admitted, up to the very eve of the revolution. It is true, the right to *tax* the colonies was denied, but this was upon a wholly different principle; it was the right of every British subject to be exempt from taxation, except by his own consent; and as the colonies were not, and, from their local situation, could not be, represented in parliament, the right of that body to tax them was denied, upon a fundamental principle of English liberty. But the right of the mother country to regulate commerce among her colonies is of a different character, and it never was denied to England by her American colonies, so long as a hope of reconciliation remained to them. In like manner, the facts relied on by Mr. Jay, that 'all the people of this country were then subjects of the King of Great Britain, and owed allegiance to him,' and that, 'all the civil authority then existing or exercised herein, flowed from the head of the British empire,' are but the usual incidents of colonial dependence, and are by no means peculiar to the case he was considering. They do, indeed, prove a unity between all the colonies and the mother country, and show that these, taken altogether, are, in the strictest sense of the terms, 'one people;' but I am at a loss to perceive how they prove that two or more parts, or subdivisions, of the same empire, necessarily constitute 'one people.' If this be true of the colonies, it is equally true of any two or more geographical sections of England proper; for every one of the reasons assigned, applies as strictly to this case, as to that of the colonies. Any two countries may be 'one people,' or 'a nation *de facto*,' if they can be made so by the facts that their people are subjects of the king of Great Britain, and owe 'allegiance to him,' and that 'all the civil authority exercised therein, flows from the head of the British empire.'

"And, so far as the rights of the mother country are concerned, they existed in the same form, and to the same extent, over every other colony of the empire. Did this make the people of *all* the colonies 'one people?' If so, the people of Jamaica, the British East Indian possessions, and the Canadas, are, for the very same reason, 'one people' at this day.

"The *general* relation between colonies and the parent country is as well settled and understood as any other; and it is precisely the same in all cases, except where special consent and agreement may vary it. Whoever, therefore, would prove that any peculiar *unity* existed between the American colonies, is bound to show something in their characters, or some peculiarity in their condition, to exempt them from the general rule. Judge Story was too well acquainted with the state of the facts, to make any such attempt in the present case. The congress of the nine colonies, which assembled at New York, in October, 1765, declared that the colonists 'owe the same allegiance to the Crown of Great Britain that is owing from his subjects born within the realm, and all due subordination to that august body, the Parliament of Great Britain.' 'That the colonists are entitled to all the inherent rights and liberties of his (the king's) natural-born subjects within the Kingdom of Great Britain.' We have here an all-sufficient foundation of the right of the crown to regulate commerce among the colonies, and of the right of the colonists to inhabit and to inherit land in each and all the colonies. They were nothing more than the ordinary rights and liabilities of every British subject; and, indeed, the most that the colonies ever contended for, was an equality, in these respects, with the subjects born in England.

"The great effort of the author, throughout his entire work, is to establish the doctrine, that the constitution of the United States is a government of 'the people of the United States,' as contra-distinguished from the people of the several states; or, in other words, that it is a consolidated, and not a federative system. His construction of every contested federal power, depends mainly upon this distinction; and hence the necessity of establishing a *oneness* among the people of the several colonies, prior to the revolution.

"In order to constitute 'one people,' in a political sense, of the inhabitants of different countries, something more is necessary than that they should owe a common allegiance to a common sovereign. Neither is it sufficient that in some particulars they are bound alike, by laws which that sovereign may prescribe; nor does the question depend on geographical relations. The inhabitants of different islands may be one people, and those of contiguous countries may be, as we know they in fact are, different nations. By the term *people*, as here used, we do not mean merely a number of persons. We mean by it a political corporation, the members of which owe a common allegiance to a common sovereignty, and do not owe any allegiance which is *not* common; who are bound by no laws except such as that sovereignty may prescribe; who owe to one another reciprocal obligations; who possess common political interests; who are liable to common political duties; and who can exert no sovereign power except in the name of the whole. Any thing short of this would be an imperfect definition of that political corporation which we call a *people*.

"Tested by this definition, the people of the American colonies were, in no conceivable sense, 'one people.' They owed, indeed, allegiance to the British king, as the head of each colonial government, and as forming a part thereof, but this allegiance was exclusive in each colony to its own government, and consequently to the king as the head thereof, and was not a common allegiance of the people of all the colonies, to a common head.[*] These colonial governments were clothed with the sovereign power of making laws, and of enforcing obedience to them, from their own people. The people of one colony owed no allegiance to the government of any other colony, and were not bound by its laws. The colonies had no common legislature, no common treasury, no common military power, no common judicatory. The people of one colony were not liable to pay taxes to any other colony, nor to bear arms in its defence; they had no right to vote in its elections; no influence nor control in its municipal government, no interest in its municipal institutions. There was no prescribed form by which the colonies could act together, for any purpose whatever; they were not known as 'one people' in any one function of government, although they were all, alike, dependencies of the British crown, yet, even in the action of the parent country in regard to them, they were recognised as separate and distinct. They were established at different times, and each under an authority from the crown which applied to itself alone. They were not even alike in their organization. Some were provincial, some were proprietary, and some charter governments. Each derived its form of government from the particular instrument establishing it, or from assumptions of power acquiesced in by the crown, without any connexion with, or relation to, any other. They stood upon the same footing, in every respect, with other British colonies, with nothing to distinguish their relation

---

* The resolutions of Virginia, in 1796, show that *she* considered herself merely as an appendage of the British Crown; that *her* legislature was alone authorized to tax her; and that she had a right to call on *her* king, who was also King of England, to protect her against the usurpations of the British parliament.

either to the parent country or to one another. The charter of any one of them might have been destroyed, without in any manner affecting the rest. In point of fact, the charters of nearly all of them were altered from time to time, and the whole character of their governments changed. These changes were made in each colony for itself alone, sometimes by its own action, sometimes by the power and authority of the crown; but never by the joint agency of any other colony, and never with reference to the wishes or demands of any other colony. Thus they were separate and distinct in their creation, separate and distinct in the forms of their governments, separate and distinct in the modifications of their government, which were made from time to time, separate and distinct in political functions, in political rights, and in political duties.

"The provincial government of Virginia was the first established. The people of Virginia owed allegiance to the British king, as the head of their own local government. The authority of that government was confined within certain geographical limits known as Virginia, and all who lived within those limits were 'one people.' When the colony of Plymouth was subsequently settled, were the people of that colony one with the people of Virginia? When, long afterwards, the proprietary government of Pennsylvania was established, were the followers of William Penn 'one' with the people of Plymouth and Virginia? If so, to which government was their allegiance due? Virginia had a government of her own, Pennsylvania a government of her own, and Massachusetts a government of her own. The people of Pennsylvania could not be equally bound by the laws of all three governments; because those laws might happen to conflict; they could not owe the duties of citizenship to all of them alike, because they *might* stand in hostile relations to one another. Either then the government of Virginia, which originally extended over the whole territory, continued to be supreme therein, (subject only to its dependence upon the British Crown,) or else its supremacy was yielded to the new government. Every one knows that this last was the case, that within the territory of the new government, the authority of that government alone prevailed. How then could the people of this new government of Pennsylvania be said to be 'one' with the people of Virginia, when they were not citizens of Virginia, owed her no allegiance and no duty, and when their allegiance to another government might place them in the relation of enemies of Virginia?

"In further illustration of this point, let us suppose that some one of the colonies had refused to unite in the declaration of independence; what relation would it then have held to the others? Not having disclaimed its allegiance to the British crown, it would still have continued to be a British colony, subject to the authority of the parent country in all respects as before. Could the other colonies have rightfully compelled it to unite with them in their revolutionary purposes, on the ground that it was part and parcel of the 'one people' known as the people of the colonies? No such right was ever claimed or dreamed of, and it will scarcely be contended for now, in the face of the known history of the time. Such recusant colony would have stood precisely as did the Canadas, and every other part of the British empire. The colonies which had declared war, would have considered its people as enemies, but would not have had a right to treat them as traitors, or as disobedient citizens resisting their authority. To what purpose then were the people of the colonies 'one people,' if in a case so important to the common welfare, there was no right in all the people together, to coerce the members of their own community to the performance of a common duty?

"It is thus apparent that the people of the colonies were not 'one people' as to any purpose involving allegiance on the one hand or protection on the other.

"As early as 1765, a majority of the colonies had met together in congress, or convention, in New York, for the purpose of deliberating on these grave matters of common concern; and they then made a formal declaration of what they considered their rights, as colonists and British subjects. This measure, however, led to no redress of their grievances. On the contrary, the subsequent measures of the British government gave new and just causes of complaint; so that, in 1774, it was deemed necessary that the colonies should again meet together, in order to consult upon their general condition, and provide for the safety of their common rights. Hence the congress, which met in Carpenter's Hall on the 5th of September, 1774. It consisted of delegates from New Hampshire, Massachusetts Bay, Rhode Island, and Providence Plantations, Connecticut, *from the City and County of New York, and other counties in the Province of New York,* New Jersey, Pennsylvania, *Newcastle, Kent, and Sussex, in Delaware,* Maryland, Virginia, and South Carolina. North Carolina was not represented until the 14th of September, and Georgia not at all. It is also apparent that New York was not represented *as a colony,* but only through certain portions of her people; in like manner, Lyman Hall was admitted to his seat, in the succeeding congress, as a delegate from the parish of St. John's, in Georgia, although he declined to vote on any question requiring a majority of *the colonies* to carry it, because he was not the representative of a colony. This congress passed a variety of important resolutions, between September, 1774, and October 22d, in the same year, during all which time Georgia was not represented at all; for even the parish of St. John's did not appoint a representative till May, 1775. In point of fact, the congress was a *deliberative and advisory* body, and nothing more; and for this reason it was not deemed important, or, at least, not *indispensable,* that all the colonies should be represented, since the resolutions of congress had no obligatory force whatever. It was appointed for the sole purpose of taking into consideration the general condition of the colonies, and of devising and recommending proper measures for the security of their rights and interests. For these objects no precise powers and instructions were necessary, and *beyond* them none were given. Neither does it appear that any precise time was assigned for the duration of congress. The duty with which it was charged was extremely simple; and it was taken for granted that it would dissolve itself as soon as that duty was performed.

"Speaking of the congress of 1774, Marshall says: 'The members of this congress were *generally* elected by the authority of the colonial legislatures, but, in *some* instances, a different system had been pursued. In New Jersey and Maryland, the elections were made by committees, chosen in the several counties for that particular purpose: and in New York, where the royal party was very strong, and where it is probable that no legislative act, authorizing an election of members to represent that colony in congress, could have been obtained, the people themselves assembled in those places, where the spirit of opposition to the claims of parliament prevailed, and elected deputies, who were very readily received into congress.' Here the *general rule* is stated to be, that the deputies were elected by the 'colonial legislatures;' and the instances in which the people acted, 'directly in their primary, sovereign capacity,' without the intervention of the ordinary functionaries of government, are given as *exceptions.*

"As to New York, neither her people nor her government had so far lost their attachment to their mother country, as to concur in any measure of opposition, until after the battle of Lexington, in April, 1775; and the only representatives which New York had in the congress of 1774, were those of a comparatively small portion of her people. It is well known, and, indeed the author himself so informs us, that the members of the congress of 1775, were elected substantially as were those of the preceding congress; so that there were very few of the colonies, in which the people performed that act in their 'primary, sovereign capacity,' without the intervention of their constituted authorities. It is of little consequence, however, to the present inquiry, whether the deputies were chosen by the colonial legislatures, as was done in most of the colonies, or by conventions, as was done in Georgia and some others; or by committees appointed for the purpose, as was done in one or two instances; or by the people in primary assemblies, as was done in *part* of New York. The circumstances under which the congresses of 1774 and 1775, were called into existence, precluded the possibility of any precise limitations of their powers, even if it had been designed to clothe them with the functions of government. The colonies were suffering under common oppressions, and were threatened with common dangers from the mother country. The great object which they had in view, was to produce that concert of action among themselves which would best enable them to resist their common enemy, and best secure the safety and liberties of all. Great confidence must necessarily be reposed in public rulers, under circumstances of this sort.

"Many of those powers which, for greater convenience, were intrusted exclusively to congress, could not be effectually exerted, except by the aid of the state authorities. The troops required by congress, were raised by the states, and the commissions of their officers were countersigned by the governors of the states. Congress was allowed to issue bills of credit, but could not make them a legal tender, nor punish the counterfeiter of them. Neither could they bind the states to redeem them, nor raise, by their own authority, the necessary funds for that purpose. Congress received ambassadors and other public ministers, yet had no power to extend to them that protection, which they receive from the government of every sovereign nation.

"Thus it appears that, in the important functions of raising an army, of providing a public revenue, of paying public debts, and giving security to the persons of foreign ministers, the boasted 'sovereignty' of the federal government was merely nominal, and owed its entire efficiency to the co-operation and aid of the state governments. Congress had no power to coerce these governments, nor could it exercise any direct authority over their individual citizens.

"Although the powers actually assumed and exercised by congress, were certainly very great, they were not always acquiesced in, or allowed by the states. Thus, the power to lay an embargo, was earnestly desired by them, but was denied by the states; and in order the more clearly to indicate that many of their powers were exercised merely by sufferance, and, at the same time, to lend a sanction to their authority, so far as they chose to allow it, it was deemed necessary, by at least *one* of the states, to pass laws indemnifying those who might act in obedience to the resolutions of that body.

"The following extract from the journals of the convention of Virginia, containing the history of this interesting event, cannot fail to be acceptable to every American reader.

" 'Wednesday, May 15th, 1776.—The convention, then, according to the order of the day, resolved itself into a committee on the state of the colony; and after some time spent therein, Mr. President resumed the chair, and Mr. Carey reported that the committee had, according to order, had under their consideration the state of the colony, and had come to the following resolutions thereupon; which he read in his place, and afterwards delivered in at the clerk's table, where the same were again twice read, and unanimously agreed to, one hundred and twelve members being present.

" ' For as much as all the endeavours of the united colonies, by the most decent representations and petitions to the king and parliament of Great Britain, to restore peace and security to America under the British government, and a reunion with that people, upon just and liberal terms, instead of a redress of grievances, have produced, from an imperious and vindictive administration, increased insult, oppression, and a vigorous attempt to effect our total destruction. By a late act, all these colonies are declared to be in rebellion, and out of the protection of the British crown, our properties subject to confiscation, our people, when captivated, compelled to join in the plunder and murder of their relations and countrymen, and all former rapine and oppressions of Americans declared legal and just. Fleets and armies are raised, and the aid of foreign troops engaged to assist these destructive purposes. The king's representative in this colony hath not only withheld all the powers of government from operating for our safety, but, having retired on board an armed ship, is carrying on a piratical and savage war against us, tempting our slaves by every artifice to resort to him, and training and employing them against their masters.

" 'In this state of extreme danger, we have no alternative left, but an abject submission to the will of those overbearing tyrants, or a total separation from the crown and government of Great Britain, uniting and exerting the strength of all America for defence, and forming alliances with foreign powers for commerce and aid in war. Wherefore, appealing to the Searcher of all hearts, for the sincerity of former declarations, expressing our desire to preserve our connexion with that nation, and that we are driven from that inclination by their wicked counsels and the eternal laws of self-preservation; resolved, unanimously, that the delegates appointed to represent this colony in general congress, be instructed to propose to that respectable body, to declare the united colonies free and independent states, absolved from all allegiance to, or dependence upon, the crown or parliament of Great Britain; and that they give the assent of this colony to that declaration, and to whatever measures may be thought proper and necessary by the congress, for forming foreign alliances, and a confederation of the colonies, at such time and in such manner as to them may seem best. Provided, that the power of forming government for, and the regulations of the internal concerns of each colony, be left to the respective colonial legislatures.

" 'Resolved, unanimously, that a committee be appointed to prepare a declaration of rights, and such a plan of government, as will be most likely to maintain peace and order in this colony, and secure substantial and equal liberty to the people.'

" It is impossible to contemplate this proceeding on the part of Virginia, without being convinced that she acted from her own free and sovereign will; and that *she*, at least, *did* 'presume' to establish a government for herself, without the least regard to the recommendation or the pleasure of congress.

"We all admit that the power and authority of the federal government, within its constitutional sphere, are superior to those of the states, in some instances; and co-ordinate in others; and that every citizen is under an absolute obligation, to render them respect and obedience; and this *simply because his own state, by the act of ratifying the constitution, has commanded him to do so.* We all admit it to be true, as a general proposition, that no citizen nor state has an independent right to 'construe,' and still less to 'control,' the constitutional obligations of that government, and that neither a citizen nor a state can 'judge,' that is, '*decide*' on the nature and extent of those obligations, with a view to control them. All that has ever been contended for, is, that a state has a right to judge of its *own* obligations; and, consequently to judge of those of the federal government, so far as they relate to *such state itself*, and no farther. It is admitted on all hands, that when the federal government *transcends* its constitutional power, and when, of course, it is not acting *within* its 'obligations,' the parties to that government, whoever they may be, are no longer under any duty to respect or obey it. This has been repeatedly affirmed by our courts, both state and federal; and has never been denied by any class of politicians. Who then is to determine whether it has so transcended its constitutional obligations, or not? It is admitted, that to a certain extent, the supreme court is the proper tribunal, in the last resort, because the states in establishing that tribunal, have expressly agreed to make it so. The jurisdiction of the federal courts extends to certain cases, affecting the rights of the individual citizens, and to certain others affecting those of the individual states. So far as the federal government is authorized to act on the individual citizen, the powers of the one and the rights of the other, are properly determinable by the federal courts; and the decision is binding too, and absolutely final, so far as the relation of the citizen to the *federal government* is concerned. There is not, within that system, any tribunal of appeal, from the decisions of the supreme court. And so also of those cases in which the rights of *the state* are referred to the federal tribunals. In this sense and to this extent, it is strictly true that the parties have not 'an independent right to construe, control, and judge of the obligations' of the federal government; but they are bound by the decisions of the federal courts, so far as they have authorized and agreed to submit to them. But there are many cases involving the question of federal power, which are not cognizable before the federal courts; and, of course, as to these, we must look out for some other umpire. It is precisely in this case, that the question who are the parties to the constitution, becomes all-important and controlling. If the states are parties as sovereign states, then it follows, as a necessary consequence, that each of them has the right which belongs to every sovereignty, to construe its own contracts and agreements, and to decide upon its own rights and powers.

"The *nullifier* contends only for the right of a state to *prevent the constitution from being violated by the general government*, and not for the right either to repeal, abrogate, or suspend it. The *seceder* asserts only, that a state is competent to withdraw from the union whenever it pleases; but does not assert that in so doing, it can repeal, or abrogate, or suspend the constitution as to the other states. Secession would, indeed, utterly destroy the compact as to the seceding party; but would not necessarily affect its obligation as to the rest. If it would, then the rest would have no right to coerce the seceding state, nor to place her in the attitude of an enemy. *It is certain, I think, they would not have such right;* but those who assert that they would—and Judge Story is among the number—must either abandon that idea, or they must admit that the act of secession does not break up the constitution, except as to the seceding state. For the moment the constitution is destroyed, all the authorities which it has established, cease to exist. There is no longer such a government as that of the United States; and, of course, they cannot, as such, either make any demand, or assert any right, or enforce any claim.

"Having disposed of this preliminary question, we now approach the constitution itself. *I affirm that it is in its structure a federative and not a consolidated government;* that it is so in all its departments, and in all its leading and distinguishing provisions; and, of course, that it is to be so interpreted, *by the force of its own terms,* apart from any influence to be derived from that rule of construction which has just been laid down. We will first examine it in the structure of its several departments.

"*The Legislature.*—This consists of two houses. The senate is composed of two members from each state, chosen by its own legislature, whatever be its size or population, and is universally admitted to be strictly federative in its structure. The house of representatives consists of members chosen in each state, and is regulated in its numbers according to a prescribed ratio of representation. The number to which each state is entitled is proportioned to its own population, and not to the population of the United States; and if there happen to be a surplus in any state less than the established ratio, that surplus is not added to the surplus or population of any other state, in order to make up the requisite number for a representative, but is wholly unrepresented. In the choice of representatives, each state votes by itself, and for its own representatives, and not in connexion with any other state, nor for the representatives of any other state. Each state prescribes the qualifications of its own voters, the constitution only providing that they shall have the qualifications which such state may have prescribed for the voters for the most numerous branch of its own legislature. And as the *right* to vote is prescribed by the state, the *duty* of doing so cannot be enforced, except by the authority of the state. No one can be elected to represent any state, except a citizen thereof. Vacancies in the representation of any state are to be supplied under writs of election, issued by the executive of such state. In all this there is not one feature of nationality. The whole arrangement has reference to the states as such, and is carried into effect solely by their authority. The federal government has no agency in the choice of representatives, except only that it may prescribe the 'times, places, and manner of holding elections.' It can neither prescribe the qualifications of the electors, nor impose any penalty upon them for refusing to elect. The states alone can do these things; and, of course, the very existence of the house of representatives depends, as much as does that of the senate, upon the action of the states. A state may withdraw its representation altogether, and congress has no power to prevent it, nor to supply the vacancy thus created. If the house of representatives were national, in any practical sense of the term, the 'nation' would have authority to provide for the appointment of its members, to prescribe the qualifications of voters, and to enforce the performance of that duty. All these things the state legislatures can do, within their respective states, and it is obvious that they are strictly national. In order to make the house of representatives equally so, the people of the United States must be so consolidated that the federal government may distribute them, without regard to state boundaries, into numbers, according to the prescribed ratio; so that *all* the people may be represented, and no unrepresented surplus be left in any state. If these things could be done under the federal constitution, there would then be a strict analogy between the popular branches of the federal and state legislatures, and the former might with propriety be considered 'national.' But it is difficult to imagine a national legislature which does not exist under the authority of the nation, and over the very appointment of which the nation, as such, can exert no effective control.

"The second argument is, that the states are not *equally* represented, but each one has a representation proportioned to its population. There is no reason apparent to me, why a league may not be formed among independent sovereignties, giving to each an influence in the management of their common concerns, proportioned to its strength, its wealth, or the interest which it has at stake. This is but simple justice, and the rule ought to prevail in all cases, except where higher considerations disallow it. History abounds with examples of such confederations, one of which I will cite. The states general of the United provinces were strictly a federal body. The council of state had almost exclusively the management and control of all their military and financial concerns; and in that body, Holland and some other provinces had three votes each, whilst some had two, and others only one vote each. Yet it never was supposed that for this reason the United provinces were a consolidated nation. A single example of this sort affords a full illustration of the subject, and renders all farther arguments superfluous.

"It is not, however, from the apportionment of its powers, nor from the modes in which those powers are exercised, that we can determine the true character of a legislative body, in the particular now under consideration. The true rule of decision is found in the manner in which the body is constituted, and that, we have already seen, is in the case before us, federative, and not national.

"We may safely admit, however, that the house of representatives is not federative, and yet contend, with perfect security, that the *legislative department* is so. Congress consists of the house of representatives and senate. Neither is a complete legislature in itself, and neither can pass any law without the concurrence of the other, and as the senate is the peculiar representative of the states, no act of legislation whatever can be performed, without the consent of the states. They hold, therefore, a complete check and control over the powers of the people in this respect, even admitting that those powers are truly and strictly represented in the other branch. It is true that the check is mutual; but if the legislative department were national, there would be no federative feature in it. It cannot be replied with equal propriety, that, if it were federative, there would be no national feature in it. The question is, whether or not the states have preserved their distinct sovereign characters in this feature of the constitution. If they have done so, in any part of it, the whole must be considered federative; because national legislation implies a *unity*, which is absolutely inconsistent with all idea of a confederation; whereas, there is nothing to prevent the members of a confederation from exerting their several powers, in any form of *joint action* which may seem to them proper.

"But there is one other provision of the constitution which appears to me to be altogether decisive upon this point. Each state, whatever be its population, is entitled to at least one representative. It may so happen that the unrepresented surplus, in some one state, may be greater than the whole population of some other state, and yet such latter state would be entitled to a representation. Upon what principle is this? Surely if the house of representatives were national, something like *equality* would be found in the constitution of it. Large surpluses would not be arbitrarily rejected in some places and smaller numbers not equal to the granted ratio, be represented in others. There can be but one reason for this: as the constitution was made by the states, the true principle of the confederation could not be preserved, without giving to each party to the compact a place and influence in each branch of the common legislature. This was due to their perfect *equality* as sovereign states.

"*The Executive.*—In the election of the president and vice-president, the exclusive agency of the states, as such, is preserved with equal distinctness. These officers are chosen by electors, who are themselves chosen by the people of each state, acting by and for itself, and in such mode as itself may prescribe. The number of electors to which each state is entitled, is equal to the whole number of its representatives and *senators*. This provision is even more federative than that which apportions representation in the house of representatives; because it adds two to the electors of each state, and, so far places them upon an equality, whatever be their comparative population. The people of each state vote *within* the state and not elsewhere; and for their own electors and for no others. Each state prescribes the qualifications of its own electors, and can alone compel them to vote. The electors, when chosen, give their votes within their respective states, and at such times and places as the states may respectively prescribe.

"There is not the least trace of national agency in any part of this proceeding. The federal government can exercise no rightful power in the choice of its own executive. 'The people of the United States' are equally unseen in that important measure. Neither a majority, nor the whole of them together, can choose a president, except in their character of citizens of the several states. Nay, a president may be constitutionally elected, *with a decided majority of the people against him*. For example: New York has forty-two votes; Pennsylvania, thirty; Virginia, twenty-three; Ohio, twenty-one; North Carolina, fifteen; Kentucky, fourteen; and South Carolina, fifteen. These seven states can give a majority of all the votes, and each may elect its own electors by a majority of only one vote. If we add their minorities to the votes of the other states (supposing those states to be unanimous against the candidate,) we may have a president, constitutionally elected, with less than half—perhaps with little more than a fourth—of the people in his favour. It is true that he may also be constitutionally elected, with a majority of the *states,* as such, against him, as the above example shows; because the states may, as before remarked, properly agree, by the provisions of their compact, that they shall possess influence in this respect, proportioned to their population. But there is no mode, consistent with the true principles of free representative government, by which a minority of those to whom, *en masse,* the elective franchise is confided, can countervail the concurrent and opposing action of the majority. If the president could be chosen by the people of the 'United States' in the aggregate, instead of by the states, it is difficult to imagine a case in which a majority of those people, concurring in the same vote, could be over-balanced by a minority.

"All doubt upon this point, however, is removed by another provision of the constitution, touching this subject; if no candidate should receive a majority of votes in the electoral colleges, the house of representatives elects the president from the three candidates who have received the largest electoral vote. In doing this, two-thirds of the states must be present by their representatives, or one of them, and then *they vote by states, all the members from each state giving one vote, and a majority to all the states being necessary to a choice.* This is precisely the rule which prevailed in the ordinary legislation of that body, under the articles of confederation, and which proved its federative character, as strongly as any other provision of those articles. Why, then, should this federative principle be preserved in the election of the president by the house of representatives, if it was designed to abandon it, in the election of the same officer, by the electoral colleges? No good reason for it has yet been assigned, so far as I am informed.

"This view of the subject is still further confirmed by the clause of the constitution relating to impeachments. The power to try the president is vested in the senate alone, that is, in the representatives of the states. There is a strict fitness and propriety in this; for those only whose officer the president is should be intrusted with the power to remove him.

"It is believed to be neither a forced nor an unreasonable conclusion, from all this, that the executive department is, in its structure, strictly federative.

"*The Judiciary.*—The judges are nominated by the president, and approved by the senate. Thus, the nominations are made by a federative officer, and the approval and confirmation of them depend on those who are the exclusive representatives of the states, this agency is manifestly federative, and 'the people of the United States' cannot mingle in it, in any form whatever.

"As the constitution is federative in the structure of all three of its great departments, it is equally so *in the power of amendment.*

"Congress may *propose* amendments, 'whenever two-thirds of both houses shall deem it necessary.' This secures the states from any action upon the subject by the people at large. In like manner, congress may call a convention for proposing amendments, 'on the application of the legislatures of two-thirds of the several states,' It is remarkable that, whether congress or the states act upon the subject, the *same proportion* is required; not less than two-thirds of either being authorized to act. From this it is not unreasonable to conclude, that the convention considered that the *same power* would act in both cases: to wit, the power of the states, who might effect their object either by their separate action as states, or by the action of congress, their common federative agent; but whether they adopted the one mode or the other, not less than two-thirds of them should be authorized to act efficiently.

"The amendments thus proposed 'shall be valid to all intents and purposes, as part of this constitution, *when ratified by the legislatures of three-fourths of the states, or by conventions in three-fourths thereof,* as the one or the other mode of ratification may be proposed by congress.' It is the act of adoption or ratification alone which makes a constitution. In the states before us the states alone can perform that act. The language of the constitution admits of no doubt, and gives no pretext for double construction. It is not the people of the United States in the aggregate, merely *acting* in their several states, who can ratify amendments. *Three-fourths of the several states* can alone do this. The idea of separate and independent political corporations could not be more distinctly conveyed by any form of words. If the people of the United States, as one people, but acting in their several states, could ratify amendments, then the very language of the constitution requires that *three-fourths of them* shall concur therein. Is it not, then, truly wonderful that no mode has yet been prescribed to ascertain whether three-fourths of them do concur or not? By what power can the necessary arrangement upon this point be effected? In point of fact, amendments have already been made, in a strict conformity with this provision of the constitution.

"So strongly were the states attached to that perfect equality which their perfect sovereignty implied, and so jealous were they of every attack upon it, that they guarded it, by an express provision of the constitution, against the possibility of overthrow. All other rights they confided to that power of amendment, which they reposed in three-fourths of all the states; but this they refused to intrust, except to the separate, independent, and sovereign will of each state; giving to each, in its own case, an absolute negative upon all the rest.*

"The object of the preceding pages has been to show that the constitution is federative, in the power which framed it; federative in the power which adopted and ratified it; federative in the power which sustains and keeps it alive; federative in the power by which alone it can be altered or amended; and federative in the structure of all its departments. In what respect then can it be justly called a consolidated or national government?

"We come now to a more particular and detailed examination of the question, 'Who is the final judge and interpreter in constitutional controversies?' Judge Story's conclusion is, that 'in all questions of a judicial nature' the supreme court of the United States is the final umpire; and that the *states,* as well as individuals, are absolutely bound by its decisions.

"Whatever comes within the legitimate cognizance of that tribunal it has a right to decide, whether it be a question of the law or of the constitution; and no other tribunal can reverse its decision. The constitution, which creates the supreme court, creates no other court of superior or appellate jurisdiction to it; and consequently its decisions are strictly 'final.' There is no power *in the same government to which that court belongs* to reverse or control it, nor are there any means *therein* of resisting its authority. So far, therefore, as the *Federal Constitution* has provided for the subject at all, the supreme court is, beyond question, the final judge or arbiter; and this, too, whether the jurisdiction which it exercises be legitimate or usurped.

"Let us now inquire *what* 'constitutional controversies' the federal courts have

---

* So absolutely is the federal government dependent on the states for its existence, at all times, that it may be absolutely dissolved, without the least violence, by the simple refusal of a part of the states to act. If, for example, a few states, having a majority of electoral votes, should refuse to appoint electors of president and vice-president, there would be no constitutional executive, and the whole machinery of the government would stop.

authority to decide, and how far its decisions are final and conclusive against all the world.

"The third article of the constitution provides, that 'the judicial power shall extend to all cases of law and equity, arising under this constitution, the laws of the United States, and the treaties made, or which shall be made, under their authority; to all cases affecting ambassadors, other public ministers and consuls, to all cases of admiralty and maritime jurisdiction; to controversies to which the United States shall be a party; to controversies between two or more states; between a state and citizens of another state; between citizens of different states; between citizens of the same state, claiming lands under grants of different states; and between a state and the citizens thereof, and foreign states, citizens or subjects.'

"The eleventh amendment provides that "The judicial power of the United States shall not be construed to extend to any suit in law or equity, commenced or prosecuted against one of the United States by citizens of another state, or by citizens or subjects of any foreign state.'

"It will be conceded on all hands that the federal courts have no jurisdiction except what is here conferred. The judiciary, as a part of the federal government, derives its powers only from the constitution, which creates that government. The term 'cases' implies that the subject matter shall be proper for judicial decision; and the *parties* between whom alone jurisdiction can be entertained are specifically enumerated. Beyond these cases and these parties they have no jurisdiction.

"There is no part of the constitution in which the framers of it have displayed a more jealous care of the rights of the states than in the limitation of the judicial power. It is remarkable that no power is conferred except what is absolutely necessary to carry into effect the general design, and accomplish the general object of the states, as independent, confederated states. The federal tribunals cannot take cognizance of any case whatever in which all the states have not an equal and common interest, that a just and impartial decision shall be had. A brief analysis of the provisions of the constitution will make this sufficiently clear.

"Cases 'arising under the constitution' are those in which some right or privilege is denied which the constitution confers, or something is done which the constitution prohibits, as expressed in the constitution itself. Those which arise 'under the laws of the United States' are such as involve rights or duties which result from the legislation of congress.

"Cases arising under treaties, made under the authority of the United States, and those 'affecting ambassadors and other public ministers and consuls' could not be properly intrusted to any other than the federal tribunals. Treaties are made under the common authority of all the states, and all alike are bound for the faithful observance of them. Ambassadors and other public ministers and consuls are received under the common authority of all the states, and their duties relate only to matters involving alike the interests of all. The peace of the country, and the harmony of its relations with foreign powers, depend, in a peculiar degree, on the good faith with which its duties, in reference to these subjects, are discharged. Hence it would be unsafe to intrust them to any other power than their own control; and even if this were not so, it would be altogether incongruous to appeal to a state tribunal to enforce the rights, the obligations, or the duties of the United States. For like reasons cases of admiralty and maritime jurisdiction are properly entrusted to the federal tribunals.

"Controversies, to which the United States shall be a party, should, upon general principles, belong only to her own courts. There would be neither propriety nor justice in permitting any one state to decide a case in which all the states are parties. In like manner, those between two or more states— between a state and citizens of another state, where the state is plaintiff (it cannot *be sued*,) and between citizens of different states, could not be entrusted to the tribunals of any particular state interested, or whose citizens are interested therein, without danger of injustice and partiality. Jurisdiction is given to the federal courts, in these cases, simply because they are equally interested for all the parties, are the common courts of all the parties, and therefore are presumed to form the only fair and impartial tribunal between them. The same reasoning applies to cases between citizens of the same state, claiming lands under grants of different states. Cases of this sort involve questions of the sovereign power of the states, and could not, with any show of propriety, be entrusted to the decision of either of them, interested, as it would be, to sustain its own acts against those of the sister state. The jurisdiction in this case is given upon the same principles which gave it in cases between two or more states.

"Controversies between a state or the citizens thereof, and foreign states, citizens, or subjects, depend on a different principle, but one equally affecting the common rights and interests of all the states. A foreign state cannot, of course, be sued; she can appear in our courts only as plaintiff. Yet, in whatever form such controversies, or those affecting the citizens of a foreign state, may arise, all the states have a deep interest that an impartial tribunal, satisfactory to the foreign party, should be provided. The denial of justice is a legitimate, and not an unfruitful, cause of war. As no state can be involved in war without involving all the rest, they all have a common interest to withdraw from the state tribunals a jurisdiction which may bring them within the danger of that result. All the states are alike bound to render justice to foreign states and their people; and this common responsibility gives them a right to demand that every question involving it shall be decided by their common judicatory.

"The tenth article of the amendments of the constitution, provides that, 'The powers not delegated to the United States by the constitution, nor prohibited by it to the states, are reserved to the states respectively, or to the people.' The powers thus reserved, are not only reserved against the federal government in whole, but against each and every department thereof. The judiciary is no more excepted out of the reservation than is the legislature or the executive. Of what nature, then, are those reserved powers? Not the powers, if any such there be, which are possessed by all the states together, for the reservation is to 'the states *respectively;*' that is, to each state separately and distinctly. Now we can form no idea of any power possessed by a state as such, and independent of every other state, which is not, in its nature, a sovereign power. Every power so reserved, therefore, must be of such a character, that each state may exercise it, without the least reference or responsibility to any other state whatever. It is incident to every sovereignty to be alone the judge of its own compacts and agreements. No other state or assemblage of states, has the least right to interfere with it, in this respect, and cannot do so without impairing its sovereignty. The constitution of the United States is but the agreement which each state has made, with each and all the other states, and is not distinguishable, in the principle we are examining, from any other agreement between sovereign states. Each state, therefore, has a right to interpret that agreement for itself, unless it has clearly waived that right in favour of another power. That the right is not waived in the case under consideration, is apparent from the fact already stated, that if the judiciary be the sole judges of the extent of their own powers, their powers are universal, and the enumeration in the constitution is idle and useless.

"The federal government is the creature of the states. It is not a party to the constitution, but the result of it—the creation of that agreement which was made by the states as parties. It is a mere agent intrusted with limited powers for certain specific objects; which powers and objects are enumerated in the constitution. Shall the agent be permitted to judge of the extent of his own powers, without reference to his constituents? To a certain extent he is compelled to do this, in the very act of exercising them, but this is always in subordination to the authority by whom his powers were conferred.

"Considering the nature of our system of government, the states ought to be, and I presume always will be, extremely careful not to interpose their sovereign power against the decisions of the supreme court, in any case where that court clearly has jurisdiction. Of this character, are the cases cited at the commencement of this inquiry; such, for example, as those between two states, those affecting foreign ministers, those of admiralty and maritime jurisdiction, &c. As to all these subjects, the jurisdiction is clear, and no state can have any interest to dispute it.

"According to the principles of all our institutions sovereignty does not reside in any government whatever, neither state nor federal. Government is regarded merely as the agent of those who create it, and subject in all respects to their will. In the states, the sovereign power is in the people of the states respectively; and the sovereign power of the United States would, for the same reason, be in 'the people of the United States,' if there were any such people, known as a single nation, and the framers of the federal government.

"The true sovereignty of the United States, therefore, is in the states, and not in the people of the United States, nor in the federal government. That government is but the agent through whom a portion of this sovereign power is exerted; possessing no sovereignty itself, and exerting no power, except such only as its constituents have conferred on it. In ascertaining what these powers are, it is obviously proper that we should look only to the grant from which they are derived. The agent can claim nothing for itself, and on its own account. The constitution is a compact, and the parties to it are each state, with each and every other state. The federal government is not a party, but is the mere creature of the agreement between the states as parties. Each state is both grantor and grantee, receiving from each and all the other states, precisely what, in its turn, it concedes to each and all of them. The rule, therefore, that the words are to be taken most strongly in favour of the grantee, cannot apply, because, as each state is both grantor and grantee, it would give exactly as much as it would take away. The only mode, therefore, by which we may be certain to do no injustice to the intentions of the parties, is by taking their *words* as the true exponents of their meaning.

"The lovers of a strong consolidated government have laboured strenuously, and, I fear, with too much success, to remove every available restriction upon the powers of congress. *The tendency of their principles is to establish that legislative omnipotence which is the fundamental principle of the British constitution, and which renders every form of written constitution idle and useless.* They suffer themselves to be too much attracted by the splendours of a great central power. Dazzled by these splendours, they lose sight of the more useful, yet less ostentatious purposes of the state governments, and seem to be unconscious that, in building up this huge temple of federal power, they necessarily destroy those less pretending structures, from which alone they derive shelter, protection, and safety. This is the *ignis fatuus* which has so often deceived nations, and betrayed them into the slough of despotism. On all such the impressive warning of Patrick Henry, drawn from the lessons of all experience, would be utterly lost. 'Those nations who have gone in search of grandeur, power, and splendour, have also fallen a sacrifice, and been the victims of their own folly. While they acquired those visionary blessings, they lost their freedom.' The consolidationists forget these wholesome truths, in their eagerness to invest the federal government with every power which is necessary to realize their visions of a great and splendid nation. Hence they do not discriminate between the several classes of federal powers, but contend for all of them, with the same blind and devoted zeal. It is remarkable that, in the exercise of all those functions of the federal government which concern our foreign relations, scarcely a case can be supposed requiring the aid of any implied or incidental power, as to which any serious doubt can arise. The powers of that government, as to all such matters, are so distinctly and plainly pointed out, in the very letter of the constitution; and they are so ample for all the purposes contemplated, that it is only necessary to understand them according to their plain meaning, and to exercise them according to their acknowledged extent. No auxiliaries are required; the government has only to go on in the execution of its trusts, with powers at once ample and unquestioned. It is only in matters which concern our domestic policy, that any serious struggle for federal power has ever arisen, or is likely to arise. Here, that love of splendour and display, which deludes so large a portion of mankind, unites with that self-interest by which *all* mankind are swayed, in aggrandizing the federal government, and adding to its powers. He who thinks it better to belong to a splendid and showy government, than to a free and happy one, naturally seeks to surround all our institutions with a gaudy pageantry, which belongs only to aristocratic or monarchical systems. But the great struggle is for those various and extended powers from the exercise of which *avarice* may expect its gratifications. Hence the desire for a profuse expenditure of public money, and hence the thousand schemes, under the name of internal improvements, by means of which hungry contractors may plunder the public treasury, and wily speculators prey upon the less skilful and cunning. And hence, too, another sort of legislation, the most vicious of the whole, which, *professing* a fair and legitimate object of public good, looks, *really*, only to the promotion of private interests. It is thus that *classes* are united in supporting the powers of government, and an interest is created strong enough to carry all measures and sustain all abuses.

" Let it be borne in mind that, as to all these subjects of domestic concern, there is no absolute necessity that the federal government should possess any power at all. They are all such as the *state* governments are perfectly competent to manage; and the *most* competent, because each state is the best judge of what is useful or necessary to itself. There is, then, no room to complain of any want of power to do whatever the interests of the people require to be done.

" Here, then, are all the powers which it is necessary that government should possess; not lodged in one place, but distributed; not the power of the state governments, nor of the federal government, but the aggregate of their several and respective powers. In the exercise of those functions which the state governments are forbidden to exercise, the federal government need not look beyond the letter of its charter for any needful power; and in the exercise of any other function, there is still less necessity that it should do so; because, whatever power that government does not plainly possess, is plainly possessed by the state governments.

" A clause in the constitution allows representation to three-fifths of the slaves.* Judge Story considers the compromise upon this subject as unjust in principle, and decidedly injurious to the people of the non-slave-holding states. Mr. John Adams was of a different opinion. He said, in the convention which framed the constitution, ' that as to the numbers of the people being taken as the index of the wealth of the state, it was of no consequence by what name you called your people, whether by that of freemen or slaves; that in some countries the labouring poor are called freemen, in others they are called slaves; but that the difference as to the state was imaginary. That five hundred freemen would produce no more profits for the payment of taxes

---

* The slaves have no voice in elections.

than five hundred slaves. Therefore the state in which the labourers are called freemen should be taxed no more than that in which the labourers are called slaves.

"*If slaves are people*, as forming the measure of national wealth, and, consequently, of taxation; and if taxation and representation be placed upon the same principle, and regulated by the same ratio, then that slaves are people, in fixing the ratio of representation, is a logical *sequitur* which no one can possibly deny.

"But it is objected that slaves are *property*, and, for that reason are not more entitled to representation than any other species of property. But they are also *people*, and, upon analogous principles, are entitled to representation as people. It is in this character alone that the non-slave-holding states have a right to consider them as has already been shown, and in this character alone is it *just* to consider them. We ought to presume that every slave occupies a place which, but for his presence, would be occupied by a free white man, and, if this were so, every one, and not three-fifths only, would be represented; but the states who hold no slaves have no right to complain, that this is not the case in other states, so long as the labour of the slave contributes as much to the common stock of productive industry, as the labour of the white man. It is enough that a state possesses a certain number of *people*, of living rational beings, we are not to inquire whether they be black, or white, or tawny, nor what are their peculiar relations among one another. If the slave of the south be property, of what nature is that property, and what kind of interest has the owner of it? He has a right to the profits of the slave's labour. And so the master of an indented apprentice has a right to the profits of *his* labour. It is true, one holds the right for the life of the slave, and the other only for a time limited in the apprentice's indentures; but this is a difference only in the *extent*, and not in the *nature* of the interest. It is also true, that the owner of a slave has, in most states, a right to *sell him;* but this is only because the laws of the state authorize him to do so. And, in like manner, the indentures of an apprentice may be transferred if the laws of the state will allow it. In all these respects, therefore, the slave and the indented apprentice stand upon precisely the same principle. To a certain extent they are both property, and neither of them can *be regarded as a free man;* and if the one be not entitled to representation, the other also should be denied that right. Whatever be the difference of their relations to the separate members of the community, in the eye of that community they are both *people*. Here, again, Mr. Adams shall speak for me; and our country has produced few men who could speak more wisely: 'A slave, may indeed, from the custom of speech, be more properly called the wealth of his master, than the free labourer might be called the wealth of his employer; but as to the state both are equally its wealth, and should therefore equally add to the quota of its tax. Yes; and consequently, they should equally add to the quota of its *representation*.'

"It is remarkable that the constitution is wholly silent in regard to the power of removal from office. The *appointing* power is in the president and senate; the president nominating, and the senate confirming. But the power to *remove* from office, seems never to have been contemplated by the convention at all, for they have given no directions whatever upon the subject. The consequence has been precisely such as might have been expected, a severe contest for the possession of that power, and the ultimate usurpation of it, by that department of the government to which it ought never to be intrusted. In the absence of all precise directions upon the subject, it would seem that the power to remove ought to attend the power to appoint; for those whose duty it is to fill the offices of the country with competent incumbents, cannot possibly execute that trust fully and well, unless they have power to correct their own errors and mistakes, by removing the unworthy, and substituting better men in their places. This, I have no doubt, is the true construction of our constitution. It was for a long time strenuously contended for by a large party in the country, and was finally yielded, rather to the confidence which the country reposed in the virtues of Washington, than to any conviction that it was properly an executive power, belonging only to the president. It is true of Washington alone, of all the truly great of the earth, that he never inflicted an injury upon his country, except only such as proceeded from the excess of his own virtues. His known patriotism, wisdom, and purity, inspired us with a confidence, and a feeling of security against the abuses of power, which has led to the establishment of many precedents, dangerous to public liberty in the hands of any other man.

"Another striking imperfection of the constitution, as respects the executive department, is found in the veto power. *The right to forbid the people to pass whatever laws they please, is the right to deprive them of self-government.*[*]

"The re-eligibility of the president, from term to term, is the necessary source of numberless abuses; at present there is no danger of this. *Presidents are now made, not by the free suffrages of the people, but by party management;* and there are always more than one in the successful party, who are looking to their own turn in the presidential office. It is too early, yet, for a monopoly of that high honour; but the time will come, within the natural course of things, when the actual incumbent will find means to buy off opposition, and to ensure a continuance in office, by prostituting the trusts which belong to it. We cannot hope to be free from the dangers which result from an abuse of presidential power and patronage, until that officer shall be eligible only for one term, a long term if you please; and until he shall be rendered more easily and directly responsible to the power which appoints him."

HONOURABLE J. C. SPENCER'S EXAMINATION OF JUDGE UPSHUR'S REVIEW OF THE CONSTITUTION OF THE UNITED STATES.

Mr. Macgregor thus introduces Mr. Spencer's answer:—"In order to comprehend the views entertained by eminent legislators in the United States of America, we consider it just to introduce into this work the following examination by a gentleman and statesman of great learning and ability of Mr. Upshur's strictures on the American constitution. Mr. Spencer is not only a profound jurist, but he has held the most important trusts in the government of his country. He was one of the most able secretaries of the treasury; an office which nearly corresponds with that of chancellor of the exchequer in England."

"Having," says Mr. Spencer, "been favoured by a friend with the perusal, in sheets, of a part of Mr. Macgregor's great work on the Progress of America, which contained the remarks of the Honourable Abel P. Upshur on the constitution of the United States, I expressed my unhesitating opinion that they were as erroneous as they were injurious; that they were calculated to produce a very false impression of the weakness of our Union, and the incapacity of our federal government to maintain itself, or to fulfil the high duties assigned to it; and that it would be equally unfortunate for us and for other

---

[*] So thoroughly is this right of the people to make the laws understood in the British parliament, that the royal disallowance of any bill is never contemplated; and, although the royal prerogative of disallowance still exists *de jure*, it has long ceased *de facto*, by *disusage*.

countries if those views should be received and accredited, as just expositions ^ of a system somewhat complicated, and therefore liable to be much misunderstood by those who had neither the means nor the leisure for its thorough investigation. I was urged to prepare a statement of the opinions of that class of our countrymen (believed to be, by far, the largest portion of the active and intelligent men engaged in such discussions,) who take a practical view of our government, and seek to ascertain its powers and duties by a reference to the plain words and fair meaning of the constitution. Under the impression that the withdrawal from the cares of public life, and the absence of professional engagements, would afford abundant leisure for such an undertaking, a partial assent was given. This having been communicated to Mr. Macgregor, he has announced that in a subsequent part of his work, a review of Mr. Upshur's remarks, by me, would be given. Under these circumstances, although the anticipated leisure has not been enjoyed, yet the desire to fulfil an implied pledge, impels me to endeavour to execute a task which should have been committed to more competent hands.

"Judging from the portions of Mr. Upshur's communication, for portions only of it are given, it would seem that he quite disapproved of our federal constitution; for while he points out what he supposes to be defects, which he severely censures, no part of it has received his unqualified approbation. To those who were acquainted with the peculiar character of his mind, this, probably, will not be surprising. A knowledge of those peculiarities will serve to explain, if it does not elucidate some of his views. Mingling very little with the world, and in a profound retirement, in a secluded part of Virginia, he indulged a naturally speculative mind to its fullest extent, in reflections upon our form of federal government, without ever having had the advantage of personally partaking in its operations.

"He had held public stations in the state of Virginia, but had held no office under the general government, nor had he ever been a member of either house of Congress, when his opinions on nullification were promulgated. He had prided himself on being one of the most high-toned federalists of the country, until about the time when the disputes with South Carolina commenced. These disputes involved deeply and extensively the interests of the southern states, who complained that their agriculture was made subservient to northern manufactures, by means of the tariff acts of Congress. Failing to secure a numerical majority in that body, they questioned its constitutional power thus to oppress them, as they said, by legislation; and having satisfied themselves of the want of such power, they next inquired into the means of resisting its exercise. This led them to what is called the doctrine of nullification; which means, according to their theory, that any one state legislature which conceives an act of the federal Congress to be unconstitutional, may *nullify* such act, by declaring it to be inoperative within the limits of the state, and by punishing, through the state tribunals, the officers who should attempt to execute it. The old maxim, that where there is a will there is generally a way, was exemplified in this case. The novel system of a federal government uniting several sovereign states in one confederacy, and under one government for certain definite purposes, afforded an ample field for the speculative tendencies of our southern statesmen; and to a man like Mr. Upshur, it was a rich mine, in which he could strike his own quarry, and pursue it at his own option. There was nothing in the institutions of ancient, or modern republics, at all similar. Neither experience nor the labours of learned or thoughtful men afforded guides to reflection, or checks to the wildest license of speculation. He entered this field warmly; and as the first step in his progress, abandoned all the political principles which forty years had enabled him to form and strengthen. He became a writer for the periodicals of the day, and contributed the principal articles to the 'Southern Review,' the champion of nullification. In the support of that cause, and in discussions, written, printed, and oral, he was engaged more or less extensively, for about eight years, when he was called to take charge of the navy department, by Mr. Tyler, from which he was transferred to the state department, and in which he remained about eight months. The communication to Mr. Macgregor, a part of which appears in his work, is but a condensation of the essays published in the 'Southern Review,' and other periodicals.

"This account of the author of the remarks which are proposed to be examined, and this history of the question he has discussed, seemed useful, if not necessary, to a full comprehension of his views. It should be added, that the nullifiers profess to derive their doctrine from Mr. Jefferson and Mr. Madison; and Mr. Macgregor has apparently fallen into the error of supposing that doctrine to constitute the great point of difference between the federalists and democrats. It is very true that these parties have differed much in their construction of the constitution, the former being latitudinarian, pushing to its utmost extent the principle embodied in the eighteenth subdivision of section eighth of the first article of the constitution, that of passing all laws necessary and proper for carrying into execution the powers vested by that instrument in the government, or in any of its departments, while the democrats have insisted on a rigid and strict construction, and have maintained that these implied powers must always be subordinate and ancillary, and can never be converted into main and principal purposes of government. But as to the remedy, for the abuse of the legislative authority, proposed by the nullifiers, the democrats, when in full possession of power, and with ample means to sustain and vindicate it, so far from supporting, rebuked and denounced it in the most significant manner. On the occasion already referred to, South Carolina asserted this reserved right to nullify a tariff act of congress, and passed laws for the purpose. General Jackson, the then president, with a vast majority of democrats in both houses of congress, adopted the most stringent measures to put down the doctrine and its abettors.

"He issued a proclamation, which received the warm approbation of the whole country, (excepting South Carolina, and a very few in some of the other southern states,) in which the doctrine was examined, and its fallacy exposed. And the misguided men who acted under it were warned to return to their allegiance; and this was followed by acts of congress of the most effective character. The incipient rebellion was crushed—by democratic men—indeed, by the democratic party.

"In truth, this doctrine of nullification is the peculiar property of a distinguished statesman of South Carolina, who has enjoyed all the highest stations in the republic but the very highest, and who has repeatedly been a competitor for that station. His own state, and some citizens of other states, whose interests are supposed to be identical with those of South Carolina, have embraced it; and although partisan writers talk about reserved rights of the states, on special occasions, the general and almost universal feeling of the country abhors and condemns it.

"In these circumstances an apology will be found for an effort to prevent any erroneous impression as to its prevalence, and to exhibit what are deemed the unfounded assumptions in Mr. Upshur's communication, by which it is sought to be sustained.

"It should be remarked preliminarily, that Mr. Madison has publicly and fully disavowed the paternity of any such doctrine, and declared his conviction of its fallacy, as well as its dangerous consequences. It was contended, by its friends, that the germ of the principle was to be found in the resolutions of the legislatures of Virginia and Kentucky, passed in 1798 and 1799, and which are known to have been prepared by Mr. Jefferson and Mr. Madison.

"These resolutions were aimed at the alien and sedition laws, enacted under the administration of the elder Adams. After denouncing these acts as unconstitutional, the resolutions declared, that if they were not repealed it would be the duty, as it was the right, of the states of the union to interpose and seek a rightful remedy. In a letter to Mr. Rives, written a few years since, Mr. Madison denies that the language or spirit of the resolutions authorizes any *separate* state to resort to any means of resistance, but that the action of the states *combined* was contemplated; and he refers to the provision of the constitution for calling a convention of all the states, on the application of two-thirds of the number, as the remedy intended.

"The reader, not particularly conversant with American politics, will find some advantage in these preliminary remarks, by their enabling him to perceive the exact position advanced by Mr. Upshur on the subject of nullification.

"Justice to him requires that it should be stated in his own words.

"He first admits that the supreme court is the proper tribunal, in the last resort, to determine whether the federal government has transcended its constitutional obligation or not, *to a certain extent;* that its decision is binding and absolutely final, so far as the court has jurisdiction over cases affecting the rights of the individual citizens, and over certain others, affecting the rights of the individual states; and that states, as well as individuals, in these cases, have not 'an independent right to construe, control, and judge of the obligations of the federal government, but that they are bound by the decisions of the federal courts, so far as they have authorized and agreed to submit to them.' So far Mr. Upshur has but expressed the clear and unequivocal import of the constitution, and the common opinion of every man in America who has ever publicly declared his opinion on the subject. It will be seen, then, that the dispute is rather about a question of fact than of principle. The principle is conceded that the jurisdiction of the federal courts is final and conclusive in all cases where such jurisdiction exists. The dispute is, whether a given case comes within that jurisdiction. If it does not, then no one has contended that the decision of the supreme court would be more effectual in determining it than that of the emperor of China; it would still remain to be settled. If the parties to the controversy should happen to be a powerful state on one side, and the federal union on the other, it must be determined by physical strength—as all controversies must be where there is no umpire, and the parties will not amicably adjust them. This is natural nullification, independent of all law, all constitutions, and all compacts; in other words, it is a revolution. If this be all that Mr. Upshur and his nullifying associates mean—that when the federal government exercises powers not delegated, no decision of the supreme court can supply the defect in the grant, and that resistance to oppression, even in a judicial form, is a right and a duty, few or none on this side the Atlantic will be found to controvert their views. And it is very immaterial whether this resistance proceeds from voluntary and temporary associations of individuals, or from an organized state government. The intelligent reader will perceive at once that this cannot be the question at issue, respecting which so much ink has been shed. The great and the real question is, *who* shall decide whether *the case presented* does or does not fall within the circle of powers, duties, and obligations of the federal government, as prescribed by the constitution? It is not as Mr. Upshur would have the reader to infer, whether a state may resist the decision of the supreme court in a case of acknowledged usurpation. But it is, whether the supreme court shall decide whether the power claimed in the given case be a usurpation or not. Now, the real object of the nullifiers is to establish the doctrine, that the states may sit in judgment upon the decisions of the supreme court, review them, like an appellate tribunal; and if any one state conceives that the federal judiciary has sanctioned a usurpation, it may of its own will, and as an incident to its sovereignty, apply the remedy of nullifying, as before explained, or may secede—withdraw from the union.

"Unwilling at the onset to state the question in this broad form, Mr. Upshur, after making the admission before quoted, says,—'But there are many cases

Involving the question of federal power which are not cognizable before the federal courts; and of course, as to these we must look out for some other umpire.' And in this case it is, as he contends, that each state has the right to construe its own contracts, and decide upon its own rights and powers. In this short extract lies the root of the whole matter; every thing is based upon the quiet and apparently simple assumption, that there are many cases involving the question of federal power, which are not cognizable before the federal courts. Now, this is utterly denied, and it is averred that in the whole history of our government, no such case has ever occurred, and from the nature of our institutions it cannot occur. In other words, it is affirmed that no case can be conceived, where federal power could be exercised of which the courts of the United States could not take *cognizance*, by means of a suit or legal proceeding presenting the question directly to them.

"If an officer of the United States forcibly collects an impost upon an imported article, the laws and the forms of proceeding enable the citizen conceiving himself oppressed to present the question by an action at law. The courts act upon individuals; if they claim to be clothed with authority for their proceedings, the extent and constitutionality of that authority necessarily come up for judgment. If the officers and process of the United States be resisted, civil actions, as well as criminal prosecutions, instantly furnish the means of determining whether such resistance was justifiable or not. By the terms of the second section of the third article of the constitution, the judicial *power* extends to *all cases* in law and equity arising under the constitution, *the laws of the United States*, and treaties made under their authority. The question discussed by Mr. Upshur supposes a law of Congress, because, without the authority of the legislative department there can be no exercise of the federal power. And as if to remove every vestige of doubt, and to provide for cases, if any should occur, which did not arise under a law of Congress, the same section provides that the judicial power shall extend 'to controversies to which the United States shall be a party,' without distinction or discrimination. How can there be any cases, then, 'involving the question of federal power,' to which 'the judicial power' of the United States does not extend, or which, in the language of Mr. Upshur, 'are not cognizable before the federal courts?'

"If this, then, be the case, as Mr. Upshur supposes, 'in which the question, who are parties to the constitution, becomes all-important and controlling,' the question itself might be dismissed as of no practical consequence; for the case itself never can occur. But although introduced in this quiet and unpretending form, the question, nevertheless, is one which lies at the foundation of the whole argument advanced by the nullifiers. Their theory is, that the government is federative—a confederation of sovereign states, and not consolidated—and that the states, the parties to the league, retain the right to construe the compact—the constitution—each for itself, and to decide upon its own rights and powers. It is for this purpose that Mr. Upshur has examined our colonial history, contending that we were not 'one people' before the adoption of our own constitution. In the sense in which he uses this term, no one will dispute his correctness. The American colonies certainly were not 'a political corporation;' and great injustice would be done to Judge Story by the supposition that he maintained such an historical untruth. Mr. Upshur has also shown, what no one had ever denied, that by the articles of confederation the several states retained their sovereignty; and he might have added, that the very weakness of the league which connected them was so apparent—its utter unfitness, either in war or in peace, to unite the common strength of the Americans, to restrain the powerful states, and to compel the reluctant to contribute equally to the common defence, was the cause, and the sole cause, of its abandonment, and of the adoption of the new constitution. The question arises under this new form of government. The inhabitants of the thirteen colonies had waged a common war, and they, unitedly as well as severally, had been acknowledged to be independent by the treaty of 1783. They united in appointing ambassadors to negotiate this treaty, and, by its terms and operation, they were not only separated from Great Britain, but were bound together in a common mass. France, Spain, and Holland, had recognised them as one people, and had sent ministers to the body, not to the several states. The body had formed treaties with those nations; it had acted as a nation, had assumed its duties and responsibilities—nay, in the very first line of the Declaration of Independence, they had called themselves 'one people.' They were, therefore, to some extent 'a people;' they were in the incipient stages of forming 'a political corporation,' and were in a condition—physically, morally, and politically—to do so. Yet Mr. Upshur remarks, that 'in the states the sovereign power is in the people of the states respectively, and the sovereign power of the United States would, for the same reason, be in the people of the United States, if there were any such people known as a single nation, and the framers of the federal government.' The historical references already made show sufficiently that there *was* a people composing the thirteen colonies, who had made themselves somewhat extensively known as a single nation, having an army and a navy, a national ensign, issuing a national currency, represented abroad by its ministers, and receiving embassies from other nations. The first condition stated by Mr. Upshur would seem to have been complied with. As to the second condition, viz. that a people known as a single nation should have been 'the framers of the federal government'—perhaps the instrument which was the work of their hands—will be allowed to be good evidence, if not conclusive, upon the point. It commences with these words: 'We, the people of the United States, in order, &c., &c., do ordain and establish this constitution for the United States of America.' It made provision for its own existence by its last article, that the ratification by nine states should be sufficient for its establishment. It was accordingly submitted to the people of the several states, not to their ordinary legislatures, but to conventions elected specially to consider the new constitution, and to adopt or reject it. This was the most expedient form in which it could be submitted to the people directly. A ballot, or a *viva voce* vote at the election polls, directly upon the various parts of the constitution, was obviously objectionable, if not wholly impracticable; and the same object was obtained by calling on the electors to choose delegates who should directly and immediately express their will. Admitting, then, that up to the time of the formation of the constitution the inhabitants of the thirteen colonies did not form a separate and distinct political corporation, perfect in its organization, and capable of maintaining itself, yet it must be apparent that they had so long associated together under a common government, had exercised unitedly so many of the functions of the national sovereignty, that they were in a condition to become integrated, and to perfect their identity; and the exact question is, what was the effect of the constitution upon them in this respect?

"There has certainly been a class of politicians who have contended that this effect was a complete consolidation, and that the federative principle was extinguished. Another class, and these are the nullifiers, maintain that the federative principle still prevails as effectually under the new constitution as it did under the articles of confederation; and that, consequently the separate states have the same right as before to construe for themselves the new compact—in other words, to set aside the decisions of the federal judiciary. There is another class, comprising, it is believed, two-thirds of the American people, who hold both these views to be extremes, and to be fallacious, and who adopt a middle course regarding the federal government as both federative and consolidated—federative in its origin, federative in reference to domestic and internal concerns, and yet consolidated; that is, an independent integer, a popular government in relation to foreign affairs, and in general to all that concerns the common interest of the people of all the states. The idea has been correctly expressed by M. de Tocqueville. 'The object was,' he says, 'so to divide the authority of the different states which composed the union, that each of them should continue to govern itself in all that concerned its internal prosperity, while the *entire nation*, represented by the union, should continue to form a compact body, and to provide for the exigencies of the people.' And the whole matter is condensed in one line: 'The United States form not only a republic, but a confederation;' and he shows that the authority of the nation is more *central* than it was in France or Spain, when the American constitution was adopted. The identity of the people of the several states, their *oneness*, as Mr. Upshur expresses it, is very clearly shown by the second section of the fourth article. 'The citizens of each state shall be entitled to all privileges and immunities of citizens in the several states.' Here is a provision that operates, not upon the states, but individually upon every citizen, clothing him with a new character, in addition to that he already possesses. It enables the citizens of Louisiana to inherit lands by descent in Massachusetts: it removes all alienage at once, and leaves no trace of a foreign feature. Without dwelling upon the first section of the same article, which gives full faith and credit in 'each state to the public acts, records, and judicial proceedings of every other state,' and which has been held by all our courts to give them the same effect in every part of the union that they have in the state where they originate, or upon the power given to Congress exclusively, of establishing the mode of making citizens of the United States; and, without adverting to various other provisions of a similar character, it must be sufficient to rest on this single section, which makes the citizen of one state a citizen of every state, to demonstrate that the union is not a mere confederacy, or league of sovereign states, but that it is an integer, a political body under a constitution which declares that treason may be committed against it by declaring war, or adhering to its enemies. It becomes quite immaterial how this result was accomplished, or who were the parties to the instrument by which it was effected. The question, and the only question, is, what is the political condition of the people under that instrument? Are they one people, or are they twenty-seven distinct people, aliens to each other?

"Contenting myself with these general views of some of the leading and prominent features of the constitution, I do not deem it necessary to follow Mr. Upshur in his examination of the *structure* of the different departments. He admits, however, that the House of Representatives is *not* federative. The ordinary course of electing a president by the votes of the people of the different states, in choosing special delegates to express their will on that subject, is also certainly not federative; while the mode of proceeding in the event of a failure to elect in the first instance, is evidently federative; and thus, in the structure of the departments, the federative and the consolidating, or central principle, are both adopted, and are applied as the nature of the power to be conferred may require.

"We may now approach more directly the true question which the nullifiers present against the residue of their countrymen, and which Mr. Upshur has rather intimated than distinctly avowed. After enumerating at some length the cases to which the judicial authority of the United States extends, he refers to the tenth amendment of the constitution, by which it is provided, that 'the *powers* not delegated to the United States by the constitution, nor prohibited by it to the states, are reserved to the states respectively, or to the people.' And he contends that these *powers* are reserved as well against the judiciary as against the other departments of the federal government; that among these powers is that of each state, judging *alone* of its own compacts and agreements; that the constitution being such a compact, each state has a right to interpret it for itself, *unless*, and then comes a most important qualification, which presents the point of the whole controversy, 'unless it (each state) has clearly waived that right in favour of another power.' Now the position advanced and maintained by all parties in America, except the nullifiers, is, that by the very terms of this compact this right of each state to interpret it for itself, has been expressly waived in favour of the federal judiciary. No language which I can employ would so clearly state this position as that of M. de Tocqueville: 'The attributes of the federal government,' he says, 'were, therefore, carefully enumerated, and all that was not included among them, was declared to constitute a part of the privileges of the several governments of the states. Thus the government of the states remained the rule, and that of the confederation became the exception. But as it was foreseen that in practice, questions might arise as to the exact limits of this exceptional authority, and that it would be dangerous to submit those questions to the decision of the ordinary courts of justice established in the states by the states themselves, a high federal court was created, which was destined, among other functions, to maintain the balance of power which had been established by the constitution between the two rival governments.' 'To suppose,' he remarks in another place, 'that a state can subsist, when its fundamental laws may be subjected to four-and-twenty different interpretations at the same time, is to advance a proposition alike contrary to reason and to experience. The object of the erection of a federal tribunal, was to prevent the courts of the states from deciding questions affecting the national interests in their own departments, and so to form a *uniform* body of jurisprudence for the interpretation of the laws of the union.' The supreme court of the United States was, therefore, invested with the right of determining all questions of jurisdiction. And to effect this purpose, can language be more clear and explicit than that of the second section of the third article? 'The judicial power shall extend to *all* cases in law and equity arising under this constitution, the laws of the United States, and treaties made, or which shall be made under their authority, to controversies to which the United States shall be a party,' &c. If it *extends* to them, it must be for the purpose of deciding them, not for the purpose of referring them to some other power or tribunal. It has already been shown it is supposed that this description necessarily comprises every case that can possibly arise, involving the exercise of the federal power. Every such case must be founded on a claim that it springs from the authority given by the constitution, and then the courts must decide whether it 'arises under the constitution.' If it does not, it must be dismissed. If it does, the courts must entertain and decide it. And it is somewhat extraordinary that this very power is conceded by Mr. Upshur in a previous part of his remarks: 'So far, therefore, as the federal constitution has provided for the subject at all, the supreme court is, beyond question, the *final* judge or arbiter; and this, too, whether the jurisdiction which it exercises be legitimate or usurped.' These are his words, and they afford a complete and perfect answer to the qualification he makes of the right of each state to interpret the constitution for itself, 'unless it has clearly waived that right in favour of another power.' If, then, the federal constitution has provided for the subject in the way he states, and if the States have assented to that provision by adopting the constitution, have they not 'waived the right of interpreting it in favour of another power?'

"But Mr. Upshur says, that it is not waived, and this, he says, is apparent from the fact 'that, if the judiciary be the sole judges of the extent of their own powers, their powers are universal, and the enumeration in the constitution is idle and useless.' Now, with deference be it said, this is very inconclusive. The liability of any power to abuse, to gross perversion, does not, in sound minds, tend in the least to prove its non-existence. The same remark, which Mr. Upshur makes in reference to the judiciary, is still more applicable to the states. If *they* are 'the sole judges of their own powers, *their* powers are universal,' and the grant of authority to the federal government, or to the judiciary, is 'idle and useless.' The question, however, still remains, whether the power has been granted? The object of all political compacts and constitutions is to produce and preserve peace, and to prevent wars, by providing a mode of final settlement peaceably, by an independent tribunal. Every umpire may err; may enlarge its jurisdiction, and take cognizance of what is not submitted to it. In the formation of a constitution, the question is open, whether it is better to incur this hazard, than the opposite one of having nothing finally settled? And this was the very question which the framers of our constitution considered, and debated and decided, and this decision having been ratified by the states, as well as by the people of the United States, it is too late to seek to evade it by questioning its wisdom.

"Mr. Upshur, however, persists in falling back on principles anterior to the constitution, instead of looking to that instrument alone; and he urges that the federal government is the creature of the states; that it is a mere agent, with limited powers, and then asks,—'Shall the agent be permitted to judge of the extent of his own powers, without reference to his constituents?' To a certain extent he is compelled to do this, in the very act of exercising them; but this is always in subordination to the authority by whom his powers were conferred.' Besides, the fallacy, as it is believed to be, that the federal government is the creature of the states, as distinguished from the people of the states, there is a fundamental error in considering the judiciary as an *agent* to exercise certain political powers—as a mere attorney, in fact, to perform certain delegated functions, and as being subordinate to the states, by whom it is intended to be implied that the judicial power was conferred. It is conceived that its functions are of a character entirely different. As its very name imports, it is to *adjudge*—not execute, nor legislate. It is the means by which disputes and controversies are to be terminated, without a resort to force. It is the contrivance of civilization, to prevent a recurrence to the law of nature. It is the last and strongest link which unites the ends of the chain of civil government, and renders that complete, which, without it, would not deserve the name of government. So far from partaking of the nature of agents, or being subordinate to the authority which conferred their powers, the judiciary are by the constitution rendered wholly independent of their constituents, who cannot revoke or annul the authority once granted; and, instead of being subordinate, they are by the same instrument placed above those who created them, and administer the law to them and to all others. Even controversies between states are subjects of their jurisdiction. What becomes then of this idea of their being agents, and bound to make 'reference to their constituents' to determine the extent of their powers?

"It will be observed, that the argument of Mr. Upshur covers the whole ground. 'True,' he says, 'the states ought to be, and, I presume, will be, extremely careful not to interpose their sovereign power against the decisions of the supreme courts in any case where that court clearly has jurisdiction.' But this involves the very point of determining whether it has jurisdiction or not; and whatever may be Mr. Upshur's opinion of certain cases being *clearly* within their jurisdiction, a state which has passed a *stop-law*, as it is termed— an act to suspend the collection of debts, or to prevent their recovery—will not be very scrupulous in its construction of one part of a constitution which interposes a check to its rashness, when it has already violated another part of the same instrument. In truth, this doctrine, that a judiciary is not 'to judge of the extent of its own powers without reference to its constituents,' at one blow prostrates that department of government in the states, as well as in the United States. For, if it be true in one case, it is equally so in the other. Mr. Upshur was himself a local judge in Virginia; but history does not record the instance of his having referred to the General Assembly of that state, which passed the laws instituting his court, and which appointed him to the office, for its directions as to the extent of his judicial jurisdiction, although many perplexing cases of that kind must have occurred before him.

"The argument, so often repeated in Mr. Upshur's remarks, that because the constitution was a compact between the states, one with the other, each must possess the right to construe it for itself, is deemed a very dangerous fallacy. 'According to our ideas, every government is the result of a compact, express or implied, by those who submit to it. In the states then the citizens who are the parties to this compact must respectively have the same right to construe it for themselves, and in a *clear* case of judicial usurpation must have the right to nullify the decision.' Before admitting such consequences it will be well to test the soundness of the premises from which they flow. Now, as remarked in General Jackson's proclamation in 1832, it is precisely because it is a compact that the parties cannot depart from it. It is an agreement, a binding obligation, entered into for mutual benefit, and upon a mutual consideration between the respective parties, that they will respectively fulfil the obligations and perform the duties which it enjoins. Each party has an interest in its performance by the other, and therefore no party can withdraw from that performance without the consent of the others. To secure this performance, all the parties have agreed upon the creation of a distinct and independent tribunal to determine their controversies, not only with each other, but with the common or federal government, and have further agreed that such determination shall be final. That tribunal is not the agent or functionary of the federal government alone. Its members must be appointed with the advice and consent of a majority of the states, expressed by their representatives in the senate. They are the umpires chosen by the federal government and the states conjointly. The very first step which that tribunal must always take when a case is presented to it, is to inquire whether it be one of those that have been agreed on to be submitted to its determination. Now the pretence that one of the parties may under this agreement revise the decision of this tribunal, and decide for itself whether a given case was subject to its jurisdiction, is to nullify not only the decision but the agreement itself. But this it has no moral or political right to do. It would be a shameful violation of not only its faith, but an outrage upon all the other parties to the compact, which they would have the unquestionable right to resent and to punish. This then would immediately bring on a war. It is to avoid this very consequence that the tribunal created to decide these controversies is armed with power to enforce its decisions; and, fortunately, it operates not on states, but on individuals, on the citizens composing the people of the United States. If a state should, through its courts, imprison or otherwise punish an officer of the United States, for executing one of its laws, the persons committing the offence would be held responsible, and to enforce that responsibility the whole power, civil and military, of all the other states, would be put in requisition. Such are the guarantees of our constitution, and that they are effectual and will be called into action whenever occasion shall require, has already been proved in a case peculiarly calculated to test their value and strength.

"With these remarks Mr. Upshur's views on the doctrine of nullification are dismissed, although the subject is far from being exhausted. Many incidental matters have been purposely omitted, with the view of engaging attention to the one single point involved. It is hoped that it will at least appear that the constitution of the United States is not the miserable rope of sand which the nullifying doctrine would render it, and that we do not hold our liberties, our rights, and our property, by the feeble tenure of the fitful caprice of a state exasperated into fury by faction, or overawed by combinations of powerful interests.

"I have no disposition to follow Mr. Upshur in his remarks upon that clause of the constitution which allows representation to three-fifths of the slaves. It is enough to say that it was one of the results of a compromise without which no constitution could have been formed. Whatever doubts of its justice or its expediency may be entertained, every good citizen will observe and obey it in its integrity.

"He also remarks upon the omission in the constitution to provide for removals from office. He might have noticed a hundred other omissions of details which necessarily flow from express provisions, or which are supplied by the usages of the country from which we borrow our language and so many of our legal and political institutions.

"He regards as a 'striking imperfection' in our constitution the existence of the veto-power, and adds the right to forbid the 'people to pass whatever laws they please, is the right to deprive them of self-government.' Can this be the view of a statesman, or even of a lawyer! The veto power, or the veto, does not forbid the people to pass what laws they please. How much more accurate and discriminating is the accomplished author of 'Democracy in America!' The veto is, as he represents it, an appeal to the people by a president, in defence of the independence which the constitution awards him. It is an appeal to the sober second thought of the representatives of the people, to re-consider the matter, and if two-thirds of both houses still believe the proposed bill to be just and constitutional, they may pass it notwithstanding the president's objections. It is a *suspensive* veto, not an *absolute* one, as in England; and without it the president would long since have been stripped of every valuable function of his office, or rendered utterly dependent on the Congress. In fifty-five years that have elapsed since the power was granted, it has not been exercised more than ten or twelve times; and in every instance but one its exercise has been sanctioned by the people.

"The re-eligibility of the president from term to term is also complained of by Mr. Upshur, and he thinks proper to add, 'Presidents are now made, not by the free suffrages of the people, but by party management.' But he has not intimated that the ineligibility of a president would have the least effect in preventing party management. A president has the same means of choosing his successor—nay, greater means than of promoting his own re-election; and we have not found less party management during the second term to which our presidents are limited by the unwritten law of public opinion, than during their first term, when they were candidates for re-election. It is obvious that exigencies may arise, such as a foreign war, which would require indispensably the continuance in power of an existing administration, that it might carry out a plan of measures it had devised. The opinion that ordinarily the same person should not serve more than once in the presidential office is becoming prevalent: and a sound public sentiment will doubtless regulate the matter as well, if not better, than it could be done by a positive provision of the constitution.

"In conclusion, I ask leave to express a deep regret that Mr. Upshur could have found nothing in the constitution of his country worthy of his commendation, and that his ingenuity should have been employed in attempting to prove it utterly defective, as the foundation of a government of laws, incapable of restraining the oppressions of powerful states, and of affording the shelter and protection which it promised to every citizen. If these remarks shall have the effect of dispelling such a reflection upon the wisdom of that distinguished body of men who calmly and deliberately weighed every suggestion that sprang from their own minds, or was suggested to them by others;

who investigated most carefully the very peculiar condition of the states, and understood their various local interests; who had felt the defects of the confederation in seven years of war and six of peace; and invoking the blessing and aid of Divine Providence, devoted themselves to their task with a fidelity, patience, and forbearance which have been the admiration of the world, and finally produced the first written constitution of government that ever emanated direct from the people themselves—a constitution venerated by the intelligence of all Europe, and enshrined in the hearts of all patriotic Americans; if that constitution shall have been in any degree cleared of the mists with which a partial, theoretic, and heated imagination had invested it, I shall be thankful, and shall feel that neither my time nor the patience of the reader has been misspent.

"(Signed)   J. C. SPENCER."

"Albany, State of New York, June 14, 1845.

THE ADDRESS OF THE SOUTHERN DELEGATES IN CONGRESS TO THEIR CONSTITUENTS.*

We, whose names are hereunto annexed, address you in discharge of what we believe to be a solemn duty, on the most important subject ever presented for your consideration. We allude to the conflict between the two great sections of the Union, growing out of a difference of feeling and opinion in reference to the relation existing between the two races, the European and the African, which inhabit the southern section, and the acts of aggression and encroachment to which it has led.

The conflict commenced not long after the acknowledgment of our independence, and has gradually increased until it has arrayed the great body of the North against the South on this most vital subject. In the progress of this conflict, aggression has followed aggression, and encroachment encroachment, until they have reached a point when a regard for your peace and safety will not permit us to remain longer silent. The object of this address is, to give you a clear, correct, but brief account of the whole series of aggressions and encroachments on your rights, with a statement of the dangers to which they expose you. Our object in making it is not to cause excitement, but to put you in full possession of all the facts and circumstances necessary to a full and just conception of a deep-seated disease, which threatens great danger to you and the whole body politic. We act on the impression, that in a popular government like ours, a true conception of the actual character and state of a disease is indispensable to effecting a cure.

We have made it a joint address, because we believe that the magnitude of the subject required that it should assume the most impressive and solemn form.

Not to go farther back, the difference of opinion and feeling in reference to the relation between the two races disclosed itself in the Convention that framed the Constitution, and constituted one of the greatest difficulties in forming it. After many efforts, it was overcome by a compromise, which provided in the first place, that representatives and direct taxes shall be apportioned among the States according to their respective numbers; and that, in ascertaining the number of each, five slaves shall be estimated as three. In the next, that slaves

---

* From the present position of political parties in the Union, the further agitation of the slavery question seems inevitable; certain leading politicians in the North and South are determined to bring the issue to a trial. Our readers will therefore desire to have for reference the manifestos and documents that state by authority the points and merits of the controversy on both sides. We shall give them as we have room.

escaping into States where slavery does not exist, shall not be discharged from servitude, but shall be delivered up on claim of the party to whom their labour or service is due. In the third place, that Congress shall not prohibit the importation of slaves before the year 1808; but a tax not exceeding ten dollars may be imposed on each imported. And finally, that no capitation or direct tax shall be laid, but in proportion to federal numbers; and that no amendment of the Constitution, prior to 1808, shall affect this provision, nor that relating to the importation of slaves.

So satisfactory were these provisions, that the second, relative to the delivering up of fugitive slaves, was adopted unanimously, and all the rest, except the third, relative to the importation of slaves until 1808, with almost equal unanimity. They recognise the existence of slavery, and make a specific provision for its protection where it was supposed to be the most exposed. They go farther, and incorporate it, as an important element, in determining the relative weight of the several States in the Government of the Union, and the respective burden they should bear in laying capitation and direct taxes. It was well understood at the time, that, without them the Constitution would not have been adopted by the Southern States, and, of course, that they constituted elements so essential to the system that it never would have existed without them. The Northern States, knowing all this, ratified the Constitution, thereby pledging their faith, in the most solemn manner, sacredly to observe them. How that faith has been kept, and that pledge redeemed, we shall next proceed to show.

With few exceptions of no great importance, the South had no cause to complain prior to the year 1819,—a year, it is to be feared, destined to mark a train of events, bringing with them many, and great, and fatal disasters, on the country and its institutions. With it commenced the agitating debate on the question of the admission of Missouri into the Union. We shall pass by for the present this question, and others of the same kind directly growing out of it, and shall proceed to consider the effect of that spirit of discord which it roused up between the two sections. It first disclosed itself in the North, by hostility to that portion of the Constitution which provides for the delivering up of fugitive slaves. In its progress it led to the adoption of hostile acts, intended to render it of non-effect, and with so much success that it may be regarded now as practically expunged from the Constitution. How this has been effected will be next explained.

After a careful examination, truth constrains us to say, that it has been by a clear and palpable evasion of the Constitution. It is impossible for any provision to be more free from ambiguity or doubt. It is in the following words:

"No person held to service, or labour, in one State, under the laws thereof, escaping into another State, shall, in consequence of any law or regulation therein, be discharged from such service or labour, but shall be delivered up on claim of the party to whom such service or labour may be due."

All is clear. There is not an uncertain or equivocal word to be found in the whole provision. What shall not be done, and what shall be done, are fully and explicitly set forth. The former provides that the fugitive slave shall not be discharged from his servitude by any law or regulation of the State wherein he is found; and the latter, that he shall be delivered up on claim of his owner.

We do not deem it necessary to undertake to refute the sophistry and subterfuges by which so plain a provision of the Constitution has been evaded, and, in effect, annulled. It constitutes an essential part of the constitutional compact, and of course the supreme law of the land. As such, it is binding on all the Federal and State Governments, the States and the individuals composing them. The sacred obligation of compact, and the solemn injunction of the supreme law, which legislators and judges, both Federal and State, are bound by oath to support, all unite to enforce its fulfilment, according to its plain meaning and true intent. What that meaning and intent are, there was no diversity of opinion in the better days of the Republic, prior to 1819. Congress, State Legislatures, State and Federal Judges, and Magistrates, and people, all spontaneously placed the same interpretation on it. During that period none interposed impediments in the way of the owner seeking to recover his fugitive slave; nor did any deny his right to have every proper facility to enforce his claim to have him delivered up. It was then nearly as easy to recover one found in a Northern State as one found in a neighbouring Southern State. But this has passed away, and the provision is defunct, except perhaps in two States.*

When we take into consideration the importance and clearness of this provision, the evasion by which it has been set aside may fairly be regarded as one of the most fatal blows ever received by the South and the Union. This cannot be more concisely and correctly stated than it has been by two of the learned judges of the Supreme Court of the United States. In one of his decisions† Judge Story said:

"Historically, it is well known that the object of this clause was to secure to the citizens of the slaveholding States the complete right and title of ownership in their slaves, as property, in every State of the Union, into which they might escape from the State wherein they were held in servitude." . . . "The full recognition of this right and title was indispensable to the security of this species of property in all the slaveholding States, and, indeed, was so vital to the preservation of their interests and institutions, that it cannot be doubted that it constituted a fundamental article, without the adoption of which the Union would not have been formed. Its true design was to guard against the doctrines and principles prevalent in the non-slaveholding States, by preventing them from intermeddling with, or restricting, or abolishing the rights of the owners of slaves."

Again:

"The clause was therefore of the last importance to the safety and security of the Southern States, and could not be surrendered by them without endangering the whole property in slaves. The clause was accordingly adopted in the Constitution, by the unanimous consent of the framers of it,—a proof at once of its intrinsic and practical necessity."

Again:

"The clause manifestly contemplates the existence of a positive, unqualified right on the part of the owner of the slave, which no State law or regulation can in any way regulate, control, qualify, or restrain."

The opinion of the other learned judges was not less emphatic as to the importance of this provision and the unquestionable right of the South under it. Judge Baldwin, in charging the jury, said:‡

"If there are any rights of property which can be enforced—if one citizen have any rights of property which are inviolable under the protection of the supreme law of the State, and the Union, they are those which have been set at naught by some of these defendants. As the owner of property, which he had a perfect right to possess, protect, and take away,—as a citizen of a sister State, entitled to all the privileges and immunities of citizens of any other State,—Mr. Johnson stands before you on grounds which cannot be taken from under him— it is the same ground on which the Government itself is based. If the defendants can be justified, we have no longer law or government."

Again, after referring more particularly to the provision for delivering up fugitive slaves, he said:

"Thus you see that the foundations of the Government are laid, and rest, on the right of property in slaves. The whole structure must fall by disturbing the corner-stone."

These are grave, and solemn, and admonitory words, from a high source.

---

* Indiana and Illinois.   † The case of *Prigg vs.* the Commonwealth of Pennsylvania.
‡ The case of *Johnson vs.* Tomkins and others.

They confirm all for which the South has ever contended, as to the clearness, importance, and fundamental character of this provision, and the disastrous consequences which would inevitably follow from its violation. But in spite of these solemn warnings, the violation then commenced, and which they were intended to rebuke, has been fully and perfectly consummated. The citizens of the South, in their attempt to recover their slaves, now meet, instead of aid and co-operation, resistance in every form; resistance from hostile acts of legislation, intended to baffle and defeat their claims by all sorts of devices, and by interposing every description of impediment—resistance from judges and magistrates—and finally, when all these fail, from mobs, composed of whites and blacks, which, by threats or force, rescue the fugitive slave from the possession of his rightful owner. The attempt to recover a slave, in most of the Northern States cannot now be made without the hazard of insult, heavy pecuniary loss, imprisonment, and even of life itself. Already has a worthy citizen of Maryland* lost his life in making an attempt to enforce his claim to a fugitive slave under this provision.

But a provision of the Constitution may be violated indirectly as well as directly, by doing an act in its nature inconsistent with that which is enjoined to be done. Of this form of violation there is a striking instance connected with the provision under consideration. We allude to secret combinations which are believed to exist in many of the Northern States, whose object is to entice, decoy, entrap, inveigle, and seduce slaves to escape from their owners, and to pass them secretly and rapidly, by means organized for the purpose, into Canada, where they will be beyond the reach of the provision. That to entice a slave, by whatever artifice, to abscond from his owner into a non-slaveholding State, with the intention to place him beyond the reach of the provision or prevent his recovery, by concealment or otherwise, is as completely repugnant to it as its open violation would be, is too clear to admit of doubt or require illustration. And yet, as repugnant as these combinations are to the true intent of the provision, it is believed that, with the above exception, not one of the States within whose limits they exist, has adopted any measures to suppress them, or to punish those by whose agency the object for which they were formed is carried into execution. On the contrary, they have looked on and witnessed with indifference, if not with secret approbation, a great number of slaves enticed from their owners and placed beyond the possibility of recovery, to the great annoyance and heavy pecuniary loss of the bordering Southern States.

When we take into consideration the great importance of this provision, the absence of all uncertainty as to its true meaning and intent, the many guards by which it is surrounded to protect and enforce it, and then reflect how completely the object for which it was inserted into the Constitution is defeated by these two-fold infractions, we doubt, taking all together, whether a more flagrant breach of faith is to be found on record. We know the language we have used is strong, but it is not less true than strong.

There remains to be noticed another class of aggressive acts of a kindred character, but which, instead of striking at an express and specific provision of the Constitution, aims directly at destroying the relation between the two races at the South, by means subversive in their tendency of one of the ends for which the Constitution was established. We refer to the systematic agitation of the question by the Abolitionists; which, commencing about 1835, is still continued in all possible forms. Their avowed intention is to bring about a state of things that will force emancipation on the South. To unite the North in fixed hostility to slavery in the South, and to excite discontent among the slaves with their condition, are among the means employed to effect it. With a view to bring about the former, every means are resorted to in order to render the South, and the relation between the two races there, odious and hateful to the North. For this purpose societies and newspapers are every where established, debat-

---

* Mr. Kennedy, of Hagerstown, Md.

ing clubs opened, lecturers employed, pamphlets and other publications, pictures, and petitions to Congress resorted to, and directed to that single point, regardless of truth or decency; while the circulation of incendiary publications in the South, the agitation of the subject of abolition in Congress, and the employment of emissaries are relied on to excite discontent among the slaves. This agitation, and the use of these means, have been continued, with more or less activity, for a series of years, not without doing much towards effecting the object intended. We regard both object and means to be aggressive and dangerous to the rights of the South, and subversive, as stated, of one of the ends for which the Constitution was established. Slavery is a domestic institution. It belongs to the States, each for itself, to decide whether it shall be established or not; and, if it be established, whether it should be abolished or not. Such being the clear and unquestionable right of the States, it follows necessarily that it would be a flagrant act of aggression on a State, destructive of its rights, and subversive of its independence, for the Federal Government, or one or more States, or their people, to undertake to force on it the emancipation of its slaves.

But it is a sound maxim in politics, as well as in law and morals, that no one has the right to do that indirectly which he cannot do directly, and it may be added, with equal truth, to aid, to abet, or countenance another in doing it. And yet, the Abolitionists of the North, openly avowing the intention, and resorting to the most efficient means for the purpose, have been attempting to bring about a state of things-to force the Southern States to emancipate their slaves, without any act on the part of any of the Northern States to arrest or suppress the means by which they propose to accomplish it. They have been permitted to pursue their object, and to use whatever means they please; if without aid or countenance, also without resistance or disapprobation. What gives a deeper shade to the whole affair is the fact, that one of the means to effect their object, that of exciting discontent among our slaves, tends directly to subvert what its preamble declares to be one of the ends for which the Constitution was ordained and established—"to ensure domestic tranquillity"—and that is the only way in which domestic tranquillity is likely ever to be disturbed in the South.

Certain it is, that an agitation so systematic—having such an object in view, and sought to be carried into execution by such means—would, between independent nations, constitute just cause of remonstrance by the party against which the aggression was directed, and, if not heeded, an appeal to arms for redress. Such being the case where an aggression of the kind takes place among independent nations, how much more aggravated must it be between confederated States, where the Union precludes an appeal to arms, while it affords a medium through which it can operate with vastly increased force and effect? That it would be perverted to such a use, never entered into the imagination of the generation which formed and adopted the Constitution; and, if it had been supposed it would, it is certain that the South never would have adopted it.

We now return to the question of the admission of Missouri into the Union, and shall proceed to give a brief sketch of the occurrences connected with it, and the consequence to which it has directly led. In the latter part of 1819 the then territory of Missouri applied to Congress, in the usual form, for leave to form a State constitution and government, in order to be admitted into the Union. A bill was reported for the purpose, with the usual provisions in such cases. Amendments were offered, having for their object to make it a condition of her admission, that her constitution should have a provision to prohibit slavery. This brought on the agitating debate, which, with the effects that followed, has done so much to alienate the South and North, and endanger our political institutions. Those who objected to the amendments rested their opposition on the high grounds of the right of self-government. They claimed that a territory, having reached the period when it is proper for it to form a constitution and government for itself, becomes fully vested with all the rights of self-government; and that even the condition imposed on it by the Federal constitution, relates not to the formation of its constitution and government, but its admission into the Union. For that purpose it provides as a condition, that the government must be republican.

They claimed that Congress has no right to add to this condition, and that to assume it would be tantamount to the assumption of the right to make its entire constitution and government; as no limitation could be imposed, as to the extent of the right, if it be admitted that it exists at all. Those who supported the amendment denied these grounds, and claimed the right of Congress to impose, at discretion, what condition it pleased. In this agitating debate, the two sections stood arrayed against each other; the South in favour of the bill without amendment, and the North opposed to it without it. The debate and agitation continued until the session was well advanced; but it became apparent towards its close, that the people of Missouri were fixed and resolved in their opposition to the proposed condition, and that they would certainly reject it, and adopt a constitution without it, should the bill pass with the condition.

Such being the case, it required no great effort of mind to perceive that Missouri, once in possession of a constitution and government, not simply on paper, but with legislators elected, and officers appointed, to carry them into effect, the grave questions would be presented, whether she was of right a State or Territory; and if the latter, whether Congress had the right, and if the right, the power, to abrogate her constitution, and disperse her legislature, and to remand her back to the territorial condition. These were great, and, under the circumstances, fearful questions—too fearful to be met by those who had raised the agitation. From that time the only question was, how to escape the difficulty. Fortunately, a means was afforded. A compromise (as it was called) was offered, based on the terms, that the North should cease to oppose the admission of Missouri on the grounds for which the South contended, and that the provisions of the ordinance of 1787, for the government of the north-western territory, should be applied to all the territory acquired by the United States from France, under the treaty of Louisiana, lying north of 36° 30' except the portion lying in the State of Missouri. The northern members embraced it; and although not originating with them, adopted it as their own. It was forced through Congress, by the almost united votes of the North, against a minority consisting almost entirely of members from the Southern States.

Such was the termination of this, the first conflict, under the Constitution, between the two sections, in reference to slavery in connexion with the Territories. Many hailed it as a permanent and final adjustment that would prevent the recurrence of similar conflicts; but others, less sanguine, took the opposite and more gloomy view, regarding it as the precursor of a train of events which might rend the Union asunder, and prostrate our political system. One of these was the experienced and sagacious Jefferson. Thus far time would seem to favour his forebodings. May a returning sense of justice, and a protecting Providence, avert their final fulfilment.

For many years the subject of slavery in reference to the Territories ceased to agitate the country. Indications, however, connected with the question of annexing Texas, showed clearly that it was ready to break out again, with redoubled violence, on some future occasion. The difference in the case of Texas was adjusted by extending the Missouri compromise line of 36 30, from its terminus, on the western boundary of the Louisiana purchase, to the western boundary of Texas. The agitation ceased again for a short period.

The war with Mexico soon followed, and that terminated in the acquisition of New Mexico and Upper California, embracing an area equal to about one-half of the entire valley of the Mississippi. If to this we add the portion of Oregon acknowledged to be ours by the recent treaty with England, our whole territory on the Pacific and west of the Rocky Mountains, will be found to be in extent but little less than that vast valley. The near prospect of so great an addition rekindled the excitement between the North and South in reference to slavery in its connexion with the Territories, which has become, since those on the Pacific were acquired, more universal and intense than ever.

The effects have been to widen the difference between the two sections, and to give a more determined and hostile character to their conflict. The North no longer respects the Missouri compromise line, although adopted by their almost unanimous vote. Instead of compromise, they avow that their determination is to exclude slavery from all the territories of the United States, acquired, or to be acquired, and of course to prevent the citizens of. the Southern States from emigrating with their property in slaves to any of them. Their object, they allege, is to prevent the extension of slavery, and ours to extend it, thus making the issue between them and us to be the naked question, Shall slavery be extended or not? We do not deem it necessary, looking to the objects of this address, to examine the questions so fully discussed at the last Session, whether Congress has the right to exclude the citizens of the South from emigrating with their property into territories belonging to the confederated States of the Union. What we propose in this connexion is, to make a few remarks on what the North alleges, erroneously, to be the issue between us and them.

So far from maintaining the doctrine which the issue implies, we hold that the Federal Government has no right to extend or restrict slavery, no more than to establish or abolish it; nor has it any right whatever to distinguish between the domestic institutions of one State or section and another, in order to favour the one and discourage the other. As the Federal representative of each and all the States, it is bound to deal out, within the sphere of its powers, equal and exact justice and favour to all. To act otherwise, to undertake to discriminate between the domestic institutions of one and another, would be to act in total subversion of the end for which it was established—to be the common protector and guardian of all. Entertaining these opinions, we ask not, as the North alleges we do, for the extension of slavery. That would make a discrimination in our favour as unjust and unconstitutional as the discrimination they ask against us in their favour. It is not for them nor for the Federal Government to determine whether our domestic institution is good or bad, or whether it should be repressed or preserved. It belongs to us, and us only, to decide such questions. What, then, we do insist on, is, not to extend slavery, but that we shall not be prohibited from immigrating, with our property, into the Territories of the United States, because we are slaveholders; or, in other words, that we shall not on that account be disfranchised of a privilege possessed by all others, citizens and foreigners, without discrimination as to character, profession, or colour. All, whether savage, barbarian, or civilized, may freely enter and remain; we only being excluded.

We rest our claim not only on the high grounds above stated, but also on the solid foundation of right, justice, and equality. The territories immediately in controversy—New Mexico and California—were acquired by the common sacrifice and efforts of all the States, toward which the South contributed far more than her full share of men,* to say nothing of money, and is, of course, on every

* Volunteers from the South—Regiments	.	.	.	.	.	.	33
" " " Battalions	.	.	.	.	.	.	14
" " " Companies	.	.	.	.	.	.	12
Total number of volunteers from the South			.	.	.	45,640
Volunteers from the North—Regiments	.	.	.	.	.	22
" " " Battalions	.	.	.	.	.	2
" " " Companies	.	.	.	.	.	12
Total number of volunteers from the North		.	.	.	23,084

Being nearly two on the part of the South to one on the part of the North. But taking into consideration that the population of the North is two-thirds greater than the South, the latter has furnished more than three times her due proportion of volunteers.

principle of right, justice, fairness, and equality, entitled to participate fully in the benefits to be derived from their acquisition. But impregnable as is this ground, there is another not less so. Ours is a Federal Government—a government in which not individuals but States, as distinct sovereign communities, are the constituents. To them, as members of the Federal Union, the Territories belong; and they are hence declared to be Territories belonging to the United States. The States, then, are the joint owners. Now, it is conceded by all writers on the subject, that in all such governments their members are all equal —equal in rights and equal in dignity. They also concede that this equality constitutes the basis of such government, and that it cannot be destroyed without changing their nature and character. To deprive, then, the Southern States and their citizens of their full share in territories declared to belong to them in common with the other States, would be in derogation of the equality belonging to them as members of a Federal Union, and sink them, from being equals, into a subordinate and dependent condition. Such are the solid and impregnable grounds on which we rest our demand to an equal participation in the territories.

But as solid and impregnable as they are in the eyes of justice and reason, they oppose a feeble resistance to a majority determined to engross the whole. At the last Session of Congress, a bill was passed establishing a Territorial Government for Oregon, excluding slavery therefrom. The President gave his sanction to the bill, and sent a special message to Congress assigning his reasons for doing so. These reasons presupposed that the Missouri compromise was to be, and would be, extended west of the Rocky Mountains to the Pacific Ocean. And the President intimated his intention in his message to veto any future bill that should restrict slavery south of the line of that compromise. Assuming it to have been the purpose and intention of the North to extend the Missouri compromise line as above indicated, the passage of the Oregon bill could only be regarded as evincing the acquiescence of the South in that line. But the developments of the present Session of Congress have made it manifest to all that no such purpose or intention now exists with the North to any considerable extent. Of the truth of this, we have ample evidence in what has occurred already in the House of Representatives, where the popular feelings are soonest and most intensely felt.

Although Congress has been in session but little more than one month, a greater number of measures of an aggressive character has been introduced, and they more aggravated and dangerous than have been for years before. And what clearly discloses from whence they take their origin, is the fact that they all relate to the territorial aspect of the subject of slavery, or some other of a nature and character intimately connected with it.

The first of this series of aggressions is a resolution introduced by a member from Massachusetts, the object of which is to repeal all acts or parts of acts which recognise the existence of slavery, or authorize the selling and disposing of slaves in this District. On question of leave to bring in a bill, the votes stood 69 for and 82 against leave. The next was a resolution offered by a member from Ohio, instructing the Committee on Territories to report forthwith bills for excluding slavery from California and New Mexico.* It passed by a vote of 107 to 80. That was followed by a bill introduced by another member from Ohio, to take the votes of the inhabitants of this District on the question whether slavery within its limits should be abolished.

The bill provided, according to the admission of the mover, that free negroes and slaves should vote. On the question to lay the bill on the table, the votes stood—for, 106; against, 79. To this succeeded the resolution of a member from New York, in the following words:

*. Since reported to the House.

" *Whereas* the traffic now prosecuted in this metropolis of the Republic in human beings, as chattels, is contrary to natural justice and the fundamental principles of our political system, and is notoriously a reproach to our country, throughout Christendom, and a serious hinderance to the progress of Republican liberty among the nations of the earth. Therefore,

" *Resolved*, That the Committee for the District of Columbia be instructed to report a bill, as soon as practicable, prohibiting the slave-trade in said District."

On the question of adopting the resolution, the votes stood—98 for, and 88 against. He was followed by a member from Illinois, who offered a resolution for abolishing slavery in the territories, and all places where Congress has exclusive powers of legislation; that is, in all forts, magazines, arsenals, dock-yards, and other needful buildings, purchased by Congress with the consent of the legislature of the State.

This resolution was passed over under the rules of the House without being put to vote.

The votes in favour of all these measures were confined to the members of the Northern States. True, there are some patriotic members from that section who voted against all of them, and whose high sense of justice is duly appreciated; who in the progress of the aggressions of the South have, by their votes sustained the guarantees of the Constitution, and of whom we regret to say many have been sacrificed at home by their patriotic course.

We have now brought to a close a narrative of the series of acts of aggression and encroachments connected with the subject of this address, including those that are consummated and those still in progress. They are numerous, great, and dangerous, and threaten with destruction the greatest and most vital of all the interests and institutions of the South. Indeed, it may be doubted whether there is a single provision, stipulation, or guarantee of the Constitution, intended for the security of the South, that has not been rendered almost nugatory. It may even be made a serious question whether the encroachments already made, without the aid of any other, would not, if permitted to operate unchecked, end in emancipation, and that at no distant day. But be that as it may, it hardly admits of a doubt that, if the aggressions already commenced in the House, and now in progress should be consummated, such in the end would certainly be the consequence.

Little, in truth, would be left to be done after we have been excluded from all the territories, including those to be hereafter acquired; after slavery is abolished in this District and in the numerous places dispersed all over the South, where Congress has the exclusive right of legislation, and after the other measures proposed are consummated. Every outpost and barrier would be carried, and nothing would be left but to finish the work of abolition at pleasure in the States themselves. This District, and all places over which Congress has exclusive power of legislation, would be asylums for fugitive slaves, where, as soon as they placed their feet, they would become, according to the doctrines of Northern assailants, free; unless there should be some positive enactments to prevent it.

Under such a state of things the probability is, that emancipation would soon follow, without any final act to abolish slavery. The depressing effect of such measures on the white race at the South, and the hope they create in the black of a speedy emancipation, would produce a state of feeling inconsistent with the much longer continuance of the existing relations between the two. But be that as it may, it is certain, if emancipation did not follow as a matter of course, the final act in the States would not be long delayed. The want of constitutional power would oppose a feeble resistance. The great body of the North is united against our peculiar institution. Many believe it to be sinful, and the residue, with inconsiderable exceptions, believe it to be wrong. Such being the case, it would indicate a very superficial knowledge of human nature, to think that after aiming at abolition systematically for so many years, and pursuing it with such unscrupulous disregard of law and constitution, the fanatics who have led the way, and forced the great body of the North to follow them, would, when the finishing-stroke only remained to be ·given, voluntarily suspend it, or permit any constitutional scruples of considerations of justice to arrest it. To these may be added an aggression, though not yet commenced, long meditated and threatened —to prohibit what the abolitionists call the internal slave-trade; meaning thereby the transfer of slaves from one· State to another, from whatever motive done, or however effected. Their object would· seem to·be to render them worthless by crowding them together where they are, and thus hasten the work of emancipation. There is reason for believing that it will soon follow those now in progress, unless, indeed, some decisive step should be taken in the mean'time to arrest the whole.

The question then is, Will the measures of aggression proposed in the House be adopted !

They may not, and probably will not be this session. But when we take into consideration that there is a majority now in favour of one of them, and a strong minority in favour of the other, as far as the sense of the house has been taken; that there will be in all probability a considerable increase in the next Congress of the vote in favour of them, and that it will be largely increased in the next succeeding Congress, under the census to be taken next year, it amounts almost to a certainty that they will be adopted, unless some decisive measure is taken in advance to prevent it.

But, if even these conclusions should prove erroneous—if fanaticism and the love of power should, contrary to their nature, for once respect Constitutional barriers, or if the calculations of policy should retard the adoption of ·these measures, or even defeat them altogether, there would be still left one certain way to accomplish their object, if the determination avowed by the North to monopolize all the territories, to the exclusion of the South, should be carried into effect. That of itself would, at no distant day, add to the North a sufficient number of States to give her three-fourths of the whole; when, under the colour of an amendment of the Constitution,·she would emancipate our slaves, however opposed it might be·to its true intent.

Thus, under,every aspect, the result is certain, if aggression be not promptly and decidedly met. How it is to be met, it is for you to decide.

Such, then, being the case, it would be to insult you to suppose you could hesitate. To destroy the existing relation between the free and servile races at the South would lead to consequences unparalleled in history. They cannot be separated, and cannot live together in peace and harmony, or to their mutual advantage, except in their present relation. Under any other, wretchedness, and misery, and desolation would overspread the whole South. The example of the British West Indies, as blighting as emancipation has proved to them, furnishes a very faint picture of the calamities it would bring on the South. The circumstances under which it would take place with us would be entirely different from those which took place with them, and calculated to lead to far more disastrous results. There, the government of the parent country emancipated slaves in her colonial possessions—a government rich and powerful, and actuated by views of policy, (mistaken as they turned out to be,) rather than fanaticism.

It was, beside, disposed to act justly toward the owners, even in the act of emancipating their slaves, and to protect and foster them afterward. It accordingly appropriated nearly $100,000,000 as' a compensation to them for their losses under the act, which sum, although it turned out to be far short of the amount, was thought at that time to be liberal. Since the emancipation, it has kept up a sufficient military and naval force to keep the blacks in awe, and a number of magistrates, and constables, and other civil officers, to keep order in the towns and plantations, and enforce respect to their former owners.

To a considerable extent, these have served as a substitute for the police formerly kept on the plantations by the owners and their overseers, and to preserve the social and political superiority of the white race. But, notwithstanding all this, the British West India possessions are ruined, impoverished, miserable, wretched, and destined probably to be abandoned to the black race. Very different would be the circumstances under which emancipation would take place with us. If it ever should be effected, it will be through the agency of the Federal Government, controlled by the dominant power of the Northern States of the confederacy, against the resistance and struggle of the Southern.

It can then only be effected by the prostration of the white race; and that would necessarily engender the bitterest feelings of hostility between them and the North. But the reverse would be the case between the blacks of the South and the people of the North. Owing their emancipation to them, they would regard them as friends, guardians and patrons, and centre, accordingly, all their sympathy in them. The people of the North would not fail to reciprocate and to favour them, instead of the whites. Under the influence of such feelings, and impelled by fanaticism and love of power, they would not stop at emancipation. Another step would be taken—to raise them to a political and social equality with their former owners, by giving them the right of voting and holding public offices under the Federal Government. We see the first step toward it in the bill already alluded to—to vest the free blacks and slaves with the right to vote on the question of emancipation in this district. But when once raised on an equality, they would become the fast political associates of the North, acting and voting with them on all questions, and by this political union between them, holding the white race at the South in complete subjection.

The blacks, and the profligate whites that might unite with them, would become the principal recipients of federal offices and patronage, and would, in consequence, be raised above the whites of the South in the political and social scale. We would, in a word, change conditions with them—a degradation greater than has ever yet fallen to the lot of a free and enlightened people, and one from which we could not escape, should emancipation take place, (which it certainly will, if not prevented,) but by fleeing the homes of ourselves and ancestors, and by abandoning our country to our former slaves, to become the permanent abode of disorder, anarchy, poverty, misery and wretchedness.

With such a prospect before us, the gravest and most solemn question that ever claimed the attention of a people is presented for your consideration: What is to be done to prevent it? It is a question belonging to you to decide. All we propose is to give you our opinion.

We, then, are of the opinion that the first and indispensable step, without which nothing can be done, and with which every thing may be, is to be united among yourselves, on this great and most vital question. The want of union and concert in reference to it has brought the South, the Union, and our system of Government to their present perilous condition. Instead of placing it above all others, it has been made subordinate, not only to mere questions of policy, but to the preservation of party ties and ensuring of party success, as high as we hold a due respect for these, we hold them subordinate to that and other questions involving our safety and happiness. Until they are so held by the South, the North will not believe that you are in earnest in opposition to their encroachments, and they will continue to follow, one after another, until the work of abolition is finished. To convince them that you are, you must prove by your acts that you hold all other questions subordinate to it. If you become united, and prove yourselves in earnest, the North will be brought to a pause, and to a calculation of consequences; and that may lead to a change of measures and the adoption of a course of policy that may quietly and peaceably terminate this long conflict between the two sections. If it should not, nothing would remain for you but to stand up immovably in defence of rights, involving your all—your property, prosperity, equality, liberty, and safety.

As the assailed, you would stand justified by all laws, human and divine, in repelling a blow so dangerous, without looking to consequences, and to resort to all means necessary for that purpose. Your assailants, and not you, would be responsible for consequences.

Entertaining these opinions, we earnestly entreat you *to be united*, and for that purpose adopt all necessary measures. Beyond this, we think it would not be proper to go at present.

We hope, if you should unite with any thing like unanimity, it may of itself apply a remedy to this deep-seated and dangerous disease; but, if such be not the case, the time will then have come for you to decide what course to adopt.

HUNGARIAN MANIFESTO.

Ladislas Teleki, Hungarian Minister of Foreign Affairs, to the French Republic.

MONSIEUR LE MINISTRE.—Events press onward. The intervention of Russia is a reality. After having gloriously résisted the armies of Austria, Hungary finds herself now upon the point of being crushed under the weight of a new Holy Alliance, reorganized on Cossack principles. The manifesto of the Czar Nicholas leaves no further doubt on this subject. The Emperor Francis Joseph publicly avows himself the ally of the foreigner who invades his states. The fact of this Russian intervention, solicited in the name of the Emperor King of Hungary, is what has, above all other things, led the National Assembly of Hungary to declare the *déchéance* of the house of Hapsburg-Lorraine, which had already violated every engagement, and broken all the compacts, by virtue of which they have, for more than three centuries, possessed the crown of Hungary.

I have given the details relative to the Hungarian question in two of my notes, presented to the Minister for Foreign Affairs of the French republic, in October, 1848, and in March of the present year, as well as in a manifesto addressed in the name of Hungary to the civilized nations of Europe, and which I had likewise the honour to present to the Minister of the republic in December, 1848.

Since then, this question has assumed greater dimensions; henceforward it has a European importance.

It now becomes my duty to sum up, in a few words, that which has relation to the just rights of Hungary in the deadly struggle which she has to bear against absolutism, and which identifies her cause with that of civilization and freedom in general.

1. *The Legal Right of Hungary.*—Hungary has ever been independent of Austria. Ferdinand I., the first Prince of the house of Austria that ever reigned in Hungary, received the crown in 1526, in accordance with an election by the Diet. He swore to maintain the constitution and the independence of Hungary. All his successors took the same oath. The crown of Hungary first became hereditary in the house of Hapsburg, in virtue of the Pragmatic Sanction, passed by the estates of Hungary, in 1687. In 1723, this settlement was extended by the Hungarian Diet to the female line of the house of Hapsburg, (second Pragmatic Sanction.) But the independence of Hungary was maintained and guarantied not less by these very acts than by

the oaths of all the kings of the house of Hapsburg-Lorraine, even down to our own days. By article ten of the year 1790, the Emperor King Leopold II., recognised Hungary as a free and independent State in its whole legislative and administrative system. Hence the article three of the year 1848, by which a parliamentary government was settled in Hungary, introduced no change in its relations to Austria. This law was no more than a development of all the foregoing laws. It was passed by a unanimous vote of the two houses in the Hungarian Diet, and was formally sanctioned by the king, Ferdinand V. All that we demanded of the house of Austria was that our charter should henceforward be a truth; our demands did not go one step beyond what had been guarantied to us in succession by all our kings.

2. *Conduct of the House of Austria.*—The house of Austria has broken all her engagements with Hungary, from the moment when, in consequence of her victory over the army of Charles Albert, in July, she felt herself strong enough to venture it. She put in force every means which could lead to her end of overthrowing the Hungarian constitution, and incorporating Hungary in her Austrian monarchy. She publicly preached revolt abroad; she raised up national hatreds among us; she excited men to pillage, to burn, to murder; she awakened the enmity of the poor against the rich; she offered the hand of friendship to all our enemies; she decreed the partition of Hungary into numerous provinces; she launched armies against us, and declared all those to be rebels who remained faithful to their country and its laws. Last of all, she has called in Russia to her aid, and has thus caused her own states to be invaded by the most dangerous of her own rivals. It is, therefore, in the exercise of a legal right, that the Hungarian Diet has decreed the *déchéance* of the house of Hapsburg-Lorraine, which has shown itself the most bitter enemy of our country. I feel an intimate conviction that Europe, that France, ought to take an interest in us; for we are at once the champions of freedom and legal order; we are the defenders of good order and of society; and it is the house of Austria which, in reference to us and to our constitution, legally guarantied, is in the state of rebellion.

3. *Hungary is the Champion of Civilization.*—This Russian intervention is totally adverse to the interests of the whole of Europe. Austria has always been looked upon as the proper bulwark of Europe against Russia. But this intervention is the death of Austria. It would be absurd to imagine that Russia marches her armies and perils her finances with the sole object of setting up a barrier against herself. Her intervention, therefore, will be nothing but a means of subjugating Austria. Besides, we know very well what are the real intentions of Russia with regard to the Sclavic populations of the Austrian empire. The Russian autocrat already looks upon himself in the light of their legitimate sovereign. Hence, when she has succeeded in reconstituting Austria after her own fashion, Russia will have pushed herself, in fact, as far as Germany: this is what must be expected, if we are crushed. Under such circumstances, will Turkey, already wounded by the occupation of Moldavia and Wallachia, have power to bear the shock of the Northern Colossus?

No! all is destined to be subdued in its turn. After having invaded Austria, Russia will have the Bosphorus. Europe will no longer possess any bulwark against her. Thus in combating the Russians, we are serving the interests of the whole of Europe.

Our army amounts to very nearly 200,000 men, perfectly drilled and disciplined, together with an imposing force of artillery. The force of Turkey is hardly inferior; and she has, besides, her fleet, and the Egyptian contingent. This strength is more than is required to resist the Russians. The intervention of Russia could not take place—at all events, could not succeed—if advantage were taken of these forces, if pains were taken to invite them. France has only to will it. Let me hope that she will not look on with an indifferent eye upon this intervention—that she will have the will to prevent it.

For the policy of Russia, at last unmasked by the manifesto of the Czar Nicholas, proves sufficiently that he looks upon himself as the natural enemy of all civilized people, and, as a final consequence, of France. It proves that in her present attack upon us, Russia is only taking up a strong position, by rendering Austria subject to herself.

Let me entreat you to take into consideration the respect for existing rights, which the national government of Hungary maintains, even against its own interest. While the Austro-Russian troops were violating the neutrality of the Turkish territory in Wallachia, the General of the Hungarian forces made it his duty to respect it; he halted his men upon the frontiers of Transylvania at a moment when, by imitating the enemy's example, and pursuing him into the Turkish territory, he could have put the Austro-Russians in a condition to do him no further mischief.

Pardon me, M. le Ministre, for having troubled you with so many details; but this was for me a sacred duty, which I could not avoid fulfilling.

I am a Hungarian—I owe myself to the cause of my country. I am the representative of her interests—it is my duty to defend them—and I do so, in the intimate conviction that the interests of all humanity are sharers in our own.

Your own feelings towards the cause I represent are a pledge that you will give a favourable reception to these lines.

Be pleased, M. le Ministre, to accept, &c.,

Comte LADISLAS TELEKI.

M. de Tocqueville, Minister of Foreign Affairs, &c.

ADDRESS OF THE CONSTITUENT ASSEMBLY OF ROME.

The following is the address of the Constituent Assembly of Rome to the Governments and to the Parliaments of France and England:

"The representatives of the free Roman people confidently appeal to the Governments and to the Parliaments of the two most free and most powerful nations of Europe.

"It is well known that we have been for many ages governed by the church, with the same special and absolute authority in all matters temporal as in spiritual, whence it happened that, amid the enlightenment of the nineteenth century, we are surrounded by the darkness of the middle ages. Civilization was combated at times with open warfare, always with the force of inertia, to such a degree that it was considered a crime in us to feel and call ourselves Italians.

"It is well known that we have, on many occasions, attempted to achieve our own liberty; but Europe has made us expiate by a harder slavery those very attempts by which other nations have been rendered glorious. At length, after our long martyrdom, the day of redemption appeared to have arrived, and we trusted to the power of ideas as well as to that of events, and to the mild character of the prince. We desired, above all things, to be Italians: this was a crime. We believed ourselves free: this was an illusion. The day came when the prince abandoned us, and we were left without government. All attempts at conciliation failed. Messages and messengers from the Parliament and the Municipality were rejected. The people awaited their time with patience, but the emigrated government no longer proffered a single word of liberty or of love. It stigmatized three millions of men with the guilt of an individual, and, when we deliberated on employing the only means which remained to us for constituting an authority which the prince had, in fact, abdicated, the priest pronounced a malediction upon us.

"It is well known that our Assembly had its origin in universal suffrage; that Assembly, exercising of necessity an imprescriptible right, decreed the dethronement of theocracy for ever, and proclaimed the republic.

"No one opposed it. The only voice of complaint arose from the theocracy which we had overthrown. And yet it is to this voice that Europe is willing to listen, and seems to forget the story of our woes, and to confound what lies within the province of spiritual authority with that which is purely temporal.

"The Roman Republic has sanctioned the independence and the free exercise of the spiritual authority of the Pope, and has thereby demonstrated to the Catholic world how profoundly deep is its conviction that the liberty of religious action should be inseparable from the supreme head of the church. To maintain this liberty in the fullest integrity, the Roman Republic adds to the moral guarantee afforded by the devotion of all our Catholic brethren the material guarantee of all the force at its disposal. But Europe is not contented with this, and it is repeated that the existence of the temporal power of the Pope is essential to Catholicism.

" For this reason we invite the Governments and Parliaments of France and England, to consider what right can be alleged by any Power, to impose any form of government whatever on an independent nation; and where is the wisdom of attempting to restore a Government by its very nature irreconcilable with liberty and civilization; a Government long since morally abolished, and actually so for upwards of five months, without any one among the clergy having attempted to set up again its fallen standard? Or where is the wisdom of resuscitating a Government universally detested, incapable of a long existence, and, on the contrary, certain to provoke continual conspiracies, disturbances, and revolutions?

"And if we assert that such Government cannot be identified and reconciled either with liberty or civilization, we have surely good grounds for such an assertion, since the experiment we have lately made of a constitution has proved how much the attempt to establish an affinity and combination between temporal and spiritual concerns has impeded its working and development. Here ecclesiastical canons nullified civil statutes; under the empire of theocracy, public education, and instruction, were the privilege and monopoly of the clergy—the ecclesiastical privilege of mortmain impeded the transmission of property. Ecclesiastics were exempted by privilege from appearing before the civil tribunals, while the laity were subject to the jurisdiction of the ecclesiastical tribunals, all which constituted a condition of things so far removed from real liberty or civilization, that any free nation must prefer the alternative of waging ten wars to enduring a single one of them. And how can Europe—so often thrown into commotion by the sacerdotal power which launched the thunders of the Church against her States—how can she expect three millions of men to submit at the present day to an authority which not only exercises its political right of temporal punishment against the offender, but even threatens damnation to his soul! Europe cannot reason herself into the belief that free institutions can be fitly carried out under a prince who can, under cover of his political power, turn the enormous authority of the priest to perplexing and disturbing consciences.

" We trust that England and France, so justly jealous of their own independence, will never willingly consent that there should exist in the centre of Italy a people neutral with respect to other nations made serfs for the sake of the rest of the Catholic world, excluded from the rights of nations, and made a mere appanage for the clergy. The Roman people claim to be masters of the Roman State. And, if Catholic nations may intervene in behalf of their religious affairs, surely they have no right to interfere with our political rights or our social pact. However neutrality may be imposed upon a whole nation, it surely cannot be imposed on the central district of a country with regard to the rest, it being impossible for this centre to have by itself a national life by the mere force of treaties or protocols.

"The representatives of the Roman people would consider it an insult to the political wisdom of the governments and parliaments of France and England, were they to doubt their acknowledging the importance of the rights and arguments herein slightly touched upon, no less than the advantage to Europe herself, who must ensure its own lasting tranquillity by securing the abolition of the government of the priesthood.

"Undoubtedly, it can never be expected of us that we should not oppose the restoration with a bold, determined, and irrevocable will; nor can Europe impute to us the threatening catastrophe that may ensue, nor the inevitable injury that a violent and bloody restoration would occasion, even to the Catholic authority of the Papacy. We are convinced that England and France will lend us both aid and counsel in order to avert such evils, and to draw closer the bond of amity in which all free nations should now be united."

For the National Assembly:

"G. GALLETTI, President.

"G. PENNACCHI,
"A. ZANOBIANCHI,
"A. FABBRETTI,
"G. COCCHI,
} Secretaries.

"Rome, April 18th, 1849."

THE FRENCH EXPEDITION TO ROME.

The following are the instructions addressed by the Government of France to its agents at Vienna and Gaeta, setting forth the motives and objects of the French in sending Gen. Oudinot and his army to Rome:

M. Drouyn de Lhuys to Admiral Cecille, communicated to Viscount Palmerston by Admiral Cecille, April 21.

PARIS, April 19, 1849.

M. L'AMIRAL: I have the honour to send you herewith copies of two despatches which I have just written, one to the Chargé d'Affaires of France at Vienna, the other to our Ambassador to the Pope, and to our Envoy at the Court of Naples, to communicate to them the reasons and the object of the expedition which is about to depart for Civita Vecchia under the command of General Oudinot. I request you to have the goodness to read them to Lord Palmerston. We doubt not that the British Government will duly appreciate a determination, the object of which is at once to maintain, as far as shall depend on us, the balance of power; to guaranty the independence of the Italian States; to secure to the Roman people a liberal and regular system of administration; and to preserve them from the dangers of a blind reaction, as well as from the phrensy of anarchy.   Receive, &c.,

E. DROUYN DE LHUYS.

(ENCLOSURE I.)
M. Drouyn de Lhuys to M. de la Cour.

PARIS, April 17, 1849.

SIR: The events which have occurred so rapidly within some weeks in the north of Italy; the movements which have been effected by the Austrian army after its very short contest with the Piedmontese army; the intention distinctly announced by Prince Schwarzenberg of interfering in all the countries of the Peninsula adjoining Lombardy; and, lastly, the decision even of the members of the conference of Gaeta, who did not think that they could agree to any of the plans suggested by our plenipotentiaries: all these circumstances have led us to think that, in order to retain in the regulation of the affairs of Central Italy the share of influence which legitimately belongs to France, and the preservation of which is essential to the maintenance of the balance of power, France ought to assume a more decided attitude. The Government of the Republic has resolved to send to Civita Vecchia a body of troops commanded by General Oudinot. Our intention in deciding on this measure has been neither to impose on the Roman people a system of administration which their free will would have rejected, nor to constrain the Pope to adopt, when he shall be recalled to the exercise of his power, this or that system of government. We thought, we more than ever think, that by the force of events, by the effect of the natural disposition of men's minds, the system of administration which the revolution of last November has established at Rome is destined soon to fall, and that the Roman people will place themselves again under the authority of the Sovereign Pontiff, provided they are secured against the dangers of a reaction. But we nevertheless think, and in this respect especially you know our language has never varied, that that authority will not take strong root, and can only strengthen itself against fresh storms by the help of institutions which may prevent the return of the old abuses, the reform of which Pius IX. had with such generous zeal begun.

To facilitate a reconciliation which would be effected on such grounds; to give to the Holy Father, and to all those who, whether at Rome or at Gaeta, are disposed to co-operate therein, the assistance which may be required to surmount the obstacles raised by exaggerated pretensions, or by evil passions: such is the object which we have assigned to our expedition.

Prince Schwarzenberg will understand, I am convinced, that, after having taken the important decision which I have the honor to announce to you, we have not wished to risk the chances of its success by the delay which a preliminary communication made to the Conference of Gaeta would have caused. The rapid progress of events made it impossible for us to temporize. Moreover, our intentions are unequivocal and cannot be suspected. What we wish is, that the Holy Father, on re-entering Rome, may find himself placed in a situation which, while it is satisfactory to him and to his people, may at the same time preserve Italy and Europe from fresh disturbances, and may not interfere either with the balance of power or the independence of the Italian States. The means to which we have recourse are, if I am not mistaken, the fittest to attain that end. They ought, then, to meet with the approbation of all friends of order and peace.

We should not, without regret, see that Austria, to whom the occupation of a considerable part of upper Italy and the victory recently obtained over the Piedmontese secure already so large a share of influence in the Peninsula, should think proper, as she has more than once intimated, to procure for herself by the occupation of Bologna, a fresh security, which, however useless to her with regard to serious interests, would serve but to disquiet and to excite men's minds. Receive, &c.,

E. DROUYN DE LHUYS.

[ENCLOSURE II.]

M. Drouyn de Lhuys to M. D'Harcourt and M. de Rayneval.

PARIS, April 17, 1849.

SIR: The determination announced to you in a despatch of the 15th inst., is at length taken, and is about to be carried into execution. A vote of the

National Assembly, passed at the close of a solemn discussion, having provided the government of the Republic with the funds which it required for that purpose, a body of troops, commanded by General Oudinot, will be despatched without delay to Civita Vecchia. The idea of the government of the Republic, in deciding upon this measure, has not been either to impose upon the Roman people a system of administration which their free will would have rejected, nor to compel the Pope, when he shall be recalled to the exercise of his temporal power, to adopt such or such system of government. We have thought, we think more than ever, that, by the force of circumstances, and in consequence of the natural disposition of men's minds, the system of administration which was founded at Rome by the revolution of November is destined shortly to fall; that the Roman people, provided it is re-assured against the dangers of a reaction, will readily place itself under the authority of the Sovereign Pontiff; and that Pius IX., on returning to his dominions, will carry back thither the generous, enlightened, and liberal policy with which he has lately shown himself to be animated. To facilitate a reconciliation which should be carried out in such a spirit; to furnish the Pope and all those who, at Gaeta as well as at Rome, are disposed to contribute thereto, with the support which they may require, in order to surmount the obstacles raised in the one sense or the other by exaggerated influences or by evil passions, such is the object which we have assigned to our expedition. Have the goodness, when announcing, in concert with M. de Rayneval, to Cardinal Antonilli the departure of the division commanded by General Oudinot, clearly to explain to him the object and the bearing of the resolution which we have now adopted. He will understand that, in order to place himself in a position to profit by it, the Pope must hasten to publish a manifesto, which, by guarantying to the people liberal institutions in conformity with their wishes as well as with the necessities of the times, shall cause the overthrow of all resistance. The manifesto, appearing at the very moment when our troops would show themselves on the coasts of the States of the church, would be the signal for a reconciliation from which only a very small number of malcontents would be excluded. You cannot insist too strongly upon the utility of, or the necessity even which exists for, such a document.

It will be easy for you to make the members of the Conference of Gaeta understand that if we have not thought fit to await the result of the deliberations of that conference before resorting to action, it is because the rapid progress of events did not allow us to do so. What we desire is, that the Pope, on returning to Rome, shall find himself in a position which, at once satisfactory for himself and for his people, shall secure Italy and Europe from new commotions, and shall not prejudice either the balance of power or the independence of the Italian States. The means to which we have recourse are, if I do not deceive myself, the best calculated for the attainment of this object. They must consequently meet with the approbation of the friends of order and of peace. Receive, &c.,

E. DROUYN DE LHUYS.

RUSSIA.

THE following ukase, relating to the Russian intervention in Hungary, has been published in St. Petersburgh:—

"By the grace of God, We, Nicholas I., Emperor and Autocrat of all the Russias, &c., declare to the nation, having, by our manifesto of the 14th of March, 1848, informed our subjects of the miseries which afflicted Western Europe, we at the same time made known how we were ready to meet our enemies wherever they might show themselves, and that we should, without sparing ourselves, in conjunction indissoluble with our sacred Russia, defend the honour of the Russian name, and the inviolability of our frontiers.

"The commotions and rebellions of the west have not since then ceased. Guilty delusion, enticing the thoughtless crowd with visionary dreams of that prosperity which can never be the fruit of wilfulness and obstinacy, has entered the east and the dominions contiguous to us, subjects of the Turkish empire, viz.: Moldavia and Wallachia. Only by the presence of our troops, together with those of Turkey, has order been restored and maintained; but in Hungary and Transylvania the efforts of the Austrian Government, distracted already by another war with foreign and domestic enemies in Italy, have not yet been able to triumph over rebellion. On the contrary, strengthening itself by hordes of our Polish traitors of 1831, and of others, foreigners, outcasts, runaways, and vagrants, the rebellion has developed itself there to a most threatening degree.

"In midst of these unfortunate events the Emperor of Austria has addressed himself to us with the wish for our assistance against our common enemies. We shall not refuse him.

"Having called to the assistance of this righteous enterprise, the Almighty Leader of battles and Lord of victories, we have commanded our armies to move forward for the extinction of rebellion, and the destruction of the audacious and evil-intentioned men, who endeavour to disturb the peace of our dominions also.

"Let God be with us, and who shall be against us?

"So—we are convinced of it—so feels, so hopes, so aspires our God-preserved nation; every Russian, every true subject of ours, and Russia will fulfil her mission.

"Given at St. Petersburgh, the 26th day of April, in the year from the birth of Christ, 1849, and the 24th of our reign."

(Signed) "NICHOLAS I."

SPEECH OF THE QUEEN OF GREAT BRITAIN.

The following is the speech of the Queen at the close of the last session of Parliament. It was read by the Marquis of Lansdowne:—

My Lords and Gentlemen:

We have it in command from her Majesty to inform you that the state of the public business enables her to dispense with your attendance in Parliament, and to close the present session. Her Majesty has directed us to express her satisfaction with the zeal and assiduity with which you have discharged the laborious and anxious duties, in the performance of which you have been occupied.

Her Majesty has given her assent to the important measure you have passed to amend the Navigation Laws, in full confidence that the enterprise, skill, and hardihood of her people will assure to them a full share of the commerce of the world, and maintain upon the seas the ancient renown of this nation.

Her Majesty has commanded us to acquaint you that the friendly character of her relations with foreign powers affords her a just confidence in the continuance of peace.

The preliminaries of peace between Prussia and Denmark have been signed, under the mediation of her Majesty; and her Majesty trusts that the convention may prove the forerunner of a definitive and permanent treaty.

Her Majesty's efforts will continue to be directed to promote the restoration of peace in those parts of Europe in which it has been interrupted.

Gentlemen of the House of Commons:

We are commanded by her Majesty to return you her thanks for the provision which you have made for the public service. The public expenditure has undergone considerable reduction within the present year, and her Majesty will continue to apply a watchful economy in every branch of the public service.

My Lords and Gentlemen:

We are commanded by her Majesty to congratulate you on the happy termination of the war in the Punjaub. The exertions made by the Government of India, and the valour displayed by the army in the field, demand her Majesty's warmest acknowledgments.

Her Majesty has observed with gratification the spirit of obedience to the laws which has been manifested by her subjects during the period which has elapsed since her majesty last addressed her Parliament.

It is the characteristic of our constitution that it renders the maintenance of order compatible with the fullest enjoyment of political and civil liberty.

The satisfaction with which her Majesty has viewed the peaceful progress of her people in arts and industry has been greatly alloyed by the continuance of severe distress in one part of the United Kingdom.—Her Majesty has observed with pleasure your liberal exertions to mitigate the pressure of this calamity; and her Majesty commands us to thank you for your unremitting attention to measures calculated to improve the general condition of Ireland.

It is her Majesty's fervent hope that it may please the Almighty Disposer of events to favour the operation of those laws which have been sanctioned by Parliament, and to grant to her Irish people, as the reward of that patience and resignation with which they have borne their protracted sufferings, the blessings of an abundant harvest and of internal peace.

OFFICIAL.

By the President of the United States.

PROCLAMATION.

WASHINGTON, Aug. 11, 1849.

THERE is reason to believe that an armed expedition is about to be fitted out in the United States, with the intention to invade the Island of Cuba, or some of the provinces of Mexico.—The best information which the Executive has been able to obtain, points to the Island of Cuba as the object of this expedition.

It is a duty of this Government to observe the faith of treaties, and to prevent any aggression by our citizens upon the territories of friendly nations,—I have therefore thought it necessary and proper to issue this proclamation, to warn all citizens of the United States, who shall connect themselves with an enterprise so grossly in violation of our laws and our treaty obligations, that they will thereby subject themselves to the heavy penalty denounced against them by our acts of Congress, and will forfeit their claims to the protection of their country. No such persons must expect the interference of this government in any form on their behalf, no matter to what extremities they may be reduced, in consequence of their conduct.

An enterprise to invade the territories of a friendly nation, set on foot and prosecuted within the limits of the United States, is, in the highest degree, criminal, as tending to endanger the peace, and compromise the honour, of this nation; and, therefore, I expect all good citizens, as they regard our national reputation—as they respect their own laws and the laws of nations—as they value the blessings of peace and the welfare of their country, to discourage and prevent, by all lawful means, any such enterprise. And I call upon every officer of this government, civil or military, to use all efforts in his power to arrest, for trial and punishment, every such offender against the laws providing for the performance of our sacred obligations to friendly powers.

Given under my hand, the eleventh day of August, in the year of our Lord, one thousand eight hundred and forty-nine, and the 74th of the Independence of the United States.

By the President,　　　　　　　　　　　　　　　　**Z. TAYLOR.**

J. M. CLAYTON, Secretary of State.

DIPLOMATIC DIFFICULTY BETWEEN THE FRENCH MINISTER AND THE U. STATES GOVERNMENT.

The following documents will explain the matter. The *whole* correspondence is voluminous.

Mr. Clayton's letter to Mr. Rush, the American Ambassador at Paris, is first given—then an extract from a note of M. Poussin to Mr. Clayton, and a letter from the same to the same, in which communications are found the offensive expressions complained of—

The Secretary of State to the Minister of the United States at Paris.

DEPARTMENT OF STATE,
WASHINGTON, June 5, 1849.

SIR: You will receive with this despatch a copy of a correspondence that has recently passed between this Department and M. Poussin, the tone of which, on the Minister's part, is regarded as offensive to the American government, and cannot, it is presumed, meet the approbation of the government of the Republic which he represents.

From these papers you will learn that, in October of last year, Commander Carpender, of the United States Navy, commanding the United States war-steamer "Iris," had the good fortune to rescue the French barque "Eugenie," of Havre, which had struck on the bank of Riso, near the anchorage of Anton Lizardo, on the coast of Mexico. Under the belief that the case was one which justly entitled his officers and men to salvage, the commander caused the rescued vessel to be moored in safety near the "Iris" until he could communicate with the consignee, Señor Gomez, at Vera Cruz; but after waiting thirty hours, and receiving no answer from the consignee, he determined to deliver, and did deliver, the barque over to the charge of her captain. In the opinion he entertained respecting the right to salvage, Commander Carpender was supported by Mr. Clifford, our Minister in Mexico, and his whole conduct was approved by that Minister.

On the 12th ultimo, M. Poussin, under instructions from his government, addressed a representation of this subject in a note to this Department, complaining, in strong terms, of what he considers to be arbitrary and illegal conduct on the part of the commander of the Iris; suggesting that that officer should be severely blamed, and asking that speedy satisfaction should be given to the just complaints of the French Republic.

The Department lost no time in placing in M. Poussin's possession the explanations of Commander Carpender, which had been obtained from the Navy Department; and, in communicating them, the hope was expressed that they would remove all misapprehension on the part of the French government in regard to the conduct of the American officer. Commander Carpender and his crew had actually saved the French barque and her crew from imminent peril, if not certain destruction; and for this signal service Commander Carpender has received, not merited thanks, but censure and indignant animadversion from the Minister of the nation to which the vessel belongs.

But M. Poussin himself was not satisfied with the explanations furnished, and without condescending to refer the matter to his government, and await their instructions, he declared the explanations to be not of a nature calculated to dispel the discontent of his government. Having also failed to bring upon Commander Carpender the severe reproof of this government for an alleged error "committed," as M. Poussin rashly asserts, "on a point involving the dignity of your [our] national marine," the Minister taunts the government of the United States with subscribing to the erroneous "doctrines" of the commander, against which doctrines he therefore proceeds to protest in the name of his government.

The attention of this government would not, perhaps, have been so strongly attracted to the tone and temper of M. Poussin, exceptionable as they are, had not that Minister, on a previous occasion, and that quite recently, made use of highly insulting language, in a note he addressed to this government under date of the 18th April last, the offensive portions of which he was afterwards indulgently suffered to withdraw. In resolving to overlook this mark of disrespect, the Department was guided by a sincere desire to omit nothing which would tend to promote the friendly and harmonious relations of the two governments. But, at the same time, not feeling disposed to countenance communications from any quarter which question or impugn the honour and dignity of the American government, the President has deemed it proper to direct me to transmit to you the accompanying correspondence, which he wishes you to submit to the French government. You will readily perceive that the language objected to, and the temper which M. Poussin has not been able to conceal, must necessarily tend to obstruct diplomatic intercourse, and are essentially calculated to embarrass rather than to promote a friendly discussion of questions that concern the honour and interests of the two Republics.

I am, sir, respectfully, your obedient servant,

JOHN M. CLAYTON.

RICHARD RUSH, Esq., &c.

Extract of a letter addressed to the Secretary of State by M. Poussin, under date of April — 1849.

Finally, Mr. Secretary of State, I said, in my note of the 30th, that M. Port quitted Puebla on the 10th of September, and did not return until the 15th of October, 1847. You answer, that this assertion of mine is not supported by any evidence, and you therefore consider yourself justified in rejecting it entirely. I shall therefore annex to this letter some documents, the mere reading of which should convince you of the reality of the statement made by me; and you will also see that the Legation of France, which would never consent to become the organ of a criminal accusation without proofs, does not venture, without proofs, to advance an assertion of a fact of the most innocent nature.

Allow me to hope, Mr. Secretary of State, that this letter may be the last of a correspondence which has been already too long, on an affair so clear. [The government of the United States must be convinced that it is more honourable to acquit fairly a debt contracted during war, under the pressure of necessity, than to avoid its payment by endeavouring to brand the character of an honest man.*]

Accept, I pray you, sir, the assurance of my high consideration.

GUILLAUME TELL POUSSIN.

Translation of a note from the Minister Plenipotentiary of France.

LEGATION OF FRANCE, }
WASHINGTON, May 30, 1849. }

SIR: I received on the 28th of May the note which you did me the honour to address to me on the same day, in answer to mine calling upon the government of the United States to disavow the conduct of Commander Carpender, of the American war steamer Iris, towards the French ship Eugenie, of Havre, which had run upon the bank of Riso, near the anchorage of Anton Lizardo.

The explanations given by Commander Carpender are not of a nature, Mr.

[* The passage in the above letter included within brackets is that which was subsequently withdrawn by M. Poussin.]

Secretary of State, such as to dispel the discontent which his proceedings have caused to my government. He considers, as he says, and he still considers, that the case was one of salvage; that the rights acquired by him as the saver of the vessel saved empowered him to keep possession of her until his extravagant pretensions were fully satisfied; but his opinions have little interest in our eyes when we have to condemn his conduct.

I called on the Cabinet of Washington, Mr. Secretary of State, in the name of the French government, to address a severe reproof to that officer of the American navy, in order that the error which he has committed on a point involving the dignity of your national marine might not be repeated hereafter.

From your answer, Mr. Secretary of State, I am unfortunately induced to believe that your government subscribes to the strange doctrines professed by Commander Carpender, of the war-steamer Iris; and I have only to protest, in the name of my government, against those doctrines.

I have the honour to be, with distinguished consideration, your most obedient servant.

GUILLAUME TELL POUSSIN.

To the Hon. J. M. CLAYTON, *Secretary of State.*

M. de Tocqueville to Mr. Rush.

[Translation.]

PARIS, AUGUST 9, 1849.

SIR: I have received with the letter, which you did me the honour to write to me on the 7th of last month, the copy of the correspondence which has taken place between the Secretary of State for Foreign Affairs of the United States and the Minister of France at Washington, upon the subject of two claims, which the latter had been charged to present to the Federal Government: one against the irregular detention of the French ship l'Eugenie, by Commander Carpender, off Vera Cruz; and the other for the purpose of asking for an indemnification in favour of M. Port, a French merchant, for the abrogation of the sale of a certain quantity of tobacco struck off to him by the commander of the American forces at Puebla.

These two affairs, having hitherto been discussed at Washington, where they are to be concluded, it is not my province to examine their merits. Besides, I am too certain of the integrity of the Government of the Union to doubt that it will ultimately acknowledge every claim founded in right; and, on its part, it cannot think that the French Government allows itself to be drawn by the desire of protecting its subjects to support pretensions the justice of which has not been demonstrated to it.

These sentiments of reciprocal confidence being of a nature to avert and prevent, in the discussions of private interests, those susceptibilities and misunderstandings which cannot fail to complicate them, we have seen with as much astonishment as regret the turn which the communications exchanged between our Envoy and Mr. Clayton have taken. Even before I had received the letter which you have written me to call my attention to them, M. Poussin had transmitted copies of them to me. I have been painfully impressed to find in that correspondence a tone of acerbity and harshness very little conformable to the friendly relations between the two countries; but I ought to say, without entering into useless recriminations, without seeking for the side whence the first injuries proceeded, it had appeared to me that this observation was not alone applicable to the letters written by the Minister of France.

M. Poussin, doubtless misconstruing some expressions in those which have been addressed to him by the Secretary of State, believed he saw in them a want of respect, for which he may have manifested his resentment with too much spirit; but if a passage of his letter of the — of April may have hurt Mr. Clayton, it seems to me that there is no longer any ground to take advantage of it against him after he has consented to withdraw it; and he has given a pretty signal proof of his conciliatory spirit in abstaining from animadversion upon an expression in the answer addressed to him by that Minister on the 21st of April, which, estimated with a certain degree of susceptibility, might have seemed to be rather an imperious summons than a diplomatic invitation.

Furthermore, sir, it is not necessary for me to tell you that I entirely concur in the opinion which you express upon not deviating in negotiations from the observances and forms of a benevolent courtesy.

I invite M. Poussin never to forget this rule in his intercourse with the Government of the United States, and I am sure that, if it be reciprocated, the observance of it will be rendered easy to him.

Receive, sir, the assurance of the high consideration with which I have the honour to be your very humble and very obedient servant,

ALEXIS DE TOCQUEVILLE.

The Secretary of State of the United States to the Minister of Foreign Affairs of France.

DEPARTMENT OF STATE,
WASHINGTON, September 8, 1849.

M. ALEXIS DE TOCQUEVILLE,
    Minister of Foreign Affairs of the French Republic.

SIR: I have received a despatch from Mr. Rush, the American Minister in Paris, of the 13th of August, covering a note from you to him, dated the 9th of that month. Both have been submitted to the President, with the correspondence to which they relate. As Mr. Rush is returning home, and Mr. Rives, who has been appointed to succeed him as Minister to France, has probably not yet arrived in Paris, I hasten to avail myself of the only means of communication between the Governments we represent, by addressing you directly on the subject of your note.

You acknowledge the receipt of the correspondence "which took place between the Secretary of State for Foreign Affairs of the United States and the Minister of France at Washington," from which it must have been obvious to your mind that the latter had repeatedly and gratuitously addressed communications to this Government highly offensive and discourteous, both in manner and in substance.

That correspondence was submitted simply to enable your Government to decide upon the proper course to be taken in regard to its own Minister. You appear to have considered the occasion as one which called upon you to construct an apology for that Minister, by indiscriminately censuring both parties to the correspondence. You were not invited to decide as an arbiter upon the mode in which the American Government conducted that correspondence, which was not only courteous and respectful in terms, but entirely unexceptionable in spirit; and you could not have failed to observe that this Department had not, in any instance, descended to recrimination, whether useless or otherwise, with Mr. Poussin.

Should the correspondence of any Minister of this Republic prove insulting to the friendly Government of France, that Government is too confident of our desire to maintain kind relations with it to doubt that the President of the United States would feel it to be a high duty to examine the complaint, and to render a prompt and proper atonement for the injury. But the issue presented in the correspondence of Mr. Poussin cannot be evaded by any charge of recriminations. If that charge can be made with any shadow of truth, let it be separately presented, and it will be promptly and most respectfully considered.

The President instructs me to say to your Excellency that, as from the whole tone of your communication to Mr. Rush, which has struck him with much surprise, it would seem that the disrespectful language of the French Minister at Washington has been received with indulgence, and held worthy of palliation by the distinguished Minister of Foreign Affairs of France, who has manifested no disposition to redress the wrong, he, as the Chief Magistrate of the United States, feels himself now at perfect liberty, and in fact constrained, with a view to preclude opportunities which might be again abused, to perform, without any further delay, an unpleasant duty, from which he had hoped his friendly appeal to the French Government would have relieved him.

This Government is the guardian of its own honour, and, as on all occasions it seeks to avoid giving cause of offence, so will it never submit to intentional disrespect. By the time this letter reaches your Excellency, Mr. Poussin will have been informed that no further correspondence will be held with him by the Executive of the United States, and that every proper facility will be afforded him, should he desire to return to France.

The President further instructs me to express to your Excellency the friendly sentiments of himself and of this Government for the President, the Government, and the People of France. He does not doubt that these kind sentiments are reciprocated by them, and he anticipates, with lively satisfaction, the arrival of Mr. Poussin's successor, with whom it will be the study of this Government to cultivate agreeable and friendly intercourse, in the terms and the spirit of mutual courtesy, which will be equally honourable to both the sister Republics.

In the mean time prompt and respectful attention will be given to any communications touching the interests of our respective countries which may be made through any other diplomatic agent whom the French Government may see fit to select.

I avail myself of this opportunity to offer to your Excellency the assurance of my most distinguished consideration.

JOHN M. CLAYTON.

DEPARTMENT OF STATE, }
WASHINGTON, September 14, 1849. }

SIR: The President has devolved upon me the duty of announcing to you that the Government of the United States will hold no further correspondence with you as the Minister of France; and that the necessity which has impelled him to take this step at the present moment has been made known to your Government. In communicating the President's determination in regard to yourself personally, I avail myself of the occasion to add, that due attention will be cheerfully given to any communications from the Government of France, affecting the interests of our respective Republics, which may reach this Department through any other channel. Your own Government will be able to explain to you the reasons which have influenced the American Executive in delaying the present communication until this period.

The President has instructed me further to say, that every proper facility for quitting the United States will be promptly given, at any moment when you may be pleased to signify that it is your desire to return to France.

I am, sir, very respectfully, your most obedient servant,

JOHN M. CLAYTON.

MR. WILLIAM TELL POUSSIN, &c.

SECOND REPORT ON THE SLAVE TRADE.

THE select committee appointed (by the House of Commons) to continue the inquiry undertaken by a committee appointed last year, to consider the best means which Great Britain can adopt for providing for the final extinction of the slave trade, and to whom the evidence taken before the said committee was referred, and who were empowered to report the evidence taken before them from time to time to the House, and who were further empowered to report their observations to the House; have further considered the matters referred to them, and have agreed to the following report:—

"That the committee which was appointed in the last session of Parliament to consider the best means which Great Britain can adopt for providing for the final extinction of the slave trade, adopted certain resolutions, which were reported to the House. In the purport of those resolutions this committee is agreed with the committee of last session.

"That a long and large experience of attempts to suppress the slave trade by a naval force, leads to the conclusion that to put down that trade by such means is impracticable.

"That over and above a return to the system of discouragement by commercial legislation, several measures have been suggested as suitable auxiliaries to the present preventive system, particularly the destruction of barracoons, the infliction of the penalties of piracy on the captains and crews of vessels engaged in the slave trade, and the enforced liberation of all slaves illegally imported into Brazil and the Spanish colonies.

"That your committee have considered whether these expedients are practically available, as they conceive that if that were the case, such expedients ought to be tried before the abandonment of the system of forcible suppression should be resolved upon. But even assuming that Great Britain either is actually entitled, or could by negotiation acquire a title, to adopt all these measures, your committee are still convinced that such a prosecution of them as could alone be effectual, would not be sustained by the general opinion of other civilized countries; would be attended with the imminent risk of very serious calamities, and would scarcely be sooner commenced than abandoned.

"Your committee are, therefore, constrained to believe that no modification of the system of force can effect the suppression of the slave trade, and they cannot undertake the responsibility of recommending the continuance of that system. Your committee are not, however, prepared to recommend the immediate and unconditional withdrawal, by Great Britain, of her contingent from that system which her influence has been so mainly instrumental in recommending to other countries, without any communication with those countries, and without any definite understanding of their views.

"Your committee are, however, of opinion, that the aim of those communications should be to release Great Britain from such treaty engagements in respect to the slave trade, as place the question of maintaining a blockading squadron beyond the free and exclusive control of British authorities.

"Your committee do not conceive that if the use of force is to be abandoned, it therefore follows that Great Britain is to become neutral or indifferent with respect to the slave trade.

"It is painful to your committee to acknowledge want of success in an undertaking to which the intelligence, the energy, and the wealth of Great Britain have been so long and so unsparingly applied—an undertaking, the success of which this country has endeavoured to ensure by great sacrifices of human life, and for which it has consented to place at constant hazard the peace of the world; but nothing can absolve your committee from the duty of recognising the truth of the case as their inquiry has brought it under view.

"It would still be the duty of the British Government to exhibit its unabated hostility to the African slave trade; to employ every means compatible with a just regard to the independence of other states to promote the mitigation of its evils, and to accelerate its final extinction; and by no means to shrink from suggesting further pacific efforts, and even further sacrifices, in the cause for which it has already toiled so much, if at any time they should be found necessary for the attainment of so happy a consummation.

"That your committee entertain the hope that the internal improvement and civilization of Africa will be one of the most effective means of suppressing the slave trade; and for this purpose, that the instruction of the natives by missionary labours, by education, and by all other practical efforts, and the extension of legitimate commerce, ought to be encouraged wherever the influence of England can be directed, and especially where it has already been beneficially exerted."

LETTERS OF KOSSUTH.

Szegedin, July 26, 1842.

A circumstance has happened to the last degree unfortunate for me, and for you, and for the whole country. Gen. Georgey writes from Comorn on July 20: "The battle at Raab is lost. The enemy will be in Buda in forty-eight hours." The government must attend to the securing of the stores, the bank, &c. I had no garrison in Pesth, and hence was unwilling to leave the bank-note machinery exposed to being carried off in case of an unfavourable event. I was therefore obliged to take it to pieces, and cause it to be transported to Szegedin (a heavy load, of at least 6,000 hundred weight of presses and matrices,) just at the time when, on account of the approach of the Russians, I was obliged to break up the apparatus at Debreczin. The erection took at least fourteen days, and for that time we fabricated no money. You therefore get nothing except the 125,000 florins, which I sent on the 9th inst. to Szolnok. I did what man could do; but I am no god, and cannot create out of nothing. For a whole year, nothing has come in: empty purses and war. At this moment, I have the following troops to maintain: in Transylvania, 40,000 men; Upper army and Comorn, 45,000; South army, 36,000; Theiss army, 36,000; Peterwardein, 8,000; Grosswardein, Arad, Szegedin, Baja, Zarander, Granzcordon, and small detachments, 10,000; in the whole, 137,000 men. Beside the reserved squadron of eighteen Huzzar regiments, seven battalions in erecting fortifications, 20,000 sick, 80,000 militia to be sustained—powder-mills, foundries, armories, boring of cannon, making of bayonets, 24,000 prisoners, the whole civil administration. This, General, is no trifle, and the bank-note apparatus has not worked for a fortnight. I ask for patience. I am not God. I can die for my country, but I cannot make a "creation." In three days, the bank will again be in order, and I can then deliver to your treasurer 20,000 florins a week. You write for 800,000 florins, and this sum is scarce a tenth part of our monthly expenses. So much for explaining our difficulties. More I cannot. Now for something very important. Bolexis and Balliach, emigrants from Wallachia, have proposed to me to form a Wallachian legion. I have accepted the offer, in general, and referred them for details to the commander-in-chief. I recommend them. The matter is of great consequence. If you should return into Wallachia, as I hope, this battalion will form the advanced guard. The effect would be incalculable. I consider it very important to announce in the proclamations that we come as friends of the Turks and Wallachians, to free them from the Russians. The Turks pursue a two-sided policy. We must compromise them.

L. Kossuth.

KOSSUTH TO COUNT BATTHYANY, MINISTER OF FOREIGN AFFAIRS.

Dear Count,—You will receive this letter from Col. Von Kalmany, who is charged to communicate my wishes to you verbally. The apprehensions I stated to you at Szegedin on June 23d have been realized. Georgey's conquest of Ofen was the last gleam of the setting sun of the republic, for immediately afterwards Dembinski was defeated in the north, and Perczel in the south; then Georgey fell into his fatal position at Comorn, and, finally, Bem was compelled to retreat before Luders. My slender hopes of being able, by resorting to extraordinary measures, to give our cause a more favourable turn, have been wholly destroyed by the shameful ingratitude of Georgey, for the revelation and execution of his plans, which I had long perceived and feared, was a treason to the cause of the nation, and inflicted on me, and through me on the republic, a death-blow. Our misfortune has cost us 200,000 cannon balls, and a flight, already become dangerous, is the grave of so many glorious victories. Our cause is now utterly lost; the immense fatigues I have lately undergone have wearied my spirits and shattered my bodily strength; I sigh for repose. My greatest consolation in my present critical position is the knowledge that those most dear to me after my native land—my family—are in safety. I go to-night with Csanyi and Hervath to Lugos, where I shall expect your verbal answer through Col. Von Kalmany. In the mean time, accept the assurance of my profound respect.

ARAD, August 11th. KOSSUTH.

LETTER OF KOSSUTH TO GENERAL BEM.

DRENKOVA, August 14th.

I am regardless of my safety. I am weary of life, as I now behold the fine edifice of my country's freedom, and with it the sanctuary of European liberty, destroyed—not by our enemies, but by our brethren. It is not, then, a cowardly love for existence that determines my departure; but the conviction that my presence has become injurious to my country. General Guyon writes that the army concentrated near Temesvar is in a state of complete dissolution. You, General, are placed *hors de combat;* Georgey is at the head of the only army which, according to his account, still exists, and he declares that he will no longer obey, but govern. I implored him to remain, at all events, patriotic and faithful to his country, and I ceded to him my place.

At this moment I am merely a simple citizen, nothing more. I have been to Lugos to ascertain the state of affairs, and to learn what could be done to continue the struggle. I found the corps of General Vecsey in good order, and animated with the best spirit, but all the others neatly dissolved. Descorf and Kmetz declared to me that their army would not fight any longer, but would retreat at the first cannon shot. I found a complete want of supplies, and we are obliged to feed by requisition—a miserable means, which renders the people our enemies. The bank, transferred to Arad, is in the hands of Georgey. I am convinced that if Georgey surrenders, the army will not stay near Lugos twenty-four hours, as it is in want of every thing. An army may provide for its existence by requisition in an enemy's country— but not in its own country! So far as regards myself, I shall never consent to measures of violence against my own people; I am ready to save them at the sacrifice of my life, but to oppress them—never.

You see then, general, the present is a case of conscience. I could not resign yesterday, and resume the reins of power to-day: If the nation and the army decide otherwise, it is different; but the army of Georgey, the bravest of all, should give its consent. If it do not, I remain a simple citizen, and as such I shall never co-operate, even passively, in measures of terrorism, of destruction, of pillage, of requisition, and of oppression towards the people.

If the army of Georgey summon me to resume power—if you succeed in executing some operation in order to secure supplies for your army without having recourse to acts of oppression—if the bank shall be free to operate, and at my disposal—under these conditions I shall respond to the call of the nation, and I shall resume the government. If not, I will never consent to do so. For me, war is not the object, but the means of saving the country. If

I do not see the possibility of obtaining that object, I will not consent to the continuation of the war merely for the sake of carrying on war. I advise you, then, as a good citizen and as a man of honour, to name a committee of representatives of the people; for the sovereign power only can dispose of the government. Send couriers to Comorn and Peterwardein to summon them, and secure the co-operation of the commandant of the fortress of Arad. This, and not my presence, is above all necessary; because, as you must have recourse to force to feed your army, I do not wish to sanction by my presence any such measures. Receive, I pray you, the assurance of my perfect consideration, &c.

Louis Kossuth.

LETTER OF GENERAL GEÓRGEY TO GENERAL KLAPKA.

Grosswardein, August 16, 1849.

My Dear Friend Klapka: Since we saw one another events have taken place which were not, indeed, unexpected, but have been decisive. The everlasting jealousy of the Government, the common jealousy of some of its members, had fortunately brought matters to the point which I foretold in April. When I had passed the Theiss at Tokay, after many honourable battles with the Russians, the Diet declared its wish that I should be commander-in-chief. Kossuth secretly appointed Bem. The country believed that Kossuth had appointed me, from the jesuitical answer which he gave to the motion of the Diet.

This knavery (spitz-buberei) was the source of all which befell later. Dembinski was beaten at Szoreg; Bem was routed at Maros-Vasarhely. The latter hastened to Temesvar, under the walls of which Dembinski had retired. He arrived on the field during the battle, restored the fight for some hours, but was then defeated in such wise that, according to Kossuth's calculation, out of 50,000 men only 6,000 remained together. The rest were all dispersed, as Vecsey announced to me. In the mean time the Austrians advanced between Arad and Temesvar. The Minister of War had given orders to Dembinski to retreat naturally to the friendly fortress of Arad, and not the hostile one of Temesvar. Dembinski, however, acted against these orders; why, I am not able to determine, But there are too many data to surmise that he did so out of jealousy toward me.

The consequence of all this was that I stood alone with the force which I had brought from Comorn, (after deducting important losses which I sustained at Waitzen, Ressag, Goromboly, Ipolica, Kesstrely, Debreczin,) threatened on the south by the Austrians, and on the north by the main force of the Russians. I had, it is true, still one retreat open from Arad through Radna to Transylvania. But, regard for my country, to which I desired, at any price, to restore peace, induced me to lay down arms. First I had called upon the Provincial Government to reflect that they could no longer serve the country helpfully, but only plunge it into deeper misfortune, and therefore they should resign. They did so, and laid down in my hands the whole civil and military power; whereupon I, as the moment was urgent, embraced the resolution, suddenly manifested, but maturely deliberated, to lay down arms unconditionally before the army of the Emperor of Russia. The bravest and most valiant of my army agreed with me, and consented. All the divisions of troops in the immediate vincinity of Arad voluntarily joined me. The fortress of Arad, under Damjanich, has declared the wish to do the same. Up to the present hour we are treated as the brave soldier has a right to expect from brave soldiers. Ponder what thou canst do and what thou oughtest to do.

Arthur Georgey.

THE

American

QUARTERLY REGISTER

AND

MAGAZINE.

Causas rerum, videt, earumque progressus. — CICERO.

Conducted by James Stryker.

DECEMBER, 1849. . . . Vol. III. No. II.

Philadelphia:

PUBLISHED BY THE PROPRIETOR,

NO. 520 CHESTNUT STREET.

1849.

WM. S. YOUNG, PRINTER.

CONTENTS.

No. II. Vol. III.

NOTE.—Hereafter the Register will be issued semi-annually, instead of quarterly, in the volume form, handsomely bound, and without any additional charge.

ERRATA.

Page 471, 21st line, "hardly"—read "badly."
Page 472, 32d line, "sight,"—read "night."
Page 473, 1st line, "suggests,"—read "suggest."

THE AMERICAN

QUARTERLY REGISTER

AND MAGAZINE.

NO. II. . . VOL. III.

DECEMBER, 1849.

HISTORICAL REGISTER.

1849,—CONCLUDED.

UNITED STATES.

WHATEVER concerns our foreign relations is viewed with a more lively interest in this country, partly from the popular character of the government, by which every man is converted into a politician, and partly, perhaps, from its federative character, whereby the interest which in most countries is divided among the numerous objects that must be cared for by a single executive and legislature, is here concentrated on the few that are exclusively cognizable by the federal government. It thus happens that our foreign concerns, which are among the few thus cognizable, are often regarded with a sensibility far exceeding their importance. Of all this, the recent correspondence between Mr. Clayton, the secretary of state, and the French minister, M. Poussin, and M. de Tocqueville, affords an apt illustration. Under the influence of this undue interest, it was predicted by that class of persons who are prone to apprehend evil, as well as those who habitually excite alarm, whether they apprehend danger or not, that points of difference which were of a personal character, and which, therefore, should be suffered to end with the individuals with whom they originated, would bring about a serious misunderstanding between two great nations bound together by so many ties of amity and mutual interest. It was even asserted that the diplomatic altercation, which ended in M. Poussin's dismission, would afford a pretext to the French government not to receive Mr. Rives, the new American minister, for no greater offence than that he had obtained for his country the best treaty that France was willing to grant; and, though he had shown his homage to liberal principles by being the first foreign minister to acknowledge Louis Philippe, after the revolutions of 1830, and had continued on the most friendly terms with the French government as long as he remained in France. His formal reception by the President of France, soon after Mr. Rush, the late minister, took his leave, has dissipated these evil auguries so far as France was concerned. The claims on the American government, preferred by M. Poussin, and which afforded him the occasion for the discourteous language complained of, are comparatively insignificant, and no doubt admit of a ready adjustment that will be satisfactory to both parties.

The controversy between the republic of Nicaragua and the king of Mosquito, whose interests the United States and Great Britain have respectively espoused, and which seemed greatly to exceed the other in difficulty and importance, has given rise to similar apprehensions; but we trust they will prove equally unfounded.

Of the precise merits of this controversy we are, as yet, very deficient in information. The exclusive right to the navigation of the river San Juan, may be found to be beyond all dispute, or it may be dependent on facts that are involved in doubt, and are now scarcely susceptible of proof. The substance of our present information on the subject may be thus stated.

When five communities, inhabiting that portion of the Mexican isthmus which lies between the 8th and the 18th parallels of north latitude, formed a federal republic under the name of "the United States of Central America," it is alleged that the greater part of the eastern coast of the isthmus within those limits was occupied by several Indian tribes, who formed no part of the new republic, but remained in the same state of savage independence as before. Even there, however, the whites had a few settlements, and among them were Matina, in Porto Rico, and the fortress of San Juan, on the northern mouth of the river of that name.

Among those tribes were the Mosquitos, a mixed breed, descended from Indians and the negroes whom English adventurers had introduced into the country when they made settlements there, but which they afterwards surrendered by their treaty with Spain in 1786, for their present colony of Honduras or Belize. By reason of this early connexion, the Mosquitos have always been under the protection of the British government, and they are said to be more advanced in civilization than the other Indian tribes. But the country originally occupied by the Mosquitos lies north of the river *Gracias à Dios*, which is itself more than 200 miles north of the river *San Juan*, and it is not known how they acquired a right to the territory occupied by other Indian tribes south of the Gracias à Dios, or how, indeed, any tribe had a claim to the San Juan, which had so long been in the exclusive possession of the whites of Nicaragua. The king of the Mosquitos has set up a claim to it, and the British government seems to have decided on upholding that claim.

In October, 1847, the Nicaraguan government declared that it did not recognise the king of Mosquito as the legitimate representative of that tribe, and still less their rights to the territory in question. They asserted their own right to the north bank of the San Juan, and added, that they would regard as an act of war on the part of Great Britain the occupation of any part of that river by the Mosquitos under its protection.

The council of state of the Mosquitos responded to this declaration that they would take possession of the territory in dispute on the first appearance of a British man-of-war. Two British ships soon afterwards arrived, and removed the Nicaraguans who were in possession of the fort at the mouth of the San Juan. The ships, passing up the San Juan, entered the Nicaragua lake, and a treaty was made between Great Britain and the Nicaraguans, by which the latter engaged not to interrupt the peaceful inhabitants on the San Juan. They refused, however, to surrender their claims to the territory. The Mosquito king, subsequently, granted to the British government the exclusive navigation of the San Juan, and he refuses to allow the Americans to execute the projected communication between the two oceans, according to the grant made by Nicaragua during the present year.

For the purpose of removing these difficulties in the way of their claims, the Nicaraguans sent an envoy to London, Señor Castellon, who also represented the republic of Honduras. A correspondence took place between this envoy and Lord Palmerston early in the current year. The British minister then declared that the British government would do nothing to indicate a doubt that Grey Town—a name they have recently given to the place formerly called San Juan —belonged exclusively to the Mosquitos. The Nicaraguan minister replied, that the Mosquito nation had no existence, and though it had, it possessed no claims to Port San Juan, which had been immemorially in the possession of Nicaragua. He was, however, willing to submit the question of right to arbitration. This offer was peremptorily rejected by Lord Palmerston, who declared that his government having come to a definite resolution on the subject, it was now impossible to recede. It has been further stated in the public journals, that the British government had negotiated for a colony of Germans to be established at fort San Juan; against which measure the Nicaraguan government was able to make no other resistance than a protest. Lord

Palmerston had previously declared that the Mosquito boundary extended from Cape Honduras to the southern mouth of the San Juan, and he instructed all British agents in America, that the British government "would not view with indifference any encroachment on their territory."

In July and August last, a correspondence took place between the secretary of the supreme government of Nicaragua, and Mr. Chatfield, the British consul general, on the subject of this grant, in which the latter states that having seen the notice of a contract between the Nicaraguan government and Dr. Brown, of New York, for a canal through the San Juan, he informs the secretary that the British government will object to any arrangement that does not provide for the debts to British subjects, which Nicaragua, in common with other states of Central America, had assumed to pay. The Nicaraguan minister protested against this invasion of his country's independence, and also against the declaration repeatedly made by the British government that it would sustain the claims of the king of Mosquito. He again declares that the Nicaraguan government does not recognise the right of the tribe of Mosquitos to erect itself into a sovereign state.

When this point of disagreement between the United States and Great Britain first occurred, it seemed not improbable that a new element would be introduced into the controversy that was much more likely to irritate and prolong it, than to soothe and settle it. This is the right which grows out of the celebrated position assumed by Mr. Monroe in his annual message to Congress in 1823, "that the American continents were no longer to be regarded as fit subjects for colonization by a European power," and "that any attempt to introduce European systems of government into any portion of this hemisphere, would be regarded by the United States as dangerous to their peace and safety." The right of President Monroe to make these declarations has been questioned on more than one ground; and though they met with an approving response from the American people, they have never yet received the formal and deliberate sanction of the national legislature. It must, however, be admitted that if such colonization or intervention should put in hazard our safety or peace, as Mr. Monroe's claim assumes, that claim would have a foundation which has always been deemed valid in Europe, and which none of its sovereigns ever failed to assert when they had sufficient power to enforce it. The only difficulty in the argument is to show that our peace or safety would be thus endangered, and that may be no small one when we regard our present strength, and the gigantic strides by which it is advancing. It is probable that this controversy will be adjusted without the necessity of resorting to a topic of so delicate a character, and so prolific of irritating discussion. We can scarcely doubt that the very lively interest which Great Britain has taken in the projected communication between the Atlantic and Pacific oceans, has arisen from the fear that her great commercial rivals would endeavour to monopolize the vast commerce which that communication will call into existence; but when she finds, as she will find, that no such claim to monopoly is asserted—that no one has had the boldness even to propose it, and that the projected canal is stipulated to be open to the ships of all nations, she will no longer deem it expedient to assert a right which is certain to be contested, and is in so many ways assailable.

The increased importance of Nicaragua, induced the government of the United States, some months since, to send a Chargé d'Affairs, Mr. Squier, to that republic. He was very cordially received by its President, and in his reply to Mr. Squier's first address he said, that "Nicaragua had long felt the necessity of sheltering herself under the bright banner of the North American confederacy." Don Herman Gildos Zepede was soon afterwards appointed a commissioner to negotiate a treaty with Mr. Squier on the subject of the proposed canal, and early in September such a treaty was concluded.

According to the principal provisions of that treaty, the contract made with David L. White, successor to Dr. Brown, on behalf of the citizens of New York, with Nicaragua, was sanctioned and confirmed. The right of the grantees to the use of the canal was to continue for eighty-five years from the time it was completed. Twelve years were allowed for its completion. The sum of ten thousand dollars was to be paid immediately to Nicaragua, and the same sum annually during the twelve years. This sum was to be afterwards increased, first twenty per cent., and then twenty-five per cent. The canal to be open to the commerce of all nations on the payment of the prescribed tolls. Thus, in consequence of the several grants by the Mosquito and Nicaraguan governments to Great Britain and the United States of the exclusive right to the navigation of the San Juan River, those nations have now become parties to this territorial question, which, at first merely local and of little seeming moment, has swelled into one of national importance.

The commercial consequence of the proposed canal has not, on the whole, been overrated; but its principal value will probably not be in that way which was first supposed. A water communication between the two oceans was long most anxiously desired, from the facility it would afford the trade with China and India; but it does not seem likely that such trade admits of a very great increase, since a small number of ships are sufficient for the transport of all the commodities that the Atlantic states would probably buy of them, or sell to them. But of the traffic between the ports on the Atlantic and those on the Pacific the probable future increase is incalculable; and for every ship which now doubles Cape Horn, to carry on such commerce, there might, in no long time, be twenty, or even fifty, if they could find a passage through the Isthmus; and the number would continue to increase with our increasing population. Our whalers, too, would be able to carry on their business at a great saving of time and expense, and the easier access to the various groupes of fertile islands in the Pacific would give an immense spring to their population, their production of articles useful to us, and their consumption of our products; and although the length of this communication between the two oceans is more than five times as long as that projected at Panama, yet by its being further north, it would shorten the distance between all the Atlantic states and the whole Pacific coast of North America, some seven or eight hundred miles; so that the communication between them by the projected canal through Nicaragua may be as expeditious, or more so, than by the projected rail-road at Panama.

Our new settlements on the Pacific, and still more the gold mines of California, have greatly stimulated the desire to facilitate the passage from the Atlantic to the Pacific. Not only have two companies been formed for this purpose—one to make a rail-road across the Isthmus at Panama, and the other a canal through Lake Nicaragua—but two conventions of delegates, from various states, assembled in the summer for the sake of furthering the stupendous project of a rail-road from the Mississippi to the Pacific. One of these met at Memphis, in Tennessee, on the 23d of October. Fourteen States were represented by nearly four hundred delegates.

Without much delay or discussion, they adopted six resolutions of the following purport:

1. That it is the duty of the general government to provide for the construction of a national road from the Mississippi River to the Pacific.

2. To facilitate the object, a competent corps of engineers should be appointed to explore and survey the several routes designated by public opinion.

3. After those surveys, the government should locate the line of the road, selecting that which is easiest of access; most favourable to national defence; most convenient to the people; is most central, and in which a rail-road is the cheapest.

4. The lands of the United States constitute the legitimate and proper fund for the construction of such a road.

5. After the construction of the main trunk from the Mississippi to the Pacific, it will be the duty of Congress to aid in the construction of such branch canals as will connect it with the northern lakes and the great thoroughfares to the Atlantic, and other points on the Mississippi and the Gulf of Mexico.

6. Congress should also provide, under liberal conditions, communications between the main trunk and all other rail-roads now made, or which may be made by the several states and territories; and while this rail-road is in progress, a present communication, by canal or rail-road, should be made between the Atlantic and Pacific at Tehuantepec, Nicaragua, or Panama; and they recommend the conveyance of the mail and military stores by such canals.

They also recommend the establishment of military posts from the confines of the Western States along the southern boundaries of our republic to the Pacific; and

That, in the event of appropriations by Congress of any considerable portion of the public lands to the construction of a rail-road from the Mississippi to the Pacific, appropriations of lands lying within the limits of the respective States should also be made to those States to aid them in their public works. All the preceding recommendations passed unanimously; but a majority of the States only—ten to fourteen—recommend for examination the route commencing at San Diego, crossing the Colorado, running along the Gila River to the Paro del Norte, and thence across Texas to its north-eastern boundary between 32° and 33° north latitude, and terminating on the Mississippi, between the mouth of the Ohio and Red rivers.

The Missouri convention, for the same object, assembled at St. Louis, on the 28th day of October. Fifteen States were there represented by near nine hundred delegates. They agreed upon an address to the people of the United States, on the importance of a rail-road between the Atlantic and Pacific. They say they do not presume to suggest the route of the proposed rail-road; but they venture to recommend a line of military posts from the Mississippi to the Pacific, and to propose, by way of compromise of the rival claims of the north, to a line from the great lakes to Oregon, and of the south, from Texas to San Diego on the Pacific, a central route, with branches to the northern, the middle, and the southern States. They conclude with proposing a general convention from all the States in Philadelphia, on the 1st Monday in April next.

The newly acquired territory of California has continued, throughout the whole of the current year, to attract adventurers in pursuit of the gold which is there so abundant. More than eight hundred vessels had left the Atlantic ports, before the 1st of December, for California; and while some of the emigrants have been amply rewarded for the toils and privations of the voyage or which their mining labours may have cost them, not a few have encountered varied sufferings and bitter disappointment. Gold cannot be obtained at the mines without labour, often of the severest and most irksome character, and since that labour cannot be purchased, each individual must be content with the small portion he can furnish to himself. Its products are somewhat precarious, and though their average is nominally large, the value is so depreciated, that they are often not more than sufficient to defray the cost of the labourer's maintenance. The merchandize carried to San Francisco at first, indeed, yielded large profits, but was afterwards so increased as to glut the market, and occasion great loss. The adventurers, however, from the western States, overland, have been the greatest sufferers from this avidity for gold. Many of those who undertook to pass the Rocky Mountains, and the desolate regions at their

base, have found themselves in danger of starvation, and have been
obliged to subsist on the cattle and horses employed for their transport.
This resource has not always proved sufficient, and their track has been
strewed with the graves of those who have been cut off by fatigue, the
want of food, or disease, as well as with the goods which the wretched
wayfarers were compelled to leave on the road for the sake of expe-
diting their journey.   The success of some of the adventurers to California may be inferred from the fact that the quantity of gold which
their labours have furnished to the mint this year has been about six millions of dollars.

On the 31st of August, deputies chosen by the people of California
assembled at Monterey, to form a Constitution.   One was accordingly
formed, prefaced with a bill of rights, and it will be submitted to Congress for their approval.

This example of a community erecting itself into a sovereign State,
and applying for admission into the Union, was followed by another
voluntary association, for a similar purpose, of far more doubtful pretensions.   The sect of the Mormons who, driven from Illinois by the
people of that State, because some of their tenets and practices were
deemed repugnant to morality, betook themselves to the extreme West,
and, after roaming to and fro, they finally seated themselves near the
Salt Lake in California, and there, constituting a community of about
20,000 souls, recently formed a political Constitution, not essentially
different from those of the other States, and boldly ask, like California,
to be admitted into the Union as a State, under the name of Deseret,
without going through the usual probation as a territory.   The condition of these applicants differs from that of all others who have preceded them, in the following particulars: They have no right to the
soil on which they have seated themselves, either by purchase, or the
direct sanction of Congress.   The population of all the western States
has been partly composed of squatters, but this is the first instance in
which the whole community was thus constituted. Again, their population
does not yet amount to one-third of the number now requisite to elect
a member to the House of Representatives, and that number will, after
the next census, be considerably augmented.   Another remarkable
feature in their application is that the boundaries which they propose
for their new State, thus occupied by a handful of people, without a
shadow of legal right, comprehends a territory equal to four or five of
the largest States in the Union.

Amidst these procedures, in open violation of existing laws, one is
struck with the love of order, and the facility of political organization,
so generally manifested by the Anglo-Saxon population of this continent.   Here are two communities free from all the restraints of government, and consequently exposed to the mischiefs of the wildest licentiousness, yet quietly, soberly, and discreetly forming a government for
themselves, to whose authority the minority, who may chance to dis-

approve the provisions of that government, yield as implicit obedience as the majority who formed it. Such a moral phenomenon could be exhibited in no other country under the sun; but here every man, from his birth, is impressed with the conviction that government is necessary to the well-being, nay, to the very existence of society; that the majority of the community have the right, as well as the power to construct and direct the machinery of such government, and that, as soon as they have carried their purpose into execution, every member of the community must obey the rules prescribed by the majority, or cease to be a member.

In September, Mr. Squier obtained from the republic of Honduras the cession of the Island of Tigre, in the Bay of Fonseca, on the Pacific, and on the 28th of that month, he gave Mr. Chatfield, the British Consul, official notice of the cession;* but eighteen days afterwards, Mr. Chatfield, in the British ship Gorgon, proceeded to take possession of the Island, in the name of her Britannic Majesty, under the pretext of debts due to British subjects, which the government of Honduras had assumed, but failed to pay. Against this high-handed proceeding, the feeble government could do nothing but protest, after denying the justice of the British claim, and alleging that it had offered to leave the matters in dispute between the two governments to the adjustment of commissioners appointed for the purpose. It is hoped that Mr. Chatfield's course was not authorized by the British government, and, though it was, that this as well as the other points at issue in Central America between the United States and Great Britain will be amicably settled in Washington by the new minister, Sir Henry Bulwer.

On the 4th of December, the members of the thirty-first Congress assembled at Washington, but they being divided, not into two parties as usual, but into some three or four, having diverse and irreconcilable views, it was found at first impracticable to choose a Speaker. Nearly three whole weeks were spent in unavailing ballotings for a presiding officer, and it was only on Saturday, the 21st, that, on the sixty-third ballot, a Speaker was chosen. It is probable that a large majority of the public, who could but partially share the feelings of the members, would rather have seen any member of the house chosen to the office, than longer to have witnessed the humiliating spectacle of the incapacity of the national legislature to take the first step in organizing itself as a deliberative assembly, and thus alarming the fears, or mortifying the pride of the friends of popular government; and calling forth the taunts and derision of its enemies.

On the 22d of December, the President's annual message was sent

---

* It has since appeared, by the publication of the treaty, that the cession was only for eighteen months, and was made expressly to save it from seizure "by some foreign inimical power." Such a cession, it is presumed, will scarcely be defended by the government of the United States.

to both Houses of Congress.   It is a plain, straight forward, business-like document, exhibiting very succinctly, but in sufficient detail, the condition of the country in all its great relations, foreign and domestic. It holds a prudent reserve on all agitating party questions, and throughout it breathes a spirit of moderation, of liberality, and of amity towards all.

Rather more than half the message is appropriated to the foreign relations of the United States.   He says that we are on friendly terms with all foreign powers, towards all of whom we have observed a strict neutrality.   He adverts to the late alterations in the British navigation laws, the effect of which, together with that of the act of Congress of March, 1817, will be to admit British vessels into the ports of the United States, with cargoes of the productions of any country, on the same terms as to duties and charges as vessels of the United States, whose ships will have like admission into the ports of Great Britain.

The slight interruption to the diplomatic intercourse between the United States and France, he remarks, has been happily terminated.

The purchase of a war steamer in the United States by the German Empire, which had been permitted by the late administration during the armistice between that Empire and Denmark, is noticed, and the course pursued by the present administration, as detailed in the preceding number of this journal, is briefly stated.   Although a minister had been sent from the United States to the German Empire, and a minister from that empire had been accredited here, he remarks that no such government as that of the German Empire had been definitively constituted; it is thought that no such union could be permanently established without the co-operation of Prussia.   If it should take place, then it would become necessary to withdraw our minister now sent to Berlin; but until then, there is no necessity to continue the mission to Frankfort.   The minister sent thither has accordingly been withdrawn.

Having heard of the expedition meditated against Cuba, the President had, in conformity with the act of April, 1818, issued a proclamation for the purpose of putting a stop to it.

The case of Rey, the foreigner, who had been clandestinely seized in New Orleans and carried off to Cuba, is noticed.   It is suggested that as there is no punishment for abductions of this character, the law should be amended.

During the late conflict between Hungary and Austria, an agent of the United States was vested with the power of recognising the independence of Hungary, as soon as she had established a permanent government.   The United States did not in any way interfere in the contest, but it seemed right that the Executive should take the first fit occasion of expressing the lively sympathies of the American people.

The claims of American citizens on Portugal had been earnestly pressed, but as yet without effect.   The distracted condition of that country for some time past has been urged as a prominent cause of the delay.   The subject would be again brought before Congress, with a view to more decisive measures.

The letters of credence to the Chargé d'Affaires from the United States to Rome had not been delivered while the papal territory was in a state of revolution.   A counter-revolution has since taken place, and the American Chargé waits to see a permanent government established before he proposes a diplomatic intercourse with it.

Congress are referred to the correspondence between the State Department and the Mexican envoy on the subject of the protocol to the treaty of Guadalupe Hidalgo.   The commissioners appointed to run the boundary line between the United States and Mexico, had entered on that duty soon after the time prescribed by the treaty, and had made some progress in the work.   It will require a further appropriation.

In the adjustment of the claims of American citizens on Mexico, he recommends the employment of counsel to protect the interests of the United States, who have assumed to pay those claims.

The civil war in Venezuela has at length been brought to a close. During its progress the rights of American citizens have been frequently violated.   The restoration of order will enable the Venezuelan government to redress these wrongs, as well as others of longer standing.

The rapid settlement of Oregon and California give new importance to our relations with the foreign countries lying on the Pacific, between whom and our settlements on the Pacific the future commercial intercourse will be very considerable.   It is, therefore, desirable to cherish our friendly relations with those countries.   The same liberal course is recommended towards all other American States.   "We may often kindly mediate in their behalf, without entangling ourselves in foreign wars, or unnecessary controversies.   Whenever the faith of our treaties with any of them shall require our interference, we must necessarily interpose."

A convention has been negotiated with Brazil for the satisfaction of American claims on that government.

The laws for the suppression of the slave trade, it is suggested, require amendment.   That odious traffic is still carried on in vessels built in the United States, which, purchased by foreigners abroad, are able to prosecute their voyages to the coast of Africa by means of the temporary sea-letter they obtain from the American consul abroad.   Congress is invited to adopt a course which, preventing such abuses of the national flag, should leave the benefits meant to be extended to navigation and commerce unimpaired.

As there is no prospect of a reunion of the five States of Central America, separate treaties have been negotiated with several of them. One has been made with the State of Nicaragua, by which both governments pledge themselves to protect a company who have contracted with Nicaragua to connect by a canal, the Atlantic and Pacific oceans. All other nations are invited to make similar stipulations. They will all enjoy the right of transit on paying the same rate of toll. The territory through which the canal shall pass, should be exempt from all foreign power or control.

The routes across the Isthmus at Tehuantepec and Panama also deserve consideration. The negotiator of the treaty of peace with Mexico was instructed to offer a large sum for the right of way at Tehuantepec, but the offer was not accepted by Mexico, probably in consequence of a previous contract for the same object. The offer would not be renewed, because such a communication should be the common right of all nations, in which case a reasonable toll to those who constructed the work would be sufficient to induce individual enterprise to undertake and complete it. The benefits which would accrue to Mexico from the canal would sufficiently remunerate her.

The railroad about to be constructed at Panama will be protected under the late treaty between the United States and New Grenada. He adds, that we should encourage every practicable route across the Isthmus.

The destiny of the Sandwich islands, as the President well observes, is on many accounts interesting to us. We could not be indifferent to their passing under the dominion of a foreign power, and it is hoped that no nation will deprive them of their independence. Though he does not mention the late outrage of a French frigate on their independence, with the seeming sanction of the French consul-general, he plainly meant to allude to it.

Passing then to the domestic concerns of the country, he states the receipts into the treasury for the year ending June 30, to be $48,830,-097.50 in money, and in funded treasury notes, $10,833,000, making an aggregate of $59,663,097.50. The expenditures in the same time were $46,798,667.82, and in treasury notes funded, $10,833,000— making an aggregate of $57,631,667.82.

According to the accounts and estimates of the treasury department, there will be deficits, occasioned by the Mexican war and treaty, in 1850 and 1851, amounting together to $16,375,214.39. He recommends Congress to give authority to borrow the sum required to cover the whole deficit, which, he remarks, is exceeded by the extraordinary expenses of the Mexican war and the purchase of California.

He recommends a revision of the present tariff, and that it should be so modified as to increase the revenue. He does not doubt the right or duty of Congress to encourage domestic industry, and he looks " to the adoption of a system which may place home labour, at last, on a sure and permanent footing," and by due encouragement to manufactures, " give a new and increased stimulus to agriculture." For the furtherance of these objects he earnestly recommends a system of specific duties.

The question of continuing the sub-treasury system is submitted to the wisdom of Congress; with a suggestion that, if it is continued, further modifications of it appear to be indispensable,

He recommends the establishment of an agricultural bureau, to be connected with the department of the interior; no direct aid having as yet been given by the general government to this "leading branch of domestic industry."

Having stated that the people of California had probably by this time formed a constitution and state government, and would soon apply for admission into the Union, he recommends their application to the favourable consideration of Congress. The people of New Mexico are likely to make a similar application. He suggests to Congress that by awaiting the action of those communities, "causes of uneasiness may be avoided." He deprecates the introduction of topics of a local character, and repeats the solemn warning of "the most illustrious of his predecessors," against furnishing "any ground for characterizing parties by geographical discriminations."

A collector had been appointed for San Francisco, under the act of Congress of last session. Before his arrival, duties had been collected under the military authority previously established. Congress is recommended to confirm these collections, and to appropriate the money for the improvement of the rivers and harbors of the territory.

Measures had been taken for the coast survey of Oregon, and for ascertaining the proper sites for light-houses in that territory and in California, now so urgently required.

Indian agencies have been transferred from Upper Missouri and Council Bluffs to Santa Fe and Salt Lake; and sub-agents have been appointed for the Gila, the Sacramento, and the San Joaquin rivers. Farther legal provisions are required for the extension of our system of Indian intercourse over the new territory.

The establishment of a branch mint in California is recommended. So is the organization of commissions to decide upon the validity of land titles in California and New Mexico. Provision should also be made for the establishment of offices of surveyor-general in New Mexico, California, and Oregon, and for the conveying and bringing into market the public lands in those territories. They should be disposed of on liberal terms, which should be especially favourable to the early emigrants. He recommends a geological and mineralogical exploration of the principal mineral deposits in California, in connexion with the linear surveys; and that the mineral lands be divided into small lots, to be sold or leased, so that a permanent property may be acquired in them.

The great mineral wealth of California, and the convenience of its ports and harbours, as well as those of Oregon, for commerce, will soon create large and prosperous communities on our Pacific coast. It is, therefore, important that a line of communication should be opened within the territory of the United States from the navigable waters of the Atlantic to the Pacific. Public opinion, as indicated by "large and respectable conventions" recently held at Memphis, in Tennessee, and St. Louis, in Missouri, points to a railroad as best meeting the wants and wishes of the country. The great importance of such a communication, as well as its enormous cost, recommend, as a preliminary measure, a careful survey of the proposed routes. Early appropriations to continue the river and harbour improvements already begun, are suggested.

The large accessions to our territory, as well as our obligations under the Mexican treaty, make an addition to our military force expedient. He commends to the notice of Congress the views of the secretary of war on the inconvenience of the rank heretofore given to brevet and staff commissions, and on the expediency of providing for retiring disabled officers, as well as an asylum for the superannuated or infirm of the rank and file. The present naval force is as large as is admissible. The re-organization of the navy, according to the suggestions of the secretary of that department, is recommended, as well as his plan for the establishment of a "retired list" for disqualified officers, and for the employment of war steamers.

The efforts to extend post-office and mail accommodations to Oregon and California, according to the act of Congress of last session, have hitherto proved ineffectual, from the high price of rents and labour in California. Further legal provision is necessary on the subject.

A further reduction of postage on letters is recommended. The late postal treaty with Great Britain is noticed, as is also the performance of the duties of the census board appointed by the act of Congress of March last. The interests of the city of Washington are especially recommended to Congress, to whose care they are assigned by the constitution.

In conclusion, he refers to the qualified negative which the constitution confers on the President, and which he says he shall consider it his duty never to exercise except "in the extreme cases contemplated by the fathers of the republic." He dwells on the value of the Union, upon the preservation of which depends "our own happiness, and that of countless generations to come;" and however assailed or threatened, he says he should use all the powers confided to him to maintain it in its integrity.

Many of the preceding views were more fully exhibited and enforced by the reports of the several departments. It appeared by that of the secretary of the treasury that the probable receipts into the treasury for the year preceding the 1st of July, 1850, together with the balance in the treasury July 1, 1849, would be $37,823,464.23, and the expenditures in the same time would be $43,651,585.94, leaving a deficit 1st July, 1850, of $5,828,121.66; and that the amount received, for the year ending July 1, 1851, (including the balance in the treasury,) would be $34,450,000, and the expenditures in the same time would be $44,997,092.73, leaving a further deficit of $10,547,092.73, making the whole deficit upward of 16 millions, to raise which a loan is recommended. The whole amount of the public debt he states to be $64,704,693.71.

The secretary discusses at some length the mooted question whether Congress has the power under the constitution of regulating commerce and levying imposts for the purpose of encouraging domestic industry, and he concludes that they have the power, and that it is wise and politic to exercise it. He notices in detail the several circumstances of the country which are favourable or unfavourable to the productions of industry, and to counteract the latter, he thinks that duties should be laid on imports sufficiently high to afford substantial and sufficient encouragement to our domestic industry, provide for the necessary increase and due security of the revenue, and ensure the permanence and stability of the system.

The modifications proposed by him to the existing tariff are, 1st, An increase of duties on articles similar to our own staples, as on cottons, hempen goods, sugar, salt, coal, woollens, iron, and hemp. 2. A return to specific duties, which he thinks are more easily assessed, more favourable to commerce, more equal, and less exposed to frauds. 3. On those articles on which ad valorem duties are retained, they should be estimated according to the market value in the principal markets of our own country at the time of arrival. 4. He objects to laying lower duties upon non-enumerated than on enumerated articles, as inviting to attempts at disguise, and favouring controversy and litigation; to different rates of duty on manufactures of the same materials; and lastly, to higher duties on the raw material than on the articles manufactured of it. For reasons given at length, the secretary thinks that the warehousing system has not been beneficially felt in the general business of the country, and that its practical operation is "a return to the system of credit upon duties, under a new name and form."

Several inconveniences of the sub-treasury are pointed out, to alleviate which some modifications of the law are suggested. A revision of the laws regulating the coasting trade is recommended, so that it may be relieved from some necessary embarrassments and delays, and subjected to modifications suited to its altered character of late years.

In July last, the number of light-houses was two hundred and eighty-eight, and of floating lights thirty-two. Of these, sixty-one are on the northern lakes and the river St. Lawrence.

Details are given relative to the structure of custom houses, and marine hospitals, in the different States.

The report of the newly created "Home Department," or the "Department of the Interior"—for it is designated both ways in the act of Congress—was, from being the first of its kind, regarded with peculiar interest. On its first topic, the public buildings, various suggestions were made for the repair or preservation of the national edifices at the seat of government, it appearing that much of the stone hitherto used is liable to disintegrate, by which the buildings are destined to an early decay, unless chemical science should suggest some means of preserving it, for which object a series of experiments is recommended.   In the notice of the patent office, it is stated that there is a large surplus fund, derived from the fees paid for patents, which the secretary suggests should be applied "to the encouragement of the inventive arts," and "to reward successful inventors."

The establishment of an agricultural bureau by Congress is recommended, on the plans adopted by the French and the Belgian governments.

In the pension office it appears that the whole number of invalid pensions now on the list is 4,115.   The number of claims for bounty land warrants filed, and to be filed, is 103,000.

It appears, by the report of the commissioner of the general land office, that the quantity of land sold in the first three quarters of 1848 was 1,418,240 acres, and in the first three quarters of 1849 it was 887,206 acres, showing a decrease of 561,034 acres.   The amount located on bounty warrants, in the first three quarters of 1848, was 1,525,200 acres, and in the first three quarters of 1849, was 2,496,560 acres, showing an increase of 971,360 acres, from which if the decrease in the number of acres sold for cash be deducted, an increase of the joint sales and locations in three-fourths of the current years is 416,325, which is considered "to mark the increase of agricultural migration." The whole number of claims for bounty lands, not yet satisfied, are estimated to require 9,631,200 acres; and as the bounty land warrants are received in the place of money in the ordinary sales of land, the receipts in cash, from the sales of the public lands, will be comparatively small, until the bounty warrants are exhausted.   The secretary thinks they will be probably absorbed, at the farthest, in three years.

Details are given respecting the geological explorations and surveys of the public mineral lands in Michigan, Wisconsin and Iowa.   To extend the laws for the disposition of the public lands, to Oregon, California and New Mexico, it will be necessary to negotiate treaties with the Indian tribes claiming title to the land, to appoint a surveyor-general, and establish land offices in each territory, and create judicial commissions to examine and settle land titles in New Mexico and California.

On the subject of the gold mines in California, the report is very copious.   It states that, under the laws of Spain, mines of the precious metal did not pass by a grant of the lands which contained them, but the same were reserved to the crown.   It is believed that the same policy was adopted by Mexico after her independence, in which case these mines are now the property of the United States, though they may be on the lands formerly granted to individuals.   By far the larger part, however, of those mines are on lands which have never been granted, and are, therefore, unquestionably the property of the United States.   These are now exposed to the unmolested intrusion of all persons, foreigners as well as citizens, who make no remuneration for the large amount of gold they find.   In order that "this rich deposit of mineral wealth should meet, in process, of time, the heavy expenses incurred in its acquisition, the secretary recommends that those mineral lands be sold or leased, on condition that all the gold found on them shall be carried to the branch mint to be established in California, a portion of which shall be paid to the United States by way of rent or seignorage.   For the lands which contain surface deposites of gold, he thinks leases will be preferable to sales.   As the market price of gold bullion in California has been but sixteen dollars per ounce, which is more than two dollars less than its real value, which he thinks is more than one-half of the amount that ought to be reserved as rent, the profit from coining, he supposes, would, to those who held bullion, induce them to carry it to the mint, and pay the rent to the public.   The property of the United States in the mines of quicksilver, which are known to exist in California, is on the same footing as its property in the gold mines.

The importance of a direct communication overland between the Atlantic and Pacific is pointed out with great clearness and force by the secretary, and he suggests that the Indian tribes, through whose country the proposed rail-road would pass, should be paid an annual sum for the right of way.   They should also be paid for the grass consumed and the game destroyed by the overland emigrants to California. If the annuities be paid them in useful articles, and implements of agriculture, they may be "turned from their roving habits and thirst for war, and gradually won over to habits of agriculture and civilization." The attention of Congress is called to the Indian tribes in Florida, in Texas, New Mexico and California, where agents ought to be appointed.   A favourable account is given of the progress made in civilization by the tribes permanently settled on our western borders.   He recommends an increase of the sum annually appropriated for the civilization of the Indians, especially since we are now brought into contact with so many more than heretofore.

The report of the secretary of the navy gives a full detail of the several squadrons in active service both at home and abroad, noticing the ships composing each, and their operations during the past year. The principal facts then noticed are as follows: Contracts, as authorized by the acts of Congress, for three steam-ships, to carry the mail between Oregon and Panama, and for the five mail steamers between New York and Liverpool, had been duly made.   Some other contracts, for the transportation of the mail by sea, and for an iron war steamer, are also mentioned.   The four first-class "sea-going steam-ships," authorized by the act of Congress of March, 1847, are in progress.

They will add greatly to the efficiency of the navy, and a further addition to the naval steam force is strongly urged.

As the number of officers of the higher ranks in the navy is greater than is necessary, a reduction is recommended, as well as a retired list of those who are disqualified for active service, by which change the other officers may be kept in active service, so necessary to give them the requisite experience and professional skill.

The attention of Congress is directed to the naval school at Annapolis, as of great value in preparing officers for the navy, but which, by some improvements that have been suggested, may be made much more efficient.

The total amount drawn from the treasury during the fiscal year, ending June 30, 1849, $18,167,906.56, from which, if a deduction be made for repayments, the sum of $16,898,542.97 is the expense of the navy and marine corps, together with all objects under the control of the naval department for the year.

Whenever the condition of the country, and the price of labour in California will justify it, the secretary recommends the establishment of a navy yard, and the construction of a dock on the Pacific for the repair and refitting of our public ships.

The value of stores and materials on hand at the navy yards for naval purposes, exclusive of ships building in ordinary, undergoing repairs and in commission, navy yards and other public lands required for the purposes of the navy, with their improvements, is $9,853,921.27."

The secretary of war states that the present strength of the army is less than the organizations provided by law. The desertions have been unusually great in California. Out of 1,200 troops in that territory, two-fifths had deserted for the gold mines in the first eight months of the year. Some suggestions are made to check desertion, and encourage enlistment. An increase of the military force, suited to the great extension of our frontier, and its increased exposure to the incursions of predatory Indian tribes. Inconveniences are stated to have arisen from the multiplication of brevet commissions, which the secretary suggests should be merely honorary distinctions, without an increase of pay, except in special cases. The inconvenience resulting "from the anomalous position of officers holding staff commissions which confer rank," is also pointed out, and a remedy suggested.

The adoption of some rule for retiring disabled officers, and the establishment of an asylum for veteran soldiers, are strongly recommended. The benefits of the military academy at West Point are warmly eulogized.

The outrages committed by the Indians in New Mexico in the course of the present year, are noticed, together with the regular troops, aided by volunteers, employed in suppressing them.

Details are given of the disturbances in Florida; of the regular force sent for the defence of the inhabitants; of the surrender of the Indian murderers; of the continued efforts to remove the Indians still remaining in Florida to the west of the Mississippi; and of the further time asked by the Indians for deliberation on the subject of their removal.

The military operations for keeping the Indians within the limits of Texas in check, and the release of many citizens, both of Mexico and the United States, who had been made captives by the Indians, are also detailed.

Some progress has been made this year in the establishment of the line of military posts on the route to Oregon, which was required by the act of May, 1845, but which had been delayed by the Mexican war.

Aid was given by the Indian agents, and the subsistence department of the army, to the overland emigrants to California. The fortifications on the Pacific, which will be indicated by the engineers now employed there in examinations and surveys, are recommended to the attention of Congress.

The anomalous condition of California had imposed on the army in that territory new and delicate functions, and among them that of collecting duties on imports until the arrival of the officers appointed by the treasury department. The military authorities there have aided the civil functionaries in preserving tranquillity. Its measures are submitted to the approbation of Congress—reference is made to the fuller details given by the several bureaus attached to the war department.

It appears by the report of the Postmaster-General, that the revenue of the post office for the last year amounted to $4,905,176, including $200,000 appropriated for mail services to the government. The expenses of the establishment, in the same time, were $4,449,049. Of the money received for postage, more than four-fifths was on letters, and less than one-fifth on pamphlets and newspapers.

There has been a great reduction in the expense of transporting the mail since 1845, the cost then being eight cents and one mill per mile; but under the operation of laws passed in 1845, the cost was reduced this year to five cents six mills per mile. The number of mail routes on the 1st of July last was 4,943, and their length was 167,703 miles.

The average annual increase of the postage is between nine and ten per cent., which is something more than three times the annual increase of the population. The excess may be referred partly to the increase of wealth, and partly to the advance of civilization.

As the postage received pays the whole expense of the mail service, it virtually pays the cost of all the letters and papers that are within the franking privilege. The postmaster-general thinks that if the public service justifies and requires this privilege, it should be paid for out of the public treasury, as other branches of the public service, so that the postage on letters may be reduced to the amount that is merely sufficient to defray the expense of the post office establishment. The matter now franked by the different departments, and by members of

Congress, would, he computes, at the present rates of postage, annually pay nearly $1,400,000. But without interfering with the franking privilege, he considers that Congress may safely abolish the ten cent postage, so as to subject all letters to the uniform rate of five cents, whatever may be the distance.

The railroad service now extends to 6,138 miles, and is constantly increasing. The cost of this mode of transportation is greater than any other, yet it may yield a greater return, as the mail is now annually transported by these routes 5,749,040 miles, out of the whole amount of 42,549,069 miles, or more than one-eighth, while the length of its routes, 6,128 miles, is not one twenty-seventh part of the length of all the routes—167,703 miles.

The mail is now carried, or soon will be, in steam ships between New York and Bremen, by way of Southampton; between Charleston and Havana; between New York and New Orleans; between Havana and Chagres; between Panama, and California, and Astoria; and between New York and Liverpool. Thirteen war steamers carry the mail on a part of these lines, the expense of which is greater than the postage received on them can support. The postmaster-general hopes, therefore, that their annual charge will not continue to be drawn from the treasury, as is now done.

The effect of the postal treaty concluded with Great Britain is, that letters on which the postage is pre-paid, pass through the mails of the two countries "in the same manner as if those countries were one." What one country receives for the other is at stated times accounted for and settled.

California has had, as yet, but to a small extent, the accommodation of post offices, in consequence of the high price of labour and rent. The great extension of business in this department requires an additional number of clerks. In 1837, the number of post offices was 11,767; it is now 17,164. The number of quarterly returns was then 48,000; it is now 73,000. The number of mail contractors was then 1,682; it is now 4,180. The length of the mail routes, which is now 167,863 miles, was then but 141,242 miles.

It appears from the official reports of the treasury department, that for the year ending June 30, 1849, the whole amount of imports from the United States was $147,857,439, and the exports, in the same time, were $132,666,955. The domestic produce consisted of

The products of the sea,	-	-	$2,547,654
" of the forest,	-	-	5,917,994
" of agriculture,	-	-	111,079,358
" of manufactures,	-	-	10,798,473

The residue of the exports consisted of foreign produce, or of articles not enumerated.

The whole tonnage of the United States, registered and enrolled, amounted, on the 30th of June last, to 3,334,015 tons.

The number of vessels built in the United States, in the same time, was 1547. Their tonnage was 256,577. .

From the relative strength of parties in Congress, and the temper already manifested by them in the house of representatives in the election of a speaker, the prospect of the present session is a gloomy one; and threatens to realize the worst anticipations formed of it. But we see no advantage.in shutting our eyes to it. By watching the signs of the approaching tempest, we neither increase nor lessen its force, but we may be better able to elude or resist it.

It is now clear that there is a majority in both houses of Congress opposed to the administration, by which its action may be impeded and even embarrassed: this, however, is but a small part of the evil with which we are threatened. The principal questions on which the parties are likely to be divided, are, 1. That of protecting manufactures. 2. The adoption of specific in, preference to *ad valorem* duties. 3. The warehousing system. 4. The sub-treasury. 5. The admission or exclusion of slaves in the newly acquired territories; and 6. The abolition of slavery in the District of Columbia.

On all these questions, except the two last, the defeated party will acquiesce with that loyal deference which the people of the United States habitually show to the will of the majority; but on the questions relative to slavery, the case is different. On these the parties disagree about those first principles which are equally independent of majorities and minorities; and that course which the majority feel themselves bound to pursue, the minority regard as an infraction of their rights. With this radical difference of parties, who have no umpire to refer to, the union of these states, and, perhaps, the practicability of self-government, will be subjected to their severest test. If no plan of compromise can be adopted, either expressly or silently, and both parties obstinately adhere to the ground they have taken, we can see no alternative but an open rupture, to be terminated either forcibly by the power of the strongest, or quietly by separation; which, it may be remarked, will only defer, but not prevent the same contests by violence.

Against this reckless conflict of the passions, there are some conservative influences which may be sufficient to preserve to these states the blessings of union, peace, safety, and happiness. In the first place, every reflecting mind is aware that all we most dearly prize in our political institutions is dependent on the union; that the natural and inevitable consequences of its dissolution must be perpetual disputes and occasional wars between neighbouring states; increased taxation to build fortifications and support standing armies, and, finally, a great diminution of civil freedom, and the subjection of the weaker states to the stronger. These considerations will induce men of both parties, who have influence as well as patriotism, to surrender the pride of opinion, and even to make some concession of right, to avert the greatest of national calamities. Then again, of the several questions which divide the two great parties of the country, the majority on one does not consist of the same individuals as the majority of another, so that the political sympathies on one question may be counteracted by the political antipathies on another, and the parties, on the most delicate and dangerous questions, be thus brought more nearly to that equilibrium which is most favourable to compromise. May they prove sufficient instruments to continue that unmatched course of prosperity which Providence has hitherto bestowed on us.

MEXICO, &c.

Notwithstanding the encouraging view taken of the Mexican finances by President Herrera in July last, the general government still has its pecuniary difficulties, to which, indeed, now that money is the great instrument of political power, as well as works of utility, all modern states are more or less exposed, whether they be rich or poor, weak or strong, despotic or free; and to avoid which is often the most onerous duty of their statesmen. In the case of Mexico, the late war naturally lessened her resources, and increased her public debt. In October last, Señor Elorriago, the minister of state, submitted to the legislature a plan of improving the public credit, of which the principal features are as follows:

The government will proceed to ascertain the amount of the public debt—excluding all claims which are not brought forward by a given time.

The debts, foreign and domestic, shall be reduced to 110 millions of dollars, bearing an interest not exceeding 6 per cent.

The government will proceed to make retrenchments and ameliorations.

It will aim to secure an income of $1,500,000, besides the interest of the debt: a system of taxation will be forthwith adopted to meet any deficiency that may arise.

It shall discharge no debt with any particular funds, or in any other respect different from the arrangement made with all the creditors of the state.

It shall create no office, make sale of no public function, or assign any higher salary than that provided by law.

It shall pay no higher interest than one-half of one per cent. monthly, and this only for sums received in specie.

The government shall report to the legislature the result of this plan, in case of its adoption, in the session of 1851 or before.

The plan was substantially adopted, and in pursuance of one of its provisions, the pay and salaries of the public officers have been generally reduced. The executive has also been permitted to anticipate as much of the next instalment of the debt due from the United States, as would be necessary to meet the deficit, estimated at $3,000,000.

It is understood that the insurgents in Sierra Madre have been entirely quelled, the troops sent against them disbanded, and that a restoration of the authority of government is nearly effected throughout the Mexican States. The more recent disorders in the States of Durango and Coahuila have been comparatively insignificant. As crime so often goes unpunished in Mexico, they are disposed to try the penitentiary system as a remedy.

The war between the whites and the Indians in Yucatan still continues. The invincible repugnance manifested by the Indians to submit to the Yucatecos, has suggested the plan of dividing Yucatan into two States, the capitals of which would be Merida and Campeache: which plan is now agitated. The Indians who now desire this division, will, it is supposed, put themselves, like the Mosquitos, under the protection of Great Britain.

HAYTI.

In Hayti, the new dignity of the Emperor Soulouque seems to have inspired no awe in his neighbours of the Dominican republic, whatever it may have done on his own subjects. In a grandiloquent proclamation issued in November by the Dominican government, it avows the purpose no longer to carry on a war of defence, but to seek the enemy "at their own threshold;" and they notice some small successes, both on sea and land, since they decided on offensive war. They have burnt one town, put the inhabitants of another to flight, and have captured a schooner, a sloop, and six boats.

The new Emperor proposes to protect the industry and the purses of his subjects by assuming the monopoly of coffee, their principal article of export, and by a tariff of prices on the principal articles of import, which no one can exceed on pain of imprisonment. The limited prices are, however, exorbitantly high, and perhaps his majesty expects to make a greater profit on the coffee he monopolizes, by reason of the very large profits he has allowed to importers. It is said that the price he pays for coffee to the grower, is 1¾ of a cent per pound.

CENTRAL AMERICA.

In the States of Central America, since the long-projected communication between the Atlantic and Pacific through their country seems about to be effected, there has been a suspension of the civil wars and commotions from which they have never before been free since their separation from Spain. The treatment which some of them have received from the British authorities on the Isthmus, which those States believe to be lawless and unjust, and which certainly was contemptuous, have, by exciting a common sympathy, conduced to the same end. The completion of the proposed canal would not only give a new importance to their country in the eyes of the world, but would add greatly to the value of their lands, and the extension of their commerce.

They all appear to be very friendly to the United States, which both
their hopes and their fears induce them to cherish as their natural pro-
tectors.   It seems highly probable that the collisions between the Nicaraguans and the Mosquito Indians about the right to the navigation
of the San Juan, and the hostile proceedings of the British at Grey-
town or San Juan de Nicaragua, on the Atlantic, and at Tigre Island
on the Pacific, will soon be settled, and after awhile forgotten, in consequence of the negotiations now going on between the American government and the British minister at Washington.

SOUTH AMERICA.

In Venezuela, though Monagas is in the undisputed authority of the
government, and now holds his ancient rival and opponent, Gen. Paez,
a close prisoner, the latter still appears to have many friends, and,
judging from past experience, it is not at all improbable that the civil
commotions which have so frequently and so long agitated this country,
will be renewed.

In the South Pacific American States, there have been lately intestine troubles as usual, but in Peru the contest for the presidency was
settled by an appeal to arms.   In November, the Congress confirmed
an arrangement made between their envoy in London and their creditors, by which the debts of 1822 and 1823 are to bear an interest of
4 per cent., which is to be annually increased half of one per cent. until
1853, from which time it is to be 6 per cent.; and a subsequent debt,
payable in 1848, is to bear one per cent. interest until 1852, and increasing as before until 1856, it is then to bear an interest of three per
cent.

In the Argentine republic, the chief subject of public interest recently has been the offer of General Rosas to resign the supreme authority, and the vehement opposition made to his proposal by the
Buenos Ayreans.   Whether he was sincere in his purpose or not, there
seems to be little doubt that he will retain the power he has so long
and so energetically wielded.

It is rumoured that a part of the Emperor of Brazil's wide-spread
domain is to be allotted to his son-in-law, the Prince de Joinville, and
that in this way a large debt due from his Brazilian majesty to Louis
Philippe is to be cancelled.   There has been an insurrection at Pernam-
buco, the second town in Brazil, and the insurgents refusing the terms
of the amnesty offered, the governor of the province was preparing to
attack them.

EUROPE.

The year being about to close let us take a *coup d'œil* at the European continent.

When we recollect the political condition of Europe but a year since,
and compare it with its present state, we can scarcely believe that the

same countries can present such a contrast within that brief term ; and the commotions of 1848, which shook almost every state of Europe, seem to us like the scenes of a troubled dream. As soon as a Parisian mob had overturned monarchy in France, backed as it apparently was, by consummate arts of state policy, and an obsequious army of more than 200,000 men, the people almost every where else determined to assert their rights, and to restrict the power of their sovereigns within the narrowest limits, if they did not deprive them of it altogether. Then we saw these same sovereigns, whose will had been the law to their people, trembling with apprehension; glad to surrender one half of their power for the sake of retaining the rest; affecting to yield willingly what they could no longer withhold; and every where sanctioning, sometimes even tendering constitutions in which the rights of conscience, the freedom of the press, the rights of self-legislation and self-taxation and universal suffrage were recognised as unquestionable rights of the people. In this upheaving of society, power and its ordinary attendants so shifted hands that the haughty tyrant and the cowering slave seemed to have changed places.

When the storm of popular enthusiasm, to which every thing at first gave way, had spent much of its force, and men found that their new-born liberty had not realized their fond expectations—that poverty, and crime, and the bad passions of man's nature, must be ever productive of his misery; and that the very love of civil freedom, which in itself is so elevated a sentiment, and has really produced so much that is pure, and noble, and useful, may lead its reckless votaries to the most barefaced injustice and the most atrocious crimes—a reaction took place. It then seemed that, in the frantic spirit of innovation engendered by civil revolution, the approved rules of law, order, and morality, were about to be subverted; and that the rights of property, which sets all the machinery of civil society in motion, and gives it endurance as well as life, were about to be abrogated. Then it was that the mass of the French nation out of the cities, and not a small number within their limits, became alarmed, and doubting the practicability of the liberal schemes of policy they had aimed at, they determined on retracing their steps to a certain point. It was thus that they preferred for their chief magistrate, one who was connected by blood and name with him by whom the glory of France had been raised to a higher point than it had ever before reached, and who was known to have inherited some of the influence of his uncle's great name. The very ambition his early life had exhibited, which so far exceeded his talents or his circumstances, and which tended to alienate the more ardent friends of republicanism, recommended him to the holders of property. Around him, therefore, they determined to rally; and the same fears of the wild excesses of the Socialists and Red Republicans—the one as unhesitating in their ends, as the other was unscrupulous in their means—that made them elect him, made them uphold him after he was elected. In his constant reference to the necessity of law and order, he aims to keep alive these fears, and thus to maintain a salutary check upon the legislature, who are aware of his influence, his hopes and his views, which though they do not approve, they dare not openly resist, lest his power should be thereby strengthened, and his ambitious purposes furthered. There are, however, other counteractions to the President's aspirations to imperial power and rank. These are parties which respectively support the claims of the two branches of the Bourbons. So far as checking the republican spirit is concerned, both those parties go hand-in-hand with Louis Napoleon. But whenever they think there is the shadow of a chance for a monarch of the "legitimate race," they will be as much opposed to the increase of the power of the president as are the republicans themselves. But for these counteractions, it is likely that Louis Napoleon would ere this have tried the strength of his advantages, and made more unequivocal demonstration of his purposes. Affairs, however, seem not likely to go on much longer in their present train; and financial difficulties at home, or foreign wars, may calm the fever that is now secretly gathering strength to manifest itself, and to give impulse and direction to a new revolution.

Republicanism in Italy and Germany, thus deprived of the countenance and support of France, was shorn of more than half its strength. The supporters of monarchical power in these countries, being in possession of office and authority, familiar with the exercise of power, and supported by the military who had not been, as in France, inoculated with sympathy for the cause of the people, profited by the change they so rejoiced to see, and were soon able to regain all they had lost. The union of all the German States—that plan of confederation which was to combine civil freedom with national grandeur, has fled like a vision. The sovereigns of Austria and Prussia seem to be reinstated in despotic power. Hungary, frustrated in her heroic efforts, first to regain her ancient rights, and failing in that, to obtain national independence, is about to be reduced lower than ever in the scale of political existence.

Italy, that seemed for awhile to have achieved emancipation from the iron rule of her sovereigns, foreign and domestic, is again subjected to arbitrary power; and the people of Sardinia, Lombardy, the Papal States, Naples and Sicily, as well as in the minor States of that beautiful peninsula, are again reduced to a seemingly hopeless servitude.

But, after all, the present may be but the second act of the great drama now going on between those who exercise political power and those who feel its pressure; and in the chain of causes and effects now in operation, we may see several other great changes before the same drama is concluded.

Prussia having a more intelligent population than any other part of Germany, the measures of the court party there are likely to be more moderate and guarded—to wear the semblance of the public good, which mankind now generally regard as the first duty of every government, whatever may be its form. Perhaps, too, it is intended that the sentiment of German nationality as well as the love of civil freedom should find safe vent in perfecting the federal constitution which the principal German States have submitted to the rest, and the provisions of which are soon to be under deliberation.

In Austria, as the army is larger, more uniformly submissive to the government, and the people are less enlightened, the Emperor is likely to be reinstated in his former power in every part of his dominions. In Hungary, indeed, the government will seek to extend its power; but there its purposes will be constantly encountering difficulty so long as the Hungarians retain the memory of their ancient rights, the heroic self-devotion by which those rights have been defended, and the cruelties with which the victors have marked their triumph. When in Poland a period of seventy-five years has not been able to efface the remembrance of her independence and her wrongs, who can suppose that the Hungarians, a people superior in intelligence, can be soon oblivious of theirs? Her oppressors show their fears upon this subject, by their anxiety that Kossuth and his brave compatriots should be delivered up. Let us now turn our attention to the separate European States.

GREAT BRITAIN.

The discontents excited in Canada by the bill to indemnify the sufferers in the late insurrection, though much mitigated, have not yet passed away, and the project to which they gave rise of annexation to the United States, still has its advocates and supporters. But the petition or memorial which the friends of annexation put forth, gave rise to a counter memorial which was signed by a yet greater number of names, and the disaffection seems likely to pass away for the time, without any lasting or visible effects. The removal of the seat of government for the Canadas from Montreal to Toronto, has doubtless contributed to increase the disaffection at the former place.

It is known that the speculative politicians of Great Britain have been, for some time, divided on the question whether colonial possessions were really profitable to a nation or not: many, of late years, insisting that they do not repay to the mother country the cost of protecting and governing them; that in some of them the expense of the military force there maintained exceeds the *gross amount* of their trade, and, consequently, must be equal to many times the *profits* of that trade. Even where they are less burdensome, the cost of defending them is considerable; and this cost, and that of the precautionary measures taken to secure their dependence and obedience, so largely deducts from the profits afforded by the monopoly of their trade, as to make the difference comparatively insignificant. They, moreover, multiply the chances of rivalship, of conflicting interests, and, finally, of war with other nations; and they distract the attention of statesmen which should be concentrated on the home interests.

A large portion, probably much the largest portion of the British nation, are not converts to this new doctrine. Multitudes are directly benefited by the colonial import or export trade; and a yet greater number regard the colonies as monuments of the nation's present power, as well as of its past prowess, and none of these are willing to surrender certain profit or glory for the chance of lower taxes. But the present ministry belong to the party who favour these economical views, and it is probably the influence of those views, as much as a prudent acquiescence in what could not be permanently prevented, which has induced the ministers to intimate to the colonial authorities in Canada that if the people of that country really desired annexation to the United States, the government would not oppose it.

The course which the British government has pursued towards the little republic of Nicaragua has been already noticed. If its purpose is merely to share in the proposed communication between the Atlantic and Pacific, and not to get the monopoly of the commerce that will there find a channel, the late measures of their Consul General, Mr. Chatfield, will be disavowed. It will make no further opposition to the grant made by Nicaragua to citizens of the United States, by which the projected canal will be open to all nations upon equal terms; and it will aid in bringing about the same great result by treaty engagements with the United States.

If the British government has not seemed to show as much moderation and forbearance towards the petty states of Nicaragua and Honduras as became a great and powerful nation, it has acted a truly noble part in supporting Turkey against the threatened hostility of Russia; and if we complain that she has not fulfilled one half of the Roman maxim of magnanimity—*parcere subjectis*—we should be prompt to give her credit for having well discharged the other—*debellare superbos.* The British ministry as well as the British people have manifested the liveliest sympathy for the Hungarians in their late glorious struggle for independence, and in the sad consequences of their defeat; and when it was known that the Emperor of Russia by his Envoy, Prince Radzivil, required of the Turkish Sultan that the Hungarians who had sought an asylum in his dominions should be given up, Sir Stratford Canning, the British Minister at Constantinople, who had been unwearied in his efforts to serve the Hungarian cause, induced the Sultan to resist the arrogant demand, by the assurance that he would probably have the support of Great Britain, even if it should lead to war. France was induced to take the same generous course, but in taking it, her President, wishing, perhaps, not to make an ungracious return for the personal civilities of the Czar, seemed rather to follow than to lead.

While this matter, of so threatening an aspect to Turkey, was pending, the Sultan's Minister of Foreign Affairs put the following queries to the British and French Plenipotentiaries then at Constantinople, to which their answers are respectively annexed:

1. Do the treaties of Kutchuck and Passarovitch authorize Russia and Austria to demand the Hungarian refugees?

Answer. No.

2. Would the refusal by Turkey be an infraction of those treaties?

Ans. It would not.

3. Would those powers, in consequence of such refusal, be justified in declaring war against Turkey?

Ans. The treaties do not admit of such a construction, and, consequently, a declaration of war would be unjustifiable.

4. In the event of such a declaration of war, would England and France assist Turkey with an armed force?

Ans. The envoys cannot guaranty such assistance without the instructions of their respective governments.

5. Are the refugees claimed by Russia, the subjects of Russia?

Ans. Some of them may be, but the generality of them are not.

6. In case the refusal by Turkey should interrupt the peaceful relations between her and the other powers, would France and England interpose to re-establish harmony between them?

Ans. Yes.

The subject being taken into consideration by the grand council of Turkey, they were unanimous in refusing to deliver up the Hungarian refugees; but as Russia seemed disposed to insist on their delivery, the English fleet, under Admiral Parker, of seven ships of the line, one frigate and three steam ships, which had been in the Levant awaiting the result of the pending negotiations, were forthwith ordered to the Dardanelles. Sir Stratford Canning was, moreover, instructed to inform the Emperor of Russia that, in case of his rupture with Turkey, England would make a common cause with her.

In the great number and vast extent of the colonial possessions of Great Britain, it can scarcely ever happen that all of them should be at once prosperous and quiet. The discontents and disturbances in Canada have been already mentioned. In Jamaica, and some of her other colonies in the West Indies and Guyana, the planters still feel the effects of struggling, under the disadvantages of dearer and insufficient labour, against the cheaper sugar of Cuba and Brazil. The exports of those colonies to Great Britain continue to decline, and their estates proportionally fall in value.

A very different cause of complaint lately arose at the Cape of Good Hope. The government, by way of lessening the expense of their convict system, decided on sending some of these outcasts of society to that settlement. But on the arrival of the ship Neptune, with several hundreds of them, in the month of September last, the liveliest commotion was excited among the inhabitants, and they determined with one voice on opposing their admission into the colony at all hazards. At a general meeting, the colonists entered into "a mutual pledge" that they would have no connexion with any one who "would assist in supporting convict felons," and would furnish no supplies to the public ships of war so long as the Neptune remained in the bay.   They insisted that the Governor, Sir Harry Smith, should send back the convicts without suffering them to land.   They declared in their public address that the convicts "must not, cannot, shall not be landed in the colony."   During the excitement, the mob attacked the house of a public officer, and committed other excesses, whereupon the Governor issued a proclamation in which he stated that such outrages should be put down by the police, and, if necessary, by the military.   The excitement among the colonists continued as late as the 27th of October, and it is said that the convicts are to be transported to Van Diemen's Land, but that, in consideration of the extraordinary privations and sufferings to which they have been exposed, most of them will be liberated when they arrive at the place of their final destination.   Perhaps, however, when the first ebullitions of popular feeling have passed away, the colonists may acquiesce in the purposes of the government.   The colony at the Cape contains somewhat more than 100,000 whites, half English and half Dutch, and 50,000 blacks.

The insurrection in Cephalonia has been entirely suppressed, and some twenty or thirty of the insurgents have been executed by Commissioner Ward under the authority of martial law, put in force after the insurrection.   The British government consents to give a popular form to the Ionian legislature.

Among the questions which now engage the public attention in England, the most prominent seems to be that of protection to the agricultural interests.   The policy of a free trade in grain seems to have lost some of the popularity which procured the repeal of the corn laws. While the agricultural class very sensibly feel the injurious consequences of the competition of cheaper corn from abroad to which that repeal subjects them, the consuming classes appear not to have equally felt the correspondent benefit.   There has, hence, been some reaction in public opinion, and public meetings are now held throughout the kingdom in favour of protection.   It is even said that the members of the cabinet are divided on this question, and that a part of them are now the advocates of a moderate duty.   It remains to be seen whether this change is one of those oscillations of public sentiment which great reforms in national policy often experience before their final success, or whether the policy of protecting domestic corn growers, which has been assailed and defended ever since the days of Adam Smith, will continue to be an unsettled question.

The provisions of the new navigation act have been reciprocated by most commercial nations; and British ships will be admitted, after the 1st of February, into the ports of the United States, Sweden, Prussia, Hanover, the Hanse Towns, Denmark, Russia, the Italian States, Greece, the Ottoman Empire, and the States of Central and South America, on the same terms as their own vessels.

Parliament is expected to meet early in February.

FRANCE.

It seems that President Bonaparte's letter to his aid-de-camp, Col. Ney, in August last, and which was apparently intended to conciliate the confidence of the republican party, manifestly a very strong one, and, judging by the elections, now on the increase, did not meet with the approbation of his cabinet; and that even those ministers who did not much object to the tenor of the letter itself, were opposed to its publication. Thus thwarted in a favourite purpose by those on whose obsequiousness he had counted, their opposition was made the occasion of an entire change of ministers. This took place in October, and a new ministry was forthwith appointed. On the 31st of October, the President informed the legislative assembly of the fact, and assigned his reasons for the change. He said, he had, in the selection of his first cabinet, appointed men of opposite opinions, and the result, instead of being amalgamation, as he had expected, had proved to be neutralization; unity of action had been prevented, and conciliation had been regarded as weakness. Adverting to his own election by so vast a popular majority, he remarked that a whole system had triumphed on the 10th of December; "for," said he, "the name of Napoleon is a programme in itself. It means order, authority, religion, welfare of the people at home, the national dignity abroad. It is the triumph of that policy, inaugurated by my election, which I seek with the support of the assembly and the people. I wish to be worthy the confidence of the nation, by maintaining the constitution to which I have sworn. I wish to inspire in the country, by my loyalty, my perseverance, and my firmness, such confidence as to give new life to business, and hope in the future."

"The letter of the constitution has, doubtless, a great influence upon the destinies of a country, but the manner in which it is interpreted has, perhaps, a far greater one. The longer or shorter duration of a government has contributed, doubtless, greatly to the stability of public affairs, but it is also by ideas and by principles that the government knows how to reassure society."

"Let us then again raise up authority, without causing alarm to real liberty. Let us calm anxiety by boldly curbing bad passions, and by giving a useful direction to all noble interests."

"Let us consolidate the principles of religion, without abandoning any thing of the conquests of the revolution, and we will save the country, in spite of factions, ambitious men, and even of those imperfections which may exist in our institutions."

The following is a list of the new ministers:

General D'Hautpoul, minister of War.

M. De Raymoal, minister of Foreign Affairs.

M. Ferdinand Barrot, minister of Interior.

M. Rouber, minister of Justice.

M. Bineau, minister of Public Works.

M. Parien, minister of Public Instruction and Worship.

M. Dumas, minister of Agriculture and Commerce.

M. Achille Fould, minister of Finances.

Admiral Romain Desfosses, minister of Marine.

It is understood that all the members of the cabinet agree in political sentiment with a majority of the legislature. This change of ministry happened very opportunely for closing the correspondence between Mr. Clayton and M. de Tocqueville, and facilitated the public reception of Mr. Rives, that took place soon afterwards, by which the way is smoothed to a complete restoration of good feeling between the United States and France. The President wishing to unite courtesy to the American minister with a salvo of what might be due to the dignity of France, remarked that as Mr. Rives came from a republic, there was no difficulty in his reception; but had he been the ambassador of a monarchical government, he could not have been received.

Nor was the letter to Colonel Ney the only manifestation of the President's wish to gain the favour of the liberal party in France. The French envoy at Constantinople has gone hand in hand with Sir Stratford Canning in his interposition in behalf of Turkey, so as to lead the world to believe that France would concur with England in taking up arms to defend Turkey against her powerful and domineering neighbour. As an earnest of her purpose, a French fleet of six ships of the line, two frigates, and two steamers, was ordered to the Dardanelles, in co-operation with the British fleet.

The great confidence which the recent measures of Louis Napoleon show that he has in his popularity, and the influence of his name, are thought by many to indicate that some great political change is meditated, especially when certain passages in his late excursions into the provinces are recollected; but perhaps his course may be merely the result of that sanguine and self-confident temper by which the French President is so strongly characterized.

The future political destiny of France still remains an insoluble problem. No one believes that things are to continue in their present state, yet no one can pronounce with any confidence what new phases her government is about to assume; and supposing she will again resort to the monarchical form, which a majority of the nation, disappointed in the past efforts to establish a republic, and apprehensive of the future, may think the safest and most suitable to France and Frenchmen, it is impossible to say whether the new dynasty is to be of one of the branches of the Bourbons, or of the Bonaparte stock. It is equally clear that the republican party, though probably a minority throughout all France, constitute a powerful party, particularly in Paris, as to numbers, energy, and talents.

Their financial budget exhibits large arrears of debt, with a prospect of increase; and between the pecuniary necessities of the government, and the fear of offending the voters, the government and the legislature find themselves not a little embarrassed. Where indirect taxes, as in France, are not sufficient to meet the public expenditure, the legislature must choose between an insufficient revenue and a discontented people. It is this inherent difficulty of reconciling public burdens with public favour, which has given such encouragement to the schemes of the socialists, according to which, governments are required to assume the functions of occupying and rewarding labour as well as of taxing it.

About the middle of August last, the French frigate Poursuivante and a steamer arrived at Honolulu, the capital of the Sandwich Islands, when M. Dillon, the French consul, demanded of the Hawaiian government, 1st, a reduction of the duties on brandies and wines, and a return of all the duties on those articles collected since 1846. 2. The same rights to Catholics as to Protestants. 3. The repeal of the law which subjects whaling ships to port charges. 4. The remission of a fine which had been imposed on the master of a whaling ship; and three days were allowed to the government to comply with these terms or reject them. On their rejection by the Hawaiian government, the French landed a body of troops, took possession of a fort, spiked the cannon, and threw them from the ramparts; and hoisted the French flag, though without taking down that of the Hawaiian government. After keeping possession of the fort for three days, they abandoned it, and their ships left the island with M. Dillon and his family. The American, British, Danish, Peruvian, and Chilian consuls protested against these acts; and the British consul offered his mediation, but it was refused by the French. It is not yet known whether the conduct of the French officers was authorized by their government, or will receive its sanction. It is delicately alluded to by General Taylor in his opening message to Congress.

General Baraguay d'Hilliers, the last military and diplomatic representative of the French government at Rome, has made a strong remonstrance against the political measures pursued by the three cardinals whom the Pope had empowered to act in his behalf, and has even threatened them with the displeasure of the French President. He went to Naples to endeavour to overcome the Pope's objections to return to Rome. Among the anecdotes circulated at Paris, it is told that when General Baraguay d'Hilliers assured Pius IX. that the French government would guaranty his safety and authority in Rome, the Pope replied, " But who will guaranty the continuance of your government?"

The proposed tax on liquors, which was taken off in May last, is still under discussion in the legislative assembly. The members are divided between the large amount of money which this tax would bring into the treasury, now so much in need of it, and the unpopularity of the tax, the effects of which would be so naturally felt in the next elections. The indications were all in favour of its passage.

There has been an insurrection in Algiers, but it has been quelled by the military force which France has there. The town of Zaatchi was taken by storm in November last.

PRUSSIA.

The chief objects of public concern in Prussia, for some months past, have been its own constitution, and that of the proposed German Confederation. The constitution which Frederick William granted to his people in December, 1848, expressly provided that it should be subject to the revision of the two legislative chambers. It has, accordingly, been so revised, and the work was expected to be brought to a close before Christmas. When, in its amended form, it has received the royal assent, and the king has sworn to support it, it will be obligatory upon him and the people. Should it be thus sanctioned, as it probably will, Prussia will have made a great advance towards a liberal and representative government.

On the scheme of German unity, the mind of the king seems to have greatly vacillated. Sometimes he appeared to be friendly to the views of the Frankfort parliament, sometimes hostile; and finally he became its decided opponent, probably, both because he was convinced that the constitution they had prepared for United Germany could not be adopted against the determined opposition of Austria, and because it was more democratic in its character than he considered safe or expedient. The great object of this assembly having thus proved a failure, and its functions having virtually ceased,* the Prussian monarch decided on making another attempt to unite the German States in a federal league under better auspices. Should the plan succeed, it would make him very popular with the whole German race, still ardently desiring a political union, and might further gratify his ambition by his becoming the head of the new confederation. All the German States have been accordingly invited to send deputies to a convention to be held at Erfurt, a fortified town in his own dominions, on the 31st of January next.

The Emperor of Austria, seeing nothing in such a confederation, but a diminution of his own rank and power in Germany, and an increase of those of his ambitious rival, has opposed this scheme as well as those which preceded it; and has formally protested against it, since, being addressed to all the German States, it is calculated to bring some of his dominions under the subjection of Prussia. The correspondence between the sovereigns of Austria and Prussia, taken in connexion with

* A new *provisional* central power for Germany has been formed, to which the archduke John, the vicar of the Empire, has given his consent, and has resigned his office. (See Chronicle.)

the presumed sentiments of both, were thought for awhile to threaten an open rupture. The prospect of that has now passed away, and a large majority, if not all the States of Germany, are expected to meet at Erfurt on the last of January, to agree on the terms of a German Confederation.

Among the rumours lately put in circulation, one is that the King of Prussia is about to resign his power in favour of his nephew, the Prince of Prussia. This report has derived some credit from the personal character of Frederick William, who is believed to be wavering in his purposes, and operated on by the impulse of the moment; and it is possible, too, that he may resign the crown of Prussia as a means of becoming the Emperor of the Confederation.

AUSTRIA.

The Emperor of Austria having, by the aid of his Russian ally, suppressed the Hungarian revolt, his next objects were to punish the offenders, and to guard against the recurrence of a similar evil. In the first of these purposes, he has exhibited a severity that has greatly shocked the feelings of mankind. General Haynau, who was appointed to this duty, so odious in general to brave men, seems to have discharged it with peculiar pleasure, and to have amply gratified the vindictive feelings of his employers. Victims were sacrificed without regard to rank, age, or sex, and the streets of Pesth were stained with the blood of some of the purest and best in Hungary. Among these, Count Batthyany, who had been formerly the Emperor's chief minister in that country, and who had taken no active part in the insurrection, was particularly regretted. To punish him for his supposed secret wishes, he was, by some refinement of reasoning, found guilty of violating "the pragmatic sanction." His large estates were forfeited, and his wealth was supposed to have contributed to his condemnation.

Not satisfied with the executions in Hungary, the Emperor united with the Czar of Russia in demanding of the Turkish Sultan the surrender of Kossuth, Bem, Dembinski, and other distinguished Hungarians who had taken refuge in Turkey. The demand, as we have seen, was refused, and it is probable that the general remonstrance of the civilized world, and yet more the active intervention of Great Britain backed by France, induced the reluctant acquiescence of these Emperors in the refusal. But their vengeance was not altogether disappointed. The Sultan, by a compromise between his honour and his prudence, or his fears, though he would not surrender the refugees, agreed to retain them under a strict *surveillance* in his dominions for a twelvemonth; and the better to enable him to do so, they were removed to Shumla, a town in the interior of Bulgaria. Under an existing treaty between Russia and Turkey, the Sultan was probably bound to deliver up the Polish insurgents, who had not embraced the Moslem faith, which many of them, it is said, have done. These refugees were marched off from Widdin to Shumla, in separate detachments, according to their respective nations, having first received a solemn and affecting address from Kossuth; and the Sultan not only provided for their necessary wants, but generously distributed a considerable sum of money among them.

Many changes, of a precautionary character, have been made by the Austrian government in the civil regulations of the country; and it is thought that more radical changes are meditated, until the civil polity of Hungary is assimilated to the rest of the Emperor's dominions. A *gens d'armerie,* or military police, has been established, whose duty it is to keep a strict watch over the Hungarian people, and to enforce many restrictions on the personal liberty they formerly enjoyed. The government has as yet met with difficulty in finding men of rank and respectability willing to undertake the execution of these new regulations; and the commissions granted for that purpose have, in many instances, been peremptorily refused. Some of the most wealthy, and among them Count Esterhazy, have sold their estates, with a view, no doubt, to their removal from the country. It will probably require a degree of lenity and firmness, not often seen united, before Hungary will again be one of the secure possessions of the Austrian empire.

The Austrian government finds another subject of solicitude and embarrassment in its finances. The expenses of the army this year are computed to have been double the amount of the public revenue; and, as usual, the difficulty of borrowing increases with the pressure of its wants. Hungary can contribute little at this time to replenish the imperial treasury. Its currency of late consisted principally of paper money, which policy had induced Kossuth to issue to a large amount, and patriotism had induced the Hungarian patriots to receive. As the present government refuses to redeem this money, and it has consequently become valueless to the holder, the loss must be a heavy one to the mass of the people. It is said that it is carefully preserved, and even buried by the peasants, in the expectation that it will be one day exchanged for gold and silver.

The relative position of Austria in Europe is greatly changed within the last two years. Not only is her supremacy in Germany greatly impaired, and even put in jeopardy, but she can no longer, for the present at least, become an obstacle to the colossal ambition of Russia; and should the Czar insist on holding Wallachia and Moldavia, and come to an open rupture with Turkey, she may find she has paid a high price for the aid of her potent neighbour, timely and efficient as it was.

RUSSIA. .

However confident the Emperor Nicholas was of quelling the insurrection in Hungary, and of again bringing that brave people under the dominion of Austria, the success of his armies seemed to have exceeded his expectations. His expressions of delight are said to have passed all bounds, and, by a ukase issued in August, the same martial honours were decreed to Prince Paskiewitch, as had previously been reserved for the emperor alone, and these honours were be paid to the victorious general even in the cities in which the emperor then resided.

The expected consequences of the Czar's successes in Hungary probably caused no small part of his exultation. His purposes hardly seemed doubtful. Having by his timely assistance to Austria, the most formidable obstacle to his further aggrandizement in Europe, neutralized her opposition, and converted for the nonce an ancient foe into a grateful friend, he seems to have thought that the time had come for him to make some demonstration of his long-settled designs against Turkey.

Pretexts are never wanting for picking a quarrel by the strong against the weak, and at first the principalities of Wallachia and Moldavia, over which Turkey and Russia have a divided sovereignty, appeared likely to afford such a pretext, but the Hungarians who have taken refuge in Turkey seem to have furnished a better. Her ambassador at Constantinople, together with that of Austria, required that Kossuth and other distinguished Hungarian exiles should be delivered up, according to the treaty of Passarowitch, well knowing that protection had been promised to them by the Sultan, and that as the demand could not be complied with without dishonour, it would be refused. It was to no purpose that explanations to justify the refusal were offered. They were disregarded, and the imperial ambassadors at once put an end to all diplomatic relations between their governments and the Porte. The Sultan then despatched an envoy, Fuad Effendi, to the Emperor of Russia to deprecate his wrath, if possible; but the effort had probably been unavailing, but for the spirited intervention of England, backed as it was by the popular sentiment in France, and to whose impulses the executive of France finally yielded. Not contented with speaking, they acted also. An English fleet of seven ships of the line, and four smaller ships, and a French fleet of six ships of the line, and fourteen smaller ships, entered the Dardanelles about the last of October, ready to defend Constantinople or attack the Russian squadron of twenty-six ships, according to circumstances. The Czar's purpose was changed, not, however, without expressing his resentment against Great Britain; and the death-struggle of Mahometanism in Europe was, for the time, postponed. Count Nesselrode, the Russian prime minister, now informed Fuad Effendi, that the Czar demanded that the Hungarian refugees should be located in the interior of Candia, or such other part of the Turkish territory as would ensure their being under the surveillance of the government.   They might even be permitted to go to France or England.   Since that time the exiles which were previously at Widdin, on the Danube, have been ordered from that place to Shumla, a town in the heart of Bulgaria.   This change, it would seem, from an address of Kossuth to his brethren in exile, is very acceptable to the Hungarians themselves.   They are there more out of the reach of Russian violence; and, as Kossuth told them, they could also more easily get back to their own country, in case of another struggle to obtain her independence.

While the superiority of Russia over Turkey must continue to increase, unless the Turkish polity and institutions undergo a radical change, yet the conquest of twenty-five millions of people, warlike and brave, and whose bravery is stimulated by all the great incentives to national animosity—by diversities of religion, language, and manners; by neighbourhood, and by ancient recollections—is no easy achievement; and Russia must have a yet larger army than she has ever sent abroad, and a yet richer treasury, before she can count upon success. Her superiority even over European Turkey, at present, is not greater than Spain has over Portugal, and not so great as France has over Belgium or Switzerland, or England over Scotland, and yet the inferior nations, though often humbled, were yet able to preserve their independence.

Russia counts as auxiliaries not only on Greece, but on all who belong to the Greek church, and she has diligently sought to obliterate or sooth the patriotic griefs of her Polish subjects for the loss of their existence as a nation, by the wider and more comprehensive sentiment of *panslavism*, which she loses no opportunity of cherishing; which she expects to bring to bear against Austria, if need be, no less than against Turkey; and which, by its opposition to the Magyars, in the late struggle of the Hungarians, has weakened the cause of Polish patriotism.

Thus checked for a time in her further progress, Russia may look to the east, and seek in Persia for further aliment to her ambition, or even to British India, to which she will be further stimulated by the recent intervention of England in behalf of Turkey.   The gallant Circassians have been at length compelled to yield to overpowering force, and the Caucasian mountains no longer present any impediment to the southern march of Russian troops into the Turkish dominions, east of the Black Sea.   But while they have thus been forced into submission, the benefit of this proof of Russia's resistless power may be outweighed by showing how difficult it is to conquer even a small community at once brave, warlike, and determined on resistance.   Nor in truth has the Czar abandoned all chance of further aggrandizement in the west.   He still holds a considerable military force, said to number 31,000 men, in Wallachia and Moldavia, and seems to evade a final

and amicable adjustment with Turkey on the subject of the Polish refugees.   Enough yet remains unsettled to be improved into a cause of
war, if, in the ever-changing circumstances and relations of European
States, war should be deemed advisable.

ITALY.

The political condition of this peninsula is apparently now very
nearly what it was in the beginning of the preceding year, though
every part has been in the interval the theatre of war or civil commotion.   In the papal states, indeed, the restoration to their former political condition has been begun, but is not yet consummated.   France
still retains her anomalous position at Rome, holding it as a conquered
city, in which she has a garrison; but all the while professing sentiments of amity and good will to its former sovereign, the Pope, whom
she urges to return to his dominions, and to resume his power.   This
he has shown himself willing enough to do by his agents, but refuses
to do in person.   He still remains a voluntary exile in the dominions
of the king of Naples, and while he has profited by the interposition
of France, attended as it was by violence and bloodshed, he seems loth
to regard the French as his benefactors; but in a late manifesto, dated
September 12, of his future plan of government, neither France, nor
her President, nor the French army are mentioned: from which it
would seem that their claims to his gratitude are no longer recognised.

In this proclamation, which being made in the Pope's name, and at
his own suggestion, is called his *propria motu*, the holy pontiff sets
forth those institutions which he thinks are calculated to ensure to his
subjects a fit portion of privileges and civil freedom.   They are,

1. A council of state, to give its advice on all bills before they are
submitted to the sovereign for his sanction.
2. A council of finance, to determine all matters relative to the
budget, or ways and means.
3. Provincial councils,—the members to be selected from lists presented by the common councils.   They are to discuss the local interests
of the province, the local expenses, &c.
4. Municipal bodies are to enjoy the widest liberty compatible with
the local interests of the communes.
5. Reforms and ameliorations in law institutions, in civil, criminal,
and administrative legislation.
6. An amnesty is to be granted under certain restrictions.

If these several establishments are created by his holiness, and responsible only to him, one cannot see that any thing whatever has been
gained to the cause of civil freedom or personal security.   Of this we
were soon furnished with an ample proof, if proof was needed.   The
three cardinals whom Pope Pius made his representatives in Rome,

issued their proclamation immediately after that of the pontiff himself, as to the amnesty which he had granted; and they excepted from it all who had taken any part in the provisional government, which exception is computed to comprehend no-less than 13,000 persons.

M. Baraguay d'Hilliers, who succeeded General Rostolan as the representative of France at Rome, lately made a visit to the Pope at Portici, with the expectation of overcoming his objections to returning to Rome, but this return, which has been announced from time to time, seems to be as uncertain as ever. He will apparently consent to no compromise either with the French government or his own people, by which he is required to concede any of his temporal power as a sovereign.

Since Venice has again been brought under subjection to Austria, she, like the rest of Lombardy, has been made to feel the heavy burden of Austrian taxation. By way of weakening or neutralizing the effects of her repugnance to her present rulers, it is said that it is intended to unite her territory with Tyrol, supposed to be the most loyal part of the Austrian dominions.

AFRICA.

Saving the partial insurrection in Algeria, which the French troops quickly suppressed, and the resistance at the Cape of Good Hope to the introduction of convicts, there is nothing on this vast region so worthy of our notice as the little colony of Liberia. The movements of its newly organized government have been thus far marked with regularity and success, and present a striking contrast to the political measures of the same race in Hayti. They have, in the last two years, received about a thousand emigrants from this country; and others are ready to embark as soon as the means of defraying the expense are provided.

Their efforts to destroy the slave trade on the coast of Africa are unwearied, and they cherish the hope that in time they will be successful. Their plan is to extend their possessions on the coast, so as to cut off all connexion between the foreign slave ships and the natives who supply them from the interior. They have enlarged their territory by the purchase of Grand Cape Mount and Sugaree, and they will soon receive further accession by the annexation of Cape Palmas, which the people of that settlement have proposed. They have also made a treaty with the British government, which has presented them with an armed cutter of one hundred and ten tons. They are exerting themselves to purchase Gallinas, part of the coast in which the slave trade has been particularly active, but the requisite sum cannot be raised without foreign aid.

When one sees the prejudices of race operating so powerfully in every part of the globe, and no where perhaps with the same force as with the blacks of Hayti, it is very creditable to the same race in Liberia that they seem to be entirely exempt from it. The white missionaries who have gone there have always been regarded with the gratitude and respect due to benefactors; and the Rev. Mr. Gurley has lately received from them a cordial welcome. They have listened to his lectures for instruction, and have shown their sense of his services by a public dinner.

All lovers of their country, whether abolitionists or slaveholders, ought to wish success to this colony; and we see with pleasure that a bill is now before the legislature of Virginia to appropriate $30,000 for the removal of free negroes to Africa.

ASIA.

In this, the largest of the four quarters of the world, there is little to arrest the attention of those who are so distant, and so little connected with them as ourselves. A great outrage has been lately committed by the Chinese at the Portuguese settlement of Macao.

In August last, six or eight Chinamen attacked Señor de Amiral, the Governor of Macao, when on horseback, accompanied by his aid. Having dragged him from his horse, they cut off his head and left hand, which they carried off. The Portuguese soldiers, in revenge, attacked and destroyed a small fort, and some lives were lost on both sides. The American, British, and French there, all offered their support to the Portuguese authority in Macao. The death of the Governor, who had been distinguished for ability and firmness, was greatly regretted.

The Chinese seas have been for some time infested with pirates, which have afforded active employment to the British ships of war, and have more especially given to Sir James Brooke a new opportunity of exhibiting his remarkable enterprise, vigour and prowess.

QUARTERLY CHRONICLE.

Oct. 1st. The drought of 1849.—Accounts from all parts of the country concurred in pronouncing the drought at this period to be the most general and the longest continued which has prevailed within the memory of the oldest inhabitant. The streams were all very low; some of them were quite dry, and many of the cotton, flour, and other mills were doing little more than a tithe of their usual amount of work. In the country vegetation was literally burnt up. Farmers could neither plough their land nor pasture their cattle, and almost all the usual autumn farming operations were suspended. The York (Pa.) Gazette of this date remarked:

"There has been no rain of any consequence for *more than a hundred days!* During all that time hardly enough has fallen to wet the surface of the earth. The streams are lower than they have been since 1822; most of the mills have ceased grinding; wells and springs are giving out that had not done so before for more than a quarter of a century; our hydrants are closed by the water company for about twenty hours out of the twenty-four. The universal petition here is for *rain.*"

The cultivation of Tea.—The cultivation of the tea plant, which was undertaken by Mr. Junius Smith, near Greenfield, (S. C.,) in 1848, has so far proved highly successful. In the fall of 1848, about five hundred plants were received from China, via London, and in December they were planted in his garden. A considerable quantity of tea seed was planted at the same time. Notwithstanding the severe winter and spring, the plants, which were left to take care of themselves, were unharmed, and are now in a flourishing condition. Several specimens of green and black plant are in bud. The tea plant buds one year, but does not fruit till the next. Next year Mr. Smith expects to pick tea, although his great object for some time to come will be to increase the quantity of his plants.

Indian Legislature.—The following announcement was made in the Cherokee Advocate:

"To-day the newly elected members to our national council or legislature will meet and organize themselves for business; after which they will be ready to receive the message of the principal chief.

"The nation is now blessed with peace and harmony, and the

greater portion of the farmers are raising a competency of the staff of life, and other produce necessary for the sustenance of nature. Our common schools are in successful operation throughout the nation, so that many of our children are now in a condition to enter the seminaries for further advancement in their education, while others of our citizens have been improving the country with the erection of machinery of one kind or other, such as saw and grist mills, &c.; and to compare our condition now with what it was some twenty or thirty years ago, one would hardly suppose that we are the same people—but we are Cherokees yet."

Scientific Intelligence.—We learn from Newton's London Journal that *zinc-white* may be employed with great advantage as a substitute for *white-lead*, for painting and other purposes. This substance is said to produce no disease allied to the painters' colic, and it is also stated to be unchangeable.

An artesian well, near Southampton, England, has lately been bored to the depth of 353 feet, the further progress having been interrupted by a rock of unusual hardness.

A liquid glue has been invented in England which has the advantage of being stronger than the ordinary glue, and always ready, and will unite wood, iron, and plaster.

The number of exhibiters at the great *scientific exposition*, recently held in Paris, was 4,532.

A French chemist has succeeded in preserving water in a sweet state by placing 1½ kilogrammes of black oxide of manganese in each cask of water containing 250 litres, equal to 6½ pounds to a butt of 108 gallons. In this manner water has been kept perfectly sweet for seven years.

Geographical Discoveries.—The South African Commercial Advertiser contains an interesting account of the discovery of a great inland lake called Ngama. It is 556 miles from Kolobeng, and the party making the discovery traversed 200 miles along the banks of a beautiful river before they came to the lake. Two large rivers run into the latter from the north. When they came to the lake, "they could not see an horizon, except one of water, on the south and west." The information is contained in a letter from Rev. Mr. Moffat.

Another important discovery of water in the wilderness has been made by Major Emory of the Topographical corps: he reports the recent appearance of a river of sweet, delicious water in the desert, between the mouth of the Gila river and the mountains. It made its appearance somewhere between the 20th of June and the 1st of July. The river is some forty feet wide, and more than waist deep, and will be an inestimable blessing to the travellers over that route, as they have heretofore suffered dreadfully with thirst, and will make this route one of the most desirable routes to California, being the only one that can be passed over in winter.

The Polar Expedition.—Sir John Richardson arrived at Ste. Marie river from a fruitless search after the lost polar expedition of Sir John Franklin, of whose dreadful fate among the icebergs of the Arctic ocean, there is left little or no room to doubt. Sir John Richardson, having failed to find even the remotest clue to the Franklin expedition, was then on his way back to England. He left there in April, 1848; and from the Saut Ste. Marie has made the voyage in canoes and boats and overland, a distance of three thousand five hundred miles and back, by the way of the Lake of the Woods, Mackenzie's river, &c. After reaching the Arctic ocean, they travelled five hundred miles along the coast. He speaks confidently of the existence of a northern passage; its practicability, he says, is another question, the summers being only from thirty to sixty days long.

The Cholera.—At this date the pestilence had generally ceased in the cities of the United States.[*] In our last number we have given accounts of its ravages. In Philadelphia, there were from May to October, 1849, 1,019 deaths, in New York, 5,017, in Boston, 616.

2d. *Indians.*—The accounts at St. Louis to this date from Chihuahua, were that the Indians in that part of the country were daily becoming more hostile towards the whites.

During the two weeks preceding the 2d of August, upwards of fifty Mexicans, and several Americans, had been killed by hostile Indians near Chihuahua.

In the middle of July, Mr. Vaughan, an American trader, was murdered by a party of Apache Indians near Sacramento. Six daring Americans immediately started in pursuit of the murderers, and succeeded in securing Mr. Vaughan's scalp and property. The Indians, who numbered about thirty, fled.

Jones, the Apache chief, offers a premium of ten horses for the scalps of each American, and thirty horses for the scalps of each Mexican officer that are brought to him.

The Arrickara Indians, a very savage tribe on the Missouri river, have joined the Apaches.

Col. Washington and his force were, at last accounts, in pursuit of them.

A later despatch from Chihuahua states that the Apaches attacked the military post of Janos, captured all the horses and cattle in the vicinity, and twenty-nine Americans, who had just arrived at that place. The Apaches approached the Americans under the pretext of seeking peace, and having lulled them into a state of fancied security, suddenly turned in hostility on them. The Americans flew

---

[*] It has since re-appeared on some of the Western rivers.

to their arms, but it was too late, and they became the prisoners of the savages.*

Several of the Apaches then went into the Presidio, a species of fort there, and proposed to the commandant to make, peace and exchange prisoners. The commandant immediately sent out couriers to all the places in the vicinity, calling for aid to defend the Presidio, and to rescue the Americans. When the intelligence reached Chihuahua, the governor sent despatches to the political chief of Canton Galena, directing him to treat with the Apaches immediately for an exchange of prisoners.

It may be recorded in this place, though somewhat out of the order of time, that in the month of November Major Green and party started in pursuit of a band of Apaches who had previously captured a Mr. and Mrs. White and child, together with eight other prisoners—all of whom were afterwards killed, with the exception of Mrs. White and child, who were still held as prisoners by the Indians. As soon as the Major and his comrades came in sight of the Indian camp, and were discovered by them, the latter became much alarmed, and after having shot Mrs. White, precipitately fled —leaving their camp equipage and two Indian children behind. The body of the lady was then taken possession of, but no trace of her child was to be found.

Early in this month *a great Indian council* was held in Minesota by Governors Ramsey and Chambers, at which 3000 of the natives were present. The object of the commissioners was to effect a treaty with the Sioux and others.

The Sandwich Islands.—Advices were received at San Francisco that the French Admiral at Honolulu had taken possession of the Fort, and held it for three days, when he abandoned it. The cause of this violent proceeding was the refusal of the king to accede to the following demands made by the French consul:

"1st. A reduction of duties on brandies and liquors of one-half, and the return of one-half of all such duties as have been collected since 1846. 2d. The same rights to Catholics and their schools as are granted to Protestants. 3d. The repeal of a law which compels whale ships, importing liquor for sale, to pay port charges. 4th. The remission of a fine imposed upon some captain of a whale ship."

The British and American consuls protested against the action of the French forces.

4th. Hungarians.—The Sultan of Turkey magnanimously refused to deliver up Kossuth and his associates, who had sought refuge in his dominions, on the demand of the emperors of Austria and Russia. From the peremptory nature of the demand, war was anticipated, and preparations were made to resist the Czar. The Sultan

* The Apaches are well armed, and their hostility is ascribed to attacks made on them by Mexicans and Americans.

reviewed 50,000 troops on the plain of St. Stefano. Gen. Bem, one of the distinguished Hungarian generals, as soon as he learned the determination of the Sultan to resist the demands of Russia and Austria, and to refuse the extradition, declared that his country was his first religion, and as the Sultan had the same enemies and friends with himself, he wished to become his subject and to serve under his flag, and that he would therefore, embrace Islamism. On embracing the Moslem faith he received the name of Murad Pacha. Kossuth pursued a different course; on being informed of the abjuration of Bem he went to the camp of the Hungarians, and informed them that the Porte resisted the demands of Austria and Russia, that France and England appeared decided to aid the Porte, and implored them not to stain by apostacy the flag of Christian Hungary, which they had always served with honor.

6th. This day, the anniversary of the death of Count Latour, was fixed upon for the *execution of Count Louis Batthyany*, late prime minister of Hungary, and of other Hungarian patriots. The names of some of those executed at this time are Count Charles Bensay, Major Louis Anlick, Count Charles Linengen,—subsequently at Pesth other executions took place—among the sufferers were Prince Woronjechi, Gerin, Havareourt, &c.

German Empire.—The vicar General, the Archduke Charles, gave his public assent to the Convention for the formation of a new provisional central power for Germany, concluded between Austria and Prussia; by which these two powers were to act in the name of all the governments until the 1st May, 1850. The Archduke offered to resign the dignity of Vicar of the German Empire, and to deposite the rights and duties conferred upon him on the 12th July, 1848, by the German Diet into the hands of the Emperor of Austria and King of Prussia. *

Hurricanes.—Several places in this country and in Europe, were at this date, visited with very severe gales.—At *New York City* the wind blew with great fury. Among the disasters occasioned by its violence, the Evening Post enumerates the following:

The destruction of the Pavilion and the beautiful Diorama of Holyrood Chapel and the Harbor of Brest, valued at from $6,000 to $7,000. These elaborate paintings, extending over a thousand feet of canvass, were torn into shreds: a new four story house was blown down —two or three churches were much injured—trees were torn up by the roots—vessels drifted from their moorings along the East and North rivers; some of the eastern steamboats were delayed in consequence of the gale, and others were compelled to put back. In *Boston* the gale was equally severe.—The walls of a new church

*This act he subsequently performed.

were prostrated.—The British brig St. John was driven on the Grampus rock, and a number of the passengers were lost. (This disaster we recorded in the last number.) At the same time a dreadful tornado was experienced at *Cape May*, N. J., by which three dwelling houses were literally torn to pieces,—and trees were twisted off at the roots.

A few days after a similar tornado visited *Terrebone*, La. Houses were destroyed, and lives lost. The Orleans Bee says, "several sugar houses, negro cabins, stables, corn cribs, out houses, &c., were prostrated to the ground, and their fragments scattered far and wide. The largest trees in the forest were wrenched from the ground as though they were but small saplings, and carried to a great distance from their original position. Those who have never seen the effect and great force of the wind, would be loth to give credence to the wondrous and disastrous effects produced by this tornado."—The English papers state that "sixty wrecks had taken place on the East Coast" early in the month of October; the Conqueror of Glasgow, on the Gunfleet Sands, keeled over and all on board perished, numbering sixteen or twenty persons. For miles the sea was literally studded with portions of her freight. Two other vessels were lost near the same spot, and all on board perished. The Dutch and Belgian mails describe the gales to have been very destructive on their respective coasts. Numerous vessels were lost. The Camilla, steamship, reports a most fearful hurricane visiting Cronstadt, and a consequent serious damage to the shipping.

Horse Racing.—The Pasha of Egypt has challenged the Jockey Club of London to run a match race of horses for £10,000 a side. It was accepted, and the race is to come off in Egypt.

9th. Great Riot in Philadelphia.—A most dreadful and sanguinary riot commenced about nine o'clock in the evening, at a tavern called the California House, kept by a colored man, who was said to be married to a white woman. The house was soon in flames, the inmates driven out and fired upon, with many other colored persons, men, women, and children, who were seen flying from their houses in extreme terror, chased by gangs, who pelted them with brickbats and fired after them with guns and pistols. Several were wounded, and it was said that more than one was killed. But this report was exaggerated. The assailants are described as being composed of the "Killers" and other similar associations of disturbers of the public peace.

Meanwhile the fire made rapid progress, but several engine and hose companies were soon upon the ground. And here a truly frightful scene occurred. The firemen, who went to the conflagration for the purpose of saving property, were fired upon, not in solitary cases, but actually in a running fire, and by volleys of several guns and pistols at once—the rioters being out in very strong force. They were also assailed with showers of brickbats, and their hose cut in every direction. In a word, the first companies that arrived, were compelled, as the only mode of avoiding wounds or death, to leave the neighborhood. Still the firing continued. One of the firemen was shot dead on the spot, and several others wounded. Shortly after midnight a body of police made their way to the scene of action—but nothing efficiently was done until the military came on the ground, headed by the Mayor; when after a partial renewal of the riot, the disturbed district was taken possession of by the authorities—cannon planted in the streets—and the mob finally quelled.

11*th*. *Fairs* —The great fair of the *American Institute*, closed with an address from Gen. Tallmadge. Among other things he stated one important fact with regard to the manufacture of *steel* in this country. By a recent American invention the best quality of steel is now manufactured directly from *iron ore*, with the use of *anthracite coal*. And this is done in a single operation, while the method practised in Europe requires some half a dozen operations to extract the iron from the ore, and run it into pigs, and then into bars, and to work it into malleable iron, and then into coarse steel, and then into refined steel. Gen. T. stated that a factory at Jersey City for the production of steel by this new method, already manufactures about one tenth of the quantity required to supply the United States. He believed the time could not be distant when our country will produce its own iron and its own steel.

The Maryland Agricultural Fair,—held at Baltimore,—was honoured by the presence of General Taylor, the President of the United States; who spent several hours in visiting all parts of the grounds and examining with great interest the herds of fine stock, agricultural productions, implements, &c. He expressed the highest gratification at the display, and by the inquiries and remarks which he made, showed the active concern and interest which he takes in all that appertains to agricultural pursuits.

The Cuba Invaders—evacuated Round Island. They were taken across to Pascagoula by Midshipman Dyer, whence forty of them took passage in the mail-boat for New Orleans, and the others, about twenty-five in number, in the steamer Mobile. No obstruction was offered by the United States vessels to their peaceful departure.

(An account of this projected expedition, will be found in the History for September.)

12*th*. *The State Constitution of California.*—Completed and submitted to the people.

The Telegraph Line to the East, completed as far as Halifax, N. S.

15*th.* *The Secretary of the Treasury,* Mr. Meredith, in relation to the alterations in the British Navigation Laws,—issued the following instructions to collectors of customs: ·

1st. In consequence of the alterations of the British Navigation Laws above referred to, British vessels from British or other foreign ports will, (under existing laws,) after the first of January next, be allowed to enter in our ports with cargoes of the growth, manufacture, or production of any part of the world.

2d. Such vessels and their cargoes will be admitted, from and after the date before mentioned, on the same terms as to duties, imposts, and charges, as vessels of the United States and their cargoes.

A Great Rail Road Convention was held at St. Louis, Mo., to take into consideration the propriety of constructing a rail road from the Mississippi Valley to the Pacific Ocean.—The convention was organized by the appointment of the Hon. Stephen A. Douglass of Illinois, as President, and of Vice Presidents corresponding with the number of States represented in Convention. The States represented were Missouri, Illinois, Iowa, Indiana, Ohio, Pennsylvania, Tennessee, Michigan, Kentucky, New York, Wisconsin, Maryland, Virginia, Louisiana, New Jersey ; the number of delegates was very large—from Missouri alone there were 464. The first business transacted was the appointment of a committee, consisting of three members from each State, to report resolutions for adoption by the meeting.

A resolution was then introduced requesting Congress to act promptly in relation to the Pacific Rail Road; whereupon—

Mr. Senator BENTON rose and read a letter from Colonel FREMONT, stating that the Convention ought not to designate any road across the Rocky Mountains, as he believed the pass between the head of the Arkansas and the Rio del Norte to be the most practicable and nearest to the Pacific. Colonel FREMONT writes. "The road would enter the basin at the southern end of the Mormon settlements, and cross by way of Humbolt river. About midway of that river's course a large valley opens into it, and *up this lies an excellent way to a low pass near the head of the lower Sacramento valley.* Before reaching this pass, a way diverging to the north affords a very *practicable valley road into Oregon,* and, in my opinion, far the best by which you can reach that country." Mr. Benton then addressed the Convention with great force and eloquence, on the importance of the road, and was repeatedly applauded. The Convention adjourned to meet in Philadelphia, in April, 1850.

16*th.* *The Island of Tigre,* in Honduras, which had been ceded to our government by Nicaragua, was seized by the British.

17th. AN INCA OF PERU.—At a meeting of the American Ethnological Society, a communication was read, which was communicated by the President of the United States, and consisted of a letter to him from a Peruvian prince, a descendant of the Incas of Peru. His name is Doctor Don Justa Sahaurauria, a canon of the Cathedral of Cusco, and is now more than ninety years of age. He claims to be the lineal descendant, in the seventh degree, from Huana Caipae, the last reigning Inca, the father of Atahualpa, who was burnt by the conquerors of Peru. The gentleman (Mr. Arnold) who transmitted the letter to the President, describes him as a fine-looking man, with a physiognomy quite different from that of the Quicha Indians, (the race peopling that part of Peru,) having a high forehead, large, regular features and a fine eye.

The letter is addressed to " the Most Excellent President of the United States of North America, from the Capital of the Sovereign Incas of Cusco, the 16th of August, 1848." He thus commences: "A Peruvian prince, the seventh in descent from the Emperor of Huaynicapac, the most immediate branch from the sovereign Incas, places himself under the protection and auspices of your Excellency, entreating that you will have the goodness to receive his homage." He then refers to the ancient prophecies which predict the loss of the kingdom, and of the restoration of the Incas by a people who shall come from Inglaterra.

19th. Florida Indians.—Gen. Twiggs met Sam Jones, Billy Bowlegs, and sixty warriors in council. They had been waiting some nine days for him. They delivered up three of the murderers, the hands of another, whom they were obliged to kill in capturing, and the fifth, Billy Bowlegs' nephew, making his escape. Gen. Twiggs spoke to them of emigrating. They seemed to take it quite kindly, but requested sixty days to decide.

Salt Lake City.—The latest accounts from the Mormon capital, at this date, state that much gold had been brought in from California.

All kinds of merchandise were scarce, and commanded high prices. There were only two small stores in the Valley, to supply a population of 15,000. Snow had fallen on all the mountains around the Valley, and at the South-west Pass it was four feet deep.

Rumours prevailed that Missouri emigrants had killed some squaws of the Snake tribe of Indians, and that they were consequently hostile to the whites, and were committing depredations wherever an opportunity offered. Subsequently they had one battle with another party of emigrants.

Popular Education.—A convention, composed of delegates from fifteen states, was held at this time, in Philadelphia, in relation to the organization and administration of a system of public instruction.

It was organized by the choice of the following officers:

The Hon. HORACE MANN, of Massachusetts, *President.*

Vice Presidents.

Joseph Henry, of Washington.

John Griscom, of New Jersey.

Samuel Lewis, of Ohio.

The Right Rev. Alonzo Potter, of Pennsylvania.

G. B. Duncan, of Louisiana.

Secretaries.

Charles Northend, of Massachusetts.

P. Pemberton Morris, of Pennsylvania.

S. D. Hastings, of Wisconsin.

Sol. Jenner, of New York.

23d. The Memphis Railroad Convention convened this day. Delegates were present from the States of Arkansas, Mississippi, Alabama, Georgia, Kentucky, Missouri, Texas, Illinois, Pennsylvania, Massachusetts, New York, Virginia, South Carolina and Tennessee.

Professor W. F. Maury was chosen *President.* Vice Presidents —Messrs. Clay, of Ala.; Mason, Miss.; Willoughby Williams, Tenn.; R. A. Watson, S. C.; Jameson, Ga.; Col. Maunsel White, La.; Gov. Drew, Ark.; Ashbel Smith, Texas; Ashton Johnston, Missouri; Benj. Dray, Ky.; John J. Tresevant, Va.; J. H. Thompson, Pa.; and L. L. Robinson, of N. Y.

The Convention was ably addressed by Professor Maury. We have noticed elsewhere, with some particularity, the proceedings of this convention, and of that held at St. Louis for a similar object.

We subjoin the resolutions on the subject of this great railroad project, passed by the *Illinois legislature:*

Resolved by the Senate, the House of Representatives concurring herein, That we cordially approve of the general proposition of connecting the navigable waters flowing into the Atlantic and those of the Pacific, by means of a national railroad.

Resolved, That Congress should encourage the construction of three branch roads, from such a point as shall be selected as the eastern terminus of said national road, one to Chicago, one to St. Louis, and one to the mouth of the Ohio river or to Memphis, by making liberal grants of land on the lines to the States respectively through which the same shall pass, to be applied by the Legislature of the respective States to the construction of said branch roads, and to no other objects or purposes whatever.

Resolved, That our Senators in Congress be instructed, and our Representatives requested, to harmonize their action with the principles set forth in the foregoing resolution.

24th. The *Pawnee Indians* were defeated by the U. S. dragoons under Lieut. Ogle, near Fort Kearney.

Hon. Abbott Lawrence, the American Minister, was received by the Queen of England.

25th. The *Great Anglo-Saxon Jubilee,* commemorative of the birth of Alfred the Great, was celebrated in England.

The Trial of G. F. Manning and his Wife, in England, for the murder of Patrick O'Connor, which had very much excited the public mind, was brought to a close by the conviction of the accused. The evidence disclosed a most deliberate and revolting murder, committed for the purpose of obtaining the property of the unsuspecting victim, with whom the wife was on terms of intimacy. Her behaviour at the trial was bold and defiant in the extreme. They were both executed.

Gen. Klapka, of Comorn, with other distinguished Hungarians, arrived in England from Hamburgh.

29th. *Murder at St. Louis*—An awful tragedy took place at Barnum's Hotel, in the city of St. Louis.

Some days previous, two young French gentlemen, calling themselves Count Gonzales de Montesqui and Count Raymond de Montesqui, arrived in that city from Chicago, and took apartments at Barnum's Hotel, representing that they were on a hunting excursion through the Western country.

Nothing particular was observed in their manners until the night of the murder; when, about 11 o'clock, as Mr. Barnum, the nephew of the proprietor of the hotel, and J. J. Macomber, the steward of the house, were retiring to their chamber, one of the Frenchmen came to the window on the gallery at the head of the stairs, and tapped lightly. Mr. Barnum pushed the curtain aside for the purpose of seeing who was on the outside, when the Frenchman fired a gun, a ball from which passed through Mr. Barnum, who is since dead, and two buckshot lodged in the arm of Mr. Macomber.

The report of firearms alarmed the lodgers of the house, and Mr. Albert Jones, a coachmaker in Third street, who roomed adjoining, rushed to the door, where he received a shot through the head, and fell dead. Two gentlemen, who had by this time reached the gallery, were struck with buckshot.

Both the Frenchmen were arrested. Their trunks were opened, and letters found in them proving them to be Parisians of wealth and family. Splendid equipments and $1,500 in German gold coin were found in their trunks.

It is said that one of the brothers is insane. They have since been indicted for the murder, and a relative or friend of high standing, has arrived from France, sent out by their family to attend to their case, bringing letters from Mr. Rives, the American minister at Paris.

The trial is expected to develop the causes which led to the commission of this bloody deed.

30th.—The French Ministry resigned, and a new cabinet was selected by the President. (See History.)

31st.—At a meeting of the Board of Regents of the University of the State of NewYork, *Hon. Garrit Y. Lansing* was elected Chancellor of the University.

NOVEMBER, 1849.

Nov. 1st. Trade to the Pacific.—The trade between the Atlantic cities and the Pacific has increased to such an extent that but few persons are likely to form a just conception of its amount. The Baltimore American contains a list of sixty-five vessels which have departed from the United States for California during the last month, (October.) The list comprises 19 ships, 16 barques, 17 brigs, and 13 schooners—all of them, except four, having sailed from cities eastward of that place. The American says:

"The greater proportion are ships of the largest class, but even by putting the average tonnage down at 300 tons, we have an aggregate tonnage of 19,500 tons, leaving the Atlantic ports in the short space of one month for our distant possessions in the Pacific. It may be safely estimated that during the month of October at least twenty-three hundred persons have left the United States by sea, bound to California."

The Boston shipping list gives the total number of vessels that have left the United States for California since the beginning of the gold excitement, at five hundred and seventy-three, as follows: ships 189, barques 175, brigs 119, schooners 83, and steamers 7. Of this number there had arrived at California, at the latest date, one hundred and sixty-seven, viz., ships 55, barques 45, brigs 35, schooners 28, and steamers 4.

Explorations in Africa.—The French surpass all other nations in the grandeur of their exploring expeditions to various parts of the world. It is now announced that the Academy of Sciences, and the Geographical society of France, have projected an expedition on a grand scale for penetrating the interior of Africa to Timbuctoo. It is to be conducted by scientific men, and will have in view the twofold purpose of extending our knowledge of this portion of the continent, and of opening new channels for French trade and commerce. It is a singular fact that, notwithstanding the several attempts by Mungo Park, Clapperton, Denham, Oudney, Lander, and Laird, for the exploration of that portion of Africa which lies between the gulf of Guinea and the Mediterranean, none have yet reached Timbuctoo and returned. The only European traveller who has reached this inland city, and returned to give an account of it, is Caille, a Frenchman, some ten years since. The expedition now projected, it is said, will have an escort of eight hundred armed Europeans, and four hundred Africans.

Liberia.—The Rev. Mr. Gurley, agent of the Colonization society, in a recent letter, thus describes the residence of the President, and the appearance of Monrovia:

"President Roberts lives in a very commodious brick house, furnished with taste and elegance, and the hospitalities of his mansion and table are set off with a refined good breeding which commends him and the republic over which he so ably presides, to the respect and confidence of visiters from the whole civilized world."

Of the appearance of the town of Monrovia, and the beauty of its ornamental trees, as well as the great improvement which has taken place, Mr. G. writes:

"The beauty of these large trees, (the orange,) loaded with fruit, as well as that of the heavily laden coffee trees, one of the handsomest trees you can imagine, with the deep green of its magnificent leaf, it would be difficult to describe.

"When I behold what has been done since my former visit to this coast, the many substantial and convenient houses and stores that have been constructed, the general aspect of health, contentment, and hope, which this people exhibit; the great good order, and respect to religion which prevails, I am impressed more than I ever was with the vast dignity and beneficence of the colonization of Africa."

2d. Steam-dried Meal.—The invention of J. R. Stafford, Esq., of Cleveland, Ohio, for steam-drying corn, is getting into high repute. He has already a contract to supply the navy with corn meal; and has published a very interesting pamphlet on the preservation of cereal grains.

The theory is, that without the presence of air and moisture, no organic body can change. The advantages claimed by the patentee for his revolving drier over all others, are, mainly, that it dries all substances without the possibility of change of quality, colour, or flavour, and removes all danger of the meal dried by that process undergoing any change under any circumstances of exposure. Mr. Stafford affirms that when grain is ground into flour or meal, and is dried by his process, by packing it into casks its cohesive properties make it impervious to air, and, being divested of internal moisture, vermin cannot exist among it; and from this cause it is susceptible of being kept in any climate an indefinite time.

The theory is sustained by incontestable facts.

Rice Culture in France.—The culture of rice has been lately introduced with success into the southern departments of France, and also into the Gironde. M. Ferry, a skilful and successful farmer of that department, at an annual agricultural festival, presented a specimen of rice which he had raised, having sowed several hectares, on which he produced a crop of thirty-five· hectolitres per hectare. As this may not be intelligible to some of our agricultural readers, it may be proper to explain that this rate of produce is about thirty-seven bushels per acre. This culture, it is stated, is about to be continued on a vast scale, and it is likely to contribute greatly to the riches of the south of France.

Cotton Culture in the East.—Specimens of cotton from Algeria have been exhibited and pronounced of good quality. The London Morning Chronicle declares the attempt to cultivate cotton in Bengal and Madras a failure. In Egypt, the introduction of cotton, now one of the greatest staples of the country, and in quality ranking nearly at the head of the Manchester market, is wholly attributable to Mehemet Ali. It is not, however, a favourite production among the fellahs; it requires too much labour and attention, and its gathering is troublesome.

5th. Railroad Accidents.—As the train of the N. York and New Haven railroad was passing Morrisania, it came in contact with a drove of cows, fifteen in number, which threw the locomotive off the track, and at the same place the express train out of New York was passing at a great speed, causing a collision of the two trains, killing eight cows, and throwing both trains off the track. The last car of the upward train contained the Marion Guard, going on a target excursion to New Rochelle. This car was nearly destroyed by the locomotive of the downward train running into it. Several members of the Guard were injured. Mr. George Bailey had his leg badly broken, and Mr. Wm. Swinnard and four others were injured in various parts of the body. We understand there was no serious injury sustained by any others in either train, but the destruction to the cars, particularly in the upward train, was very great. The 2d, 3d, 4th, and 5th passenger cars were nearly destroyed, and the 1st and 2d cars of the downward train were more or less injured.

At Whitehaven, in England, a remarkable railroad accident occurred. A locomotive, by some mismanagement, passed the station, ran through the outer wall of the house of a Mr. Pennington, and through another wall into his back parlour. A little girl, his daughter, was at the same time sitting singing in the kitchen, when the engine passed over her, causing immediate death. The engine, on dashing into the parlour, knocked the fire-grate out of its place, throwing the burning contents over the forehead and breast of a little boy eight years old.

The Lake Trade.—There arrived this day at Buffalo, N. Y., fifteen steamers, two propellers, two brigs, and twenty-one schooners, bringing 160,000 barrels of flour, 49,000 bushels of wheat, 800 live hogs, 2,500 boxes of cheese, and large quantities of other produce. The propeller Illinois was on her way down with 4,445 barrels of flour, and 2,114 bushels of wheat, equal to 580 tons of merchandise; and the steamer Empire State was on her way down with 7,000 barrels of flour, said to be the largest cargo ever brought by one vessel.

In 1825, there were but 30 or 40 small craft, and one steamboat on Lake Erie. In 1845, there were on the lakes 60 steam vessels, and 320 brigs and schooners. In 1846, the amount of merchandise transported was 3,861,088 tons. The value of the lake commerce in 1847 was $141,000,000. There are now six large states in the vicinity of these lakes, containing between four and five millions of inhabitants.

6th. Mr. Rives, the American minister, was presented to the President of France.

Sir James Ross returned to England from an unsuccessful expedition to the Arctic regions in search of Sir John, Franklin.

The government of *the Pasha of Egypt* neglects the prosecution of the improvements made by the great Mehemet Ali.

10th. The steamer *Empire city* arrived at N. York with half a million of California gold.

The nomade *tribes of Zaatcha,* in Africa, defeated by the French; 3,000 camels, and 10,000 sheep captured.

Amnesty granted by Louis Napoleon to the June insurgents.

12th. The *ship Caleb Grimshaw* was destroyed by fire at sea. She was 987 tons burden, and had a cargo valued at $200,000, with a large number of passengers, stated at more than three hundred. The fire was between decks, and the hatches were kept down for several days, until they were relieved by Capt. Cook of the British barque Sarah, and all were saved. Sixty of the passengers had left on a raft the second day of the fire, but they were picked up. A part of the time the wind blew high.

13th. The State Prisoners in France.—The trial of these persons terminated in the acquittal of eleven, a sentence of transportation for life against seventeen, for conspiracy to destroy the government and excite civil war, and three others, on account of extenuating circumstances, were let off with five years' imprisonment. The conduct of the prisoners, while being sentenced was dignified and manly; the entire party, after hearing the sentence, rose and cried, "Vive la Republique Democratique et Sociale!"

It will be remembered that the leaders of the conspiracy of the 13th June, found means to effect their escape. Of the eleven persons sentenced to transportation, seven are, however, members of the legislative assembly, and Col. Guinard held a high command in the artillery of the National Guard. It is said that Albert (*ouvrier*) and Barbes, who were convicted at Bourges, in March, of treason, committed on the 15th May, 1848, will share the fate of these later offenders, and that they will all be shipped off together to Fort Zaouzzee or the Marquesas.

Venezuela and Paez.—From the Havana Faro Industrial, we derive the intelligence that a great number of the principal families, most probably the friends and adherents of Paez in the late troubles, are about leaving Venezuela, and emigrating to Cuba and Mexico. This, however, is the ordinary custom with a defeated party, in all the Spanish American Republics, owing to the intolerance which each triumphal junta displays towards its opponents.

The castle of Cumana, where General Paez is imprisoned, has been put in a state of thorough repair at an expense of $4000.

Dr. Angel Quintero, formerly secretary, and the constant friend of Paez, attracts attention by the serenity and firmness which he has displayed. Misfortune has elevated his soul.

Major General Scott was received at Richmond, Va., with great honour, as a "distinguished son of Virginia, the hero of two wars, and of nine great battle-fields." It is stated that some fine toasts and speeches were given. The Governor drank to General Scott, "The most distinguished son of Virginia living." Counsellor Patton gave, "To the hero of two wars and three pacifications." General Scott made an appropriate reply.

14th. Indian Troubles on Lake Superior.—The Indians and half-breeds, under the command of Allen and Argus Macdonnell, and Wharton Metcalfe, drove the Quebec Mining Company from their location. The assailants were well armed, and took possession of the whole establishment. The Indian party offered to relinquish on the payment of their claims. One hundred troops were subsequently ordered on. The M'Donnells were arrested at Saut Sté Marie, and a detachment was sent on to take possession of the mines at Mica Bay, and to arrest the other leaders.

A Fowl Fair at Boston.—This novel exhibition took place at the public garden. The Boston Courier thus notices it:

"The first exhibition of the 'fowl sects' took place yesterday at the public garden. The show of articles was numerous, and the attendance of visiters large. Considering the short time employed in the preparation for the fair, there has never been any thing of the kind more successful. Every spectator must be struck with the variety and fine condition of these specimens of the feathered creation. The collection comprises almost every thing of the kind that has been domesticated in this country, amounting to nearly 700 individuals. Among the rarer birds are English pheasants, carrier pigeons, swans,'China geese, and summer ducks. There is a venerable old goose belonging to Col. Jacques, of Charlestown, which for progeny and profit may hold up her head with any thing that ever went to grass. *Five thousand* of her descendants have been sold at a large price."

Grand Funeral Pageant.—The military and civic display in the City of New York, in honor of the remains of Gen. Worth, Col. Duncan and Major Gates, heroes of the Mexican War, was probably the most magnificent that has ever been made in this country. The procession was grand and imposing—the remains were placed in coffins, rich and gorgeous; on these were the swords of the deceased, crossed. They were drawn on hearses decorated with waving plumes. The houses in the principal streets were hung with black drapery—the flags of the shipping were half mast.—The military of the city and adjoining towns united in the solemn pageant. Many distinguished men were present to do honor to the illustrious dead —A funeral oration was delivered by John Van Buren, Esq., and after three volleys were fired over the remains, they were removed to the Governor's room in the City Hall, and there kept until the next day,—when Gen. Worth's body was buried in Greenwood Cemetery;—Col. Duncan's was carried to Cornwall, Orange Co., his native place; and Major Gates to Governor's Island.

15th. Steamboat Explosion.—The steamboat *Louisiana,* Capt. CANNON, bound for St. Louis, loaded with a valuable cargo, and having on board a large number of passengers, had rung her last bell, and was just backing out from the wharf at the foot of Gravier street, when the whole of her boilers burst with a tremendous explosion, which resounded throughout the city. The concussion was so great that it shook the houses to their foundations for many squares distant. The Louisiana was lying along side the steamer Bostona, Capt. Dustin, at the time of the disaster, and the steamer Storm, Capt. Hopkins, had just arrived from Louisville, coming in on her starboard side. The upper works of these two boats were complete wrecks, their chimneys having been carried away, and their cabins stove in and shattered in some places to atoms. The violence of the shock operating on the boilers was tremendous. A part of one of them, a mass of considerable size, was hurled with inconceivable force on the levee. It cut a mule in two, and killed a horse and the driver of a dray to which the animals were attached. It was one of the most terrible catastrophes of the kind on record. The loss of life was very great, and under the most appalling circumstances. From fifty to seventy were killed at once, and many were wounded.

Death of the Queen of Madagascar.—A Mauritius journal mentions the death of Ranavalo Marigaeka, Queen of Madagascar. This event, there was reason to hope, would put an end to the difficulties which had hitherto existed, as her son, who succeeds to the throne, is a Christian, and likely to pursue a more liberal and more tolerant policy than that followed by his mother, of whom England and France had so much reason to complain. The journal states that the Sacklaves had made an eruption into the French possession of Nossi-Bè, killed almost the whole of the garrison, and forced the inhabitants to take refuge on board the vessels in the roadstead. The French vessels on the station were concentrating in order to take vengeance for this attack. The death of this cruel Sovereign will give a new turn to the affairs of Madagascar. This is the woman who decreed that her subjects should *forget the name of Jesus Christ!*

16th. Circassia.—Advices from St. Petersburgh of the 16th November state that the division of the Russian army under Prince Dolgoruki had succeeded in storming and sacking the Circassian fortress of Tshoek. The Circassians are stated to have lost as many as 3,000 men, while the loss of the Russians is quoted at 50.

Missionaries in Syria.—Outrages have recently been committed by the Maronite Population on the Christian Missionaries, near Tripoli. The matter was referred to Beyrout, and also to the Porte, and the Sultan has taken active measures to prevent a recurrence of the outrage. Twenty-six of the chief Moslem rioters are now at Beyrout, a detachment of troops from that place having surrounded Tripoli, and commanded the citizens to deliver them up within twenty-four hours, in default of which, they threatened to fire upon the town. The ringleaders were accordingly surrendered.

African Missionaries.—A great effort is about to be made in England, by some of the Missionary Societies, to extend their operations into Africa, and the Colonial Bishopric's Fund Committee have intimated their intention of erecting Sierra Leone into an episcopal see at the earliest possible opportunity. It is desired by some influential persons that the new prelate should be one of Africa's sable sons—'a real black bishop,'—as Mr. Stowell expressed it. There is some probability of this suggestion being carried out.

Artificial Leeches.—The *Journal des Debats* describes an important discovery, which occupies the attention of the French scientific world. It is a mechanical leech, invented by M. Alexander, a civil engineer, already celebrated for his useful discoveries. All the scientific bodies, after satisfactory trials, have caused this leech to be adopted in all the hospitals; having proved not only the immense economy of its use, but, what is better, the decided advantage which it has over the natural leech, often so scarce, always repugnant to the patient, and sometimes dangerous.

17th. The Arctic Expedition.—Captain Sir James Ross and Captain Sir John Richardson met in London. The latter arrived in an American packet. They were also met by Captain Kerr, of the whaler Chieftain, who brought the story of the Esquimaux respecting Sir John Franklin. Neither Ross nor Richardson have discovered any traces of Sir John Franklin, Capt. Crozier, Captain Fitz James, and their brave and gallant companions.

The Cholera.—This dreadful disease has again manifested itself on the Western rivers. At this date a number of deaths occurred on board the steamer Constitution, bound to St. Louis from New Orleans; other cases have been mentioned. It seems to have manifested itself principally among the emigrants.

The Church in Borneo.—An account of the ceremony of laying the first beam of the missionary church at Sarawak has just been received. The celebrated Rajah of Sarawak, Sir James Brooke, with his suite, and the naval officers, and English residents, were present on the occasion.

20th. Slave Trade.—The French government have notified to the British cabinet their intention of withdrawing the twenty-six cruisers which have been placed on the coast of Africa for the suppression of the slave trade, pursuant to a convention signed by the Duke de Broglie, May 29, 1845.

23d. Two sailors were executed on board the U. S. frigate Savannah, at San Francisco, for mutiny.

25th. A very distressing and melancholy case of *desertion of husband and children* by a lady, occurred at Niagara Falls. From letters written at the time, and from parts of her dress found on the bridge, it was believed that she had thrown herself into the rapids. But it was subsequently ascertained that she had left during the night with a paramour, and gone South. The lady is Mrs. Miller, the wife of an officer of the army. She had heretofore borne an irreproachable character, and evinced a strong attachment to her children.

28th. Wonders of the Telegraph.—"We were present," says the editor of the National Intelligencer, "a few evenings ago at the Coast Survey astronomical station, on Capitol Hill, which was put in telegraphic connexion with Cincinnati, for the purpose of determining the longitude between the two places. The electrical clocks in this city and Cincinnati having been introduced into the completed circuit, *every beat* at Cincinnati was recorded at *almost the same instant* on Saxton's revolving cylinder in this city, and every beat of the clock here was recorded in like manner upon Mitchell's revolving plate at Cincinnati. At the moment a star passed the meridian at Washington, by the touch of a key the record of the passage was made upon the disc at Cincinnati, as well as upon the cylinder at the Washington station, and the difference of the time of the two clocks would of course indicate the difference of longitude. The distance between the two cities, it must be recollected, is upwards of five hundred miles; this distance was annihilated, and events happening at the one were instantly recorded by automatic machinery at the other."

29th. A day of general thanksgiving throughout the United States.

DECEMBER, 1849.

1st. The Planetary System.—As one of the signs of the progress of science, which we feel bound to chronicle, is the opinion lately expressed by Sir J. Herschell, that it is impossible any longer to attempt the explanation of the movements of all the heavenly bodies by simple attraction, as understood in the Newtonian theory, these comets, with their trains, perversely turned *from* the sun, deranging sadly our systematic views. Nor are there (writes Humboldt,) any constant relations between the distances of the planets from the central body round which they revolve and their absolute magnitudes, densities, times of rotation, eccentricities, and inclinations of orbit or axis. We find Mars, though more distant from the sun than either the Earth or Venus, inferior to them in magnitude; Saturn is less than Jupiter, and yet much larger than Uranus. The zone of the telescopic planets, which are so inconsiderable in point of volume viewed in the series of distances commencing from the sun, comes next before Jupiter, the greatest in size of all the planetary bodies. Remarkable as is the small density of all the colossal planets which are farthest from the sun, yet neither in this respect can we recognise any regular succession. Uranus appears to be denser than Saturn, and, though the inner group of planets differ but little from each other in this particular, we find both Venus and Mars less dense than the Earth, which is situated between them. The time of rotation increases, on the whole, with increasing solar distance; but yet it is greater in Mars than in the Earth, and in Saturn than in Jupiter. After other remarks of the same character, he adds: "The planetary system, in its relation of absolute magnitude, relative position of the axis, density, time of rotation, and different degrees of eccentricity of the orbits, has, to our apprehension, nothing more of natural necessity than the relative distribution of land and water on the surface of our globe, the configuration of continents, or the elevation of mountain chains. No general law, in these respects, is discoverable either in the regions of space or in the irregularities of the crust of the earth."

The fall of Zaatchi.—This place is in the midst of a desert, in the province of Constantine, in Africa. A handful of Arabs established themselves here, and for some time resisted the entire French army. They fought with a desperation and courage never perhaps surpassed, until they were overpowered by numbers, and fell, fighting to the last. On the final assault, the French swept all before them, and the whole city is now desolate.

Murder of Dr. Parkman at Boston.—On the 23d November. Dr. Parkman, who was a wealthy citizen of Boston, disappeared very suddenly. A large reward was offered to whoever should find him, and for a week all efforts were fruitless. His continued absence induced his friends to suppose that he was murdered, and a further reward of $1000 was added to the $3000 already offered for his discovery. Suspicion at length pointed to the medical college in North Grove Street, and implicated Dr. John W. Webster, Professor of Chemistry in Harvard University, a gentleman of most excellent character, who had held the professorship for several years. Dr. Parkman was last seen going to the college, whither, it was supposed, he went for the purpose of collecting a demand which he had against Professor Webster, whom he had somewhat exasperated by the means he had used to collect it. It was said too that Prof. W. admitted that Dr. Parkman had called, and that he had paid him $450. Dr. P. was not seen again alive. Professor Webster had kept his rooms locked during the week, and a dense smoke was seen issuing from his chimney. Urged by these circumstances, Mr. Ephraim Littlefield, who had charge of the college buildings, broke into the private vault under the laboratory of Dr. Webster, and found a leg and part of the trunk of a human body. On the further examination in Prof. W.'s laboratory there were found, in the ashes of the furnace, parts of a human skull and jaw, and teeth filled in a peculiar manner, as Dr. P.'s were, and particles of gold and silver, supposed to be parts of a watch; in a tea-chest, a bloody knife which corresponded with stabs found in the body; in another chest, all the parts of the body not previously discovered, except the head, feet, and arms. On putting the several parts of the body together, it appeared to be that of Dr. Parkman. Other evidences of identification were discovered, and the family of Dr. Parkman recognised and claimed the remains as his.

Professor Webster was arrested, and at the time of his arrest was dreadfully agitated; but soon regained composure of manner, and subsequently evinced perfect self-possession and calmness. The coroner's jury sat for several days with closed doors, and after examining a large number of witnesses, rendered a verdict that Dr. Parkman was killed by Professor Webster. The grand jury have found a bill for wilful murder. Notwithstanding the strong circumstances against him, the friends of Prof. W., and they are many, express their convictions of his innocence

Professor Webster's family consists of a wife and four daughters, and his house was distinguished as the seat of hospitality. He himself was mild, kind, and unassuming—his character free from stain, and was amongst the very last men who would be thought capable of committing so horrible a crime.

3d. The *first session of the thirty-first Congress* commenced this day.

In *the Senate* the Vice President, Hon. Millard Fillmore, took the chair, forty-one members being present. Mr. Underwood presented the credentials of the Hon. Henry Clay, of Kentucky, and Mr. Mangum those of Hon. James Shields, of Illinois. The House not being organized, no further business was transacted by the Senate.

In *the House of Representatives* the roll was called, and 223 members were found to be in attendance. The House proceeded to the election of speaker. On the first ballot, Howell Cobb, of Ga, had 103 votes, and Robert C. Winthrop, of Mass., 96 votes—four efforts were made that day with similar results, and no candidate having received a majority of all the votes, the House adjourned.

The *Supreme Court of the United States* was opened in the Capitol. Present, Chief Justice Taney, and Associate Justices M'Lean, Wayne, Catron, Daniel, Woodbury, Nelson, and Grier. Justice M'Kinley absent.

The celebrated police officer, *Jacob Hays,* now in his eightieth year, was appointed, for the forty-ninth time, high constable of New York.

5th. The *New York Canals* were closed. The amount of tolls collected last year was $3,245,662; this year the amount collected is $3,259,210 30, which is an increase of $13,548 30. And in the mean time the work of enlargement has been studiously and advantageously progressing. The expense of repairs has been diminished, and the canals are left in better order for resuming navigation than they have been at the close of any former season.

7th. Brig. Gen. Garland assumed command of the military post at San Antonio,—the position occupied by Gen. Worth at the time of his death.

8th. The steamer Crescent City arrived at New York from Chagres, with $1,000,000 in California gold.

10th. The Ohio arrived, bringing from Chagres $500,000 in gold.

12th. Lieut. Beale, of the navy, arrived as the bearer of despatches to the government from San Francisco, and bringing with him a copy of the constitution of California.

This is the gentleman who, when pursued by the Indians, so generously gave up his horse to a soldier who begged him to save his life for the sake of his wife and children, and thus apparently surrendered up all hope of preserving his own life; but was providentially rescued.

14th. The Capitol of Alabama.—This beautiful edifice was destroyed by fire. The archives of State were all saved.

The mercury at *St. Paul's,* Minesota, was 20° below Zero.

15th. The Fair for all Nations.—This grand assemblage proposed by Prince Albert is to be held at a future day, yet to be named. In a recent paper we find this notice:—"A large and highly respectable meeting, presided over by the Lord Mayor, took place at Egyptian Hall, London, relative to the proposed exhibition of the industry of all nations in that city, during the ensuing year. The best feeling was evinced towards the plan of the projectors, and it was proposed to raise by subscription the sum of £20,000 to distribute in premiums. All nations are invited, without distinction or preference, and the promoters of the design feel no misgiving of the possibility of raising £100,000 or more for the general expenses of the exhibition."

16th. The Hungarian Exiles.—Ladislaus Ujhazy, the Ex-Civil Governor of Comorn, and his companions, arrived in New York—among them were several distinguished officers, and the celebrated Mademoiselle Apolonia Jagella, who so heroically devoted herself to the care of the wounded, during the struggles and battles in Hungary. Previously to leaving Europe, Gov. Ujhazy addressed a letter to the President of the United States announcing the determination of the exiles, "to seek a permanent resting-place for themselves, their wives and children, upon the friendly shores of America."—And asking from the citizens of the United States, " nothing but that hospitality which they are always ready to extend to the unfortunate victims of despotism, and which it would be their first duty to deserve at their hands." After their arrival, he received the following response from Gen. Taylor.

" Sir:—I have duly received your letter of Nov. 2d, from London, announcing the determination of yourself and comrades to seek an asylum in America.

The people of this republic have deeply sympathized with the Hungarians in their recent struggle for constitutional freedom, and in the calamities which have befallen their unhappy land; and I am sure that I but speak the universal sentiment of my countrymen, in bidding you and your associates a cordial welcome to our soil, the natural asylum of the oppressed from every clime. We offer you protection and a free participation in the benefits of our institutions and our laws, and trust that you may find in America a second home.

I am, with high respect, your sincere friend,

Z. TAYLOR.

LADISLAUS UJHAZI.
Late Governor of Comorn, in Hungary.

17th. California,—State Organization, &c.—By the arrival of the steamer Empire City in New York, which brought $2,000,000 in gold, we have recent news from California. On the 17th December the legislature was fully organized, and on the 20th, the governor, Peter H. Burnet, was inaugurated, the oath of office being administered by the Chief Justice.

The constitution had been adopted by the people of California by a vote of 12,061 out of 15,000, the whole number of votes polled. The election took place in the rainy season, and great numbers of voters could not reach the polls.

The message of the governor was sent to both houses on the 21st, and 10,000 copies in English, and 2,000 in Spanish, were ordered to be printed.

An election of United States senators, and of representatives in Congress, took place immediately after the organization of the house, and resulted in the choice of Col. J. C. Fremont, and Dr. Wm. M. Gwinn, as senators, and of George W. Wright, and Edward Gilbert, as representatives in Congress. The following are the State officers:

Governor—Peter H. Burnet. *Lieut. Governor*—John M'Dougal. *Secretary of State*—William Van Voorhies. *Treasurer*—Richard Roman. *Comptroller*—J. S. Houston. *Attorney General*—Edward J. C. Kewen. *Surveyor General*—Charles J. Whiting. *Chief Justice*—S. C. Hastings. *Associate Justices*—H. A. Lyon, Nathaniel Bennett.

Thus this new state seems to be completely organized, and ready for admission into the Union, and its senators and representatives either on the way to or at the seat of the general government, before the question of its admission has been decided by Congress.

The accounts state that a very destructive fire had occurred at San Francisco on the 24th, causing the destruction of property to the amount of a million and a half of dollars. A fire had also, on the same date, broken out at Stockton, and caused the loss of $150,000 worth of property.

A party of armed Chilenos, numbering 200, had attacked a few Americans in the diggings, killing three, and severely wounding

others. A party of Americans had started from Stockton to revenge
the injury, and it was feared it might lead to a serious outbreak.

A large number of persons having disputed the title of John A.
Sutter to the lands which he holds under Mexican grants, have actually seized and "squatted" upon lots in Sacramento city.

The mines are nearly abandoned for the present, owing to the
heavy falls of rain and snow.

18*th*. News received of the *destruction of a formidable fleet* of
pirate junks on the coast of Borneo by Sir James Brooke, the Rajah
of Sarawak, and 400 men killed.

Bloody Affrays.—Had we room and inclination to do so, we
might chronicle a number of murderous conflicts which have occurred in broad day-light in the streets of our cities and towns
within the current quarter. Bound, however, to exhibit the evil
with the good, that we may present true pictures of the times, we
take two of the first that come to hand as specimens of the revolting
scenes that have been enacted within the quarter.

At St. Louis, two persons, Wimer and Thomas, both men of respectable standing, quarrelled, and meeting in the street, drew re-
volvers and fired at each other, and then closed in a hand to hand
struggle. Wimer being the strongest, obtained the advantage, and
beat his antagonist over the head with a pistol. Thomas, whilst held
down, drew a small pistol and shot Wimer through the body, who
fell, exclaiming "I am killed." He died that night. This affair
happened in the afternoon, and many persons by.

At Shreveport, La., Dr. Green and Mr. Hester, who had previously been on an intimate footing, met at the hotel; the latter immediately struck the former, and was about drawing a knife, when
Dr. Green exclaimed that he was not armed. He was told to go
and arm himself, and they separated. For a day or two, hostile
messages passed between them, when Mr. Hester, without notifying
any person, so far as known, went to the back door of Dr. Green's
room, pushed it open, and instantly fired twice at the doctor, one of
the shots taking effect in his side. Dr. Green sprang to his feet,
pistol in hand, and fired at Mr. Hester, the shot taking effect also
in his side. He then threw his pistol, striking Mr. H. on the head,
drew a bowie knife, stabbed him four or five times—once in the
breast, and Mr. Hester fell and immediately expired. Dr. Green
lived till 2 o'clock that night.

The Mission of Peace and Good Will.—In contrast with such
bloody conflicts, and as another part of the picture, we record an account received at the same time of the labours of a worthy missionary in New England, performed in the spirit of Christian philanthropy, who has, during the past year, looked after hundreds of sick
sailors, seen that the destitute were clothed, assisted many a poor boy

with means to return to his almost broken-hearted mother and put on board our whale ships 382 Bibles, 1,148 testaments, and about 10,000 tracts and pamphlets.

At Onondagua Castle, Oneida county, N. Y., the pagan Indians still residing there celebrated the rite of sacrificing the White Dog. The customary victim was immolated on the flaming altar, with all the formality and circumstance of ancient usage among the Iroquois, in presence of the pagan portion of the nation, and of a numerous body of white persons, spectators!

21st. The British steamer Hecate, came up the Potomac to Washington, having on board *Sir Henry L. Bulwer,* the British minister, and his family.

About the same time *Mr. Donelson,* late minister to the Germanic confederation, arrived at Washington.

22d. Woolsey & Co.'s sugar refinery was destroyed by fire in New York. The loss on the sugar was $200,000—on the machinery $300,000—on the buildings $50,000—total, as estimated, $600,000, only a small portion of which was insured, as the company had lately let a policy of $250,000 on the property run out. Nearly five hundred hands are thrown out of employment by this calamity.

In Cincinnati, the pork house of Pugh & Co. was destroyed by fire, with the loss of $100,000. There was $70,000 worth of lard in the buildings, and 3000 hogs uncut.

The Convention in Kentucky for the revision of the constitution, finished its labours. The new instrument provides for the election of judges by the people; and the right of the owner to the slave is declared "as inviolable as the right to any other property."

In the House of Representatives of the United States a Speaker was chosen, after a struggle of nearly three weeks between the contending parties, by the adoption of the plurality rule, as proposed by Mr. Stanton of Tennessee. On the sixty-third vote, Mr. *Howell Cobb,* of Georgia, received 102 votes, and Mr. *Robert C. Winthrop,* of Massachusetts, 100 votes, when the former was declared duly elected Speaker; and on being conducted to the chair by Messrs. Winthrop and M'Dowell, addressed the House as follows:

Gentlemen of the House of Representatives:

It would be useless to disguise the fact that I feel deeply embarrassed in taking this chair under the circumstances attending my election.

I am conscious of the difficulties by which this position is surrounded at the present time.

The peculiar organization of this body, as exhibited in our proceedings since we first met—the nature and character of the various important and exciting questions of public policy which will engage our attention during the present session of Congress, conspire to render the duties of the office peculiarly embarrassing, onerous, and responsible.

I may be permitted, therefore, to ask in advance your generous aid and support in the effort I shall make firmly, faithfully, and impartially to discharge its duties.

The country has been looking with anxiety to our efforts to effect an organization. The people will continue to regard with intense interest every step we take in our legislative course. Our duties will be laborious, our responsibilities great. Let us, then, in view of these considerations, invoke, in the discharge of these duties, a patriotism as broad as the Union, and as comprehensive as the nature and character of her various interests and institutions. Guided by this spirit, under the blessing of Heaven, our action will result in the continued prosperity of our common country.

Accept, gentlemen, my grateful acknowledgments for the honour you have conferred on me in selecting me as your presiding officer during the present Congress.

24*th.* Both houses of Congress being now organized for the transaction of business, the President, at a quarter past one o'clock, transmitted by the hands of his private secretary, Col. Bliss, his annual message.

The 229th anniversary of the landing of the pilgrims on Plymouth Rock was celebrated in New York.

25*th.* The steamer Empire City arrived from Chagres at New York with nearly half a million of dollars in California gold.

STATISTICS.

—

CALIFORNIA.

The following statement of the present condition, productions, climate, population, &c., of California, was recently communicated by T. O. Larkin, Esq., navy agent at Monterey, to a gentleman of Boston.

Mr. L. has resided in the region which he describes for eighteen years; and "his statement," says the Boston Journal, "may be regarded as the result of matured observation and a thorough knowledge of every thing bearing upon the interests of the country."

1st. The population of California in July, 1846, was about 15,000, exclusive of Indians; in July, 1849, it is about 35,000 to 40,000. The Americans are the lesser half of the people. From July to January, 1850, probably 40,000 Americans, by land and water, will reach this country; and after September the Europeans will commence arriving here. By January, 1850, we shall number 80,000 to 100,000 people, and in 1851 from 175,000 to 200,000.

2d. The character of the natives prior to July, 1846, was proverbial for inactivity, indolence, and an unwillingness to learn or improve. They had no wish or desire to indulge or enjoy themselves in any new or foreign customs, and they were happy, and kind and hospitable to all strangers. Foreign residents, happily situated among the natives, improving their advantages, gradually became men of property, and many of them have married into some of the principal families in California. The American emigrants arriving here in future will be composed of our most restless, active, and ambitious countrymen. No faint heart will leave his home to essay a journey of ten thousand miles, when at the journey's end only the most active and bold will be able to hold their way. Very many of our emigrants are Mexicans and South Americans—labourers (*peons*,) of the most abject class—mild and inoffensive in their general manners, who are guided with ease. They are, however, slothful, ignorant, and from early life addicted to gambling. They will sleep under the canopy of a tree, and enjoy themselves to the full if they have a blanket or a sheet with which to enwrap themselves; and they are content if they have only paper cigars to last them a week, and a monte bank to resort to at will. This class of men are brought by their employers from Chili, Peru, and Mexico. The employers are men of ease and urbanity, who will in time take their departure from this country, most of their labourers or peons remaining behind to live and die here.

3d. The climate of the sea-coast of California is healthy. At San Francisco, in the afternoons, during six months of the year, there is so much wind as to make the town a disagreeable one to reside in. At this great and rapidly-settling sea-port, four-fifths of the imports of California arrive, which are mostly sent up the Sacramento and San Joaquin rivers. One of the novel features of San Francisco now is, that *gold* is actually being picked up in the streets! Natives of the Sandwich Islands and Chili are seen daily engaged in this occupation. Whether it is dropped from people's pockets and rough leather purses, or is produced by the recent constant employ of carts, with iron tires, which have superseded those tireless, broad-wheeled affairs, previously in use, I am unable unadvisedly to say. The town of Santa Cruz is warm, and extremely healthy; and, for timber and grain, it possesses advantages over any other town in California. Benicia is a newly-formed town on the straits of Carquines, thirty miles from San Francisco, and about the same from the sea. This place is more subject to cold and wind than Monterey, but not so much so as San Francisco. It is the chief point of passing from one end of California to the other. Its ferry will at some future day be of immense value, and the income constitutes an education fund for the school of Benicia. Before the resources of the Sacramento and San Joaquin valleys were known, the town of San Francisco was considered to be one of the greatest importance, the more so as it was said no large vessel could go any higher up. Many merchant ships and men-of-war have gone to and returned in safety from Benicia. The location and advantages of the place now promise that it will soon be of the first importance. It may be the meeting-place of ships from the sea and of steamers from the river, which matter time and scientific men will soon determine.

The town of Sonoma, twenty miles from Benicia, with the valleys of the Napa and Suisun nearly adjacent, offers inducements of the highest order to the most lazy of our roaming emigrant families. In the Sonoma, Napa, and Suisun valleys the land is good, the country healthy, and the temperature is never very cold in winter, snow being seen only on the highest mountains. This part of the country contains the best of grazing land, many places being covered with clover and with wild oats. Cattle and horses lose flesh but a trifle in the winter; hogs, perhaps, not at all. In California, prior to 1846, not one horse or hog out of one hundred ever eat grain, and not one bullock out of one hundred thousand has yet done so; yet the horses and cattle are always serviceable. The proper time for killing cattle is from May to September; June and July are the best months. Wheat produces well. It is sowed from October to January, and cut from June to August. The yield is large, say thirty to sixty fold. Beans, corn, and wheat keep four years or more; fruits and vegetables less time than they do in the Atlantic States.

Twenty miles above Benicia some enterprising American gentlemen are laying out three towns, called Montezuma, Suisun, and New York. The banks of the river, as far up as these points, are without a doubt healthy. As California becomes populated, these new towns will contain their fair proportion of inhabitants, and there will be heard the busy hum of Yankee enterprise. On the San Joaquin there is a town laid off under the name of Stockton, which has now some hundreds of traders and wagoners living in tents. Lumber being landed in San Francisco and Benicia from Oregon and foreign ports, and held at two hundred and fifty to three hundred dollars per one thousand feet, and the price being much enhanced when it reaches the highest points of boating, there must for a time be a drawback to building within the limits of the placer locations. Higher up the San Joaquin, proposals are out to build two small towns, in which people are purchasing house lots at low prices. At Captain Sutter's Fort, and extending to his embarcadera, there is a town called Sacramento City, with a thriving and numerous population of little less than a thousand people already. Several brigs and barques of light draught have reached this town, and also Stockton. On Feather river there are projections of a township. The people on the upper Sacramento river, Bute creek, Feather, Yerba, Americanos, Cosumnes, and Moquelemes (the last two members of the San Joaquin,) rivers, and their vicinity, must depend at present on Sacramento City for supplies; the remainder of the rivers, lower branches of the San Joaquin, on Stockton; the upper branches on Monterey; Sacramento City and Stockton, by steamboats, will receive their supplies from Benicia and the town of San Francisco.

Monterey may be considered at the present time the most pleasant place for a *residence* in California. The growth and prosperity of the town is slow, and there is but little business doing in it. The new emigration have not taken the prospects of the place in hand. By land it is nearer the placer than San Francisco. In Monterey the same wearing apparel and bed-clothes are worn throughout the year. The Americans and English only use chimneys within their houses for comfort; the natives have no desire for them.

The Pueblo of San Jose, between Monterey and Benicia, and fifty miles from San Francisco, is situated in one of the most pleasant and healthy valleys in California. It is well watered, and for twenty miles north and south there is a perfect carriage road, with barely a mound of earth to lift a wheel. Its advantages for gardens, fruits, and grains are of the highest order. It only waits those who are soon to be its owners, and it will flourish in all its destined beauty and luxuriance. From Monterey to San Diego, every twenty to thirty miles there are large broken down missions, each so pleasantly located that they will entice people to settle near them.

The port of San Luis Obispo is half way from Monterey to Santa Barbara. It is an unsafe port in winter, and has an extensive farming country around it, but is not very well watered.

Santa Barbara is a small town, pleasantly located, surrounded by mountains, but affords little inducements to the present settler.

San Pedro is the port of the Pueblo of the Angels, twenty-seven miles distant. This Pueblo is one of the better cities of California, equal to the upper Pueblo, and far preferable to it for grapes and wines. It is perhaps equal for vintage to any part of the world. The present stirring times and people have not yet reached this valley; land has, therefore, risen but little in value here. The rich placers urge every new comer to the north; but time will soon send thousands to this Pueblo, to Santa Barbara, and to Monterey. The heat and unhealthy climate of the San Joaquin valley and of part of the Sacramento, with the cold there prevalent in winter, must check the future settlement of those valleys.

The following are the prices of grain, vegetables, animals, &c., in California, July, 1846, and July, 1849:

	July, 1846.	July, 1849.
Horses,	$20 to 50	$70 to 300
Mules,	15 to 40	50 to 200
Steers, 4 years old,	6 to 8	10 to 20
Yoke of oxen,	15 to 30	50 to 150
Hogs,	5 to 20	10 to 30
Cow and calf,	7 to 12	13 to 30
Wild mares,	2 to 4	5 to 20
Sheep,	1½ to 2	2 to 4
Fanned wheat, 2 bushels,	2 to 4	3 to 5
Do. corn,	1¼ to 3	4 to 6
Barley,	1½ to 2	5 to 10
Beans,	3 to 4	5 to 7
Flour, per 100 lbs.	6 to 8	variable.
Bullocks' hides,	$2 each	75c to 1
Tallow, per 100 lbs.	6	4 to 5
Labourers, per month,	15 to 30	60 to 100
Mechanics, do.	25 to 60	100 to 260
Seamen, do.	12 to 20	75 to 125
	October and November, 1848.	July, 1849.
Flour, per barrel,	26	6 to 8
Salt pork, do.	60 to 80	20 to 30
Brown sugar,	25c.	8 to 10c
Coffee,	12 to 14c	8 to 10c
Lumber, per 100 feet,	$100	$300
Prints, piece of,	$8 to 10	$3 to 4
White and brown sheeting,	7 to 9	2 to 3

Prices are at a much higher rate at the placers.

Country lands, including those for planting and grazing, are selling at from 50 cents to $3 per acre. Many a square mile (of 640 acres,) in the Sonoma and Napa valleys have been sold at 500 to $2,000. They are steadily on the rise in value. The old padres had each an orchard, which are now destroyed, and I know of but few instances of individuals who possess them.

The placer of the Sacramento embraces almost the whole of the branches of the river on the east side. The most remarkable now worked is the upper part of the river known as Reading rancho, and on Feather river, above Larkin rancho, and Yerba, Bear, and Dry creek. Feather and Yerba are the richest. There are three branches of the American river which join the Sacramento near Sutter's Fort, which have produced much gold. In the vicinity of the American there are many rich placers; in the ravines and valleys on each branch of the San Joaquin, gold has been found. These rivers irrigate slightly a large country of some three hundred to four hundred miles in length and breadth. Almost every spot that has been dug into has produced the precious metal in a greater or less quantity, and all over twenty carats fine. The only well known quicksilver mine is ten miles from the Pueblo of San Jose, on the rancho of the Berezera family and Grove Cook's. The land which is now worked was, in January, 1846, taken from the owners by the Mexican law of denouncement, namely: A person gives information to the nearest alcalde that on such a place there is a valuable mine, and the informer files a memorial and deposites a piece of the ore. He has then some thirty days to excavate and to dig at least thirty feet deep in the mine. By the expiration of ninety days he must have performed certain conditions, and by survey, and the personal attendance at the land of the alcalde, obtain judicial possession. If this is all done within a certain limited time, he then as owner holds the right to work the mine. Should the denouncer quit the work a certain number of months, he is liable to lose his right. In the winter of 1845–6, two California labourers offered to show Don Andres Castanoras, of Mexico, a silver mine; and on his examining it, he pronounced it at once cinnabar. He proceeded immediately to denounce the spot, laid his plan off in twenty-four parts or shares—gave away twelve, and retained twelve. He then returned to Mexico. There he rented the mine for sixteen years to Alexander Forbes, Esq., of Tepic, who has purchased many of the shares, some at $1,000 each, and is now working the mine, but not extensively. Mr. Forbes was a wealthy man, of no family, and seventy years of age. His cares, great wealth, and the responsibility of his quicksilver mine, give him much trouble. On Mr. Cook's land there are other locations containing rich deposites of cinnabar, that will produce a heavy per cent. of quicksilver. A pinch of pounded quicksilver ore dropped on a red hot iron will produce a vapour; by covering it with a tea-cup, the inside of the cup will be coated with a smoky substance, similar to that produced by the burning of a lamp. By rubbing this carefully over the inside of the cup with the finger, several globules of quicksilver will be brought into existence. There is, without a doubt, silver and lead in California in some quantities. I have seen a little of each. Coal is known to exist, but I am inclined to think is not of much account in quantity or quality.

I am of the opinion that the production of gold in the California placers will this year exceed that of 1848. The individual gains will not be so large, nor will so much be obtained in proportion to the number of people employed. Americans who had been some time on the Sacramento had every influence over the wild Indians, and each man to this day has from ten to thirty Indians at work on the upper streams. They protect, feed, clothe, and attend to the wants of these Indians.

On the lower rivers the whites and Indians are destroying each other. It is said that the emigrants from Oregon commenced this bad business, and the loss will be severe. Less gold will be produced, and, through the disturbance, the sale of much clothing, &c., to the Indians on the rivers will be prevented.

The whites, who are now or may be industriously employed this year in digging and washing the golden sands, will obtain from one to three ounces of gold per day; next year less, from the large number of labourers, and from the ground being so much worked over. Some who arrive here will never go far from the first port they land at, and many will return to the settlements after only two or three weeks passed in digging. The majority of these, if they seek for it, can obtain lucrative employment all over California as merchants, mechanics, clerks, storekeepers, farmers, hotel and innkeepers, &c, in towns and on the public roads, keeping coaches and stages, stables and boarding-houses, running launches and wagons, cutting firewood for housekeepers, ships and steamboats, and not be liable to summer sickness in the placer.

Timber is plenty, and much of it is softer than the white pine of Maine. Tools are very cheap. Live cattle for meat and for working are not high. One-inch boards bring $150 per M feet at the pit. This must, even this year, offer inducements for many labourers. Merchandise is very rapidly falling in value. Prior to the exchange of flags (July 7, 1846,) in Monterey, the maritime duties had averaged $85,000 a year, paid into the Mexican customs of Monterey. In April, 1849, the amount received by the American collectors for one month was over one hundred thousand dollars. The foreign goods received into the territory were chiefly from Boston; a proportion from Mazatlan, Valparaiso, and Oahu. The prices were almost stationary year after year. In 1846 and 1847, goods fell in value. In June, 1848, commerce began to feel the effects of the discovery of the placer, while from June to October, 1848, lands fell in price, foreign merchandise sold at unheard-of prices, and continued high until May, 1849. Country lands have now risen in value, and town lots advanced thousands per cent., and this day are yet advancing, while merchandise is now suffering a rapid decline in prices. Bricks, ready-made frame houses, and lumber yet command the highest prices. The shippers of merchandise in our Atlantic States since January, 1849, while they saw one-tenth of their vessels chartered or purchased for California, and twenty millions of dollars invested in those vessels and their cargoes, were convinced that this department was to receive from 100,000 to 200,000 emigrants this year. These estimates were the minimum and maximum. At the same time they became participators in the supplies for two or three millions of people. They were far better judges of the number of emigrants, and the supplies sufficient, than residents of California could be. The excitement has gone throughout Great Britain, and is now agitating other parts of Europe. What is the result of all this? Large fleets of merchant vessels are laid up in the bays and rivers of San Francisco for want of seamen, and there is an immense sacrifice of mercantile property. There will not this year be sufficient warehouses to store the goods on the way for this country, nor can owners afford to pay the storage. Many of the owners will be present with their goods, depending on a prompt sale to satisfy their own wants, or to pay their debts. This itself will force the sale of much property, and without this the prospect for 1850 will not warrant owners or consignees to keep on hand goods for sale. A quantity will go to Oahu, San Blas, Mazatlan, Callao, and Valparaiso; some may even return to the Atlantic States. I do not believe that the goods landed here in September up to January (ensuing) from Europe will, in every instance, bring much more than sufficient to pay duties and other charges, leaving out any reference to first cost.

In this extraordinary position of affairs, the state of the emigrants is of primary importance, especially of that portion composed of women and children.

Many will arrive destitute, and death will do his work among them. Houses cannot be obtained for one-half of this vast increase of people, nor will all provide themselves with a tent or even bush shed. The cold will not incommode the new comers, except those who may go to the mountainous parts of the Sacramento and Joaquin. In January and February, however, the rain will fall. As a general thing the climate is advantageous to the coming thousands, and in the course of time, with the immense and peculiar prospects before us, a large proportion, after some individual cases of suffering, will settle themselves, and subsequently obtain a gradual improvement of their state and situation. The want of schools must be felt for some time to come, at least within the vicinity of the placers. Monterey, Pueblo de San Jose, San Francisco, and Benicia have each a good school, paying the preceptor $1,800 to $2,000 a year. These towns have also each a Protestant clergyman settled among them. The towns of Monterey, San Jose, Santa Barbara, and Pueblo de los Angelos have each Catholic churches, with Mexican padres, and are well attended. The whole territory of California has scarcely a public building, exclusive of the town of Monterey, which contains two that were built prior to 1846. This town has also a wharf, built in 1845, and some buildings and a fortification, erected under the command of Colonel Mason in 1847 and 1848, and a fine stone building for a school and court-house, and state convention, built under the alcaldeship of Walter Colton, Esq.

The prospects of California are flattering in the prospective, more so than of any other new State in our rapidly extending Union. The climate of most parts of it is mild and congenial, yet changeable. The Sacramento and San Joaquin are prolific of ague and fever of the worst forms, and rheumatic complaints on the coast are prevalent. The mornings are invariably the most pleasant on the sea coast, especially at Monterey and San Francisco —the nights throughout the country are cool. At Santa Barbara and the lower Pueblo there is experienced little or no fog. The town of San Diego, now without trade, is of little consequence; at that place the climate is the mildest and most salubrious in all Alta California.

The rivers throughout this territory are low most of the year, and can be passed. Rains in November increase until February—they then decrease until April. During the summer rain may fall once in the course of five or six years, but not sufficient to saturate the ground. In the months of December and January, rain is the most copious. From the drought in the summer months, vegetation becomes much parched. On some ranchos (farms) the grass fails for the cattle at the driest season. The farmers are always desirous that some rain should fall in April to moisten their land just previous to their planting beans, corn, and potatoes. A person not acquainted with the soil and climate of California, would doubt its capacity to produce any grain without summer showers; yet wheat produces abundantly. Gardens in towns require wells, excepting at the two Pueblos and Sonoma, where there are good streams of water, the country adjacent to which is best adapted to grazing. The Government have here horses and mules, kept up and fed on barley and wild oats, cut in May and June; individuals will also do the same. Oats and clover grow spontaneously over the country, and within the reach of every man. Formerly horses and bullocks were worked but a few days and then turned out to graze as many weeks, when these animals sold for ten to fifteen dollars each, and breeding mares from two to three dollars. This plan to a Californian presented its advantages. The American farmer will do more work and to more advantage with four or five horses and twenty or thirty cows and steers than the natives do this day with hundreds or thousands of stock.

Eggs are from $1 to $2 a dozen; hens $2 to $4 each; turkeys $4 to $8 a piece; butter $1 to $1.50 a pound; potatoes, by the pound, 6 to 8 cents; turnips and cabbages, etc. still higher—opening other advantages to farmers than raising cattle. But few or none have engaged in supplying towns with the fruits of gardens, orchards, and the rich products of the dairy. This will all be done at less prices, but at very remunerating ones, even when the golden sands of California have been turned over and over again—washed and re-washed, and its soil delved deep into for the precious metal until nearly valueless. For some years, however, the labours of the hard-working and frugal gold-digger will yield him fair compensation, if he can avoid the chills and fever of July, August, and September.

The whites have, in several instances, destroyed Indians in the placer, who, in their turn, have retaliated. This warfare will continue until the wild man and owner of the placer is exterminated. This may cause the people to have more tame Indian servants, as they will seek the towns where many get constant employ. The real cause of the shedding of blood is the too common enmity of the white man towards the aboriginals of our country; while too many, caring only to get a good share of the riches of the placer, as free laborers, look tamely on the atrocities they may see perpetrated. Before 1850 the two very distinct races will be separated into parties in the placer by the Spanish and English languages, being the vernacular of each, and they will very likely be brought into fierce and deadly conflict. Those of Spanish extraction far outnumber the Americans, though this will not be considered worth a thought by the latter. Numbers opposed to them in battle array or in commerce are not counted, and when brought into collision with Yankee ingenuity are subverted or overthrown. However, the Americans in this country will in a short period outnumber the foreigners; and from the present time Mexican and South American emigration hitherward must decrease, and by 1851 the emigrants from Europe will not outnumber our own countrymen.

In all this astonishing influx of people we have a practical illustration of the fact that the absence of good laws cannot stagnate commerce or crush the energies of the people. Each alcalde of the different jurisdictions has some form, mode, and practice of administering law. There are Mexican laws in print, in theory, but in practice little is known of them by the judges or justices—of course less by the people. Yet peace and good order is fairly sustained, and murder and robbery is not of hourly occurrence. Where there is no known code of law lawyers can have but little business. By the time there is business for them the present attorneys who are in this country will, by having other means of making a fortune, be able to live like the mass of the people.

General Riley, as Governor of California, has, in a proclamation, requested or recommended the people of California to meet in all their respective towns the first day of August next, to choose for each different district a judge, prefect, two sub-prefects, and an alcalde, and a certain number of delegates, to meet in Monterey in September, 1849, to organize and frame some laws and a constitution for the country, with the expectation of sending a Delegate to Congress, and asking admission into the Union as a State. The opinion of the old and new inhabitants of California will be divided, the former holding the belief that it properly comes under his lawful jurisdiction, and the latter that, on account of his holding one office, and that in a military capacity, he is no way constitutionally empowered to convene the inhabitants for the transaction of any civil affairs, much less in a business of such moment as is involved in the present exigency. In the sequel, however, I presume the majority of the people will acquiesce in his proclamation; and, if it is assented to by the people of California, will, by November, have fair prospects of possessing, laws, judges, and requisite legal officers, and a form of civil government. The citizens of Monterey have, by their unanimous vote, agreed to support the proclamation of Governor Riley and carry out its provisions, recommending others throughout California to do the same. The Pueblo of San Jose have passed the same resolution.*

* The Convention above alluded to has been held.

A passage round Cape Horn, from an Atlantic to a Pacific port, occupies from four to six months. The shortest trip on record is that of the "Grey Eagle," in one hundred and seventeen days to San Francisco; the "Col. Fremont" came in one hundred and twenty-seven days; one hundred and fifty is a fair calculation. This voyage is as safe and pleasant as those performed by sea and land; it occupies two, in some cases three, months more time. It has not the variety of a sea and land voyage, but a person has less risk of reaching his port of destination. The expense is $150 to $300, the passenger having to provide himself with bedding only. A trip via Chagres and Panama costs $250 to $600, the two steamers charging $175 and $200 to 400. The time occupied ought not to be more than forty days; in 1850 it will probably be less. At present but few reach here via Panama under sixty to seventy days from New York or New Orleans. Those who arrive here, as thousands have, in sail vessels from Panama, have been sixty to one hundred days in coming this distance. The passage to Vera Cruz is easy; and, if the Mexicans have mules and horses to sell at Vera Cruz, or in the vicinity, a traveller mounted may reach San Blas in twenty to forty days. At first he will be somewhat worn, perhaps nearly broken down, but in a week his spirits will be on the ascendant, and he will be able to pursue his way tolerably pleasantly. The travelling expenses on the road from Vera Cruz to San Blas or Mazatlan, will be about $1 50 to $2 50 per diem for man and mule. A laughing, happy, and contented traveller can get along with the Mexicans in his own way, and at his own prices—*if* he but please the people, they will please him. At present, and I think hereafter, the supply of vessels for passengers from San Blas and Mazatlan to California will correspond to the demand. The charge for passage $75 to $200; the time occupied twenty-five to forty-five days.

The overland route from the frontier of Missouri to the Sacramento valley is now so well known that a very correct estimate may be made of the time required, and the means necessary, to perform it with ease and safety. A family carrying with them only such things as are necessary for the road, may calculate on making it in four and a half months. About the 1st to the 10th of May is a suitable time for leaving the Missouri frontier, and this would bring them into California from the middle to the end of September. Light but strong wagons, with mules, especially in the present condition of the road, are the most reliable and convenient means of travelling. Grass is at its best during the season, which will be occupied by the journey, and the mules may always be kept picketed near the place of encampment, and consequently less risk will be incurred of their being stolen, and no time lost in hunting them up in the morning. The road being now well known the travelling may be regulated, and the animals never forced into extraordinary journeys, but make their average day's travel uniformly, and regularly have grass and water. The best way to travel is to start at sunrise and halt again, remaining at rest during the middle hours of the day, completing the day's march in the afternoon. This gives the animals abundant time to rest and eat, and in this way they will go through in good order.

House rooms in San Francisco, eight feet by ten to fifteen by twenty, are $30 to $500 per month each. Houses at present being over 100 per cent. on cost a year for rent. Board is $2 to $3 a day, without a room. There is a new hotel, containing sixty rooms, now finished in the town of San Francisco. The owner has spared neither time, trouble, nor funds in making this building of a superior order, in all its parts and branches. The passage in a launch from San Francisco or Benicia to Stockton, or Sacramento city, is $15 to $30, and it occupies two to three days. Thence travellers take a horse, mule, or wagon, or go on foot, as they may prefer, to the placer. Freight in the launches is $4 to $6 per barrel; thence to the placer in wagons $10 to $50 has to be paid.

Although there are many advantages in California over some of our other territories, and a wide field of enterprise for a new beginner, I would earnestly advise all those who are well situated at their places of nativity or adoption to remain as they are. To a young man, not yet in business, with little or uncertain prospects in our Atlantic or Middle States, I would say, try California; more especially if he is bold, active, restless, and ambitious, and not inclined to *dissipation.* Sickness he will be liable to here as elsewhere, even without exposure in the placers. *If he know one card or one wine from another where he was educated, raised, or brought up, in California he will soon know the whole pack, and become a perfect connoisseur of liquors.* This will alter for the better as society becomes established. For a farmer, mechanic, or merchant, with ordinary prospects in any other State, to break up for the purpose of coming out, with the view of bettering his condition in California, is, I think, if not utopian, at least hazardous. My several official letters up to 1849, which have been published throughout the United States, were written for the use of the different Departments in Washington, to which I was at the time attached, and not for publication. On reception by the chiefs of those Departments they were at their disposal. When despatched from California to Washington I had no expectation of their being published, and no one in this country could then have had any idea that our "placers" so soon, or even in any length of time, were to affect our whole Union and a part of Europe. In June and July, 1848, the American residents in California, especially the land owners, were apprehensive that the placers would prove an injury to them; the value of town lots, it was supposed, were more depreciated thereby than any thing else, but the contrary effect on real estate in town and country is now experienced, and in fact in every class of property, and in every line of business throughout the Territory. The busy hum of incessant activity, and the enterprise of an industrious, go ahead, Yankee population, now reverberates throughout the northern part of Alta California, and will soon extend from latitude 49 to 32 on the Pacific, and embrace the whole length and breadth of the country—of Oregon and California.

POPULATION OF CALIFORNIA.

From the Alta California of November 29.

In an article published in the Alta California of the 2d of July last, we stated the probable population of the country at that time at 30,000 souls. As the recent election has failed to bring out more than *one-quarter* of the legal voters in the country, and as the hopes which that contest held out of approximating to the number of inhabitants, have failed, we have thought it proper and necessary to give the following statistics. They are made up, in some instances, from actual records, in others from the best estimates we have been able to procure.

The population of California on the first day of January, 1849, may be set down as follows, viz.:

Californians, say	13,000
Americans,	6,000
Foreigners,	5,000
Total,	24,000

From that time down to the 11th of April, 1849, there were a great many arrivals by sea, and a few by land. If we set down the arrivals by sea in round numbers at 5,000, (of which one-half were Americans,) and the arrivals by land (principally from Sonora and Lower California) at 1,000, we shall then have the following result, viz.:

Californians,	.	.	.	.	.	.	13,000
Americans,	.	.	.	.	.	.	9,000
Foreigners,	.	.	.	.	.	.	9,000
Total,	.	.	.	.	.	.	31,000

From the 12th of April down to the present time, (November 28, 1819.) we are enabled to give, through the politeness of Edward A. King, Harbour Master, reliable statistics of the arrivals by sea. They are as follows:

Months.	American.	Foreign.	Male.	Female.	Total.
April,					
May, }	3,944	1,942	5,677	209	5,886
June,					
July, . . .	3,000	614	3,565	49	3,614
August, . .	3,384	509	3,806	87	3,893
September, .	4,271	1,531	5,680	122	5,802
October, . .	2,655	1,414	3,950	119	4,069
November, .	1,746	490	2,155	81	2,236
Total, . .	19,000	6,500	24,833	667	25,500

In the article before alluded to, which we published in July last, we stated the then probable population at 30,000. Subsequent experience, and travel through the country, has convinced us we were then in error. We were anxious at that time not to go beyond the mark in our estimate, but in the extremity of our care we undoubtedly fell far below it.

Admitting, then, that, on the 11th day of April last, there were 31,000 inhabitants in the country, as above stated, if we add thereto the 25,500 arrived by sea, as shown by the table above, we have a total of 56,500. To this must be added the sum of 6,000 Mexicans, who came into the country by land, and of which probably 2,000 still remain. Further than this, there have run away from the several vessels now in this port, at least 3,000 seamen; there have arrived at other ports in California 500 souls; and there have come into the country by the Santa Fe and southern route, at least 2,000. These figures give the following result as the present population of the country, derived from all sources except the emigration over the Rocky mountains.

Californians, .	.	.	.	.	.	13,000
Americans, .	.	.	.	.	.	32,500
Foreigners, .	.	.	.	.	.	18,500
Total,	.	.	.	.	. .	64,000

The number of the emigration by way of the "Plains," is variously estimated at from 30,000 to 40,000. Our own impression is, that it will not be found to vary much from 30,000. Adding that number to the figures above, and we have a total of 94,000 souls, as follows:

Americans, .	.	.	.	.	.	62,500
Californians,	.	.	.	.	.	13,000
Foreigners, .	.	.	.	.	.	18,500
Total,	.	.	.	.	.	94,000

There cannot be a doubt that the figures given above are below the mark; and we have no hesitation in saying, and we think the figures will bear us out in the assertion, that the population of California now exceeds *one hundred thousand.*

STATISTICS OF OREGON.

(*From letters of* ISRAEL MITCHELL *and* ACHILLES DE HARLEY.)

Each of the three great divisions of Oregon have their peculiarities. The east is almost a desert, destitute of timber, burnt by excessive droughts, and the soil is wholly of volcanic formation, lava, leached ashes, lime, &c. The Blue Mountains, however, have much good land and timber, and will some day no doubt be inhabited by a healthy and happy people. Middle Oregon is a good soil in general, and the best grazing country, I suppose, on earth. Though apparently not half so luxuriant as the prairies of the Mississippi valley, the grass is more nutritious, and in many places it is so thick as to form a mat, which, to a person walking through or over it, seems like walking over a bed; and there is one kind as salt as brine. Timber, however, is scarce; much of the country will lie waste, but it will pasture millions of stock; and even now many of the Indians count their horses by hundreds, if not by thousands.

The middle district is bounded on the west by the Cascade Mountains, which are covered with a timber of which you can have no idea. Pine, red, yellow, and white fir, hemlock, spruce, cedar, &c., rise in straight and uniform trunks from the height of one hundred to one hundred and fifty feet, in many instances, to the first limbs, and then tapering from one hundred to one hundred and fifty feet to a sharp point. At other places the limbs commence nearer the ground. The most remarkable undergrowth is the vine maple. It grows in bunches, each bunch containing five or ten shoots of the size of a man's thigh. They grow ten or fifteen feet high, then turn down, and grow into the ground again, branch out again, and so continue the process, rendering it impossible to pass through on horseback, and sometimes even on foot. I have literally crawled through them, and not been on the ground for hundreds of yards, and sometimes have not been able to see the ground, so thick is the undergrowth below, nor see any object thirty feet from me on any side. These cases are not common, though there are many places of miles in extent, in the neighbourhood of the most dense settlements we have, where the foot of the white man never trod. So you need not be surprised when I tell you that Western Oregon has never yet been to any great extent explored, most of the travel from place to place being by water.

The great valley of the Walamette (pronounced Wa-*lam*-ette, accenting the second syllable) is a most beautiful prairie. There is considerable timber, and what are here termed fern openings and oak openings. The fern openings are where the fire has killed the greater portion of the timber, and the fern has grown up to the detriment of all other herbs and grasses. The oak openings are covered with grass, as with you. There is very little waste land in West Oregon—even the mountain lands are a good soil, free of rock, and seldom very steep. Like all mountain countries there is much good water; mill sites abound. The quantity of sawing timber is immense. There are many places where, I verily believe, 1,000 logs may be cut from an acre that will average 500 feet to the log. Now, for a moment, cast your eye to our market. China, Australia, and all the islands of the Pacific, are almost destitute of timber, and rely alone on Oregon for supplies. Our facilities for manufacturing are unrivalled on earth. Our stock is raised and fatted with less labour than that of any other country. A state of health and energy unknown in the Mississippi valley is experienced by our inhabitants, and we might and should be a happy people; but the variety of tempting lucrative employments that present themselves, make it difficult what to choose or where to locate, and there is a continual change of business. There is a great want of capital, and little competition. Were I able to give you the number of our producers, our exports would exceed belief. I will state, however, that they exceed $500 for every able-bodied white male citizen in Oregon. I know of more than 15,000 barrels of flour having been shipped, 5,000,000 feet of lumber, 1,000 barrels of salmon, and a large quantity of butter, cheese, &c. The products of 1848 more than doubled that of any former year, and those of 1849 would no doubt have exceeded it had not the gold mania broke out and nearly depopulated the whole country. About three-fourths of the whole population of Oregon are gone to the mines. Some, however, have returned to cultivate their farms, most of whom intend to go back again. The quantity of coin and gold in the country has become so great that every thing is uncommonly high. A good labouring man gets $50 per month. Large farms are deserted, and even mills lay idle.

The following is the account given of the INDIAN TRIBES in Oregon.

1st. The *Makaw*, or Cape Flattery Indians, are warlike, occupying the country about Cape Flattery and the coast for some distance to the southward, and eastward to the boundary of the Halaam, or Noostlalum lands. They number about 1,000 souls. They live by fishing, hunting, and the cultivation of the potato.

2d. The *Noostlalums* consist of eleven tribes or septs, living about the entrance of Hood's canal, Dungeness, Port Discovery, and the coast to the westward. They are warlike, and their relations with the white inhabitants of Oregon and with the Hudson's Bay Company are doubtful. They live by fishing, hunting, and the cultivation of the potato. Their numbers are: males, 517; females, 461; children under ten years, 467; slaves, 40; total, 1,485.

3d. The *Soquamish* are a warlike tribe of Indians, whose relations with the whites and with the Hudson's Bay Company are friendly. They occupy the country about Port Orchard and neighbourhood, and the west side of Whidby's Island. Males, 150; females, 95; children under 12 years, 210; slaves, 64; total, 519. They live by labour.

4th. The *Homamish, Hotlimamish, Squahsinawmish, Sayhaywamish,* and *Stitchassamish,* are peaceable tribes, numbering about 500, who subsist by fishing and labour. They reside in the country from the Narrows along the western shore of Puget's Sound to New Market.

5th. The *Tuanoh* and *Skokomish* tribes reside along the shores of Hood's canal. They number about 200, are peaceable, and subsist by fishing and labour.

6th. The *Squallyamish* and *Pugallipamish* are situated in the country about Nesqually, Pugallippi, and Sinuomish rivers. Males, 200; females, 220; children under 12 years, 190; slaves, 40; total, 550. They are peaceable and friendly, and live by labour and fishing.

7th. The *Sinahemish* is a peaceable and friendly tribe, subsisting by labour, fishing, and hunting. They live on the Sinahemish river (falling into Possession Sound) and the southern extremity of Whidby's Island. Males, 95; females, 98; children under 12 years, 110; slaves, 30; total, 333.

8th. The *Snoqualimich* are a warlike tribe, part of whom are hostile to the whites. They occupy the country along the Snoqualimich river and the south branch of the Sinahemish river. They subsist by fishing and hunting. Males, 110; females, 140; children under 12 years 90; slaves, 8; total, 348.

9th. The *Skeysehamish* occupy the country along the Skeysehamish river and the north branch of the Sinahemish. They number about 450; are peaceable and friendly, and subsist by fishing and hunting.

10th. The *Skadjets* are a peaceable and friendly tribe, living by farming, fishing, and hunting. They reside in the country on both sides of the Skadjet river, and on the north end of Whidby's Island. Males, 160; females, 160; children under 12 years of age, 180; slaves, 10; total, 506.

11. The *Nooklummis* live around Bellingham's bay. They are a warlike people, subsisting by farming, fishing, and hunting; and their relations with the white inhabitants of Oregon and with the Hudson's Bay Company are doubtful. Males, 60; females, 50; children under 12 years, 90; slaves, 22; total, 222.

12. The *Staktomish* inhabit the country between Nisqually and Cowlitz and the head waters of Chehaylis river. Males, 50; females, 56; children under 12 years of age, 80; slaves, 18; total, 204. This tribe is peaceable and friendly, and subsist upon roots and fish.

THE ISLAND OF CUBA.

(The following interesting statistical account is taken from sources entitled to credit.)

This island is now a great object of interest, not only to the American people, but to all the world. Half a century ago, the Chevalier de Marbois foretold that Cuba could never remain a colony, being worth more intrinsically than many a European kingdom. The development of the resources of that island, in spite of a bad administration of execrable laws, has sufficed to call attention to the system existing in the "Queen of the Antilles."

From a work on Cuba—that of Turnbull, usually considered the most authentic and the most reliable authority—we are induced to make the following digest of the principles which appear to actuate the government of the island. The vast extent of Cuba, the largest island of the western hemisphere, has made it necessary to divide it into civil, judicial, military, and ecclesiastical jurisdictions. The civil jurisdiction is divided into two provinces, with separate governors, altogether independent of each other in theory. The eastern extremity of the island is under the charge of a governor of Santiago de Cuba, while the western is under the control of a captain general de San Cristobal de la Habana. In civil functions these two officers are altogether distinct and independent, though in military affairs the first has an *ex officio* command. It has sometimes happened that the *gefe* of the eastern end has had no rank, the troops being commanded by an officer purely military. The captain general must, however, whatever may be the army rank of the first officer of the forces, be second only to the orders of the Spanish crown. At Matanzas, Trinidad, Puerto Principe, and Cienfuegos, are also officers, with the title of *gobernador*, or GOVERNOR, the duty of whom, however, is merely judicial. Subordinate to these are the *capitanes a guerra*, relics of the old contests with the aboriginal inhabitants. The captain general is the supreme military authority of the whole island, and chief of the *real audiencia*, the seat of which is the city of Havana. In every city of the island there are also perpetual courts, known as *ayuntamientos perpetuos*, and in the rural districts *jueces pedaneos*, appointed by the local governors. The latter are rather commissaries of police than judges, being charged with a general surveillance of the law and order of their districts.

The ayuntamiento of Havana once consisted of four corregidors. This number was afterwards increased by two, and ultimately to eight, a commissioner promoting the crusades and another officer having been added. The commissioner residing in Spain, in 1834 and 1835, eclipsed the magnificence of the representatives of first-rate powers, and his *deputado* in Havana left all the Cuban noblesse far behind him. Ultimately Havana became a city, and the corregidors were raised to twelve, one of whom was the alferez, real or royal standard bearer; a second the chief alguacil: the third an officer of the *Santa Hermandad*, so celebrated by Gil Blas; a fourth the public administrator; a fifth holds an untranslatable office as *Receptor de Penas de Camara;* and a sixth is the keeper of the archives, treasures, &c. Several of the corregidors hold their office by hereditary right, among whom is the *Padre de Menores,* who, however, has no deliberative voice.

At present, therefore, the ayuntamiento of the Havana consists of twelve *Corregidores;* two *Alcaldes ordinarios,* elected annually; two *Alcaldes de la Santa Hermandad,* also elected annually; one *Mayor provincial;* one *Alferez Real;* one *Alguacil Mayor;* one *Sindico procurador del comun,* named by the corporation to serve for a year, beginning and ending at the same dates with the term of service of the Alcaldes. In former times these officers were chosen by the inhabitants at large; but latterly the system has degenerated into a sort of self-election by the permanent members of the ayuntamiento. Besides these there are a *Mayor domo de proprios,* an *Escribano,* and other subordinate functionaries.

At the meetings of this body the captain general presides; in his absence one of the three *Tenientes Letrados,* or subaltern chiefs, and in their absence, also, one of the *Alcaldes ordinarios.* On the admission of the members of the corporation, they are bound to take the same oath which is administered to the Spanish military orders of Santiago, Alcantara, and Calatrava, which is, to defend the purity of the Conception of the Holy Virgin.

The secular tribunals of Havana are, that of the captain general, assisted by the auditor de guerra in military affairs, and in civil matters the *Asesores generales.* The *Alcaldes generales* have also cognizance of civil and military disputes, and even the *ayuntamiento* has original jurisdiction in cases where the *res in lite* is less than $300 in value. In such cases this body proceeds on instruction from its own subordinates, the *Tenientes Letrados* and *Alcaldes ordinarios.*

There is also a commercial tribunal, consisting of a *prior, consuls,* a *consultor,* and an *escribano,* whose jurisdiction extends only to mercantile affairs; but before any one can address himself to this tribunal, he must first go before the *Juez Avenidor,* whose duty is like that of the *Judge de Paix* in France, to endeavour to conciliate the parties and prevent litigation.

The name Cuba is an aboriginal one, and was in use when Columbus discovered the Island in 1492. Cuba is the most westerly of the group of Islands known as the Antilles, and not only the largest in the Carribean Sea, but larger than all the other West India Islands together. Its greatest length, following the curves, is 800 miles; its breadth is very irregular, varying from 135 to 25 miles; and it is estimated that there are, on its coast, at least fifty ports and anchorages, safe and easy of access. Of these, the harbor of Havana is the finest in the world. The entrance is very narrow, but opens into a magnificent bay, capable of accommodating a thousand ships of the largest class, and there is at all times such depth of water, that vessels of the largest tonnage come up to the quay.

The island is traversed through its whole length by a range of mountains, some of which attain the elevation of 8,500 feet; and the interior is well watered by numerous fresh and rapid streams, which take their rise in the mountains. These streams abound in fine fish, and formerly brought down in their beds no inconsiderable quantity of gold dust. The shores are low and flat, and this peculiarity is presented, that along the line of coast, there are innumerable lagoons, which, during the spring tides, are filled with sea water, from which are collected large quantities of salt, for the consumption of the inhabitants.

The climate of Cuba is dry and warm; the seasons are divided into *rainy* and *dry;* and the warmest months are July and August, when the mean temperature is from 80 deg. to 82 deg. The general range of the thermometer in summer on the lowlands is 90 deg. to 95 deg. Fahrenheit; the coldest months are January and December, when the cold is represented to be 10 deg. less than under the equator. There is an alternation of land and sea breezes, which, in the dry season, render the weather cool and agreeable. The coast is considered unhealthy, the interior the reverse. Travellers speak in the highest terms of the interior of Cuba, and depict in glowing language, the beauty of the scenery, the verdure of the foliage and herbage, and the soft and balmy character of the atmosphere. The elevated position of the interior, its salubrious air, and perpetually genial climate, attract valetudinarians from all parts of the world.

The area of Cuba has been estimated at 37,000 square miles. The population is estimated at 1,400,000; of which, 610,000 are whites, 190,000 are free coloured, and 600,000 slaves. The imports in 1847 were $32,389,119, of which $7,049,976 were from the United States. The exports during the same period were $27,998,770, of which $12,394,877 were to the United States. In 1848, the number of arrivals at its ports was 3,740, and the number of clearances 3,446. The amount of American tonnage employed in the trade with Cuba is 479,673 tons.

Cuba has 195 miles of railroad completed and in successful operation, and 61 miles in the course of construction. About two-fifths of its surface are cultivated. Of the remaining three-fifths, now unused, one is probably worthless, leaving one-half of its agricultural resources undeveloped. The climate is so genial that it yields two crops a year of its productions. It also abounds in materials for manufacturing purposes, and its mountains contain mines of copper which are worked to considerable advantage.

At one time the island of Cuba yielded to the Spanish crown a net revenue of four millions of dollars. At present, perhaps, it is not so lucrative a possession. The trade from Cuba to the Baltic is very great, and most of it is carried on in American bottoms.

COMMERCE OF ASIA.

The trade of Europe and America with Asia is already immense, and must, by the laws of human intercourse, increase at a very rapid rate. We propose to exhibit some of the particulars of the trade with Asia.

The following table comprehends the ships, tonnage, and men, employed by Europe and the United States in the import trade with the Pacific:

	Ships.	Tonnage.	Men.
England,	877	329,404	16,698
United States,	329	111,180	6,998
France,	117	36,040	2,048
Antwerp,	7	2,860	125
Bremen,	6	1,800	100
Hamburg,	10	5,000	200
Netherlands,	188	97,231	5,150
Russia,	50	25,000	1,000
Totals,	1,584	608,515	32,319

The outward bound or export trade is about the same. We see at once that this is already a very great commerce. The British trade is mainly to the East India company's possessions—to Mauritius, to New Holland, and to China. The United States' trade is in the South Seas and to China. The Dutch trade is chiefly with the islands of Java and Sumatra. Let us now proceed to *value*, and see if we can approximate the value of the Asiatic trade by sea.

The following are the *imports* into Great Britain from beyond the Cape of Good Hope, taken several years since:

Imports from the East Indies, ...	$47,553,000
From Mauritius, Java, Sumatra, New Holland, &c., . .	24,933,000
From China, ...	13,040,775
Aggregate imports, ...	85,526,775
Exports, ...	59,187,000
Imports into France, ...	16,300,000
Exports, ...	8,238,000
Imports into the Netherlands, ...	23,527,390
Exports, ...	4,702,130
Imports into the United States, ...	11,438,400
Exports, ...	5,433,800

We find, then, the following aggregate of imports and exports with the Asiatic ports yearly:

Imports, ...	$136,892,565
Exports, ...	77,560,705
Aggregate, ...	214,453,270

Here we have a commerce with Asia, on the part of Great Britain, the United States, France, and the Netherlands, amounting several years since to more than two hundred millions of dollars per annum! We have no doubt that it has since greatly increased in consequence of the opening of the China trade.

The British trade with Canton alone amounted, in the year 1838, to *twenty-four millions* of dollars. The capital invested in ships alone for the Asiatic trade by the British amounts to more than *thirty millions* of dollars!

The facts we have given constitute a mere rough outline of the present trade, and a glance at what it may become. Commerce and human intercourse are the great civilizers, humanizers, and equalizers of the human race. A railroad across the American continent would do more to increase civilization and freedom than all that government can do. The steam chariots, crossing the North American Andes, will carry with them light, knowledge, and Christianity. The Asiatic will become accustomed to them, and far over the plains of Tartary the banner of the cross will speed with victorious flight.—*Cincinnati Chronicle.*

REPORT FROM THE ADJUTANT GENERAL OF THE ARMY TO THE SECRETARY OF WAR.

WAR DEPARTMENT, ADJUTANT GENERAL'S OFFICE,
Washington, Nov. 30, 1849.

SIR: Pursuant to your instructions of September 5th, I respectfully submit the following annual report, together with the usual returns of the army, viz.:

1. Organization of the army of the United States as established by law,   A.
2. General return of the army, - - - - - - -   B.
3. Position and distribution of the troops in the eastern division,   -   C.
4. Position and distribution of the troops in the western division,   -   D.
5. Position and distribution of the troops in the Pacific division,   -   E.
6. Return of the troops employed in suppressing Indian hostilities in Florida,   F.
7. Exhibit of the number of recruits enlisted from October 1, 1848, to September 30, 1849, - - - - - - - -   G.

I. The authorized military establishment consists of 870 commissioned officers, and 8,940 non-commissioned officers, musicians, artificers, and privates, and is constituted as follows:

Designation of regiments and corps.	Commissioned officers.	Non-commissioned officers, musicians, artificers & priv's.	Aggregate
General officers,	3		3
General staff. { Adjutant General's department,	14		14
Inspector General's department,	2		2
Judge Advocate of the army,	1		1
Quartermaster's department,	43		43
Commissary General's department,	8		8
Medical department,	95		95
Pay department,	28		28
Corps of engineers,	43		43
Corps of topographical engineers,	36		36
Ordnance department,	37		37
Military storekeepers,			17
Two regiments of dragoons,	70	1,230	1,300
One regiment of mounted riflemen,	35	765	800
Four regiments of artillery,	208	2,600	2,808
Eight regiments of infantry,	272	4,192	4,464
One company of engineer soldiers, (sappers, miners, and pontoniers,)		100	100
Ordnance sergeants,		53	53
Aggregate of the authorized military establishment,	*895	8,940	9,852

It will be seen that the authorized force, (troops of the line,) consists of 2,100 cavalry, officers and men; 2,808 artillery, of which eight companies are organized as light artillery, and 4,464 infantry—making, in the aggregate, 9,372.

The latest returns show 9,003 men in service, including recruits and men unassigned, being 216 more than authorized; but returns from distant regiments not being later than July and August, it is estimated that there is a *deficiency* of 500. The reported strength of all the regiments is 7,974, or 813 less than the establishment.

The number of enlisted men of the ordnance department in service, according to the last returns, is 535. The number is not restricted by law.

II. The number of major generals having been reduced, as contemplated by the act of July 19, 1848, to one, Major General Scott, general-in-chief, in accordance with the President's instructions, resumed command of the army on the 11th of May, 1849, and established his head-quarters at the city of New York.

The number of brigadier generals having, in like manner, been reduced to two, Brigadier Generals Wool and Twiggs (major generals by brevet) have been assigned to the command respectively of the eastern and western geographical divisions.

---

* The actual number of commissioned officers is 870;—25 hold commissions both in the staff and line, are counted twice, and should be deducted from the number 895, obtained by adding the full number allowed to each regiment and corps. This number (895) does not include the military storekeepers, (17,) but these are accounted for in the column of "aggregate."

THE TREASURY ESTIMATES.

ESTIMATES OF APPROPRIATIONS.

In pursuance of the joint resolution of January 7th, 1846, which makes it the duty of the secretary of the treasury to cause the estimates of appropriations, which he is by law required to prepare and submit to Congress, to be printed, and copies of the same to be delivered to the clerk of the house of representatives in time for distribution at the commencement of each session, estimates of additional appropriations required for the service of the fiscal year ending June 30, 1850, and for the fiscal year ending June 30, 1851, were placed on the tables of the members of the house. From this volume we extract the summary of the additional appropriations required for 1850 and the summary of the appropriations asked for 1851.—*Washington Republic.*

TREASURY DEPARTMENT, }
November 16, 1849. }

SIR: Agreeably to the joint resolution of Congress of the 7th January, 1846, I have the honour to transmit, for the information of the house of representatives, printed estimates of additional appropriations proposed to be made for the service of the fiscal year ending the 30th June, 1850, amounting to $1,696,851 47

All of which is on account of the civil list, foreign intercourse, and
  miscellaneous, including expenses of collecting revenue from
  customs and lands, from 1st January to 30th June, 1850.

To the estimates is added a statement showing—

The indefinite appropriations for the service of the last three quarters of the fiscal year ending the 30th June, 1850, made by former
  acts of Congress, of a permanent character, amounting to .   4,539,458 81

Viz.:

Civil list, foreign intercourse, and miscellaneous,	$584,580 41
Pensions,	255,000 00
Interest, &c., public debt, and treasury notes, .	3,700,878 40

                                       $6,236,310 28

I am sir, very respectfully, your obedient servant,

W. M. MEREDITH,
Secretary of the Treasury.

Hon. Speaker of the House of Representatives.

—

TREASURY DEPARTMENT, }
November 16, 1849. }

SIR: Agreeably to the joint resolution of Congress of the 7th January, 1846, I have the honour to transmit, for the information of the house of representatives, printed estimates of the appropriations proposed to be made for the fiscal year ending June 30, 1851, amounting to   . $33,697,159 15

Civil list, foreign intercourse, and miscellaneous, in-cluding payment to be made to Mexico under the 12th article of the treaty, expenses of collecting the revenue from customs and lands, census of 1850, public buildings, and expenses of courts,	$12,812,480 29
Army proper, &c.,	5,866,127 00
Military academy,	199,298 47
Fortifications, ordnance, &c.,	1,647,446 00
Internal improvements, surveys, and light-houses,	1,164,080 00
Indian department,	998,739 17
Pensions,	1,433,893 00
Naval establishment,	9,575,078 00

To the estimates are added statements showing—

1. The appropriations for the fiscal year, ending the 30th June, 1851, made by former acts of Congress, of a permanent character, amounting to . . 5,648,410 24

Viz.:

Civil list, foreign intercourse, and miscellaneous,	724,560 14
Arming and equipping the militia, . .	200,000 00
Civilization of Indians, ...	10,000 00
Pensions,	473,000 00
Interest on public debt, ...	3,742,951 13
Purchase of stock of the loan of 1847, . .	492.898 97

2. The existing appropriations which will be required to be expended in the fiscal year ending the 30th June, 1851, amounting to . . 5,656,530 34

Viz.:

Civil list, foreign intercourse, and miscellaneous,	472,519 21
Army proper, &c., ...	2,230,747 97
Fortifications, ordnance, &c., . .	168,000 00
Internal improvements, surveys, &c., . .	83,123 38
Indian department, ...	903,971 36
Pensions, ...	20,117 00
Naval establishment, ...	1,778,051 42

44,997,092 72

3. There is also to be added to the estimates a statement of the several appropriations, which will be carried to the surplus fund, amounting to $502,170 02

Accompanying the estimates are sundry papers furnished by the treasury, war, navy, and interior departments, containing references to acts of Congress, &c., on which the estimates are founded.

I am, very respectfully, your obedient servant,

W. M. MEREDITH,
Secretary of the Treasury.

Hon. Speaker of the House of Representatives.

TREASURER'S STATEMENT.

Showing the amount at his credit in the Treasury, with Assistant Treasurers and designated depositaries, and in the mint and branches, by returns received to Monday, the 24th December, 1849; the amount for which drafts have been issued, but were then unpaid, and the amount then remaining subject to draft; showing also the amount of future transfers to and from depositaries, as ordered by the Secretary of the Treasury.

In what place.	Amount on deposite.	Drafts heretofore drawn, but not yet paid, though payable.	Amount subject to draft.
Treasury U. S., Washington, D. C., - -	$260,286 85	37,124 50	223,162 35
Assistant Treasurer, Boston, Massachusetts, -	1,215,218 05	167,719 97	1,047,498 08
Assistant Treasurer, New York, New York, -	3,380,104 74	1,220,808 38	2,159,296 36
Assistant Treasurer, Philadelphia, Pa., - -	891,188 45	29,802 11	861,386 34

In what place.	Amount on deposite.	Drafts heretofore drawn, but not yet paid, though payable.	Amount subject to draft.
Assistant Treasurer, Charleston, S. C.,	134,461 48	39,742 51	94,718 97
Do. New Orleans, La.,	390,902 95	322,463 28	68,439 67
Do. St. Louis, Missouri,	281,621 35	87,303 58	194,317 77
Depositary at Buffalo, N. Y.,	13,429 94	466 22	12,963 72
Do. Baltimore, Md.,	19,319 82	5,905 73	13,414 09
Do. Richmond, Va.,	9,777 89	1,890 67	7,887 22
Do. Norfolk, Va.,	7,378 63	5,236 00	2,142 63
Do. Wilmington, N. C.,	3,655 70	2,631 50	1,024 20
Do. Savannah, Ga.,	34,041 51	15,956 30	18,085 21
Do. Mobile, Alabama,	49,145 29	26,582 80	22,562 49
Do. Nashville, Tenn.,	14,631 77	10,858 52	3,773 96
Do. Cincinnati, O.,	82,425 28	3,583 02	78,842 26
Do. Pittsburg, Pa.,	456 77	318 07	138 70
Do. Cincinnati, O., (late)	3,301 37	32 00	3,269 37
Do. Little Rock, A., Bert.	12,703 94	360 00	12,343 94
Do. Jeffersonville, Ia.,	78,720 11	26,702 22	52,017 89
Do. Chicago, Illinois,	8,169 41	1,926 26	6,243 15
Do. Detroit, Mich.,	24,864 14	11,242 44	13,621 70
Do. Little Rock, Lincoln,	18,717 56	6,174 15	12,543 41
Do. Little Rock, Wilson,	4,101 14	42 93	4,058 91
Suspense account, $2,064 41		2,064 41	
Mint of the United States, Philadelphia, Penna., -	841,150 00		841,150 00
Branch mint of the U. States, Charlotte, N. C., -	32,000 00		32,000 00
Do. Dahlonega, Ga.,	26,850 00		26,850 00
Do. New Orleans, La.,	100,000 00		100,000 00
	2,064 41 7,938,624 84	2,026,937 57	5,913,751 68
Deduct suspense account, -		-	2,064 41
Net amount subject to draft, -		-	$5,911,687 27

Treasurer's Office, Dec. 28, 1849. ●

UNITED STATES MINT.*

Statement showing the deposites of California gold at the mints:

Year.	MINTS.		
	Philadelphia.	New Orleans.	Total.
1848, . . .	$44,177		$44,177
1849, . . .	5,481,439	666,080	6,147,519
Total, . . .	$5,525,616	$666,080	$6,191,696

* We are indebted to Dr. R. M. Patterson, for these statements of the deposites and coinage at the mint and branches in the year 1849:

Statement of deposits of Gold and Silver in the mints, exclusive of California gold, for 1849.

	MINTS.				
	Charlotte, N.C.	Dahlonega.Ga.	New Orleans.	Philadelphia.	Total.
GOLD.					
U.S. coins, old stand'd.			3,902	37,318	41,220
Foreign coins, . .			437,130	4,483,091	4,920,221
U. S. Bullion, . .	390,732	252,974	677,985	5,767,092	7,088,783
Foreign Bullion, .			6,728	186,223	192,951
Total gold, . .	390,732	252,974	1,125,745	10,473,724	12,243,175
SILVER.					
Foreign coins, . .			1,242,552	873,448	2,116,000
Foreign bullion, .			78,477	132,699	211,176
U. States Bullion, including silver parted from gold, . .				39,112	39,112
Total silver, :			1,321,029	1,045,259	2,366,288
Total deposites, .	$390,732	$252,974	$2,446,774	$11,518,983	$14,609,463

COINAGE.

	MINTS.				
	Charlotte, N. C.	Dahlonega, Ga	N. Orleans	Philadelphia.	Total.
GOLD.					
Eagles, pieces,			23,900	653,618	677,518
Half eagles, "	64,823	39,036		133,070	236,929
Quarter eagles,	10,220	20,945		23,294	44,459
Dollars, . .	11,634	21,588	215,000	688,567	936,769
Value of gold,	361,299	244,130$\frac{50}{100}$	454,000	7,948,332	9,007,761$\frac{50}{100}$
SILVER.					
Dollars, pieces,				62,600	62,600
Half dollars, "			2,310,000	1,252,000	3,562,000
Quarter dollars,				340,000	340,000
Dimes, "			300,000	839,000	1,139,000
Half dimes, "			140,000	1,309,000	1,449,000
Value of silver,			1,192,000	922,950	2,114,950
COPPER.					
Cents, pieces,				4,178,500	4,178,500
Half cents, "				39,864	39,864
Value of copper,				41,984$\frac{32}{100}$	41,984$\frac{32}{100}$
Total coinage in pieces, . .	86,677	71,569	2,988,900	9,519,513	12,666,659
Total coinage in value, . .	$361,299	$244,130$\frac{50}{100}$	$1,646,000	$8,913,266$\frac{32}{100}$	$11,164,695$\frac{82}{100}$

Statement of the coinage at the mint and branches to the close of the year 1849 :

MINTS.	Operations commen'd.	GOLD.		SILVER.	
		Pieces.	Value.	Pieces.	Value.
Philadelphia, . .	1793	11,725,426	63,470,612	176,801,491	64,091,211.30
New Orleans, . .	1838	2,551,895	15,768,990	34,551,830	11,490,253.00
Charlotte, . .	1838	560,937	2,381,689		
Dahlonega, . .	1838	842,189	3,727,910		
Aggregates, . .		15,680,447	$85,349,201	211,353,321	$75,581,464.30

MINTS.	Operations commen'd.	COPPER.		TOTAL COINAGE.	
		Pieces.	Value.	Pieces.	Value.
Philadelphia, .	1793	128,913,641	1,251,734.52	317,440,558	128,813,558.42
New Orleans, .	1838			37,103,725	27,259,243.00
Charlotte, . .	1838			560,937	2,381,689.00
Dahlonega, .	1838			842,189	3,727,910.00
Aggregates, .		128,913,641	$1,251,734.52	355,947,409	$162,182,400.42

TAXATION OF UNITED STATES PROPERTY WITHIN THE STATES.

THE PORTLAND CUSTOM-HOUSE AND PHILADELPHIA MINT CASES.

The action of the supreme court upon these cases renders it proper that the public should be apprized of the questions involved in them. For a series of years prior to 1843, the city of Portland, under the laws of Maine, assessed a tax upon the United States custom-house, warehouse, and wharf in that city, which the collector paid, to avoid a forced collection. The attorney-general, Mr. Legare, having expressed an official opinion that this and all other taxes imposed upon property held by the United States for similar purposes, were illegal, the United States brought a suit in the United States circuit court to recover back the moneys thus paid. On the trial, the circuit judges were divided in opinion upon the constitutionality of the law imposing this tax, and certified their division to the supreme court for instructions. The case was argued two years since by Mr. Clifford, attorney-general, for the United States, and Mr. Evans for the city of Portland.

The court held the question under advisement until the last term, with the view of hearing the argument in the Philadelphia Mint case, before making a decision. The latter case was this: The city of Philadelphia, under the laws of Pennsylvania, as she claimed, assessed taxes upon the mint in that city, and under them brought a suit against Isaac Roach, then treasurer of the mint, as the occupant of the mint buildings, and recovered a judgment in the local court, which was affirmed by the supreme court of that state, on which the United States brought a writ of error to the United States supreme court, to test the validity of the law under which the tax had been assessed. The case was argued last winter by Mr. R. H. Gillet, then solicitor, and Mr. Attorney-General Toucey, for the United States, and Mr. Brewster for the city of Philadelphia.

On consultation, the supreme court ordered a re-argument at the present term, of the two causes together, upon the single question of the validity of the two statutes under which the taxes had been imposed. The two causes were argued a few days since, by Mr. Gillet and Attorney-General Johnson, for the United States, and by Mr. Evans for Portland, and Mr. Brewster for Philadelphia. It was contended on the part of the United States, that whatever the government purchased, or provided, under the constitution, in the execution of the powers conferred upon the national government, could not be taxed by the states, because by such taxation the state could destroy whatever was thus provided, or expel it from the state, which makes the state power supreme, and would enable it to exclude the authority of the national government from its territories.

It is further contended, that by thus taxing the instruments necessarily provided to coin money and collect revenue, Maine and Pennsylvania, in effect, imposed taxes upon her sister states, who contributed to the expense of providing them. And that if the custom-houses and mints could be taxed, ships employed by the navy, and the war and post-office departments, ship materials, arms, ammunition, and provisions, and the mail establishment, might also be taxed.

On the other side, it was contended that a state possessed the eminent domain within itself, and might impose taxes, by general law, upon property within it, over which it had not conferred exclusive jurisdiction upon the United States. And that the United States, like other proprietors holding lands under the laws of a state, were bound to pay their share of the expenses incurred in administering the laws which protected such property; and that if it were otherwise, the national government might monopolize property, and thus prevent it from taxation, to the injury of the state, and to the destruction of state rights.

To this it was replied, that the power of eminent domain was limited under our system of government, and a state could only tax what she might take and apply to her own public use; but the power which would authorize her to take possession of the custom-house and mint, and use them for poor-houses, or quartering state troops would be destroying necessary constitutional instruments; and that if the United States purchased and paid for real estate on which to make erections, it placed in the hands of the former owner taxable means in its stead; and that the states accepted the United States constitution upon the condition that its powers might be executed, without molestation, whenever necessary, of which the national government, as often held by the supreme court, must judge, unless these necessary buildings were exempt when Congress had ordered their erection, the laws passed empowering the United States constitution would not be supreme, as provided in that instrument.

On consultation, after this argument, the judges of the supreme court, eight being present, were equally divided in opinion, and, consequently, no opinion could be given as the judgment of the court upon the constitutional question involved. The Portland case was remitted to the circuit court to be disposed of without instructions. The mint case is left as it came to the supreme court, and, consequently, the judgment of the court below stands affirmed, and the tax upon the mint is to be collected. Whether the Portland taxes are to be recovered back, is a question now pending, and to be disposed of in the circuit court, by Justice Woodbury and Judge Ware, of Maine.—*N. Y. Post.*

INTEREST AND USURY LAWS.

In an article on Interest, published in the Banker's Magazine, the writer makes the following statement for the purpose of exhibiting the advantages that would result from a repeal of the laws limiting the rate of interest: "The case of Holland furnishes a practical and striking proof of the correctness of the theory we have been endeavouring to establish. It is an undoubted fact, that the rate of interest has been, for a very long period, lower in Holland than in any other country in Europe; and yet Holland is the only country in which usury laws are altogether unknown, where capitalists are allowed to demand, and borrowers to pay any rate of interest. Strictly speaking, this applies only to the state of Holland previously to the revolution in 1795. The enactments of the Code Napoleon were subsequently introduced; but it appears from the report of the parliamentary committee on the usury laws, that they have not, in any instance, been acted upon. Notwithstanding all the violent changes of the government, and the extraordinary derangement of her financial concerns in the course of the last twenty years, the rate of interest in Holland has continued comparatively steady. During the whole of that period, persons who could offer unexceptionable security have been able to borrow, at from three to five and a half per cent.; nor has the average rate of interest charged on capital, advanced on the worst species of security, ever exceeded six or seven per cent., except when the government was negotiating a forced loan. The general rate of discount in Holland is from four to five per cent., and occasionally from three to three and a half per cent., but very seldom lower. During the revolution it had been at six and seven per cent., and even at eight; but this was generally owing to some *forced financial operation* on account of the government, and was never of long duration. The following is the average rate of discount at Amsterdam and Rotterdam from 1795 to 1817:

```
1795—4,  4½, 5,  6.                     1807—4,  4½, 5,  6.
1796—4,  4½, 5,  6.                     1808—4,  3½, 4½, 5,  6.
1797—4,  4½, 5,  5½, 6,  9, 12.         1809—4,  4½, 5,  6.
1798—4,  4½, 5,  5.                     1810—4,  4½, 5,  6.
1799—3,  4,  4½, 5.                     1811—3,  3½, 4,  5.
1800—4,  4½, 5,  6.                     1812—3,  3½, 4,  5.
1801—4,  4½, 5,  6.                     1813—3,  3½, 4,  5,  6.
1802—4,  5,  5½, 6.                     1814—4,  5,  5½, 5,  6,  6½.
1803—4,  5,  5½, 6.                     1815—5½, 6,  6½, 7.
1804—4,  4½, 5,  5½, 6.                 1816—5,  5½, 6,  6½, 7.
1805—4,  5,  5½, 6,  9.                 1817—5,  5½, 6.
1806—4,  4½, 5,  5½, 6,  9.
```

"The Bank of Amsterdam never discounts at a higher rate than five per cent.; but they discount at a lower rate, and vary their discounts according to the abundance of capital, never exceeding five per cent., and occasionally as low as two and a half and three." (Mr. Holland's evidence, *Report of the Committee on the Usury Laws*, p. 45.) But in this country, where the law declares that no more than five per cent. shall be taken, the rate of interest for capital advanced on the best landed security has, in the same period, varied from five to sixteen or seventeen per cent., or *five* times as much as in Holland. Surely this ought to put to rest all doubts as to the impolicy and the inefficiency of the usury laws.

LEGAL RATE OF INTEREST IN FRANCE.

In France the usury laws were abolished at the revolution; and it is distinctly stated, that their abolition *was not attended by any rise of interest.*— Storch, *Economie Politique,* tome iii. p. 187. According to the *Code Napoleon,* only six per cent. interest is allowed to be taken in commercial affairs, and five per cent. when money is advanced on the security of real property. There is not, however, any difficulty in evading this law. The method resorted to for this purpose is to give a *bonus* before completing the transaction, or, which is the same thing, to frame the obligation for the debt for a larger sum than was really advanced by the lender. None of the parties particularly interested can be called to swear to the fact of such a *bonus* being given; so that the transaction is unimpeachable, unless a third party, who was privy to the settling of the affair, can be produced as a witness. The Bank of France never discounts at a higher rate of interest than five per cent., but sometimes at a lower rate.

IN HAMBURG.

In Hamburg the rate of interest is quite unrestricted; or, if there be a written law restraining it, it has become altogether obsolete. The rate, therefore, varies according to circumstances. Occasionally it has been at seven, eight, and even ten per cent.; and in 1799, a period of great mercantile embarrassment and insecurity, it was as high as fourteen per cent. Generally, however, the rate of discount on good bills does not exceed four or five per cent. *Report on Usury Laws,* p. 46.

IN RUSSIA.

In Russia the legal rate of interest is six per cent. But as Russia is a country capable of much improvement, and where there are very great facilities for the advantageous employment of capital, the market rate of interest is invariably higher than the statute rate, and the law is as constantly as it is easily evaded.—*Ibid.* and Storch, tome iii. p. 207.

IN AUSTRIA.

At Trieste, and throughout the Austrian empire in general, the usual rate of interest is fixed by law at six per cent.; but capital can seldom be obtained for less than eight or ten per cent.—See Report, *ubi supra.*

IN LEGHORN.

At Leghorn the ordinary rate of interest is a half per cent. per month, or six per cent. per annum; but there is no law to prevent the taking of a higher rate.

IN SPAIN.

In Spain the ordinary rate of interest is six per cent.; but no law exists against taking a higher rate, and it seldom falls below five, or rises above seven per cent.

IN THE UNITED STATES.

In the United States legal interest is fixed at six per cent.; but the market rate fluctuates from ten to twelve per cent. Efforts, Mr. Birbeck informs us, are now making in various parts of the Union, particularly in Virginia and North Carolina, to do away the restraints on usury, which, as he justly observes, "operate merely as a tax on the needy borrower."

RAIL ROAD STATISTICS, &c.

(*From the Daily Advertiser.*)

During the financial embarrassments now passing away, as we trust, so much has been said and written, especially in the money articles of the public presses, of the rapid extension of railroads, and of their injurious consequences to other branches of business, it may be the part of wisdom to take a dispassionate view of the subject, and to know if the forebodings of croakers and other timid minds have sufficient foundation to justify their depressing anticipations.

For this purpose we propose to present some statistics, and institute some comparisons, which may tend to allay, in a degree, the apprehensions now rife in our community from such sources.

In England, where the railroad fever has seriously affected the pecuniary interests of vast multitudes of speculators, there is just ground of alarm, because that country, with its already overgrown population and limited area of land, may not be in a position to justify such immense outlays for this branch of improvement.

The population of England, *proper*, excluding Wales, Scotland, &c.,
may be reckoned at something near, ... 16,495,058
Of Wales, Scotland, and other dependencies at home, . . 10,336.047
That of the United States at 21,250,000

			Acres.	Sq. miles.
The area of land in England proper, at	.	.	32,243,200 or	50,380
"	"	Wales, Scotland, &c.,	. . 42,444,800 or	66,320
"	"	the United States, . .	938,000,000 or	1,450,000
"	"	new territories, including Texas,'	1,192,971,510 or	1,861,110

In the former there is not much room for great progress in these particulars, while in the latter there are boundless resources. The increase of inhabitants in the first is about 1 4-10 per cent, per annum, and in the last, that is the United States, 3 3-10 per cent.

The valuation of property, real and personal, in Great Britain, is very great, and here the comparison is against us, but then she has incurred an immense debt amounting to 3,800 millions of dollars, which is a very great drawback upon her prosperity.

The valuation of property in the United States exceeds 8,298,000,000 dollars. The public debt of the general government and the several states, 285,911,554 dollars.

A country, like individuals, should be estimated in its property to be worth just what may remain after discharging all its liabilities. A large portion of the property of England is personal, and consists of the government scrip, in the form of consols, annuities, and bills of exchequer. Heavy burdens are therefore imposed upon the property and people, to enable government to provide for its interest, sinecures, and unavoidable expenses for the support of its administration. "Her revenues for these objects amount to 270 000,000 of dollars, exclusive of poor rates, the church, local taxation, India," &c., annually.

In order, however, to form an estimate, so far as the cases can be made analogous, we will take the old thirteen states and Vermont, where rail roads have become more extended than in the new states. Here are, in area of land, 251,255,360 acres, or 403,124 square miles.

In England and dependencies, as before stated, 74,668,200 acres, or 116,700 square miles.

The population in these fourteen states, by estimation, is . 12,028,633
" in England, &c., ... 26,381,105

Thus is shown great disparity in capability of improvement, both in extent of territory and accumulation of population, for it must be remembered the increase here is more than twice as much as it is there.

The amount of railways in Great Britain, so far as we have authentic information, is about 4,400 miles in use to January, 1849.

3,000 miles in progress of construction.
6,200 miles chartered, but will not be built at present.

Total, 13,500 miles, with capitals of $1,422,000,000.

The amount already absorbed there exceeds 827,000,000 dollars for these works, and "we find that in twenty-two months (from January 1, 1847, to October 30, 1848,) there has been paid by British shareholders no less than £75,000,000, or $333,300,000 to the railway companies, and nearly the whole of this has been expended." Large, *very large* sums go for preliminary expenses, excise, and customs for taxes, and yet most of the great roads now amalgamated paid from 6 to 8 per cent. dividends in June, 1848.

The railways in the portion of the United States referred to above, and now in operation, extend to 5831 miles, and there is no prospect of rapid extension at this time. The cost has amounted to $182,843,966, but a little more than half the sum that has been expended in Great Britain within the last *twenty-two months*. This statement may not be *perfectly* accurate, on account of the constant progress in these works, but is derived from reliable sources, and is an approximation to the truth.*

The magnitude and continual accumulation of business in our country to justify these enterprises, can hardly be grasped by the mind at once. As one instance of its importance, we will state "that the value of the produce of the Mississippi valley annually set afloat upon its 16,674 miles of navigable waters, is estimated at $262,825,620, and if the returns are only reckoned as of equal value, we have a grand aggregate of 526 millions of dollars, as the worth of the products and merchandise afloat on these inland waters, while our whole imports from and exports to foreign countries, do not exceed 306 millions of dollars." Chains of railroads are built, and in progress of building, to bring much of this produce to the Atlantic ports, thus saving time in transportation, and avoiding many risks. In view of these matters, then, who will say we are going "too fast and too far," and although much money is required, it is not extinguished by these works, but like tools it may be used to accomplish the purpose, and then returned to be used for other departments of business.

INCOME, EXPENDITURE, AND EXPORTS OF GREAT BRITAIN.

LONDON, Nov. 9, 1849.

The following comparative statement of the public income of Great Britain, for the three last years, is abridged from an official return:

Customs and excise.	1846.	1847.	1848.
Spirits, foreign,	£2,426,927	£2,499,810	£2,747,594
British,	5,949,151	5,235,489	5,455,475
Malt,	5,084,650	4,456,738	5,225,072
Hops,	280,265	440,403	392,381
Wine,	1,892,242	1,704,319	1,732,295
Sugar and molasses,	4,050,418	4,504,650	4,741,272
Tea,	5,112,005	5,066,494	5,329,992
Coffee,	756,838	746,436	709,632
Tobacco and snuff,	4,319,088	4,263,702	4,350,733
Butter and cheese,	224,832	243,191	246,194
Currants and raisins,	470,263	427,889	478,662
Corn,	723,600	13,912	767,668
Silks,	235,377	217,613	274,506
Paper,	798,814	768,934	750,864
Soap, candles, and tallow,	1,055,724	974,642	1,090,853
Coals, (sea borne,)	1,653	4,053	4,183
Bricks, tiles, and slates,	638,422	681,329	455,846

* In the North British Review for August we find the following table:

Railroad traffic in Great Britain.

Years.	No. of passengers.	Receipts from passengers.	Years.	Receipts from goods.	Total receipts from goods and passengers.
1843,	23,466,896	£3,110,257	1843,	£1,424,932	£4,535,189
1844,	27,763,605	3,439,294	1844,	1,635,380	5,074,674
1845,	33,791,253	3,976,341	1845,	2,233,373	6,208,719
1846,	48,796,983	4,725,216	1846,	2,846,353	7,565,569
1847,	51,352,163	5,149,002	1847,	7,362,884	8,512,886
1848,	57,965,070	5,720,382	1848,	4,213,169	9,933,551

	1846.	1847.	1848.
Timber, - - -	1,133,627	993,465	737,235
Excise licenses, - -	1,086,155	1,091,563	1,103,436
Sundries, - - -	1,044,405	1,150,682	1,043,280
Stamps, - - -	7,675,921	7,671,325	6,785,050
Assessed and land taxes,	4,474,462	4,553,862	4,506,461
Property tax, - -	5,543,682	5,612,654	5,485,164
Post office, - - -	1,963,857	2,181,017	2,143,650
Crown lands, - -	394,482	430,763	362,501
China money, &c., -	1,095,026	325,342	1,033,776
Excess of expenditure over income, - - -		2,860,138	1,034,919
Total income, - -	£58,427,891	£59,230,415	£58,290,734

As we hear a great deal about the objects on which our immense revenue of nearly sixty millions sterling is expended, it may not be uninteresting to take a bird's-eye view of the subject.

Objects of expenditure.		1846.	1847.	1848.
Charges of collecting the public revenue,		£2,817,777	£2,848,494	£2,836,788
Charges arising from the public debt,		28,077,967	28,141,532	28,563,517
CIVIL GOVERNMENT.				
Civil list, royal privy purse, salaries and tradesmen's bills,	£371,800			
Allowance to members of the royal family and Prince Leopold,*	290,000			
The lord lieutenant of Ireland's establishment,	26,209			
Expenses of the houses of Parliament, including printing,	102,407			
Civil departments, including superannuation allowances,	520,933			
Other annuities, pensions, and allowances,	271,007			
		1,582,356	1,598,809	1,584,491
Judicial departm't, and police and criminal prosecutions,		1,693,019	2,074,277	2,327,541
Diplomatic departm't, salaries, disbursements and outfits,		350,818	346,945	325,852
Forces.—Army,	£7,803,464			
Navy,	6,699,699			
Ordnance,	2,361,534			
		16,864,697	18,502,148	17,645,695
Bounties for promoting fisheries,		11,519	16,979	12,513
Public works,		1,015,273	988,999	858,327
Post office, expenses of collection and other charges,		1,128,442	1,186,215	1,392,944
Miscellaneous,		2,041,135	3,526,027	3,442,966
Total expenditure,		£55,583,023	£59,230,416	£58,990,734

* Now king of Belgium. He does not receive any thing; the balance of the annuity granted to him is, after paying the annuities, &c., due to the servants of the late Princess Charlotte, paid back to the exchequer. The sum so repaid last year was £36,000.

A more detailed account of the public expenditure, shows that the amount paid to charitable institutions for the last three years was £157,524, £237,646, and £297,189, respectively. Of the latter sum, the establishment for the administration of the poor laws cost

tration of the poor laws cost	£202,975
There was spent in Ireland,	41,387
For Greenwich Hospital, &c., in England,	33,200
For vaccine establishment,	2,000
Polish exiles,	9,308
Toulonese and Corsican emigrants,	2,000
Protestant dissenting ministers, and poor French refugee clergy and laity,	6,319
	£297,189

The increasing demands of education, science, and art, is leading to a gradual annual increase of the expenditure under this head, which, we trust, few will be found to complain of. The total amount for the last three years was £341,216, £353,307, and £392,696, respectively. The latter amount was appropriated as follows:

To the British Museum,	£57,230
Steam navigation to India,	50,000
Salaries to certain professors in Cambridge and Oxford,	2,006
University of London,	4,171
Public education, Great Britain,	86,000
Education in Ireland,	115,000
Irish academies, societies, and colleges,	22,951
Maynooth college,	26,360
Universities of Scotland,	9,896
Museum of Economic Geology, London,	10,798
Expense of the National Gallery, London,	1,099
Astronomical expenses,	6,304
Inspectors of anatomy, England,	881
	£392,696

BRITISH EXPORTS.

A lately published parliamentary document presents the following facts. The total declared value of British and Irish produce and manufactures exported from the United Kingdom to various countries, was, in 1847, £58,842,377, in 1848, £52,849,448.

	1847	1848
The British colonies took	£14,588,397	£12,654,183
The United States took	10,974,161	9,584,909
The Hanseatic Towns	6,007,366	4,669,250
Holland,	3,017,423	2,823,558
France,	2,554,823	1,024,521
Russia,	1,844,543	1,925,226
Turkey,	2,576,989	2,858,179
China, Hong Kong,	1,503,969	1,445,959
Brazil,	2,568,804	2,067,302
Mexico, and Central and South America, (ex. Brazil,)	2,505,855	3,761,743
Foreign West Indies,	1,410,221	1,010,138
All other countries,	9,290,366	9,024,780
	£58,842,377	£52,849,448

A return has been published of the exports of British machinery and mill work for the year ending the 5th of January, 1849. From this it appears that the quantity taken by Russia was more than double that by any other country, the declared value in her instance being £312,712, while Spain, which comes next, figures for £98,142. Italy is the third on the list, being for £83,561; then the Hanseatic towns for £58,128, France £35,197, Brazil £29,201, Holland £27,611, the East Indies £26,997, Turkey £26,124, Mexico £25,807, Java £21,965, and Egypt £20,143. All the other countries show amounts under £20,000. The general total is £817,656.

A similar return with regard to hardwares and cutlery shows the total amount exported to have been £1,860,150, of which the enormous proportion of £777,964 was taken by the United States. Canada and the other North American colonies stand next, but only for £95,966. The general total to our colonies, including Australia for £79,103, is about £363,000. The Hanse Towns figure for £82,030, Brazil £73,473, Russia £61,664, France £51,583, the foreign West Indies £48,590, Holland £40,201, Italy £36,129, Peru £29,056, Chili £27,034, Mexico £23,476, Belgium £22,908, Spain £22,779, and Turkey £20,182.

THE COTTON TRADE OF GREAT BRITAIN.

(Condensed by the Inquirer from tables in the London Times.)

The imports of cotton for several periods within the last forty-four years.

In 1806.	Bales.	In 1816.	Bales.
American,	124,939	American,	166,077
Brazil,	51,034	Brazil,	123,450
East Indies,	7,787	East Indies,	30,670
West Indies, &c.,	77,978	West Indies, &c.,	49,235
Gross,	261,738	Gross,	369,432
In 1826.	Bales.	In 1836.	Bales.
American,	395,852	American,	764,787
Brazil,	55,590	Brazil,	148,715
East Indies,	64,699	Egyptian,	34,953
Egyptian,	47,621	East Indies,	219,493
West Indies,	18,188	West Indies, &c.,	33,506
	581,950		1,291,374
1846.	Bales.	1849.	Bales.
American,	932,000	American,	1,477,727
Brazil,	84,000	Brazil and Portugal,	163,768
Egyptian,	59,600	Mediterranean,	72,651
East Indies,	49,400	East Indies,	182,167
West Indies, &c.,	9,000	Demarara, West Indies, &c.,	9,114
	1,134,100	Total,	1,905,427
		Total in 1848,	1,739,997
		Increase of import in '49,	165,430

STOCKS AT THE CLOSE OF THE YEARS 1848 AND 1849.

	Pounds.
Total unconsumed January 1, 1850, . . .	240,325,000
" January 1, 1849, . . .	220,198,000

STOCKS IN PORTS, &c.

Stock in the ports 1st Jan., 1849, . . .		498,600
" Dealers and Spinners' hands, England, .	93,000	
" " " Scotland, .	7,000	
		100,000
Import in 1849, ...		1,905,400
		2,204,000

EXPORTS AND CONSUMPTION IN 1849.

Export to the continent and Ireland—152,300 American; 16,800 Brazil and West India; 84,600 East India; 500 Egyptian, ...		254,200
Taken for consumption of England and Scotland from the ports, ...		1,590,400
Consumed in England, 1,494,100, or 28,694 bags per week.		
Consumed in Scotland, 96,300, or 1,852 bags per week.		
Remaining on hand in ports Jan. 1, 1850, . .		559,400
In dealers and spinners' hands, England, . .	90,000	
" " Scotland, . .	10,000	
		100,000
		2,504,000

QUOTATIONS OF COTTON IN LIVERPOOL.

At the close of the week, ending January 26, 1849, the prices were as follows:

Upland fair, .	$4\frac{1}{4}$d. to $4\frac{5}{8}$d.		Maranham, .	$4\frac{1}{4}$d. to $5\frac{1}{4}$d.	
N. O. fair, . .	$4\frac{1}{2}$ " $4\frac{7}{8}$		Egyptian, . .	$4\frac{3}{4}$ " $8\frac{1}{2}$	
Sea Island, . .	7 " 20		Surat, . .	$2\frac{3}{4}$ " 4	
Pernambuco, .	$4\frac{7}{8}$ " 6		West India, .	4 " 6	

For the week ending December 20th, 1849, the prices were as follows:

Upland fair, .	$6\frac{3}{8}$d. to $6\frac{1}{2}$d.	Maranham, .	$5\frac{1}{2}$d. to $6\frac{1}{2}$d.
N. O. fair, .	$6\frac{1}{8}$ " $6\frac{3}{4}$	Egyptian, . .	6 " 9
Sea Island, .	$9\frac{1}{2}$ " 20	Surat, . .	$3\frac{7}{8}$ " 5
Pernambuco, .	$6\frac{1}{8}$ " $7\frac{1}{4}$	West India, .	5 " 7

We also notice a statement of the extreme prices in each year, from 1806 to 1849. We quote a single kind, "upland," for a few years:

UPLAND "GOOD."

1806, . .	15d. to $21\frac{1}{2}$d.	1821, . .	10d. to $11\frac{1}{2}$d.
1811, . .	$12\frac{1}{4}$ " 16	1829, . .	$6\frac{1}{4}$ " 7
1817, . .	20 " $23\frac{1}{4}$	1836, . .	$10\frac{1}{8}$ " 12

SOUTHERN MANUFACTURES.

We find in the *Telegraph*, published at Columbia, S. C., an interesting article setting forth in a forcible manner a great many facts and figures to show that the true policy of the South is to enter, to some extent, into manufacturing. The article is ably written, and its facts are as interesting at the North as at the South. The writer says:

"If we trace the cause of the depression of the price of the Southern staple, we will find that it is principally owing to an over-production; this over-production originates from too much labour being thrown into one particular channel. Diversify labour, by manufacturing a portion of that surplus staple at home, and the benefit will be two-fold—first, by rendering that portion of the labour thrown off from the old channel more productive, and next by being enabled to realize a better price for the remaining part which we have for exportation.

"Experience has long proven that a crop of cotton of 1,800,000 bales will bring, under ordinary circumstances, quite as much money to the planter as a crop of 2,500,000 bales. The reason of it is very apparent. If we raise but 1,300,000 bales, after taking out half a million of bales, which is required at present for domestic consumption, we have but 1,800,000 bales for exportation. This amount is barely enough to supply the wants of the foreign manufacturer —the consequence is, that, according to the laws of supply and demand, he has to pay more for it than if the quantity were larger. But the crop of late years has averaged very near 2,500,000 bales, and we are compelled to throw two millions of bales on the market of the world, which, being more than the demand calls for, has the effect of causing the price of it almost entirely to be regulated by foreign manufacturers and speculators.

"But the culture of cotton has been pushed of late years to such an extent that, without a failure, 2,500,000 bales is likely to be an average crop for the future; and the question arises, how is the price to be raised, and the welfare of the South to be permanently effected? The answer is at hand. Let the South manufacture a portion of her cotton herself, and the object in view will be accomplished.

"To explain this matter, let us assume that the South would adopt this policy, and each of the cotton-growing States, ten in number, would manufacture but 50,000 bales yearly; this would give us a consumption of 500,000 bales in the South; add to this the amount consumed in the Northern States, say 500,000 bales more, and it will give us a home consumption of 1,000,000 bales.

"Now let us see the result of it. In the place of exporting now, with a full crop, about two millions of bales, we would then export but one and a half millions. The effect of thus diminishing our export one half million bales yearly would be, that we would no longer be compelled to cast ourselves at the mercy of foreigners to beg a purchaser; we could, in fact, regulate the price of it ourselves; and in the place of six to seven cents, being now the extent we can obtain, nine to ten cents would then be the average price.

"It must be admitted that there is perhaps no portion of the face of the earth which abounds so much with all the elements of greatness, and no people possess more means at their command to become wealthy and independent than the people of the South; yet how little have they taken advantage of it?

"It must be likewise admitted that the cotton planter, under present circumstances, has to work harder, and receive less remuneration for the amount of capital which he has invested, than any other class of men; and, while the very staple which he produces enriches almost every one, he himself is the least benefited by it.

"The reason of this is very obvious. Every bale of cotton he sells more than triples in value from the time it leaves him till he buys it back again, if it be even cotton shirting. If he receives $25 per bale, the manufacturer, with not half as great an outlay of capital as it takes to raise a bale of cotton, receives at least $50 to manufacture it into goods; he creates, therefore, more than twice as much wealth, with not half as much capital as the cotton planter.

"To fortify this position it is only necessary to refer to statistics whose authority is indisputable. McCulloch, in his Encyclopedia of Commerce, published in London in 1847, estimates the amount of American cotton consumed by British manufacturers at about 500,000,000 pounds. The present average value of cotton in England is about nine cents per pound, and the aggregate cost of this cotton to the British manufacturer is, therefore, about $45,000,000. At this rate, the highest amount the American cotton planters can receive, would be, (after taking the expenses off,) say seven cents per pound, the sum of $35,000,000.

"According to the estimate of the same author, the value of British cotton manufactures in 1847 was about £42,000,000, or nearly $186,000,000. It is estimated that the amount of capital invested in the business is about the same as the value of the product per annum. As the American cotton constitutes about four-fifths of the entire cotton consumed by the manufacturers in England, the capital required to manufacture the same will be about $150,000,000, and the product about the same. It will thus be seen that, through the combination of British capital and skill, $150,000,000 is produced out of the cotton for which the American planter receives but $35,000,000; and that, after taking off the raw material, the amount of wealth thus created by the British cotton mills is the net sum of $115,000,000.

"Now, let us estimate the amount of capital the American cotton planter will have to invest to produce the same cotton. Allowing about 200 pounds to be the product of an acre, it would require about 2,500,000 acres to produce it, which we will estimate at an average cost of $15 per acre, making about $37,500,000. To produce this, it will take at the rate of 2,000 per hand, about 250,000 slaves, at $500 each, making the value of the slaves about $125,000,-000. Thus the land and slaves, together with necessary items, such as farming utensils, mules, horses, cotton-gins, buildings, &c., would exceed the sum of $170,000,000. In making a comparison in the matter, the case stands thus: the planter invests $170,000,000 to produce about $35,000,000 worth of cotton; the British manufacturers employ a capital of $150,000,000, and produce about $115,000,000 worth of goods, after having paid for the raw material.

"So much for the productiveness of British capital in manufacturing American cotton, and American capital in producing it.

"Again: the British manufacturers employ about 540,000 operatives. To work up the American cotton, it will take about four-fifths of that number, say 432,000 hands; divide the above $115,000,000 among them, and they will have $266 as the value of production per hand; divide the net receipts of $35,000,000 among 250,000 hands, you will have $140 per hand for producing; less by $122 per annum for each hand in the production of the article than is realized by manufacturing it.

"If we come nearer home, we will find the case to be precisely the same. In five of the New England States—New Hampshire, Massachusetts, Maine, Rhode Island, and Connecticut—the capital employed in the business is estimated to be about $50,000,000, and the product about $45,000,000 per annum. Deduct 33⅓ per cent. for the cost of the raw material, labour excepted, say $15,000,000, and you have as the net product of industry $30,000,000, being the actual creation of wealth, in the five States, by the manufacturing of cotton.

"The total cotton crop in the United States for 1848 is estimated at about

1,000,000,000 pounds. If it average six cents per pound, it will bring $60,-000,000. To produce this, it requires, according to the basis assumed, a capital of $340,000,000.

"In order that the Southern planter should create wealth as fast as the Northern manufacturer, in proportion to the amount of capital employed, the crop of 1848 should have brought $200,000,000 in the place of sixty million of dollars.

"I have said at the outset, that the Southern States possess the capacity to manufacture at least 500,000 bales of the raw material. This would be consumed in the manufacture of coarse fabrics, with which the South could defy competition. I will now examine what effect this policy would have. I have already shown that a permanent advance in cotton would be bound to follow, say from two to three cents; to be very limited, let us say at two cents per pound; it would give the South 2,000,000 of bales, allowing four hundred pounds to the average weight per bale, at least an increase of 16,000,000 yearly.

"The 500,000 bales which we would manufacture ourselves would be worth, at $25 per bale, about $12,500,000. As the raw material usually costs about one-third of the manufactured goods, the product of it would be about $37,-000,000, leaving $25,000,000 for the labour and profit to the manufacturer; and if we add to this the $16,000,000, the South would become $41,000,000 richer every year."

WASHINGTON NATIONAL MONUMENT.

Condensed statement of the receipts and expenditures of J. B. H. Smith, Treasurer of the Washington National Monument Society, from 1st January, 1849, to 31st December, 1849, inclusive, to wit:

RECEIPTS.

Received from Hon. E. Whittlesey, the general agent,	-	$9,486 15
Do.	interest on stocks,	2,193 65
Do.	sale of stocks, -	48,734 65
Do.	George Watterston, collector for city of Washington,	295 15
Do.	Mrs. Anna M. Thornton, her subscription,	20 00
Do.	E. W. Fletcher, through Thomas Ritchie, Esq.,	1 00
Do.	exchange on Virginia paper, -	75 00
		60,805 60
Add balance in bank of Washington, on settlement, the 31st December, 1848,		420 88
		$61,226 48

EXPENDITURES.

Paid during said period, per resolutions of the board of managers, and on drafts of the building committee, for expenses of materials, and construction of the monument, per vouchers numbered 1 to 210,	$60,628 82
Paid discount on uncurrent money,	4 06
Paid bank of Washington expenses of collection,	42 38
Balance to credit of treasurer in the bank of Washington the 31st December, 1849,	551 22
	$61,226 48

January 1, 1850.   J. B. H. SMITH, *Treasurer.*

THE DECLARATION OF INDEPENDENCE.

A list of the signers of the declaration, with the times of their birth and death, the State represented by each, and their several ages when they executed the instrument.[*]

Name.	State.	Born.	Age.	Died.
Samuel Adams,	Mass.	1722	54	1803
Robert Treat Paine,	"	1731	45	1814
John Adams,	"	1735	41	1826
John Hancock,	"	1737	39	1793
Elbridge Gerry,	"	1744	32	1814
Stephen Hopkins,	R. I.	1707	69	1785
William Ellery,	"	1727	49	1822
Josiah Bartlett,	N. H.	1729	47	1790
Matt. Thornton,	"	1714	62	1803
William Whipple,	"	1730	46	1785
Oliver Wolcott,	Conn.	1726	50	1797
Roger Sherman,	"	1721	55	1793
Sam. Huntington,	"	1732	41	1796
Wm. Williams,	"	1731	45	1811
Ph. Livingston,	N. Y.	1716	60	1768
William Floyd,	"	1734	42	1821
Lewis Morris,	"	1726	50	1798
Francis Lewis,	"	1713	63	1802
Fran. Hopkinson,	N. J.	1737	39	1790
John Hart,	"	1715	66	1780
Abraham Clark,	"	1726	50	1794
Richard Stockton,	"	1730	46	1781
John Witherspoon,	"	1722	54	1794
Benj. Franklin,	Penn.	1706	70	1790
James Smith,	"	1718	58	1806
Benjamin Rush,	"	1745	31	1813
George Clymer,	"	1739	37	1813
Robert Morris,	"	1733	43	1806
George Ross,	"	1710	46	1799
George Taylor,	"	1716	60	1781
John Morton,	"	1724	52	1777
James Wilson,	"	1742	38	1798
George Reid,	Del.	1734	42	1798
Cæsar Rodney,	"	1730	46	1783
Thomas M'Kean,	"	1734	42	1817
Charles Carroll,	Md.	1737	39	1832
Thomas Stone,	"	1743	33	1787
William Paca,	"	1740	36	1800
Samuel Chase,	"	1741	35	1811
Thomas Jefferson,	Va.	1743	36	1815
Benj. Harrison,	"	1745	31	1799
Francis L. Lee,	"	1734	42	1794

[*] The first motion to declare the colonies independent was made by Richard Henry Lee, of Virginia, on the 7th June, 1776, and the resolution to that effect was debated with great ability. The committee appointed to prepare the declaration which consisted of Jefferson, Adams, Franklin, Sherman, and Livingston, reported on the 1st July, and on the 4th July, 1776, the paper received the assent of all the delegates.

Name.	State.	Born.	Age.	Died.
Richard H. Lee,	Va.	1732	44	1794
George Wythe,	"	1726	50	1806
Thos. Nelson, jr.,	"	1738	38	1789
Carter Braxton,	"	1736	40	1797
John Penn,	N. C.	1741	35	1788
Joseph Hewes,	"	1730	46	1779
William Hooper,	"	1742	34	1790
Thos. Lynch, jr.,	"	1740	36	1789
Arthur Middleton,	"	1733	43	1788
Edward Rutledge,	"	1740	36	1800
Thomas Haywood,	"	1746	30	1809
Button Gwinnett,	Ga.	1732	44	1777
George Walton,	"	1740	36	1804
Lyman Hall,	"	1730	45	1791

GOVERNMENTS OF AMERICA FOR 1850.

(For the following statement we are indebted to the N. Y. Tribune:)

Governments.	Population.*	Capitals.	Chief Executives. Names.	Titles.
NORTH AMERICA.				
Iceland, Danish,	15,000	Reikiavik,		Sliftaman.
Greenland,	56,000	Uppernavik,		
Miquelon, &c., French,	100	St. Pierre,		Governor.
Russian America,	6,000	New Archangel,		do.
New Britain,	162,686	York Factory,	Sir George Simpson,	Manager.
Canada west,	723,087	Toronto,	Lord Elgin,	G. Gen of B. N. A.
Canada east,	768,334			
New Brunswick,	290,000	Fredericton,	Sir E. W. Head, Bt.	Lieut. Gov.
Nova Scotia, &c.,	276,903	Halifax,	Sir John Harvey,	do.
Prince Edward's Island,	62,678	Charlotte Town,	Sir D. Campbell,	do.
Newfoundland,	91,264	St. Johns,	Sir J. G. LeMerchant,	Governor.
United States of America,	22,000,000	Washington,	Zachary Taylor,	President.
United States of Mexico,	7,000,000	Mexico,	José J. D. Herrera,	do.
Honduras, British,	4,000	Balize,	C St. J. Fancourt,	Superintend't.
Guatemala,	935,000	N. Guatemala,	—— Paredes,	President.
Salvador,	362,000	San Salvador,	Dor. Vasconcelos,	do.
Nicaragua,	400,000	Leon,	—— Munos,	Dictator.
Costa Rica,	198,000	Cartago,	Jose M. de Castro,	President.
Honduras,	308,000	Chiquimula,	Juan Leado,	do.
Mosquitia,	40,000	Blewfields,	Jamaso I.	King.
Total,	31,632,054			
WEST INDIES.				
Hayti, St. Domingo,	700,000	Port Republican,	Faustin L. Soulouque	Emperor.
Dominica,	200,000	San Domingo,	Buenaventura Baez,	President.
Cuba, Spanish,	1,315,796	Havana,	Conde de Alcoy,	Capt Gen.
Port Rico,	357,086	San Juan de P. R.		do.
Jamaica,	360,000	Spanish Town,	Sir Charles Grey,	Gov. Gen.
Trinidad,	47,000	Puerto d'Epana,		Lieut. Gov.
Tobago,	15,000	Scarborough,		do.
Grenada, &c.,	49,000	St. George,		do.
St. Vincents, &c.,	28,500	Kingstown,		do.
Barbadoes,	115,000	Bridgetown,		Governor.
St. Lucia,	16,000	Castries,		Lieut. Gov.
Dominica,	20,000	Rosean,		do.
Antigua,	36,980	St. Johns,		Governor.
Nevis,	19,800	Charleston,		Lieut Gov.
St. Christophers, &c.,	31,300	Basseterre,		do.
Virgin Islands,	7,000	Tortola,		Lieut. Gov. of St Christophers.
Bahamas,	20,000	Nassau,		Governor.
Turks' Island,				Lieut. Gov.
Bermudez' Island,	14,000	Hamilton,		Governor.
Gaudaloupe, &c., French	135,000	Basseterre,		do.
Martinique,	119,700	Port Royal,		do.

* Chiefly only approximate.

Governments.	Population.	Capitals.	Chief Executives.	
			Names.	Titles.
Caracoa, Dutch,	14,000	Wilhelmstadt,		Stadtholder.
Santa Cruz, &c., Danish,	44,000	Christianstadt,		Governor.
St. Bartholomew's, Swedish,	15,000	La Carenage,		do.
Total	3,680,162			
SOUTH AMERICA.				
Venezuela,	1,060,000	Caraccas,	Jose Tadeo Monagos,	President
New Grenada,	1,687,000	S. Fé de Bogota,	Jose Hilaro Lopez,	do.
Ecuador,	600,000	Quito,	Gen. Ascasubi, [*]	do.
Bolivia,	1,700,000	Chuquisaca,	Gen. Belzu,	do.
Peru,	1,373,000	Lima,	Ramon Castilla, [†]	do.
Chili,	1,200,000	Santiago,	Manuel Bulnes,	do.
Argentine Republic,	675,000	Buenos Ayres,	Juan M. de Rosas,	Governor.
Uruguay,	140,800	Montevideo,	Joaquim Sudrez,	President.
Paraguay,	250,000	Ascension,	—— Lopez,	Dictator.
Brazil,	5,200,000	Rio Janeiro,	Pedro II.	Emperor.
Guayana, British,	96,500	Georgetown,		Governor.
Guayana, Dutch,	6,500	Paramaribo,		Gov. Gen.
Guayana, French,	18,000	Cayenne,		Governor.
Patagonia,	—?	——	Native Chiefs.	
Total	13,946,000			

[*] Assumed the Presidency in October, 1849, on the failure to elect one by the Congress. General Elizalde and Don Norva were the candidates. Ascasubi had been elected Vice President, and Roca, the late President, retired.

[†] The election of a new President is at hand. Vivanco and Echenique, (the latter President of the council,) are the candidates.

STATE FINANCES.

PENNSYLVANIA.

Extract from the last message of Governor Johnston.

The consideration of the legislature is respectfully invited to the financial condition of the commonwealth.

The present funded debt is as follows:—

6 per cent. loans,	$2,041,022 51	
5 per cent. "	37,336,716 90	
4½ per cent. "	200,000 00	
		$39,577,739 41

Unfunded debt, to wit:

Relief notes in circulation, (without interest,)	$663,164 00	
Interest certificates outstanding,	179,422 91	
" " unclaimed,	4,448 38	
" on certificates to be added when the same shall be funded or paid,	11,294 34	
Domestic creditors, (on settlement,)	85,104 88	
		$933,434 51

Amount of canal, railroad, and motive power debts, contracted prior to Dec. 1, 1848, and unpaid by the appropriations of the last session, ... 63,239 53

Total indebtedness of commonwealth, Dec., 1849, . . $40,574,413 45

The funded debt on the 1st Dec., 1848, was	$39,393,350 24	
Unfunded debt,	1,081,386 69	
Amount of canal, railroad, and motive power debt contracted prior to December 1, 1848,	367,642 38	
		$40,842,379 31

Amount of public debt paid during the year 1849, exclusive of the
sum paid commissioners of the sinking fund, . . . $267,965 86
Amount paid during the year 1849 to the commissioners of the
sinking fund, ... 227,513 53

Amount appropriated during the year 1849 towards payment of public debt, - $495,479 39

In exhibiting the operations of the treasury for the last fiscal year, the sum of
$130,000, borrowed on special loan for the avoidance of the Schuylkill inclined
plane, and included in the aggregate of the public debt in December, 1849, should
be added to the above stated sum of $495,479 39.

The amount of receipts at the treasury during the year ending Dec.
1, 1849, is $4,433,688 65
The amount of expenditures during the same period, is . 4,084,771 80
Balance in the treasury on Dec. 1, 1848, . . . 577,290 39
"   "   "   1849, . . . 926,207 24
Amount paid to commissioners of the sinking fund, to January 1,
1850, $227,513 53, with which was purchased of the funded debt,
and transferred to the commonwealth, . . . 253,500 00
Difference between the indebtedness of the state on the 1st Dec.,
1848, and Dec. 1, 1849, ... 267,965 86

Total amount of public debt paid during the year, . $521,465 86

NEW YORK.

Extract from the recent message of Gov. Fish.

At the close of the fiscal year, ending on 30th of September 1849,
the general fund debt amounted to . . . $6,389,693 32
The canal debt, ... 16,505,345 67

Total "direct" debt, ... $22,895,038 99

Toward the payment of which debt there was on hand—
A surplus of the general fund debt sinking fund of . $13,515 16
A surplus of the canal fund debt sinking fund of . . 209,877 01

$214,392 17

Included in the amount of canal debt above stated, is the sum of $90,822, which
was payable prior to the close of the fiscal year, but had not then been presented
for redemption. The interest on this had ceased from the time when it became
payable;—the funds for its redemption being on hand awaiting the call of the
holders of the stock. Since the close of the fiscal year, $77,917 of this amount
have been redeemed.

The revenue of the general fund, exclusive of the annual appropriation of
$200,000, from the surplus canal revenues, made by the constitution, and in-
cluding a temporary loan to the treasury of $15,000, was . $792,451 69
The canal revenues were 3,442,906 62

Aggregate revenue, ... $4,235,358 31

The payments on account of the general fund during the year, amounted to
$842,228 49, leaving a surplus of the revenue on hand, on 30th September, of
$113,279 22.

The payments out of the canal revenues were:

1. Expenses of collection, superintendence, and ordinary repairs, $685,803 91
2. Appropriations made by article 7 of the constitution, toward the sinking funds, and to defray the necessary expenses of the government, ... 1,850,000 00

  Total payment, ... $2,535,803 91

This amount of payments deducted from the canal revenues of the year, leaves the sum of $907,102 71, applicable to the completion of the Erie canal enlargement, the Genesee valley, and Black river canals.

The receipts from canal tolls, during the year, show an increase of nearly $225,000 over those of the year preceding; the expenses of repairs, &c., have been nearly $170,000 less.

The general fund debt exceeds the amount stated last year by the sum of $400,000. $385,000 of this amount constitute the sum directed by chapter 225 of the laws of the last session, to be paid to the use of the canal fund, to repay the principal and interest of the amount stated to have been paid from the canal fund to the general fund after the first of June, 1846, beyond the amount limited by the constitution.

VIRGINIA.

Extracted from the annual message of Gov. Smith.

Receipts and expenditures for the year ending 30th September, 1849.

RECEIPTS.

The balance in the treasury on the 1st of October, 1848, .	$104,247 72
The receipts principally arising from the usual sources of revenue,	689,841 00
Dividends on bank stock owned by the state, . .	164,291 00
Eighteen months' interest on bond due the state by the James river and Kanawha company, ...	24,178 08
Interest due Washington monument fund, and including a small portion of principal, ...	2,930 39
From the general government, on account of revolutionary claims paid by the state, and refunded, ...	93,586 80
Total revenue, ...	$1,079,074 99

EXPENDITURES.

The usual and ordinary expenses of government, . .	$574,153 88
Interest of the public debt, ...	63,297 04
Board of public works to meet interest on public debt, .	175,000 00
Public roads, under special acts, ...	17,233 00
Literary fund, as directed by law, revolutionary half pay claims received from the general government, . . .	77,216 00
Lunatic hospitals for new improvements, &c., . .	41,754 04
Various disbursements, not ordinary expenses of government,	14,932 95
Warrant issued prior to 1st October, 1848, . . .	63
	$963,586 84
Deduct warrants unpaid on the 1st October, 1849, . .	207 97
Total disbursements, ...	963,378 87
Receipts into the treasury, ...	1,079,074 99
	$115,696 12

It is estimated that there will be a surplus on hand at the close of the present fiscal year, Sept. 30, 1850, of upwards of $187,000, unless expenditures not now anticipated should be sanctioned by the legislature.

SOUTH CAROLINA.

From the message of Gov. Seabury.

Rate interest, and date of loan.				Amount now owing.	When payable.	Where payable.
6 per cent. R. R. loan, 1839,			.	$176,328 71	1850	Charleston.
6	"	"	" .	176,328 71	1852	Charleston.
5	"	Fire loan, 1839,	.	486,666 67	1858	London.
6	"	"	" .	482,722 20	1860	Charleston.
5	"	"	" .	488,808 88	1868	London.
6	"	"	" .	325,808 90	1870	Charleston.
6	"	Randolph stock,	.	10,000 00	1850	Charleston.
5	"	Railroad bank capital,		46,714 34	1859	Charleston.
3	"	Revolutionary,	.	117,438 40	At pleasure.	Charleston.

$2,310,896 81

The resources of the bank of South Carolina, (the capital of which was pledged in 1820 for the redemption of the debt,) applicable to the payment of this debt, amount to $3,888,368 60, which is an excess of available assets over the liabilities of the state of $1,532,843 99, or over two and a half millions, if the sum of $1,051,000, received from the federal government on deposit, be included.

MASSACHUSETTS.

The annual message of Gov. Briggs gives the revenue of the state for the past year at $540,658, the expenditures $601,604. The receipts are less than the amount estimated, in consequence of a falling off in the auction tax, and in the tax on alien passengers, cut off by a decision of the supreme court of the United States, that the tax was unconstitutional. The charges during the year for the support of state paupers exceeds $90,000. The debt of the state is $1,085,000; her property $1,722,258, not including lands in Maine, $1,500,000, and claims on the general government, $181,000. Her school fund is $903,000.

ALABAMA.

The report of F. S. Lyons, bank commissioner, was laid before the legislature. From this document it appears that the foreign debt created to establish the state bank and branches, amounted, two years ago, to $9,170,555 55. Since that time the interest has been punctually paid, and the principal of the debt has been reduced to about $5,600,000. Besides this, there is now in the hands of the commissioner about $500,000 more of specie funds, to be applied in reduction, and the prospect of a further reduction of $1,000,000 out of the funds of the bank. The collections actually made from the bank assets since February, 1846, have amounted to over $5,000,000 in cash.

OHIO.

From the message of Governor Ford.

The condition of the state finances is thus stated.

Receipts from every source during the year, . . .	$2,511,119 37
Disbursements, ...	2,176,681 04
Total amount of domestic bonds redeemed and cancelled during the year 1849, ...	199,386 25
Balance applicable to the payment of the state debt, .	$433,365 16

It will be seen (says the Governor) by this statement of the condition of the finances, that under the present system, after discharging all the general requirements of the state, the interest on our public debt has been punctually paid, and a large balance annually applied to the extinguishment of that debt.

The receipts from the canals and public works during the year, ending November 15th, 1848, were	$773,554 37
The receipts from the same source during the year, ending November 15th, 1849, are	731,173 50
Making a difference of	$42,380 87
Balance of the receipts over the expenditures applicable to the redemption of state bonds,	$334,438 33
Add appropriations for the redemption of state bonds in the hands of fund commissioners on the 15th November, 1848,	298,312 08
Total amount applicable to the redemption of the state debt during the year 1849, exclusive of the balance of $426,451 87, in the treasury on the 15th November, 1848,	632,751 41
There has been redeemed by the treasurer and cancelled during the year 1849, domestic bonds to the amount of	$131,650 25
The fund commissioners have also redeemed and cancelled and delivered to the auditor domestic bonds to the amount of	67,376 00

The Governor says:—"The decrease is not so great as was at one time apprehended, from the general stagnation of business throughout the whole country, produced by the prevailing epidemic, and by reason of the very extensive failure of the wheat crop in the state. Considering these two causes of decrease, the result shows the growing importance of our public works, and the generally increasing wealth and resources of the state."

INDIANA.

The following extracts are from the message of Gov. Dunning.

"It is a source of gratification to be enabled to state that our financial condition still continues to improve. It is the most unerring evidence of the increasing prosperity of the country. The ordinary expenditures of the state government for the fiscal year ending on the 31st day of October, 1849, were $74,469 89. The ordinary expenditures for the current fiscal year, are estimated by the auditor of state at $72,000. The amount of revenue paid into the state treasury during the last year, on all accounts, was $441,650 22, which exceeds the amount paid the previous year $28,901 49.

With reference to the public debt of Indiana, Gov. Dunning says:

"In 1847, when the arrangement of the state's indebtedness was made with her creditors, the debt, inclusive of interest, was $11,045,000. There has been surrendered and converted into new stock, to 1st July last,	$9,530,000
Since July 1st,	33,000
Making,	$9,563,000

Leaving yet to come into this arrangement 1,488 bonds, or $1,488,000. These bonds are held in Europe and in this country, and are coming in gradually. I am informed by the agent of state that he entertains but little doubt that all will be surrendered so soon as arrangements can be made by the holders to obtain the assent of parties interested. I am induced to concur in opinion with this officer for the additional reason that the holders must be satisfied that the state will not soon (if ever) make any different arrangement for their liquidation.

"The semi-annual interest due to our creditors under the two acts of the Legislature of 1846 and 1847, providing for the settlement of our state debt, was punctually paid at the Indiana Agency in the city of New York, on the 1st of July last, amounting to $95,300. A portion of this sum, say $79,000, was borrowed of the commissioners of the Sinking Fund and of the banks."

CHURCH STATISTICS.

MISSIONARY OPERATIONS.

There are in Northern India, 100 missionaries, and 184 native assistants. Thére are connected with these missions, 130 schools, 10,576 scholars, and 2,240 church members. The interior of India, for many hundred miles square, had never been visited by any Christian Missionary; but Southern India and Ceylon had been, comparatively, highly favoured, having been much earlier subjected to British sway. Within the last fifty years, eight different religious denominations have planted missions around the coast, and in the Southern interior.

The Church Missionary Society, is the most efficient missionary organization in the world; the Wesleyan Missionary Society, (London,) scarcely second; the London Missionary Society; the Gospel Propagation Society of the High Church party, which was doing a noble work in India; the English Baptists; the Free Church of Scotland; the American Baptists, and our brethren of the American Board, who had accomplished great things in that region.

These societies have in Southern India and Ceylon, 171 missionaries, 612 native assistants, 956 schools, 29,258 scholars, and 11,695 church members.

CLERICAL.

Among the facts of our times is the great diminution which has taken place in the number of clerical persons in proportion to the amount of population. This is true in Protestant, Greek, and Roman Catholic countries. The statistical work of Mons. Moreau de Jonnés furnishes the following particulars on this subject:

"In France, in 1757, there were 40,000 curates, 60,000 other priests, 100,000 monks, and 100,000 nuns—being a total of 300,000, or 1 to every 67 inhabitants. But, in 1829, the entire clerical order had decreased to 108,000 members; that is, 1 to every 280 inhabitants. This is a decrease of more than four-fifths. At Rome, in 65 years, the decrease has been three-fifths. In Portugal, in 31 years, the falling off has been five-sixths. In Bavaria, in 28 years, the decrease has been the greatest; out of every 23 only 1 is left. In Sicily, in 51 years, the decrease has been one-half. In six of the states of Europe the Roman Catholic clergy, including priests, monks, and nuns, has decreased 855,000 in the last sixty years! In Russia, where the Greek church is the prevailing denomination, the decrease has been, in 33 years, more than one-third."

The same important process has been going on in half Protestant and Protestant countries, as is shown by the following facts: In Switzerland, in 37 years, the decrease has been one-third. In England, in 133 years, nearly two-thirds. In Denmark, in 20 years, more than one-half. In Sweden, in 60 years, one-third.

SOUTHERN BAPTIST CHURCH embraces 220 associations, 4,672 churches, 2,341 ministers, and 383,728 church members, in the states of Maryland, Virginia, North Carolina, South Carolina, Georgia, Florida, Alabama, Mississippi, Louisiana, Texas, Missouri, Arkansas, Kentucky, Tennessee, and the District of Columbia.

ROMAN CATHOLIC CHURCH.

The Roman Catholic Almanac for 1850, states there are now in the United States 3 archbishops, 24 bishops, 1,082 priests, and 1,078 churches—an increase of 1 bishop and 105 priests within the past year. Of these priests, 52 were ordained in the United States. If California and New Mexico be included, the Catholic priests are 1,411 and the churches 1,133. The Catholic population of the Union is estimated at 1,473,350, or if Upper California and New Mexico be included at 1,523,350.

METHODIST EPISCOPAL CHURCH OF THE SOUTH.

There are in the connexional union of the Church, nineteen annual conferences, covering the Southern states and the Indian territory. The general superintendence of the whole is in the hands of four bishops; the regular pastoral and missionary work is in the care of 1,476 travelling preachers, being an increase during the past year of 73. The total number of superannuated preachers is 108, and of local preachers, 3,026, a decrease of 116, though some of the conferences give no returns. The total number of members is 491,786, namely, whites, 354,258; coloured, 134,153; Indians, 3,375, exhibiting upon the returns of last year the large increase of 26,233.

CHRISTIAN MISSIONS AND WAR.

By a volume recently published in London, entitled "The Year Book of Christian Missions," it appears that there are no less than twenty-five large denominational societies in the several protestant countries of Europe and America, devoted entirely to foreign missions. Of these, nine are found on the continent, ten in England and Scotland, and six in the United States. The aggregate amount annually expended by these societies for the objects of their organization, is estimated, in round numbers, at £592,000, of which about £32,000 are contributed on the continent, £460,000 in England and Scotland, and £100,000 in the United States. "The enterprise," says an American writer, "is the offspring of the noblest and most comprehensive form of Christian charity; and though now scarcely half a century old, even in its oldest operations, it has produced the most magnificent results, and is already beginning to change the destinies of the human race." It is a fact of sad significance, however, that the sum total of all the contributions of protestant Christendom to this enterprise, though liberal, and yearly increasing, seems small when compared with the annual contributions of Christian nations to enterprises of an opposite character. For instance, these Christian nations of Europe and America expend every year, in preparations for war, £200,000,000. This amount, when compared with "the most comprehensive form of Christian charity," stands thus:

For preparations for war, *per day*, 548,000*l.* For preaching the gospel of peace to the heathen, 1,640*l.* If we compare the results of Christian missions with the desolating effects of war, the subject is presented in the most striking light   Take a single instance of the latter in the wars between France and the allies.

The La Presse states that as the result of the various conscriptions made in France between the years 1791 and 1813, we find that *four millions five hundred thousand* Frenchmen were blown to pieces by cannon, brought down by musketry, impaled upon bayonets, or cut down by broadswords and sabres. The London Times follows up the above calculation, and computes the loss sustained by the allies at *ten millions of men*, cut to pieces in the prime of life!

MISCELLANEOUS STATISTICAL ITEMS.

THE VINEYARDS OF FRANCE.

The New Orleans Bulletin, in an article on wines, says:

"France enjoys the richest vegetable gifts of the Creator—'corn, oil, and wine,'—in the greatest abundance. She is the vineyard of the earth. From the Moselle and Champagne of the north, to the Lunel and Frontignac of the southern provinces, some four millions of acres are in vineyard. The produce is valued at over twenty-two millions sterling. Bordeaux alone exports 50,000 pipes. The oldest vineyards are those of Champagne. Their excellence was famous in the fourteenth century, when the king of Bohemia, visiting France to negotiate a treaty with Charles VI., first tasted the nectarious draught at Rheims. After spinning out his treaty as long as he could, he gave up all that was required in order to prolong his stay and luxuriate upon Champagne dinners.

"The banks of the Marne are most celebrated for champagne, and some twenty-six millions of gallons are grown in the arondissements of Chalons, Rheims, Vitry and Epernay. The best vineyards cultivate only the *black grape*—the red champagne of *Bouzy*, and the white of *Sillery*—which last comes from the blackest grape, named after the soil, being the best. These choice varieties are chiefly monopolized in Paris and London, though plenty of the *brand* may be found in all our taverns. The colouring matter is only in the skin, as all pulps are the same. Inferior qualities are chiefly owing to difference of *site* and soil, the treatment being in all cases alike. The rose-coloured champagne, (which connoisseurs abroad never drink when they can get any other,) though sometimes coloured by the skin, is generally tinged with red wine or elderberry juice. The finest varieties are usually in perfection after three years' cellaring; but they do not lose in delicacy for even ten or twenty years. In calculating profits, the merchants allow a large per centage—from three to four per cent.—for breakage from the effervescence, in July and August. It was recently reported that M. Moet, of Epernay, had some sixty thousand bottles stored in his solid limestone cellars—cellars not subject even to the vibration of the pavements.

"The varieties of the vine are innumerable; they have a thousand in France alone. But we are unable to trace its history; the wild plant is lost, like the parent stock of the wheat. Both came, doubtless, from the east; and both, like every other good thing, have followed the star of empire westward, and we already have the 'corn and wine' of the Rhine on the banks of the Ohio. Seventy kinds of native vines have been enumerated, and cultivation is naturalizing the choicest clusters of sunny France."

———

The official report made at the present meeting of the Grand Lodge of the United States by the Grand Secretary, presents the following facts:

"The Order has prospered and spread greatly in the various States and Territories of the Union. The whole number of Lodges at present is 1,712; initiated during the year, 23,350; suspensions, 6,726; expulsions, 848; Past Grands, 13,514; Past Grand Masters, 188. Total revenue of the subordinate Lodges, $880,389 32. Number of contributing members, 133,401; brothers relieved, 19,035; widows relieved, 1,687; brothers buried, 1,162; amount paid for the relief of brothers, $272,174 50; for relief of widowed families, $33,392 33; for education of orphans, $6,732 25; for burying the dead, $51,636 65. Total amount for relief, $363,943 95.

"The number of Lodges in Maryland at present is 66; initiated during the year, 1,501; suspensions, 441; expulsions, 14; revenue of Lodges, $65,982 46; contributing members, 8,592; brothers relieved, 1,805; widowed families relieved, 195; number of brothers buried, 90; amount paid for the relief of brothers, $17,434 50; for the relief of widowed families, $7,793 95; amount paid for the education of orphans, $2,216 12; amount paid for burying dead, $6,540 16.

"In the District of Columbia the whole number of Lodges is 13; initiations, 116; suspensions, 175; expulsions, 1; revenue of the Lodges, $6,971 91; total amount of relief given during the year, $3,841 73.

"The Grand Secretary reports the receipts of the Grand Lodge for the fiscal year to have been $13,989 41. All appropriations and current expenses of the year have been paid, leaving a balance in their treasury, on the 13th instant, of $1,169 92, which will be much increased by the ordinary receipts of the session.

"The finances of the Grand Lodge of the United States continue in a prosperous condition. The invested funds amount to $12,817."

BOSTON WATER WORKS.

The great reservoir of the Boston Water Works is completed, and filled with the Cochituate water. Three million gallons are contained in the ample basin of the structure. The depth of this basin is 15 feet 8 inches, its sides respectively measure 177, 168, 166, and 157 feet, and the mean area of water when full is 27,726 square feet. The floor on which this immense body of water, supplied by two pipes, each thirty inches in diameter, will rest at an elevation far above the tops of most houses in the city, is not supported by pillars, but by fourteen massive walls, from forty to sixty-one feet high and twelve feet thick, with a coping broad enough to drive a coach upon, which is reached by a spiral staircase of stone. This mighty fabric, the Courier says, has used up 15,600 cubic yards of granite and 9,000 of concrete. In all, it includes about 50,000 cubic yards of masonry, weighing not less than 70,000 tons. For the last six months the materials have been raised at the rate of 250 tons per day.

THIRTY-FIRST CONGRESS.*

SENATE.

President—Hon. MILLARD FILLMORE, Vice President of U. S.
Secretary—ASBURY DICKENS.

MEMBERS.

MAINE, Hannibal Hamlin, J. W. Bradbury.—NEW HAMPSHIRE, John P. Hale, Moses Norris, jr.—VERMONT, Samuel S. Phelps, William Upham.—MASSACHUSETTS, Daniel Webster, John Davis.—RHODE ISLAND, Albert C. Greene, John H. Clarke.—CONNECTICUT, Roger S. Baldwin, Truman Smith.—NEW YORK, Daniel S. Dickinson, William H. Seward.—NEW JERSEY, William L. Dayton, Jacob W. Miller.—PENNSYLVANIA, Daniel Sturgeon, James Cooper.—DELAWARE, John Wales, Presley Spruance.—MARYLAND, James A. Pearce, Thomas G. Pratt.—VIRGINIA, James M. Mason, Robert M. T. Hunter.—NORTH CAROLINA, Willie P. Mangum, George E. Badger.—SOUTH CAROLINA, John C. Calhoun, A. P. Butler.—GEORGIA, John M. Berrien, W. C. Dawson.—ALABAMA, William R. King, Jeremiah Clemens.—MISSISSIPPI, Jefferson Davis, Henry Stuart Foote.—LOUISIANA, S. U. Downs, Pierre Soule.—ARKANSAS, William K. Sebastian, Solon Borland.—TENNESSEE, Hopkins L. Turney, John Bell.—KENTUCKY, Joseph R. Underwood, Henry Clay.—OHIO, Thomas Corwin, Salmon P. Chase.—MICHIGAN,

---

* At pages 120, 121, &c., of the second volume, with the tables of the late and present executive governments, we gave the lists of senators and members of the house of representatives as far as they could be ascertained at the time. We now insert the corrected lists.

Lewis Cass, Alpheus Felch.—INDIANA, Jesse D. Bright, James Whitcomb.—
ILLINOIS, Stephen A. Douglas, James Shields.—MISSOURI, Thomas H. Benton,
David R. Atchison.—FLORIDA, David Yulee, Jackson Morton.—TEXAS, Thomas
J. Rusk, Samuel Houston.—IOWA, George W. Jones, Augustus C. Dodge.—
WISCONSIN, Henry Dodge, Isaac P. Walker.

CALIFORNIA has chosen John C. Fremont and William M. Gwinn, as senators,
to take their seats on the admission of the state into the Union.

HOUSE OF REPRESENTATIVES.

Speaker—Hon. HOWELL COBB.
Clerk—THOMAS J. CAMPBELL.

MEMBERS.

MAINE, Thomas J. D. Fuller, Elbridge Gerry, Rufus K. Goodenow, Nathaniel
S. Littlefield, John Otis, Cullen Sawtelle, Charles Stetson.—NEW HAMPSHIRE,
Harry Hibbard, Charles H. Peaslee, Amos Tuck, James Wilson.—VERMONT,
William Hebard, William Henry, James Meacham, Lucius B. Peck.—MASSA-
CHUSETTS, Charles Allen, George Ashmun, James H. Duncan, Orrin Fowler,
Joseph Grinnell, Daniel P. King, Horace Mann, Julius Rockwell, Robert C.
Winthrop, Vacancy.—RHODE ISLAND, Nathan F. Dixon, George G. King.—CON-
NECTICUT, Walter Booth, Thomas P. Butler, Chauncey F. Cleveland, Lorenzo P.
Waldo.—NEW YORK, Henry P. Alexander, George R. Andrews, Henry Bennett,
David A. Bokee, George Briggs, James Brooks, Lorenzo Burrows, Charles E.
Clarke, Harmon S. Conger, William Duer, Daniel Gott, Herman D. Gould,
Ransom Halloway, William T. Jackson, John A. King, Preston King, Orsamus
B. Mattison, Thomas M'Kissock, William Nelson, J. Phillips Phœnix, Harvey
Putnam, Gideon Reynolds, Elijah Risley, Robert L. Rose, David Rumsey, jr.,
William A. Sackett, Abraham M. Schermerhorn, John L. Schoolcraft, Peter H.
Silvester, Elbridge G. Spaulding, John R. Thurman, Walter Underhill, Hiram
Walden, Hugh White.—NEW JERSEY, Andrew K. Hay, James G. King, Wm.
A. Newell, John Van Dyke, Isaac Wildrick.—PENNSYLVANIA, Chester Butler,
Samuel Calvin, Joseph Casey, Joseph R. Chandler, Jesse C. Dickey, Milo M.
Dimmick, John Freedley, Alfred Gilmore, Moses Hampton, John W. Howe,
Lewis C. Levin, Job Mann, James X. M'Lanahan, Henry D. Moore, Henry Nes,
Andrew J. Ogle, Charles W. Pitman, Robert R. Reed, John Robbins, jr., Thos.
Ross, Thaddeus Stevens, William Strong, James Thompson, David Wilmot.—
DELAWARE, John W. Houston.—MARYLAND, Richard J. Bowie, Alexander Evans,
William T. Hamilton, Edward Hammond, John B. Kerr, Robert M. McLane.—
VIRGINIA, Thomas H. Averett, Thomas H. Bayly, James M. H. Beale, Thomas
S. Bocock, Henry A. Edmondson, Thomas S. Haywood, Alexander R. Holladay,
James M'Dowell, Fayette M'Mullen, Richard K. Meade, John S. Millson, Jere-
miah Morton, Richard Parker, Paulus Powell, James A. Seddon.—NORTH CARO-
LINA, William S. Ashe, Joseph P. Caldwell, Thomas L. Clingman, John R. J.
Daniel, Edmund Deberry, David Outlaw, Augustine H. Sheppard, Edward Stan-
ley, Abraham W. Venable.—SOUTH CAROLINA, Armistead Burt, William F. Col-
cock, Isaac E. Holmes, John M'Queen, James L. Orr, Daniel Wallace, Joseph
A. Woodward.—GEORGIA, Howell Cobb, Thomas C. Hackett, Hugh A. Haral-
son, Thomas Butler King, Allen T. Owen, Alexander H. Stephens, Robert
Toombs, Marshal J. Welborn.—ALABAMA, Albert J. Alston, Franklin W. Bow-
don, Williamson R. W. Cobb, Samson W. Harris, Henry W. Hilliard, David
Hubbard, Samuel W. Inge.—MISSISSIPPI, Albert G. Brown, Winfield S. Fea-
therston, William M'Willie, Jacob Thompson.—LOUISIANA, Charles M. Conrad,
John H. Harmanson, Emile La Sere, Isaac E. Morse.—OHIO, Joseph Cable,
Lewis D. Campbell, David K. Carter, Moses B. Corwin, John Crowell, David
T. Disney, Nathan Evans, Joshua R. Giddings, Moses Hoagland, William F.
Hunter, John K. Miller, Jonathan D. Morris, Edson B. Olds, Emery D. Potter,
Joseph M. Root, Robert C. Schenck, Charles Sweetzer, John L. Taylor, Samuel
F. Vinton, William A. Whittlesey, Amos E. Wood.—KENTUCKY, Linn Boyd,

Daniel Breck, George A. Caldwell, James L. Johnson, Humphrey Marshall, John C. Mason, Finis E. M'Lean, Charles S. Morehead, Richard H. Stanton, John B. Thompson.—TENNESSEE, Josiah M. Anderson, Andrew Ewing, Meredith P. Gentry, Isham G. Harris, Andrew Johnson, George W. Jones, John H. Savage, Frederick P. Stanton, James H. Thomas, Albert G. Watkins, Christopher H. Williams.—INDIANA, Nathaniel Albertson, William J. Brown, Cyrus L. Dunham, Graham N. Fitch, Willis A. Gorman, Andrew J. Harlan, George W. Julian, Joseph E. M'Donald, Edward W. M'Gaughey, John L. Robinson.—ILLINOIS, Edward D. Baker, William H. Bissell, Thomas L. Harris, John A. M'Clernand, William A. Richardson, John Wentworth, Thomas R. Young.—MISSOURI, William V. N. Bay, James B. Bowlin, James S. Green, Willard P. Hall, John S. Phelps.—ARKANSAS, Robert W. Johnson.—MICHIGAN, Kinsley S. Bingham. Alexander W. Buel, William Sprague.—FLORIDA, E. Carrington Cabell.—TEXAS, Volney E. Howard, David S. Kaufman.—IOWA, Shepherd Leffler, William Thompson.—WISCONSIN, Orsamus Cole, James D. Doty, Charles Durkee.—OREGON, S. R. Thurston.—MINNESOTA, Henry H. Sibley.

CALIFORNIA has sent as representatives, to take their seats on the admission of the state, George W. Wright and Edward Gilbert.

THE SPEAKERS OF THE HOUSE.

Since the organization of the government under the constitution adopted in April, 1789, the following have been speakers of the house of representatives:

Congress.	Commenced.	
1	April, 1789,	Frederick A. Muhlenburg, Pa.
2	Oct., 1791,	John Trumbull, Conn.
3	Dec., 1793,	F. A. Muhlenburg, Pa.
4	Dec., 1795,	Jona. Dayton, N. J.
5	May, 1797,	do.
6	Dec., 1799,	Theo. Sedgwick, Mass.
7	Dec., 1801,	Nathaniel Macon, N. C.
8	Oct., 1803,	do.
9	Dec., 1805,	do.
10	Oct., 1807,	Joseph B. Varnum, Mass.
11	May, 1809,	do.
12	Nov., 1811,	Henry Clay, Kentucky.
13	May, 1813,	{ do. do. resigned. Langdon Cheeves, S. C.
14	Dec., 1815,	Henry Clay, Ky.
15	Dec., 1817,	do.
16	Dec., 1819,	{ do. resigned. John W. Taylor, N. Y.
17	Dec., 1821,	Philip P. Barbour, Va.
18	Dec., 1823,	Henry Clay, Kentucky.
19	Dec., 1825,	John W. Taylor, N. Y.
20	Dec., 1827,	Andrew Stevenson, Va.
21	Dec., 1829,	do.
22	Dec., 1831,	do.
23	Dec., 1833,	{ do. resigned. John Bell, Tennessee.
24	Dec., 1835,	James K. Polk, Tenn.
25	Sept., 1837,	do.
26	Dec., 1839,	Robert M. T. Hunter, Va.
27	May, 1841,	John White, Ky.
28	Dec., 1843,	John W. Jones, Va.
29	Dec., 1845,	John W. Davis, Indiana.
30	Dec., 1847,	Robert C. Winthrop, Mass.
31	Dec., 1849,	Howell Cobb, Geo.

BIOGRAPHICAL SKETCHES.

(Prepared for the Register.)

We commence in this section of the work a series of notices of prominent men, which we design to continue throughout the succeeding volumes.

It is not our intention, in the prosecution of this plan, to write eulogies of distinguished characters, or to set down all they have done, and written, or spoken: we merely propose to make a record, in a statistical form, in which will be noted the principal events of their lives,—the steps by which they have advanced to their present positions.

We introduce, first, the sketches of officers of the general government, and members of Congress, so far as we are at present possessed of authentic materials for the purpose, and as specimens of our plan. In the next volume we shall continue the series, with notices of the other senators, members of the cabinet and representatives, and in every successive volume add to the record similar sketches of all the public men of the country distinguished by station, services, or talents.

Gen. ZACHARY TAYLOR, President of the United States, was born in Orange county, Virginia, in 1790. His father, Col. Taylor, served in the war of the revolution, and in 1790 emigrated from Virginia to Kentucky, where he bore a conspicuous part in the labours and struggles of the early settlers.

In May, 1808, Zachary Taylor was commissioned as a Lieutenant in the 7th Regiment of U. S. Infantry. In 1812 he was made captain, and placed in command of Fort Harrison on the Wabash. When the war with Great Britain commenced, the fort was attacked by 400 Indians, and for his successful defence of it, he was brevetted major. After that war, he received the rank of colonel, and during the Black-Hawk war in 1832, distinguished himself at the battle of Bad-axe, which resulted in the capture of Black-Hawk and the Prophet.

In 1836, he was ordered to Florida in command of a separate column, and in December, 1837, fought at the battle of Okee-cho-bee, which resulted in the total defeat of a large body of the Indians. In May, 1845, Texas was annexed to the Union, and in the August following, General Taylor, then in command of the first department of the army, proceeded with a portion of his troops to Corpus Christi. On the 11th of March, 1846, he took up his line of march for the Rio Grande, where he arrived on the 28th. On the 12th of April, he was summoned by the Mexican general to evacuate his posts on the river, which he refused to do. On the 1st of May he left his intrenchments opposite Matamoras, to open the communication with Point Isabel. On the 8th of May, on his return to relieve Fort Brown, which was bombarded by the Mexicans, he was encountered by 6000 of the enemy at Palo Alto, whom he defeated. His own force consisted of 2100 men. The next day, the 9th, he again met them at Resaca de la Palma, and after a hard-fought battle routed them with great slaughter, and took possession of Matamoras. These two signal victories, obtained with such disparity of force, produced an enthusiastic admiration of Gen. Taylor, and of his gallant companions in arms. On the 21st and 22d of September, he assaulted Monterey, a fortified city in Mexico, which, after a desperate resistance, capitulated. On the 22d February, 1847, with a force consisting of 5000 men, (Gen. Wool being second in command,) he encountered the Mexicans at Buena Vista, under Santa Anna, 20,000 strong, and totally defeated them. On the 14th February, 1849, on an examination of the electoral votes for President and Vice President, he was declared duly elected President of the United States, and was inaugurated the 4th of March following.

Hon. MILLARD FILLMORE, Vice President of the United States, was born in Summer Hill, Cayuga county, New York, Jan. 7th, 1800. His father, Nathaniel Fillmore, is a farmer, still living in Erie county, New York. Mr. Fillmore spent four years, in early life, in working at the clothier's trade, and during that time devoted all his leisure hours to reading and study. At the age of nineteen he attracted the notice of Judge Wood, of Cayuga county, who took him into his office. In 1821, he removed to Buffalo, and entered a law office, teaching for his maintenance until the year 1823, when he was licensed to practise in the court of common pleas. In 1827, he was admitted an attorney of the supreme court of the state of New York. In 1829 he was elected a member of the assembly from Erie county, and was twice re-elected. He was elected to Congress in the fall of 1832, and after the expiration of his term resumed the practice of his profession. In 1836 he was again sent to Congress, and was subsequently re-elected for another term. During this session, he was placed at the head of the committee of ways and means. In 1844, he was nominated by the whig party as their candidate for governor. In 1847, he was elected comptroller of the state. In 1848 he was elected Vice President of the United States, and on the 4th March, 1849, he entered upon the duties of the office.

———

Hon. WILLIAM MORRIS MEREDITH, Secretary of the Treasury, was born in the city of Philadelphia on the 8th June, A. D. 1799. He was educated at the University of Pennsylvania, and was admitted to the degree of Bachelor of Arts in that institution at the annual commencement in July, 1812, when he took the second honour, and delivered the valedictory oration. He studied law in the office of his father, the late William Meredith, Esq., and was admitted to the bar in December, 1817, and immediately commenced the practice of the law. In this pursuit he was eminently successful, and occupied a high position in the profession. In October, 1824, he was elected one of the representatives of the city of Philadelphia in the legislature of Pennsylvania, and continued to serve in that capacity, (with a short intermission,) till the spring of 1828. In 1833, he was elected a member of the select council of Philadelphia, and in the ensuing year succeeded the Hon. Joseph R. Ingersoll as president of the council. This office he continued to hold till March, 1849, when he resigned it on being appointed Secretary of the Treasury of the United States. He was elected one of the representatives of the city of Philadelphia in the convention which met in 1837, to revise the constitution of the commonwealth of Pennsylvania, and served in that body till its final adjournment in 1838.

———

Hon. THOMAS CORWIN, Senator from Ohio, was born in Bourbon county, in the state of Kentucky, on the 29th July, A. D. 1794. His father removed with his family to the Miami valley in Ohio, then the north-western territory, in the year 1799. He was brought up like all others in that new country, at constant hard labour, in clearing the woods and cultivating the earth. His scholastic education was such as could be had at a common school as then-taught, the opportunities of which he enjoyed at intervals up to his 14th year. In the year 1813 he received a severe injury, which disqualified him for hard labour. He studied law, was admitted to the bar in 1817. In 1818, he was appointed public prosecutor for the county he resided in, which place he held eleven years. He was elected to the Ohio legislature in 1822, and again in 1823. He then declined a re-election. In 1829 he was again induced to take a seat in the Ohio legislature. In 1830 he was elected to the House of Representatives in Congress, and served his district for ten years without interruption. In July, 1840, he was nominated for Governor of Ohio by the whig party. He resigned his seat in Congress in May, 1840, was elected governor of Ohio, and served out the term. In 1844 he was elected to the senate of the United States.

Hon. ALBERT C. GREENE, Senator from Rhode Island, was born April 15, 1791, in Rhode Island. His father was the youngest brother of the celebrated Gen. Greene of the revolutionary army. He studied law in the city of New York in the office of the late George Brinckerhoff, and was admitted to practice in May, 1812. He passed the next winter at the law school in Litchfield, Conn., and commenced the practice of the law at East Greenwich, Kent county, R. I., where he married; and in 1815 was elected a representative in general assembly from that town, and was re-elected semi-annually to the same office until 1824. He was speaker of the house of representatives of Rhode Island for several years, and also held the office of major general of the state. In 1824 he was elected attorney general of the state, and was annually re-elected to the same office until 1843, when, on the adoption of the present constitution, he declined a nomination. Whilst holding this office, he distinguished himself on the celebrated trial of the Rev. E. K. Avery for murder. Having removed to Providence in 1834, Gen. Greene was elected senator from that city when he relinquished the office of attorney general in 1843, and was re-elected in 1844. In January, 1845, he was elected U. S. senator for six years, from the 4th of March, 1845. General Greene lost his only son on board the ill-fated steamer Lexington, which was burnt on Long Island sound.

Hon. HENRY CLAY, Senator from Kentucky, is a native of Hanover county, Virginia, and was born 12th April, 1777. His father was a clergyman, and died during the revolutionary war. The scantiness of his means, in early life, obliged him to submit to manual labour and personal sacrifices, but by his energy and talent he overcame all hinderances. In 1793, becoming acquainted with Chancellor Wythe at Richmond, Va., he commenced the study of the law, and in 1797, bearing a license to practise, he removed to Lexington, Kentucky. His rise to distinction in his profession was very rapid. In December, 1806, he was elected to the senate of the United States for an unexpired term. In 1808 he became a member of the Kentucky legislature. In 1810, he took his seat again in the senate of the United States to supply a vacancy. In 1811 he was elected a member of the house of representatives, and was chosen speaker of that body. In 1814 he was sent as one of the commissioners to Ghent, to negotiate a treaty of peace. On his return he was again sent to Congress, and chosen speaker in 1815 and 1817. In 1818 he made his celebrated speech in favour of the recognition of the independence of the South American republics. In 1823 was again elected speaker of the house, and in 1824 made a speech in favour of the protection of American industry. In 1824 he was a candidate for the presidency. Of the electoral votes, Mr. Adams received 84, Mr. Crawford 49, Gen. Jackson 99, and Henry Clay 37. Mr. Adams was chosen President by the house of representatives, and Mr. Clay accepted the office of secretary of state, March 4, 1825. In 1831 he was elected to the senate of the United States. In 1832 he was again a candidate for the Presidency, when Gen. Jackson was re-elected. In 1833 he brought forward the celebrated tariff compromise bill, which passed both houses. In 1836 he was re-elected senator. On the 31st March, 1842, he resigned his seat in the senate. In May, 1844, was again nominated for the presidency by the whig party—Mr. Polk being the democratic candidate. The latter received 170 electoral votes, and Mr. Clay 105. In February, 1847, Mr. Clay lost his son, Col. Henry Clay, who was killed fighting valiantly at the battle of Buena Vista. In December, 1849, he again took his seat in the senate of the United States.

Hon. DANIEL S. DICKINSON, Senator from New York, was born at Goshen, Conn., Sept. 11th, 1800, and removed with his father to the State of New York in 1806. He learned a mechanic's trade, but did not pursue it after he attained his majority. He then devoted himself to study, and was strictly and literally a self-taught man. He acquired the knowledge of surveying without the aid of a teacher, and practised it extensively. He also obtained, in the same manner, a proficiency in mathematics and languages, and was, for a number of years, a successful teacher of youth. He studied law and was admitted to practice in the courts of New York in 1828, and in the course of five years after his admission, had a very lucrative and extensive business. He was elected to the Senate of New York, in 1836, and served four years in that body—was elected Lieut. Governor, in 1842, which office he held until Dec. 1844, when he was appointed a senator in Congress, by the executive of the state, to fill the vacancy (for one session) occasioned by the resignation of N. P. Tallmadge. On the assembling of the Legislature, he was elected for the residue of the term, and subsequently, during the same session, for the term of six years, from the 4th of March, 1845. Mr. Dickinson was one of the state electors for President and Vice President in 1844, and voted for James K. Polk and George M. Dallas.

Hon. WILLIAM C. DAWSON, Senator from Georgia, was born in the county of Greene, in the state of Georgia—and is the descendant of one of the very first settlers of that part of middle Georgia. In the same county he now resides. He was educated at the University of his native state. The first year of his manhood, he was the clerk of the House of Representatives of the General Assembly of the state, was twice a delegate to the convention to amend the constitution; was senator to the state Legislature; and was elected four successive times as a Representative in the Congress of the United States. During his service in Congress, (1841,) he was the nominee of the Whig party for Governor, was defeated in consequence of the vote he gave in the extra session of Congress, 1841, to tax tea and coffee, and perhaps for other causes, though that was probably the chief cause. Immediately thereafter he resigned his seat in Congress. In 1845 he was appointed one of the Judges of the Supreme Courts of the state, in 1847 he was chosen one of the senators in Congress.

Hon. ROBERT C. WINTHROP, late Speaker of the House of Representatives, was born in Boston, 12th May, 1809. His father was Lieut. Gov. Thomas L. Winthrop, lineal descendant in the fifth generation of John Winthrop, first Governor of Massachusetts. His mother was Elizabeth Bowdoin Temple, daughter of Sir John Temple, and grand-daughter of Gov. James Bowdoin of Massachusetts. Mr. Winthrop graduated at Harvard college in 1828, studied law with Hon. Daniel Webster, and was elected to the Legislature of Massachusetts in 1834. He was a member of the House for six years, three on the floor, and three years as speaker. Elected to Congress in 1840, he has been re-elected from that time to this—was chosen speaker of the House of Representatives, at the commencement of the 30th Congress, and was the Whig candidate for speaker during the late protracted contest, and defeated on a plurality vote, by two votes. He is a member of the Massachusetts Historical Society, American Academy of Arts and Sciences, and American Antiquarian Society, and received the degree of LL. D. at Bowdoin college in 1849. He delivered an eloquent and able address at the laying of the corner-stone of the Monument to Washington, 4th July, 1848, and is the author of several literary and historical addresses on other occasions.

Hon. JEREMIAH CLEMENS, Senator from Alabama, was born at Huntsville, Alabama, Dec. 28th, 1815, and educated at the Alabama University, Tuscaloosa—Elected to the Alabama Legislature from Madison (the county of his birth) in 1839, 1840, and 1841. He went to Texas as Captain of a volunteer company, in the spring of 1842, and was elected Lieut. Col. of Volunteers on the frontier of Texas in July 1842. Returned to Alabama and became a member of the Legislature in 1843, and Democratic elector of president in 1844. He was again elected the same year to the Legislature. Appointed Major 13th Infantry, March 3d, 1847. Promoted to Lieut. Col. 9th Infantry, July 16th, 1847. By the reduction of the army at the close of the Mexican war, he was discharged from service. Elected to the United States Senate, Nov. 29th, 1849.

Hon. ROGER SHERMAN BALDWIN, Senator from Connecticut, is a son of Simeon Baldwin, formerly a representative in Congress, and judge of the Supreme Court of Connecticut, and a grandson of Roger Sherman, who signed the declaration of independence, was a member of the convention which formed the constitution, and a senator of the United States from Connecticut.

Mr. Baldwin was born at New Haven in 1793, and was graduated at Yale College in 1811. He immediately commenced the study of law, at the law school in New Haven, then recently established by Seth P. Staples, Esq., and subsequently attended the lectures at the law school in Litchfield, Connecticut, under Judges Reeve and Gould, where he was admitted to the bar in 1814. Having established himself in practice at New Haven, he devoted himself exclusively to his professional pursuits.

In 1837 he was elected a member of the senate of Connecticut, and was re-elected in 1838. In 1841 and 1842 he represented New Haven in the house of representatives in the state legislature. In 1844 he was chosen Governor of Connecticut, and again in 1845, when he declined being a candidate for re-election.

In November 1847, on the death of the Hon. Jabez W. Huntington, he was appointed by governor Bissell, in the recess of the legislature, to fill the vacancy thereby occasioned in the senate of the United States; and at the session of the general assembly in May, 1848, he was appointed for the residue of the unexpired term of his predecessor.

Hon. JESSE D. BRIGHT, Senator from Indiana, was born December 18th, 1812, at Norwich, Chenango county, state of New York. At the age of seven years, emigrated with his father and family to Madison, state of Indiana, where he was educated, and where he has ever since resided.

At the early age of nineteen, he was admitted to the bar. His progress professionally and politically was rapid, and marked with signal success. When in his twenty-second year, he was elected by the people to the office of probate judge, which place he resigned in 1839, on receiving the appointment of marshal of the U. S. for the district of Indiana. From this office Mr. Bright was removed by president Tyler, ten days before the annual election in 1841, and was immediately announced, without his knowledge or previous assent, as a candidate for the state senate. And the same district that had given the then executive of the U. S. a majority of 700 votes, elected Mr. Bright by a decided majority. In 1843 he was nominated by a state democratic convention for the office of Lieut. Governor and was elected by greatly more than his party vote. In 1845 Mr. Bright was chosen by the unanimous vote of his political friends, to represent his state in the senate of the U. S. for the term of six years.

Hon. WILLIAM UPHAM, Senator from Vermont, was born in Leicester, Massachusetts, August 5th, 1792, and commenced his education at the Academy in that place. He removed with his father to Montpelier, Vt., in 1803, and there continued his studies until 1809, when he entered the office of the Hon.

Cyrus Ward of Montpelier, as a student at law, remained in Mr. Ward's office one year, then entered the office of the Hon. Samuel Prentiss, and continued his legal studies until Dec. 1812, when he was admitted to the bar. Mr. Upham commenced the practice of the law at Montpelier, Vt., in 1813, and obtained a high reputation at the bar. He was elected a member of the legislature of his adopted state in the years 1827, 1828 and 1830, and state's attorney in 1828. In October 1842 was elected to the senate of the United States for the term of six years, from and after the 3d March 1843. And in October 1848 was elected to the United States senate for another term of six years, ending the 3d March 1855.

———

Hon. STEPHEN ARNOLD DOUGLAS, Senator from Illinois, was born at Brandon, Vermont, April 23d, 1813, and is the son of Dr. Stephen A. Douglas, formerly of Rensselaer county, N. Y., who died in July 1813. In early life he worked upon a farm, and afterwards, at the cabinet-making business; but his health failing, upon the marriage of his sister to Mr. Julius N. Granger of Ontario county, New York, he removed thither, and entered the Academy of Canandaigua. Afterwards, he commenced the study of the law with Mr. Hubbell. In the spring of 1833 he left Canandaigua, and started westward, for the purpose of establishing himself in business. His first location was in Cleveland, Ohio, but after being there a short time he was taken sick, and confined to his bed a whole summer. On his recovery he left Cleveland, and with slender means, he sought employment at Cincinnati, Louisville, and other places, until he was successful in obtaining the place of teacher of a school at Winchester, near Jacksonville, Illinois, in December, 1833. He soon acquired means sufficient to open a law office, and in the course of one year from that time, was so successful in his profession as to be chosen by the legislature state's attorney. In 1836 he was elected a member of the legislature of the state of Illinois. In all the leading measures for the improvement of the state, he took an active part. He was appointed register of the land office at Springfield; and in December, 1840, he was appointed secretary of state of Illinois. In 1841 he was elected a judge of the supreme court; and in 1843 a member of the congress of the United States, and re-elected in August 1846; and in 1847 he was elected to the senate of the United States, for the term of six years.

———

Hon. WILLIAM LEWIS DAYTON, Senator from New Jersey, was born on the 17th February 1807, at Baskenridge, New Jersey. He is of the family of Daytons who settled in Elizabethtown at an early period, and one of whom, Jonathan Dayton, was speaker of the house of representatives in the fourth congress.

Wm. L. Dayton was educated at the Academy in Baskenridge, and at Princeton College, where he was graduated in 1825. He pursued legal studies with Gov. Vroom, and was admitted to the bar in 1830. For seven years he practised law in Monmouth county, and was then, at the age of thirty, elected by the Whig party to the upper house of the New Jersey legislature. He was very soon after appointed a judge of the supreme court of the state; but after having occupied that station for three years with great credit, he resigned it, and returned to the practice of his profession. In 1842 he was appointed by Gov. Pennington to fill the vacancy in the United States senate, occasioned by the death of Mr. Southard. In 1845 he was elected for the full term of six years. He made an able speech in favour of the ratification of the Mexican treaty.

———

Hon. HOPKINS L. TURNEY, Senator from Tennessee, was born the 3d of Oct. 1797, in the state of Tennessee, where he has resided ever since. His father died when he was about six years old, leaving but a small estate, and a large family. He was bound out to learn the tailoring business, but did not serve out his term, and received no classical education. In 1818 he volunteered and served a tour of five months in Florida against the Seminole Indians, under General Andrew Jackson. In 1825 he was elected a member of the legislature of Tennessee, and was afterwards three times re-elected. In 1837 he was elected a representative in congress, and subsequently, re-elected twice, and then voluntarily retired. In 1844 he was on the Democratic electoral ticket for the state at large, when he canvassed the state, and in 1845, was elected by the legislature to his present position in the United States senate.

———

Hon. SAMUEL L. PHELPS, Senator from Vermont, was born in Litchfield, Connecticut, on the 13th of May, A. D. 1793. Entered Yale college in Sept. 1807, and graduated Sept. 1811. Spent the ensuing winter at the law school at Litchfield, and in May, 1812, emigrated to Vermont, and continued the study of his profession in the office of the Hon. Horatio Seymour. In the summer of 1812, he was drafted in the militia, and in September, was ordered to the frontier. Served in the ranks until November, when he received the appointment of district paymaster in the United States service, occupied that place for a time, and returned to the study of his profession—was admitted to practice in the superior courts, in December, 1814—and continued in the practice of his profession at Middlebury, where he has ever since resided. In 1827, was a member of the Council of Censors of Vermont—in 1831, was elected to the Legislative Council, and during the session of the legislature of that year, was elected to the bench of the supreme court He filled that station for seven years under seven successive elections,—in 1838, was elected to the senate of the United States, and in 1844, re-elected for six years, from the 4th of March, 1845.

———

Hon. JACOB COLLAMER, Postmaster-General of the United States, was born at Troy, N. York, and is the son of a soldier of the revolution. He removed to Vermont at an early age, and after pursuing a course of study at the college at Burlington, he was graduated there in 1810. He studied law, made the frontier campaign of 1812 as a lieutenant of militia, and was admitted to the bar in 1813. He pursued his profession in the counties of Orange and Windsor with much success until 1833, when he was elevated to the bench of the supreme court of the state. In 1843 he was elected to represent his district in the Congress of the United States, and was re-elected in 1844, '46, and '48. Whilst on the bench he was chosen a member of a convention for revising the constitution of the state. In March, 1849, he was appointed by President Taylor, Postmaster-General.

———

Hon. HANNIBAL HAMLIN, Senator from Maine, was born in Paris, Maine, Aug. 27, 1809, where he resided until the spring of 1833. His early life was devoted to labour on a farm in the summer, while his winters were employed in prosecuting English and classical studies. In 1828 he commenced the study of law with his oldest brother. In the winter following, his father having died, he returned home, and for two years took charge of the farm on which his mother lived. He then purchased an interest in a paper called the Jeffersonian, in Paris, and entered the office as a compositor. The year after, he returned to the study of the law, and in the winter of 1833 was admitted to the practice. Settled in Hampden, Maine, (where he now resides,) and was a successful practitioner. He was elected a member of the Maine legislature for 1836, '37, '38, '39, '40, and '41, and was speaker of the house of representatives in 1837, '39, and '40. Was elected in 1843 a representative in Congress, and was re-elected in 1844, and for four years was an energetic and industrious member of the house. In 1848 he was elected a senator in Congress to fill the vacancy occasioned by the death of John Fairfield. He is now at the head of the committee on commerce.

Hon. TRUMAN SMITH, Senator from Connecticut, was born Nov. 27th, 1791, at Roxbury, Connecticut. His father, Phineas Smith, was a farmer, an elder brother of the late Nathaniel Smith, judge of the supreme court of Connecticut, and of Nathan Smith, who died in Washington in Dec., 1835, a member of the Senate of the United States. Mr. Truman Smith graduated at Yale college in 1815, was admitted to the bar in 1818, settled at Litchfield, Connecticut, in the practice of the law the same year, where he still continues to reside. He was elected a member of the house of representatives of the general assembly of Connecticut in the years 1831, 1832, and 1834, was elected a member of Congress in 1839, re-elected in 1841, in 1845, and in 1847. In the spring of 1848 he was elected a member of the senate of the United States for the term of six years from the 4th March, 1849.

Hon. S. U. DOWNS, Senator from Louisiana, was born in Tennessee in 1801; emigrated, when a boy, to Louisiana; was sent back to Tennessee to complete his academic studies; then entered the University of Transylvania, and graduated with distinction. He was admitted to the bar in 1825. He soon after became involved in politics, political discussions, and attracted public attention by his essays and speeches in favour of popular rights, the extension of the right of suffrage, the limitation of the judicial tenure of office, the election of governor and other state officers by the people, and the extinction of chartered monopolies. He is the author of an able argument published in 1844 in favour of the annexation of Texas. Gen. Downs has been successively chosen a member of the convention for remodelling the state constitution, a brigadier general of the state, a state senator, elector of president and vice president, United States district attorney, and finally elected to the senate of the United States. He is member of the judiciary committee, and chairman of the committee on private land claims, and prepared the minority report from a select committee on the admission of California.

Hon. ALPHEUS FELCH, Senator from Michigan, was born at Limerick, Maine, on the 28th September, 1806, and was left an orphan at the age of three years. He was prepared for college at the academy in Exeter, N. H., under the instruction of Dr. Abbott. He entered Bowdoin college in September, 1823, and graduated in September, 1827—studied law, and was admitted to the bar in the fall of 1830. He practised law in Maine until June, 1833, when he removed to Monroe, Michigan, in the month of August following; where he pursued his profession. At the election in 1835, Mr. Felch was chosen a member of the state legislature. In the following year he was re-elected. He opposed the general banking law of the state, under the provisions of which the country was afterwards flooded with worthless bank paper. In February, 1838, he was appointed a bank commissioner, which office he held until March, 1839, when he resigned it and returned to his professional business. In February, 1842, he was appointed auditor general of the state. In this office he continued only about one month, when he received the appointment of judge of the supreme court. In the summer of 1845, against his expressed wishes, he was nominated by the democratic state convention as a candidate for the office of governor, and was elected. In February, 1847, he was elected by the legislature to the senate of the United States for the term of six years. He resigned the office of governor, and took his seat in the United States senate on the first Monday of December, 1847.

Hon. HOWELL COBB, Speaker of the house of representatives, was born Sept. 7, 1815, at Cherry Hill, Jefferson county, Georgia. He is the son of Col. John A. Cobb, who removed from Granville county, North Carolina, to Georgia, at an early age. Howell Cobb was educated at Franklin college, the University of Georgia, and was graduated in 1834. He was married in the year 1835 to Mary Ann Lamar, daughter of Col. Zachariah Lamar, of Georgia, and was admitted to the bar in 1836. He was elected solicitor general of the western district of Georgia in 1837, holding the office for three years; was elected to Congress under the general ticket system in 1842, and re-elected from his present district successively in '44, '46, and '48. On the 22d December, 1849, after a contest of three weeks between the different parties in the house of representatives, he was elected speaker of that body by the vote of the democratic party.

Hon. JAMES W. BRADBURY, Senator from Maine, is a native of the county of York, state of Maine, and son of Dr. James Bradbury, a physician of eminence. He graduated at Bowdoin college, Brunswick, in that state, in 1825, in a class distinguished for the eminent men it has produced; amongst them the late Hon. Jer. Cilley, Prof. Longfellow, Rev. Dr. Cheever, and others. On leaving college, he was employed one year as an instructer of the academy at Hallowell, and afterwards studied law with Judge Shipley, late of the U. S. senate, and Hon. Rufus M'Intire, and, on his admission to practice, removed, in 1830, to Augusta, Maine, the place of his present residence, and the capital of the state, and devoted himself exclusively to the practice of the law until elected to the United States senate in 1846, being then in his forty-first year. He was a delegate to the democratic national convention of 1844, which assembled at Baltimore, and nominated Mr. Polk for the presidency. Placed that year at the head of the electoral ticket, and president of the electoral college of the state, he cast his vote for Mr. Polk.

Hon. LEWIS CASS, Senator from Michigan, was born at Exeter, New Hampshire, 9th October, 1782, and is the son of Major Jonathan Cass, a gallant soldier of the revolution. He taught a school for some time, when he was eighteen years old, and then started on foot across the Allegheny mountains, and established himself at Marietta in the north-west territory. He studied law with Hon. R. J. Meigs, and in 1802 was admitted to practice at the bar. His success was speedy, and in 1806 he was elected a member of the legislature from Muskingum county. In 1807 he was appointed by Mr. Jefferson marshal of the United States for the district of Ohio, in which office he continued five years. On the breaking out of the war with Great Britain in 1812, Mr. Cass was chosen colonel of a regiment of Ohio volunteers. On the 12th July, he crossed with the army of Gen. Hull into Canada, and being detached on separate service, he had a skirmish with the British force near Malden, in which he was successful. At the surrender of Detroit by Hull, 15th August, 1812, Cols. Cass and M'Arthur were included in the capitulation. The ensuing winter, on being exchanged, he was appointed brigadier general in the army of the U. States. On the 5th October, 1813, he was at the battle of the Thames with Gen. Harrison, when the British and Indians under Proctor were defeated. In 1813, he was appointed by Mr. Madison governor of Michigan. He removed to Detroit—was re-appointed governor of the territory, as his terms expired, under seven successive administrations, and was engaged in the negotiation of several important Indian treaties. His duties on the frontier were arduous, and ably discharged. In 1831 he was appointed secretary of war in the cabinet of Gen. Jackson. In 1836 he left the cabinet and went to France as minister plenipotentiary. In 1844 he was elected to the senate of the United States. In 1848 he was nominated as the democratic candidate for the presidency by the Baltimore convention, and re-signed his seat in the senate. Of the votes of the electoral college, he received 127—Gen. Taylor 163. He was subsequently re-elected by the legislature of Michigan to the senate of the United States.

Hon. THOMAS HART BENTON, Senator from Missouri, was born in the county of Orange, North Carolina, and is about sixty-six years of age. His ancestors were patriots of the revolution of 1775, and the family of the Harts, from whom he is descended on his mother's side, were among the most active of the early settlers of Kentucky. Col. Benton removed, about the year 1815, from Tennessee to Missouri, having already at that time distinguished him-self at the bar. In 1820, he was elected to the senate of the United States by the legislature of Missouri, before its formal admission into the Union. The admission of the representatives from that state did not take place until the year after their election. He has been in the senate of the United States from that period until the present time without any intermission. One of his first efforts as a debater was made in 1823, on the mode of the presidential election. He was in the opposition during the term of Mr. Adams, but sus-tained the administrations of General Jackson and Mr. Van Buren. His powers as a debater were exhibited in the famous veto debate of 1832, in which Mr. Clay and others bore a conspicuous part.

He has advocated with much zeal a specie currency, and the disconnexion of the government with banking institutions.

In 1837, he carried through the senate the famous "expunging resolution," striking from the journal of the senate the memorable resolution condemning Gen. Jackson for the removal of the deposites.

In 1840, he proposed the armed intervention of Florida. In 1844, he con-tended against the Rio Grande boundary of Texas, and introduced a bill fixing the boundary line from the desert prairies of the Nueces to the parallel of 42° north. In 1844, he was re-elected to the senate, after having been twenty-four years in that body. In 1845, he was chairman of the military committee. In Jan., 1847, he was nominated, in Missouri, for the presidency, but he imme-diately repressed the movement in his favour. In March following, he was appointed by President Polk a major general in the army of the United States, which office he declined accepting. Col. Benton has been a close student—is a good Spanish scholar, and has amassed, as a statesman, a vast amount of information. He is the father-in-law of Col. Fremont, the newly elected se-nator from California.

Hon. DANIEL WEBSTER, Senator from Massachusetts, was born in Salisbury, New Hampshire, in 1782. His father was a farmer, and had served in both the French war and the war of the revolution. Mr. Webster received his early instruction from Dr. Abbott, principal of the Exeter academy, where Mr. Cass and other distinguished men laid the ground-work of their educa-tion. He afterwards entered Dartmouth college, and was graduated in 1801. He was compelled, by the circumstances of his family, to labour for his own support, and his professional studies were often interrupted. He entered the office of Mr. Gore, in Boston, and in 1805 was admitted to practice at the bar. He first pursued his profession at Boscawen, in his native state, but after the death of his father, in 1807, he removed to Portsmouth, where, coming in con-flict with that distinguished lawyer, Hon. Jeremiah Mason, his mind first de-veloped its wonderful powers. In 1812, he was elected a representative in Congress from New Hampshire. In 1816 he retired from Congress, and went to Boston to pursue his profession, and for six or eight years devoted himself exclusively to the law. In 1820, he was a member of a convention of delegates to revise the constitution of Massachusetts. In the same year he delivered his celebrated address at the 200th anniversary of the landing at Plymouth. In 1822, he was elected from Boston a member of the house of representatives of the United States, and in 1826, he was elected to the senate of the United States to supply a vacancy which had occurred. In January, 1830, Mr. Webster made his famous constitutional argument in the senate in answer to Gen. Hayne of South Carolina. In 1833 he was re-elected to the senate. In 1839, he visited Europe. In March, 1841, he entered the cabinet of President Harrison as secretary of state, and continued in office during the administration of Mr. Tyler until May, 1843. In 1842, he negotiated, at Washington, on the part of the United States, with Lord Ashburton, on the part of Great Britain, the important treaty by which the dispute in relation to the north eastern boundary was adjusted. Mr. Webster, in 1845, returned to the senate of the United States, of which he is still a member.

———

Hon. John Caldwell Calhoun, Senator from South Carolina, was born March 18th, 1782, in Abbeville district, South Carolina. His grandfather emigrated from Ireland to Pennsylvania in 1733. The family afterwards removed to Virginia, but upon Braddock's defeat, they went to South Carolina in 1759, where they established themselves in "Calhoun's settlement." He commenced his studies under Dr. Waddell, at the age of thirteen, but owing to a disorder of his eyes, incurred by severe application, he was obliged to abandon books, and turning his attention for awhile to rural pursuits, contracted the fondness for agriculture which he has ever since evinced. In 1800, he re-commenced study, and in 1802 entered Yale college, then under the presidency of Dr. Dwight. He studied law at the Litchfield law school, and in 1807 commenced the practice of the profession. In 1811 he entered Congress, was placed at the head of the committee on foreign affairs, and was one of the leading members who sustained the war measures of that period. He was, subsequently, at the head of the committee on currency, and reported a bill for the establishment of a national bank. In 1817, he was appointed by Mr. Monroe secretary of war. At the expiration of Mr. Monroe's second term, Mr. Calhoun was elected vice president of the United States, with Mr. Adams as president, and was re-elected vice president when Gen. Jackson came into office. He now began to assert the doctrine of state rights, —which has since been called nullification—assuming the right of a state to declare an act of congress null and void; and at the call of his state resigned his office of vice president, and entered the senate of the United States in 1834. In 1842, he resigned his seat in the senate, and in March 1844, accepted the office of secretary of state, in place of Judge Upshur, who was killed on board the Princeton; and as secretary advocated the annexation of Texas. In 1845, he left the office at the commencement of Mr. Polk's administration, and in 1846, was re-elected to the United States senate. He was opposed to a rupture with Great Britain on the question of right to Oregon, and also to its organization as a territory. He is the author of the celebrated address from the southern delegates, in congress, to their constituents, on the subject of slavery.

———

Hon. William Henry Seward, Senator from New York, was born in Orange county, New York, May 16th, 1801, and is the son of the late Dr. Samuel Seward, an eminent physician, and grandson of Col. Seward who served in the war of the revolution.

In 1816, Mr. Seward entered Union college, and was graduated in 1820. He afterwards studied law with John Anthon in New York, and with John Duer. and Ogden Hoffman in Goshen, N. Y. He was admitted to the bar in 1822, and soon after established himself in Auburn, in the practice of his profession. In 1828, he presided over "the young men's convention," said to be the first political organization of the kind in the United States. In 1830, he was elected to the senate of the state of New York, by the votes of the Whig party, in a district which had previously given majorities for the adverse party. He took an active part in the most prominent subjects of legislation, such as the abolition of imprisonment for debt, the extension of internal improvements, &c. In 1838, he was nominated and elected governor of the state of New York, and was re-elected to the same office in 1840. At the expiration of this term he declined a re-nomination, and returned to his profession. In 1849, he was elected, and took his seat in the senate of the United States.

Hon. Solon Borland, Senator from Arkansas, was the youngest of three sons of Dr. Thomas Borland, and born in Nansemond county, Virginia, on the 8th August, 1811. He removed with his father into North Carolina, in 1823, and to the western district of Tennessee, in 1836. In 1843, he went to Arkansas, where he has resided ever since. He received no regular collegiate education, but studied medicine, and attended a course of lectures in the University of Pennsylvania, Philadelphia, and commenced practice in 1834, in North Carolina. While residing at Memphis, Tennessee, he attended another course of medical lectures at the Louisville (Ky.) Institute, where he was graduated in March, 1841. He then went to Arkansas, by invitation of the democratic central committee of that state, to establish and conduct, as editor, the Arkansas Banner newspaper. Was elected by the Arkansas Legislature, at the session of 1844–5, presidential elector. Appointed by the governor Adjt. Genl. of Arkansas, in Nov. 1844. Resigned that appointment, and raised a company for the Mexican war in May, 1846. Was elected major of the Arkansas mounted regiment at its organization. He was taken prisoner at Encarnacion, Mexico, by General Minon, January 23d, 1847, whence he was marched to the city of Mexico, and kept a prisoner until the 1st of August, when he effected his escape, and joined the American army at Contreras, just as the place was captured. United himself to Gen. Twiggs' command, and was in the ranks at the taking of Churubusco. Major Borland then joined General Worth as volunteer aid-de-camp, on 8th September, at the beginning of the battle of Molino del Rey, and continued with him in that capacity while he was at Tacubaya, through the battles of Chapultepec, San Cosmo, and the city of Mexico. He left the army, and returned home in December, 1847. About the 1st April following, he was appointed by the Governor of Arkansas to the United States senate, to fill the vacancy created by the appointment of A. H. Sevier, commissioner to Mexico, and was, subsequently, elected to the same place, for six years, from the 4th March, 1849.

Hon. James Cooper, Senator from Pennsylvania, was born in Frederick county, Maryland, 8th May, 1810. His father was a native of Pennsylvania, and removed to Maryland in 1767. The pecuniary embarrassments of his parents prevented the execution of their wish to educate him, until he had nearly attained the age of eighteen years. In 1827, he was taught the Latin and Greek languages, and about two years afterwards, was sent to St. Mary's College, at Emmettsburgh; and thence removed to Washington College, Pennsylvania, where he was graduated. In 1832, he commenced the study of the law, under the direction of Thaddeus Stevens, Esq., at Gettysburg; and after reading the usual term, was admitted to the bar. He commenced the practice of his profession in Gettysburg, and was immediately successful. In October, 1838, he was elected to congress, and re-elected in 1840. In March

1843, his term of service in congress expired, and in the autumn of the same year, he was elected to the legislature of Pennsylvania, where he brought forward measures for the redemption of the faith of the state. He was re-elected to the legislature in 1844. He was again elected to the legislature in 1846. He was, subsequently, appointed attorney general by Governor Johnston, and held the office until the meeting of the legislature on the 1st January, 1849. In 1848, he was again elected to the legislature, and in 1849, was elected to the United States senate for the term of six years.

Hon. JACOB W. MILLER, Senator from New Jersey, is a native of Morris county, N. J., and is now in the forty-ninth year of his age. He is of German lineage; his grandfather emigrated from Germany to the colony of New Jersey, a few years before the commencement of the revolution. Mr. Miller received a classical education preparatory to entering college, but at the age of sixteen was induced to abandon study, and to engage in mercantile pursuits. After three years he resumed study, and entered a law office. In Sept. 1823, he was admitted to the bar, and commenced practice at Morristown, in his native county, where he has ever since resided, and has acquired an extensive and lucrative business. In 1832, he was elected a member of the state legislature, from the county of Morris; previous to this year the county had supported the administration of Gen. Jackson; but at this election a change was effected, and there was a Whig majority in the legislature. The next year, Mr. Miller declined a re-election, and returned to the practice of his profession. In 1839, he was again called upon to represent his native county in the state senate or council. This was the year of the famous New Jersey contested election in the house of representatives. Mr. Miller defended the state authorities in a speech delivered on the occasion. The next year he declined a re-election, and again returned to his profession. In the winter of 1841, he was chosen United States senator for six years, (the term of his predecessor, General Wall, having expired,) and first took his seat as senator, on the 4th March, 1841. At the expiration of his first term, he was re-elected by a unanimous vote of his party to his second term, which commenced on the 4th March, 1847.

(These sketches will be continued in the succeeding volumes of the Register.)

(ORIGINAL COMMUNICATIONS.)

THE TENURE OF LAND.

BY A. G. JOHNSON, ESQ.

(Concluded from page 432, Vol. II.)

After a careful consideration of the facts which we have given, we think no candid reader will deny that the tenure of land has an important influence upon the people and government of every country, and that the condition and character of the former, and the form, spirit, and duration of the latter are intimately connected with, and modified by the laws regulating the ownership, transfer, and inheritance of land. We now proceed to the discussion of some of the questions which grow out of the subject.

And first, are large or small farms most favourable to production?

In India, where the land was divided into small allotments, cultivated by the owners who could not alienate their estate; where pasturage was excluded, and agriculture was aided by a religious prohibition of animal food; where the only tax was a fixed tribute paid by a district to the native prince or Rajah; and the existence of caste prevented the degradation of the higher, or the elevation of the lower classes, the fertility of the earth was tasked to the uttermost, and no other country ever supported so dense a population to a square mile.

In ancient Egypt, while the priests were agriculturists, and each had his parcel of land; while even the warrior caste, the hereditary soldiers of the state, formed a standing army of farmers, each possessing his inalienable acre; while every inhabitant of the thronged cities had a distinct allotment of the Nile's alluvion, the production of the country was more than sufficient for its over dense and well-ordered population, and the people of other lands, in times of scarcity and famine, found "corn in Egypt." In that age, too, were raised the obelisks, the pyramids, the cities, and temples,

"Of which the very ruins are tremendous."

Palestine, which in the days of Abraham was a common pasture-field for the flocks and herds of the shepherd patriarchs, subsequently, under the agrarian law of Moses, and the system of universal tillage produced by its operation, and while the periodical restoration of the land to its original proprietors preserved a certain equality among the citizens of the commonwealth, became fertile, populous, and powerful, and never again knew a time of scarcity and famine like that which drew Jacob and his sons into Egypt. Its agricultural system was the

recuperative power, which renewed the strength and wealth of the
nation after its destroying civil wars, and the desolating invasions of
the Assyrian and Persian conquerors. This system, which gave vitality to the nation, was not wholly broken up till the destruction of Jerusalem, and the dispersion of the Jews by Vespasian and Titus. Since
that time the plains of Palestine have been the battle-fields where the
Roman and Parthian, the Byzantine emperors and Arabian caliphs,
the Crusader and Saracen, have struggled for faith and for dominion.

Greece was never very populous, and whenever the citizens of the
leading states became too numerous for their agricultural resources, a
swarm would be sent forth to seek a habitation elsewhere. The coasts
of Asia Minor and Italy, the islands of the Mediterranean, the shores
of the Adriatic and Black Seas, were settled by Grecian colonies. Colonization, and incessant wars at home or abroad, relieved Greece of
its supernumerary citizens. The land owned by the aristocracy, and
cultivated by slaves, did not produce enough to sustain the population.
Poverty and idleness was the lot of the great mass of freemen, and the
demagogue who would obtain their suffrages had to feed as well as
flatter them.

After the destruction of Carthage, the agriculture of Italy no longer
sufficed to support its population. Sicily became the granary of Rome.
The senators monopolized all the wealth of the state; the population
of the city was chiefly composed of slaves and freedmen; the citizens
were enlisted in the legions, and employed in constant aggressive wars.
At every interval of peace they clamoured for a division of the land
acquired by their valour, but usurped by the nobility. War withdrew
from the walls of the city the turbulent freemen, and enabled the aristocracy to add to their own possessions, and at the same time feed the
populace from the spoils of the world. Their power lasted till the last
nation of the civilized world submitted to their sway, and then passed
into the hands of Cæsar. Henceforth, senators and citizens, patrician
and plebeian, wore the same yoke. Cæsar crushed the empty shell of
the commonwealth—Roman liberty had perished long before.

In Holland, which is more densely populated than any other country in Europe, the land is minutely divided for agricultural purposes.
Vast lakes and morasses are drained, and kept dry by means of pumps
worked by wind-mills and steam engines. The drained lands are
called *polders.* Nearly all the agricultural land of the Netherlands is
thus redeemed from the water by the operation of wind-mills. It is
said that there are in Holland 9000 of these mills, and that each mill
drains 600 acres. This vast system of drainage is accomplished in
two ways. Companies are formed under the authority of government,
who build dykes, erect mills, make the land dry, and then divide it
among themselves, or sell it to others. Or, if the work is too great
and expensive for private enterprise, the government undertakes the
drainage, as in the case of the Harlaem sea, and then sells the land,

the purchasers being bound to maintain the dykes, and keep it dry at the common expense. All newly poldered land is exempt from taxation for twenty years. These poldered lands are divided into lots, and cultivated by the owners, or farmed out to tenants.

In England, Scotland, and Ireland, the people all, nominally, enjoy personal freedom. The agricultural labourers are neither serfs or slaves. But, as in the Sclavonian countries, there is a privileged nobility who are the great land-holders and hereditary rulers of the country. Almost all the cultivated land is leased from year to year, or for short periods, at enormous rents. In England, the mass of the people is employed in mercantile, mechanical, or manufacturing business. The products of agriculture meet with a quick and certain sale. A deficiency is readily supplied by importation from America, or the continent. But owing to the fact that the commerce and manufactures of England give employment to so large a number of the poor and landless, the agricultural labourers bear a less proportion to the whole population than in any other country in the world. The land is not subdivided into such small farms, and the profit to the lessees is greater than if they were compelled to lease smaller tracts. But these farmers have to furnish all the stock, all the implements of husbandry, pay all the taxes, and then an enormous rent for the privilege of cultivating the land.

The people of Ireland have no commerce, no manufactures. Agriculture is their sole business. The land is leased in small allotments, and at such high rates that nothing but good health and good weather will enable the tenant to live; the failure of either exposes him to starvation. The rental of Ireland is the running issue which drains the life-blood of the nation. Most of the land owners live abroad, and their income goes to pay the interest on mortgages, or is spent in the dissipations of London and Paris. If the potato crop fails, a famine is inevitable. Not because the land has not yielded its increase abundantly, but because every thing but the potato goes to the landholder, and rent and tithe are exacted to the utmost farthing. During the late horrible famine, the exports of grain from Ireland were of more value than all the contributions of the charitable.

In France, when from any cause there happened to be a more equable distribution of land than at other periods, the age was characterized as the time of the good Louis Eleventh, or the good Henry Fourth. The epochs thus distinguished, happen to be when the crusades or civil wars had destroyed and impoverished the aristocracy, and they were obliged to sell their land to the rich merchants and farmers. In 1792, the constituent assembly abolished all feudal rights and tenures. Laws were passed by which real estate was divided equally among heirs, male and female, and the right to devise it by last will and testament denied. The code Napoleon did not materially alter these laws. The result of this new distribution of land and pro-

perty was seen throughout France.   An excessive stimulus was every
where imparted to French industry.   Notwithstanding the expense of
Napoleon's wars, France incurred no national debt, and after the
slaughter and carnage of twenty-five years, she was more populous in
1815 than in 1790.   The proprietors of land number about half of
the population, and however sorely the *ouvriers* of Paris and the manufacturing cities may suffer for want of work and bread, the rural
population was never so well fed, so well clothed, and independent.

Probably the most profitable cultivation in the world may be found
on the baronial estates of Germany; in Saxony, Silesia, Moravia, Wir-
temberg, Bohemia, Hungary.   But whose is the profit?   The baronial lord's.   For him the serf and the peasant toil.   He lives in luxury
and magnificence, while they have a bare subsistence.   All the surplus
production of these great estates, over and above what is essential for
the most frugal maintenance of the serf or peasant, is sold for the benefit of the great landholder, and his is all the profit.   The fine wool
of the estates of the princes Lichnowsky and Esterhazy finds its way
into the looms of Holland, France, and England, whilst the poor peasant and serf, whose labour and care have produced the staple of the
soft fabrics, is clad in the coarsest stuffs.   The value of his production
goes into the coffers of Lichnowsky and Esterhazy, and supplies the
funds to maintain their castles and palaces in splendour and magnificence.

An important inquiry connected with this subject, is whether a nation
of small proprietors is as capable of conducting a defensive war as a
nation of large landholders.

During the middle ages, when the serfs were unarmed, and all battles were but contests between armed horsemen, no military defence of
the open country was possible, and the only places of safety were castles and fortresses, built with high walls and battlements upon inaccessible precipices.   Before the musket and pistol equalized the strength
of men, and rendered defensive armour useless and cumbersome; before
the Swiss farmers at Morgarten had annihilated the splendid cavalry
of Charles the Bold of Burgundy, it was thought that peasants and
labourers could not make soldiers.   From the days of Charlemagne to
the French Revolution, was there ever a war waged for the rights of
the people, except the defensive wars of the Swiss mountaineers?

Was not the weakness of Poland, and is not the liability of all Sclavonian countries to be overrun by invasion, owing to the fact that the
cultivators of the soil have no interest, and take no part in any war?
The nobility, too, are ninety-nine hundredths of them landless, and
poor, improvident, proud, and purchasable, and gold is as efficacious
in making traitors in council and field, as Philip found it in opening
the gates of Grecian cities.

Who does not remember and admire the unflinching and unconque-
rable resistance of the German Tyrolese to the French invaders, and

the terrible defeat and murderous slaughter with which they repulsed every effort to subdue their hills and valleys? Allison tells us that these men have *homes* as well as wives.

In our revolutionary war, the only portions of the country permanently occupied by the British, were the cities, and the only cities held for any length of time were those surrounded by territory owned by large landholders. Howe was driven from Boston by a swarm of the small proprietors of New England, and Burgoyne was surrounded by farmers from the east, each of whom brought his rifle or musket, with which he had been accustomed to make war upon the inhabitants of the forest.

In our recent war with Mexico, who anticipated so easy a conquest? Why was it possible for six thousand men to penetrate to Monterey, and for twelve thousand to march through a populous country to the city of Mexico? May we not solve the mystery of Mexican weakness, and explain the facility of American conquest by the fact that the land of Mexico is the property of a few great proprietors, whose avarice, selfishness, pride, and ambition, are the bane of the government, while the mass of the people is a lack-land, poverty-stricken, ignorant, superstitious, degraded, amalgamation of Indian, Negro, and Spanish races, whose labour is perpetually mortgaged to the aristocratic landholders, a legal relation equivalent in its debasing tendencies to slavery or serfage?

Another question connected with the subject is, the danger which statesmen have apprehended, that the usurpation of a popular demagogue could not be so well resisted by a people among whom the land was minutely divided, as by a people among whom there was a class whose great wealth and consequent power could hold in check, and overawe the ambitious. The fact that every aristocratic government, except England, whether its executive head was a consul, an hereditary, or elective king, has gradually changed into an unlimited and unmixed despotism, ought to stagger these doubters, and put an end to such apprehensions.

As France and the United States are the only countries in which, to abolish all titular distinctions, and promote the distribution of land and the general diffusion of property, have been the great aims and object of governmental policy, it is in their history and fate that this problem is to be settled.

The question was so ably discussed by the Hon. Daniel Webster in a speech delivered as long ago as 1821, in the Massachusetts convention for altering the constitution, that we will quote his remarks, calling the attention of our readers to the remarkable *conjecture*, contained in the last paragraph, and which has proved to be a prophecy fulfilled.

"A most interesting experiment of the effect of a subdivision of property, on government, is now making in France. It is understood that the law regulating the transmission of property in that country, now divides it, real and personal, among all the children, equally, both sons and daughters; and that there is, also, a very great restraint on the power of making dispositions of property by will. It has been supposed that the effect of this might probably be, in time, to break up the soil into such small subdivisions that the proprietors would be too *poor* to resist the encroachments of executive power. I think far otherwise. What is lost in individual wealth, will be more than gained in numbers, in intelligence, and in a sympathy of sentiment. If, indeed, only one or a few landholders were to resist the crown, like the barons of England, they must of course be great and powerful landholders, with multitudes of retainers, to promise success. *But if the proprietors of a given extent of territory are summoned to resistance, there is no reason to believe that such resistance would be less forcible, or less successful, because the number of such proprietors should be great. Each would perceive his own importance, and his own interest, and would feel that natural elevation of character which the consciousness of property inspires. A common sentiment would unite all, and numbers would not only add strength, but excite enthusiasm.* It is true that France possesses a vast military force under the direction of an hereditary executive government; and military power, it is possible, may overthrow any government. *It is in vain, however, in this period of the world, to look for security against military power to the arm of the great landholders.* That notion is derived from a state of things long since past; a state in which a feudal baron, with his retainers, might stand against the sovereign, who was himself but the greatest baron, and his retainers. But at present, what could the richest landholder do against one regiment of disciplined troops? Other securities, therefore, against the prevalence of military power must be provided. Happily for us, we are not so situated as that any purpose of national defence requires, ordinarily and constantly, such a military force as might seriously endanger our liberties.

"In respect, however, sir, to the recent law of succession in France, to which I have alluded, I would, presumptuously perhaps, hazard a conjecture that if the government do not change the law, the law, in half a century, will change the government; and that this change will be, not in favour of the power of the crown, as some European writers have supposed, but against it. Those writers only reason upon what they think correct general principles in relation to this subject. They acknowledge a want of experience. *Here, we have had that experience; and we know that a multitude of small proprietors, acting with intelligence, and that enthusiasm which a common cause inspires, constitute not only a formidable, but an invincible power.*"

We will, also, add a quotation from St. Pierre, the author of the popular "Studies of Nature." A law preventing the "unbounded accumulation of landed property," since his day, established for France, removes the cause of his "astonishment."

"If wealthy families were permitted to purchase the lands lying commodiously for them, such bargains would speedily become fatal to the state. I have often been astonished that there is no law in France to prevent the unbounded accumulation of landed property. The Romans had censors, who limited the extent of a man's possession to seven acres, as being sufficient for the subsistence of one family. By the word *acre* was understood as much land as a yoke of oxen could plough in one day. As Rome increased in luxury, it was increased to five hundred; but even this law was soon infringed, and the infraction hurried forward the ruin of the republic. Conquerors have always met with feeble resistance in countries where property is unequally divided. Overgrown estates destroy the spirit of patriotism in those who have every thing, and those who have nothing."

The last two sentences contain a volume of wisdom for the citizens and statesmen of our country.

All governments have assumed to fix and define the tenure of land, to prescribe the forms of its transfer, and to regulate its descent by inheritance, and the effects of the different laws of tenure may be tolerably well estimated from the facts and illustrations which we have presented.

From the aforegoing examination of this important subject, it seems to follow that the best interests of mankind will be promoted by general laws favouring a diffusion of property. We are not prepared to say whether it would be wise to fix any limit to individual accumulation. But we have no doubt of the wisdom of restricting the power of devising by last will and testament within very narrow limits, and of forbidding all devises to eleemosynary institutions and organizations. Gifts, during life, to a limited extent, of land, and to any amount of personal property, should be permitted. And, probably, the exemption of a homestead, of certain dimensions, without reference to value, (dimension being certain, and value variable,) to every family from sale upon execution, and from liability or incumbrance of any kind, would be the best possible cure and preventive of pauperism.

A government organized upon the representative system, recognising no distinctions whatever among its citizens, providing by wise laws for such a diffusion of property as would obviate the evils of excessive accumulation on the one hand, and total deprivation on the other, would probably produce the consummation so devoutly to be wished, the security of life, liberty, and the pursuit of happiness.

THE ANCIENT CHEROKEE TRADITIONS AND
RELIGIOUS RITES. •

DEXED

(BY JOHN HOWARD PAYNE, ESQ.[*])

The variations in the religious system of the Cherokee appear to have been of very ancient date; but to have consisted in the objects more than in the outward ceremonies of worship, and there does not appear in any instance to have been adoration paid among them to images; on the contrary, it is asserted that an idolater of an image would always have been laughed at as a fool.

We proceed to notice some of the principal imaginations upon this subject, into which the natives are represented as having wandered.

Some say that a number of beings were engaged in creating all things. The sun was made first. The intention of the creators was to have people live always. But the sun, when he passed over, told them there was not land enough, and that people had better die. At length, the daughter of the sun being with them, was bitten by a snake and died. The sun on his return inquired for her, and was told that she was dead. He then consented that people might live always, and told them to take two boxes and go where her spirit was, and bring it back to her body, charging them, that when they had got her spirit they must not open the box till they arrived at the place where the body was. They did so, but just before they arrived, they concluded to open the box so as to look in and see her, and then shut it again; but while doing this, the spirit escaped, and then the fate of all men was decided that they must die.[†]

It is also stated that anciently the Cherokee supposed a number of beings, more than two, some have conjectured three, came down and made the world. They then attempted to make a man and woman of two rocks. They fashioned them, but while attempting to make them live, another being came and spoiled their work so that they could not succeed. They then made a man and a woman of red clay, and being made of clay, they were mortal; but had they been made of rock, they would have lived for ever. Others, however, ascribed their mortality to another cause. Soon after the creation, it is said, one of the family was bitten by a serpent and died. All possible means were used to bring back his life, but in vain. Being overcome in this first instance,

([*] We have been kindly furnished with these very curious traditions gleaned by the learned author during his residence in the Cherokee country, where he had the best opportunity of learning the history of the early faith, superstitions, and customs of these Indians. Mr. Payne contemplates furnishing, at no distant day, a work which he has commenced on this subject, embracing an account of ancient festivals, rites, and religious theories, which must prove highly interesting and valuable.)

† Yv, wi, yo, ku.

the whole race were doomed to follow, not only to death, but to eternal misery. These beings having created the earth, the man and woman, then made the sun and moon, and constituted them gods, to have the entire control and management of every thing then made, and proceed in the work till the creation was complete. These beings having employed seven days in their work, returned to their own place above, and paid no farther attention to the earth they had created. Of their place above, no one has any knowledge but themselves.

It was by others declared that the supreme creators having in seven days created the sun and moon, and given form to the earth, returned to their own abode on high,—a place known only to themselves,—where they remain in entire rest—leaving the sun and moon to finish and rule the world, about which they gave themselves no further concern. Hence, whenever the believers in this system offer a prayer to their creator, they mean by the creator either the sun or moon. As to which of these two was supreme, there appears to have been a wide difference of opinion. In some of their ancient prayers they speak of the sun as a male, and consider, of course, the moon as a female. In others, however, they invoke the sun as the female, and the moon as the male; because, as they say, the moon is vigilant and travels at night. But both sun and moon, as we have before said, are addressed as the creator. A prayer to the moon as the creator, will be found in a future page among the ceremonies in conjuring against a drought, where he (the moon) is supplicated to cast certain beads around the neck of his wife, the sun, and darken her face, that clouds may come from the mountains. While, in one of the most ancient prayers, to be repeated early in the morning, when going to the water, the sun—designated under the title of creator—is implored to grant them a long and blissful life here, as their only place of happiness; and in many instances a request is added to this creator to take their spirit and bear it with him until he has ascended to the meridian, that is, until noon, and then restore it to them. The same prayer, with the exception of the last clause, was also repeated at night. The expression, *a, ke, yv, ku, gv,—squa, ne, lv, nv, hi*, sun, my creator, is also often found among their ancient prayers; as we have elsewhere mentioned concerning the supplication for assistance in obtaining the love of a desired female; and indeed it is plain that the sun was generally considered superior in their devotions. To him they first appealed to give efficacy to the roots and herbs they sought for medicine. If, however, the plants failed to cure, they considered the moon—not the sun—as having caused the sickness, and so turned for succour to the moon. Nevertheless, at every new moon, as will be found in our notices upon that subject, they paid special homage to the moon, entreating him, as they then expressed themselves, to take care of them during his term.

Besides the sun and moon, they had many inferior deities; but the sun and moon were considered as supreme over the lower creation, and all the rest as having been made by them, subject to their direction, and employed in their service.   To each special duties were prescribed.

The most active and efficient agent appointed by the sun and moon to take care of mankind, was supposed to be fire; when, therefore, any special favour was needed, it was made known to fire, accompanied by an offering.   It was considered as the intermediate being nearest to the sun, and received the same sort of homage from the Cherokee as the same element did from the eastern magi.   This was extended to smoke.   Smoke was deemed fire's messenger, always in readiness to convey the petition on high.   A child, immediately after birth, was sometimes waved over fire.   Children would be brought before fire, and its guardian care entreated for them.   Hunters, also, would wave their moccasins and leggings over fire to secure protection from snakes; and it was a custom, in very remote times, for the same reason, to put chickens, as soon as hatched, into a kind of open basket and wave them over fire.

There are old Cherokee who consider fire as having first descended direct from above.   Others pretend that after crossing the wide waters, they sent back for it to the man of fire, from whom a little was conveyed over by a spider wrapped in her web.   It was thenceforth, they say, kept in their original national heptagon, or rather in a hole or cave dug under it; but this edifice being captured by enemies and destroyed, the fire was lost; although many suppose it only sunk deeper in the ground to avoid unhallowed eyes, and still exists there.   Since its disappearance, new fire has always been made at particular times, and with various ceremonies, which are mentioned under their appropriate heads elsewhere, and are continued to the present hour.

It is also stated among the older Cherokee that the creator,—supposed in this case to mean *Te, ho, waah*,—who supervises the affairs of the universe, and whose abode is in the centre of the sky immediately over head, in the beginning directed certain lines to points upon the earth, which white men express by the words north, south, east, and west.   To each of these respective points he sent newly created beings of a different colour.   In the north was placed the blue man; in the west, the region which is called the region of the setting sun, the black man was placed, who is called *Ewe, kah, waisk, hee*,—the fearless; and to the south was sent the white man, the man of purity and peace,—but the first, and the original of all, was the red man; he was placed in the east, (supposed to signify the sun.)   These first four beings are now existing on high as the vicegerents of the great supreme, and the mediators between him and their posterity, of whom the red man (the sun) was the first created.   To these four beings is power now given over the world, as agents of the great being of all.   To each one of them our first supplications are to be addressed in regular succession.   Whatever is addressed to the black man, the fearless, will forthwith be attended to; and for all that relates to goodness, the white man is to be invoked; but over all of them the creator reigns supreme, enthroned above in the centre of these four points. His eye at once beholds them and us. He knows every thing which each and all in this world can do or think; and he best knows what may for each be best. To him, after first invoking the man of the east, (the sun,) and the man of the north, and the man of the west, and the man of the south, to him, the greatest and the head of all, must be offered up our final, and the most fervent of our prayers.*

The beginning of one of these prayers was with much difficulty drawn by the writer of these pages from one of the most aged and intelligent of the Cherokee, who is since dead. He was in the habit of using it himself, and regarded it with special veneration. Of course it is impossible to render it literally into English; but where it has become necessary to convey the meaning by paraphrase, it has been done after conscientious study and consultation with natives well versed in our tongue. Brief as the passage is, it contains, in the original, some words of the "old language," which we have already referred to, and which words are now grown obsolete. Among them, not the least remarkable is "Ho, yannah," with which it commences. The supplicant ascended by himself, at sunrise, to the top of a high mountain, and there began a long invocation, as follows:

"Hoyannah to thee, oh, almighty one! Hear my prayer; the prayer of him who is of the acorn (by another interpreted holly) clan! I have purified my feet from the dust of the earth on which I am a dweller, until they are white enough to bear me to the high places, even above the tree tops, where I may commune with thee undisturbed by aught which can interrupt my attention; for there, minds encounter no obstruction from the things of the world, but can look straight at thee, and behold thee clearly. Shake not from thee our minds, oh, almighty one! ours of the seven clans of the red clay. Thou hast already driven off from him who now supplicates before thy throne the power of the evil bewilderer of slumbering hearts; and in so doing, for mine thou hast shown love. Continue that guardian love, oh, almighty one! and suffer not my heart to fall away from its devotedness to thee!"

In the foregoing, something of the sun worship, as stated at the beginning of this section, would seem to be traceable; but with modifications. Here, for example, the supreme intelligence still directly supervises human affairs, which is not supposed in the earlier form. The other beings who share with the red man (the sun) in the government of the earth, it is somewhat difficult to explain. It is found, however, and especially of late years, that almost every one of those in the nation who bears the name of conjurer, forms his own mythology, and falsifies the earlier. Thus it happens that the four beings just

---

* *Siot, ah, tow, eh,* through two interpreters, to the author.

invoked as men, are sometimes prayed to as four dogs,—the great black dog of the west, and so on.

Various other fantastical imaginations are found among the Cherokee; from which we proceed to select those which appear to be the least recent.

A female, for example, is held in special honour, and identified with Indian corn or maize. Most of the all night dances refer in some way to her, as did some of the ceremonies in the green corn festival. A legend in relation to her will be given in another place. A female called "the woman of the east," is also mentioned with much reverence. Allusion will be found to her in an appropriate part of our proposed work.

Thunder was adored; or rather thunders, for there was supposed to be many, stationed, or dwelling, in different places, each charged with a specific duty. A very exemplary Cherokee, after having fasted seven days, it is said, went to the top of a stupendously high mountain while it was thundering, and there saw the beings whence the thunder came.[*]

They paid a sort of veneration to the morning star also; but rather as an object of fear. They say that long ago a very wicked conjurer committed murders by witchcraft. The Cherokee combined to slay him. Hearing of their purpose, the conjurer gathered his shining instruments of mischief, and flew upward to a certain height, where, pausing, his apparatus made him seem a star. He then became fixed to his position in the sky, and is prayed to, and assists all who desire to kill others by witchcraft; or bewitches any proposed victim, and does the killing for the applicant himself.

The cluster, usually termed the seven stars, was regarded with peculiar reverence. We have not met with any prayers addressed to it, but there is a wild legend of its having sprung from a family of eight boys, brothers, who were wont to steal into the town council house and beat the drum which was kept there for public solemnities. Some of the elders of the tribe reproving them, they took offence, and seizing the drum, darted upward with it, beating it in defiance as they ascended. On the way, however, one of them came down with a fall so hard that his head struck deep into the ground. He was transformed into a cedar. The tree is to stand for ever. It has the peculiar property that whenever bruised or cut, it bleeds like a human being. The rest of the seven brothers mounted as high as they desired, and then became seven stars. This narrative is, no doubt, allegorical, but no clue can be found to its signification now.

There are many other celestial objects denominated ancients, and varying in figure, colour, and office. They are said to be stationed in different parts of the firmament, and prayers are frequently directed to them. May not these have been at first distinguished persons, whom after death the people deified?

[*] The same worship also existed in Peru.

Certain birds and creeping things also received homage; but only as intermediators, never as objects of direct power or worship.

A curious account of a very remarkable crystal,[*] or divining stone, used in ancient times by the Cherokee, is given in the introduction to the chapter on festivals. The author remarks: "We have thought it convenient that it should be preceded by some particulars regarding a sort of talisman which was uniformly employed on all solemn occasions, and for which no title more significant occurs to us than that of the divining crystal. Under this name, therefore, we propose to relate all that we have gathered upon the subject."

The divining crystal formed a very essential part of the apparatus of the ancient Cherokee priest; and though it does not seem to have been always a portion of his dress, it was indispensable to his vocation. The Cherokee name for it was *Ooh,*[†] *lúng, sah* TAH, which signifies, *Light that pierces through,* as through a glass. Light, simply, is *I, ka, ka, ti;* but *Ooh, lung, sàh, tah,* is more significant, and implies both a light piercing quite through what it falls upon, and a light conveying through the substance of which it is composed instruction to the observer. So sacred was this stone, that it was death for any one who had not been sanctified and initiated for the purpose, to touch it. The priest would sometimes wear it on his breast suspended by a string, but always hidden from view,—the *Oole, stool, eeh,* at the *Ah, tawh, hungh, nah,*—that is, propitiation, or cementation festival, as will be seen in a future page, and the *Aska, yu, gu, sti, qua,* or great warrior alone excepted. The latter hung it by a string round his neck, wrapped in a weasel skin, dressed entire. If the warrior was killed in battle, it was the first aim of his own warriors to snatch the crystal from his bosom and guard it reverently; but it was the first object of the foe to wrench it away and crush it between two stones. All who carried the talisman, the great warrior, as we have before said, only excepted, concealed even the knowledge of the place about them where it was worn. Such as were not borne about the person of a priest, were treasured up in a holy box or ark, or carefully folded in seven deers' skins.

Accounts are given of five different sizes of this talisman. It was in shape a hexagon, and composed of crystalline quartz; but many persons fancy that this was only a substitute for diamond, which, in the earlier times is said to have been its material. How the supposed magical properties were imparted to it is not explained; we only know that each priest was possessed of one, and that all sizes were consulted with equal confidence, and held in equal honour.

The larger of these crystals was used for divining the results of war. The ceremonies on those occasions will be described under their appropriate heads.

---

[*] Similar crystals were sacred among the Australians.—See Gray's Australia, Vol. II.

[†] The first syllable pronounced like the *ho* in the word who.

The crystals used by civil priests were of a size smaller than the one employed in divinations regarding war. The former were devoted to ascertaining whether sickness was to be apprehended either by an individual, or family, or town. When sought for that purpose, a sacrifice was first offered. This being over, the stone was so set either upon seven deers' skins folded, or on a post covered with fawn skin, or in some crevice of a house, as to catch the first rays of the morning sun. If the omen were favourable, a bright and unclouded blaze would appear in the stone; but if unpropitious, the stone would look blue and smoky, and just as many would die as appeared lying in its right side. The crystal was consulted for the same purpose by the people, in large bodies, on certain occasions. For example, on the great moon, as it is called; that is, the first autumnal moon, at which the ancient Cherokee commenced their civil year. This time being come, before sunrise in the morning, the priest of each town would gather all the men, women, and children of the place into one building, and seating them in rows with their faces turned towards the east, would open a crack in that side of the place, and so set his divining crystal there as to catch the rays of the rising sun. Receding about four feet, with his eyes rivetted on the stone, and his face turned towards the sun, he would make a prayer. As he would pray, it is asserted that the crystal became brighter and brighter, till a brightness as dazzling as that from a mirror with the glare of midday full upon it, would first strike the under side of the roof, and then moving back and forth, and then descending lower and lower; it would at length glance towards the people as they sat. Over such as were to die before the return of another quarterly new moon, the light would pass, without the least illumination of their persons. Credible witnesses of this superstition aver that they have actually known instances wherein this brightness has failed to rest on those it passed among, who have all died before the termination of the following three months. During these ceremonies, the priest never touches the crystal; he simply stands by and repeats his prayers.

The crystal used for recovering things lost or stolen, was less than either of the former. After setting the talisman in the sun, and praying for instruction, the priest would see the object in it, together with the thief.

That employed in reference to hunting was of a still lesser size. After an appropriate prayer, and an advantageous adjustment of the crystal in the morning sunlight, if a buck were to be killed, it would be seen in the stone; if a doe, a tinge of blood would appear; but if nothing, there would be no change. When used during the actual chase, it would be fixed on a stool at the river bank, covered with seven folded deer skins; and success was inferred from the appearance in it of a multitude of deers' horns; or failure from that of few or none.

The smallest crystal of the five was employed to ascertain the length of life. If the inquirer was to attain old age, a figure would be seen in it with gray hair and a long white beard.

CONSTITUTIONAL HISTORY.

CONSTITUTION OF NEW YORK.

BY HON. B. F. BUTLER.

The change from one system of social economy to another is often accomplished by convulsions as great as those which mark the first transition from chaotic confusion to a state of established order. We are apt to expect some decay in prevailing forces, some dissolution of existing restraints, before those that are destined to succeed them can assume vitality and vigour; between the laws that have just expired and those that have just been created, an interval without law; a pause to commemorate the passage from the one era to the other, by its independence of both; a period of disorganization unchecked by past legislation or present authority; a crisis of abuse which previous wrongs could scarcely justify, and subsequent reforms hardly atone for. But the change which we are now contemplating has been accompanied by no such disastrous effects. It has proceeded with much of the physical stillness and something of the moral grandeur which attend the great processes of nature. Demanded by the exigencies of a free people: controlled by their active will; established by their deliberate sanction; whatever may be our individual opinions as to its present value or possible results, it is a fresh illustration of the force and dignity of republican institutions. It teaches, with a new emphasis of cheering encouragement and significant warning, the great lessons of American freedom—change without violence; progress without disorder; revolution without anarchy.

As we look more closely at the new edifice, and its various parts, we are instinctively led to compare it with that in whose place it stands. Nor are we content thus to limit our examination. We would visit the original foundation; trace the history of the successive superstructures; and note the times and the persons, when and by whom, the corner stones were laid, and the several fabrics erected or demolished, altered or renewed. We would mark the form and style of each, and make some attempt to ascertain its value, and to determine the merits of its authors.

Aside from the pleasure which a liberal curiosity may derive from these inquiries, they answer one of the highest ends of historical research. The organic laws of a community, and the changes which from time to time are made in them, are the most authentic proofs of its civilization—the most instructive monuments of its progress * * *
' At the commencement of the revolutionary struggle, the wants and impulses of the times brought into existence, in this colony as well as in the others, governments by congresses and committees, informal and temporary, in character and duration. As the conflict went on,

and the hope of reconciliation with the king and parliament declined, the patriots and sages who, at first, thought only of defending their natural and chartered liberties, were forced to contemplate the prospect of a final separation, and to provide for the ground of absolute independence. Accordingly, on the 15th of May, 1776, a resolution was passed by the Continental Congress, then sitting at Philadelphia, by which it was recommended to the respective assemblies and conventions of the United Colonies, where no government sufficient to the exigencies of their affairs had been established, to adopt such government as should, in the opinion of the representatives of the people, " best conduce to the happiness and safety of their constituents in particular, and America in general."

Of the thirteen original colonies, all, except Connecticut and Rhode Island, pursued the course thus recommended. The charters of these two colonies reserved to the crown no control over the acts of internal policy emanating from the colonial legislative bodies, nor even any share in the executive power; the acts of the former did not require the royal sanction, and the latter was chosen by the colonists themselves; nothing, therefore, was necessary to their convenient action as states, but the casting off of their dependence on Great Britain.

The constitution of Virginia, which was the first in the order of time, was adopted on the 12th of June, 1776. New Jersey, Maryland, and North Carolina, following her example, completed their constitutions during the same year. The constitution of New York was the fifth in the series; having been finally adopted on the 20th of April, 1777.

The Provincial Congress of New York, elected in April, 1776, assembled in the city of New York, a few days after the passage of the resolution of the Continental Congress, mentioned above.

They proceeded, without delay, to consider this resolution. It was fully discussed, and on its true grounds. It was treated as involving, substantially, the question of independence. Gouverneur Morris, then a delegate for the county of Westchester, appears, though one of the youngest members, to have taken a leading part in this debate; and, as may be seen by the extracts from his speech, in the work of Mr. Sparks, he strongly argued the duty and necessity of abandoning, for ever, the phantom of reconciliation, and of seeking peace, liberty, and security by a new and independent movement. Being, however, of opinion, that the Congress had not the power to enter on the plan of a new government, he proposed that a committee should be appointed, to draw up a notice to the people, recommending the election of delegates, for the express purpose of assembling and forming a new government. Other members thought, and of this opinion was a majority of the house, that the subject should be referred to a committee, to consider and report thereon; and a resolution to this effect was accordingly adopted. The committee, on the 27th of May, reported, that the right of framing or new-modelling civil government belonged to the people; and that as doubts existed of the authority of the Provincial Congress to form a new government, the people should be called together to express their sentiments on the subject, by the usual mode of election.

This report is worthy of special notice, as one of the earliest and most explicit expositions of the doctrine of the popular sovereignty put forth in this state. It was approved by the Congress; and on the 31st of May, this body passed a series of resolutions prepared by Mr. Jay, calling on the people of the several counties to elect deputies to a new Congress, with power to establish a form of government.

The general movement towards independence, was now proceeding with such strength and swiftness, that before the sense of the people of New York could be taken, the Provincial Congress was obliged to anticipate, in some degree, the action it had invited.

The convention of Virginia had passed a resolution on the 22d of May, instructing the representatives of Virginia in the Continental Congress, to bring forward and sustain a proposition for declaring the United Colonies *free and independent states.*

On the 7th of June, the delegates from Virginia made such a motion, which was discussed on the 8th and 10th. As it then appeared, (to use the language of Mr. Jefferson,) "that the Colonies of New York, New Jersey, Pennsylvania, Delaware, and Maryland, were not matured for falling from the parent stem, but they were fast advancing to that state; it was thought most prudent to wait awhile for them, and to postpone the final decision to the first of July, but that this might occasion as little delay as possible, a committee was appointed to prepare a Declaration of Independence."

This committee reported on the 28th of June; and, as is well known to every American, the immortal declaration was adopted on the 4th of July.

In the mean time, delegates had been elected in the several counties of this state, who were to meet in the city of New York on the 8th of July Before that day, Sir William Howe arrived at Sandy Hook with a British fleet and army; and the city of New York, which had for some time been occupied by Washington and the American troops, became the immediate centre of the great military operations about to ensue. The new Congress, unable to assemble in the city, came together at White Plains, and at the moment of its meeting, received official notice of the decisive step which had been taken at Philadelphia. Its first acts (July 9th) were to pass, by unanimous vote, a resolution approving the Declaration of Independence, and to order its publication throughout the State. It then changed its title from that of the "Provincial Congress of the Colony of New York," to that of the "Convention of the representatives of the state of New York;" and in view of the new exigencies pressing upon the country, immediately took measures for relieving the city, and for maintaining, by military power and by all the influence it could exert, the cause of liberty and independence.

These duties compelled the convention to defer its entrance on the special labour for which it had assembled, until the 1st of August, when a committee was appointed to draw up and report a constitution. JOHN JAY was the chairman of this committee; and the duty of preparing the draft appears to have been assigned to him. But he was also chairman of the committee of safety appointed by the convention, and with his associates in both bodies, was engaged day and night in the toils and cares of that most perilous conjuncture.

The convention, acting sometimes in this character, and sometimes as a general committee of safety, watching the progress of military events, and migrating from place to place, sat, successively, at White Plains, Haerlem, Fishkill, and finally, from February, 1777, to May in that year, at Kingston. While at Fishkill, the members supplied themselves with arms and ammunition for their defence in case the British or their armed adherents, of whom there were many, should assail them in their retreat. Like the high-souled Hebrew leader and his brave companions, these equally fearless builders "had every one his sword girded by his side, and so builded."

On the 12th of March, 1777, the committee reported the draft of a constitution, which, on the 20th of April, 1777, was adopted by the convention. Though more than a month intervened between the report and the final vote, the convention was compelled to give to the subject a very hurried consideration. Mr. Jay, the chief author of the draft, ascribes to this circumstance the striking out of some provisions which he regarded as important, and the insertion of others which he deemed objectionable.

The constitution, as finally adopted by the convention, bears, on its face, many of the intellectual and moral traits of its principal author. It begins with a preamble in which are set forth in explicit terms, the causes which demanded the erection of a new government; the several steps taken for the purpose, under the sanction of the continental Congress, by the people of New York; and the authority of the convention to represent them in this solemn and momentous work. Among other things, it recites at large the Declaration of Independence, and the unanimous resolution of the convention of the 9th of July, 1776, approving the declaration and pledging the colony to its support. As a consequence of this measure and of the other matters thus recited, the preamble concludes, that all power whatever, in the state of New York, " hath reverted to the people thereof; " and that the convention having been appointed by their suffrages and free choice, is authorized to institute and establish for the good people of the state, a new form of government.

By its first article the constitution declared, that no authority should, on any pretence whatever, be exercised in the state, but such as should be derived from, and granted by the people.

It then proceeded to vest the legislative power in a senate and assembly—the members of the former body, twenty-four in number, being chosen from four senate districts into which the state was divided, for four years, from and by the freeholders of the district respectively, possessed of freeholds of the value of £100 ($250) over and above incumbrances; and of the latter, who were to be at least seventy in number, for one year, from and by the inhabitants of the respective counties, possessing freeholds of the value of twenty pounds, or renting tenements of the yearly value of twenty shillings and paying taxes. Provision was made for increasing both branches with the increase of population, but the senate was never to exceed one hundred, nor the assembly three hundred.

The executive power was vested in a governor, and as his substitute, a lieutenant governor, to be chosen by ballot, by and from the freeholders qualified to vote for senators, for three years; and the judicial, in a chancellor, and judges of the supreme court, and first judges of counties, to hold respectively during good behaviour until the age of sixty years, and in other courts, judges and inferior magistrates, holding at the pleasure of the appointing power.

A court of last resort and for the trial of impeachments, was formed on the principle of the English house of Lords, and of the colonial council. It was to be composed of the lieutenant governor, the senators, the chancellor, and the judges of the supreme court; the chancellor having no voice in the determination of appeals from his decrees, nor the judges in that of writs of error.

The appointing power was vested in a council of appointment; consisting of four senators selected annually by the assembly, who, with the governor, were to form the council. To this body was given the power of appointing and removing, at pleasure, all officers in the state, except the chancellor, judges of the supreme court and first judges of counties.

To prevent the passage of laws inconsistent with the spirit of the constitution, or with the public good, there was established, a council of revision, composed of the governor, the chancellor, and the judges of the supreme court, in which was vested the power of negativing all acts passed by the senate and assembly; the *veto* of the Council being absolute, except when the bill should be repassed by a vote of two-thirds of each house.

The constitution, after reciting that the opinion had long prevailed among the people of New York, that voting by ballot would tend more to promote the liberty and freedom of the people, than voting *viva voce*, directed the legislature after the termination of the war, to prescribe by law the mode of voting for senators and representatives in the house of assembly, by ballot; with power to recur to the former mode, if, after a full and fair experiment, it should be thought best so to do. But during the war with Great Britain, all votes for those officers, were to be given *viva voce*.

It was provided that such parts of the common law of England, and of the statute law of England and Great Britain, and of the colony of New York, as, together, formed the law of the colony on the 19th day of April, 1775, (the day of the battle of Lexington,) should continue subject to alteration by the legislature, to be the law of New York; except that all such parts of the common and statute law, as might be construed to establish or maintain any particular denomination of Christians, or their ministers, as well as those which concerned the allegiance before yielded to, and the sovereignty claimed by the king of Great Britain, or were otherwise repugnant to the constitution, were expressly abrogated and rejected.

Grants by the king of Great Britain, after the 14th of October, 1775, were declared to be void; but those made by him or his predecessors, before that day, were preserved.

To prevent frauds upon the natives, the power of making Indian purchases was so limited, as to make the authority and consent of the legislature necessary to their validity.

Besides abrogating such parts of the common and statute law as gave any preference to any particular church, the constitution also expressly declared, that the free exercise and enjoyment of religious profession and worship, without discrimination or preference, should be *for ever* allowed within the state, TO ALL MANKIND. This clause was preceded by a preamble, expressed with remarkable energy and point:

"We are required," (say the convention as their reason for the article,) "we are required, by the benevolent principles of rational liberty, not only to expel civil tyranny, but also to guard against that spiritual oppression and intolerance, wherewith the bigotry and ambition of weak and wicked priests and princes have scourged mankind."

In contrast, as has been thought in later times, with this liberality, is the next clause, in which, after reciting that "the ministers of the gospel are, by their profession, dedicated to the service of God and the cure of souls, and ought not to be diverted from the great duties of their function," the constitution provides, that "therefore, no minister of the gospel, or priest of any denomination whatsoever, shall, at any time hereafter, under any pretence or description whatever, be eligible to, or capable of holding, any civil or military office or place within this state."

The constitution contained no formal bill of rights; but besides the full protection of religious freedom already mentioned, the right of trial by jury was made inviolate; acts of attainder, except for crimes committed during the then existing war, were prohibited; no person was to be disfranchised, unless by the law of the land or the judgment of his peers; quakers were to be excused from military service on paying an equivalent in money; freedom of debate in the legislative bodies was secured; parties impeached, or indicted for crimes were to be allowed counsel as in civil cases; town officers and other officers before eligible by the people, were to continue so; and the legislature were forbidden to institute any new court, except such as should proceed according to the course of the common law.

Finally—the legislature were authorized to pass naturalization laws; but persons of foreign birth were to take an oath of allegiance to this state, and to abjure all allegiance and subjection to all and every foreign potentate and state, in all matters ecclesiastical as well as civil.

The freehold qualification required of voters for governor, lieutenant-governor and senators, was found, as the population of the state increased, to operate injuriously. Large portions of the people, many of them persons of great intelligence and possessed of personal property, or of interests in lands less than freeholds, far exceeding the value of the freehold demanded by the constitution, were, so far as regarded the choice of these officers, practically disfranchised. The injustice and impolicy of this exclusion attracted more and more of the public attention, and in the year 1820, became a prominent topic of discussion. As relief could only be obtained by an amendment of the constitution, and as there was then no way of effecting such an amendment but by the call of a convention, the friends of reform made this measure their rallying point, and pressed it with such earnestness, that on the 13th of March, 1821, an act recommending a convention of the people of the state, was passed by the legislature.

This act authorized the taking of the sense of the electors on the question whether a convention should be held; and in case of a decision in the affirmative, provided for the choosing and assembling of delegates. Such being the decision, a convention was accordingly chosen, and in August, 1821, it entered upon its duties.

The delegates to this body immediately resolved to take up the whole constitution, with the view not only of making the particular amendments so loudly called for by their constituents, but of giving the instrument a thorough revision. It soon became evident, that to carry out the views of the convention, it would be necessary to prepare an entirely new constitution. This was accordingly done; and the instrument, on being submitted to the people, was approved by a large majority of votes, and came into full effect on the first of January, 1823.

By this instrument, which was arranged in a lucid order, and expressed, for the most part, in a neat and perspicuous style, the general frame of the government was retained; but the changes in some of its most material arrangements were many and important.

The number of the senators was retained at 32, and the term of service was unaltered; but the number of the senate districts was doubled, the state being divided, for the election of senators, and also for judicial purposes, into eight districts. The house of assembly was fixed at 128. The numbers of these two branches, as thus settled, still remain.

The compensation of members of the legislature was permanently fixed; they were prohibited from receiving civil appointments from the governor and senate, or the legislature; officers of the federal government were prohibited from sitting in either house; and the legislature were empowered to remove, by a vote of two-thirds of the assembly, and a majority of the senate, the highest judicial officers. All these provisions have been retained in the constitution of 1846.

The term of service of the governor and lieutenant-governor was reduced to two years; the council of revision was abolished; and the qualified *veto* power, before possessed by that board, vested in the governor. These provisions remain in force.

The right of suffrage, (except as to persons of colour,) was placed on a new and enlarged basis. The freehold qualifications prescribed by the constitution of 1777 were abolished; but the payment of taxes, or some equivalent contribution to the public service, was still required. In 1826, this article was amended so as to require only citizenship, inhabitancy, and residence—thus introducing, in effect, universal suffrage, which yet exists.

Men of colour (except when citizens of three years' standing, owners of freeholds of the value of $250, and tax payers,) were prohibited from voting. This arrangement, though a provision for its alteration was separately submitted, by the convention of 1846, to the decision of the people, remains unaltered.*

* At the time of framing the constitution of 1777, there were few or no free persons of colour, possessed of the qualifications required of voters, within the state; and the question, whether the right of suffrage should be confined to *white* persons, seems not to have arisen. By the act of February 22d, 1788, new facilities were provided for the manumission of slaves. Under its operation, the number of free persons of colour continued to increase from year to year; and as these persons, when possessed of the requisite qualifications, were entitled to vote, the number of electors of colour increased in almost equal proportion, though it remained small until after 1817. The act of March 29th, 1799, provided for the gradual abolition of slavery, by declaring that every child born *after* the 4th of July, 1799, of a slave, should be free—if a male, on attaining the age of 28 years, and if a female, on attaining the age of 25. By this law, a large number of persons of colour became free in 1817; and thus the number of coloured voters was largely increased. The act of March 31st, 1817, declared that after the 4th of July 1827, every coloured person born *before* July 4th, 1799, should be free—thus completing the abolition of slavery within this state. The convention of 1821—in view of the rapid increase of free coloured persons, by the operation of these laws, and by immigration from other states, and of the inexpediency of intrusting the right of suffrage to a class practically ineligible to even the humblest office, and doomed by positive enactment, as well as the stronger law of public opinion, to a degrading social inferiority—thought it necessary to insert in the constitution the prohibitory clause mentioned in the text; and the like reasons, it may be presumed, led to the rejection of the amendment submitted by the convention of 1846. As a consequence of their exclusion from the list of voters, the constitutions of 1821 and 1846 carefully provide, that persons of colour shall not be subject to direct taxation, unless seised and possessed of real estate sufficient to entitle them to vote.

It was provided that all elections by the citizens should be by ballot, except for such town officers as might, by law, be directed to be otherwise chosen. This provision is retained.

The appointing power was placed on an entirely new footing. The council of appointment was abolished. Militia officers, except a few of the highest grades, were made elective. The appointment of the higher judicial officers was assigned to the governor with the consent of the senate. Justices of the peace were to be appointed by the boards of supervisors and the county judges; a provision which was altered in 1826, when these officers were made elective.

The secretary of state, and other state officers, were to be appointed by the senate and assembly. Sheriffs, coroners, and clerks of counties were made elective; and they so continue.

The higher courts were empowered, as in the constitution of 1777, to appoint their own clerks. Local officers were, in some cases, made appointable by local authorities, and a discretionary power was given to the legislature, to fix the manner in which officers not specially provided for in the constitution should be elected or appointed. In the exercise of this power, the appointment of many administrative officers was afterwards devolved, by law, upon the governor and senate—thus greatly enlarging the patronage of the former, and making more close the connexion of the latter with the appointing power.

All these provisions, except such as gave the appointing power to the people, or to local authorities, have been swept away by the constitution of 1846.

The constitution of 1821 retained the court of chancery, the supreme court, and the court for the correction of errors, as established in 1777; except that the judges of the supreme court were relieved from circuit duties.

The official tenure of the higher judicial officers, as fixed by the constitution of 1777, was retained; but they were made removeable by joint resolution of the senate and assembly, to be passed with the concurrence of two-thirds of the latter, and a majority of the former. The like power of removal is contained in the constitution of 1846.

For the trial of issues of fact, and of criminal cases, and for such equity jurisdiction as the legislature might assign to them, eight circuit judges were created. This arrangement was soon found to be inadequate, and as the state increased in population, the deficiency became more and more apparent, until, in 1845, it formed one of the chief necessities for calling a new convention.

The provisions of the constitution of 1777 for the security of personal rights were retained; but as they were not deemed sufficiently comprehensive, several new sections, mostly taken from the first amendments to the constitution of the United States, were added. These provisions, thus enlarged, are repeated in the constitution of 1846.

Provision was wisely made for further amendments without the agency of a convention. Amendments might be proposed in either house. If agreed to by a majority of the members elected to each house, and by two-thirds of each house of the legislature next elected, they were then to be submitted to the people; and if ratified by a majority of the electors, to become a part of the constitution. In the mode thus prescribed, several amendments, some of which have been alluded to, were adopted by successive legislatures, approved by the people, and thus added to the constitution.

The convention of 1846, had its origin in the failure of certain amendments on the subject of state debts and liabilities, proposed in 1844, to obtain, in the following year, the assent of *two-thirds* of each house, though they commanded that of a *majority* of each.

These amendments were directed to two objects: *First*, to confirm the pledges and guarantees of the memorable act of 1842, "to provide for paying the debts and preserving the credit of the state;" and *secondly*, to limit and control the debt-contracting power of the legislature. They had called out so general a discussion, and had been so favourably received by large portions of the people, and there was also so general a conviction that the judiciary establishments required a thorough re-organization, that the legislature of 1845, on the failure of the proposed amendments to receive the constitutional majority, passed an act recommending a convention to revise the constitution; and directing the question, whether such a convention should be held, to be submitted to the people at the annual election in November, 1845. In the event of an affirmative decision, an election for delegates was to be held in April, 1846, and the delegates then elected were to assemble in June, 1846, for the execution of their trust.

The people having decided for a convention, delegates were chosen and assembled. The result of their labours appeared, in due time, in the form of a new constitution, which, having been approved by a large majority of the people, is now, as to all matters within the circle of state sovereignty, the supreme law of the state, and of the three millions of souls dwelling within its bounds.

All the provisions of the constitution of 1821, with the amendments made to it, by which the right of suffrage, and other civil rights, were extended or more fully secured, are preserved in this instrument. It contains, in addition, many new provisions of the like nature, conceived in a still larger spirit of democratic liberty, and giving new efficacy and vigour to the popular will.

Thus—the governor is no longer required to be either a native citizen or a freeholder; the general power of appointment before vested in him and the senate, is given directly to the people; and the legislature are authorized to confer on the board of supervisors, in the several counties, such further powers of local legislation and administration as they may prescribe. By these changes, and by other like provisions, the central power before existing at the seat of government is broken up; the number of elective officers much increased; and the immediate agency of the people in the practical administration of the government, very greatly enlarged.

The principle of these changes receives its boldest illustration in the establishment of an entirely new judiciary, elective in all its parts, and for short terms of service.* Clerks of courts, and district attorneys, and all judicial officers of cities and villages, are also to be chosen in the same way. The secretary of state, comptroller, treasurer, and attorney general, instead of being appointed by the senate and assembly for three years, are also to be chosen by the people, and to hold for but two years. A state engineer and surveyor, canal commissioners, and inspectors of state prisons, are also to be chosen, and for short terms, by the people.

All county officers, whose appointment is not otherwise provided for, are to be elected by the people, or to be appointed by the boards of supervisors, as the legislature may direct: and they may also direct all city, town, and village officers, whose appointment is not otherwise provided for, to be chosen by the electors of their respective municipalities.

Along with these proofs of undoubting confidence in the people, there is displayed, throughout the whole instrument, a jealousy of their representatives, which has led to the forbidding of some powers before possessed by the legislature, and to the limiting of others yet intrusted to that body. The principle of responsibility on the part of legislators and of other public agents, is also more fully developed by bringing

* Art. 6. The court for the correction of errors, the court of chancery, the supreme and circuit courts, and, except in the city of New York, the county courts, as they existed under the constitution of 1821, are all abolished. In lieu of them, the constitution of 1846 creates, *first—a court of appeals,* to consist of eight judges, four to be elected by the electors of the state for eight years, and four to be selected from the class of justices of the supreme court having the shortest time to serve:—*Secondly—a supreme court,* having jurisdiction in law and equity, to consist of thirty-two justices, to be chosen in eight separate districts, the electors of each district choosing four; the justices first chosen to be classified, so that one justice in each district shall go out of office every two years; but every justice afterwards chosen is to hold for eight years; general terms of the court to be held, in the several districts, by three or more of the justices; and special terms of the court, and circuit courts, to be held by any one or more of the justices, any one or more of whom may also preside in courts of oyer and terminer;—and, *thirdly, a county court,* of civil jurisdiction, in each county, (except in New York, where the court of general sessions, the court of common pleas, and the superior court, are left in existence subject to the direction of the legislature,) to be held by a single judge, chosen by the electors of the county for four years, which judge may be charged, by the legislature, with equity jurisdiction in special cases, and, in certain counties, with the duties of surrogate, and, with two justices of the peace, may hold courts of sessions of criminal jurisdiction. Art. 6. §§ 2, 3, 4, 6, 12, 14; Art. 14. § 12. It is much to be regretted that the new method of appointing judicial officers should be associated at its commencement with a judicial system, in many respects, not well arranged. The elections of 1847 have fully sustained the confidence reposed by the convention of 1846 in the capacity of the people to select upright and able judges; but there seem to be defects in the system which no amount of ability or integrity in the judges can entirely overcome, and which will soon demand material and extensive changes.

them nearer to the people, by giving greater publicity to their proceedings; and by subjecting such proceedings and their authors, at shorter intervals, to the public judgment.

Thus—the senators, instead of being chosen for four years, and in large districts, are to be chosen for only two years, and in single districts. A like change is made in regard to the assembly, the members of which are also to be elected in single districts.

The governor is required annually to communicate to the legislature each case of reprieve, commutation, or pardon granted by him, with its particulars.

The compensation of members of the legislature, as before provided, is not to exceed three dollars a day; and it is also now added, that such pay shall not exceed, in the aggregate, three hundred dollars for per diem allowance, except in proceedings for impeachment, and except that the members may also be paid for their attendance at extra sessions convened by the governor.

No bill can be passed unless by the assent of a majority of all the members elected to each branch; and the yeas and nays, in every case, are to be entered on the journal. Private and local bills are to embrace but one subject, and that is to be expressed in the title.

The legislature are absolutely prohibited from granting divorces; from authorizing lotteries, or allowing the sale of lottery tickets; and from sanctioning, in any manner, the suspension of specie payments by banks or bankers. They may authorize the forming of banking and other corporations under general laws; but corporations are not to be created by special act, except for municipal purposes, and where the object cannot be attained under general laws. Dues from corporations are to be secured by the individual liability of the corporators, and by other means to be prescribed by law.

But the most important of the new provisions, especially as affecting the power and duties of the legislature, are those which relate to the funds, property, and credit of the state.

It was, as we have seen, in the anxieties of the people touching this great interest, that the convention had its birth. Accordingly, on this point, the provisions of the constitution are most thorough and explicit. To secure to its true uses the public property; to prevent the increase of the existing state debt; to provide for its full and early payment; and to guard, in future, the resources and credit of the state against debt, improvidence, and hazard—these were the chief ends which the convention laboured to accomplish. Wise and worthy ends, all, I think, must admit them to be; however any may doubt as to some of the details of which I am to speak.

The provisions of the constitution of 1821, making the capital of the common school fund inviolate, are retained, and are extended to the literature and United States deposite funds. The revenues of the literature fund are to be applied exclusively to academies. Of the revenues of the United States deposite fund, $25,000, annually, are to be appropriated in aid of the common school fund.

The canal fund and its revenues are made the subject of regulations still more careful and minute. After paying ordinary expenses and repairs, there is set apart, out of these revenues, in each year, the sum of $1,300,000, until 1855; and from that time the sum of $1,750,000, in each year, as a sinking fund, to pay the canal debt, until it shall be wholly paid. Of the surplus revenues, $350,000 in each year, until payment of the entire canal debt is provided for, and after that period, $1,500,000 in each year, are to be set apart, as a sinking fund, to pay the general fund debt. From the same source, there is made a further annual appropriation, of not exceeding $200,000, for the use of the general fund, in defraying the expenses of the state; and the remainder of the surplus canal revenues is to be applied by the legislature to the completion of the Erie canal enlargement, and the Genesee and Black river canals.

There are some further provisions of a prospective nature, to meet certain contingencies; but it is expressly provided, that if the sinking funds for the payment of the canal debt, and the general fund debt, or either of them, prove insufficient to satisfy the public creditors, as their claims become payable, the legislature shall, by taxes, so increase the revenues of these sinking funds, as to make them sufficient perfectly to preserve the public faith.

Thus much for the past and the present; let us now look at the provisions for the future.

Laws appropriating public moneys are only operative to authorize payments of such moneys for two years. Every law making a new appropriation, or continuing or reviving an appropriation, must distinctly specify the sum appropriated, and the object to which it is to be applied; and it shall not be sufficient for such law to refer to any other law to fix such sum. The like provision is made in respect to every law imposing, continuing, or reviving a tax; and on the final passage in either house of every such act, and of every act creating a debt or charge, or making, continuing, or reviving any appropriation of public or trust money or property, or releasing, discharging, or commuting any claim or demand of the state, three-fifths of all the members elected to the house are required to be present to constitute a quorum; and the question is to be taken by ayes and noes, which are to be entered on the journals.

The credit of the state is not, in any manner, to be given or loaned to, or in aid of, any individual, association, or corporation.

The legislature may authorize the contracting of debts to meet casual deficits or failures in the revenues, or for expenses not provided for; but such debts, direct and contingent, singly, or in the aggregate, cannot, at any time, exceed one million of dollars; and they may also contract debts to repel invasion, suppress insurrection, or defend the state in war. With these exceptions, no debt can be contracted on behalf of the state, unless authorized by a law for some single work or object, to be distinctly specified therein; and such law must provide for imposing and collecting a direct annual tax sufficient to pay the interest on the debt as it falls due, and to pay the principal within eighteen years. On the final passage of every such law, the question is to be taken in a special form; and, moreover, before the law can take effect, it must have been submitted to the people at a general election, and have received a majority of all the votes cast for and against it. Whenever any such law shall have been duly passed by the legislature and approved by the people, it may be repealed by the legislature; but the tax imposed by it is irrepealable so far as may be necessary to pay any debt contracted under it.

In hereafter organizing cities and villages, the legislature are so to restrict their power of taxation, of contracting debts, and of loaning credit, as to prevent the abuse of these powers.

The instrument exhibits an earnest desire on the part of its framers to reform and simplify the practice of the law, and to render the administration of justice less dilatory and expensive than heretofore. Admission to practice in all the courts is secured to every male citizen of good moral character, possessing the requisite learning and ability; provision is to be made by law for enabling parties in civil cases to waive a jury trial; testimony, in equity cases, is to be taken in like manner as in cases at law; witnesses are not to be unreasonably detained; and no person is to be incompetent as a witness on account of his opinions on religious subjects. Provision is to be made for the speedy publication of all statute laws, and of such judicial decisions as the legislature may deem expedient.

Tribunals of conciliation for the decision of controversies voluntarily submitted may be established by law.

To secure further reforms in the methods of procedure, the legislature, at their first session after the adoption of the constitution, are to appoint commissioners to simplify and abridge the rules of practice, pleadings, forms, and proceedings of the courts.

But the views of the convention were not limited to a mere improvement in the forms of procedure. They contemplated a bold, and, in the judgment of some, a startling innovation in our system of jurisprudence; for the legislature are also directed to appoint commissioners to reduce, into a written systematic code, the whole body of the law, or so much, and such parts thereof, as they shall think practicable or expedient. The two boards thus provided for, have, accordingly, been appointed, and are now engaged in the performance of their difficult, but important and honourable tasks.

The guarantees for the security of life, liberty, and property, contained in the former constitutions, are continued, and with some additional safeguards in respect to property when taken for public use.

To ensure the soundness and stability of the circulating medium, all bank notes are to be registered, and ample security is to be required for their redemption in specie; the stockholders in every banking association or corporation, after the first of January, 1850, are to be individually responsible to the amount of their stock, respectively, for all its debts contracted after that day; and in case of the insolvency of any bank, the bill-holders are to have preference in payment over all other creditors.

In another matter of much importance to the interests of trade, a great and long-needed reform has been effected. All offices for the weighing, measuring, or inspecting of any merchandise, produce, or commodity, are abolished; and no such office can hereafter be created.

In view of the unfitness of long leases of agricultural lands, to the genius of our government, and the habits and temper of our people, and moved probably by facts of recent occurrence—too familiar to require, and too discreditable to allow me to dwell on them—the constitution provides, that no lease or grant of such lands for a longer period than twelve years, hereafter made, shall be valid; and it declares that all fines, quarter sales, and other like restraints upon alienation, hereafter reserved, shall be void.

Some other new provisions, of a miscellaneous nature, deserve to be mentioned.

The constitution of 1821 authorized the passing of laws excluding from the right of suffrage persons convicted of infamous crimes. The constitution of 1846 authorizes the extension of such laws to persons convicted of bribery or larceny. It also authorizes the passing of laws depriving persons making, or interested in, bets or wagers on any election, of the right to vote at such election.

The secretary of state, and other state officers, the judges of the court of appeals, and the justices of the supreme court, are to receive fixed compensations, which can neither be diminished nor increased during their continuance in office; and they are not to receive to their own use, fees or perquisites of office. This latter prohibition is also extended to all judicial officers, except justices of the peace.

In addition to the power of removing officers for official misconduct, contained in the constitution of 1821, the constitution of 1846 directs provision to be made by law for the removal, in such cases, of certain of the new officers hereafter to be elected at the general elections.

Two omissions remain to be mentioned—the one—of a provision contained in the constitution of 1821 requiring the assent of two-thirds of the members elected to each branch of the legislature, to bills creating, altering, or renewing corporations—and the other—of the provision, contained in the constitutions of 1777 and 1821, rendering ministers of the gospel, and priests of every denomination, ineligible to any civil or military office. Experience had clearly shown the inexpediency of the first named of these provisions, and the omission of the last obliterates an anomalous distinction. It may, however, be questioned whether the theoretic equality now secured to the clergy will, in the long run, be found of as much practical benefit to them or to their flocks, as both have heretofore derived from the distinct recognition, in the two former constitutions, of the sacred character and preeminent usefulness of the clerical profession.

The new constitution, like that of 1821, contains a distinct recognition of the power of the people to alter or abrogate, as they may find occasion, in part or in whole, their existing government, and to establish new systems in its place; and it closes with a most emphatic avowal, not only of their right, but of their duty, at frequent intervals, to examine the principles, and to scrutinize the working of their organic laws. For this purpose, in addition to the former mode of amendment, through the action of the legislature, approved by the people, it is now provided, that at the general election to be held in the year 1866, and in each twentieth year thereafter, and at such other times as the legislature may direct, the question, whether there shall be a convention to revise and amend the constitution, shall be submitted to the people, and if a majority of the electors decide in the affirmative, the legislature, at its next session, shall provide, by law, for the election of delegates to such convention.

ASSOCIATION OF IDEAS.* •

(BY PROFESSOR G. TUCKER.)

It is a familiar truth that our thoughts, however erratic and irregular they may seem to be, obey certain fixed laws, and that in their most capricious wanderings, even in the wildest flights of imagination,

* I have chosen to use this term, by which that mental faculty which is ever joining thought to thought, has been familiarly known ever since Locke's Essay was published, notwithstanding the objections that Brown and others have made to it. The first of these objections—that the faculty applies to *feelings* as well as *ideas*, is well founded if we regard the present limited sense in which the word "idea" is taken; but it must be recollected that Locke used it in a far more extensive sense, and in fact applied it to all our mental acts whatever—to *sensations* and *emotions* as well as mere *conceptions*. The impropriety of the expression, therefore, growing out of one of those mutations of language that time is ever producing, it hardly seems worth while to change it on that account after it had obtained general use, no more than it has been to lay aside the terms *sun-rise* and *sun-set*, since the Copernican theory has shown us that they were founded in error.

But the second objection, to wit: that the term "association" has been suggested by a false theory, which it is calculated to propagate and confirm, rests on a gratuitous and very questionable assumption of Dr. Brown's. I am decidedly of opinion that in this he is mistaken, and that one mental act never did, and never can, suggest another, unless the two have been previously associated, either directly, themselves, or indirectly by their signs, by language or other indicia. If any such case can be shown, then the preceding theory of repetition must fall to the ground. If none can be shown, then the term "association" as indicating the material fact in producing the phenomenon, is better than that of "suggestion" proposed by Brown.

there is the same natural connexion between the conjoined ideas as exists in any process of reasoning.

This connexion between the thoughts that spontaneously spring up in our minds, and which is commonly termed "the association of ideas," has been a favourite theme with those who have speculated on our mental operations, from the days of Aristotle, who seems first to have noticed the connexion, to the present day. Yet when we consider how much has been written on this curious and interesting subject, it is remarkable that more has not been added to the brief hints thrown out by the Greek philosopher.

Some, for example, have merely repeated and expatiated on Aristotle's views; some have noticed the connexion between the ideas of a series, without mention of Aristotle; while others again, observing the same silence, have, by expanding and illustrating his views, obtained the credit of originating the theory of the connexion or association of ideas. Thus, Sir James M'Intosh, according to Coleridge, affirmed, in the lectures delivered by him at Lincoln's Inn Hall, that "the law of association, as established in the contemporaniety of the original impressions, formed the basis of all true psychology; and that ontological or metaphysical science not contained in such psychology, was but a web of abstractions and generalizations. Of this prolific truth, of this great fundamental law he declared Hobbes to have been the original *discoverer*, while its full application to the whole intellectual system we owe to David Hartley; who stood in the same relation to Hobbes, as Newton to Kepler; the law of association being that to the mind which gravitation is to matter."

Coleridge himself, however, denies the claims both of Hobbes and Hartley; and he thus succinctly and perspicuously explains Aristotle's theory:

"Ideas, by having been together, acquire a power of recalling each other; or every partial representation awakes the total representation of which it had been a part. In the practical determination of this common principle, to particular recollections, he admits five agents or occasional causes: 1st. Connexion in time, whether simultaneous, preceding, or successive; 2d. Vicinity, or connexion in space; 3d. Interdependence, or necessary connexion, as cause and effect; 4th. Likeness; and, 5th. Contrast. As an additional solution of the occasional seeming chasms in the continuity of reproduction, he proves that movements or ideas possessing one or the other of these five characters had passed through the mind as intermediate links, sufficiently clear to recall other parts of the same total impressions with which they had co-existed, though not vivid enough to excite that degree of attention which is requisite for distinct recollection, or as we may aptly express it, *after-consciousness*. In association, then, consists the whole mechanism of the reproduction of impressions in the Aristotelian psychology. It is the universal law of the passive fancy, and *mechanical* memory; that which supplies to all the other faculties their objects, to all thought the elements of its material."

The recent editor of Reid's works, Sir William Hamilton, while he denies Coleridge's competence to expound Aristotle, agrees with him in his reverence for that philosopher, whom Hamilton pronounces to be at once "the founder and finisher" of the theory of association—at once "the Copernicus, the Kepler, and the Newton of the intellectual world."

Without stopping to maintain that the opinions of Professor Hamilton at once exaggerate Aristotle's merit and do injustice to later psychologists, especially to one of his predecessors, Dr. Thomas Brown, I will remark that the result of all preceding inquiries on the subject of association consists in maintaining the following principles: to wit:

That in all our trains of thought, whether we remember, imagine, or reason, the mind cannot pass from one idea or feeling to another, except by certain principles of connexion between the conjoined thoughts or feelings, which are sometimes said to be three, sometimes four, and are occasionally extended to five; and which are all comprehended under contiguity of time or place, resemblance, and contrast.

That whenever any thought or feeling is presented to the mind, it suggests another related to it in one of the before mentioned ways; that is to say, every thought or feeling suggests some other thought or feeling which either bears a resemblance to it, or is contrasted with it, or was formerly in the mind at the same time or in the same place as the suggesting thought.

The residue of the theory of association consists in showing how these principles of connexion sometimes manifest themselves in memory, sometimes in imagination; why one particular association or set of asiociations suggest themselves in preference to others; and in what way the associating faculty has influence on our tastes, opinions, and conduct.

While some metaphysicians have extended the principles of connexion to five, by separating contiguity of time from contiguity of place, and in the former distinguishing casual connexion in time from cause and effect, others have reduced them to two; and Brown attempted to reduce them all to one—*proximity* or contiguity of time.

It is the object of the following remarks to show that they may all —proximity included—be referred to a more general or elementary law, of which the principles of connexion specified by Aristotle and others are mere corollaries.

It is a law both of the material and the sentient parts of our nature, that whatever body or mind has once done, they find it easier to do again, and have a propensity to repeat. This tendency to a repetition of our former acts is what is meant when we speak of the force of habit; of which some examples may be given, and first, of the body.

Our appetite for food recurs in most force at the hour at which we have been accustomed to gratify it. This may in part be referred to the wants of our animal system, but not altogether, for often if the customary hour be passed by without food, the appetite is lessened, or even ceases altogether.

So as to sleeping and waking. These changes of our sensitive state are apt to recur at the usual hour, though the previous state may have been different from our previous usage.

We require the same quantity of salt, sugar, or other condiment in our food and drink that we have previously used. The great diversity among individuals as to the quantities used, and even with the same individual at different times, can be referred only to the law of habit.

- In like manner persons accustomed to the use of tobacco, opium, alcohol, or other stimulant of the nervous system, have a craving for them which is altogether the creature of habit.

So the act of masticating our food being commonly preceded by a sight of that food and accompanied by a copious flow of saliva, it follows that whenever we see savoury food, the saliva is apt of itself to flow, as one of the train of sensations and acts of which the sight of food is the first.

It is by the same law of habit that certain diseases and states of the body are apt to return at the same hour every day, or every other day, or every week, &c., which physicians call *periodicity.*

To this, too, we must refer that unconscious repetition of little gestures or movements of the limbs or features which the French call *tic;* and so likewise the very frequent use which some persons make of particular words.

Again: we are accustomed, in all quick vibratory motions of our hands, to move both in the same direction and with the same celerity. It is therefore with some difficulty that we can give to the two hands quick simultaneous motions that are entirely different. To effectuate it, we must make repeated trials, so as to superinduce a new habit; and this, too, though either hand may separately perform such motions with ease.

It is to the same influence that we must attribute much or most of the skill which practice gives in writing, playing on a musical instrument, or in the use of tools. A part of this acquired talent no doubt arises from our profiting by experience to correct former errors or failures, but nothing less than the law in question will explain the extraordinary ease and celerity that practice commonly gives, which fact we recognise by calling it *expertness.*

This tendency to repetition is quite as strong in the *mind*, as in the body; and it would perhaps be still more manifest if we were as much in the habit of looking at our mental as our bodily operations.

Whatsoever has been presented to any one of our senses, so as to produce sensation, that same mental act the mind immediately copies or repeats when the object is no longer present. In other words, what

we see, hear, feel, &c., we naturally remember, for every act of remembrance is neither more nor less than a repetition of the mind's former act—the only difference between the two being that the copy is
less vivid and distinct than the original.　To know the difference, one
has only to look at a visible object—a chair, for example—and close
his eyes; the image of the chair will there be present to his mind
exactly as it was at first, except that it will be more faint and shadowy.
So if I pronounce some words, as " the declaration of independence,"
the mind again hears the same succession of sounds, only they are,
compared with the original, as a whisper to ordinary speech: and so of
the other senses.　It must, however, be remarked that while the mind
repeats its impressions, *immediately after it has received them*, by its
own inherent powers, it *subsequently* requires a first impression to be
given to it.　But in this case, as soon as a part of a former series of
thoughts is presented to it, it forthwith, by the same self-copying tendency, completes the whole series; as the electric fluid passes along the
whole conducting wire the moment it touches a point of that wire.[*]
In all these cases the action of the brain, of the nerves, or whatever
part of the system it may be which precedes thought, is precisely similar to that which took place at first, except that it is of less force or
intensity.

In a word, a river does not more naturally run in the channel its
waters have previously formed, or a stone fall to the ground, than the
mind of man repeats its previous impressions or states.

As a consequence of the mind's thus accurately repeating or copying
its former states, it copies all parts of the impression which are simultaneous or co-existent, in the same order of juxtaposition, as when they
were first perceived, and those parts that are not co-existent in time,
in the same order of succession.　In the first class of objects—co-
existent sensations—its copies may be assimilated to daguerreotype
pictures in delicacy and fidelity; in the second class—sensations in
succession—to a faint and distant echo.

This repeating tendency of the mind has different degrees of intensity, according to circumstances, which seem to be principally, if not
wholly, there.

1st. *The copy is most lasting and distinct when the original impression was most forcible.*　A bright colour, a loud sound, a pungent
taste, &c., are better remembered, that is, are more apt to be repeated,
than weaker sensations.

2d. *The repeating tendency is strengthened by every repetition.*

---

[*] In these references to the physical world, I do not mean to identify the operations of the mind with those of matter ; but offer them merely by way of illustration
from some seeming resemblance.　It is indeed not improbable that those changes in
our corporeal system which always precede thought, obey the same laws as the matter (in its subtler forms) that is cognizable by our senses; but, supposing that they
do, the *modus operandi* of these material agencies on the sentient principle we are
utterly ignorant of, and must ever remain so.

What we have often seen or often heard, is thereby better remembered. By this process of. repetition, children are taught to remember more, and more accurately.

3d. *It is strongest immediately after the impression, and becomes weaker by time.* A longer sentence, or a greater number of lines, for example, can be remembered, immediately after they are heard than an hour afterwards; and in an hour than a day afterwards. These weak impressions are like writing on sand—the last nearly effaces those which preceded it.

4th. *It is most strong and enduring when it is accompanied by any feeling of pleasure or pain.* We seldom forget a favour, and never an insult or injury.* The poet or orator who most pleases us is best remembered. Passion or lively feeling seems to have the same effect on our minds as heat has on wax; it fits them for receiving accurate and distinct impressions: and if one takes a distant retrospect of his past life, he will find that the pictures which are still reposited in his memory consist altogether of his past joys or sorrows, of his fears, or vexations, of his hopes or triumphs. Of the countless multitude of thoughts that have passed through his mind scarce a vestige remains but of those that have been embalmed by emotion. It is because this sensibility decreases with years, that old men hardly remember recent occurrences.

5th. *It is also of importance that the succession of perceptions should not be too much confounded or intermingled with different feelings and other vivid perceptions.* Whatever is communicated with clearness and distinctness will be far better remembered than that which has been stated confusedly. Hence, in very exciting scenes, as in cases of personal rencounter, in which death ensues, the variety of lively ideas and feelings which then supervene in the mind of the spectator, prevent that accurate repetition of what has been witnessed in the precise order of time and place in which they occurred, just as water ceases to be a faithful mirror as soon as its surface is ruffled: and this is the reason why, in courts of justice, reputable witnesses of very exciting scenes are often mistaken, and are found to contradict each other. Particular parts of such scenes may indeed be repeated or remembered with the liveliness of a perception experienced but the moment before, but there is not the same truth and fidelity as to the order of succession.

6th. *Where an idea has been associated with many others it is more likely to be remembered.* Hence, those who view a subject technically, or scientifically, or philosophically, remember it longer and remember it better than those who view it only in its casual relations. By these aids old people may remember some things better than most young ones. So the extraordinary memory which princes often have for faces and names; or which a dairy-maid has for her cows; a shep-

---

* Our sensibility to pain is more intense than that to pleasure; but happily for us it is far less frequently put in requisition.

herd for his sheep; a drover for his cattle; and a clerk for his papers, is the consequence of their habit of making nicer discriminations, and of their having more links of association. Each one is a new anchor, as it were, to prevent the mind from being borne away by the intervening currents of scenes and incidents.

These laws of the repeating faculty or modifying circumstances, which determine its relative strength in each particular case, having all degrees of intensity, and acting sometimes together and sometimes in conflict, are capable of being infinitely compounded, and thus give a boundless variety to the mind's repetitions of its previous impressions.

The tendency of the mind to repetition, thus modified, is capable of explaining all the phenomena of conception, memory and imagination; and it shows why it is that all conjoined thoughts, whether co-existent or successive, are related either by contiguity of time or place, resemblance or contrast: in other words, that those principles of connexion are not ultimate facts, as has been supposed, but are all referrible to this repeating tendency, as I shall now attempt to show.

First, As to *contiguity* or *proximity* of *place.* If we admit the self-repeating tendency of the mind, then objects perceived at the same place will be afterwards mutually suggestive. Thus, I have seen an individual—say the late Mr. Duponceau in that chair*—the two objects being parts of the same visual impression. A sight of the chair alone, giving a mental impulse similar to that formerly experienced, the mind goes on and completes the picture, that is, the former train, by suggesting the idea of Mr. Duponceau. So if I hear the letters A, B, C, having previously heard them followed by D, E, &c., these last letters rise spontaneously in my mind, by reason of its tendency to repeat its former motions or changes. So if I have heard the words, January, February, the mind, by the same inherent tendency, adds March, &c.

Second, Proximity or *contiguity* of *time.* By the process of repetition sight suggests the ideas of sleep, artificial light, suspension of business. In like manner, if any remarkable event has occurred on the 4th of July, the idea of the day may suggest that event, or the idea of the event may suggest the day. So any scene that occurred when the cholera prevailed, for example, or at Christmas, may be renewed or repeated by the mind, on the suggestion of those periods of time when they severally took place. It is to this form of the repeating process that we owe the faculty, or rather the uses of language. For, whenever we have heard the name of an individual, or an object, that is, heard certain sounds conjoined with the sight or conception of such person or object, their presence immediately suggests the name, and the name suggests the person or object. Thus, the sight of the ordinary covering for the head suggests to us the word *hat;* to a Frenchman it suggests the word *chapeau;* to a Spaniard, the word *sombrero;*

* This paper was read before the American Philosophical Society.

these different words suggests to these different persons the same object, for such must be the consequence of the mind's repeating its former series of motions or changes. It is in this way that cause and effect mutually suggest each other, they having the same connexion in time as exists between a name and its object, with this difference, that in the latter case the connexion is casual, while that between cause and effect is necessary and invariable.

Third, Resemblance. This principle of association is as familiar to all as the preceding. The sight of a portrait reminds us of the absent original. Nay, one person reminds us of another by a resemblance in a single feature, or gesture, or mode of speech. A piece of red sealing-wax may cause us to think of blood, or the wild poppy, &c., and this is equally the result of the self-copying tendency of the mind, when objects resemble each other they put the mind in the *same*, that is, in a precisely similar state. It is only by our instinctive consciousness of this similarity between our present and past mental states, that we ever perceive resemblance. A former series, containing the resembling object, being thus begun, the mind completes it, and thus is suggested what was formerly associated with that object. In this way, the sight of sealing-wax, producing in my mind the *same* (that is, precisely similar) action or change as the sight of blood, may repeat or renew a scene in which I witnessed the shedding of human blood, or mayhap the blood of an ox. So the aquiline nose of John may, by the like process of repetition, remind me of Thomas, with whose image a like aquiline nose was previously conjoined, and made a part of the series which constituted that image.

The difference between the cases of resemblance and proximity is rather apparent than real. In both cases the mind receives a precisely similar impression to one previously received, which gives it the impulse that causes it to repeat its former state. The only difference between them is, that in the case of *proximity* this similar impression is produced by the *same* object, seen at different times or places, while in *resemblance* the similar impression is produced by *similar*, but *different* objects.

Similarity has generally been considered as an elementary principle of connexion by psychologists; but Mr. Mill has endeavoured to reduce cases of resemblance to the class of proximity, because like things are often seen together at the same place, or at the same time, as trees in an avenue or wood, sheep in a flock, &c., but as this is not always true, the explanation is unsatisfactory. Thus, the red sealing-wax may remind us of blood, though the two were never before seen together; or a perfect stranger may remind us of a friend or acquaintance; and, putting the mind in the same state, either of the resembling objects may start the train with which the mind has been associated; precisely as in the case with proximity.

Fourth, Contrast. How this principle of association is a consequence of the self-copying tendency of the mind, is less obvious, but it is equally certain. What do we mean by *contrast?* Certainly objects of the same class, but differing as much as objects so closely related can differ in a single particular. Thus, high and low; good and bad; vice and virtue; pleasure and pain; north and south; light and darkness; day and night; wet and dry; yes and no—which are the first examples of contrast that chance to present themselves to my mind—show the closest affinity between the contrasted objects or conceptions. They stand in the relation of negative and affirmative; and commonly each one may be expressed by a negation of the other. They have usually been present to the mind at the same time, or rather in immediate succession; for, in the ever recurring wants and occasions of life, if we wish for, or like the one, we fear or dislike the other. In our objection to *darkness* we desire *light*. In wanting *dry weather*, we dread *rain*, or wanting *rain*, fear a *drought*. In feeling *cold*, we wish for *heat*. In flying *poverty*, we wish for *wealth*. In seeking an *affirmative* answer, we are fearful of a *negative*, and so on. These contrasts, that is, opposite affinities, having been always, or at least generally, in the mind together, the one, as in other cases of proximity, naturally suggest the other. Our thoughts habitually oscillating from one contrasted object to the other, as in the case of cause and effect, whenever one of them is presented, the mind, by its self-copying tendency, naturally passes to the other.

But it is alleged that contrast may be a principle of suggestion when the contrasted objects never have been present to the mind together—or even present at all. The sight of a giant, for instance, may suggest the idea of a dwarf, though the observer may never before have seen either a giant or a dwarf. Dr. Brown admits the fact, and, on the supposition that contrast is not an original principle of suggestion or association, he offers this explanation of it. Contrasted objects, he says, are striking deviations from the ordinary course of nature, and from this common feature one may suggest the other—thus in fact reducing this relation to that of *resemblance.* The solution would be plausible, if contrasts were always, like that of the giant and dwarf, deviations from the ordinary course of nature; but it so happens that most contrasts are of the most frequent and familiar recurrence; as day and night, wet and dry, high and low, great and small, &c. How then, it may be asked, can a giant suggest a dwarf to one who had never before seen either? This seeming difficulty is explained by the fact that the link of connexion by which the mind passes from thought to thought is sometimes between the objects themselves, and sometimes it is only between their *signs*, that is, the words by which they are indicated. Puns, rhymes, alliterations, are all examples of this class of associations. Now, although the spectator may never before have seen either a giant or a dwarf, he was familiar with the contrasted terms of high and low; little and great; and seeing a very tall

and large man, and then according to our general habit of embodying
our thoughts, in the habitual signs of those thoughts, that is, on his
thinking, in language, that the giant was *tall* or *high*, these words
would, by reason of the former habitual connexion in his mind between
high and *low*, naturally suggest the word *low* or *little*, &c., and thus
the mind would pass from the idea of a very tall man, or a giant, to
that of a very low or small man, a dwarf.

That our contrasts are often merely verbal, appears from the fact
that some words have more than one contrast; and while one of these
would be suggested to one man, another would be suggested to another. Thus, *right* is sometimes contrasted with *wrong*, and sometimes with *left*. To a lawyer, the word "right" would be more
likely to suggest the word "wrong," than "left;" but to a soldier on
drill, the same word would suggest "left" rather than "wrong."
Thus, too, *man* is sometimes contrasted with *brute;* sometimes with
woman; sometimes with *boy;* and sometimes with *horse;* and the word
would be apt to suggest that particular contrast to each individual with
which he had been most familiar. So *bread* might be contrasted with
meat by a commissary; with *wine* by a minister of the sacrament; and
with *water* by a jailer; for the mind of each would repeat its former
train of thought in which *bread* had formed a part.

It thus appears, that whether our thoughts be connected by proximity of time or of place, by resemblance or contrast, they are always
copies of the mind's former trains; and that in consequence of this, its
inherent self-copying tendency, the adjoining thoughts of every mental
train must come under one of these relations, since they comprehend
every class of conjoined ideas or feelings. In the cases of proximity
and contrast, the mind being made to begin its process of repetition by
a recurrence of the same object as formerly; and in the case of resemblance, by a different object. In other words, the mind being able,
by its inherent powers, only to repeat itself, when it passes from idea
to idea, the succeeding idea must always be suggested by the preceding
one, perceived on some former occasion, which preceding one might
have been produced either by the same object, as in the cases of proximity and contrast, or by a different object, but capable, by resemblance, of producing the same state of the mind.

When the succeeding trains of thought follow in the same order of
time and place as that in which they were originally perceived, we call
the copies acts of the *Memory*. When the trains are made up of what
has been perceived at different times and places, we call them acts of
the *Imagination*. All our conceptions of the future, if they at all vary
from the past, are of the latter character. If I think of my dinner yesterday, as it actually was, it is *memory;* if I think how much better it
had been if of canvass-back ducks, it is *imagination*.

But how is it that the mind, with its tendency to repeat its former
acts or movements, does not always copy them in the same order of

time and place? In other words, why does it sometimes imagine rather than remember?

The answer is to be found in those several circumstances or laws which give to the repeating faculty its relative strength for each particular occasion, as recency, frequency of repetition, being accompanied by emotion, &c. The mind obeys whichever of these modifying circumstances has the greatest influence, and *that one* may suggest something which occurred at another time or place, so as to make a train that had no exact prototype, in which case the train is fancy or imagination. Thus, the sight of that portrait may remind me of Mr. Jefferson;* and having recently heard his opinions cited relative to the late war with Mexico, and felt a lively interest in the subject, my mind may be more strongly disposed to think of what would probably have been his views of the war: that is, it may be more strongly drawn to this new train than to copy any former one in which that statesman was an actor. So from the same predominance of feeling, whether of surprise, or sense of injustice, the absence of the statues of Brutus and Cassius, in the funeral procession of Junia, the wife of the one and the sister of the other, caused those individuals to be more strikingly before the minds of the spectators than the twenty other illustrious men whose images were present. *Sed præfulgebant Cassius atque Brutus, eo ipso, quod effigies eorum non visebantur.* Here imagination prevailed against the senses; that is, the train of thought produced by the associating faculty was more lively than that suggested by actual vision, just as if we were to see a complete alphabet, with the exception of a blank space for a single letter, and our minds should think, as they easily might, more of the omitted letter than of those in sight.

Since every thought may suggest many things to which it had previous relations by proximity or resemblance, the mind is led to one or the other of these remembrances by the influence of the modifying circumstances that have been mentioned. Its process in making the selection is very well explained by Dr. Brown, by the operation of what he calls "the secondary law of suggestion," and which are virtually comprehended in those circumstances that give to the repeating faculty its precise degree of activity and force. These same circumstances which give to the memory this or that direction, do also divert or turn it from memory to imagination.

As the mind cannot pass from idea to idea, that is, carry on a train of thought, except by copying its previous impressions, this same faculty of association furnishes all the materials of our profoundest speculations, and of our simplest acts of reasoning, no less than those of memory and imagination.

Thus, whenever this faculty has suggested a proposition, that is to say, has affirmed or denied somewhat of something, either the predi-

---

* His portrait is in the Hall, with those of other Presidents of the Society.

cate or the subject of that proposition, by means of the same faculty, suggests a second *proposition* having a common link with the first, whereupon the mind intuitively sees the conclusion.   Suppose, for example, that the idea of *commerce* being presented to the mind, the associating or repeating faculty suggests that of *wealth*, as one of its proximate effects.   Then, either wealth or commerce, by the ever ready agency of the same repeating faculty, may suggest a second proposition.

In the first case, the reasoning, reduced to syllogistic form, would be as follows:

> *Commerce* is productive of national *wealth.*
> *Wealth* is favourable to *luxury and the arts:*
> Therefore, commerce is favourable, &c.

In the second case, by a like process, the reasoning would be in this mode:

> *Commerce* is productive of national *wealth.*
> *Commerce* has flourished most in *free States.*
> Therefore, civil freedom is not inconsistent with national wealth.

And so through all the moods and figures of which human reason is capable.

In conclusion, I would remark, that according to the simple view of the associating faculty here taken, there seems to be no difference between the mental operations of memory and recollection, except that in the last we watch the operations of our mind in order that when, in its ceaseless repetitions, it may chance to light upon the fugitive thought we are in pursuit of, we may profit by it.   But in both cases the mind copies its former states, and obeys the same laws.   It, therefore, is not to be believed that if Aristotle had distinctly seen that there were the same principles of connexion in both, or that the mind, in no train of thought whatever, could pass from idea to idea, except by one of the connecting links he had mentioned when treating of recollection, he would not have expressly stated it; nor, if he had seen, as Brown did, that memory and imagination were merely modes of the same faculty of association, that he would have treated of them in different parts of his work, without the slightest notice of their kindred character; and, lastly, were we to concede to his brief and somewhat obscure views on this branch of psychology, that very liberal and favourable interpretation which Sir William Hamilton has given, it is still quite clear that he did not perceive that all the mental operations and phenomena of which he separately treats could be resolved into the mind's repetition of its own operations.   It is as unnecessary to his glory, as it is unjust to others, to deny all merit to succeeding inquirers.

MIST AND CLOUDS.

(In Vol. II. of the Register, page 477, will be found a brief article under this title, explaining the phenomena of mist and clouds. We now copy from the National Intelligencer, the following communication of the learned Dr. Robert Hare, in opposition to the theory there stated—a duty we owe to the cause of science.)

Strictures on an article entitled Mist and Clouds, in the American Register for June last. By ROBERT HARE, M. D., *Emeritus Professor of Chemistry in the University of Pennsylvania, and Associate of the Smithsonian Institution.*

I have had much pleasure and have received much valuable information in reading "Stryker's American Register" for June. I object to the article on Mist and Clouds as tending to convey erroneous ideas. In that article it is stated that, agreeably to Sir Humphrey Davy, mists and clouds are produced by the "*radiation of vapour;*" and, moreover, it is alleged that mist, when "negatively electrified," deposites vapour more quickly, forming a heavy sort of dew.

The idea that vapour, when negatively electrified, deposites dew more copiously can only be true when the bodies which it moistens are differently electrified. I cannot understand why the deposition should be greater when the dew is negative and the bodies positive than when these are negative and the dew positive. In either case, the attraction is reciprocal, and the action and reaction equivalent.

Not less new to me is the suggestion that vapour can be "*transferred by radiation,*" though it be well known that it may give out heat by radiation, so as to be refrigerated and condensed.

Agreeably to the received Daltonian theory, water being present in excess, the amount of vapour in any given space will be directly as the temperature, whether air be present or not; in other words, it will be no less plentiful in a receiver replete with air than in one exhausted by an excellent air pump.

A mist or fog invariably results when air saturated with moisture at any temperature is refrigerated. Of course it ensues whenever air and water, at different temperatures, are brought into contact. The vapour due to the temperature of the water, when this is the warmer of the two, in rising into strata of the air too remote from the water to be sufficiently warmed by it, must be condensed by refrigeration. When the air is the warmer, the vapour with which it may be saturated, giving out its heat to the water by radiation or circulation, is of course converted into a mist or fog. Thus a wind blowing over the Gulf Stream is consequently warmed and supplied with an excess of vapour, which condenses on reaching the cooler aquatic region between the banks of Newfoundland and the neighbouring coast of North America.

The moisture which, in the state of vapour during autumnal

days, rises into the atmosphere; being condensed during the succeeding chilly nights, subsides as a fog, which is more or less dense and extensively prevalent in proportion to the difference between the temperature of the day and night. Clouds are caused by rarefaction as well as cold. This explains their being formed when air, saturated by moisture, reaches a certain elevation, where the atmospheric temperature and pressure and density are diminished. Moreover, at the moment of rarefaction, air robs the moisture of its heat and precipitates it as a fog. This was adverted to by Davy, in his elements, as the cause of clouds. It is just at the point where cold and rarefaction concur to condense the contained vapour that clouds are seen usually flitting above us.

It is well known that the surface of a vessel of cold water, exposed in a warmer atmosphere, becomes covered by a dew. The greater the quantity of aqueous vapour mingled with the air, the less the refrigeration requisite to produce this deposition. The highest temperature at which this dew can be obtained is called the dew point; and in proportion as this dew point, determined by a thermometer, is higher, the vapour is more abundant. Obviously, precisely the same reduction of heat which induces dew on a refrigerated surface would produce a fog or cloud, were it to take place in an adequate mass of air containing aqueous vapour.

Whenever a given weight of air is augmented in bulk, it must of course occupy a proportionally greater space, and will, in consequence, receive a quantity of aqueous vapour commensurate with the additional space. Consistently, an opposite change in its dimensions will have the opposite effect; so that, if saturated with vapour, a portion of this must be condensed commensurate with the space of which it may be deprived.

If, while the bulk of air remains unchanged, another portion of air, equally moist, be superadded to it, so as to increase proportionally the density of the resulting aggregate, all the vapour associated with the additional air will precipitate as fog or as rain.

As is it universally admitted that similarly electrified particles recede from each other proportionably to the intensity of the charge by which they may be affected, it seems inevitable that a charge of electricity must occasionally augment the bulk of extensive portions of the atmosphere, and thus cause more vapour to be associated with them; and that when discharges take place of electricity, so as to neutralize the excitement, the moisture held, in consequence of the excitement, must be precipitated. Thus, the air under the influence of electricity may be compared to a sponge under that of the hand, by which it may be made, by alternate pressure and relaxation, to receive and give out the water with which it may be contiguous.

I am under the impression that this agency of electricity is not sufficiently recognised by the meteorologists, if it has not entirely escaped them.

WINTER QUARTERS IN THE ARCTIC CIRCLE.

The approach of winter in the Arctic Circle is attended with many interesting changes. Snow begins to fall as early as August, and the whole ground is covered to the depth of two or three feet before the month of October. Along the shores and bays the fresh water, poured from the rivulets, or drained from the thawing of former collections of snow, becomes quickly converted into solid ice. As the cold augments, the air deposites its moisture in the form of a fog, which freezes into a fine gossamer netting, or spicular icicles, dispersed through the atmosphere, and extremely minute, that might seem to pierce and excoriate the skin. The hoar frost settles profusely, in fantastic clusters, on every prominence. The whole surface of the sea steams like a lime-kiln, an appearance called *frost-smoke*—caused as in other instances of the production of vapour, by the water being still relatively warmer than the incumbent air. At length, the dispersion of the mist, and consequent clearness of the atmosphere, announce that the upper stratum of the sea itself has cooled to the same standard; a sheet of ice spreads quickly over the smooth expanse, and often gains the thickness of an inch in a single night. The darkness of a prolonged winter now broods impenetrably over the frozen continent, unless the moon chances at times-to obtrude the faint rays, which only discover the horrors and wide desolation of the scene. The wretched settlers, covered with a load of bear skins, remain crowded and immured in their hut, every chink of which they carefully stop against the piercing cold; and, cowering about the stove or the lamp, they seek to doze away the tedious night. Their slender stock of provisions, though kept in the same apartment, is often frozen so hard as to require to be cut by a hatchet. The whole of the inside of their hut becomes lined with a thick crust of ice; and if they happen for an instant to open a window the moisture of the confined air is immediately precipitated in the form of a shower of snow. As the frost continues to penetrate deeper, the rocks are heard at a distance to split with a loud explosion. The sleep of death seems to wrap the scene in utter oblivious ruin.

Sir Edward Parry has thus beautifully described this effect: "The sound of voices, which, during the cold weather, could be heard at a much greater distance than usual, served now and then to break the silence which reigned around us; a silence far different from that peaceable composure which characterizes the landscape of a cultivated country; it was the death-like stillness of the most dreary desolation, and the total absence of animated existence."

During the winter at Melville Island people were heard conversing at the distance of a mile. This was no doubt, owing to the density of the frigid atmosphere, but chiefly to the absence of all obstruction in a scene of universal calm or darkness.

Melville Island was discovered on September 4th, 1819. Here Parry and his companions pushed forward, but soon found their course arrested by an impenetrable barrier of ice. They waited a fortnight, in hopes of overcoming it; and, about the 20th, their situation became truly alarming. The young ice began rapidly to form on the surface of the waters, retarded only by winds and swells; so that the commanding officer was convinced that, in the event of a single hour's calm, he would be frozen up in the midst of the sea. No option was, therefore, left but to return, and to choose between two apparently good harbours, which had been recently passed on Melville Island. Not without difficulty he reached this place on the 24th, and decided in favour of the more western haven, as affording the fullest security: but it was necessary to cut his way two miles through a large floe (a small expanse of salt-water ice) with which it was incumbered. To effect this arduous operation the seamen marked with boarding-pikes two parallel lines, at the distance of somewhat more than the breadth of the larger ship.

They sawed, in the first place, along the path tracked out, and then by cross-sawing, detached large pieces, which were separated diagonally, in order to be floated out; and sometimes boat sails were fastened to them, to take advantage of a favourable breeze. On the 26th, the ships were established in five fathoms water, at about a cable's length from the beach. For some time the ice was daily cleared round them. But this was soon found to be an endless labour, and they were allowed to be regularly frozen in for the winter.

The usual winter protection for the vessels is covering in the deck. Sometimes a house is erected on the shore, with blocks of ice, which soon become a solid concrete mass, which, being a slow conductor, checks the access of cold. It was necessary to be very economical of fuel, the small moss and turf which could be collected being too wet to be of any use. By placing the apparatus for baking in a central position, and by several other arrangements, the cabin was maintained in a very comfortable temperature; but still, around its extremities and the bed places, steam, vapour, and even the breath, settled first as moisture and then as ice. To remove these annoyances became, accordingly, a part of their daily employment. To keep the men's minds in a lively and cheerful state, plays were performed, Lieutenant Beechy being nominated stage-manager, and the other gentlemen coming forward as amateur performers; the Arctic management and the North Georgian Theatre were very popular. The officers had another source of amusement in the *North Georgian Gazette*, of which Captain Sabine became editor, and all were invited to contribute to this chronicle of the frozen regions. Even those who hesitated to appear as writers, enlivened the circle by good-humoured criticisms:

> Thus pass'd the time,
> Till through the lucid chambers of the south
> Look'd out the joyous sun.

It was on the 4th of November that this great orb ought to have taken his leave; but a deep haze prevented them from bidding a formal farewell, and from ascertaining the period to which refraction would have rendered him visible; yet he was reported to be seen from the mast head on the 11th. Amid various occupations and amusements the shortest day came on almost unexpected, and the seamen then watched with pleasure the twilight gradually strengthening at noon. On January 28th none of the fixed stars could be seen at that hour by the naked eye; and on February 1st and 2d, the sun was looked for, but the sky was wrapt in mist; however he was perceived from the main-top. Throughout the winter, the officers, at the period of twilight, had taken a regular walk for two or three hours; not proceeding, how-ever, further than a mile, lest they should be overtaken by a snow-drift. There was a want of objects to diversify this promenade. A monotonous surface of dazzling white covered land and sea; the view of the ships, the smoke ascending from them, the sound of human voices, which through the calm cold air was carried to an extraordinary dis-tance, alone gave animation to this wintry scene.

On March 16, the general attention was turned to the means of ex-trication from the ice. By May 17, the seamen had so far cut it from around the ships as to allow them to float; but in the sea it was still immovable. By the middle of June there were channels in which boats could pass; yet throughout this month and the following the great covering of ice in the surrounding sea remained entire, and kept the ships in harbour. On the 2d of August, however, the whole mass, by one of those sudden movements to which it is liable, broke up and floated out.—*London Illus. Times.*

THE SUPREMACY OF NATIONAL LAW.

(From the Hon. D. Webster's Speech, at the New Hampshire Festival.)

"We have all had our sympathies much enlisted in the Hungarian effort for liberty. We have all wept at its failure. We thought we saw a more rational hope of establishing independence in Hungary than in any other part of Europe where the question has been in agitation within the last twelve months; but despotic power from abroad inter-vened to suppress it.

"And, gentlemen, what will come of it I do not know. For my part, I feel more indignant at recent events connected with Hungary than at all those which passed in her struggle for liberty. I see that the Emperor of Russia demands of Turkey that the noble Kossuth and his companions shall be given up,—and I see that this demand is made in derision of the established law of nations. Gentlemen, there is some-thing greater on earth than arbitrary or despotic power. The light-ning has its power, and the whirlwind has its power, and the earth-

quake has its power.   But there is something among men more capable
of shaking despotic power than lightning, whirlwind, or earthquake—
that is the threatened indignation of the whole civilized world.   Gentlemen, the Emperor of Russia holds himself to be bound by the law of
nations, from the fact that he treats with nations—that he forms alliances; he professes in fact to live in a civilized age and to govern an
enlightened nation.   I say that if, under these circumstances, he shall
perpetrate so great a violation of natural law, as to seize these Hungarians and to execute them, he will stand as a criminal and malefactor
in the view of the law.   The whole world will be the tribunal to try
him, and he must appear before it and hold up his hand and plead and
abide its judgment.

The Emperor of Russia is the supreme law-giver in his own country,
and for aught I know, the executor of it also.   But, thanks be to God,
he is not the supreme law-giver or executor of the national law, and
every offence against that is an offence against the rights of the civilized
world, and if he breaks that law in the case of Turkey, or in any other
case, the whole world has a right to call him out and to demand his
punishment.

Our rights as a nation are held under the sanction of national law—
a law which becomes more important from day to day—a law which
none who profess to agree to it, are at liberty to violate.   Nor let him,
nor let any one imagine, that mere force can subdue the general sentiment of mankind.   It is much more likely to extend that sentiment and
to destroy that power which he most desires to establish and secure.

Gentlemen, the bones of poor John Wickliffe were dug out of his
grave seventy years after his death, and burnt, for his heresy, and his
ashes were thrown upon a river in Warwickshire.   Some prophet of
that day said:

> "The Avon to the Severn runs,
> The Severn to the sea,
> And Wickliffe's dust shall spread abroad,
> Wide as the waters be."

If the blood of Kossuth is taken by an absolute, unqualified,
unjustifiable violation of national law, what will it appease—what
will it pacify?   It will mingle with the earth—it will mix with the
waters of the ocean—the whole civilized world will snuff it in the
air, and it will return with awful retribution on the heads of those vio-
lators of national law and universal justice.   I cannot say when, or in
what form; but depend upon it, that if such an act take place, the
thrones and principalities and powers must look out for the consequences.

And now, gentlemen, let us do our part—let us understand the
position in which we stand as the great republic of the world at the
most interesting era of the world.   Let us consider the mission and
the destiny which Providence seems to have designed us for, and let
us so take care of our own conduct, that with irreproachable hands

and with hearts void of offence we may stand up whenever and wherever called upon, and with a voice not to be disregarded, say this shall not be done—at least not without our protest.

THE PRESS.

Conspicuous among the agencies which serve as pioneers in human progress, and without which science would be comparatively useless, is an untrammelled Press. It is the pillar and the cloud to direct the footsteps, and serves to perfect all that is grand in design, pure in motive and mighty in achievement. Its warning notes summon the soldier to the field of battle, and send terror and alarm to the wrong-doer and usurper. It strikes with Ithuriel's spear the high and the haughty in the moment of their impious daring, and stoops down to console and relieve the most abject of mortals. It has gone out to all nations upon its mission of light, bearing with it the standard of civilization, knowledge, commerce, arts and universal liberty. It takes to itself the wings of the morning and flies to the uttermost parts of the earth, diffusing joy and intelligence, and unites in bonds of amity and interest children who play around the beams of the morning and the setting sun. It imparts freshness and vigour to free and happy institutions, and quickens the pulsations of liberty. It elevates the patriotism of the statesman, and nerves the mailed arm of the warrior in the hour of battle. It enters within the domestic circle, that bower of earthly paradise, diffusing its salutary influences, and dries up the mourner's tears by teaching the consolations of religion.

What though it has transcended its high and its holy functions, and by its excesses abridged its power for good; it is yet equal to the reformation of its own abuses. Like the swollen stream, gathering blackness and fury and overflowing its boundaries, it will anon subside into its own healthful channel—be purified by the freedom of its own current, and roll onward to fertilize and bless the extended domain of humanity. Though petty despots have stretched out their puny sceptres over it, and prescribed limits beyond which it should not pass, it flows onward upon its errand of mercy, bearing upon its proud waves the tidings of civil and religious liberty to all mankind.

Thrice happy day, when barbarism and ignorance shall no longer degrade and afflict devoted man; when all shall meet together around the sacred home-hearth, like children of a common father; when all shall bask alike in the warm sunlight of their Maker; when all shall drink together at the pure gushing fountain of liberty; when man shall no longer lord it over his fellow man; when charity shall not be locked up in the icebergs of the heart, but spring up at every step from the best instincts of humanity; when vice and tyranny shall live only in the remembrance of the wrongs they have done to mar the page of history and darken the shadows of tradition. (*Senator Dickinson.*)

NOTICES OF BOOKS.

———

THE HORTICULTURIST AND JOURNAL OF RURAL ART AND RURAL
TASTE. EDITED BY A. J. DOWNING, Author of Landscape Gar-
dening, &c., published by Luther Tucker, Albany.

We have received the third volume of this valuable work, embracing
the twelve monthly numbers, from July, 1848. The study of horticulture has assumed of late years much importance, and a work so replete
with information, as is the journal of Mr. Downing, cannot fail to attract general attention. The Editor seems to have communicated an
interest to the subject which it did not before possess, and to enter into
the field of rural improvement with a determination to excel all his
predecessors. He does not confine himself to the garden and its
products, but takes a wide range among all the objects that give
beauty to the landscape and enhance the value of country life. Plans
of gardens and villas and cottages, descriptions of lawns and meadows,
of trees, fruits and flowers—accounts of horticultural exhibitions, of the
advances of the art in this country, and the experiments and improvements in Europe, and hints and directions in whatever concerns the
proper arrangement and management of the garden, are all put together
in these numbers with a taste and skill that evince both study and
genius. We were struck with the description at page 164 of the
meadow park, *at Geneseo,* of James S. Wadsworth, Esq. (the largest
landholder, we believe, in Western New York,) whose father and uncle
settled at Geneseo in 1790, and accumulated the immense estate
now held by the Wadsworth family. The picture of this park given
by Mr. Downing is truthful, we know, and we make a short extract that
our readers may form some conception of its extent and beauty.

"The whole of that part of the valley embraced by the eye—say a thousand
acres, is a *park* full of the finest oaks—and such oaks as you may have dreamed
of, (if you love trees) or, perhaps, have seen in pictures by Claude Lorraine, or
our own Durand; but not in the least like those you meet every day in your
woodland walks through the country at large. Or rather, there are thousands of
such as you may have seen half a dozen examples of in your own country.

"And they are not only grand, majestic, magnificent, noble trees—these oaks,
—but they are grouped and arranged just as you, a lover of the beautiful, and we,
a landscape-gardener, would have had them arranged, if we had had the taste of
Sir Humphrey Ripton and the wand of an enchanter, and had attempted to make
a bit of country after our own heart.

"No underwood, no bushes, no thickets; nothing but single specimens or
groups of giant old oaks, (mingled with, here and there, an elm,) with level
glades of broad meadow beneath them! An Englishman will hardly be convinced that it is not a park, planted by the skilful hand of man hundreds of years
ago.

"This great meadow park is filled with herds of the finest cattle—the pride of the home-farm. The guest at Geneseo takes his seat in the carriage, or forms one of a party on horseback, for the afternoon drive over the '*flats*,' as the Geneseo valley is called.

"Thus in reality, you follow no roads,—none are needed, indeed; for the surface of the great meadow park, for the most part, is so smooth and level that you drive here and there, to any point of interest, as you please. To us, first of all, the trees themselves,—many, beautiful in their rich masses of foliage; many, grand in their wonderful breadth of head and branches; and some, majestic and venerable in their great size and hoary old age. Near the bank of the river still stands the great oak* '*Big Tree*,' under which the first treaty was signed between the Indians and the first settlers of Geneseo. Its enormous trunk measures 65 feet in circumference. It still wears a healthy crown of leaves, and is preserved with all the veneration which an object that awakens the sentiment of antiquity inspires in a new country. Not far from it stands the stump of a contemporary, destroyed a few seasons before by the elements. The annual rings of its trunk tell the story of *nine hundred years' growth!*

"What is the solution, you ask, as you resume your drive again, of the mystery of this peculiar growth of trees in this great natural park? Has nature, who usually sows bushes and briers in thicket and underwood amid the forest, taken it into her head to set an example here to planters of parks, and allowed only gigantic trees and broad meadows to extend, seemingly, to the horizon?

"The tradition ran thus: This beautiful valley was a favourite hunting ground of the Indians. In order that they might render it as perfect as possible for this purpose, they were in the habit, every year, at the proper season, of lighting fires. These fires swept over the whole surface, and destroyed all the lesser forest growth. The trees which survived, grew on, larger and larger every year, until at length the whole reached the condition of a great park, as it was transferred to the white man.

"There are many beautiful features in the scenery of the broad state of New York; but there is no picture of sylvan or pastoral scenery daguerreotyped in our memory, at once so fair, and so grand, as the meadow park at Geneseo."

A Theoretical and Practical Treatise on Algebra, by H. N. Robinson, A. M., formerly Professor of Mathematics in the U. S. Navy. Published by *Erastus H. Pease & Co., Albany, and Jacob Ernst, Cincinnati.*

A Treatise on Astronomy, Descriptive, Physical and Practical, *by the same author and same publishers.*

The methodical and perspicuous arrangement which characterize these valuable treatises, cannot be too highly commended. One of the greatest errors observable in most of the elementary class books daily issued from the press, for the use of schools and academies, is the want of definitions and illustrations in simple and intelligible terms, and of such an arrangement of the several parts of the work as will cause the least confusion in the mind of the student. First principles should be briefly and lucidly stated, so that there can be no possibility of a mistake,

* "Big Tree" was the name of the Indian chief, of the tribe which originally lived in this part of the Geneseo country. The old chieftain has long since gone to the eternal "hunting ground" of his fathers; but the tree, which was venerable in his earliest youth, still survives him, and preserves his memory.

and examples and illustrations of rules and theories should be so chosen as to fix the whole subject on the mind, and thus to make the way clear as the pupil advances. Such, however, is not often the case in these days of progress. Metaphysical theories abound in books that should be simple and elementary in all their parts. We have arbitrary rules leaving too much to the black-board and maps, and the directions of the teacher; we have language even difficult to be understood by adults, which is used for explanation to boys and girls, and sometimes a seeming confusion in the arrangement of the subject (especially in geographies) by which the young mind is bewildered, and flounders amongst the mass without obtaining any permanent benefit.

Professor Robinson seems to have avoided confusion in arrangement as well as abstruseness in theory. His treatise on *Algebra* is both theoretical and practical; the explanations are easily understood, and the rules and modes of operation direct, clear and brief. As an example of the former, he remarks, under the head of subtraction:

"We do not approve of the use of the term subtraction as applied to Algebra, for in many cases subtraction appears like addition, and addition like subtraction. We prefer the use of the term *difference*. What is the difference between 12 and 20 degrees of north latitude? This is subtraction. But when we demand the difference of latitude between 6 degrees north and 3 degrees south, the result appears like addition; for the difference is really 9 degrees, the sum of 6 and 3. This example serves to explain the true nature of the sign *minus*. It is merely an opposition to the sign *plus*; it is counting in *another direction*; and if we call the degrees north of the equator *plus*, we must call those south of it *minus*, taking the equator as the *zero* line. So it is on the thermometer scale—the divisions above zero are called *plus* and those below *minus*. Money due to us may be called plus; money that we owe should then be called minus—the one circumstance is directly opposite in effect to the other. Indeed we can conceive of no quantity less than nothing, as we sometimes express ourselves."

This is very plain, and can be easily understood by any pupil who has progressed as far as the study of Algebra. The author has maintained this simple and clear method which is adapted to all capacities throughout his whole volume of three hundred pages, thus making it a useful treatise and text book for schools and universities. Nothing is left in obscurity and doubt. From the first principles of the science to the higher degrees of equations, embracing Sturm's theory and Horner's method, there is manifest a steady and skilful effort to bring every thing to the comprehension of the student.

The Treatise on Astronomy is, without doubt, a valuable addition to its class. The chief merits of the work "are brevity, clearness of illustration, anticipating the difficulties of the pupil, and removing them, and bringing out all the essential points of the science."

Professor Robinson informs us, and we believe he is right, that there is a class of works on Astronomy, "which consist of essays and popular lectures," but from which "little substantial knowledge can be gathered, for they do not *teach* astronomy; as a general thing they only *glorify* it." "There is also," he remarks, "another class, in which most of the important facts are recorded; such as the distances, magnitudes and motions of the heavenly bodies; but how these facts became known is rarely explained: this is what the true searcher after science will always demand, and this book is designed expressly to meet that demand." He proceeds to state the design of the work in the following terms:

"In the first part of the book we suppose the reader entirely unacquainted with the subject; but we suppose him competent to the task—to be, at least, sixteen years of age—to have a good knowledge of algebra, geometry and trigonometry —and then, not until then, can the study be pursued with any degree of success worth mentioning. Such a person and with such acquirements as we have here designated, we believe, can take this book and learn astronomy in comparatively a short time; for the chief design of this work is to teach whoever desires to learn; and it matters not where the learner may be, in a college, academy, school or a solitary student at home and alone in the pursuit."

CROLY'S BRITISH POETS.—A beautiful edition of this work has recently issued from the press of *Phillips, Sampson & Co., Boston.* It is ornamented with some handsome engravings, among which is the gentle face of Cowper's mother, of whom the poet wrote:

"Oh that those lips had language!
  Their own sweet smile I see,
The same that oft in childhood solaced me"—

There is a picture too representing the cavaliers as they are seen riding,

"Over hill, over valley, o'er dale and o'er down"—
—"There's Derby and Cavendish, dread of their foes:
"There's Erin's high Ormond and Scotland's Montrose."

This volume of Croly is well deserving of a place in every library. From the quaint rhymes of Chaucer to the sweet stanzas of Hemans, there is a selection of the choicest beauties of the British poets, presenting a faithful exhibition "of their styles of thought and language."

HUME'S HISTORY OF ENGLAND, AND MACAULAY'S HISTORY, by the same publishers. These cheap and well executed editions of popular and valuable works are worthy of high commendation. Five volumes of the first have been received and two of the last. The publishers state that "Hume will be comprised in six volumes. Two volumes of the continuation of Macaulay, having been published, the balance will be issued in uniform style, immediately on their appearance in London."

In examining one of the volumes of Macaulay, we happened to open it at the graphic description of the person and punishment of the infamous informer, Titus Oates, who was tried and convicted of perjury in the reign of James II., and though some of our readers have seen it before, we cannot resist our inclination to introduce in this place a brief extract.

"On the day in which he was brought to the bar, Westminster Hall was crowded with spectators, among whom were many Roman Catholics, eager to see the misery and humiliation of their persecutor. A few years earlier his short neck, his legs uneven as those of a badger, his forehead low as that of a baboon, his purple cheeks, and his monstrous length of chin, had been familiar to all who frequented the courts of law. He had then been the idol of the nation. Wherever he had appeared men had uncovered their heads to him, the lives and estates of the magnates of the realm had been at his mercy. Times had now changed; and many, who had formerly regarded him as the deliverer of his country, shuddered at the sight of those hideous features on which villany seemed to be written by the hand of God.

"It was proved, beyond all possibility of doubt, that this man had, by false testimony, deliberately murdered several guiltless persons. He was convicted on both indictments. He was sentenced to be stripped of his clerical habit, to be pilloried in the Palace Yard, to be led round Westminster Hall with an inscription declaring his infamy over his head, to be pilloried again in front of the Royal Exchange, to be whipped from Aldgate to Newgate, and, after an interval of two days, to be whipped from Newgate to Tyburn.

"This rigorous sentence was rigorously executed. On the day on which Oates was pilloried in Palace Yard, he was mercilessly pelted and ran some risk of being pulled in pieces. On the following morning he was brought forth to undergo his first flogging. At an early hour an innumerable multitude filled all the streets from Aldgate to the Old Bailey. The hangman laid on the lash with such unusual severity as showed that he had received special instructions. The blood ran down in rivulets. For a time the criminal showed a strange constancy: but at last his stubborn fortitude gave way. His bellowings were frightful to hear. He swooned several times; but the scourge still continued to descend. When he was unbound, it seemed that he had borne as much as the human frame can bear without dissolution. James was entreated to remit the second flogging. His answer was short and clear: 'He shall go through with it, if he has breath in his body.' An attempt was made to gain the queen's intercession; but she indignantly refused to say a word in favour of such a wretch. After an interval of only forty-eight hours, Oates was again brought out of his dungeon. He was unable to stand, and it was necessary to drag him to Tyburn on a sledge. He seemed quite insensible; and the Tories reported that he had stupified himself with strong drink. A person who counted the stripes on the second day, said that they were seventeen hundred. The bad man escaped with life, but so narrowly that his ignorant and bigoted admirers thought his recovery miraculous, and appealed to it as a proof of his innocence. The doors of the prison closed upon him. During many months he remained ironed in the darkest hole of Newgate."

Titus Oates lived after the infliction of this terrible punishment twenty years. At the revolution the tide of popular favour set in his favour, and he received a pension of £1000.

We have also received from Phillips, Sampson & Co., the illustrated edition of SHAKSPEARE'S DRAMATIC WORKS, now in the course of publication. They state their object to be, "to prepare an edition from the highest authorities and in the most elegant form; not too much encumbered with comments, nor so destitute of them as to be obscure to the general reader."

They have followed the reading of the text of the folio edition of 1623, and acknowledge their indebtedness to Mr. Singer for the preliminary remarks. The typography and the ornamental parts of the work are admirable. The head of Miranda pre-fixed to the Tempest is exquisitely designed and finished. An American edition of the plays of the great English dramatist in this form disincumbered of useless notes—elegant and accurate—is a desideratum. It is surprising that such perfect copies of the works of Shakspeare should be preserved, when it is considered how careless he was himself of their preservation, leaving them in the hands of stage-managers when he retired from the world, apparently regardless of its applause, and unconscious of the power and value of his productions.

HOME RECREATIONS, MARY HOWITT'S TALES AND STORIES, THE CA-
RAVAN, FIRESIDE FAIRIES, HEARTS AND HOMES, from the press of
D. *Appleton & Co., New York.*

These works are all got up with the usual good taste and accuracy of the publishers; and the matter is mostly designed for the instruction and entertainment of youthful readers. The first,—*Home Recreations,* by Grandfather Merryman,—is a collection of "Tales of Peril and Adventure, Voyages and Travels, Biography, Manners and Customs, Poetry, &c."—The *Tales and Stories* by Mary Howitt, are in the best style of that practised and entertaining writer. They have the great merit of simplicity of language and purity of thought—and whilst boys and girls take delight in reading them, the moral lessons are so mixed up with the entertainment that they never fail to instruct. *The Caravan* is a collection of tales, translated from the German by G. P. Quackenbos. If the judgment of our young friends, who have read them, is to be relied on, they are pleasant and interesting stories which do credit to the author. Of the *Fireside Fairies,* or *Christmas at Aunt Elsie's,* we also hear the opinion universally expressed, that this volume has met the approbation of "the little people for whom it was expressly designed." It has, therefore, accomplished its object, which, we learn from the preface, is so "to deck familiar, yet important truths, and the home duties of every day life in the drapery of fiction," as to reach the mind of the child. *Hearts and Homes* is a tale by a distinguished writer, Mrs. Ellis, which needs not our opinion or encomium to make it acceptable to the public.

RECOLLECTIONS OF DEPARTED FRIENDS. By the *Rev. Wm. Berrian,*
D. D., Rector of Trinity Church. New York: Stanford and
Swords.

We are indebted to the author for a copy of this well written, and, to us, deeply interesting volume. It contains a series of brief notices of his personal friends, who have died in the faith. Among them are the names of John Henry Hobart, Cornelius R. Duffie, Robert Troup, Jacob Lorillard, Thomas Lyell, John C. Rudd, David B. Ogden, and others; all of whom are well known to New Yorkers, and some of whom have a reputation for talent and worth, wide as the Union.

Dr. Berrian is an able and agreeable writer, and his descriptions of character are truthful and impressive. Of Mr. Duffie, whom we remember as a classmate, highly esteemed, he thus writes:

"His piety was of the most engaging character; for while he was careful to adorn the doctrine of Christ by the strictness and purity of his life, yet there was such a gentleness in his manners, such sweetness of temper, such lowliness of heart, and unaffected modesty in his carriage, as represented religion in her own meek and winning air, and gave a powerful and persuasive influence to his example."

Referring to the advanced age and unimpaired faculties of David B. Ogden, the eminent jurist, he uses this language:

"We are apt to think that at that age all the purposes of life are accomplished, that active exertion is at an end, that desire has failed, that this mortal existence itself, on the conditions with which it must be held, would soon become a burden, . . . it was not so in respect to our departed friend, . . . there was a freshness of feeling in him which is but seldom found in so old a man; a cheerfulness of spirit which, in despite of the vexations and trials of life, was an unfailing source of comfort to himself, and which shed perpetual sunshine on those around him."

His intellectual strength and his piety are thus described:

"The peculiar and characteristic distinction of his logical mind was considered to consist in its clearness, consecutiveness and force, in seizing upon the general bearing and the strong points of every case, and urging it with the utmost precision and energy to its just conclusion. . . . The levity, ungodliness and skepticism, which he had met with in his promiscuous intercourse with the world produced not the slightest effect upon his devout and well ordered mind; and having all rational ground for his faith as a Christian, he received its holiest mysteries, and most incomprehensible truths with the meekness and simplicity of a child."

MEMOIRS OF THE LIFE OF WILLIAM WIRT. By *John P. Kennedy.* Lea and Blanchard. Philadelphia.

We received a copy of this popular work at so late an hour as to be unable to do justice to its merits by more than a general notice. The established reputation of Mr. Kennedy as an author, and the success of his work, which has already passed to a second edition, are sufficient guarantees of its value. He has exhibited the incidents in the life and the character of the highly gifted William Wirt with a master's hand. We question whether any contemporaneous biography will be read more generally or with more interest, as the author has been able to interweave with the narrative so many of the familiar letters of Wirt and is friends—all of which abound with brilliant thoughts, sound philosophy, or touching expressions of affection and duty. Mr. Wirt was one of those instances of successful talent so often seen in this country. The son of a tavern-keeper at Bladensburgh, he rose to high rank in his profession—electrified the public by his brilliant eloquence on the trial of Aaron Burr—enjoyed the personal friendship of Jefferson, Madison and Monroe, and became Attorney General of the United States.

THE ANGLO-SAXON. Published in London by Longman & Co. Edited by the Author of Proverbial Philosophy. Agent in Philadelphia, Mr. Moore, 193 Chestnut Street.

We are indebted to the politeness of the Rev. Dr. Lyons for the numbers of this new, original and elegant periodical. Its grand design, as declared in the prospectus, is to promote "unity and brotherly good will" among Anglo-Saxons, and all of Anglo-Saxon origin and relationship throughout the globe. In one of the numbers some light is thrown upon the meaning of that comprehensive appellative "Anglo-Saxon," which of late has come so generally into use.

"By Saxon race, (says Dr. Knox,) I mean the classic German of antiquity, now represented with more or less admixture by the Norwegian, Swede, Dane, Hollander, &c. . . . The insular Saxon is an offset from the continental; occupies England as distinct from Wales, the eastern coasts of Scotland and of Ireland. In America he is already paramount lord of all the northern portion—there the Saxon, true to his nature, has changed his name; he calls himself an 'American.' . . . The Anglo-Saxon in England stands on neutral ground. Anxious for the *statu quo* throughout the world, he dreads continental wars. His fleets are ever ready to support dynasties. As a merchant, he intermeddles every where; as a Saxon, his colonies continually threaten revolt. It is the same with Holland, also (peopled by) a thoroughly Saxon race —the twin-brothers in fact of the Saxon English."

A map is given in the first number, on which are marked the parts of the earth's surface under the rule of the Anglo-Saxon race, and the population of those portions is set down at 188,177,763. This is a wide field for the diffusion of those principles of concord and amity which Mr. Tupper proposes in his magnificent scheme. We regret we have not room for a longer notice; but we heartily wish him success. Certainly he has given us four numbers full of beautiful engravings, replete with interesting matter, and in which we have facts and theory, philosophy, religion and poetry, admirably combined. As an example of the latter, we select the following specimens:

"The blended memories of the good and great,
Whom time has harmonized in excellence,
Are a fair meeting field—let angry hate
And jealous emulance be banished thence,
With sordid creed, and bigot self-pretence.
Thoughts that are holy, actions that are brave—
Counsels of wisdom, words of influence—
These are the sureties that are strong to save."

"———————— when most forlorn,
In darkest hours of pain and anguish,
No wild despair, or faithless scorn,
Shall bid all Hope within me languish.
What tho' from earthly fount may flow
No solace for a heart self-broken!
Yet prayer avails—and none so low
For whom God's goodness has no token."

OBITUARY NOTICES.

SEPTEMBER, 1849.

Sept. 4th. At Palermo, on board the U. S. frigate Constitution, Capt. JOHN GWINN, of the Mediterranean squadron. He was a native of Maryland, and entered the naval service of the United States in 1809.

6th. At Brahan Castle, England, EDWARD STANLEY, D.D., Bishop of Norwich, aged 70.

11th. In the city of Mexico, General MARIANO PAREDES, President of Mexico, at the commencement of the late war.

19th. At Woodbury, N. J., JONAH CATTELL, aged 91, a venerable soldier of the revolution, who fought at the battle of Princeton.

20th. In California, on the Upper Sacramento, Capt. W. H. WARNER, of the Topographical Engineers. He was murdered by a party of Indians, who shot him down whilst he was leading a command, eight arrows having entered his body, and one passing entirely through it.

In Germany, STRAUSS, the celebrated musical composer. It is said that thirty thousand persons attended his funeral.

OCTOBER.

Oct. 1st. In France, at Fontenay, M. JEAN BAPTISTE ROBILLARD, aged 113 years. He retained his faculties to the last.

In Saxony, at Raudnitz, Madame SCHRŒDER, one of the first tragediens in Germany, at the advanced age of 84. The emperor, Francis I., had her portrait painted and placed in the imperial museum.

In England, Admiral Sir EDWARD OWEN, at the age of 78, a distinguished officer.

4th. In Philadelphia, Penn., DANIEL FITLER, Esq., formerly High Sheriff of the city and county.

6th. At the Washington Hospital, Baltimore, EDGAR A. POE, Esq. He was a poet of singular originality and power—of rare genius, great scholarship, and a caustic and severe critic, as well as writer in other departments of pure literature. At about 38 years of age, he terminated a life of those trials to which genius is too often subject.

7th. In Texas, near the Colorado river, Lieut. MONTGOMERY P. HARRISON, (grandson of the late President of that name.) He was killed by the Indians. He had ridden out from camp on the afternoon of that day alone, for the purpose of ascertaining the proper road. No Indian signs had previously been seen, and no Indians were supposed to be near. He was found pierced in many places with arrows, and shot, as is supposed, with his own pistol.

11*th*. At Porte Grande, Island of St. Vincent, Commander Gordon, of the U. S. navy. He had been in command of the African squadron.

At Vernon, N. Y., Capt. STEPHEN BRIGHAM, at the age of 96. He served at Bunker Hill.

14*th*. At Hardwicke House, England, Dr. COPPLESTONE, Bishop of Llandaff, aged 73. He was distinguished for his classical attainments, and his excellent private life.

16*th*. In California, Captain HERMAN THORN, of the U. S. army, drowned in crossing the Colorado river, near Gila.

20*th*. At Windsor, Vermont, Hon. JONATHAN H. HUBBARD, aged 81 years. He was a representative in Congress for several years, and a judge of the supreme court.

At York, Penn. Rev. ROBERT CATHCART, D.D. He was probably the oldest minister in the Presbyterian church, having attained the age of 90.

25*th*. In New Hampshire, on the White mountains, Mr. FREDERICK STRICKLAND, an English gentleman, about thirty years of age, and heir to large estates, who had been travelling for some months in this country. He separated himself from his companions, lost his way, and perished on the mountains.

26*th*. At Boston, Mass., CHARLES E. HORN, at the age of 63—an eminent composer of music.

At Exeter, New Hampshire, BENJAMIN ABBOTT, LL.D., at the age of 87. He was extensively known as the principal of Exeter Academy, at which Daniel Webster, Lewis Cass, and other distinguished men were educated.

27*th*. In Baltimore county, Md., TOBIAS E. STANSBURY, 93 years old. He lived and died in the place where he was born. From the opening events of the revolutionary war, down to within a very recent period, he participated actively in national and state affairs, was repeatedly a member of the legislature, and presided as speaker of the house of delegates.

At Geneva, N. Y., Major DAVID B. DOUGLASS, Professor of Mathematics and Natural Philosophy in Geneva College. He entered the army at an early age, and distinguished himself in the battles of Lundy's Lane and Fort Erie. After the war, he took a leading part in re-organizing the military academy, and remained a professor there until 1830, since which he has been extensively employed in civil engineering on some of the principal works in the United States, and was, for several years, acting president of Kenyon college. He prepared the plans and estimates of the Croton aqueduct. He was a gentleman of great worth, of polished manners, and sincere piety.

29th. At Albany, N. Y., Dr. PETER WENDELL, Chancellor of the Regents of the University of New York, and the oldest resident physician in that city, in the 64th year of his age. He was widely known, and highly respected for his intelligence, probity, and usefulness.

30th. At Shoreham, Vt., Hon. SILAS JENISON, for several years governor of that State.

In Paris, FREDERICK FRANCIS CHOPIN, at the age of 39. He was born near Warsaw, and was one of the most remarkable musicians in the world. Chopin shunned public performances. His delight was to have around him a circle of musicians and pupils who would listen to his ravishing strains as he sat extemporizing and inspired at the piano.

NOVEMBER.

Nov. 1st. At New Haven, Conn., Hon. ELIZUR GOODRICH, LL.D. at the age of 89.

Mr. Goodrich was one of the very few survivors among the men who figured in public life under the administrations of Washington and the elder Adams. Indeed, since the death of the late Albert Gallatin, he is believed to have been the eldest survivor among the members of Congress during that period.

At Kingston, Rhode Island, SYLVIA TORRY, at the age of 112. Her youngest child lived with her, and was 87.

4th. At Waterloo, Ill., Rev. PETER ROGERS, in his hundredth year. He was one of Washington's life guards in the war of Independence, and perhaps the last of that noble band.

16th. In Germany, Prince LEOPOLD ALEXANDER HOHENLOHE, Bishop of Sardica, Grand Provost and Canon of the Chapter of Groswardein, Hungary, and Mitred Abbot of St. Michael of Gaborjau, was a scion of the Waldenburg branch of the ancient and illustrious German family of Hohenlohe. The prince was born August 17, 1794, and very early in life devoted himself to the service of religion. His fervour and piety were so ardent, and his prayers in behalf of the sick and afflicted proved so frequently successful, that many believed that he was gifted with a miraculous power. Some five and twenty years ago, this supposed divine attribute created a great sensation, and became the universal theme of conversation. The subject was then much and seriously discussed on both sides. Since that little or nothing has been heard of the prince, who, it appears, shrank from the strange publicity given to him, and confined himself subsequently to the zealous and exemplary performance of his high clerical and episcopal functions.

Prince Hohenlohe, whatever might be the faith in his miracles, was much esteemed and beloved for the mildness and benevolence of his disposition; and his death is very generally regretted.

24*th.* In England, Lady Charlotte Lindsay, an accomplished and highly gifted woman, the last surviving child of the celebrated statesman, Lord North. She was one of the household of Caroline, Princess of Wales.

26*th.* In Rhode Island, Mrs. Henshaw, the mother of Bishop Henshaw, at the age of 79. She was devotedly pious, and anticipated death with calm composure. On the day of her death, she withdrew to her room, apparently well, and in fifteen minutes after she was found by one of her daughters seated in the same arm chair in which her husband had died in 1825—her spectacles on—the Bible and Prayer-Book on the stand before her—not a limb, feature or muscle moved, perfectly life-like; but her heart had ceased to beat.

27*th.* At Macon, Georgia, Gen. Duncan J. Clinch. He was for many years an officer in the United States army. He served with high distinction in the war of 1812, was retained as a colonel upon the reduction of the army at its close, soon acquired a brevet as brigadier general, and with that rank, commanded in Florida in 1835-6, at the commencement of the Seminole war. He was truly a hero at the battle of Withalacoochee. He was afterwards a member of Congress, and recently a candidate for Governor of Georgia.

He was "a soldier without reproach, and an honest man."

At Roxbury, Mass., Joseph Adams, in the hundredth year of his age.

December.

Dec. 1*st.* In England, Ebenezer Elliott, the celebrated "corn-law rhymer," and devoted friend of humanity, at the age of 70. If Scott be the poet of Tweedside, and Wordsworth of the Lakes, to Elliott, assuredly, belong the heights and dales of Yorkshire—and, yet more, its "broad towns," in which manufacture is unable to destroy or efface the elements of poetry that lie in the human heart, "with all its dreams and sighs."

At Canonsburgh, S. C., Capt. John Williamson, of the U. S. army. He was a native of N. Jersey, and an accomplished officer.

In England, William Charles Keppel, Earl of Albemarle, at

an advanced age. He succeeded to the peerage when he was only six months old.

3*d*. At Newport, R. I., Hon. WILLIAM HUNTER, LL.D. He was in the senate of the United States, and in 1834 he accepted from Gen. Jackson the appointment of Chargé d'Affaires to Brazil, and in 1841 he was made minister plenipotentiary at that court, where he remained till 1844.

Recently, at Brussels, M. VERBEYEST, the most celebrated book collector in Europe, perhaps in the world. He had founded a very curious establishment, consisting of a house of several stories, and as high as a church, and disposed so as to contain about 300,000 volumes, arranged according to their subjects.

In England, ADELAIDE, Queen Dowager, at the age of 58. She was a daughter of the Duke of Saxe Meiningen, and her baptismal name was Adelaide Louisa Theresa Caroline Amelia. She was married in 1818 to William IV., then Duke of Clarence, eight years after his separation from Mrs. Jordan, the actress. She was recommended to the prince by the Queen mother, for her many amiable qualities and domestic virtues. A large portion of her annual allowance from the British exchequer has been devoted to deeds of charity and Christian benevolence, and an elegant English church in the island of Malta, remains, with other works of the kind, to commemorate her piety. She was a devoted wife to the late king, and though better fitted for private domestic life, she never failed to command the respect of all, even in the gay circles of the court.

In York, WILLIAM ETTY, a great modern painter. Like Rembrandt and Constable, he was a miller's son, and made his first sketches with chalk on the mill floor. He travelled and studied much in Rome, Venice, Florence, and France. His art was to him a source of unalloyed happiness.

In England, two of the heroes of the peninsular war, Sir GEORGE ANSON, and Sir JOHN ORMSBY VANDELEUR, who fought at Salamanca, Vittoria, Rodrigo, and Waterloo, under "the iron Duke."

5*th*. At Philadelphia, Penn., WILLIAM SHORT, in the 91st year of his age.

He was a native of Virginia, and educated in the same class with Chief Justice Marshall,—was secretary of legation to Mr. Jefferson —was Chargé to the French republic, and was the first citizen of the United States nominated and appointed to a public office under the federal constitution. During the administration of General Washington, who evinced for him high personal regard, he was successively appointed minister resident at the Hague, and commissioner, and subsequently minister to Spain.

9*th*. At Boston, JOHN BROMFIELD, Esq. He bequeathed $205,000 to charitable institutions.

At Cooperstown, N. Y., Judge Morehouse, of the 6th judicial district—an upright and highly esteemed man.

12th. In London, Sir MARK ISAMBERT BRUNEL, Vice President of the Royal Society and of the institution of civil engineers, a native of France. He built the Bowery theatre, New York, furnished plans for canals, invented the circular saw for cutting veneers of valuable woods, built steamboats, and was the engineer of the tunnel under the river Thames, London.

20th. In Washington county, N. Y., WILLIAM MILLER, "the prophet of the Millerites," at the age of 68. He was a native of Pittsfield, Mass., and during the last war with England, served as a captain of volunteers on the northern frontier. He began to speak in public assemblies upon the subject of the millennium in 1833, and in the ten years which preceded the time which he had set for the confirmation of all prophecy, he laboured assiduously in the middle and northern states, averaging, it is said, nearly one sermon a day for more than half that period. He was uneducated, and not largely read in even the common English commentaries; his views were absurd, and supported but feebly; yet he succeeded in building up a sect of some thirty or forty thousand disciples, which disappeared rapidly after the close of the "day of probation" in 1843, after which time Mr. Miller himself did not often advocate or defend his views in public.

25th. At San Francisco, California, GEORGE H. VAIL, Esq., of Troy, N. Y., at the age of 30. He was a young man of noble qualities of heart and head—of intelligence and talent of the first order. He contributed to this work the interesting articles on China and the opium trade.

POETRY.

THE ARK.

(*From the Anglo-Saxon.*)

What is it floats upon that world of seas—
Without an anchor, and without a guide?
From the strange sight each sea-born monster
 flees,
And the mad wave turns harmless from its side.

It is the sanctuary of life floats there,
Safe amidst torrents, cradled on the waves—
The Hand that made a delug'd world despair,
Unseen protects it, and 'midst ruin saves.

The strife is o'er—no more the ark of peace
Lay on the bosom of the avenging flood;

For at His word, who bade " the waters cease,"
On the bare summit of the mount it stood.

And is it so? Great God of power and grace,
That thus thy terrors did thine ark enfold,
Is it 'midst vengeance on a fallen race
That we thy miracles of love behold?

Then fearless thro' the world's tempestuous
 sea,
Saviour of men, to Thee my spirit flies—
Thy timid wounded dove will haste to Thee,
And from thy shelt'ring hand to heaven arise!

ADDITION TO GRAY'S ELEGY.

The following lines were published many years ago anonymously. in a Rhode Island paper. The author, who was the Rev. James D. Knowles, believed that Gray had not given to the subject of his muse enough of religious character to render the charm complete; hence he wrote these verses to follow the stanzas in the elegy beginning with the words—

  " Far from the maddening crowd's ignoble stir."

No airy dreams their simple fancies fired,
 No thirst for wealth, no panting after fame;
But truth divine sublimer hopes inspired,
 And urged them onward to a nobler aim.

From every cottage, with the day arose
 The hallowed voice of spirit-breathing prayer;
And artless anthems, at the peaceful close,
 Like holy incense charmed the evening air.

Though they, each tome of human lore un-
 known,
 The brilliant path of science never trod,
The sacred volume claimed their hearts alone,
 Which taught the way to glory and to God.

Here they from truth's eternal fountain drew
 The pure and gladdened waters day by day,
Learned since our days are evil, fleet and few,
 To walk in wisdom's bright and peaceful
 way.

In yon lone pile, o'er which has strangely passed,
 The heavy hand of all destroying time,
Through whose low mouldering aisle now
 sighs the blast,
 And round whose altars grass and ivy climb.

They gladly thronged their grateful hymns to
 raise,
 Oft as the calm and holy Sabbath shone;
The mingled tribute of their prayers and praise
 In sweet communion rose before the throne.

Here, from those honoured lips, which sacred
 fire
 From heaven's high chancery hath touched
 to hear
Truths which their zeal inflame, their hopes
 inspire,
 Give wings to faith, and check affection's
 tear.

When life flowed by, and like an angel, death
 Came to release them to the worlds on high,
Praise trembled still on each expiring breath,
 And holy triumph beamed from every eye.

Then gentle hands their "dust to dust" consign;
 With quiet tears the simple rites are said;
And here they sleep, till at the trump Divine,
 The earth and ocean render up their dead.

A SISTER'S LOVE.

More constant than the evening star,
  Which mildly beams above—
That diadem—oh! dearer far
  A sister's gentle love!

Brighter than dew drop on the rose,
  Than nature's smile more gay—

A living fount which ever flows,
  Warmed by love's pure ray.

Gem of the heart! Life's gift divine,
  Bequeathed as from above,
Glad offering at affection's shrine—
  A sister's holy love!

JUDGE GENTLY.

Oh, there has many a tear been shed,
  And many a heart been broken,
For want of a gentle hand stretched forth,
  Or a word in kindness spoken.

Then oh, with brotherly regard,
  Greet every son of sorrow,
So from each tone of love his heart
  New hope, new strength, shall borrow.

Nor turn, with cold and scornful eye,
  From him who hath offended,

But let the harshness of reproof,
  With kindest tones be blended.

The seeds of good are every where,
  And, in the guiltiest bosom,
Should, by quickening rays of love,
  Put forth their tender blossom.

While many a tempted soul hath been
  To deeds of evil hardened,
Who felt that bitterness of grief,
  The first offence unpardoned.

LET US GIVE THANKS.

BY ELIZA COOK.

Let us give thanks, with grateful soul,
  To Him who sendeth all;
To Him who bids the planets roll,
  And sees a "sparrow fall."
Though grief and tears may dim our joys,
  And care and strife arrest,
'Tis man, too often, that alloys
  The lot his Maker blest:
While sunshine lights the boundless sky,
  And dew drops feed the sod—
While stars and rainbows live on high—
  Let us give thanks to God.

We till the earth in labour's health,
  We plant the acorn cup:
The fields are crowned with golden wealth,
  The green tree springeth up;
The sweet, eternal waters gush
  From fountain and from vale;
The vineyards blush with purple flush,
  The yellow hop leaves trail;
And while the harvest flings its gold,
  And cowslips deck the sod—
While limpid streams are clear and cold,
  Let us give thanks to God.

The flower yields its odour breath,
  As gentle winds go past;
The grasshopper that lurks beneath,
  Chirps merrily and fast;
The ring-dove coos upon the spray,
  The larks full anthems pour;
The bees start with a jocund lay,
  The waves sing on the shore;
Hosannas fill the wood and wild,
  Where human step ne'er trod;
And nature, like an unweaned child,
  Smiles on its parent, God.

Say, brothers, shall the bird and bloom
  Thus teach, and teach in vain?
Shall all the love-rays that illume,
  Be lost in clouds of pain!
Shall hearts be dead and vision blind
  To all that mercy deals?
Shall soul and reason fail to find
  The shrine where instinct kneels?
Ah, no!—while glory lights the sky,
  And beauty paints the sod—
While stars and rainbows live on high,
  Let us give thanks to God.

DOCUMENTS.

STATE PAPERS.

PRESIDENT'S MESSAGE.

MESSAGE OF THE PRESIDENT OF THE UNITED STATES TO BOTH HOUSES OF THE THIRTY-FIRST CONGRESS, DECEMBER, 1849.

Fellow-Citizens of the Senate and House of Representatives:—Sixty years have elapsed since the establishment of this government, and the Congress of the United States again assembles to legislate for an empire of freemen. The predictions of evil prophets, who formerly pretended to foretell the downfall of our institutions, are now remembered only to be derided, and the United States of America, at this moment, present to the world the most stable and permanent government on earth.

Such is the result of the labours of those who have gone before us. Upon Congress will eminently depend the future maintenance of our system of free government, and the transmission of it unimpaired to posterity.

We are at peace with all the nations of the world, and seek to maintain our cherished relations of amity with them. During the past year, we have been blessed, by a kind Providence, with an abundance of the fruits of the earth; and, although the destroying angel for a time visited extensive portions of our territory with the ravages of a dreadful pestilence, yet the Almighty has at length deigned to stay his hand, and to restore the inestimable blessing of general health to a people who have acknowledged his power, deprecated his wrath, and implored his merciful protection.

While enjoying the benefits of amicable intercourse with foreign nations, we have not been insensible to the distractions and wars which have prevailed in other quarters of the world. It is a proper theme of thanksgiving to Him who rules the destinies of nations, that we have been able to maintain, amidst all these contests, an independent and neutral position towards all belligerent powers.

Our relations with Great Britain are of the most friendly character. In consequence of the recent alteration of the British navigation acts, British vessels from British and other foreign ports, will, (under our existing laws,) after the first day of January next, be admitted to entry in our ports, with cargoes of the growth, manufacture, or production of any part of the world, on the same terms, as to duties, imposts, and charges, as vessels of the United States with their cargoes; and our vessels will be admitted to the same advantages in British ports, entering therein on the same terms as British vessels. Should no order in council disturb this legislative arrangement, the late act of the British Parliament, by which Great Britain is brought within the terms proposed by the act of Congress of the 1st of March, 1817, it is hoped, will be productive of benefit to both countries.

A slight interruption of diplomatic intercourse which occurred between this government and France, I am happy to say, has been terminated, and our minister there has been received. It is, therefore, unnecessary to refer now to the circumstances which led to that interruption. I need not express to you the sincere satisfaction with which we shall welcome the arrival of another envoy extraordinary and minister plenipotentiary from a sister republic, to which we have so long been, and still remain, bound by the strongest ties of amity.

Shortly after I had entered upon the discharge of the executive duties, I was apprized that a war steamer, belonging to the German empire, was being fitted out in the harbor of New York, with the aid of some of our naval officers, rendered under the permission of the late secretary of the navy. This permission was granted during an armistice between that empire and the kingdom of Denmark, which had been engaged in the Schleswig-Holstein war. Apprehensive that this act of intervention, on our part, might be viewed as a violation of our neutral obligations, incurred by the treaty with Denmark, and of the provisions of the act of Congress of the 20th of April, 1818, I directed that no further aid should be rendered by any agent or officer of the navy; and I instructed the secretary of state to apprize the minister of the German empire, accredited to this government, of my determination to execute the law of the United States, and to maintain the faith of treaties with all nations. The correspondence, which ensued between the department of state and the minister of the German empire, is herewith laid before you. The execution of the law and the observance of the treaty were deemed by me to be due to the honour of the country, as well as to the sacred obligations of the constitution. I shall not fail to pursue the same course, should a similar case arise with any other nation. Having avowed the opinion, on taking the oath of office, that, in disputes between conflicting foreign governments, it is our interest, not less than our duty, to remain strictly neutral, I shall not abandon it. You will perceive from the correspondence submitted to you, in connexion with this subject, that the course adopted in this case has been properly regarded by the belligerent powers interested in the matter.

Although a minister of the United States to the German empire was appointed by my predecessor in August, 1848, and has, for a long time, been in attendance at Frankfort-on-the-Maine; and, although a minister appointed to represent that empire was received and accredited here, yet no such government as that of the German empire has been definitively constituted. Mr. Donelson, our representative at Frankfort, remained there several months, in the expectation that a union of the German states, under one constitution or form of government, might, at length, be organized. It is believed by those well acquainted with the existing relations between Prussia and the states of Germany, that no such union can be permanently established without her cooperation. In the events of the formation of such a union, and the organization of a central power in Germany, of which she should form a part, it would become necessary to withdraw our minister at Berlin; but while Prussia exists as an independent kingdom, and diplomatic relations are maintained with her, there can be no necessity for the continuance of the mission to Frankfort. I have, therefore, recalled Mr. Donelson, and directed the archives of the legation at Frankfort to be transferred to the American legation at Berlin.

Having been apprized that a considerable number of adventurers were engaged in fitting out a military expedition, within the United States, against a foreign country; and believing, from the best information I could obtain, that it was destined to invade the island of Cuba, I deemed it due to the friendly relations existing between the United States and Spain—to the treaty between the two nations—to the laws of the United States, and, above all, to the American honour, to exert the lawful authority of this government in suppressing the expedition and preventing the invasion.

To this end, I issued a proclamation, enjoining it upon the officers of the United States, civil and military, to use all lawful means within their power. A copy of that proclamation is herewith submitted. The expedition has been suppressed. So long as the act of Congress, of the 20th of April, 1818, which owes its existence to the law of nations, and to the policy of Washington himself, shall remain on our statute-book, I hold it to be the duty of the executive faithfully to obey its injunctions.

While this expedition was in progress, I was informed that a foreigner, who claimed our protection, had been clandestinely, and, as was supposed, forcibly carried off in a vessel from New Orleans to the island of Cuba. I immediately caused such steps to be taken as I thought necessary, in case the information I had received should prove correct, to vindicate the honour of the country, and the right of every person seeking an asylum on our soil to the protection of our laws. The person alleged to have been abducted was promptly restored, and the circumstances of the case are now about to undergo investigation before a judicial tribunal. I would respectfully suggest, that although the crime charged to have been committed in this case is held odious as being in conflict with our opinions on the subject of national sovereignty and personal freedom, there is no prohibition of it, or punishment for it, provided in any act of Congress. The expediency of supplying this defect in our criminal code is, therefore, recommended to your consideration.

I have scrupulously avoided any interference in the wars and contentions which have recently distracted Europe.

During the late conflict between Austria and Hungary, there seemed to be a prospect that the latter might become an independent nation. However faint that prospect at the time appeared, I thought it my duty, in accordance with the general sentiment of the American people, who deeply sympathized with the Magyar patriots, to stand prepared, upon the contingency of the establishment by her of a permanent government, to be the first to welcome independent Hungary into the family of nations. For this purpose I invested an agent, then in Europe, with power to declare our willingness promptly to recognise her independence in the event of her ability to sustain it. The powerful intervention of Russia, in the contest, extinguished the hopes of the struggling Magyars. The United States did not, at any time, interfere in the contest; but the feelings of the nation were strongly enlisted in the cause, and by the sufferings of a brave people, who had made a gallant though unsuccessful effort to be free.

Our claims upon Portugal have been, during the past year, prosecuted with renewed vigour, and it has been my object to employ every effort of honourable diplomacy to procure their adjustment. Our late Charge d'Affaires at Lisbon, the Hon. George W. Hopkins, made able and energetic, but unsuccessful efforts to settle these unpleasant matters of controversy, and to obtain indemnity for the wrongs which were the subjects of complaint. Our present Charge d'Affaires at that court will, also, bring to the prosecution of these claims ability and zeal. The revolutionary and distracted condition of Portugal, in past times, has been represented as one of the leading causes of her delay in indemnifying our suffering citizens. But I must now say it is matter of profound regret that these claims have not yet been settled. The omission of Portugal to do justice to the American claimants has now assumed a character so grave and serious, that I shall shortly make it the subject of a special message to Congress, with a view to such ultimate action as its wisdom and patriotism may suggest.

With Russia, Austria, Prussia, Sweden, Denmark, Belgium, the Netherlands, and the Italian States, we still maintain our accustomed amicable relations.

During the recent revolutions in the papal states, our Charge d'Affaires at

Rome has been unable to present his letter of credence, which, indeed, he was directed by my predecessor to withhold until he should receive further orders. Such was the unsettled condition of things in those states, that it was not deemed expedient to give him any instructions on the subject of presenting his credential letter different from those with which he had been furnished by the late administration, until the 25th of June last, when, in consequence of the want of accurate information of the exact state of things, at that distance from us, he was instructed to exercise his own discretion in presenting himself to the then existing government, if, in his judgment, sufficiently stable; or, if not, to await further events. Since that period, Rome has undergone another revolution, and he abides the establishment of a government sufficiently permanent to justify him in opening diplomatic intercourse with it.

With the republic of Mexico it is our true policy to cultivate the most friendly relations. Since the ratification of the treaty of Guadalupe Hidalgo, nothing has occurred of a serious character to disturb them. A faithful observance of the treaty, and a sincere respect for her rights, cannot fail to secure the lasting confidence and friendship of that republic. The message of my predecessor to the house of representatives, of the 8th of February last, communicating, in compliance with a resolution of that body, a copy of a paper called a protocol, signed at Queretaro, on the 30th of May, 1848, by the commissioners of the United States and the minister of foreign affairs of the Mexican government, having been a subject of correspondence between the department of state and the envoy extraordinary and minister plenipotentiary of that republic accredited to this government, a transcript of that correspondence is herewith submitted.

The commissioner on the part of the United States for marking the boundary between the two republics, though delayed in reaching San Diego by unforeseen obstacles, arrived at that place within a short period after the time required by the treaty, and was there joined by the commissioner on the part of Mexico. They entered upon their duties, and, at the date of the latest intelligence from that quarter, some progress had been made in the survey. The expenses incident to the organization of the commission, and to its conveyance to the point where its operations were to begin, have so much reduced the fund appropriated by Congress, that a further sum, to cover the charges which must be incurred during the present fiscal year, will be necessary. The great length of frontier along which the boundary extends, the nature of the adjacent territory, and the difficulty of obtaining supplies, except at or near the extremes of the line, render it also indispensable that a liberal provision should be made to meet the necessary charges during the fiscal year ending on the 30th of June, 1851. I accordingly recommend this subject to your attention.

In the adjustment of the claims of American citizens on Mexico, provided for by the late treaty, the employment of counsel, on the part of the government, may become important for the purpose of assisting the commissioners in protecting the interests of the United States. I recommend this subject to the early and favourable consideration of Congress.

Complaints have been made in regard to the inefficiency of the means provided by the government of New Grenada for transporting the United States mail across the Isthmus of Panama, pursuant to our postal convention with that republic, of the 6th of March, 1844. Our Charge d'Affaires at Bogota has been directed to make such representations to the government of New Grenada as will, it is hoped, lead to a prompt removal of this cause of complaint.

The sanguinary civil war with which the republic of Venezuela has for some time past been ravaged, has been brought to a close. In its progress, the rights of some of our citizens resident or trading there have been violated.

The restoration of order will afford the Venezuelan government an opportunity to examine and redress these grievances, and others of long standing, which our representatives at Caraccas have, hitherto, ineffectually urged upon the attention of that government.

The extension of the coast of the United States on the Pacific, and the unexampled rapidity with which the inhabitants of California, especially, are increasing in numbers, have imparted new consequence to our relations with the other countries whose territories border upon that ocean. It is probable that the intercourse between those countries and our possessions in that quarter, particularly with the republic of Chili, will become extensive and mutually advantageous, in proportion as California and Oregon shall increase in population and wealth. It is desirable, therefore, that this government should do every thing in its power to foster and strengthen its relations with those states, and that the spirit of amity between us should be mutual and cordial.

I recommend the observance of the same course towards all other American States. The United States stand as the great American power to which, as their natural ally and friend, they will always be disposed first to look for mediation and assistance, in the event of any collision between them and any European nation. As such, we may often kindly mediate in their behalf, without entangling ourselves in foreign wars or unnecessary controversies. Whenever the faith of our treaties with any of them shall require our interference, we must necessarily interpose.

A convention has been negotiated with Brazil, providing for the satisfaction of American claims on that government, and it will be submitted to the senate. Since the last session of Congress, we have received an envoy extraordinary and minister plenipotentiary from that empire, and our relations with it are founded upon the most amicable understanding.

Your attention is earnestly invited to an amendment of our existing laws relating to the African slave trade, with a view to the effectual suppression of that barbarous traffic. It is not to be denied that this trade is still, in part, carried on by means of vessels built in the United States, and owned or navigated by some of our citizens. The correspondence between the department of state and the minister and consul of the United States at Rio de Janeiro, which has from time to time been laid before Congress, represents that it is a customary device to evade the penalties of our laws by means of sea-letters. Vessels sold in Brazil, when provided with such papers by the consul, instead of returning to the United States for a new register, proceed at once to the coast of Africa, for the purpose of obtaining cargoes of slaves.

Much additional information of the same character has recently been transmitted to the department of state. It has not been considered the policy of our laws to subject an American citizen, who, in a foreign country, purchases a vessel built in the United States, to the inconvenience of sending her home for a new register, before permitting her to proceed on a voyage. Any alteration of the laws, which might have a tendency to impede the free transfer of property in vessels between our citizens, or the free navigation of those vessels between different parts of the world, when employed in lawful commerce, should be well and cautiously considered; but I trust that your wisdom will devise a method by which our general policy, in this respect, may be preserved, and at the same time the abuse of our flag, by means of sea-letters, in the manner indicated, may be prevented.

Having ascertained that there is no prospect of the re-union of the five States of Central America, which formerly composed the republic of that name, we have separately negotiated with some of them treaties of amity and commerce, which will be laid before the senate.

A contract having been concluded with the State of Nicaragua, by a company composed of American citizens, for the purpose of constructing a ship canal through the territory of that State, to connect the Atlantic and Pacific oceans, I have directed the negotiation of a treaty with Nicaragua, pledging both governments to protect those who shall engage in and perfect the work. All other nations are invited by the State of Nicaragua to enter into the same treaty stipulations with her, and the benefit to be derived by each from such an arrangement, will be the protection of this great inter-oceanic communication against any power which might seek to obstruct it, or to monopolize its advantages. All States, entering into such a treaty, will enjoy the right of passage through the canal on payment of the same tolls.

The work, if constructed under these guarantees, will become a bond of peace, instead of a subject of contention and strife, between the nations of the earth. Should the great maritime states of Europe consent to this arrangement, (and we have no reason to suppose that a proposition so fair and honourable will be opposed by any,) the energies of their people and ours will co-operate in promoting the success of the enterprise. I do not recommend any appropriation from the national treasury for this purpose, nor do I believe that such an appropriation is necessary. Private enterprise, if properly protected, will complete the work, should it prove to be feasible. The parties who have procured the charter from Nicaragua, for its construction, desire no assistance from this government beyond its protection; and they profess that, having examined the proposed line of communication, they will be ready to commence the undertaking whenever that protection shall be extended to them. Should there appear to be reason, on examining the whole evidence, to entertain a serious doubt of the practicability of constructing such a canal, that doubt could be speedily solved by an actual exploration of the route.

Should such a work be constructed, under the common protection of all nations, for equal benefits to all, it would be neither just nor expedient that any great maritime state should command the communication. The territory through which the canal may be opened ought to be freed from the claims of any foreign power. No such power should occupy such a position that would enable it hereafter to exercise so controlling an influence over the commerce of the world, or to obstruct a highway which ought to be dedicated to the common uses of mankind.

The routes across the Isthmus, at Tehuantepec and Panama, are also worthy of our serious consideration. They did not fail to engage the attention of my predecessor. The negotiator of the treaty of Guadalupe Hidalgo was instructed to offer a very large sum of money for the right of transit across the Isthmus of Tehuantepec.

The Mexican government did not accede to the proposition for the purchase of the right of way, probably because it had already contracted with private individuals for the construction of a passage from the Guasacualco river to Tehuantepec. I shall not renew any proposition to purchase, for money, a right which ought to be equally secured to all nations, on payment of a reasonable toll to the owners of the improvement, who would, doubtless, be well contented with that compensation and the guarantees of the maritime States of the world, in separate treaties negotiated with Mexico, binding her and them to protect those who should construct the work. Such guarantees would do more to secure the completion of the communication through the territory of Mexico, than any other reasonable consideration that could be offered; and as Mexico herself would be the greatest gainer by the opening of this communication between the Gulf and the Pacific ocean, it is presumed that she would not hesitate to yield her aid, in the manner proposed, to accomplish an improvement so important to her own best interests.

We have reason to hope that the proposed rail-road across the Isthmus of Panama will be successfully constructed, under the protection of the late treaty with New Grenada, ratified and exchanged by my predecessor on the

10th day of June, 1848, which guaranties the perfect neutrality of the Isthmus, and the rights of sovereignty and property of New Grenada over that territory, "with a view that the free transit from ocean to ocean may not be interrupted or embarrassed," during the existence of the treaty. It is our policy to encourage every practicable route across the Isthmus, which connects North and South America, either by rail-road or canal, which the energy and enterprise of our citizens may induce them to complete; and I consider it obligatory upon me to adopt that policy, especially in consequence of the absolute necessity of facilitating intercourse with our possessions on the Pacific.

The position of the Sandwich Islands, with reference to the territory of the United States on the Pacific; the success of our persevering and benevolent citizens who have repaired to that remote quarter in Christianizing the natives and inducing them to adopt a system of government and laws suited to their capacity and wants; and the use made by our numerous whale-ships of the harbours of the islands as places of resort for obtaining refreshments and repairs, all combine to render their destiny peculiarly interesting to us.

It is our duty to encourage the authorities of those islands in their efforts to improve the moral and political condition of the inhabitants; and we should make reasonable allowances for the difficulties inseparable from this task. We desire that the islands may maintain their independence, and that other nations should concur with us in this sentiment. We could, in no event, be indifferent to their passing under the dominion of any other power. The principal commercial states have in this a common interest, and it is to be hoped that no one of them will attempt to interpose obstacles to the entire independence of the islands.

The receipts into the treasury for the fiscal year ending on the thirtieth of June last, were, in cash, forty-eight millions eight hundred and thirty thousand ninety-seven dollars and fifty cents, (48,830,097 50,) and in Treasury notes funded, ten millions eight hundred and thirty-three thousand dollars, (10,833,000,) making an aggregate of fifty-nine millions six hundred and sixty-three thousand ninety-seven dollars and fifty cents, (59,663,097 50,) and the expenditures, for the same time, were, in cash, forty-six millions seven hundred and ninety-eight thousand six hundred and sixty-seven dollars and eighty-two cents, (46,798,667 82,) and in Treasury notes, funded, ten millions eight hundred and thirty-three thousand dollars, (10,833,000,) making an aggregate of fifty-seven millions six hundred and thirty-one thousand six hundred and sixty-seven dollars and eighty-two cents, (57,631,667 82.)

The accounts and estimates which will be submitted to Congress in the report of the Secretary of the Treasury, show that there will probably be a deficit occasioned by the expenses of the Mexican war and treaty, on the first day of July next, of five millions eight hundred and twenty-eight thousand one hundred and twenty-one dollars and sixty-six cents, (5,828,121 66,) and on the first day of July, 1851, of ten millions five hundred and forty-seven thousand and ninety-two dollars and seventy-three cents, (10,547,092 73,) making in the whole a probable deficit, to be provided for, of sixteen millions three hundred and seventy-five thousand two hundred and fourteen dollars and thirty-nine cents, (16,375,214 39.)

The extraordinary expenses of the war with Mexico, and the purchase of California and New Mexico, exceed in amount this deficit, together with the loans heretofore made for those objects. I therefore recommend that authority be given to borrow whatever sum may be necessary to cover that deficit. I recommend the observance of strict economy in the appropriation and expenditure of the public money.

I recommend a revision of the existing tariff, and its adjustment on a basis which may augment the revenue. I do not doubt the right or duty of Congress to encourage domestic industry, which is the great source of national as well as individual wealth and prosperity. I look to the wisdom and patriotism of Congress for the adoption of a system which may place home labour at last on a sure and permanent footing, and, by due encouragement of manufactures, give a new and increased stimulus to agriculture, and promote the development of our vast resources, and the extension of our commerce. Believing that to the attainment of these ends (as well as the necessary augmentation of the revenue and the prevention of frauds,) a system of specific duties is best adapted, I strongly recommend to Congress the adoption of that system, fixing the duties at rates high enough to afford substantial and sufficient encouragement to our own industry, and at the same time so adjusted as to insure stability.

The question of the continuance of the sub-Treasury system is respectfully submitted to the wisdom of Congress. If continued, important modifications of it appear to be indispensable.

For further details and views of the above, and other matters connected with commerce, the finances and revenues, I refer to the report of the Secretary of the Treasury.

No direct aid has been given by the general government to the improvement of agriculture, except by the expenditure of small sums for the collection and publication of agricultural statistics, and for some chemical analyses, which have been, thus far, paid for out of the patent fund. This aid is, in my opinion, wholly inadequate. To give to this leading branch of American industry the encouragement which it merits, I respectfully recommend the establishment of an Agricultural Bureau, to be connected with the Department of the Interior. To elevate the social condition of the agriculturist, to increase his prosperity, and to extend his means of usefulness to his country, by multiplying his sources of information, should be the study of every statesman, and a primary object with every legislator.

No civil government having been provided by Congress for California, the people of that territory, impelled by the necessities of their political condition, recently met in convention for the purpose of forming a constitution and state government, which, the latest advices give me reason to suppose, has been accomplished; and it is believed they will shortly apply for the admission of California into the Union as a sovereign state. Should such be the case, and should their constitution be conformable to the requisitions of the constitution of the United States, I recommend their application to the favourable consideration of Congress.

The people of New Mexico will also, it is believed, at no very distant period, present themselves for admission into the union. Preparatory to the admission of California and New Mexico, the people of each will have instituted for themselves a republican form of government, "laying its foundations in such principles, and organizing its powers in such form as to them shall seem most likely to effect their safety and happiness."

By awaiting their action, all causes of uneasiness may be avoided, and confidence and kind feeling preserved. With a view of maintaining the harmony and tranquillity so dear to all, we should abstain from the introduction of those exciting topics of a sectional character which have hitherto produced painful apprehensions in the public mind; and I repeat the solemn warning of the first and most illustrious of my predecessors, against furnishing "any ground for characterizing parties by geographical discriminations."

A collector has been appointed at San Francisco under the act of Congress extending the revenue laws over California; and measures have been taken to organize the custom-house at that and the other ports mentioned in that act, at the earliest period practicable. The collector proceeded overland, and advices have not yet been received of his arrival at San Francisco. Meanwhile it is understood that the customs have continued to be collected there by officers acting under the military authority, as they were during the administration of my predecessor.

It will, I think, be expedient to confirm the collections thus made, and direct the avails (after such allowances as Congress may think fit to authorize,) to be expended within the territory, or to be paid into the treasury, for the purpose of meeting appropriations for the improvement of its rivers and harbours.

A party, engaged on the coast survey, was despatched to Oregon in January last. According to the latest advices, they had not left California; and directions have been given to them, as soon as they shall have fixed on the sites of the two light-houses, and the buoys authorized to be constructed and placed in Oregon, to proceed without delay to make reconnoisances of the most important points on the coast of California, and especially to examine and determine on sites for light-houses on that coast, the speedy erection of which is urgently demanded by our rapidly increasing commerce.

I have transferred the Indian agencies from upper Missouri and Council Bluffs to Santa Fe and Salt Lake; and have caused to be appointed sub-agents in the valleys of the Gila, the Sacramento, and San Joaquin rivers. Still further legal provisions will be necessary for the effective and successful extension of our system of Indian intercourse over the new territories.

I recommend the establishment of a branch mint in California, as it will, in my opinion, afford important facilities to those engaged in mining, as well as to the government in the disposition of the mineral lands.

I also recommend that commissions be organized by Congress to examine and decide upon the validity of the present subsisting land titles in California and New Mexico; and that provision be made for the establishment of offices of surveyor general in New Mexico, California, and Oregon, and for the surveying and bringing into market the public lands in those territories. Those lands remote in position and difficult of access, ought to be disposed of on terms liberal to all, but especially favourable to the early emigrants.

In order that the situation and character of the principal mineral deposites in California may be ascertained, I recommend that a geological and mineralogical exploration be connected with the linear surveys, and that the mineral lands be divided into small lots suitable for mining, and be disposed of, by sale or lease, so as to give our citizens an opportunity of procuring a permanent right of property in the soil. This would seem to be as important to the success of mining as of agricultural pursuits.

The great mineral wealth of California, and the advantages which its ports and harbours, and those of Oregon afford to commerce, especially with the islands of the Pacific and Indian oceans, and the populous regions of Eastern Asia, make it certain that there will arise, in a few years, large and prosperous communities on our western coast. It therefore becomes important that a line of communication, the best and most expeditious which the nature of the country will admit, should be opened within the territory of the United States from the navigable waters of the Atlantic or the Gulf of Mexico to the Pacific.

Opinion, as elicited and expressed by two large and respectable conventions lately assembled at St. Louis and Memphis, points to a railroad as that which, if practicable, will best meet the wishes and wants of the country. But while this, if in successful operation, would be a work of great national importance, and of a value to the country which it would be difficult to estimate, it ought also to be regarded as an undertaking of vast magnitude and expense, and one which must, if it be indeed practicable, encounter many difficulties in its construction and use.

Therefore, to avoid failure and disappointment; to enable Congress to judge whether in the condition of the country through which it must pass, the work be feasible, and if it be found so, whether it should be undertaken as a national improvement, or left to individual enterprise; and in the latter alternative, what aid, if any, ought to be extended to it by the government, I recommend, as a preliminary measure, a careful reconnoisance of the proposed several routes by a scientific corps, and a report as to the practicability of making such a road, with an estimate of the cost of its construction and support.

For further views on these and other matters connected with the duties of the home department, I refer you to the report of the secretary of the interior.

I recommend early appropriations for continuing the river and harbour improvements which have been already begun, and also for the construction of those for which estimates have been made, as well as for examinations and estimates preparatory to the commencement of such others as the wants of our country, and especially the advance of our population over new districts, and the extension of commerce, may render necessary. An estimate of the amount which can be advantageously expended within the next fiscal year, under the direction of the bureau of topographical engineers, accompanies the report of the secretary of war, to which I respectfully invite the attention of Congress.

The cession of territory made by the late treaty with Mexico, has greatly extended our exposed frontier, and rendered its defence more difficult. That treaty has also brought us under obligations to Mexico, to comply with which a military force is requisite. But our military establishment is not materially changed as to its efficiency from the condition in which it stood before the commencement of the Mexican war. Some addition to it will therefore be necessary; and I recommend to the favourable consideration of Congress an increase of the several corps of the army at our distant western posts, as proposed in the accompanying report of the secretary of war.

Great embarrassment has resulted from the effect upon rank in the army heretofore given to brevet and staff commissions. The views of the secretary of war on this subject are deemed important, and if carried into effect will, it is believed, promote the harmony of the service. The plan proposed for retiring disabled officers, and providing an asylum for such of the rank and file as from age, wounds, and other infirmities, occasioned by service, have become unfit to perform their respective duties, is recommended as a means of increasing the efficiency of the army, and as an act of justice due from a grateful country to the faithful soldier.

The accompanying report of the secretary of the navy presents a full and satisfactory account of the condition and operations of the naval service during the past year. Our citizens engaged in the legitimate pursuits of commerce have enjoyed its benefits. Wherever our national vessels have gone, they have been received with respect, our officers have been treated with kindness and courtesy, and they have, on all occasions, pursued a course of strict neutrality, in accordance with the policy of our government.

The naval force at present in commission is as large as is admissible, with the number of men authorized by Congress to be employed.

I invite your attention to the recommendation of the secretary of the navy on the subject of a reorganization of the navy in its various grades of officers, and the establishing of a retired list for such of the officers as are disqualified for active and effective service. Should Congress adopt some such measure as is recommended, it will greatly increase the efficiency of the navy, and reduce its expenditures.

I also ask your attention to the views expressed by him in reference to the employment of war-steamers, and in regard to the contracts for the transportation of the United States' mails, and the operation of the system upon the prosperity of the Navy.

By an act of Congress passed August 14, 1848, provision was made for extending post-office and mail accommodations to California and Oregon. Exertions have been made to execute that law; but the limited provisions of the act, the inadequacy of the means it authorizes, the ill adaptation of our post-office laws to the situation of that country, and the measure of compensation for services allowed by those laws, compared with the prices of labour and rents in California, render those exertions, in a great degree, ineffectual. More particular and efficient provision by law is required on this subject.

The act of 1845, reducing postage, has now, by its operation during four years, produced results fully showing that the income from such reduced postage is sufficient to sustain'the whole expense of the service of the Post-Office Department, not including the cost of transportation in mail steamers on the lines from New York to Chagres, and from Panama to Astoria, which have not been considered by Congress as properly belonging to the mail service.

It is submitted to the wisdom of Congress, whether a further reduction of postage should not now be made, more particularly on the letter correspondence. This should be relieved from the unjust burden of transporting and delivering the franked matter of Congress, for which public service provision should be made from the treasury. I confidently believe that a change may safely be made, reducing all single letter postage to the uniform rate of five cents, regardless of distance, without thereby imposing any greater tax on the treasury than would constitute a very moderate compensation for this public service; and I therefore respectfully recommend such a reduction.

Should Congress prefer to abolish the franking privilege entirely, it seems probable that no demand on the Treasury would result from the proposed reduction of postage. Whether any further diminution should now be made, or the result of the reduction to five cents, which I have recommended, should be first tested, is submitted to your decision.

Since the commencement of the last session of Congress, a postal treaty with Great Britain has been received and ratified, and such regulations have been formed by the Post-Office Departments of the two countries, in pursuance of that treaty, as to carry its provisions into full operation. The attempt to extend this same arrangement, through England, to France, has not been equally successful; but the purpose has not been abandoned.

For a particular statement of the condition of the Post-Office Department, and other matters connected with that branch of the public service, I refer you to the report of the Postmaster General.

By the act of the 3d of March, 1849, a Board was constituted to make arrangements for taking the seventh census, composed of the Secretary of State, the Attorney General, and the Postmaster General; and it was made the duty of this Board "to prepare and cause to be printed such forms and schedules as might be necessary for the full enumeration of the inhabitants of the United States; and also proper forms and schedules for collecting in statistical tables, under proper heads, such information as to mines, agriculture, commerce, manufactures, education, and other topics, as would exhibit a full view of the pursuits, industry, education, and resources of the country."

The duties enjoined upon the census board, thus established, having been performed, it now rests with Congress to enact a law for carrying into effect the provision of the constitution which requires an actual enumeration of the people of the United States within the ensuing year.

Among the duties assigned by the constitution to the general government is one of local and limited application, but not, on that account, the less obligatory; I allude to the trust committed to Congress, as the exclusive legislator and sole guardian of the interests of the District of Columbia. I beg to commend these interests to your kind attention. As the national metropolis, the city of Washington must be an object of general interest; and, founded as it was under the auspices of him whose immortal name it bears, its claims to the fostering care of Congress present themselves with additional strength. Whatever can contribute to its prosperity must enlist the feelings of its constitutional guardians, and command their favourable consideration.

Our government is one of limited powers, and its successful administration eminently depends on the confinement of each of its co-ordinate branches within its own appropriate sphere. The first section of the Constitution ordains that "all legislative powers therein granted shall be vested in a Congress of the United States, which shall consist of a Senate and House of Representatives." The executive has authority to recommend (not to dictate) measures to Congress.

Having performed that duty, the executive department of the government cannot rightfully control the decision of Congress on any subject of legislation, until that decision shall have been officially submitted to the President for approval. The check provided by the constitution, in the clause conferring the qualified veto, will never be exercised by me, except in the cases contemplated by the fathers of the republic. I view it as an extreme measure, to be resorted to only in extraordinary cases—as where it may become necessary to defend the executive against the encroachments of the legislative power, or to prevent hasty and inconsiderate or unconstitutional legislation.

By cautiously confining this remedy within the sphere prescribed to it in the cotemporaneous expositions of the framers of the constitution, the will of the people, legitimately expressed on all subjects of legislation, through their constitutional organs, the senators and representatives of the United States, will have its full effect. As indispensable to the preservation of our system of self-government, the independence of the representatives of the States and people is guarantied by the constitution; and they owe no responsibility to any human power but their constituents.

By holding the representative responsible only to the people, and exempting him from all other influences, we elevate the character of the constituent and quicken his sense of responsibility to his country. It is under these circumstances only that the elector can feel that, in the choice of the law-maker, he is himself, truly, a component part of the sovereign power of the nation. With equal care we should study to defend the rights of the executive and judicial departments. Our government can only be preserved in its purity by the suppression and entire elimination of every claim or tendency of one co-ordinate branch to encroachment upon another.

With the strict observance of this rule and the other injunctions of the constitution—with a sedulous inculcation of that respect and love for the union of the States, which our fathers cherished, and enjoined upon their children, and with the aid of that over-ruling Providence which has so long and so kindly guarded our liberties and institutions, we may reasonably expect to transmit them with their innumerable blessings to the remotest posterity.

But attachment to the union of the States should be habitually fostered in every American heart. For more than half a century, during which kingdoms and empires have fallen, this Union has stood unshaken. The patriots who formed it have long since descended to the grave; yet still it remains, the proudest monument to their memory, and the object of affection and admiration with every one worthy to bear the American name.

In my judgment its dissolution would be the greatest of calamities, and to avert that, should be the study of every American. Upon its preservation must depend our own happiness and that of countless generations to come. Whatever dangers may threaten it, I shall stand by it and maintain it in its integrity, to the full extent of the obligations imposed, and the power conferred upon me by the constitution.

WASHINGTON, December 4th, 1849.   Z. TAYLOR.

REPORT OF THE SECRETARY OF THE TREASURY.

TREASURY DEPARTMENT, }
December 1849. }

The Secretary of the Treasury reports:

RECEIPTS AND EXPENDITURES.

The receipts and expenditures for the fiscal year ending 30th June, 1849, were:

Receipts from customs, ... $28,346,738 82
Do.   do.   public lands, . . , . 1,688,959 55
Do.   do.   miscellaneous sources, . . . 1,038,649 13
Do.   do.   avails of Treasury notes and loans in specie, 17,755,750 00
Do.   do.   do.   funded, ... 10,833,000 00

$59,662,097 50
Add balance in the Treasury July 1, 1848, . . . 153,534 60

$59,816,632 10
The expenditures for the same fiscal year
  were, in cash, ... $46,798,667 82
Treasury notes funded, . . . 10,833,000 00— $57,631,667 82

Leaving a balance in the Treasury July 1, 1849, . $2,184,964 28
  as appears in detail by accompanying statement A.

ESTIMATES.

The estimated receipts and expenditures for the fiscal year ending 30th June, 1850, are :
Receipts from customs—1st quarter, by
  actual returns, . . . $11,643,728 54
Receipts from customs—2d, 3d and 4th
  quarters, as estimated, . . . 19,856,271 46— $31,500,000 00
Receipts from public lands, . . . 1,700,000 00
  Do.   do. miscellaneous sources, . . . 1,200,000 00

$34,400,000 00
Receipts from avails of loans in specie, . . $399,050 00
  Do.   do.   do.   in Treasury notes funded, 839,450 00— 1,238,500 00

Total receipts, ... $35,638,500 00
Add balance in the Treasury, July 1st, 1849, . . 2,184,964 28

Total means as estimated, ... $37,823,464 28

EXPENDITURES, VIZ.:

The actual expenditures for the first quarter, ending 30th of September, 1849,
  were, ... $8,904,829 96
As appears in detail by accompanying
  statement B.
The estimated expenditures during the
  other three quarters, from the 1st of Oct.,
  1849, to 30th June, 1850, are:
Civil list, foreign intercourse and miscel-
  laneous, . . . 10,330,116 62
Expenses of collecting revenue from cus-
  toms, ... 1,925,000 00
Expenses of collecting revenue from lands, 113,850 00
Army proper, &c., . . . 8,245,039 80
Fortifications, ordnance, arming militia, &c., 1,997,420 93
Internal improvements, &c., . . 77,072 36
Indian Department, . . . 859,963 73
Pensions, ... 682,630 77
Naval establishments, . . . 6,814,783 43
Interest on public debt and Treasury notes, 3,700,878 40— $43,651,585 94

Deficit 1st of July, 1850, ... $5,828,121 66

The estimated receipts and expenditures for the fiscal year commencing July 1, 1850, and ending June 30, 1851, are:

Receipts from customs,	. . . . .	\$32,000.000 00
Do. do. public lands,	. . . .	2,150,000 00
Do. do. miscellaneous sources,	. . .	300,000 00
Total estimated receipts,	. . . . .	\$34,450,000 00

The expenditures during the same period, as estimated by the several departments of State, Treasury, War, Navy, Interior, and Postmaster General, are:—

The balances of former appropriations which will be required to be expended this year, ...	\$5,656,530 34
Permanent and indefinite appropriations, . .	5,643,410 24
Specific appropriations asked for this year, . . .	33,697,152 15
	\$44,997,092 73

This sum is composed of the following particulars:—

Civil list, foreign intercourse and miscellaneous, .	11,088,724 64
Expenses of collecting revenue from customs, . .	2,750,000 00
Expenses of collecting revenue from lands, . .	170,835 00
Army proper, &c., ...	8,296,183 44
Fortifications, ordnance, arming militia, &c., . .	2,015,446 00
Internal improvements, &c., ...	1,247,203 38
Indian department, ...	1,912,710 53
Pensions, ...	1,927,010 00
Naval establishment, ...	11,353,129 64
Interest on Treasury notes and public debt, .	3,742,951 13
Purchase of stock of the loan of 28th January, 1847, .	492,898 97
.	\$44,997,092 73

Deficit July 1, 1851, ...	\$10,547,092 73
Do. July 1, 1850, ...	5,828,121 66
Total deficit, 1850 and 1851, ...	\$16,375,214 39

Prior to the first of July last, the expenses of collecting the revenue from customs were paid out of the accruing revenue at the several ports, and only the balance came into the treasury; of course the receipts at the treasury, actual and estimated, were of the net revenue after deducting all expenses.

By the act of 3d March last, the system was changed from and after 1st July, 1849, and, accordingly, the receipts, actual and estimated, from that date, are of the gross revenue, and estimates are submitted of the expenses of collection.

The alteration thus made in the law must prove to be salutary, as the attention of Congress will be annually drawn to the expenditures under this head, and they will be enabled to limit them in a spirit of economy as severe as the exigencies of the public service will admit.

Notwithstanding the great increase of the business of the country, the act of 17th June, 1844, has prevented any addition to the number of inspectors, gaugers, weighers, measurers, or markers, (in any district then established,) since its passage, except ten inspectors at New Orleans, per act 3d March, 1845, and the consequence is, that at all the large ports the number of inspectors is insufficient for the discharge of the duties of those offices, and the prevention of breaches or evasions of the revenue laws.

These duties have been greatly increased by the establishment of the warehousing system, and the difficulties thereby enhanced without any provision for increasing the number of officers to meet the emergencies of the new service. In addition to the temporary "aids to the revenue" appointed by some of the collectors under the authority of the act of 1799, I have been compelled to meet in part the emergency thus occasioned by authorizing, at the ports of New York, Boston, New Orleans, Philadelphia, Baltimore, and Bristol, R. I., the employment of thirty-two additional clerks to act as storekeepers, and relieve from attendance upon the warehouses that number of inspectors, in order that they might attend to their appropriate duties; and have declined assenting to requests for similar authority from other ports, only because the necessity did not appear to be of so urgent a character as to make it impossible to await the action of Congress on this subject.

The establishment of new collection districts in Texas and California, and the probable necessity of creating more, will of course make an addition to the expenses heretofore incurred, as well as to the revenue to be received.

The preventive service is amalgamated by our system with the service of collection. There are now 110 collection districts in the United States. Of this number, eighteen are maintained at the public expense, not having collected any revenue during the past year. There are thirty-six at which the revenue collected is not sufficient to meet the annual expenses, and but fifty-six at which the gross revenue exceeds the expenses.

Under these circumstances, I submit the estimates herewith presented (marked C) of the expenses of collecting the revenue from customs on the present scale of service, submitting to the wisdom of Congress the question of reducing that scale, and the mode of such reduction. I annex to the report copies of letters (marked T) received from collectors of the customs on the subject. In my judgment, no reduction is practicable, consistently with the security of the revenue; on the contrary, I have no doubt that the force should be increased.

I deem it proper to invite the early attention of congress to the appropriation required for the second half of the current fiscal year, for which a separate estimate is submitted, (C,) as required by the 3d section of the act of 3d of March last. The entire revenue from customs being paid into the public treasury, and remittances made to each collector for all the expenses of collection, very great embarrassment would result if the necessary appropriations were delayed.

Under the provisions of the 6th section of the act of 3d March last, I present herewith a "statement of the amount of money expended at each custom house in the United States during the fiscal year ending the 30th June last, and also the number of persons employed, and the occupation and salary of each person, at each of the said custom-houses during the period aforesaid," (marked D.)

It will be seen, from the statement referred to, that full complement of officers for twenty-four revenue vessels were charged upon the revenue. The number of officers has been reduced to sixteen of each grade.

PUBLIC DEBT.

Annexed will be found table marked (E), in compliance with the 22d section of the act of the 28th of January, 1847, containing the information required thereby, respecting the issue, redemption, purchase, and resale of treasury notes.

As required by the first section of the act of the 10th August, 1846, a statement is appended (marked E E) showing the amount of treasury notes paid within the preceding year under the provisions of that act.

Statement (F) shows the payments into the treasury on account of the loan of 1848.

The public debt amounted, on the 1st of October, 1848, agreeably to table (O) annexed to the last report of my predecessor, to the sum of $65,778,450 41. Since that time, $1,073,756.70 of the debt has been redeemed and extinguished by the purchase of stocks, &c. Of the amount thus redeemed and extinguished there were—on account of the debt of the cities of the District of Columbia assumed by the act of 20th May, 1836, $60,000; on account of the old funded and unfunded debt, $5,089 58; of treasury notes purchased at par and received in payment for lands and customs, $2,150; of military bounty scrip, $233,075; of the stock of 1842, $80,700; of the stock of 1843, $136,000; of the stock of 1848, $260,000; of the stock of 1847, $382,500; which last was paid for out of the land fund, and purchased by Hugh Maxwell, Esq., collector of New York, with the aid (kindly afforded) of C. W. Lawrence, Esq., the late collector of that port, whose resignation had, at that time, just taken effect, and who had acquired some experience in similar operations, from having been employed in them by the government in the previous year. See statement hereto annexed marked (G.)

The public debt now amounts to the sum of $64,704,693 71, which will be redeemable as follows:—

Parts of the old funded and unfunded debt on presentation,	$122,735 10
Debts of the district cities assumed by Congress, $60,000, payable annually,	960,000 00
Five per cent. stock, per act of August, 1846, redeemable 9th August, 1851,	303,573 92
Five per cent. loan, of 3d March, 1843, redeemable 1st July, 1853,	6,468,231 35
Six per cent. loan of 22d July, 1846, redeemable 12th November, 1856,	4,999,149 45
Six per cent. loan of 15th April, 1842, redeemable 31st December, 1862,	8,198,686 03
Six per cent. loan of 28th Jan., 1847, redeemable 1st Jan., 1868,	27,618,350 55
Do. do. do do do.	149,828 00
Six per cent. loan of 31st March, 1848, redeemable 1st July, 1868,	15,740,000 00
Treasury notes issued prior to 1846, payable on presentation; if converted into stock, under the act of January, 1847, will be redeemable 1st July, 1868,	144,139 31
	$64,704,693 71

WAYS AND MEANS.

It will be observed, that there is estimated a deficit on the 1st July next of $5,828,121 66, and on the 1st July, 1851, of $10,548.092 73; making, in the whole an estimated deficit of $16,375,214 39, to be provided for, arising from the expenses of the war and treaty with Mexico.

In order to aid in forming an estimate of the expenses occasioned by the war with Mexico, I have directed a statement to be prepared, which is hereto annexed, (marked H.) showing the excess of the expenses of the army proper for three years from 1st April, 1846, to 1st April, 1849, over those for the three years immediately preceding; and the excess of the expenses of the navy proper for two and a half years from 1st April, 1846, to 1st October, 1848, over those for the two and a half years immediately preceding.

The excess of army expenditures thus ascertained was,	$58,853,993 41
The excess of navy expenditures,	4,751,627 90
Making together the sum of,	$63,605,621 31
The increase of debt by the loans and treasury notes authorized by the acts of July 22, 1846, 28th January, 1847, and March 31, 1848, was	49,000,000 00
The difference between these sums, viz.:	$14,605,621 31

was of course paid out of the revenue (including balance on 1st April, 1846, and

$563,061 39 premiums on loans) towards the extraordinary military and naval expenses of the war.

In addition to these expenses, (without taking into the calculation sundry smaller items,) the number of military land warrants issuable under the act of 11th February, 1847, and the act of August 10, 1848, is to be taken into consideration. Under those acts, 65,171 warrants for 160 acres each, and 5,219 for 40 acres each, have already been issued. Claims to the amount of 9,000 have been suspended or rejected, and it is estimated that the number of claims yet to be presented will amount to 17,000. (See statement marked (I,) hereto annexed.)

The whole amount of warrants issuable under the act above mentioned, may, therefore, be estimated as equal to 90,000 of 160 acres each, which, at $200 each, will amount to $18,000,000. Of course, until these warrants shall be exhausted, a large proportion of the revenue from sales of public lands must be thereby diverted.

My predecessor estimated the revenue from public lands, for the last fiscal year, to be received at the treasury, at $3,000,000.

The actual receipts at the treasury from that source in the year ending 30th of June, 1848, were $3,328,642 56.

During the calendar years 1847 and 1848, and three-quarters of 1849, there were located for patents on military bounty land warrants 5,025,400 acres, amounting, at $1 25 per acre, to the sum of $6,281,750, viz.:

In 1847, 239,880 acres,		$ 299,850 00
In 1848, 2,288,960 acres,		2,861,200 00
¾ of 1849, 2,496,560 acres,		3,120,700 00
5,025,400		$6,281,750 00

See Statement marked (J.)

The receipts at the treasury from sales of public lands during the last fiscal year were $1,688,959 55.

It is not probable that additional sales would have been made to the full extent of the number of acres located under the military bounty land warrants, but I think it may be safely considered that this source of revenue may be taken at nearly $4,000,000, of which a part is absorbed by the land warrants; a part, say $1,657,050, (that being the amount paid and payable during the present fiscal year,) is applied to the payment of interest on the loan and treasury notes, under the act of January 28, 1847; and the remainder is pledged to the extinguishment of the debt created under that act. I estimate $2,000,000 per annum of the revenue from lands as diverted by the land warrants and the extinguishment of debt.

During the last fiscal year there were paid, under stipulations in the treaty with Mexico, sums amounting in all to $7,629,108.

Public debt to the amount of $790,566 39 (including treasury notes received for customs and lands,) was also paid off or purchased out of the general funds of the treasury and extinguished, besides $382,500 of the stock and treasury notes issued under the act of 1847, purchased out of the land fund and cancelled. See statement marked (K.) Of these sums, $890,175 was new debt contracted since the commencement of the war.

The balance in the treasury, on the 1st of July, 1849, was $2,184,964 28.

The aggregate of these sums, viz.:

Balance in the treasury on 1st July, 1849,		$2,184,964 28
Payments under the treaty,		7,629,108 00
Payments out of general fund on account of debt,		790,566 39
Land fund diverted,		2,000,000 00
Amounting to,		$12,604,638 67

and would have made a balance in the treasury to that amount on the 1st July,

1849, had none of them been applied to the extraordinary purposes above designated.

During the current fiscal year there will be required, in May next, for the payment of an instalment to Mexico, $3,540,000, and the land revenue estimated as diverted, will be 2,000,000 dollars, making together 5,540,000 dollars, which, added to the aforesaid sum of 12,604,638 dollars and 67 cents, would make 18,144,638 dollars and 67 cents, from which deducting the estimated deficit on the 1st July, 1850, of 5,828,121 dollars and 66 cents, would have left an estimated balance in the treasury, on that day, of 12,316,517 dollars and one cent. Adding to that balance the instalment to Mexico, due in 1851, 3,360,000 dollars, and the revenue from lands diverted, 2,000,000 dollars, would make an aggregate of 17,676,517 dollars and one cent; from which deducting the estimated deficit on the 1st of July, 1851, 10,547,092 dollars and 73 cents, would have made an estimated balance in the treasury, on that day, of 7,129,424 dollars and 28 cents.

I have gone into this detail for the purpose of showing that the resources of the country are ample, that the estimated deficit will have arisen from the extraordinary expenses of the war and treaty with Mexico, and that the justly high public credit of the United States is not endangered by the fact that, in this position of affairs, a new loan will be required.

Under these circumstances, I propose that authority be given to raise such sum, not exceeding $16,500,000 as may be found necessary from time to time, by the issue of stock or treasury notes, on such terms of interest (not exceeding six per cent.) and re-payment, as the president in his discretion shall, previous to their being issued, think fit to order.

Authority has already been given by the act of March 3d, 1849, to issue stock for $3,250,000 appropriated to carry into effect the 15th article of the treaty with Mexico.

To provide for the payment out of the revenue of the instalment which will be due to Mexico in the fiscal year ending 30th June, 1852, to secure the raising of a fund for the gradual extinguishment of our heavy public debt, and to place the revenue on a sure basis of sufficiency for all the expenditures of the government, it will be necessary to adopt measures for increasing the revenue; and the most available means to that end are to be found in raising the duties on imports. That an economy as rigid as may be found compatible with the necessities of the country will regulate the appropriations, under existing circumstances, cannot be doubted.

In proposing some alterations in the existing tariff, with a view, as well to the necessary augmentation of the revenue as the encouragement of industry, I think it right to present distinctly the views entertained on the latter subject, in the hope that a course may be adopted by the wisdom and patriotism of Congress which may tend to harmonize discordant feelings and promote the general prosperity.

I. I entertain no doubt of the rightful power of Congress to regulate commerce and levy imposts and duties, with the purpose of encouraging our own industry. In selecting for adoption one of two proposed regulations of commerce, it would appear to be clearly the right of Congress to choose that one which would, in its opinion, be most salutary to the country; and, in like manner, in laying imposts and duties, it would seem that the endeavour ought to be to regard the interests of the whole people, not as little, but as much as possible.

It is not a question of assuming a power not expressly granted by the constitution, on the ground that it may tend to the attainment of a general end therein expressed. Here the power to regulate commerce, and the power to levy and collect duties, are expressly given, and the only question is, whether they ought or ought not to be exercised with a view to the general good.

It seems to me, that to exercise these or any other powers with any other view, would be a misuse of power, and subversive of the legitimate end of government.

I find no obligation written in the constitution to lay taxes, duties or imposts, at the lowest rate that will yield the largest revenue.

If it were true, that a duty laid on a given article with a view to encourage our own productions is unlawful, because it may operate, by discouraging importation, as a partial prohibition, the proposition would be equally true of every duty laid with that intent, whether it were above or below the maximum revenue rate. But, as under the power to regulate commerce, it is competent for Congress to enact a direct and total prohibition of the importation of any article, it can be no objection to an act levying duties, that it may operate in partially preventing importation. Whether it be wise or just so to levy duties, is another question. What I mean to say now is, that there is no prohibition of it in the constitution. The proposition is maintained, as universally true, that the express grant of a power to Congress gives to that body the right of exercising that power in such manner as, in its opinion, may be most conducive to the advantage of the country.

As instances of the exercise of the power of regulating commerce, may be mentioned the prohibition of importations, except at designated ports; the prohibition of the coasting trade to all foreign vessels, and to all American vessels, not licensed and enrolled; the prohibition of certain trade to foreign vessels under the navigation act of 1817; the prohibition of certain trade to American vessels by the non-intercourse act, and of all trade by the embargo act; the drawback on the re-exportation of foreign goods; finally, the prohibition of the introduction of adulterated drugs into the country by the act of 26th July, 1848.

Under the power to levy taxes, duties and imposts, I refer to the discriminating tonnage duties on foreign vessels, the discriminating duties on their cargoes, the preamble to the first law imposing duties passed under the constitution, and the enactments of most of the subsequent ones.

These enactments show that at most or all periods of our history the views which I have expressed appear to have been sustained and acted on.

II. All legislation designed to favour a particular class to the prejudice of others, or to injure a particular class for the benefit of others, is manifestly unwise and unjust. Nothing can be more destructive of the true interests of the country than such legislation, except the refusal of really salutary legislation, under an erroneous impression that it might favour one class to the prejudice of others, while in fact the denial of it injures all classes, and benefits nobody.

III. As every producer in one branch of useful industry is also a consumer of the products of others, and as his ability to consume depends upon the profits of his production, it follows that to give prosperity to one branch of industry is to increase that of the rest. Within each branch of industry there will be individual rivalry; but among the several branches of useful industry there must always exist an unbroken harmony of interest.

No country can attain a due strength of prosperity that does not by its own labour carry its own productions, as nearly as possible, to the point necessary to fit them for ultimate consumption. To export its raw material and re-import the articles manufactured from it, or to neglect its own raw materials and import the articles manufactured from that of another country, is to pretermit the means which nature has provided for its advancement.

For instance, we exported, during the fiscal year, ending 30th June, 1849, raw cotton to the value of about sixty-six millions of dollars. If that cotton had been spun and woven at home, (supposing its value to be increased four-fold by manufacture,) it would have produced a value of about one hundred and ninety-eight millions in addition. What would have been the effect of this increased production on the prosperity of the country?

This question would not be completely answered by merely pronouncing the added value of one hundred and ninety-eight millions of dollars to be a large profit to the manufacturer, any more than the question of the effect of the production of wheat would be answered by deducting the cost of seed wheat from

the value of the crop, and pronouncing the remainder to be a large profit to the farmer.

The manufacture of cotton cloth is begun with the planting of the cotton—it is carried to a certain point by the planter, and then taken up and perfected by the spinner and weaver. The planter and manufacturer are not engaged in different branches of industry, but in the same—the one commences the process which the other completes. Cotton-seed of insignificant value, being by regular stages of labour developed and brought to the form of cotton cloth, has acquired a value of about two hundred and sixty-four millions.

The planting States have added many millions to the annual productions of the country by the culture of cotton. By continuing the process, they could quadruple that addition.

The planter would then have a market at his door for all his produce, and the farmer would, in like manner, have a home market for his. The power of consumption of not only breadstuffs, but of every article useful or necessary in the feeding, clothing, and housing of man, would be vastly increased—the consumer and producer would be brought nearer to each other—and in fact a stimulus would be applied to every branch of productive industry.

It is gratifying to know that the manufacture of cotton has already been introduced into several of the planting States (see document marked (W) hereto annexed,) and it ought not to be doubted will rapidly be extended.

The manufacture of iron, wool, and other staples would lead to similar results. The effect would be a vast augmentation of our wealth and power.

Upon commerce the effects might be expected to be, if possible, still more marked. It is not enough to say that no country ever diminished its commerce by increasing its productions—and that no injury would therefore result to that interest. There would probably be not only a great increase in the amount, but an improvement not less important in the nature of our commerce.

Of the immense addition that would accrue to our internal and coasting trade, (which in every country form the great and most valuable body of commerce,) it is unnecessary to do more than merely speak in passing—but it may be well to offer a few remarks on foreign commerce.

Commerce is the machinery of exchange. It is the handmaid of agriculture and manufactures. It will not be affirmed that it is ever positively injurious—but it will be more or less useful as it co-operates more or less with the productive industry of the country. The mere carriage of commodities by sea or land is necessarily profitable only to the carrier, who is paid for it. It may be useful or not to others, according to circumstances. The farmer finds a rail-road a great convenience, but he understands that it is better employed in carrying his crop than in carrying away his seed-wheat and manure.

The commerce which should consist in carrying cotton-seed abroad, to be there grown, would not be so useful as that which is now occupied in exporting the raw cotton grown at home. We should easily understand, also, that the commerce thus employed would be much more limited in amount and much less profitable to the carriers than what we now have. Yet our present commerce is, in fact, of the same nature with that above described. The seed bears to the cotton the same relation which the cotton bears to the cloth. If we now export cotton of the value of about sixty-six millions, the same cotton, when converted into cloth, would make an export of some two hundred and sixty-four millions, or some two hundred and forty-five millions after deducting the fifteen or twenty millions which would be required for our own consumption, (in addition to the portion of our present manufactures consumed at home,) and our imports would be thereby in like manner increased.

England, at this moment, derives a large portion of her power from spinning and weaving our cotton. When we shall spin and weave it ourselves, make our own iron, and manufacture our other staples, we shall have transferred to this country the great centres of wealth, commerce, civilization, and political, as well as moral and intellectual power.

At present, we are far from having the amount of foreign commerce which is due to our position, as a vastly productive country, with an extensive coast, good harbours, great internal water-courses, and a people unsurpassed in maritime skill and enterprise.

Our annual products were estimated by my predecessor in this department, at three thousand million dollars, while our average exports are about one hundred and thirteen millions, and our imports about one hundred and six millions, making together two hundred and nineteen millions, exclusive of gold and silver and of foreign commodities imported and re-exported. An eminent British authority estimates the annual creation of wealth in Great Britain and Ireland, at between two thousand one hundred, and two thousand two hundred millions. If we add, for articles omitted by him, between three and four hundred millions, we shall have a total of two thousand five hundred millions.

The British exports and imports amount annually to about five hundred and twenty millions, exclusive of gold and silver, and of foreign commodities imported and re-exported. If their foreign trade were brought down to our scale upon this estimate, it would be reduced to about one hundred and eighty-three millions. If ours were raised to their scale, it would reach about six hundred and twenty-four millions.

Estimating the population of Great Britain and Ireland at thirty millions, and our population at twenty-one millions, their foreign trade averages $17 33 for each individual; ours $10 42. If their foreign trade were no greater than ours, in proportion to population, it would be reduced from five hundred and twenty to three hundred and twelve millions. If our foreign trade were as great in proportion to population as is theirs, it would be swelled in amount from two hundred and nineteen to three hundred and sixty-four millions.

A leading cause of the existing difference is to be found in the fact that Great Britain exports chiefly what she has first brought to the form in which it is ready for ultimate consumption; it is at the stage of its highest value, and her market is almost co-extensive with the civilized world.

All history shows that where are the workshops of the world, there must be the marts of the world, and the heart of wealth, commerce and power. It is as vain to hope to make these marts by providing warehouses, as it would be to make a crop by building a barn.

IV. Whether we can have workshops to work up, at least, our own materials, must depend upon the question, whether we have or can obtain sufficient advantages to justify the pursuit of this kind of industry.

The circumstances favourable to production in this country may be stated to be: 1st. Facility in procuring raw materials. 2d. Abundance of fuel. 3d. Abundance of food and other articles necessary for the sustenance and housing of the labourer. 4th. The superior efficiency of the labourers in comparison with those of other countries.

The circumstances supposed to be unfavourable to our production may be thus classed—

1st. Want of capital.

2d. Dearness of our labour as compared with that of other countries.

3d. Insecurity by exposure to the influence of violent and excessive fluctuations of price in foreign markets, and to undue foreign competition.

1st. Capital, which is but the accumulated savings of labour, is believed to be abundant among ourselves for any purpose to which it can be profitably applied. It is more divided than in some other countries, and associations of capital are therefore more common among us than elsewhere. It will be increased by the labour of every successive year, and for investments reasonably secure, it will flow in whenever required, as it has always heretofore done, from other countries where it may exist in greater abundance. The amount of capital required for a large production is not enormous. The whole capital, for instance, employed in the establishment and support of iron works in England and in Wales, in 1847, has been estimated at less than one hundred millions of dollars; the annual production then being about one million two hundred thousand tons.

2d. The difference between the price of labour here and in Great Britain, is certainly great, and, it is to be hoped and expected, will never be diminished by a reduction of wages here. The difference has been estimated at an average of thirty-three per cent. Probably the average difference is much more than that: in some branches, such as the manufacture of iron, it is certainly much greater. This difference is in part compensated by the disadvantages under which the foreign manufacturer is placed by the necessity in some branches of procuring his raw material from a great distance, or transporting a heavy article of production (such as iron) to a distant market. In addition, he is pressed by a heavy burden of taxation. The greater efficiency of our labour is to some extent an additional compensatory element. This includes the greater capacity for acquiring skill, the superior general intelligence, the higher inventive faculty, the greater moral and physical energy, both of action and endurance, which our people possess in comparison with the foreign labourer.

Better fed, clothed, housed and educated—conscious of the ability to lay up some capital annually from his savings—encouraged to invest that capital in the enterprise in which his labour is engaged—enjoying practically greater civil and political liberty, looking forward to an indefinite future in which, through his own good conduct and example, he may expect each successive generation of his descendants to be better circumstanced than its predecessor, it cannot be doubted that these advantages add greatly to the efficiency of the American labourer. The precise extent to which they go towards compensating the difference in the price of labour, it is difficult to define. The efficiency of our labour may be expected to increase with the increase of reward to the labourer.

In many of the New England factories, the labourers are encouraged to invest their surplus earnings in the stock of the company by which they are employed, and are thus stimulated, by direct personal interest, to the greatest exertion. It may be expected that this system will be introduced into other branches in which it may be found practicable, tending, as it does, so powerfully to elevate the labourer, increase production, and practically instruct all men in the great truth of the essential harmony of capital and labour.

3d. Capital flows freely at home and abroad in every productive channel in which it can flow safely, and will even incur great hazards, if they be such as its owner may hope to meet by the care and circumspection of himself or others to whom he has confided its management. But if he knows that skill, industry, and economy cannot avail him, and that, in addition to all the contingencies of rivalry and markets, he is to be further exposed to dangers arising from causes quite beyond his control or counteraction, he will hold back. The vacillations which have occurred in our policy have no doubt deterred a large amount of capital from investment in industrial pursuits. The encouragement offered on one day, and on the faith of which fixed investments have been made, which are exposed to loss by the withdrawal of that encouragement on the next, is in fact substantial discouragement. And the insecurity resulting from the repetition of such acts has been seriously detrimental.

4th. The fluctuations in the foreign markets have, for many years, been such as seem to denote an unhealthy and feverish state of business. They are not in the natural course of a wholesome trade. They seem to betoken a change in existing arrangements, and the apprehension of such change is also evinced in the efforts now making in England to sustain the British manufacturer, by putting at hazard other important branches of industry. The competition of new establishments with very large ones already in existence abroad, and in which the price of labour is lower, is evidently not an equal competition.

The capital fixed in machinery, furnaces, &c., cannot be changed, and the work of production will not cease until the price shall have been reduced to a point very little above the cost of materials, labour and repairs. Of course where the lower price is paid for labour there will be a larger margin for reduction by the sacrifice of part of the profit; and where a great accumulation is in hand of the avails of the business of former years, the owner may find it his interest for a while to sell his commodity at less than the actual cost, if by that means he can drive out his rival, looking, of course, to subsequent reimbursement (at least) when he shall again have the control of the market.

This known necessity of the position of foreign manufactures of course tends to discourage new, as well as to defeat the successful operation of existing investments of capital here, in similar enterprises.

To counteract the influence of these unfavourable circumstances, which, so long as they continue, must greatly retard our advancement, limit our foreign commerce, and prevent the due progress of industry, I propose that the duties on the staple commodities, (whether raw material or manufactured articles,) in which foreign nations compete with our own productions, be raised to a point at which they will afford substantial and sufficient encouragement to our domestic industry, provide for the necessary increase and due security of the revenue, and insure the permanence and stability of the system. Experience has, I think, shown this to be a wise, just, and effectual mode to promote new and revive languishing branches of industry, provided the selection of the objects be wisely made and limited to those productions for which the country is naturally adapted.

We have been, perhaps, too long hesitating and vacillating on the threshold of a great career. The want of stability in the course of legislation, and other disturbing causes, have heretofore occasioned inconveniences. The short duration of some of the tariff acts—the great expansion of the currency which occurred during their operation—the Compromise act, (a result of what was believed to be a political necessity,) which, whatever its effects on existing establishments, undoubtedly discouraged new adventurers—and, finally, the unexpected repeal of the act of 1842; these circumstances have certainly been of a retarding character.

Yet it is impossible not to observe that, at every favourable moment, vast movements in advance have been made, and that the ground thus gained has not been entirely lost. It is believed that every article, the manufacture of which has been established here, has, after that establishment continued gradually to diminish in price, and that, without a corresponding reduction in the wages of labour, which, indeed, could not be diminished by reason of an increased demand for it. Statements are annexed, marked (L,) exhibiting some instances of this result.

These facts lead irresistibly to the conclusion that our labour becomes so much more efficient by use, acquired skill, enlarged establishments, and new facilities derived from inventions, that the difference in price between it and the foreign labour, however serious an obstacle to successful competition, will become less so with every year of our activity in the same branches of industry; and that it by no means follows that labour must be worse paid because its products are sold cheaper; or, that because labour is better paid, its products must be sold dearer.

All that is wanting is a general determination that industry shall be encouraged and supported in the home production and manufacture of iron, wool, cotton, sugar, and our other staples, and that the legislation necessary to sustain it shall be firmly adopted and persevered in.

I will proceed to state the nature of the modifications which it appears expedient to make in the existing tariff, and, if required, will hereafter present a plan in detail.

1. The rates of duty are, in my opinion, too low, especially on articles similar to our own staples. I conceive that the revenue has suffered materially from this circumstance. Indeed, I am compelled to believe that it would have been greatly diminished but for the extraordinary demand for our bread-stuffs and provisions, produced by the famine in Europe in 1847, and to a great extent continued by the short crop abroad in 1848. (See statement marked M, hereto annexed.) Even under these favourable circumstances, the average revenue from woollens, cottons, hempen goods, iron, sugar, hemp unmanufactured, salt, and coal, has fallen under the act of 1846 from $14,162,507 to $13,392,624 50, taking the average from the receipts of 1845–6, and those of 1848–9; being an average diminution of $769,982 50, as will be seen by the table marked (N,) hereto annexed; the loss of annual revenue being as follows:

On cottons,	-	-	-	-	-	-	$918,894 00
On hempen goods,	-	-	-	-	-	-	61,794 50
On sugar,	-	-	-	-	-	-	181,741 50
On salt,	-	-	-	-	-	-	348,438 00
On coal,	-	-	-	-	-	-	70,030 00
							$1,580,898 00

The gain as follows:

On woollens,	-	-	-	-	-	-	$355,592 50
On iron,	-	-	-	-	-	-	415,240 00
On hemp unmanufactured,	-	-	-	-	-	-	40,083 00
							$810,915 50

The very small increase on the staples of woollens, iron, and unmanufactured hemp, compared with the vast injury occasioned to our production, and the diminution thereby of our power of consumption, cannot fail to attract attention; while on the other articles named the revenue and productions have both suffered materially. It is believed that the revenue could be greatly increased by increasing the duties on these and other articles.

2. I propose a return to the system of specific duties on articles on which they can be conveniently laid. The effects of the present ad valorem system are twofold, viz. on the revenue and on our own productions. Experience has, I think, demonstrated that, looking exclusively to the revenue, a specific duty is more easily assessed, more favourable to commerce, more equal, and less exposed to frauds than any other system. Of course such a duty is not laid without reference to the average cost of the commodity. This system obviates the difficulties and controversies which attend an appraisement of the foreign market value of each invoice, and it imposes an equal duty on equal quantities of the same commodity. Under the ad valorem system, goods of the same kind and quality, and between which there cannot be a difference in value in the same market at any given time, nevertheless may often pay different amounts of duty. Thus the hazards of trade are unnecessarily increased.

To levy an ad valorem duty on a foreign valuation equably, at the different ports, is believed to be impossible. That the standard of value at any two ports is precisely the same at any given time is wholly improbable. The facilities afforded to frauds upon the revenue are very great, and it is apprehended that such frauds have been and are habitually and extensively practised. The statements annexed, (marked O,) to which I invite especial attention, exhibit in a strong light the dangers to which this system is necessarily exposed.

As the standard of value at every port must at least depend upon the average of the invoices that are passed there, every successful attempt at undervaluation renders more easy all that follow it. The consequences are, not only that the revenue suffers, that a certain sum is in effect annually given by the public among dishonest importers as a premium for their dishonesty, but that fair American importers may be gradually driven out of the business, and their places supplied by unknown and unscrupulous foreign adventurers. As long ago as 1801, Mr. Gallatin urged the extension of specific duties on the ground now repeated—of the prevention of undervaluation. In his report of that year he used the following language: "Without any view to an increase of revenue, but in order to guard, as far as possible, against the value of goods being underrated in the invoices, it would be eligible to lay specific duties on all such articles now paying duties ad valorem, as may be susceptible of that operation." At that time specific duties were already laid on spirits and wines, sugar, molasses, tea, coffee, salt, pepper, steel, nails and spikes, hemp, coal, cordage, and several other articles.

The 8th section of the act of 30th July, 1846, made it the duty of the collector, within whose district merchandise may be imported or entered, to cause the dutiable value of such imports to be appraised, estimated, and ascertained in accordance with the provisions of existing laws.

By the 2d section of the act of 10th August, 1846, it is provided that, "in appraising all goods at any port of the United States heretofore subjected to specific duties, but upon which ad valorem duties are imposed by the act of the thirtieth July last, entitled 'an act reducing the duty on imports and for other purposes,' reference shall be had to values and invoices of similar goods imported during the last fiscal year, under such general and uniform regulations for the prevention of frauds or undervaluations as shall be prescribed by the secretary of the treasury."

It will be observed that these last recited provisions do not authorize the levying of duties on the value of similar merchandise in any preceding year, but merely a reference to such value and the invoices, for the purpose of aiding in the ascertainment of the value at the time fixed by existing laws. That time was, by circular issued by my predecessor, dated 6th July, 1847, determined to be the time of the shipment of the goods. My predecessor issued three circulars, calling the attention of the officers of the customs to the provisions of the 2d section of the act of the 10th August, 1846; one dated the 11th and one the 25th of November, 1846, and the last the 26th December, 1848, and there can be no doubt exhausted all practicable means for preventing undervaluations and frauds, so far as they could be checked by treasury instructions and regulations. These efforts have been continued by the department; but the radical faults of the system are such that no vigilance, sagacity, or regulations, it is believed, have been or can be found effectual for the purpose.

In England it is believed to have long been a settled point that specific or rated duties (which are ad valorem on an assumed value) are in every respect better for revenue and trade than any other system.

The effect of the existing system on production is also striking, (see documents marked — annexed.) It tends to aggravate the great fluctuations in price which are so injurious to trade as well as industry.

When prices abroad are very high, the duty is high also; and when prices fall to a very low point, the duty is low in proportion. It is a sliding scale of the worst kind. If the duty forms a part of the price, it renders the extremes of fluctuation more remote from each other by a per centage on the range equal to the rate of the duty. If the fluctuation abroad be from $50 to $20, the range is of course $30. A specific duty of $15 would leave the range still $30. But at an ad valorem of 30 per cent., the highest point would be $65 and the lowest $26, making a range of $39. On every account I strongly recommend a return to the system of specific duties on all articles to which they can be conveniently applied.

3. On those articles on which an ad valorem duty is retained, I recommend that it be levied on the market value in the principal markets of our own country

at the time of arrival. It would be easier to ascertain at our 'ports such market value, than it is to ascertain what was that of a foreign country at a past time. Every importer should declare the value of his goods, and by giving the option to the government to take them at the value thus declared, or levy the duty on the actual value, it is probable that comparatively few cases of undervaluation would occur. In connexion with this subject, and as a measure tending to the prevention of fraud, error, and want of uniformity of valuation at the various ports of our extended coast, 1 would recommend the appointment of appraisers at large, whose duty it shall be to visit, from time to time, the different custom-houses, interchange views, superintend the mode of appraisals, and suggest such practical reforms as may be deemed necessary to a just and equal enforcement of the revenue laws. The provisions of the constitution, which require that all duties and imposts shall be uniform throughout the United States, cannot, even with a home valuation, be fully and effectually enforced in practice without some system of general supervision, more perfect in this respect than any that can be established under the existing provision of law, which merely gives to the secretary of the treasury authority to direct the appraisers for any collection district to attend in any other collection district for the purpose of appraising, any goods, wares, and merchandise imported therein.

4. The laying a lower duty upon non-enumerated articles than is imposed upon those which are enumerated, leads to attempts at disguise, and to controversies and unnecessary litigation, which would be avoided by making the duty on non-enumerated articles higher than on the others.

Different rates of duty on manufactures of the same material are also inconvenient, and the same remark applies to the different rates imposed upon the manufactures of wool and manufactures of worsted.

The effect of laying the same or a higher rate of duty on the raw material than is imposed on the manufactured article, too evidently tends to injure our industry in competition with that of other countries, to require more than a passing observation.

WAREHOUSES.

A statement is herewith presented, (marked P.) showing the expenses incurred during the last *fiscal* year in the execution of the act of the 6th August, 1846, "to establish a warehousing system," from which it will be seen they amount to $194,634,66 beyond all the receipts from storage, &c. To this sum there are to be added many charges for rent, labour, clerk hire, stationery, &c., that do not appear in these accounts, but justly belong to them.

This subject is one of great embarrassment to the department. Congress has not made any provision for these expenses, unless they are embraced in the appropriation for the expenses of collecting the revenue from customs. To a large extent, they are incurred without the receipt of any revenue whatever; and, in order to meet the provisions of this act, and grant all its facilities to commerce in the several districts, it must continue to impose an annual charge upon the treasury. This act provides that, in all cases where the duties upon imported merchandise are not paid within the period allowed by law, or whenever the importer shall make entry for warehousing the same, the said merchandise shall be taken possession of by the collector and deposited in the public stores, or in other stores to be agreed on by the collector and the importer. It appears also to be contemplated by the act that the storage shall be at the usual rates at the port of importation.

The act of 3d March, 1841, requires "that all stores hereafter rented by the collector, naval officer, and surveyor, shall be on public account, and paid for by the collector as such."

These requirements of law have imposed upon this department the necessity of making ample provision for large quantities of merchandise in advance of their arrival, and of securing the attendance of competent officers, clerks, and labourers, to take charge of the same. The experience of three years fully proves that the receipts from storage at the usual rates, and no other should be charged, will not defray the expenses of the system.

A statement is also presented, (marked Q.) showing the value of dutiable merchandise re-exported from 1821 to 1849, from which it will be seen that the total amount of such exports during that period was $298,716,670, or an annual average of $10,128,161.

From the 1st December, 1846, to 30th June, 1849, the aggregate exports of dutiable merchandise from warehouse amounted to $7,213,810, or an annual average of $2,792,439. In these exports from warehouse there is included the merchandise that was imported from foreign countries and transported to Canada; also the wheat, wheat-flour, &c., that have been transported from Canada, and the salted fish, &c., from other British North American provinces intended for shipment from our ports to foreign countries.

During the three years preceding the enactment of the warehousing act, viz. in 1844, 1845, and 1846, the total exports of dutiable merchandise amounted to - - - - - $14,656,816

During the three following years, 1847, 1848, and 1849, these exports amounted to - - - - - - 17,556,182

The increase of exports, which appears from this statement, to the extent of more than two millions of dollars, is made up of the wheat, flour, fish, &c., from the British North American provinces, and merchandise transported under the transportation act of 3d March, 1845, before referred to.

From the returns made to this department, and the quarterly statements published, it is believed to be apparent that the operation of the warehousing act has not been beneficially felt in the general business of the country.

The only descriptions of merchandise that will bear unnecessary and circuitous transportation are the more valuable articles of manufactures, and these have not, to any considerable extent, sought a deposite in our warehouses with a view to re-exportation. Experience every where demonstrates that the commodities which may with advantage be deposited in public warehouses are mainly such as are needed for the consumption of the country for food or manufacture. With the present frequent and rapid communications by steam with all parts of the commercial world, it cannot reasonably be expected that merchandise to any extent will be sent to our warehouses to await an export demand.

As an illustration of these remarks, reference is made to the published quarterly statements of the value of the merchandise in all the public warehouses, (see table hereto annexed marked R.) from which it will be seen that the largest amount at the end of any quarter was - - - $7,830,010 00

And the average amount at the end of each quarter was - 5,742,166 00

Also, that the largest amount of duties payable on this merchandise at the end of any quarter was - - - 2,501,394 35

And the average amount at the end of each quarter was - 1,800,100 52

From these several statements it appears that the practical operation of the warehousing act is a return to the system of credit upon duties, under a new name and form.

The fifth section of the act of 3d March last, provides "that all imports subject to duty, and whereon the duties are not paid when assessed, shall be deposited in the public warehouse, from whence they may be taken out for immediate exportation under the provisions of that act, at any time within two years; and, on payment of the duties, may be withdrawn for consumption within the United States at any time within one year; but no goods subject to duty shall be hereafter entered for drawback, or exported for drawback, after they are withdrawn from the custody of the officers of the customs."

The effect of this section, if rigidly construed, would be to deprive the importer of the privilege of the transportation of merchandise under bond from one district to another, and of re-warehousing the same, under the provisions of the second section of the warehousing act, and thereby deprive a large portion of our citizens of any participation in its benefits.

Under the belief that this was not the intention of Congress, no such instructions have been issued.

SUB-TREASURY.

The question of the expediency of continuing the system established by the act entitled "An act to provide for the better organization of the treasury, and for the collection, safe keeping, transfer, and disbursement of the public revenue," approved 6th August, 1846, is respectfully submitted to the wisdom of Congress. Experience has demonstrated some of the requirements of the act to be productive of great inconvenience—if, indeed, there be not some which, under the influence of strong necessity, are often violated.

Disbursing officers, to whom drafts for large sums are issued, are, by existing arrangements, obliged to receive the full amount of said drafts at one payment from the proper assistant-treasurer, while their expenditures must be made in small sums from time to time. The custody of the money is thus forced upon them, without any provision for its convenience, or even safety. If the money is to be disbursed at points distant from the place where it is received, the burden of transferring it is in like manner imposed on them. If they adopt the usual and customary mode of keeping and transferring money, they violate the law. If they undertake themselves its custody and carriage, they incur great risk and responsibility.

The actual carriage of coin from place to place, in the same town, is burdensome; especially in those southern ports where silver is the coin chiefly in use.

The number of clerks authorized by law to be employed is believed to be much too limited.

To alleviate some of the inconveniences attending the system, I respectfully suggest, if it is to be continued—

1st. That any person having a draft on an assistant-treasurer be permitted to deposite his draft with the assistant-treasurer, and draw for the amount from time to time in such sums as he may desire, upon his own orders, payable to any person or persons; provided, that the whole amount of the draft should be actually drawn within a short period, say two weeks after the deposit of the draft.

2d. That any disbursing officer having a draft on an assistant-treasurer should be permitted to deposit such draft, and draw for the amount in like manner; provided that each order should be presented for payment within two weeks after its date. These provisions would, it is believed, effectually prevent the checks or orders being used as currency.

The proposed system would render necessary an increase of the force employed in the offices of the several assistant-treasurers, and ought to be accompanied by an increase of compensation.

The inconvenience arising from the accumulation of coin at points where it is not required for the public service, is very great; but it seems to be inseparable from the system itself. To pay a public creditor with a draft on a remote office, which he cannot sell but at a discount, or collect in person without a journey, would be unseemly, and the government has no means itself of making transfers in such cases, other than the despatch of special messengers, at some expense and much risk of loss.

The insecurity of the actual custody of the public money—confided, as it is, at the several points, to the vigilance and fidelity of one assistant-treasurer, and he inadequately compensated—is a subject which should attract the serious attention of Congress.

MISCELLANEOUS.

By the third section of the act of 3d March, 1849, questions arising in respect to the refunding of duties collected in Mexico, or the remission of penalties imposed, on the ground that the collection was improper or the penalties wrongfully enforced, are referred to the decision of the secretary of the treasury. I respectfully submit that, as these duties and penalties were collected and imposed by officers of the army and navy, the right to determine the propriety of their collection or imposition would be better vested in the departments of war and the navy. In some, probably many of the cases, appeals were originally taken by the parties interested to the head of one or the other of these departments, and these appeals in some way formally or informally disposed of. It is embarrassing for the secretary of the treasury to determine how far that disposition is to be considered as intended to be final, and, if so intended, how far it is his duty under the law to re-open the case and decide it anew.

In consequence of the recent alteration of the British navigation laws, British vessels, from British or other foreign ports, will, (under our existing laws,) after the first day of January next, be allowed to enter in our ports with cargoes of the growth, manufacture, or production of any part of the world, on the same terms as to duties, imposts, and charges, as vessels of the United States and their cargoes.

I deem it proper to invite the consideration of Congress to the existing provisions of law regulating the coasting trade of the United States, with a view to such modifications thereof as may be deemed expedient and proper to meet the altered condition of that trade which has arisen since the law regulating it was passed.

The law by which this trade is now regulated was enacted on the 18th of February, 1793, and its essential provisions have not been changed by subsequent legislation. Within the period elapsed since the date of the law, Congress is aware that great and important changes have taken place in the magnitude, character, and medium by which the coastwise and interior commerce of the country is carried on, owing to the increased facilities of transportation by the use of steam power, without any corresponding changes in the law to meet the altered condition of the trade. Hence a rigid enforcement of the existing requirements of the law produces much delay and vexatious embarrassment to persons engaged in the prosecution of the trade, besides in some cases, particularly where carried on by the use of steam power, proving seriously detrimental to their interests, and thus presenting a just appeal for some further legislation on the subject.

It is confidently believed that some of the requirements of the law might be dispensed with, and others changed or modified, so as to relieve the trade from existing restrictions and embarrassments, without hazarding the security of the revenue.

Should Congress feel disposed to act upon this subject, the department will, if so required by that body, submit views and recommendations in detail calculated, in its opinion, to accomplish the object desired.

The operations of the coast survey, under the superintendence of Professor Bache, have been diligently and successfully prosecuted during the past season, with satisfactory results in the respective branches of this important national work. The report of the superintendent, containing a detailed account of the extension of the work during the season, and its present condition, will be submitted to Congress at an early period of the session.

Our lighthouse establishment has gradually enlarged until it has become one of great magnitude and importance. In July last it numbered two hundred and eighty-eight lighthouses and thirty-two floating lights. Of these, sixty-one are located upon the shores of the northern lakes and river St. Lawrence. Additional lights have since been erected under appropriations made by the act of 3d March last, and others are in process of erection, a special report of which will be submitted to Congress without unnecessary delay.

Due attention has been given to the various local works provided for in appropriations placed at the disposal of the department by acts of the last and previous sessions of Congress for the erections of custom-houses, marine hospitals, and for providing the facilities contemplated by Congress for the preservation of life and property from loss by shipwreck.

The custom-house structure at New Orleans has progressed throughout the past season without interruption, and as rapidly as was deemed prudent with due regard to the massive character and general nature of the work. The foundations have been laid, and the walls on the four sides of the building carried up to the plinth course of granite, which has been completed around the entire structure. The unexpended balance of the appropriation for this work will not, it is believed, prove sufficient to carry on the same beyond the close of the present month. It is therefore recommended that additional means be provided by Congress at an early day for the continuous prosecution of the work.

The structures for similar objects at Savannah, Georgia, and Eastport, Maine, are also in a state of forwardness. In the former case the walls of the basement, and of the principal story, are completed, and the walls of the second story will be ready for the cornice by the first of February next, and, in the opinion of the superintendent, the whole structure will be completed in August, 1851. The custom-house at Eastport has advanced to the flooring of the second story, which has been laid, and the building covered in temporarily for the winter. A custom-house building at Portland, in the state of Maine, has been purchased, as provided for in the general appropriation act of the last session. The purchase of the buildings for a similar purpose at Erie, Pennsylvania, as contemplated by the same act, has not been made for want of an act on the part of the legislature of that state giving its consent to the purchase, as required by the joint resolution of Congress of the 11th September, 1841.

Some unavoidable delay has occurred in completing the purchase of the site selected by my predecessor for the proposed custom-house structure at Charleston, South Carolina, occasioned by the requisite investigation and preparation of the title and transfer of the property. It is now completed, and, having been approved by the Attorney General, the proper conveyances have been duly executed, and the purchase-money paid. Proposals have also been invited for suitable designs, or plans, with specifications and estimates for the contemplated building.

The edifices erecting for marine hospitals at Cleveland, Ohio, Pittsburgh, Pennsylvania, and Louisville, Kentucky, are so far advanced as to warrant the belief that they will be ready for the reception of patients in the month of July or August next. But little progress has been made in the buildings designed for the same object at Chicago, Illinois, Paducah, Kentucky, and Natchez, Mississippi, preliminary examinations having delayed the commencement of the work until late in the season. Nothing has been done towards the erection of the hospital edifices for which appropriations were made at St. Louis, Missouri, and at Napoleon, Arkansas. In the one case, because of the failure to secure a title to the site formerly purchased for the object at St. Louis, and the impracticability of procuring another in time to commence the building consistently with the joint resolution of Congress dated 10th September, 1841. In the other, because of the insalubrity of the site heretofore selected at Napoleon, and the hazard to which the structure would be exposed from the overflow of the waters.

In connexion with the subject of marine hospitals, I would remark that experience has fully demonstrated that the resources of the fund arising under the acts of 16th July, 1798, and 3d May, 1802, for the relief of sick and disabled seamen, with the aids from time to time derived from the bounty of Congress, are inadequate to meet the demands of relief. As a necessary consequence, the department is compelled to adhere to restrictions imposed by my predecessors in office, and to follow their example in like expedients, often arbitrary in character and partial in operation, yet essential to the proper control of the expenditures. In view of these embarrassments, of the increased charges likely to arise from the establishment and organisation of public hospitals, and looking to the favourable regard heretofore entertained for the claims of men who, by their labours and perils in peace and war, contribute so largely to the wealth and power of the nation, means are asked in the estimates sufficient to provide for their destitution and sickness in all the ports of the Union.

The moneys placed at the disposal of the department for providing means for the preservation of life and property, by the act of 3d March last, with the exception of a portion expended for similar facilities at the west end of Fisher's Island, in Long Island Sound, contiguous to the place of the wreck of the steamer Atlantic, have been applied to that part of the coast of New Jersey lying between Little Egg Harbour and Cape May, and to that part of the coast of Long Island lying eastward of the entrance into New York bay; and have been expended in the construction of life-boats and cars, the erection of houses at appropriate distances from each other for their preservation, in the purchase of mortars, carronades, rockets, &c., and other approved apparatus for communicating with stranded vessels.

In giving effect to the humane and munificent intentions of Congress, as manifested in successive appropriations for these purposes, the department has had the active co-operation of the " Life-Saving Benevolent Association of New York," and of the Board of Underwriters of Philadelphia.

Fuller details, in regard to the works thus specially referred to, will be found in papers marked V.

Communications have been addressed to the department showing the danger to be apprehended to the hospital building at Cleveland, from the sliding or falling in of the bank facing the lake, and urging the immediate expenditure of a portion of the moneys appropriated for the structure in a way calculated to arrest the further encroachment of the water. Yielding to these appeals, a sum not exceeding one thousand dollars was authorized to be applied in the way proposed. A further appropriation for the object is needed, and is respectfully recommended.

By the act of 12th of August, 1848, six thousand dollars were appropriated for the erection of a beacon light on the South-west Ledge, in the harbour of New Haven, Connecticut, or for the removal of the ledge, as the department should deem best. In the belief that the interests of commerce dictated the removal of the obstruction so as to admit the passage of vessels drawing sixteen feet water, rather than the erection of the light, measures were taken to contract for the work; but, as the offers exceeded the appropriation by several thousand dollars, the undertaking has been postponed until adequate means are provided by Congress.

I transmit for the information of Congress an exhibit (marked S) showing the business and coinage of the mint at Philadelphia from 1st January to 1st November, 1849.

The statements of the accounts of the mint, as required by the 7th section of the act of 1792, and the assays of foreign coins required by the acts of 10th April, 1806, 25th and 28th June, 1834, and 2d March, 1843, will be transmitted in a future communication.

Reference is made to statement marked E, for the information required by the 22d section of the act of 28th January, 1847.

The mineral resources of our recently acquired possessions in California have opened an extensive field for the development of American enterprise. Some thousands of our countrymen, in the pursuit of profitable labour and advantageous commerce have found their way thither; and already vast regions, heretofore unpeopled and unexplored, are contributing to the metallic wealth of the world. Constituting as they now do a portion of our territory, it is due to our fellow-citizens who inhabit them that their industry and enterprise should be cherished by wholesome laws. First in importance, as respects its commercial and financial bearing, the establishment of a branch of the mint of the United States at San

Francisco is recommended. Next, the erection of lighthouses on head-lands, and beacon lights and buoys to conduct vessels into the principal ports and harbours. Third, the establishment of a marine hospital. Anticipating the favourable action of Congress on the subject of the establishment of lights, beacons, and buoys, instructions have been given to the officer directing the operations of the coast survey, to cause such examinations and reports to be made as may be necessary to determine upon appropriate locations for such structures.

Respectfully submitted,

W. M. MEREDITH,
Secretary of the Treasury.

REPORT OF THE SECRETARY OF WAR.

War Department, Washington, November 30, 1849.

Sir: I have the honour to present the following report of the operations of this department during the past year:

The returns and statements of the adjutant-general, herewith, exhibit the strength and distribution of the military force. Agreeably to these returns, the present strength of the army is less than the organization provided by law. The deficiency arises from the discharges, deaths, and desertions which have taken place, and the difficulty of immediately supplying the want by new enlistments. The desertions have been most numerous in California, where the temptations to embark in more lucrative pursuits and the facilities for the sudden acquisition of wealth are so greatly multiplied. Out of a force of twelve hundred regular troops in that territory since the 1st of January, the desertions within the first eight months have equalled two-fifths of that number. The policy adopted by the commanding officer of granting short furloughs to the troops in small numbers, for the purpose of enabling them to work for their individual benefit at the *placers*, had the effect to check desertions to a degree, but the emergencies of the service, and the limited number of troops for duty, prevented the measure from being carried out to the extent desired, and the evil of desertions consequently continues to exist.

The recruiting of the army is regulated by the casualties in the service, so that the enlistments can at no time exceed the total fixed by law. The delays in receiving these returns of casualties will always keep the actual force considerably below the legal standard: According to the practice which has long prevailed, the great majority of enlistments is made in the northern Atlantic cities and the adjacent interior towns, whence the recruits are sent to the general depot for instruction, and finally distributed to the southern and western posts, according to the wants of the service. It necessarily follows that considerable time intervenes between the enlistment of the recruit and his presence with his company. Independently of this loss of time and service, and the fatal influence which a change of climate not unusually produces on the health of the recruit, his transportation and subsistence constitute a heavy expenditure. To remedy these disadvantages, and to encourage enlistments, in the vicinity of troops serving at frontier and remote stations, especially in California, Oregon, and New Mexico, it is recommended that a bounty be allowed to each recruit enlisted at or near such stations, equal to the cost of transporting and subsisting a recruit from the general depot to the place of such enlistment. To guard against desertions and promote good conduct, it is proposed that the bounty should be divided into instalments, so that their several amounts would be increasing annually according to length of service, and the largest amount be paid to the soldier on his discharge. This bounty would also be a strong inducement to old soldiers to re-enlist in their respective companies, an object always deemed of importance to the service.

It has been found impracticable to carry into effect the provisions of the act of 14th of August, 1848, which authorizes an increase of the rank and file of certain regiments by transfers from others of the same arm; the present organization being too limited, and the difficulty of keeping the several companies up to their legal complement too great, to hazard a further reduction, with a due regard to the discipline and efficiency of the several corps. The protection of our frontier lines previous to the late war with Mexico, was then deemed a task equal to the capacity of the army. The additions recently made seem to impose the necessity of increasing the military force, in order that its strength may be adequate to the wants which the vast extension of our territorial limits require. One territory, New Mexico, is almost surrounded by numerous tribes of predatory Indians, and open at all points to their incursions. The perils which are thus presented retard the growth of frontier settlements, which, in their infancy, are attended with severe privations, demanding the exercise of the highest courage and energy of the pioneer. Exposure to the rapine of the savage should not be a superadded evil. The duty of the government is to afford protection. To enable it to do this effectually, it is submitted that the numerical strength of each company at the several military posts on our western frontier be increased to seventy-four privates, and that a part of the infantry be mounted as emergencies arise. This plan for increasing the defence of our frontiers, is respectfully presented as combining the greatest economy and security. Without a larger regular force, the executive will find the occasions frequent and necessary to make requisitions on the militia of the states, who are called into service for short periods, with injurious interruptions in their ordinary avocations, as well as great expense to them and the government. Experience has shown that for the preservation of peace and public tranquillity on our borders, the presence of a strong military force restrains the warlike inclinations of the Indians, whilst its absence has sometimes involved the government in protracted and costly wars.

Great embarrassment has heretofore arisen from the supposed actual rank which brevet commissions confer. Their recent multiplication will increase the difficulties and inconveniences to which the military service has been exposed. Apart from the conflicting claims of officers holding brevet commissions, it may be affirmed that instances frequently occur when pay is paramount to rank, and when the brevet rank itself cannot, in legal contemplation, take effect. In the case of staff officers who have no command, and who can exercise none except by special assignment, these brevet commissions are only honorary distinctions; and, examined closely, this is the basis on which rest all brevets. The presumption is reasonable and just that every officer performs his required duty, and he who does more is entitled to honourable reward. It is then respectfully submitted whether the object, in authorizing this class of commissions, is not accomplished by retaining them as honorary distinctions, and restricting the officers holding them to their lineal rank and pay, according to the commissions by which they are mustered in their respective regiments and corps. If any exceptions be made to the rule here proposed, it is believed that, in view of the more efficient discipline and service of the troops, brevet rank and pay should exist only when volunteers and militia are united with the regular army; or, when the officers having brevet commissions are detailed for duty by special assignment with difficult or expensive commands in remote departments or divisions. According to law, brevet rank takes effect in detachments composed of different corps, but from the liberal construction which has heretofore been given to the articles of war, it would seem that every garrison at each of our numerous and widely-extended posts is considered a detachment from the main army, without any definite conception of the locality where its main body is concentrated.

Another inconvenience resulting to the service is the anomalous position of officers holding staff commissions which confer rank. These officers are not considered by established usage as eligible to the command of troops unless specially assigned, whilst at the same time they claim exemption from the orders of their juniors in the line who succeed to such commands. This state of things is calculated to injure the service by a suspension, for the time being, of the functions of the staff officers in cases where a junior line officer exercises the command; to obviate which it is suggested that a law be enacted requiring officers of the general staff serving with troops to execute according to their respective duties all orders emanating from the senior officer of the line which may relate to the discipline, police, and good order of his command, and for which he alone is responsible.

The necessity of adopting some rule for retiring disabled officers from the army, is more apparent at this time than at any former period of its history. The injurious effects of a foreign war, prosecuted in a climate unfavourable to health, and the casualties inseparable from a contest remarkable for the disparity of the opposing forces, have added to the list of those disabled from age, or other causes, and greatly increased the number of ineffective officers. To retain them would but impede that activity and efficiency which the protection of our recently extended frontiers necessarily demands from the army; to discharge them without suitable provision, crippled and worn out in the public service, would be unjust and ungrateful. In order to preserve the efficiency of the army, and without doing violence to a sense of justice towards this deserving class of officers, it is respectfully suggested that the President be authorized to place on the retired list such as in his judgment may be disqualified from age, wounds, or other disability, with an allowance equal to the pay proper of their respective grades. An effective check on the exercise of this power would be found in a legal inhibition, declaring that no officer shall be retired until the senate shall have confirmed the nomination of his successor. The number of officers to be comprehended in the list of those who may, with advantage to the public service, be retired, will probably not exceed twenty-five; the sum of whose pay will be less than fifteen thousand dollars annually.

I also respectfully recommend to favourable consideration the plan of providing an asylum for the comfort and repose of veteran soldiers, on whom time and the perils of an arduous service have produced their natural or accidental effects, and I take leave to express my concurrence in the views of the commanding general of the army on this subject. Should the suggestions of that officer be not approved, it is then submitted that some plan of benevolence and gratitude be commenced under the sanction of Congress, which shall require all disbursing officers of the army to receive and account for such sums as may be voluntarily contributed for this object. It is not doubted that at some future day a fund will be thus realized, which, judiciously employed, will supply this essential want, and accomplish a purpose which will be universally approved.

The effective power of the army is deemed to be inseparably connected with the military academy at West Point. As one of the means of national defence, it is not only the best, but one of the cheapest; unless the rule be inverted which admits that the most efficient corps are commanded by the most skilful officers. Having its organization on popular basis, and diffusing its benefits equally to all sections of the Union, this institution may be safely commended to the care and patronage of the government, not less for the brilliant achievements of its graduates, than their happy example to others who are to follow them.

The outrages committed by the Indians in New Mexico have been of a serious character, resulting in the massacre of several of the inhabitants, and depredations upon the property of the settlers to a considerable extent. The troops in that territory have been constantly occupied during the past year in giving protection to the settlements, and in pushing their scouts against the hostile and marauding bands. These duties have been performed with alacrity and zeal, but not without privation and suffering on the part of troops operating in a broken and difficult country, during the heats of summer and amidst the almost impassable snows of winter. In the several affairs which took place, the Indians were generally encountered in superior numbers, and always routed with considerable less in killed and wounded. The attacks of these marauding bands becoming more frequent as the spring opened, and often resulting in the murder of our citizens, the commanding officer, in order to afford greater protection than could be given by the limited regular force under his command, called into service an auxiliary volunteer force. Four companies of this description of troops were engaged for six months, and distributed so as to protect the lives and property of the inhabitants most exposed to attack.

In September, a movement was made against the Navajoe Indians in their stronghold at the Canon of Cheille which resulted in a treaty with that nation, on terms similar to those granted to other tribes upon our frontiers, and the surrender of several captives.

Attempts were made under the orders issued from this department, in May last, to open communications with the Indians remaining in Florida, with a view to ascertain their feelings in respect to emigration. Whilst the officer charged with the instructions was endeavouring to obtain interviews with the several chiefs in the vicinity of Charlotte Harbor, acts of violence and murder were committed by a small band of the tribe upon the settlements on Indian river and Pease Creek, which had the effect to frustrate, for a time, any effort at negotiation. On receiving intelligence of these outrages, from some of the inhabitants who had fled from the scenes of violence, arrangements were immediately made by the commanding officers at St. Augustine, Tampa Bay, and Key West, to afford that protection within their means which the circumstances demanded. Prompt measures were also taken by this department to send re-enforcements to the troops in Florida, with a view to control the Indians, in case it should appear, as this department did not then suppose, that these outrages had been dictated by a general feeling of hostility on the part of the several tribes. The number of troops thus collected in Florida within the month of September, was upwards of seventeen hundred, officers and men, a force deemed sufficient to give confidence to the inhabitants, and to promote the emigration of the Indians.

Upon renewing the efforts to negotiate with the Indians, the principal chiefs, with their sub-chiefs and warriors, were met in council. They at once agreed to deliver up the offenders, (five in number,) whom they represented as having committed the murders without the sanction or knowledge of any chief, and in opposition to the wishes of the Indians. Three of these have since been surrendered. Of the remaining two, one, in attempting to escape, was killed by the Indians, the other effected his escape; but his early capture and surrender have been promised by the chiefs. On the subject of emigration, the Indians requested time for deliberation, and a meeting in council has been arranged for a subsequent day. The policy which has been pursued, and which will probably be continued for the removal of these Indians to their brethren west of the Mississippi, will be seen in the correspondence which accompanies this report.

During the past spring and part of the summer, the troops in Texas had become greatly reduced in effective strength by the ravages of the cholera, which prevailed there to such an extent as to retard, in some measure, contemplated military movements, having for their object the establishment of a line of posts for the protection of the frontier settlement against the attacks of hostile bands. The frequency of these attacks, and the difficulty of covering so extended a frontier with the very limited disposable regular force, distributed in small commands at points remote from each other, made it necessary for the commanding general in Texas to avail himself of the authority, previously given, to call upon the executive of that State for three companies of mounted militia. Orders have been given for the discharge of those additional companies, and also those in New Mexico, as soon as the exigencies under which they were called into service shall have ceased to exist, and it is recommended that appropriations be made by Congress to pay them for the time they have been employed. No recent disturbances in Texas have been reported, and from the proffers of peace which have been lately made by the Camanche nation, through their newly elected head chief, with manifestations of the most friendly dispositions towards the United States, and a determination by them to abstain from any further depredations upon our citizens, it is believed that the regular troops in that country will be sufficient for any emergency likely to arise. The operations in New Mexico and Texas, have resulted in the recovery of many of the captives previously made by the Indians, several of whom have been restored to their homes in Mexico, agreeably to the provisions of the late treaty with that republic.

The department was prevented by the demand for troops in Mexico, during the recent war, from effecting much in respect to the establishment of military posts on the route to Oregon, required by the act of the 19th May, 1846, beyond the selection of the first station on the Platte river, now Grand Island, known as Fort Kearny. Within the last spring, arrangements were made to place the regiment of mounted riflemen, originally designed for this service, upon the route. Early in May, the regiment moved from Fort Leavenworth, and proceeded via Fort Kearny to Fort Laramie, and, after establishing at that point the second military station, continued its march in the direction of Oregon. By the last intelligence received, the regiment had passed beyond Fort Hall, on the upper waters of the Columbia river, and doubtless, ere this, it has reached its ultimate destination, after having established the intermediate station between Fort Laramie and the Pacific, and giving escort to a large number of emigrants.

To hasten and ensure the arrival of the officers connected with the customs in California, as well as of a navy agent for the port of San Francisco, and certain Indian agents transferred to, and sub-agents appointed for, the territories of New Mexico and California, an order, under your direction, was given to the proper department to furnish to them transportation at public expense. About the same time, information reached the department that a large number of emigrants had assembled at or near Fort Leavenworth, and who, in their long journey to their new and distant homes on the Pacific, would probably encounter the increased wants which their numbers were well calculated to produce. Accordingly, the officers of the subsistence department with a like direction were ordered to relieve all cases of distress in the wilderness, without disclosing the benevolent purpose of the order.

In connexion with the subject of providing the necessary means for the defence of our distant territories, the erection of fortifications for the protection of such of our harbors on the Pacific as may be indicated by the board of engineer officers at present engaged in making examinations and surveys for these objects, is respectfully recommended.

At an early period after the appropriation was available for surveys required to be made west of the Mississippi, and extending to the Pacific ocean, necessary instructions were given, and several routes suggested and directed to be examined. The reports of the several corps engaged in this service will be furnished as soon as received. In the mean time, the instructions issued from this department are respectfully submitted.

The estimates submitted for the improvements of harbors and rivers refer to works which have heretofore received the sanction of Congress. In respect to other and new works, it is presumed that, in accordance with a safe usage, no appropriations will be made without previous surveys and estimates by competent officers.

Should Congress make appropriations in conformity to the estimates, it is believed that the amount could only be judiciously applied under the supervision of the corps charged with the superintendence of public works of this class. An excess of appropriation materially varying the estimated amount, would impose the necessity of increasing the corps of Topographical Engineers, which is not recommended.

In the interval of time between the proclamation of peace with the republic of Mexico and the period when our revenue laws were extended over Upper California, a large amount was collected by the officers of the army, as duties on importations into the several ports of that territory. The same system has been continued by these officers up to the arrival of the authorized agents of the treasury; who, doubtless, before this time, have superseded the military officers employed in this extraordinary service. The order given by the commander of the Pacific division required the collections to be continued till the military officers were superseded by the proper officers of the treasury, and the amounts thus realized should be subject to the final decision of Congress. It is respectfully recommended that their acts be affirmed. The officers, however, should be required to account fully, through the appropriate department, for all sums collected by them, and such disbursements allowed as may be deemed necessary and proper for the maintenance and support of the anomalous government of that territory.

The peculiar condition of the territories of California and New Mexico, in respect to their internal governments, and the absence of any clearly defined authority by Congress for this object, has imposed delicate and difficult duties on the army. One of its assigned duties is to aid civil functionaries, when required, in the preservation of public tranquillity. But it is believed that the civil authority, so far as it had its origin in political power, in a great measure disappeared by the transfer of the sovereignty and jurisdiction from Mexico to the United States. The military regulations established for their government during the war, were superseded by the return of peace. A large concourse of foreign emigrants, not familiar with our institutions and habits, has been assembled in one of the territories and engaged in a pursuit eminently calculated to produce collisions and bloodshed. Amidst all these difficulties, the army, aided by the confirmed habit of self-government in which the American citizen is reared, has protected these territories from general or unusual disorders. I respectfully submit a copy of the correspondence on this subject sent from and received at this department.

The reports herewith of the chiefs of the several bureaus connected with this department, will exhibit in detail their respective operations, and to which I respectfully invite attention. The duties of these branches of the military service have been performed with accustomed fidelity, zeal, and ability.

Respectfully submitted,

GEO. W. CRAWFORD,

To the President. Secretary of War.

REPORT OF THE SECRETARY OF THE NAVY.

Navy Department, Dec. 1, 1849.

Sir: I have the honour to present to you the annual report of the condition and operations of this department of the public service.

The home squadron, under the command of Commodore Parker, consists of the flag-ship frigate Raritan, Capt. Page, the sloop-of-war Albany, Commander Randolph, the sloop-of-war Germantown, Commander Lowndes, the steamer Vixen, Lieutenant Commanding Ward, the steamer Water-Witch, Lieutenant Commanding Totten, and the schooner Flirt, Lieutenant Commanding Farrand. The steamer Alleghany, commanded by Lieutenant Hunter, was temporarily attached to this squadron, but has been recently withdrawn and placed in ordinary at the Washington navy yard. The sloop-of-war Saratoga, Commander Nicholson, has also been withdrawn, and placed in ordinary at Norfolk.

The vessels of the home squadron have been actively employed among the West India islands, in the Gulf of Mexico, and along the Atlantic coast.

The squadron in the Pacific ocean, under the command of Commodore Jones, consists of the flag-ship Ohio, Commander Stribling, the frigate Savannah, Captain Voorhees, the sloop-of-war St. Mary's, Commander Johnsten, the sloop-of-war Warren, Commander Long, the sloop-of-war Preble, Commander Glynn, the sloop-of-war Falmouth, Commander Pettigru, the sloop-of-war Vandalia, Commander Gardner, the sloop-of-war Vincennes, Commander Hudson, the store-ship Fredonia, Lieutenant Commanding Neville, the store-ship Southampton, Lieutenant Commanding Handy, and the steamer Massachusetts. The razee Independence, bearing the broad pennant of Commodore Shubrick, returned from the Pacific ocean on the 26th of July last, after distinguished and important service in the war with Mexico. The vessel was taken out of commission. The sloop-of-war Dale, Commander Rudd, also returned from the Pacific; she reached New York on the 23d of August, and was placed in ordinary. Orders have been given for the return of the Ohio, the Preble, and the store-ship Southampton, in consequence of the expiration of the periods of enlistment of their crews. On the 12th of January, 1849, Commodore Jones was ordered to exchange the Ohio for the Savannah as his flag-ship; the Ohio was ordered to proceed, under the command of Capt. Voorhees, to China, to relieve Commodore Geisinger in the command of the East India squadron, and Commodore Geisinger was ordered to return to the United States in the Ohio, by the way of Bengal. The terms of service of a large number of her crew having expired, it was deemed expedient to revoke that order, and instructions were accordingly sent to Commodore Jones, on the 23d of June, to direct the immediate return of the Ohio by the way of Cape Horn; she sailed from the coast of California on the 15th of September, on her passage home. Captain Voorhees has proceeded to China in the sloop-of-war St. Mary's, for the purpose of relieving Commodore Geisinger, who will return to the United States in that vessel; but, in the event of his having left the station, under a permission granted by the department on the 16th February, the St. Mary's will be retained and constitute a part of the squadron under Commodore Voorhees. The Falmouth sailed from the United States on the 16th of May, the Vandalia on the 5th of September, and the Vincennes on the 13th of November, with orders to join the command of Commodore Jones in the Pacific. The store-ship Supply, Lieutenant Commanding Kennedy, is under orders, and will shortly sail with supplies and stores for the squadron in the Pacific. Commodore Jones reports that the crews of the vessels under his command have been greatly reduced by desertions, and by the expirations of terms of service of the men; he states also that there exists an unwillingness to re-enlist for the navy. The temptations held out by the prospect of obtaining gold, and the great demand for seamen, render it impossible to enlist men on the coast of California for the navy pay of from $10 to $12 per month, while the merchant service is paying from $85 to $150 in the same ports. The evils resulting to the naval service from these causes are severely felt. Great efforts have been made to remedy them, and every exertion that authority and discipline could enforce, has been made with but partial success.

The squadron in the Mediterranean sea, under the command of Commodore Morgan, consists of the flag-ship razee Independence, Commander Blake; the frigate Cumberland, Captain Latimer; the frigate Constitution, Captain Conover; the steamer Mississippi, Captain Long; the sloop-of-war Jamestown, Commander Mercer, and the store-ship Erie, Lieutenant Commanding Porter. The frigate St. Lawrence, Captain Paulding, has also joined this squadron.

The force now employed in the Mediterranean is believed to be larger and more efficient than at any previous period in our history, with the exception, perhaps, of the years 1804 and 1805, during the Tripolitan war.

The steamers Princeton, Commander Engle, and Alleghany, Lieutenant Commanding Hunter, were ordered home from the Mediterranean in consequence of the reports of the necessity for extensive repairs. The Princeton has, since her return, undergone a strict and careful survey by a board of competent and skilful officers; their report condemned her as unworthy of repairs. She was, therefore, broken up, and such portions of her as were unserviceable for naval purposes were ordered to be sold. The schooner Taney also returned from the Mediterranean. This vessel belongs to the treasury department, and, on her arrival, was turned over to that department; there being, however, no vessel of the navy at my command calculated for the service contemplated by the 2d section of the act making appropriations for the naval service, approved March 3d, 1849, viz. for testing new routes and perfecting the discoveries made by Lieutenant Maury, in the course of his investigations of the winds and currents of the ocean, the Taney was again received and assigned to that service. Lieutenant Walsh, an officer well qualified for the duty, was intrusted with the command, detailed instructions were prepared for him, and he proceeded in their execution on the 26th of October.

The death of Commodore Bolton, which occurred at Genoa on the 22d of February, rendered it necessary to order a senior captain to the command of the Mediterranean squadron. Commodore Morgan was selected; he sailed from the United States in the steamer Mississippi on the 7th of June. Important considerations made it necessary, in the judgment of the department, to increase the force in the Mediterranean. By active exertions, two vessels, in addition to the Mississippi, (the razee Independence and the frigate Cumberland,) were despatched; the former sailed on the 26th of July, and the latter on the 10th of August. The store-ship Erie, Lieutenant Commanding M'Blair, returned from the Mediterranean on the 11th of July, and on the 5th of September she was again despatched, under the command of Lieutenant Porter, with supplies for the squadron.

By the death of Commodore Bolton, the late Captain Gwinn was left the senior officer in this squadron; his reports show that the vessels of his command were actively employed under circumstances requiring the exercise of prudence and discretion to prevent embarrassments with belligerent powers. I am happy to say that our commerce has been fully protected, and friendly intercourse has not been interrupted. Information has reached the department of the death of Captain Gwinn, which occurred at Palermo on the 4th of September, 1849. The reports from Commodore Morgan, since he took command of the squadron, are highly satisfactory. The duty assigned him has been promptly performed, and the condition of his command reflects credit upon the service.

The squadron on the coast of Brazil, under the command of Commodore Storer, consists of the flag-ship frigate Brandywine, Captain Boarman, and the sloop-of-war St. Louis, Commander Cocke. The brig Perry, under the command of Lieutenant Tilton, returned from this station on the 10th of July, and was put under repairs for further service. The store-ship Supply, commanded by Lieutenant Sinclair, returned from Brazil on the 4th of September. The store-ship Lexington, Lieutenant Commanding Mitchell, will sail in a few days with supplies for the squadron. It was the purpose of the department to increase the force on this station, and with this view the sloop-of-war John Adams, under the command of Commander Powell, sailed from the United States in June, with orders to report to Commodore Storer, as a part of his command; but it became necessary to relieve the sloop-of-war Decatur, on the coast of Africa, and on the 29th of July, orders were issued to transfer the John Adams from the Brazil to the African station. The Decatur was ordered home on a report of the surgeon of the fleet relative to the health of the crew, and because the terms of service of a large number of the men had expired. The vessels under the command of Commodore Storer have been usefully employed in the suppression of the slave trade, in protecting our commerce, and rendering efficient service to vessels of the United States.

The squadron on the coast of Africa, under the command of Commodore Gregory, consists of the flag-ship sloop-of-war Portsmouth, Commander Peck; the sloop-of-war Yorktown, Commander Marston; the sloop-of-war John Adams, Commander Powell; the brig Porpoise, Commander Gordon; the brig Bainbridge, Commander Slaughter; and brig Perry, Lieutenant Commanding Foot. The sloop-of-war Decatur, Commander Byrne, returned from the coast of Africa on the 15th of November. The brig Perry sailed from the United States on the 27th of November. The store-ship Relief, commanded by Lieutenant Totten, sailed from New York on the 26th of October, with supplies for the squadrons on the coast of Africa and in the Mediterranean. The brig Porpoise will return to the United States on the arrival out of the Perry.

In the month of August last the department was informed by Commodore Cooper that ill-health prevented his longer remaining on the coast of Africa in command of the squadron, and asked to be relieved. Orders were accordingly issued detaching him, and the command was assigned to Captain Gregory. Before the departure of the latter officer, Commodore Cooper arrived at New York in the Portsmouth, (the flag-ship of the squadron,) in low health. The command was immediately transferred to Captain Gregory, and he was ordered to proceed forthwith to the coast of Africa. Events, however, transpiring at the seat of government early in the month of September, rendered it proper to change for a time the destination of the Portsmouth, and orders were given on the 17th of September for Captain Gregory to proceed to the Mediterranean with despatches for Commodore Morgan; and, after performing that service, to repair to the station assigned him on the coast of Africa. The Portsmouth sailed from New York on the 20th of September.

The reports received from Captain Paulding of the frigate St. Lawrence, while in the North Sea, are very satisfactory. His continuance there during the winter being considered unnecessary, orders were sent to him on the 13th of September to proceed with the frigate to winter in the Mediterranean, and to report to Commodore Morgan. Should it be deemed advisable to keep up a force in the North Sea and the Baltic, vessels from the Mediterranean will be despatched in the spring on that service.

The squadron in the China Seas, under the command of Commodore Geisinger, consists of the flag-ship sloop-of-war Plymouth, Commander Gedney, and the brig Dolphin, Lieutenant Commanding Ogden. The sloop-of-war Preble was temporarily attached to this squadron; she has returned to the Pacific, and orders have been sent to Commodore Jones for her return to the United States. It is gratifying to state that the small force employed in the East Indies has been eminently useful to the commercial interests of our country in extending information, cultivating friendly relations, and affording protection to American seamen in that quarter. In a recent despatch, received from Commodore Geisinger, the important fact is stated that coal of an excellent quality is found at the island of Formosa, in a convenient position, and in abundance for the wants of steam navigation between California and China.

I am happy to report that no interruption has occurred to the fair and legal commercial pursuits of our citizens abroad. Wherever our national vessels have been shown, they have been received with marked respect, and our officers have been treated with kindness and courtesy; they have on all occasions pursued a course of steady neutrality, in accordance with the policy of our government and in compliance with the instructions of this department.

Under the 3d section of the act of the 3d of March, 1849, the secretary of war transferred to the navy department the following steamers, viz: the Massachusetts, Edith, Telegraph, Alabama, Fashion, Monmouth, New Orleans, and Major Tompkins. At the time of the transfer the Massachusetts and Edith were in the Pacific ocean, on special service connected with the war department; the others were at New Orleans. All these steamers were purchased during the war with Mexico for the transportation of troops and supplies for the army. With the exception of the Massachusetts and Edith, they were wholly unfit for general naval purposes; their retention was expensive, and as they were rapidly deteriorating in value, orders were given for their sale. The Alabama, New Orleans, and Major Tompkins have been sold and the proceeds paid into the treasury. The Fashion has been returned to the war department for the transportation of troops and supplies to Florida. The Telegraph and Monmouth remain to be sold. The Edith was wrecked and totally lost on the 24th of August last on the coast of California.

Under a provision of the act making appropriations for the naval service, approved March 3d, 1849, viz.: "that a competent officer of the navy, not below the grade of lieutenant, be charged with the duty of preparing the nautical almanac for publication," Lieutenant Davis has been selected to superintend the work. The preliminary arrangements have been commenced, and I have no doubt, from the eminent qualifications of this officer, the work will progress with all the rapidity practicable, where so great accuracy and precision are required. The report as to the manner in which Lieutenant Davis proposes to execute the important duty intrusted to him, and the progress made, will be found herewith transmitted.

The practical experiments authorized by the same act, for testing the capacity and usefulness of the electro-magnetic power as a mechanical agent for the purposes of navigation and locomotion, have, in accordance with the act, been intrusted to Professor Charles G. Page. The experiments are in progress; when they are completed, the result will be reported to Congress.

The act of August 3d, 1848, directed the secretary of the navy to cause the observations to be made recommended by the American Philosophical Society and the Academy of Arts and Sciences. The necessary instruments have been procured and are on their way to Santiago in Chili, under the charge of two passed midshipmen. Lieutenant Gillisa, the officer selected to superintend the observations, left the United States in August last, to proceed by the way of Chagres and Panama, to the point selected. No report has been received from him. He is instructed to advise the department from time to time of the progress made in the duty assigned him.

Under the act of congress of the 3d of March, 1847, contracts were made with E. K. Collins and his associates, for the transportation of the mail between New York and Liverpool; with A. G. Sloo for the transportation of the mail from New York and New Orleans, touching at Charleston, (if practicable,) Savannah and Havana, and from Havana to Chagres; and with Arnold Harris for the transportation of the mail from Panama to Astoria, in Oregon, to connect with the mail from Havana to Chagres across the Isthmus.

The three sea-steamers under the contract for the Panama and Oregon line were accepted before the close of the year 1848. It is believed they are actively employed in the service required by the law establishing the line. No provision is made, either by the law or under the contract, for the command of the steamers on this line by officers of the navy, nor for passed midshipmen to serve as watch officers. There have been no reports made to this department of the services rendered by the steamers on this line.

The contractors for the Liverpool line engaged with the department to build five steamships, of not less than two thousand tons measurement, for the transportation of the mail between New York and Liverpool; the first of the steamships to be ready to perform the service in eighteen months from the date of the agreement, (1st November, 1847,) and three others as soon thereafter as each may be required to take its place in the line; that the fifth should be commenced and built as early as may be practicable thereafter. By the 7th section of the act approved March 3d, 1849, the secretary of the navy was authorized so to modify the contract as to postpone the commencement of the mail service stipulated to be performed until the 1st day of June, 1850, which has accordingly been done. The officer superintending the construction of the vessels expresses the opinion that the Atlantic will be the first in readiness; that it is possible she may sail some time in the following month of January; the Pacific will be ready by the first of March; that two others will probably not be completed earlier than the first of August, 1850; and that a contract has been entered into by Mr. Collins for the frame of the fifth vessel. No information has yet been received of the probable period of her final completion. The department is informed that the contractors are making exertions to complete their vessels, to enter upon the service for which they are designed, by the time stipulated.

The contractor for the New Orleans and Chagres line bound himself to establish a line of steamships, to consist of at least five vessels, for the transportation of the United States mail from New York to New Orleans twice a month and back, touching at Charleston, (if practicable,) Savannah and Havana, and from Havana to Chagres and back, twice a month; that two of the steamships should be completed and ready for service on the first day of October, 1848, and should be of the burden of not less than fifteen hundred tons; that, should the secretary of the navy determine to employ a steamer of not less than six hundred tons burden for the service between Havana and Chagres, in lieu of one of the five steamers of not less than fifteen hundred tons burden, then the contractor agreed to construct a steamship complete in all respects for performing the service, and answering all the conditions required by the law. The contractor further bound himself to complete and have in readiness for service the two remaining steamships by the first day of October, 1849; that the line of steamships should be kept up by alterations, repairs, or additions, (of approved character,) fully equal to the exigencies of the service, and the faithful accomplishment of the purposes intended by the law; that the vessels should be in full and entire operation on the first of October, 1849; that each and all of the said steamships should be commanded by an officer of the navy of the United States, not below the grade of lieutenant, to be selected by the contractor with the approval and consent of the secretary of the navy; that the officers should be accommodated on board thereof, in a manner becoming their rank and station, without charge to the government of the United States; and further agreed to receive on board of each of said steamships, and accommodate in a manner suitable to their rank without charge to the government, four passed midshipmen of the United States navy, to serve as watch officers. In December last, before any of the vessels under this contract were completed, the contractors, desirous to meet the wishes of the department, proposed to place on the route, temporarily, the ocean steamer Falcon, and she was accepted until the steamships to be constructed under the contract should be ready to take their places on the line; the department reserving the right to terminate the arrangement whenever it should think proper to do so. In view of the facts that no vessel of this line has been completed, that the demands of our citizens require every facility for the transmission of the mails and for the transportation of passengers on this route which can be afforded, I have not thought proper to discontinue the service, and the Falcon has been, and continues to be, actively and usefully engaged between New Orleans and Chagres. When the steamships contracted for shall be accepted for service, or when, from any other cause, the department deems it proper to dispense with the services of the Falcon, notice will be given to the proprietors in accordance with the agreement under which she is now employed. But one steamship built under this contract has been reported as ready for the service, either by the contractor or his assignees, and that has not been accepted. Commodore Perry, the superintending agent, reported on the 17th of September that the Ohio was not then coppered, and consequently cannot be considered as finally completed according to contract. The Ohio has, since that date, been placed, by her owners, on the line between New York and New Orleans, and sailed on the 20th of September on her first trip without being accepted by the department. The contractor, some days before the sailing of the Ohio, informed me that she would commence the mail service on the 20th of September, and asked that the watch officers provided by law should be sent on board. The vessel not having been completed according to the contract, I did not accept her in fulfilment thereof, and declined to order the officers to the service as suggested. To prevent, however, any embarrassment or delay in the movements of the vessel, the officers were ordered to report to Commodore Perry, to be assigned to duty in the event of the completion of the Ohio according to the agreement, and with permission, if she were not so completed, to join the ship on such terms as might be agreed upon between themselves and the proprietors. The vessel not having been completed, Commodore Perry declined to order the passed midshipmen to duty on board of her, and the terms which were proposed by the proprietors not being such as could be accepted by those officers, they did not join the ship. The vessel has gone on her third trip and has not yet been completed, and I have no positive assurances that she will be finished on her return a third time to New York. The Georgia is progressing rapidly, and may be ready in January next. The construction of the other vessels for this line has not been commenced.

By a contract of assignment, made on the 3d day of September, 1847, A. G. Sloo assigned his contract made with the United States to George Law, Marshall O. Roberts, and Bowes R. M'Ilvaine, upon certain trusts declared in a deed dated the 17th of August, 1847, and the assignees and trustees have proceeded in the contracts with the United States. Difficulties have arisen between these parties which have led to a law-suit now pending in the courts of New York. The department regards this litigation as well calculated to embarrass and postpone the final completion of the other vessels, if not to endanger the ultimate fulfilment of the contract with the government.

The law under which these vessels are constructed does not clearly and distinctly define the powers and rights of the government over them. While the proprietors have been willing to receive on board the passed midshipmen, they have nevertheless claimed the right to prescribe their duties, and to assign them their positions; and while the passed midshipmen are received as watch officers, the executive duties of the ship and her navigation may be confided to others selected by the proprietors. I, therefore, urgently invite the attention of Congress to the law under which the contract was made, to the service in which the vessels are to be engaged, and to the condition of the contract itself, that, should it be deemed advisable to extend the terms, then it may regulate the whole subject by some distinct and unequivocal legislation.

After a careful consideration of this subject I cannot withhold the expression of an opinion adverse to embarking any further in the proposed union of public and private means in this system of ocean steamers, as calculated to promote the interest of the navy. Whatever may be the view which Congress may entertain as to the policy of transporting the United States mail, and affording facilities for the transportation of passengers and freight in the manner proposed by such a system, I entertain a decided opinion that if it should be regarded as the mode and manner which Congress has determined on for increasing the naval force of the United States, it will be found in the end entirely subversive of the object which it intends to promote. To the extent to which the present contracts have committed the faith of the government, and to the extent of the obligations under the contracts, they are of course strictly to be regarded and scrupulously to be performed. Yet, as a naval establishment, I deprecate any further extension of the system, as fraught with incalculable mischief to the navy, and involving immense expenditures of public money. All must appreciate the great importance of rapid, regular, and safe transmission of our mails to all quarters of the world, and all are sensible of the great commercial advantages that must result therefrom. The contracts already made, and the sums already appropriated, are fully adequate to a thorough test of the experiment. I believe, however, it is a subject that should in the future be left to the competition of private enterprise. I feel assured that in the struggle American enterprise and American industry will eventually be successful; for a naval establishment, that which we are most in need of, is an independent naval steam force, of such extent and of such magnitude as the wisdom and liberality of Congress may think sufficient, and the necessities of the country may require.

Those governments from whose examples the present system was adopted, have immense independent steam navies, in which a proper military education and discipline are secured to the officers and men, and upon which they mainly rely for their naval strength and power. Until we have provided a steam power for our navy adequate for our protection, I cannot but consider it as premature and unwise to regard the proposed system as answering the necessities and wants of the government for a naval establishment.

Congress has heretofore, in its liberality to the navy, and in view of the necessity of an independent force, expended vast sums of money in establishing navy yards, and in the construction of docks and machinery of all kinds for the accommodation and equipment of vessels for its service. Thus there is afforded every facility required for the maintenance of the navy; and the large quantities of stores and materials which, under the former policy of the government have been procured and are now at its command, afford the means of building and equipping vessels better adapted to the naval service, and on terms more economical than can be furnished from any other quarter. While the policy may have been wise to collect and prepare these materials in time of peace, so as to be at our command in periods of difficulty and emergency, the great change that has occurred in the condition of our country no longer renders it necessary to the same extent. Most of the materials required in the construction and outfit of a fleet, to any extent whatsoever, are to be found every where throughout the country, and no emergency can arise when a deficiency need be apprehended. To retain those on hand is unnecessary; they are constantly deteriorating, and the constant improvements in the construction and equipment of vessels render it unwise to continue the present system of accumulation. The interest of the government would be promoted by discontinuing contracts for most of the materials we now possess, and by converting those on hand, as they may from time to time be required, to the repairs and outfits of the vessels now in the service, and to the construction of such others as our necessities require. It would therefore seem proper and economical to avail ourselves of the advantages now at our command, and apply the materials now in store to such an extension of our naval force as is desired.

The sums appropriated by Congress, and included in the navy appropriations, for the transportation of the United States mail between New York and Liverpool, between New York and New Orleans, and Havana and Chagres, and between Panama and Astoria, are as follows, viz.:

By act approved August 3, 1848,	$874,600
By act approved March 3, 1849	874,600
Total sum appropriated,	$1,749,200
Of which there has been drawn from the treasury the sum of	681,500
Leaving unexpended the sum of	$1,067,700

The amount drawn from the treasury, viz. $681,500, was to make the advances to the contractors authorized by the act approved August 3, 1848. No advance, however, has been made to either of the contractors for mail steamers by this department since the month of May last. Prior to the 4th of March, 1849, the amount of one year's service of the New York, New Orleans, and Chagres line had been advanced to the proprietors, since which no money has been drawn from the treasury on account of that line of steamers, the department not feeling itself at liberty, under the law and the circumstances, to make advances beyond the amount of one year's service. For the Liverpool line advances have been made amounting to $142,500, in equal sums, on the steamers Atlantic and Pacific, which advances are secured by liens on the vessels.

A contract was made, under the authority granted by the act of Congress of April 14, 1842, with Robert L. Stevens, for the construction of a war steamer, shot and shell proof, to be built principally of iron, upon the plan of the said Stevens; and the sum of $250,000 was appropriated towards carrying the law into effect. The contract bore date the 10th of February, 1843; the time for its completion expired two years after the date of the contract. Nothing appears to have been done under this contract; no plan was furnished; the construction of the iron war steamer was not commenced. The contract was renewed on the 14th of November, 1844, and the time extended for completing the vessels two years from that date. Some preparation was made under the second contract, and a portion of the materials was procured, but no plan was submitted by the contractor, and the secretary of the navy withheld all payments after December, 1845. Thus the matter rested until the 9th of September, 1848, when a third contract was made with Mr. Stevens, and four years from that date were given for the completion of the iron war steamer. No precise plan has yet been submitted by the contractor to the department, and no progress has been made in the construction of the vessel beyond the purchase and delivery of certain quantities of iron. Under these circumstances I declined to pay bills for iron presented in July last, and further payments under this contract will not be made. The matter, however, is submitted to Congress for its decision. Of the sum appropriated for this object, there is now in the treasury an unexpended balance of $183,521 22, which it is believed should have been carried to the surplus fund. A report in this case, prepared by the chief of the Bureau of Construction, &c., is herewith submitted.

The 13th section of the act of Congress of August 3, 1848, authorizes the secretary of the navy to cause persons in the naval service or marine corps, who shall become insane while in the service, to be placed in such lunatic hospitals as, in his opinion, will be most convenient and best calculated to promise a restoration to reason. I do not think it advisable to remove the insane of the navy or marine corps from the navy hospitals to private institutions. The skill and acquirements of the medical officers of the navy, and the comforts and advantages to be afforded by the navy hospital fund, are believed to be ample for all the beneficent purposes designed by Congress for those unfortunate persons. The number of insane persons at present in the navy hospitals is but twelve, and this number, it is believed, will not be greatly increased. The reports of the attending surgeons represent most of the cases as beyond the hope of amendment.

A joint resolution of the 9th of May, 1848, authorized the secretary of the navy, if. in his opinion, it was advantageous to the public interest, to make contracts for a term not exceeding five years for the purchase of American water-rotted hemp for the use of the United States Navy, provided it could be had of equal quality with the best foreign hemp, and at a price not exceeding the average price of such hemp for the last five years. After the passage of this resolution all purchases in open market were suspended, and no foreign hemp has been purchased since that period. No advertisement for supplies of hemp under the resolution was published until the 4th of March last. On that day proposals were invited for the delivery of a quantity of about five hundred tons annually for a term not exceeding five years. Under this advertisement several offers were made; the form of the bidding, however, was decided to be erroneous, and not according to the law. All the bids were rejected, and the department determined not to enter into contracts thereon. Prior to the passage of the resolution, purchases of hemp had been made, and contracts were in existence at its date, for the delivery of considerable quantities. There were in store at the navy yard at Boston, on the 30th of September last, 762 tons of hemp, of which 600 tons were of foreign growth and preparation. At the period of the passage of the resolution an opinion was entertained that the heavy expenses to be incurred in preparing for the production of the finer qualities of water-rotted hemp deterred our farmers and hemp-growers from entering into contracts for a single year's supply for the navy, and hopes were entertained that an extension of the terms of contracts to a longer period would induce the farmers and growers to enter into contracts with the government, and that such extension of time would justify the necessary outlay to be incurred in the erection of the machinery and fixtures required for its thorough preparation. That such was the design of the resolution, and such the hopes of its friends and advocates, there can be no doubt. Experience, however, has not realized these expectations. The farmers and hemp-growers have evinced an unwillingness to enter into contracts, and numerous petitions and communications, remonstrating in the strongest terms against the proposed plan, have been forwarded to the department. But two bids were offered by the hemp-growers, and they were for small quantities, not exceeding twenty-five tons per year. Bids were offered by others than those engaged in the growth and preparation of the article, proposing to supply the entire quantity annually required for the use of the navy for the term of five years. Under the authority vested in the department by the resolution, had there been no objection to the legality of the bids themselves, it would have declined entering into contracts for the supply necessary for the next five years; as the result of such contract, if made, would have been to create an absolute monopoly in the hands of a single individual, or of an association, of the entire supply of water-rotted hemp for the navy, to the exclusion of farmers and growers, for whose benefit the resolution was obviously intended. The department is convinced that the object contemplated by the resolution cannot be attained under the existing provisions. Such alterations and limitations should be made as will prevent a monopoly, and which will secure the supply of hemp for the navy to those actually engaged in its growth and preparation.

The opinion is entertained that if the government will make known its willingness and determination to purchase American water-rotted hemp *alone*, if it can be procured at a price not exceeding the average price paid for the last five years for foreign hemp, that quantities adequate to the wants of the navy, and of a quality greatly superior to the foreign hemp, would be prepared and offered by the farmers of the West at such points as would suit the convenience of the government.

The encouragement designed by the resolution was intended to reach the agricultural interest, and, by a regular and constant demand for all that may be required for the navy, afford the opportunity for fair experiment in the preparation at home of an article essential to the protection and prosperity of the country.

The buildings in connexion with the ropewalk at Memphis will shortly be completed. A steam-engine and all other machinery required for the manufacture of cordage has been contracted for; the machinery is already completed, the steam-engine is in a state of forwardness. The ropewalk and machinery will be ready to commence operations for the manufacture of cordage by the end of the month of June, 1850.

The plan proposed will greatly promote the objects intended by Congress, as well as the interest and convenience of those engaged in the preparation of hemp. The extensive manufacture of cordage at Memphis will render it necessary that considerable quantities of hemp should be delivered at that point. It can be reached with facility and cheapness by the farmers themselves, who will attend the inspection and delivery.

Under the direction of the bureau of Ordnance and Hydrography a series of experiments in gunnery have been in progress during the past summer at the navy yard in Washington; they have proved eminently successful in their results, and are of great importance to the service. A system has been prepared for regulating the inspection, proof, and preservation of ordnance and ordnance stores, and of instruction in all matters relating to gunnery and its practice afloat.

The observations, calculations, and experiments at the observatory, the preparation of maps and charts, the rating and regulating of chronometers, have been zealously continued. The urgent demands which are constantly addressed to the superintendent for scientific information, for charts and sailing instructions, evince the increasing confidence every where felt by our commercial community in the skill, accuracy, and science with which the observatory is conducted.

A joint commission of engineer and navy officers was organized in November, 1848, for the purpose of making an examination of the coast of the United States lying on the Pacific ocean, with reference to points of defence and occupation, to security and accommodation of trade and commerce, and for naval and military purposes. The board left the United States during the last winter and arrived in California in April. The insufficiency and inadequacy of the means at the disposal of the board, and the unsettled state of the country, have entirely prevented the prosecution of the examination, and no report has been made on the various important subjects committed to its charge. I regret that it has not been in the power of this board to furnish accurate information as to the most eligible point for the location of a naval depot and establishment. The condition of our public ships (as well as of our numerous merchant ships engaged in a rapidly extending and lucrative commerce in the Pacific ocean, its remoteness from the Atlantic cities, and the long and perilous voyage around Cape Horn) renders some adequate and proper means for their repair on the coast of California absolutely necessary. Whenever the condition of that country and the prices of labour will justify the undertaking, the establishing of a navy yard, and the construction of a dock or marine railway for the refitting and repair of our vessels, are earnestly recommended.

The accounts authorized to be settled under the act of 3d March, 1849, and under the joint resolution of the same date for the relief of pursers in the navy, have all been presented and received the necessary action of this department, except those of pursers who have not yet returned to the United States.

In execution of the 3d section of the act of 3d of August, 1848, for the construction of floating dry-docks, basins, and railways, at the navy yards at Kittery, Philadelphia, and Pensacola, contracts were entered into by the department with Messrs. Gilbert and Secor and Messrs. Dakin and Moody. The contractors have commenced their operations, and have so far advanced with the works as to furnish evidence of their ability to complete their contracts within the specified periods. The time for the completion of the work at Kittery will expire before the termination of the next fiscal year. In order that the department may be enabled to meet its engagements under this contract, it will be necessary that the entire amount estimated to complete the dock, &c., viz. $300,000, should be appropriated. The time for the completion of the dock at Philadelphia also terminates during the next fiscal year, and an appropriation of the sum of $371,242 is asked for to discharge our obligations to the contractors. The dock at Pensacola has been commenced, and considerable progress has been made in its construction. By the terms of the contract, the work is to be completed by the 1st of May, 1851. The amount which will be due upon its completion is $414,320, and an appropriation for that amount is also asked.

The 8th section of the act of March 3d, 1849, repeals "the law authorizing the appointment of prize agents," and provides that all money remaining in the hands of prize agents and all proceeds of prizes hereafter accruing shall be deposited in the treasury, to be distributed under the direction of the secretary of the navy. In conformity with this act the individuals who were acting as prize agents were called upon to deposite in the treasury the prize money remaining in their hands. These directions have been generally complied with by officers of the navy acting as prize agents. In one or two cases private citizens, who had been appointed prize agents, refused to make the required deposite, upon the ground that, as they held powers of attorney to receive shares of prize money, and had actually received the amounts due from the proper officer of the prize court, they were not legally accountable for the funds in their hands, except to their constituents, or to the courts in which the awards were made. The amounts which have been deposited are now in course of distribution by the fourth auditor of the treasury, under the direction of this department.

There have been no acts of Congress authorizing the appointment, or regulating the duties or compensation of prize agents. The act for the better government of the navy, approved April 23, 1800, provides for the apportionment of prize money, and recognises the office of prize agents. An act approved April 16, 1816, directs that the shares of prizes belonging to the captors shall be paid to the parties entitled, or to their authorized agent or agents, upon the order of the proper court in term, or of the judge or judges in vacation. A special act of Congress of March 3, 1823, directs that certain prize agents who should not account for prize moneys which had been intrusted to them should "not receive from the treasury of the United States any salary or compensation" to which they may have been entitled. The right of appointing prize agents does not appear to have been considered as vested by any general law or usage in the navy department, but in the captors, subject to the recognition of the prize courts; and their compensation has been derived from a commission or per centage (not regulated by law) upon the amount to be distributed, which commission was deducted by them before payment of the shares. With regard to the prize agents appointed during the recent war with Mexico, it appears that the department expressly disclaimed any control over them, and it is not known that any bonds were required of them by the captors or prize courts for the faithful discharge of their duties. The consequence of the absence of well-understood legal provisions on this subject, has been that the department has experienced some difficulty in obtaining full and accurate information as to the disposition of the proceeds of prizes, and the returns which were required from the prize agents are still imperfect. Under the new law, however, no such difficulty need hereafter occur in ascertaining and protecting the rights of seamen, and of the government. The captures made at sea during the recent war were few in number, and of inconsiderable value, consisting chiefly of small coasting vessels.

A revision and republication of the various laws passed for the government of the navy and of the general orders of this department urgently demand attention. The laws have been passed at various times, and the general orders of the department, which constitute the larger portion of the rules and regulations for the government of the navy, have been promulgated at different periods, and exist in a detached and undigested form. A proper revision of them and an accurate and concise digest is much needed. Measures will be taken at the earliest moment to effect this object, by means of a board of intelligent and experienced officers.

Attention is most respectfully asked to our interest in the Pacific ocean and to the increasing obligations the government is under to protect and cherish it. The principle has become a settled one in the American mind, that the government is bound to afford at all times its countenance and aid to every citizen, wherever he may be, in the prosecution of the lawful and honourable enterprise of commerce or of trade. To do less is to fall short of the objects and the ends for which it was created. As within the limits of our jurisdiction at home, the obligation is imperative to extend the protection of our laws and the means necessary to enforce them to every citizen, so beyond that jurisdiction the obligation is equally strong to afford him that protection to which, by the laws of nations and the principles of justice, he is entitled abroad.

Within a short period, we have added an extent of sea-coast to our possessions of more than nine hundred miles, embracing many good and one of the best harbors in the world, possessing immense mineral wealth, attracting to its shores the inhabitants of all nations, and inviting to it the commerce and trade of every climate. Crowds of emigrants are daily arriving and becoming American citizens; large numbers of our own citizens, closely connected with us in every relation of life, have gone thither, and will doubtless shortly constitute an important portion of our republic. From their remoteness and the difficulty of access, except by sea, their safety and prosperity depend mainly on the protection of our naval power. The trade of the Pacific is now the great commercial prize for which the world is contending. The competition is one in which our country is engaged against all others. The trade of China and the Pacific ocean, from the natural advantages which we possess, if properly fostered by the government, will be easily appropriated to ourselves in a fair and generous competition. Activity and energy will make it what it ought to be—an American commerce and an American trade. A steam navy is necessary to maintain our rights, and to afford the protection to our commerce required in this competition. While a just regard to the rights of all, to the present condition and pecuniary resources of our country, do not authorize unreasonable expenditures for the maintenance of the navy, our safety, honour and interest, wholly forbid a penurious restriction of the means necessary for its proper, uniform, and judicious increase.

By an act of Congress approved March 3d, 1847, an appropriation was made for building and equipping four first-class sea-going steamships, which are now in progress of completion. I have given directions for their early preparation and outfit. The Saranac will shortly be ready for sea; the San Jacinto will be ready for service in the spring; the other two will be completed during the ensuing summer. The amount heretofore appropriated, it is believed, will be adequate to complete them. They will add greatly to the force, to the efficiency, and to the usefulness of our navy; and I respectfully submit to Congress the propriety of further appropriations for such additions to our steam force as may be deemed proper.

As a measure of deep interest to the prosperity of the navy, I ask attention to its present organization. The numbers of officers in the higher grades are greater than are required, either for the vessels now in commission, for the number of men authorized by Congress to be employed, or for any increase of force afloat which may reasonably be expected. The numbers in the respective grades are disproportioned to each other. Its present organization retards promotion. Age, infirmity, and want of employment have disqualified many for the performance of active professional duties. These evils are felt and acknowledged by all who have a just regard for the prosperity and honour of the service.

The difficulty lies in suggesting a remedy, which, while it will relieve the country from unnecessary burdens and at the same time operate justly and liberally on those who have devoted large portions of their lives to the service, will afford regular and constant occupation to those who are retained, increase their energy and activity, and hold out to all the indispensable stimulus to honourable ambition, the prospect of promotion at a period of life when each is best qualified to discharge the duties required of him. Whatever may be the extent of our naval force, or the number of officers retained in the service, the largest proportion possible of the officers should be kept in active professional employment, to acquire and ensure the requisite experience and professional skill which will render them efficient for command when an emergency may arise, and to make them really and truly the nucleus capable of any and every expansion which the future exigencies of the country may require.

As the only practicable means of accomplishing these results, I recommend to Congress a reduction of the numbers in the various grades of officers to that point which will secure a sufficient number in each for such a naval force as Congress may determine is necessary and proper, and that provision be made for a retired list for such officers as are disqualified for active service, on such terms and with such pay as may be thought liberal and just.

Should Congress deem it proper to adopt such a system, it is believed a plan can be prepared which will meet the approbation of a large proportion of the officers themselves, and which will greatly reduce the expenditure of our naval establishment.

I respectfully invite attention to the naval school at Annapolis. During the last year it has been under the superintendence of Commander Upshur, who has devoted himself with zeal to the discharge of his duties. Experience had disclosed many defects in its organization and suggested many improvements which might be readily effected without materially increasing the expenditure for the institution. In the month of October a board of officers was directed to revise and amend the regulations with a view to re-organize the school, conforming it, as nearly as the two branches of the service would permit, to the West Point Academy. The board discharged the duty in a manner highly acceptable and satisfactory to the department, and the hope is entertained that, under the system thus provided, the future discipline, instruction, and management of the school will be promoted and advanced, and its beneficial influence on the efficiency and usefulness of the service greatly increased. In the education, discipline, and professional experience of a corps of officers, can we alone evince a just and proper appreciation of the maxim that we should "in time of peace prepare for war."

Under the authority given by the 9th section of the act of August 3d, 1848, transfers have been made from certain heads of appropriation to those which were deficient, amounting to $747,533 30, most of which must be restored to the heads from which the transfers were made, to effect which a special account of the moneys transferred will be laid before Congress, and an appropriation will be asked to supply deficiencies in the appropriations for the naval service for the fiscal year ending the 30th of June, 1850.

I have the honour to submit herewith the reports from the several bureaus of this department, together with the estimates for the naval service and for other objects placed under the control of the department for the fiscal year ending on the 30th of June, 1851; the gross amount of which is $9,203,356 15, from which should be deducted the sums for special objects, namely:

For transportation of the mail,	•	•	•	$874.600 00
For dry dock at New York,	—	•		180,000 00
For floating docks,	•	—	•	1,085,562 00
For improvement of navy yards,	•	•:	•	845.966 00
For nautical almanac,	•	•	•	• 12,850 00

Amounting to the sum of - • • • - $2,998,978 00
And leaving for one year's expense of the naval service
the sum of - • - • • - - $6,204,378 15

The total amount drawn from the treasury during the fiscal year ending the 30th of June, 1849, as shown by the statement of appropriations for the naval service prepared by the second comptroller of the treasury, is $13,167,968 86; from which deduct re-payments $2,269,623 99, and the sum of $10,898,342 87 is shown as the expense of the navy and marine corps, and including all objects placed under the control of the navy department for that year.

The unexpended balance in the treasury of the appropriations for the naval service and marine corps on the 30th of June, 1849, was $2,039,798 13, all of which will be required to meet the outstanding obligations due from the appropriations made for that year.

The value of stores and materials on hand at navy yards for naval purposes, exclusive of ships building, in ordinary, undergoing repairs and in commission, navy yards and other public lands required for purposes of the navy, with their improvements, is $9,853,921 27.

The report of the commandant of the marine corps, together with the estimates for its support during the fiscal year 1850 and 1851, are also submitted herewith. An increased appropriation is asked for to meet the pay of twelve officers of that corps who had been dropped at the termination of the war with Mexico, and who were re-appointed by the President under the authority of an act in their behalf passed at the last session of Congress, and to provide the estimated amount of $30,000 to pay the three months' extra pay to the non-commissioned officers, privates, and musicians of the corps, who served with the army in the war with Mexico. Two battalions of this corps, under the separate commands of Lieut. Col. Watson and Major Harris, were detached from the navy and transferred to the army to serve with it under the command of Major-General Scott. The portion thus detached was clearly within the provisions of the joint resolution of Congress passed on the 10th of August, 1848. Another portion of the corps, attached to and employed in those vessels of the United States despatched to the coast of Mexico to aid in subduing the cities and forts of the enemy and in conquering the country, presented their claims and asserted their right to the bounty land and extra pay provided by that resolution. The payment of these demands having been refused, and doubts existing as to the true construction of the law, I thought proper to refer the question to the attorney-general. In answer to my inquiry, he has expressed the opinion that the entire portion of the corps, whether serving on land or on board ship on the Mexican coast in the war with Mexico, is to be considered within the true meaning of the resolution of the 10th of August, 1848, as having "served with the army in the war with Mexico," and entitled to the bounty land and other remuneration therein provided.

No adequate provision has heretofore been made for the discharge of these claims, and an estimate has therefore been prepared.

I have the honour to be, very respectfully, your obedient servant,

To the PRESIDENT.   WM. BALLARD PRESTON.

REPORT OF SECRETARY OF THE INTERIOR.

DEPARTMENT OF THE INTERIOR, December 3, 1849.

SIR: The act to establish the department of the interior was passed at the close of the last session of Congress, when the attention of that body was occupied by a large accumulation of public business, in consequence of which it was left, in some respects, imperfect. The department is named in the title "A Home Department," but the body of the act provides that it shall be called "The Department of the Interior." The title of the act, being the part last adopted in the process of enactment, is believed to express the intention of Congress as to the name, but the language of the act itself being impera-tive, I felt constrained to conform to it in the adoption of a seal, and in all other official acts.

Important duties, requiring much clerical labour, were transferred from the President, and from the state, the treasury, and the war departments, to the department of the interior. The act provides for the appointment of a secre-tary and a chief clerk, but directs the employment of no other clerks, except in the provision, "That the President of the United States, on the recommen-dation of the said secretary of the interior, may transfer from the treasury de-partment proper to the department of the interior such clerks in the office of the secretary of the treasury as perform the duties over which the supervision and control are given by this act to the secretary of the interior."

It was, however, ascertained, on careful examination, that there was no clerk who could be transferred, by virtue of this provision; for, although some part of the duties of several clerks, employed in the office of the secretary of the treasury, was transferred to this department, yet there was not a transfer of all, or even the principal part, of the duties of any one clerk. Therefore, on taking charge of the new department, I found that there were onerous du-ties, running into much detail, enjoined by law to be performed, and no means provided to enable me to perform them. A great proportion was current bu-siness, which required attention from day to day, and would not bear post-ponement. Pressed, therefore, by the necessities of the public service, I felt it incumbent on me to employ such clerical aid as would enable me to orga-nize the department, open its books, and keep up the current business, until Congress should make permanent provision for the full and regular discharge of all its duties. For this temporary purpose, I took from the general land office two clerks, from the Indian office one, from the pension office one; and, in addition thereto, employed five—three of them at agreed salaries of eigh-teen hundred, fourteen hundred, and twelve hundred dollars respectively, subject to the approval of Congress; the other two at the usual per diem wages. There will be needed, as a permanent force in the department proper, ten clerks, whose compensation in the aggregate is estimated at fourteen thou-sand two hundred dollars.

In addition to his various administrative duties, there are referred to the head of this department from the pension office, the general land office, and the office of Indian affairs, many cases for judicial decision, involving the exa-mination of evidence, and the determination of questions of law. The deci-sion of these cases, many of them of great magnitude and importance, require all the time, care, and research which are due to the safe and proper exercise of judicial functions. For many years there was a solicitor pertaining to the general land office, whose office was abolished in 1812. But since that time the acts of Congress giving bounty lands to soldiers who served in the Mexi-can war, have greatly increased the number of legal questions arising in that bureau, while those from the pension office, under the same acts and other laws conferring pensions and military bounties, are very numerous and often difficult. The number of private land claims, and questions arising out of our

Indian intercourse, will be also greatly increased by the extension of our settlements to Oregon and the accession of California, and New Mexico. From all these sources will arise an amount of judicial duty sufficient to require the undivided time and attention of an able law officer, and which cannot be promptly and well discharged by the head of a department engaged in his daily administrative duties. In my opinion, therefore, the public service would be promoted by the creation of the office of solicitor of the department of the interior, which officer should be charged with the examination and decision of these various cases and claims.

The act establishing the department of the interior was passed so immediately before the adjournment of Congress that no provision was or could be embodied in the general appropriation act for its support. In the law by which it is established there is a provision directing that a portion of the contingent fund of the office of the secretary of the treasury should be transferred to the office of the secretary of the interior. Under this provision the sum of four thousand dollars has been so transferred, leaving an estimated deficit to cover expenses incurred, and which must be incurred in said office, in the past and present fiscal years, of thirty-four thousand seven hundred and thirty-seven dollars and sixty-eight cents, for which an early appropriation will be desirable.

PUBLIC BUILDINGS.

In applying the appropriation for the painting and repairs of the capitol, it became necessary to examine with care the condition of the walls, and to remove such portions of the stone as were crumbling or falling off in scales, that the coat of paint might be laid upon a sound and solid surface. On this examination it was found that many of the stones, especially those near the base of the building, were disintegrated at the surface, and some were so much and so deeply affected that it was necessary to remove them. The capitol is a massive building, its walls are thick, and maintain a certain equality of temperature, changing slowly with the changes in the temperature of the air. In a change from cold to warm, the walls remain for a time cold, and there is condensed upon them a portion of the moisture of the atmosphere, as upon a pitcher containing ice water in a sultry day. The stone being very porous, readily absorbs the moisture, and the natural cement which seems to be slowly soluble in water, is dissolved or otherwise loses its adhesive power, and the stone crumbles to sand. A thick coat of paint, carefully applied from time to time, has been resorted to to preserve, and no doubt tends to preserve the building; but unless some other and more permanent protection be resorted to, it is destined to early dilapidation. If left wholly unprotected from atmospheric action for one-fifth of the time that marble structures are known to have stood, this noble edifice would become a mound of sand.

The treasury building and the present patent office building are of the same material, and, having been in no manner protected, already show signs of decay. The cornice of the treasury building, which exposes a heavy mass of stone to atmospheric action, begins to be moss-grown; and pieces of the moulding of the patent office building have crumbled and fallen. Besides its tendency to disintegration on exposure, the stone in its best condition is weak, offering little more resistance to a crushing force than common brick. These buildings cannot, with all possible care, be long preserved by the means at present adopted. But if the stone, as it stands in the walls, could be rendered permanently and absolutely impermeable to moisture, the principal difficulty would be removed; and this may perhaps be done by some means known to the arts, or which may be discovered by experiment. For this purpose I would recommend that specimens of the stone be carefully analyzed, and that a series of experiments be tried, with a view of finding some chemical agent, the application of which will prevent its absorption of moisture, and thus strengthen and render it durable.

In consequence of the defective quality of this stone, and of reports from committees of Congress in 1837 and 1839 condemning it, I thought proper to direct that the wings of the Patent Office building should be constructed of a different material. After full consideration, a white marble, from a quarry in Baltimore county, Maryland, was selected. It is a strong stone, resisting about three times as great a crushing force as the sandstone of the front building. All the practicable tests which were applied show it to be durable. It is a material of great beauty, and it will be easier to make the front building correspond with it in colour, than with the gray gneiss, or any other strong and durable stone of mixed or varied colours, which could be readily procured. The work on the eastern wing is considerably advanced. Something has been done on the foundation of the western wing; but the whole appropriation has been expended, and it is important to the progress of the work that a further appropriation for its continuance be made at an early day.

In order to make room for the foundation of the eastern wing, it became necessary to remove a part of the conservatory in which is kept the rich collection of tropical plants that were selected and preserved with so much skill and care by Capt. Wilkes and the scientific gentlemen who accompanied him on the exploring expedition. The appropriation which could be applied to that object being insufficient to erect a new building adapted to the purpose of their permanent preservation, it was thought best to remove that part of the structure which interfered with the foundation of the Patent Office, and rebuild it in a cheap manner, so as to preserve the plants until Congress might fix upon a spot on which a permanent building should be constructed, and select adjacent grounds for the cultivation of the hardier plants of the collection.

Something has been done within the present season towards enclosing and protecting the waste and neglected portions of the public grounds; but, owing to the limited appropriation for that object, but little in planting or adorning them. And in carefully looking over the best planted portions of the grounds, near the President's mansion, and about the capitol, it cannot but be observed how meager is the collection of trees and shrubs, both native and exotic. In planting the newly enclosed grounds, this defect ought to be remedied, at least as to those of our native forests, of which many varieties, and some of them the most beautiful and the best fitted for plantations and lawns, have been wholly neglected. A rich variety of exotics, though desirable, is of less importance, as there are within the temperate zone on the eastern continent but few trees or shrubs which have not their congeneric on this, of at least equal luxuriance and beauty.

Should Congress think fit, at an early day, to make the requisite appropriation, considerable progress may be made in the coming season in collecting choice varieties of forest trees and shrubs, and planting and improving the grounds.

The report of the Commissioner of Public Buildings will show the expenditures already made on the various improvements under his care, and also in the work thus far done on the wings of the Patent Office building, together with an estimate of deficiencies for the present, and necessary appropriations for the next fiscal year.

PATENT OFFICE.

The Patent Office, which marks the progress and collects the results of the inventive genius of the American people, is an object of increasing interest and importance. The skilful and ready application of the accumulated stores of human knowledge, especially the natural sciences, to the wants and purposes of man, is a distinguishing characteristic of the present age. Not but that the discoveries of science are pressed as vigorously and with as great intellectual power in this as in the past, but the present is especially marked by the practical application of every thing known, and which becomes known, to the daily wants and uses and purposes of life.

In this noble struggle for the earliest attainment of the useful in the arts, this pressing forward to the amelioration of the condition of man, the increasing of his comforts and lessening his toils by the application of science to the improvement of his industrial pursuits, that country will be foremost in which enlightened mind is most generally and most immediately brought into contact with operative labour.

It is in that fortunate concurrence of pursuits, where the hours of labour in the workshop are made to alternate with those of study and research, that there are cultivated matured minds like those of Franklin, Rittenhouse, Watt, and Davy, rich in inductive science, and ready in its application to all that is useful or ennobling. Many of the best and ripest minds of our own country belong to this class of operative students, and have long been and are still devoting themselves with signal success to scientific discoveries and mechanical improvements and inventions.

There is, as a matter of course, among the inventions of the day, mixed with the well-directed and the useful, much that is wild and visionary, and therefore abortive; and sometimes, perhaps, the vague and, for the present, useless foreshadowing of important future discoveries. But the aggregate value of the labour and study of the class of inventors is beyond all estimate. They have proved themselves benefactors to their country, and are entitled to the especial consideration and care of the government. The report of the Commissioner of Patents, which will be presented at an early day, will show a large surplus fund accumulated from their contributions, a part of which was appropriated at the last session of Congress "towards the erection of the wings of the Patent Office building." No part of this addition is considered necessary for the use of that office. Instead of thus directing this fund to a general purpose of the government, it would seem but just to apply it as the commissioner recommends, or in some other manner, that the wisdom of Congress may suggest, for the encouragement of the inventive arts and the reward of successful inventors.

AGRICULTURAL BUREAU.

The agricultural interest stands first in importance in our country, and embodies within itself the principal elements of our national wealth and power; and it should be with us as it has been and is with all other prosperous civilized nations, a leading object of public care and patronage. The principal nations of Europe have their agricultural boards, known by various names, under the direction of men of high scientific attainments, supported out of the revenues, and connected with the administration of the government; and, to borrow the language of the Father of his country in his last annual message: "This species of establishment contributes doubly to the increase of improvement, by stimulating to enterprise and experiment, and by drawing to a common centre the results every where of individual skill and observation, and spreading them thence over the whole nation. Experience accordingly has shown that they are very cheap instruments of immense national benefit."

No direct aid has been extended by our government to agriculture, except by the yearly collection and publication, through the Patent Office, of some agricultural experiments and statistics, and recently the analysis of some soils and vegetable productions. The means thus applied, though useful in their results, are wholly inadequate.

To meet the great object fully, and give to this leading branch of American industry the aid which it so well merits, I respectfully suggest the establishment of an Agricultural Bureau, connected with this department, but separated from the Patent Office. The expense would be small compared with the end to be accomplished.

If this suggestion should meet with the approbation of Congress, and the organization of the bureau become a subject of consideration, much aid may be derived from consulting the systems adopted by France and Belgium, both of which have done much towards the advancement of agriculture as a science. Belgium, it is believed, has the best organized agricultural department, and, partly owing to this, partly to the natural fertility of its soil, the best cultivated and most highly productive country in Europe.

PENSION OFFICE.

The amount of business in the Pension Bureau is large. The number of invalid pensioners has increased during the last year nine hundred and eighty-nine. The whole number now on the list is four thousand one hundred and fifteen.

The amount of claims for bounty land warrants filed prior to the 5th of
November last was about 83,000
Of these there have been suspended or rejected about 9,000.
The number which remain to be filed may be estimated at . 20,000
_____
Making an aggregate of 103,000

PUBLIC LANDS.

It will be seen by the report of the commissioner of the General Land Office, that the surveys of public lands have been pressed forward with diligence and energy, so as to bring new and good lands into market sufficient to supply the wants of emigration.

The quantity sold for cash in the first three quarters of the year
1848 was . . . . 1,448,240.51 acres.
In the first three quarters of 1849, . . . 887,206.40 "

Showing a diminution of . . . . 561,034.11 "
The amount located by bounty warrants in the first three quarters of 1848 . . . . . . 1,525,200 acres.
In the first three quarters of 1849, . . . 2,496,560 "

Showing an increase of . . . . 971,360 "
And making together an aggregate increase over the sales and
locations of the first three quarters of the preceding year of 410,325.89 acres.

This small advance in the aggregate of sales indicates very accurately the gradual increase of agricultural migration. Our admirable land system, which was devised by the founders of the republic, and modified from time to time as experience indicated changes, which would adapt it more perfectly to the wants of the people, has been thus far effectual, and will, while it is preserved, be effectual in preventing alike large monopolies of land and speculations injurious to those who purchase for cultivation. The capitalist cannot purchase up the national domain, and while the United States continues to be a vender in the market, prices are necessarily kept down to her minimum. Hence land is now seldom purchased on speculation, and even those who hold the bounty land warrants for sale do not find it profitable to locate them, for they are not thereby enhanced in value. Generally, the farmer who emigrates prefers to select his own farm out of a wider area of good land, rather than to take, at a little larger price, the selection of another. These warrants, therefore, add little to the annual sales of the public lands. The soldiers do not generally locate them; but they are used, where money would otherwise be used, as a means of payment.

The claims for bounties, under the acts of February 11, 1847, and 10th
August, 1848, as shown above, are, in round numbers . . 83,000
Estimated numbers yet to be filed 20,000
_____
Making in the aggregate 103,000
Of these, 2,922 have been satisfied in money, and 70,390 have
been allowed—to be satisfied in land—which will require 10,636,120 acres.

And should there be but 100,000 valid claims, as is estimated,
then there will remain 26,688 unsatisfied claims, which, if
settled in land, will require a further quantity of . 4,020,480 acres.

Making in all . . . . 14,656,600 "

Prior to 1st of October last there had been located with these
Mexican war warrants . . . . 5,025,400 "

Leaving yet to be located . . . . 9,631,200 "

The proportion of warrants used instead of purchase money in the ordinary sales will probably absorb them in the three next ensuing years, and sooner, if they take the place of cash generally in the current sales. Until the bounty warrants are exhausted, the receipts in cash from the sales of the public lands must be comparatively small.

The attention of this department was early directed to the continuation of the geological exploration and surveys of the mineral lands in Michigan, Wisconsin, and Iowa. On the 12th of April, about the opening of the season for field operations, Dr. Charles T. Jackson, the principal geologist, who had conducted in person the survey of the mineral lands in Michigan, resigned his situation, and recommended the appointment of his two assistants, Mr. J. W. Foster and Mr. J. D. Whitney, Jr., to finish the work. In a few days, however, he asked leave to withdraw his resignation. After looking into the progress of the work, and considering the time which it had required for its execution thus far, I was convinced that he could not, by any effort which it was reasonable to require of him, conduct the field work in person and prepare a report of what he had already done, and what was yet to be done, in time for it to be laid before Congress at their coming session. I therefore dispensed with his farther services in the field, and instructed him to finish his analysis of the minerals collected, and prepare a report of the work done by him in the two preceding years. This report has been recently received, and will accompany that of the commissioner of the general land office. It will be found to contain much historical information touching the early explorations of the country bordering on Lake Superior, with a full and able description of the geological relations and character of the rich deposites of native copper on Isle Royal and Keeweenaw point.

The magnetic observations of Dr. Locke, one of the assistant geologists charged with that service by Dr. Jackson, will be regarded with peculiar interest. The magnetic energy which manifests itself at different points on the earth's surface, by its action on the needle in different directions, and with different degrees of force, giving to it what are called its dip, its declination, and its intensity; the diurnal variations of each of these, the variations of each of them in long periods of time, and the manner in which they are affected by meteorological and electrical phenomena, have for many years past been objects of great interest to science, and of careful observation on almost every part of the earth's surface accessible to civilized man. Our linear surveyors and our topographical corps, in their survey of Lake Superior, have found it necessary to observe the magnetic action so far only as regards the declination of the needle, or its direction toward or variation from the true pole. The observations of Dr. Locke, which accompany Dr. Jackson's report, are therefore all that we have in that region which regards the magnetic force in its various manifestations, and it is matter of regret that they could not have been longer continued and further extended.

The residue of the field work of this district was intrusted to Messrs. Foster and Whitney, who have pressed it forward with much diligence and industry. Their report is not yet completed, but the synopsis and the geological maps which they have returned, and which will accompany the report of the com-

missioner of the general land office, are highly satisfactory to the department
and creditable to themselves. Their maps designate by quarter sections the
lands on which valuable mineral deposites are found, so that the agricultural
lands within the mineral region can now be offered for sale pursuant to law.

Dr. Owen, the geologist for Wisconsin and Iowa, has furnished all the data
necessary to enable the land office to bring into market the mineral lands of the
Chippewa district in Wisconsin, and he has extended his exploration and survey
over not only the northern parts of Iowa and Wisconsin, but Minesota also as
far north as the United States boundary line, and west a short distance beyond
the Red river of the north. His report, which is in course of preparation, will, it
is believed, be not only a valuable contribution to science, but contain also the
best information which we have of the agricultural capabilities and the mineral
wealth of the extensive district of country which he has explored. A further
appropriation will be necessary to enable him to complete the analysis of minerals
which he has collected, and to prepare his report.

PUBLIC LANDS IN OREGON, CALIFORNIA, AND NEW MEXICO.

No provision has yet been made to extend the laws for the disposition of the
public lands in the territories of Oregon, California, and New Mexico. The
public interest would seem to require that this should be done at an early day.
To carry it into effect the negotiation of treaties with the Indian tribes who claim
title to the lands, the creation of the office of surveyor general in each of those
territories, and the establishment of land offices in convenient districts, will be
necessary, accompanied with the usual appropriations for surveys.

Nothing beyond this, or out of the ordinary course of things, will be required,
in providing for the disposition of the lands in Oregon, except the adjustment of
a few titles of British subjects, provided for by the treaty of August 5th, 1846,
which may be referred to the judges of the territory, and some generous provision
for the early emigrants, in consideration of the hardships which they encountered
in the first settlement of this distant and exposed frontier.

New Mexico has long been settled, and portions of the land in that territory
are held by titles granted by Spain, or by Mexico since her separation from the
Spanish monarchy. It will be necessary to establish a judicial commission to
examine and settle these titles, so far as they are subject to doubt or controversy.
A large proportion of them is, it is believed, of ancient date and evidenced by
long and uninterrupted occupancy.

In California such commission will be more especially necessary. Many of
the older grants in that territory, of considerable extent, have been resumed by the
sovereign authority, and are now held under new grants, which require examination. Many important and commanding points are claimed under very recent
grants of a questionable character; and but a part of the public records were, at
the time of our last advices, in the possession, or within the knowledge of the
proper authorities. There is, however, a large amount of land in this territory,
held by grants of unquestionable validity, and some of them, especially those
granted for pasturage, are large, covering many square leagues in extent. A
considerable amount also is held by inchoate titles, regular and fair in their in-
ception, but which have not been perfected. These titles, where commenced in
good faith, by concession from the Spanish or Mexican authorities, ought to be
favourably regarded, especially if followed by possession. In no case should
the occupant of the soil suffer injury, by the transfer of the sovereignty to the
United States. This consideration has induced Congress to confirm inceptive
grants, even where the conditions were not fulfilled, in all cases where it could
reasonably be supposed that the government which made the grant would have
waived or allowed further time for their performance.

This liberal consideration ought not, however, to be extended to doubtful
grants of positions on the bays, islands, and head lands, which, when acquired,

were known to be necessary to the United States, as sites for forts, light-houses, or other objects of a national character. It is understood that titles of some kind, generally not valid without the confirmation of Congress, have been procured, and are claimed, to some of these points, which, if confirmed to and made the property of individuals, must be purchased back at a very large price. The right of the United States to such sites, where valid, ought to be at once asserted; and every spot necessary to the use of the government should be selected and separated from the general mass of public lands, and reserved from sale, and from the operation of the pre-emption laws, as they shall be extended to that territory.

MINERAL LANDS IN CALIFORNIA.

It is understood that a few of the larger grants cover, to some extent, the mines of gold and quicksilver.

By the laws of Spain these mines did not pass by a grant of the land, but remained in the crown, subject to be disposed of according to such ordinances and regulations as might be from time to time adopted. Any individual might enter upon the lands of another to search for ores of the precious metals, and, having discovered a mine, he might register, and thus acquire the right to work it on paying to the owner the damage done to the surface, and to the crown, whose property it was, a fifth or tenth, according to the quality of the mine. If the finder neglected to work, or worked it imperfectly, it might be denounced by any other person, whereby he would become entitled.

This right to the mines of precious metals, which by the laws of Spain remained in the crown, is believed to have been also retained by Mexico while she was sovereign of the territory, and to have passed by her transfer to the United States. It is a right of the sovereign in the soil as perfect as if it had been expressly reserved in the body of the grant; and it will rest with Congress to determine whether, in those cases where lands duly granted contain gold, this right shall be asserted or relinquished. If relinquished, it will require an express law to effect the object; and if retained, legislation will be necessary to provide a mode by which it shall be exercised. For it is to be observed that the regulation permitting the acquisition of a right in the mines by registry or by denouncement was simply a mode of exercising by the sovereign the proprietary right which he had in the treasure as it lay in and was connected with the soil. Consequently, whenever that right was transferred by the transfer of the entire domain, the mode adopted for its exercise ceased to be legal, for the same re   on that the Spanish mode of disposing of the public lands in the first instance   sed to be legal after the transfer of the sovereignty.

Thus it appears that the deposites of gold, wherever found in the terri   , are the property of the United States. Those, however, which are known   exist upon the lands of individuals are of small comparative importance, by far the larger part being upon unclaimed public lands. Still our information respecting them is yet extremely limited; what we know in general is, that they are of great extent and extraordinary productiveness, even though rudely wrought. The gold is found sometimes in masses, the largest of which brought to the mint weighed eighty-nine ounces. They are generally equal to the standard of our coin in purity, and their appearance that of metal forced into the fissures and cavities of the rocks in a state of fusion. Some, however, are flattened, apparently by pressure, and scratched as if by attrition on a rough surface. One small mass which was exhibited had about five parts in weight of gold to one of quartz, intimately blended, and both together bouldered, as to form a handsome rounded pebble, with a surface of about equal parts quartz and gold. A very large proportion of the gold, however, is obtained in small scales by washing the earth, which is dug up in the beds of the streams, or near their margin. A mass of the crude earth, as taken at random from a placer, was tested by the director of the United States mint at Philadelphia, and found to contain 264½ grains of gold, being, in value, a fraction over $10, to 100 lbs. of earth. It cannot, however, be reasonably supposed that the average alluvial earth in the placers is so highly auriferous.

No existing law puts it in the power of the Executive to regulate these mines, or protect them from intrusion. Hence, in addition to our own citizens, thousands of persons, of all nations and languages, flock in and gather gold, which they carry away to enrich themselves, leaving the lands the less in value by what they have abstracted; and they render for it no remuneration, direct or indirect, to the government or people of the United States. Our laws, so strict in the preservation of public property that they punish our own citizens for cutting timber upon the public lands, ought not to permit strangers, who are not and who never intend to become citizens, to enter at pleasure on these lands and take from them the gold which constitutes nearly all their value.

Some legal provision is necessary for the protection and disposition of these mines, and it is a matter worthy of much consideration how they should be disposed of so as best to promote the public interest and encourage individual enterprise. In the division of these lands regard should be had to the convenience of working every part of them containing gold, whether in the alluvion merely or in the fixed rocks. And, that such division may be made in the best manner practicable to promote the general interest and increase the value of the whole, a geological and mineralogical exploration should be connected with the linear surveys, which should be made with the assistance and under the supervision of a skilful engineer of mines.

The mining ordinances of Spain provide a mode of laying out the mines which applies only to districts where veins of ore occur in the rocks, and where it is to be mined by following the metalliferous dike or stratum in the direction of its dip and along its line of strike. But the gold which is found in the alluvion in California is continuous over a great extent of country, and it may be wrought upon any lot having surface earth and access to water. This district may be, therefore, divided into small lots with a narrow front on the margin of the streams, and extending back in the form of a parallelogram. Where gold is found in the rocks *in situ* the lots to embrace it should be larger, and laid off according to the Spanish method with regard to dip and strike. But so various are the conditions under which the precious metals may be found, by a careful geological exploration, that the mode of laying off the ground cannot be safely anticipated, but must be left to the direction, on the spot, of a skilful engineer, whose services will be indispensable.

The division, disposition, and management of these mines will require much detail; but, if placed on a proper footing, they may be made a source of considerable revenue. It is due to the nation at large that this rich deposite of mineral wealth should be made productive, so as to meet, in process of time, the heavy expense incurred in its acquisition. It is also due to those who become the lessees or purchasers of the mines that they should be furnished by the government with such scientific aid and directions as may enable them to conduct their operations, not only to the advantage of the treasury, but also with convenience and profit to themselves. This scientific aid cannot be procured by individuals, as our people have little experience in mining, and there is not in the United States a school of mines, or any in which mining is taught as a separate science.

If the United States sell the mineral lands for cash, and transfer at once all title to the gold which they contain, but a very small part of their value will probably be realized. It would be better, in my opinion, to transfer them by sale or lease, reserving a part of the gold collected as rent or seignorage.

After mature reflection, I am satisfied that a mint at some convenient point will be advantageous to the miner, and the best medium for the collection and transmission of the gold reserved. Gamboa, a Spanish author of much science and practical observation, and at one time president of the Royal Academy of Mexico, strongly recommended the establishment of a mint in their principal mining district, as a means of collecting and transmitting the rents reserved by the crown, and especially to give a legitimate currency to the miners, that they might not be compelled, from necessity, to barter their bullion, in violation of law. The same reasons would apply here with equal force.

When the land is properly divided, it will, in my opinion, be best to dispose of it, whether by lease or sale, so as to create an estate to be held only on condition that the gold collected from the mine shall be delivered into the custody of an officer of the branch mint. Out of the gold so deposited there should be retained, for rent and assay, or coinage, a fixed per cent, such as may be deemed reasonable, and the residue passed to the credit of the miner, and paid to him at his option in coin or stamped bullion, or its value in drafts on the treasury or mint of the United States. The gold in the mine, and after it is gathered until brought into the mint, should be and remain the property of the United States. The barter, sale, gift, or exportation of any portion of it before it shall have been delivered at the mint, and so coined, or assayed and stamped, or its concealment with intent to avoid the payment of rent or seignorage, should involve a forfeiture of the gold itself, and also of the mine. The terms of lease or sale should be favourable to the miner, and the law should be stringent to enforce the payment of seignorage and rents.

So far as the surface deposites extend, I am of opinion that leases will, for yet a further reason, be preferable to sales of the lands. If sold, they will pass at once into the hands of large capitalists; if leased, industrious men without capital may become the proprietors, as they can work the mines and pay the rent out of the proceeds. But where gold is found in the rocks in place the case is different. These must necessarily fall at once into the hands of large capitalists or joint stock companies, as they cannot be wrought without a heavy investment.

Some persons, whose opinions are entitled to much weight, apprehend difficulty in collecting the rents, if the mode of disposition which I suggest be adopted; but this, I think, is without a full consideration of the condition of the country and the means of enforcement. Gold, unless coined or stamped at the mint, could not circulate in California against a legal provision, and subject to a penalty such as is suggested. It could not be carried across the continent without risk of loss or detection, which would make the value of insurance equal to the rent. In any other direction it must pass the ports of California, and be there liable to detection.

Since the discovery of the mines, gold in California has not ranged higher than $16 per ounce; its actual value is a fraction over $18. The difference between its true value and the highest price at which it has sold, or would probably ever sell, except to houses transacting an open, regular, and legal business, is therefore *one ninth*, being more than half the amount that ought to be reserved as rent or seignorage.

If the penalty suggested above should be provided for an attempted evasion, and the ordinary advantages given to the officer or other person who should detect the fraud, as in case of smuggling, it would not be the interest of any one to become a dealer in the prohibited article at a small profit and great risk; nor would the miner risk a sale at a small advance of price, to be obtained at the hazard of a heavy forfeiture. The absolute security of the lawful business, the safety of the fund when deposited in the treasury of the United States, and the small profit and great risk of attempted frauds, would be reasonable security against them.

The property of the United States in the mines of quicksilver, derived from

Spain through Mexico, with the eminent domain, is, as I have shown, the same as that to the gold, already considered. Indeed, the laws of Spain asserted more sternly, and guarded more strictly the rights of the crown to that metal than to gold and silver. This arose from the scarcity of quicksilver, it being found in sufficient quantities to be worth mining in but few known places on the globe; while its necessary use, in separating silver from its matrix, makes it an essential ingredient in silver mining operations.

The deposite of quicksilver, known to exist in California, is a sulphuret of mercury, or native cinnabar. The stratum of mineral, several feet in thickness, has been traced for a considerable distance along its line of strike. The specimens assayed at the mint range from 15.5 to 33.35 per cent. of metal; it is easy of access, and is mined and reduced without difficulty. So much of the mine as has been traced is situated on a ranch, to which the title is probably valid; and since the United States took possession of the country an attempt has been made to acquire title to the mine by *denouncement.* This proceeding is, for the reasons that I have already given, invalid. It, therefore, remains for Congress to determine whether they will relinquish or assert the title of the United States in this mine.

ROAD TO THE PACIFIC.

The population of California, already considerable in numbers, is rapidly increasing by immigration. Adventurers, attracted there in search of gold, are gradually forming a fixed population, and must, in the nature of things, soon draw after and connect with them the ordinary accompaniments of social life. Its mining will become a regular branch of productive industry, employing many hands and much machinery, and affording the necessary encouragement on the spot to the building up of work shops and the exercise of the mechanic arts. It has already a considerable commerce, which is constantly increasing, and must soon become extensive, not only with our own country and Europe, but with China and the Pacific Islands, including Japan, whose ports it is believed will be opened to the admission of its gold. This concurrence of favourable elements among which should be included the agricultural and manufacturing capacities of Oregon, will cause to spring up, with a rapidity heretofore unexampled, large and prosperous communities on our Pacific coast.

Some means of communication across the continent, through our own territory, from the Atlantic to the Pacific, a road which can be passed over with reasonable speed and safety, is necessary to meet the wants of our citizens on either coast, and is equally necessary to aid the government in controlling the Indian tribes of the intermediate country, and in protecting from their depredations our two lines of frontier settlements, which will now gradually approach each other. Opinion, as expressed and elicited by two large and respectable conventions, recently assembled at St. Louis and Memphis, points to a railroad as that which would best meet the wants and satisfy the wishes of our people. But what that road will be, and where and by whom constructed, must depend upon the action of Congress, founded on such information as a careful reconnoissance of the country by a scientific corps may furnish.

INDIAN AFFAIRS.

The wild tribes of Indians, who have their hunting-grounds in the great prairie, through which our emigrants to California pass, have, during the present year, been more than usually pacific. They have suffered our people to pass through their country with little interruption, though they travelled in great numbers, and consumed, on their route, much grass and game. For these the Indians expect compensation, and their claim is just. The prairie is their pasture-field; the buffalo their herds, and if used by us they ought to be paid for. I concur in the recommendation of the commissioner of Indian affairs, that treaties be negotiated with these tribes, stipulating for the right of way through their country, and the use of grass and game, paying them therefor small annuities in useful articles of merchandise, and agricultural implements and instruction. By these means we may gain their good will and have a guarantee for their good conduct, in their dependence upon us, which will soon become habitual, for the annuities, and the fear of their loss, in case of transgression. And by these means, and with the aid of religious and benevolent societies, they may be, perhaps, turned from their roving habits, their thirst for war and bloodshed allayed, and they may be gradually won over to agriculture, and ultimately to civilization.

This is the more important, as the time is at hand when the herds of buffalo, which are now rapidly disappearing, will be insufficient to supply them with subsistence.

A band of the Seminoles, who remained in Florida under the temporary arrangement made with them in 1842, have been since that time in the care of the military. It was proposed to transfer their supervision to this department for the purpose of effecting their peaceable removal, and a sub-agent was appointed to take charge of them. But, before he entered upon the effective discharge of his duties, a marauding party of the band attacked and murdered some of our citizens, and burnt and destroyed their property. It was therefore deemed necessary at once to protect the adjacent settlements by a military force, and the sub-agent thereby becoming unnecessary, his services were dispensed with, and these Indians again placed under the sole supervision of the department of war.

A portion of the Indians in Texas were, in the early part of the season, guilty of an outbreak of a more extensive and serious character. Before they could be checked they ravaged a large extent of country along the Rio Grande, committing a number of murders, taking several women and children captive, and destroying and carrying off a considerable amount of property. The marauders were driven back and chastised by a military force.

I would especially invite attention to the necessity of some arrangement with the state of Texas by which the laws of the United States regulating Indian intercourse may be extended to the tribes within her limits. Until such an arrangement can be made the pacification of this department will be, for many reasons, ineffectual to secure that extensive frontier from depredation, or give the protection stipulated by treaty to the adjacent provinces of Mexico.

It is important that, at as early a period as practicable, a suitable number of agents should be authorized, and the necessary appropriations made by Congress, to enable the department properly and efficiently to manage our Indian affairs in the territories of Oregon, California and New Mexico, and to restrain the Indians of the two latter territories from committing depredations upon the citizens of Mexico.

No special provision having been made with respect to our Indian intercourse in Oregon, three sub-agents were appointed by the late administration last year for the Indians there; from whom, or from the governor, who is ex-officio superintendent of Indian affairs, no reports have yet been received.

In consequence of a like omission to make provision for California and New Mexico, two agents, occupying less important positions, were transferred—one to the vicinity of the Great Salt Lake, in California, and the other to Santa Fe; and three sub-agents in addition were appointed for the Indians at other points in those territories. These agents were instructed to report fully, as early as practicable, in relation to the locality, numbers, character, and habits of the Indians, in order to put it in the power of the department to lay before Congress such information as would enable that body to adopt proper measures in regard to them. In consequence of the great distance and the difficulty of communication, no reports from them have been received, except a brief communication from the agent to the Great Salt Lake, which will accompany the report of the commissioner on Indian affairs.

Most of the tribes permanently located on our western borders, particularly the more southern, continue steadily to advance in civilization, and in all the elements of substantial prosperity. The establishment of manual labour schools, in charge of missionary societies of various religious denominations, is working a great moral and social revolution among several of the tribes; and if the department had the means of extending the benefits of these institutions to those more destitute, who have no funds set apart by the treaty for these purposes, it would no doubt be productive of like happy results. With this view, and in consideration of the great addition to the Indian population, with whom we are brought into contact by the settlement of Oregon, and the accession of California and New Mexico, I would recommend that the annual appropriation for the civilization of the Indians be increased. For a particular detail of our Indian intercourse during the past year, I refer to the accompanying report of the commissioner of Indian affairs, whose suggestions and recommendations I fully approve.

I have the honour to be, very respectfully, your obedient servant,

To the President of the United States. **T. EWING**

REPORT OF THE POSTMASTER GENERAL.

Post Office Department, December 3, 1849.

Sir: The number of post offices in the United States at the close of the year ending June 30th, 1849, was 16,747; there having been 921 established, and 333 discontinued within the year; making an increase within the year of 588.

The number of postmasters appointed within the year ending June 30th, 1849, was 6,333. Of that number—

2,782 were appointed in consequence of resignations.
   183 were appointed in consequence of deaths.
   284 were appointed in consequence of changes of site of office.
2,103 were appointed in consequence of removals.
     11 were appointed in consequence of commissions expired and not renewed.
     26 were appointed in consequence of commissions renewed.
     23 were appointed in consequence of becoming presidential, by income exceeding $1,000.
   921 were appointed in consequence of new offices.

In 1845 important changes were made by law in the postage and mail service of the United States. One of those changes was a large reduction of postage; another, and almost equally important one to the pecuniary condition of this department, consisted in directing all mail service to be let to the lowest bidder, irrespective of the mode of conveyance, and abolishing the previous regulations requiring the new contractor to take the stage stock of his predecessor. This single regulation reduced the contracts of 1845 in New England and New York, the first section let under that law, more than $250,000. Another law of 1845 was that requiring a classification of the railroad service, and fixing the maximum prices of those classes. The effect of these laws greatly diminished the price of mail transportation, and aided in bringing so soon the expenses of the service within the income derived from the reduced postage; so that now, though the amount of service is very greatly enhanced, its expense bears no corresponding proportion. The mail contracts, which are for four years, are made one section in each year; so that the whole service had undergone the process of reduction under the operation of those laws in June, 1848. Therefore, the condition of the department is, as it was expected to be, found most favourable as to its expenses at the close of the year ending June 30th, 1849. The actual cost for each mile the mail was transported in the year preceding June, 1845, was eight cents one mill, and under the operation of the laws of 1845 the cost per mile of the mail transportation in June last was five cents six mills; making a difference of two and a half cents per mile, being more than one-quarter.

The number of mail routes in the United States on the first day of July, 1849, was 4,943, and the number of contractors 4,190. The length of these routes was 167,703 miles.

On those routes the mail was transported 42,547,069 miles at the cost of $2,428,515, which makes the average cost of transporting the mail last year five cents six mills per mile. To this should be added the transportation of the foreign mail by Southampton to Bremen, and the mail from Charleston and Savannah to Havana, and also the transportation of the mail across the isthmus of Panama; all which is done at the expense of this department, to the amount of $255,692.

The extent and cost of this service of the past year, as compared with that of the year preceding, will be seen by the following tabular statement, and by reference to the report of the First Assistant Postmaster General, hereto appended:

Mail Service of 1848 and 1849 compared.

		1848.		1849.	
		Miles.	Cost.	Miles.	Cost.
Length of post routes	-	163,208		167,703	
Annual transportation, mode not specified	- - -	17,774,191	$751,500	18,573,364	$777,415
Ditto	coach -	14,555,188	796,992	15,025,552	736,710
Ditto	steamboat	4,385,800	262,019	4,083,976	278,650
Ditto	railroad	4,327,400	584,192	4,861,177	635,740
Total annual transportation within the U. S.	- -	41,012,579	2,394,703	42,544,069	2,428,515
Route agencies and mail messengers	- - -		54,063		61,513

The gross revenue for the year ending June 30, 1849, amounted to $4,905,176.28, derived from the following sources:

From letter postage, including stamps sold	-	-	-	$3,882,762 62
From newspaper and pamphlet postage -	-	-	-	819,016 20
From fines	-	-	-	43 75
From miscellaneous items	-	-	-	3,254 21
From dead-letter money sold	-	-	-	99 50
				4,705,176 28

From the appropriation made by the 12th section of the act of 3d March, 1847, for mail services to the government   -   -   200,000 00

$4,905,176 28

The expenditures during the year were:

For transportation of mails	- - -	$2,577,407 71
For compensation to postmasters	- -	1,320,921 34
For ship, steamboat, and way letters	- -	36,174 45
For wrapping paper	- - -	23,936 03
For office furniture	- - -	4,219 69
For advertising	- - -	61,813 32
For mail bags	- - -	20,276 38
For blanks	- - -	20,802 71
For mail locks, keys, and stamps	- -	4,586 50
For mail depredations and special agents	-	21,223 00
For clerks for offices (the offices of postmasters)		317,218 36
For miscellaneous payments	- -	70,437 89
For post office laws and regulations	- -	31 75
		$4,479,049 13

Excess of gross revenue for the year   -   -   -   - $426,127 15

The appropriations made under the 12th section of the act of 3d March, 1847, remaining in the treasury undrawn, exclusive of the appropriation for the past year, already noticed, amounted to　-　　-　　265,555 55

$691,682 70

Thus showing the sum of $691,682 70 unexpended of the past year, including the former appropriations granted to this department for the transportation of free matter of the departments.

Estimates for the current year ending June 30, 1850.

The provisions of the laws of 1845 for reducing the cost of mail service having produced their entire effect on all the contracts (as all have now passed under their influence) before the commencement of this year, it was expected that in the further contracts a clear and decided advance of cost would ensue. This expectation was in some measure verified by the letting to contract last spring the northern section, including New England and New York. The aggregate cost for the service was at that letting much increased. The whole cost for service in that section, under the contracts made in 1845, including agencies, was $531,412

The whole cost for service in that section by the contracts of 1849, is　628,393

Making an increase of　-　-　-　-　-　-　96,981

One cause of this is that more service is now contracted for there to be done. Instead of 10,919,174 miles of transportation per year, 11,568,825 miles is performed, being an increase of 649,651 miles per annum. Another cause, and the greatest, perhaps, is owing to the change of mail service from coaches to the many newly finished railroads in that section, which is a much more expensive service. The service, in that section, in carriages or on horseback, which was open to free competition, has now been let at even a more reduced rate than before, and amounts only to about three cents for each mile the mail is transported. On the other hand, in the railroad and steamboat service, where monopoly excludes competition, the expense is increased, and the transportation amounts to nine cents for each mile the mail is carried, even under the law of 1845, fixing a maximum of price to the classes of service.

The expenses of the service of the department for the current year, ending with June next, will, therefore, be increased by the amount of increase in the eastern section, $96,981; also by the cost of new routes in other sections, ordered by Congress, $57,333, and by extensions and improvements, ordered by the department, about $28,083, to which must be added a probable sum of $50,000 for California, and a sum to meet other contingencies of $25,000. These additions to the expenses of the service of the last year will constitute the amount of the current expenses of this year, as thus stated:

Expenditures as last year - - - - -	$4,479,049 13
Additions.—Excess of cost of service in eastern section -	96,981 00
New routes let in other sections - - - -	57,333 00
New service ordered - - - - - -	28,083 00
Expenses for California - - - - -	50,000 00
Expense of mail across Isthmus - - - -	5,692 00
Publishing new edition of Post Office laws - - -	8,000 00
Other miscellaneous items - - - - -	25,000 00

Whole expenditures of the service of the department for current year $4,750,138 13

To meet this expenditure, in addition to the $200,000 appropriated by virtue of the 12th section of the act of 1847, to pay for the franked matter of the department, the entire reliance is on receipts from postage. It becomes necessary to estimate that amount. This cannot with safety be done by taking the income of the past year, and adding thereto the same per cent. of increase *that* year shows on the preceding. The effect from reduction of postage had passed, and the two preceding years showed little more than the regular and natural increase, keeping pace with the growth of the country. The great increase of the last year was unnatural, and owing to temporary causes of disturbance which have passed by. Some more safe basis of estimation must be found.

To exhibit separately the increase in the revenue derived from letter postage and from printed matter, the following comparison is instituted between the past and the preceding year:

	Year ending June 30, 1848.	Year ending June 30, 1849.	Rate of increase.
Letter postage including stamps sold,	$3,350,304	$3,882,762	15 9-10
Newspaper and pamphlet postage, -	767,335	819,016	6 7-10
Aggregate, - - - -	$4,117,639	$4,701,778	14 2-10

It will be observed that the letter postage increased in the past year 15 9-10 per cent., and that the aggregate increase is 14 1-5. The rate of increase upon letters being extraordinary, and much beyond the natural growth of our population and business, and being double that of the previous year, it cannot be expected to continue, especially as the causes to which it is mainly attributable have ceased to operate.

These were the retaliatory postage act of the 27th June, 1848, which was superseded by the postal treaty with Great Britain in February, 1849, and the greater frequency of correspondence induced by the presidential canvass in the fall of 1848. In estimating the revenue for the current year, it will therefore be necessary to assume something like the natural increase of the revenue as the basis of the calculation. To ascertain as nearly as may be what is that natural rate of increase, I take the aggregate revenue from postages, year by year, since the reduction on the 1st July, 1845, and show what has been the annual rates of increase, thus:

Year ending—	Postages on letters, newspapers and pamphlets,	Amount of increase.	Rate of increase.
June 30, 1846, - - -	$3,443,840		
" 1847, - - -	3,832,117	$388,277	11 27-100 per ct.
" 1848, - - -	4,117,639	285,522	7 43-100 "
" 1849, - - -	4,701,778	584,139	14 20-100 "
Average of the 3 years from 1846,			10 96-100 "
Average of 1847 and 1848, -			9 35-100 "

The average of the years 1847 and 1848 appears to be 9 35-100 per cent., and of the three years ending 30th June, 1849, nearly eleven per cent.; but as it has been shown that there were temporary causes operating to increase unnaturally the postages of the year ending 30th June, 1849, it is deemed safest to take 9 per cent. as the rate, omitting the fraction, and the revenue of 1848 as the basis for estimating the revenue for the year ending 30th June, 1850, thus:

Revenue from postages for year ending June 30, 1848 - - -	$4,117,639 00
Add nine per cent. - - - - - - - - -	370,587 00
Revenue for year 1849 by natural increase - - - - -	$4,488,226 00
Add nine per cent. - - - - - - - - -	403,940 00
Probable revenue for year ending June 30, 1850 - - - -	$4,892,166 00
To this add balance on hand June 30, 1849 - - - - -	691,682 70
Appropriation for free matter for departments for year ending June 30, 1850 - - - - - - - - - - -	200,000 00
	$5,783,848 70
Deduct expenditures before stated - - - - - -	4,750,138 13
	$1,033,710 57

This amount will be subject to a still further reduction of about $175,000, payable to Great Britain for the balance of postage collected for the past and current year -   -   -   -   -   -   175,000 00

Leaving a balance on 30th of June, 1850, of   -   -   -   - $858,710 57

RATE OF POSTAGE.

It seems long to have been the received principle in this department that its expenses should be always kept within the income furnished by postage, and all exertions at the improvement and extension of the service are to be limited to and fall within such receipts. The opinion of the community without the department is believed to be, that the general post-office, being for the dissemination of intelligence and advancement of business, is not a proper subject of taxation—that no burden for public service should lean upon it, and that the rate of postage should only be such as will pay the expense of the care, conveyance, and delivery of the matter on which the postage is laid. These views are in no way incompatible, and may both be successfully regarded, provided a reasonable compensation be made to the department for the service it performs by those for whose benefit such service is required.

It must be quite obvious that there can be no practicable method of ascertaining the expense of mail service on each particular letter or paper, as it fluctuates with the cost in each different section of the country; but what is the proper proportion of each class of service may be settled with a good degree of justice, if when ascertained it is to bear its fair proportion, and that only.

The classes of service now required are three: the care, transportation, and delivery—1st, of letters—2d, of newspapers and pamphlets—3d, matter carried without compensation. It is by postage on the two first classes of service that the whole expenses of the department are now sustained.

The whole number of letters charged with postage passing through the mails the past year, reckoned on the postage received, agreeably to a basis heretofore approved, amounted to sixty-two millions. On all these letters the postage collected was $3,882,762; on newspapers and pamphlets, $819,016.

It is well known that the postage on the newspapers and pamphlets, in proportion to their weight and numbers, is in a very great degree less than the letter postage; so that they do not pay their proportion of the expenses of the service. It, therefore, follows that the letter postage pays now, not only for its own cost, but also for what the paper postage falls short of its proportion, and also for all the other operations and services of the department, including the expense of all the matter carried for the public without pay from government. This brings us to inquire what is the extent of this class of service rendered without pay from the employers. First, what is the nature and amount of this franked matter? The heads of the different departments frank all the mail matter sent from their respective departments, and receive free all to them directed. Under the act of 1845, an account was kept by the post-office of the city of Washington, of all such matter *received* by the departments for the year ending June 30, 1846, but no account of the matter *sent* from them. The postage on that received, at the present rate, was $250,383 83, and the amount as then estimated at the treasury on the matter sent would be fully equal, so that the same then amounted to $500,767 66. (Ex. Doc. 64, 2d Ses. 29 Cong.) In 1847 this mode of payment was abolished, and the only provision since for this service rendered to the executive departments, is an appropriation of two hundred thousand dollars per annum. It is always to be recollected that no amount of appropriation, however large, to pay for franked matter, will ever in any degree relieve the letter or paper postage, so long as such postage actually pays the whole expense of the department, whereby such appropriation remains as surplus undrawn from the Treasury.

But the principal part of the franked matter, for which no payment is made to the department, consists in the letters, papers, and documents franked by the members of the senate and house of representatives. The amount of this matter cannot be ascertained with entire accuracy, as much is forwarded of which no account is kept.

By a report from the clerk's office of the house of representatives, it appears that, during the two sessions of the 30th Congress, ending in March last, the extra number of public documents for distribution was 370,350, and their weight was 467,762 pounds. Printed speeches folded for members to frank, 6,584,500, which are estimated at one ounce each, 411,531 pounds; though one-half of this shows the annual amount of this matter from the house of representatives the two past years. This does not include the written correspondence of the members, or the mail matter by them received. No report direct from the senate is received, but by a report from the post-office in this city, it appears that during the year ending June 30th, 1849, the number of free written mail matter sent,

was - - - - - - -	484,210
Received, - - - - -	819,293
Making, - - - - - -	1,308,503
Printed Senate speeches, 397,630 ⎱ - -	568,345
" " documents, 170,715 ⎰	
House documents, - - - -	3,448,250
	5,320,098

The letter postage and pamphlet postage, to which this matter would have been subject, if not franked, is computed by that report at $792,709.

It should be recollected that the post-office department is not only required to mail and transport this matter, after requiring the hire of additional coaches and teams, but is also subject to the actual payment of money contributed entirely by the letter postage in this manner. By law, two cents each is allowed every postmaster for the delivery of a free letter or package, if his income does not exceed $2,000 per annum. The proportion of these free papers, delivered by postmasters of $2,000 income, will not exceed one-tenth. Two cents each on the foregoing number, deducting one-tenth, was $95,161, which is actually paid to postmasters for delivering this free matter, out of money received for letter postage. Thus, it appears that for the delivery of nine-tenths of the millions of printed speeches franked and transported in the mails without compensation, (the printing of which cost about one cent each,) there is paid two cents each, not by the person who sends or by the person who receives it, or by the country as for a public service, but by those who pay postage on their private correspondence.

It rests entirely in the wisdom of Congress to decide whether this franking by its members is a valuable *public service*, proper to continue, and it is not intended to make any remark on that topic. Were it abolished, there would probably be very much less of such matter printed; but the postage on the remainder, together with that on the correspondence of the members, and the relief of the expense of the transportation and delivery of this franked matter, would enable the department to sustain itself, though the postage was materially reduced on letters. But if Congress continue this franking, as a valuable public service, it is but just and proper that the letter correspondence, by a reduction on its postage, be relieved from its support, and that provision be made therefor in the same manner that other branches of public service are sustained.

Another great additional demand of public service by the post-office department without compensation is made this year—that is, the transmission of all the blanks, returns, and correspondence required in taking the census of 1850. Three thousand reams of these blanks are already engaged.

It has been said that the newspaper and pamphlet postage is not in proportion to the cost of their transportation; but it is not, therefore, to be understood that any increase of that postage. is proposed. It has long been regarded as sound public policy to promote the circulation of these publications by cheap postage, and it may be advisable to proceed further in this policy, especially in promoting their circulation in the vicinity of their places of publication, provided no decided injustice be done to the postmasters within that same vicinity.

It would be desirable to have a fixed sum granted from the treasury for this public service, as to free matter, and then the postage so reduced and arranged as to provide for the remainder; but that course is impracticable, as the money from the treasury cannot be drawn until that from postage is first exhausted; and, therefore, the only safe way is to make reductions of postage from time to time, until justice is produced by leaving a balance to be annually drawn from the treasury, equivalent to the public service performed; and no extent of reduction which does not produce this effect is sufficient so long as public service is required to be performed free of postage.

What should be the degree or measure of the reduction of postage at this time, is entirely a question to be settled by Congress, but it is proposed respectfully to submit what would be the probable effect of one measure of reduction.

The most obvious and prominent feature now in our postage is the double price, ten cents, charged on all single letters carried over three hundred miles. The reduction of this ten cent postage, and charging all single letters at five cents each, would much simplify the manner of accounting, and render the same both more facile and perfect, would remove the dissatisfaction arising from the great difference in the postage in different offices, even in the same vicinity, but separated by this arbitrary line, and would promote and encourage the correspondence and intercourse by mail between the most distant parts of the country, which most need and demand it, in precise proportion as their other means of intercommunication are slow and unfrequent.

The next inquiry is, what would be the effect of this reduction on the receipts from postage, and how would it affect the treasury?

It is not possible from any returns or data in the department to ascertain, with much precision, the number of letters passing annually in the mail under this charge of ten cents. Even if the number of ten cent letters were actually known, it would still be impossible to determine how many of them were ten cent letters from being double. Thence arises the great difference in the estimate of loss of revenue from such a reduction as was presented in the report of the postmaster-general last year, to wit, $715,187, and that of the first assistant, $306,738.

From a careful examination now made of the data in the department, it is estimated that the whole number of charged letters sent through the mails the past year was 62,000,000; and of this number, about 15,500,000 were subject to the ten cent postage on account of distance. If then the reduction were to bring no more letters into the mail, the diminution of revenue therefrom the first year would be $775,000. It is already shown that the surplus on the first day of July last was $691,682 70; and that on the first of July next will be $858,710 57; which will undoubtedly increase in future years by natural accumulation and by increase of the number of letters arising from this reduction. It therefore follows that such reduction will, in the first year, occasion no charge on the treasury, and it is extremely uncertain whether its operation can ever produce that effect. A brief trial of this experiment will show its effect, and if it should not produce any important draught on the treasury, then further reductions of postage should be made. Whether any further reduction should be made, and a corresponding provision from the treasury adopted until after this has been tested by experiment, is respectfully submitted. Should the reduction now recommended produce, on experiment, a successful result without heavy charge on the treasury, the next step should probably be a reduction of the five to three cents postage on single letters, *if prepaid.*

RAILROAD SERVICE.

This is a constantly increasing service. In the current year the length of railroad routes is 6,138 miles, being an increase within two years of 1,149 miles; and it is almost daily increasing, as new roads are being completed. On these routes the mail is now transported 5,749,040 miles annually. It is true that this service is done with more despatch than the same amount of service in any other way, yet it is at much greater cost. The law of 1845, requiring this service to be classed, and fixing the maximum compensation, has in some degree reduced the cost. There is one feature of this service which frequently embarrasses the operations of the department. In all the ordinary mail contracts, provision is made that the time of arrival and departure and connexion of the mails is subject to the order of the department. This feature has never been admitted by the railroad proprietors to be inserted in their contracts. It is provided in them that if any change is made without their consent, they may abandon the contract. This often deprives the department of the power to make such changes and improvements in the time of the transportation of the mails as the public convenience requires, and subjects it to censure by those who know not this circumstance.

FOREIGN MAIL SERVICE.

The mail service by the way of Southampton to Bremen has been, under the contract with this department, carried the past year by the steamships Washington and Hermann for the sum of two hundred thousand dollars, and the gross amount realized in postage from that service for the year ending October 4th was $61,114. 20. The gross amount from 1st June, 1847, to October 4th, 1848, was $29,082. 51.

Notice has recently been received from the proprietors that this service will be suspended until February next, in order to make the necessary repairs now required for the safety of these steamships.

The mail from Charleston, via Savannah, to Havana, under the contract with this department, has been carried, since the 18th October, 1848, in the steamer Isabel, with a good degree of regularity, at the cost of $35,086. 22. No other foreign mail is carried by contract with this department.

By a contract with the Navy department, made by direction of law, provision was made for carrying a mail twice in each month between New York and New Orleans, via Charleston, Savannah, and Havana, and also for like transportation between Havana and Chagres. This was entered upon in December, 1848, and has been partially performed. Under a like contract with the navy department, steamships are carrying the mails on the Pacific, between Panama and California, once in each month. By a treaty, the government of New Grenada is bound to transport the mail across the Isthmus. This service, more particularly on the Atlantic and across the Isthmus, has been very imperfectly performed, and the connexions have been very unsuccessful. This the department has not been able entirely to remedy, the contractors not being within its control. Exertions have, however, been continued, and such arrangements have been made and assurances received, as to give a good degree of confidence that, with the co-operation of the navy department, the mails will hereafter receive regular despatch through this entire route of great and increasing importance.

By the present organization of the post-office department, established in 1836, the mail service of the United States is sustained by appropriations entirely from the money derived from postage.

Congress, by the act of March 3, 1847, entitled "An act providing for the building and equipment of four naval steamships," entered on the policy of encouraging the erection by individuals of war steamers, so that, on the emergency of a war, they might be ready for public use. Contracts were ordered and made by the navy department for three lines of war steamers; one from New York via Havana to New Orleans, and from Havana to Chagres, and one from Panama to California and Astoria, and one between New York and Liverpool; all which, requiring thirteen war steamships, were to carry the mail, and to receive, when completed, the sum of $874,000 per annum from the treasury. Whether this policy is to be continued or extended, is entirely a question for Congress; but it seems proper to observe that any change by which this shall be declared *mail service*, and this great additional demand be made a claim on the income from postage, will greatly embarrass and derange the operations of the department. So great is the cost of building and-sustaining these vessels, and so small the postage to be derived therefrom, that it will, if so ordered, defeat the present system of sustaining the mails within this country; put an end to all extension of its accommodations, all reduction of postage, and all improvement of its condition. It is much to be hoped that no proposition so disastrous in its consequences will be entertained. In any course Congress may think proper to pursue in relation to those war steamers, their support, while continued, must be drawn from the treasury, as provided when adopted, and as is now done.

The transportation of the mail across the Isthmus, being in a foreign country, is the proper subject-matter of a treaty, and is not within the power of this department. It is, however, respectfully suggested that this service, now done by the government of New Grenada, is very tardily and carelessly performed, and the compensation under the treaty probably inadequate. Reliable information has been received that they would willingly yield up this service. A new arrangement should immediately be made by treaty, if practicable, permitting this service to be performed by ourselves, but guarantying its protection there, and placing it under the direction of this department. The amount required by the treaty to be paid to New Grenada for carrying that mail, being in no other way provided for by Congress, has been paid by this department up to this time.

No steamship has yet been despatched on the mail service from New York to Liverpool under the contract with the navy department, but is expected soon to be done.

Since the last session of Congress, the postal treaty with Great Britain has been carried into full operation by regulations settled in pursuance of the treaty by this department and the post-office department of that country, which regulations have been promulgated. The leading feature of that arrangement is, that letters on which the postage is wholly prepaid, or on which none is paid, pass through the mails between the two countries, and are despatched and delivered in the same manner as if those countries were one; and an account is kept in each of the postage collected for the other, which is periodically settled. The effect of this is, that, while the sea service is almost entirely performed by the British steamships, the sea postage belonging to them makes the balance in accounting largely against us. The operation of this is no injury, as we actually receive all we pay, but it is stated, in order to explain, that now all this postage goes into the account of postage received in this department, and to swell its apparent amount, when it is subject always to the annual reduction of this balance payable to Great Britain. Whenever our mail steamships shall perform service between New York and Liverpool, which is soon expected, it will tend to correct this balance. The efforts to extend this arrangement through England to France have not been successful.

MAIL SERVICE IN CALIFORNIA.

By the third section of the act of Congress entitled "An act to establish certain post routes, approved August 14, 1848," the postmaster-general was authorized to appoint postmasters at places on the Pacific, in California, and to appoint agents for making arrangements for the establishment of post-offices and conveyance of mails in California and Oregon. Under this act, as early as November, 1848, a postmaster was appointed for San Francisco, and agents were appointed and sent on that business. That postmaster entered on his duties, and for a time attempted their discharge, but finding, as he writes, no sufficient income for the expense of room and assistance, or even for his support, he resigned. No report from those agents has ever been received. In April last another agent was sent, who immediately departed and entered upon his duties; and also another postmaster for San Francisco, who has also arrived there; and from information received from them and others, there is good reason to believe that all reasonable exertions are being made to give to the people there all the mail facilities the limited means legally applicable will afford.

The laws regulating the post-office duties and service are in many respects ill adapted to the circumstances and condition of that country. Many letters have been sent there for persons passing the overland route; and, if the same were to be treated as dead letters at the end of the second quarter after their arrival, they would be sent back before these persons would arrive there. Indeed, the sending as dead letters to the department here those letters mailed from one office to another in California, would be worse than useless. No sufficient pecuniary means are at the command of the department for this service.

The price of labour or personal service, and the rent required for office room, are such that no allowance now authorized by law can secure a post office in California. Nor can the mails be transported within the country for any compensation which the postage received there will furnish. No sufficient returns have been received by which to determine the expense of what has already been done, but it fully appears that provision must be made, much beyond the yield of the postage there, to meet the cost of even a very limited supply of mail accommodation in that country. This subject requires the early attention of Congress, and at the same time provision should be made for extending mails to Oregon and New Mexico.

OPERATIONS WITHIN THE DEPARTMENT.

As our country expands in dimensions, and our settlements extend in area; as our population increases in density, and business in activity, the service of the mail must have a corresponding advancement; and it follows unavoidably that the business and labour within the department are every year rapidly augmenting, demanding from time to time addition of force for their performance. In 1836, the department was re-organized, and by law a much less number of clerks provided for than had theretofore been used. In putting that organization in operation, it was immediately found impracticable to proceed with such reduced force only, and temporary clerks to the number of eight were employed in 1837. These were continued by temporary appropriations until 1842, when by law they became permanent; but no provision has been made for any additional clerks since 1837. Such, in the mean time, has been the progress of the service, and such the increase of business, that the pressure on the clerks has become so great, and delays so unavoidable, as absolutely to require now additional force, or the public service must suffer. The pressure is on all the bureaus of the department. In the contract office, where the care and arrangement of the mail service is extending in daily demand, and where the extent of correspondence is permanently the greatest. In the appointment office, business increases with the increase of the number of offices. In the financial bureau, under the third assistant, the labour is much increased, as to that branch falls the care of the dead letter office, and the receipts and charge of the quarterly returns.

In the last year there were received 2,100,000 dead letters, all of which have been opened and examined. Of these, 4,964, containing money to the amount of $32,067, have been registered, and the same sent out for delivery to the owners, and 998 letters containing other enclosures of value. The inspection office, whose duties include all matters relating to the performance or failure of mail service, all depredations on the mail, and also the supply of mail bags, locks and keys, is a branch increasing in direct ratio with the general service. In this office alone, during the past year, there were received 134,436 communications. The number of supposed depredations reported was 1,226, which were supposed to include $169,107. Twenty-nine depredators were arrested, and the amount of money reclaimed or otherwise accounted for was $77,779.

To show the great increase of service and the consequent demand for the increase of force in the department, the following comparative statement is made:

In 1837 the number of post offices was 11,767, now 17,164—four hundred and seventeen having been established since June last.

No. of dead letters in 1837,	.	900,000, now	.	.	.	. 2,100,000
No. of quarterly returns in 1837,	48,000, now	.	.	.	.	73,000
No. of mail contractors	"	. 1,682, now	.	.	.	. 4,190
Length of routes	"	. 141,242 miles, now	.	.	.	. 167,703
Ann. mail transportation	"	32,597,806 miles, now	.	.	.	42,544,069

The number of communications received at the department annually cannot be less than 370,000.

To perform this service the present force is inadequate, and it has been found absolutely necessary to employ temporary clerk service, compensation for which should be made, and which necessity, it is hoped, will be prevented by some permanent provision for supply, that the public service may not suffer.

AUDITOR.

A most important branch of the post office department is, by the organization of 1836, committed to the auditor; not only that of auditing all claims for service, but more particularly that of keeping the accounts and collecting all moneys derived from postages or otherwise.

The manner in which this has been performed, as appears by his report hereto annexed, is satisfactory evidence as well of the efficiency of the system as of energy and success in its execution.

I have the honour to be, with great respect, your obedient servant.

J. COLLAMER,
Postmaster General.

To THE PRESIDENT OF THE UNITED STATES.

CONSTITUTION OF THE STATE OF CALIFORNIA.

PROCLAMATION TO THE PEOPLE OF CALIFORNIA.

The delegates of the people assembled in convention have formed a constitution, which is now presented for your ratification. The time and manner of voting on this constitution, and of holding the first general election, are clearly set forth in the schedule; the whole subject is therefore left for your unbiassed and deliberate consideration.

The prefect (or person exercising the functions of that office,) of each district, will designate the places for opening the polls, and give due notice of the election, in accordance with the provisions of the constitution and schedule.

The people are now called upon to form a government for themselves, and to designate such officers as they desire to make and execute the laws. That their choice may be wisely made, and that the government so organized may secure the permanent welfare and happiness of the people of the new state, is the sincere and earnest wish of the present executive, who, if the constitution be ratified, will, with pleasure, surrender his powers to whomsoever the people may designate as his successor.

Given at Monterey, California, this 12th day of October, A. D., 1849.

(Signed)   B. RILEY,
Brevet Brig. Gen. U. S. A., and Gov. of California.

(Official)   H. W. HALLECK,
Brevet Captain, and Secretary of State.

CONSTITUTION.

WE, the People of California, grateful to the Almighty God for our freedom, in order to secure its blessings, do establish this Constitution.

ARTICLE I.—DECLARATION OF RIGHTS.

Section 1. All men are by nature free and independent, and have certain inalienable rights, among which are those of enjoying and defending life and liberty, acquiring, possessing and protecting property, and pursuing and obtaining safety and happiness.

2. All political power is inherent in the people. Government is instituted for the protection, security, and benefit of the people; and they have the right to alter or reform the same, whenever the public good may require it.

3. The right of trial by jury shall be secured to all, and remain inviolate for ever; but a jury trial may be waived by the parties, in all civil cases, in the manner to be prescribed by law.

4. The free exercise and enjoyment of religious profession and worship, without discrimination or preference, shall for ever be allowed in this state: and no person shall be rendered incompetent to be a witness on account of his opinions on matters of religious belief; but the liberty of conscience, hereby secured, shall not be so construed as to excuse acts of licentiousness, or justify practices inconsistent with the peace or safety of this state.

5. The privilege of the writ of *habeas corpus* shall not be suspended, unless when, in cases of rebellion or invasion, the public safety may require its suspension.

6. Excessive bail shall not be required, nor excessive fines imposed, nor shall cruel or unusual punishment be inflicted, nor shall witnesses be unreasonably detained.

7. All persons shall be bailable, by sufficient sureties; unless for capital offences, when the proof is evident or the presumption great.

8. No person shall be held to answer for a capital or other infamous crime, (except in cases of impeachment, and in cases of militia, when in actual service, and the land and naval forces in time of war, or which this state may keep with the consent of congress in time of peace, and in cases of petit larceny under the regulation of the legislature,) unless on presentment or indictment of a grand jury, and in any trial in any court whatever, the party accused shall be allowed to appear and defend in person and with counsel, as in civil actions. No person shall be subject to be twice put in jeopardy for the same offence; nor shall he be compelled, in any criminal case, to be a witness against himself, nor be deprived of life, liberty, or property, without due process of law; nor shall private property be taken for public use without just compensation.

9. Every citizen may freely speak, write, and publish his sentiments on all subjects, being responsible for the abuse of that right; and no law shall be passed to restrain or abridge the liberty of speech or of the press. In all criminal prosecutions or indictments for libels, the truth may be given in evidence to the jury; and if it shall appear to the jury that the matter charged as libellous is true, and was published with good motives and for justifiable ends, the party shall be acquitted; and the jury shall have the right to determine the law and the fact.

10. The people shall have the right freely to assemble together, to consult for the common good, to instruct their representatives, and to petition the legislature for redress of grievances.

11. All laws of a general nature shall have a uniform operation.

12. The military shall be subordinate to the civil power. No standing army shall be kept up by this state in time of peace; and in time of war no appropriation for a standing army shall be for a longer time than two years.

13. No soldier shall, in time of peace, be quartered in any house, without the consent of the owner; nor in time of war, except in the manner to be prescribed by law.

14. Representation shall be apportioned according to population.

15. No person shall be imprisoned for debt, in any civil action on *mesne* or final process, unless in cases of fraud: and no person shall be imprisoned for a militia fine in time of peace.

16. No bill of attainder, *ex post facto* law, or law impairing the obligation of contracts shall ever be passed.

17. Foreigners who are, or who may hereafter, become *bona fide* residents of this state, shall enjoy the same rights in respect to the possession, enjoyment, and inheritance of property, as native-born citizens.

18. Neither slavery, nor involuntary servitude, unless for the punishment of crimes, shall ever be tolerated in this state.

19. The right of the people to be secure in their persons, houses, papers, and effects, against unreasonable seizures and searches, shall not be violated; and no warrant shall issue but on probable cause, supported by oath or affirmation, particularly describing the place to be searched, and the persons and things to be seized.

20. Treason against the state shall consist only in levying war against it, adhering to its enemies, or giving them aid and comfort. No person shall be convicted of treason, unless on the evidence of two witnesses to the same overt act, or confession in open court.

21. This enumeration of rights shall not be construed to impair or deny others retained by the people.

ARTICLE II.—RIGHT OF SUFFRAGE.

Sec. 1. Every white male citizen of the United States, and every white male citizen of Mexico, who shall have elected to become a citizen of the United States, under the treaty of peace exchanged and ratified at Queretaro, on the 30th day of May, 1848, of the age of twenty-one years, who shall have been a resident of the state six months next preceding the election, and the county or district in which he claims his vote thirty days, shall be entitled to vote at all elections which are now or hereafter may be authorized by law: Provided, that nothing herein contained, shall be construed to prevent the legislature, by a two-thirds concurrent vote, from admitting to the right of suffrage, Indians, or the descendants of Indians, in such special cases as such a proportion of the legislative body may deem just and proper.

2. Electors shall, in all cases except treason, felony, or breach of the peace, be privileged from arrest on the days of the election, during their attendance at such election, going to and returning therefrom.

3. No elector shall be obliged to perform militia duty on the day of election, except in the time of war or public danger.

4. For the purpose of voting, no person shall be deemed to have gained or lost a residence by reason of his presence or absence while employed in the service of the United States; nor while engaged in the navigation of the waters of this state, or of the United States, or of the high seas; nor while a student of any seminary of learning; nor while kept at any almshouse, or other asylum, at public expense; nor while confined in any public prison.

5. No idiot or insane person, or person convicted of any infamous crime, shall be entitled to the privileges of an elector.

6. All elections by the people shall be by ballot.

ARTICLE III.—DISTRIBUTION OF POWERS.

The powers of the government of the State of California shall be divided into three separate departments: the legislative, the executive, and judicial; and no person charged with the exercise of powers properly belonging to one of these departments, shall exercise any functions appertaining to either of the others, except in the cases hereinafter expressly directed or permitted.

ARTICLE IV.—LEGISLATIVE DEPARTMENT.

SEC. 1. The legislative power of this state shall be vested in a senate and assembly, which shall be designated the legislature of the state of California; and the enacting clause of every law shall be as follows: "The people of the State of California, represented in Senate and Assembly, do enact as follows."

2. The sessions of the legislature shall be annual, and shall commence on the first Monday of January, next ensuing the election of its members; unless the governor of the state shall, in the interim, convene the legislature by proclamation.

3. The members of the assembly shall be chosen annually, by the qualified electors of their respective districts, on the Tuesday next after the first Monday in November, unless otherwise ordered by the legislature, and their term of office shall be one year.

4. Senators and members of assembly shall be duly qualified electors in the respective counties and districts which they represent.

5. Senators shall be chosen for the term of two years, at the same time and places as members of assembly; and no person shall be a member of the senate or assembly who has not been a citizen and inhabitant of the state one year, and of the county or district for which he shall be chosen, six months next before his election.

6. The number of senators shall not be less than one-third, nor more than one-half, of that of the members of assembly; and at the first session of the legislature after this constitution takes effect, the senators shall be divided by lot, as equally as may be, into two classes; the seats of the senators of the first class shall be vacated at the expiration of the first year, so that one-half shall be chosen annually.

7. When the number of senators is increased, they shall be apportioned by lot, so as to keep the two classes as nearly equal in number as possible.

8. Each house shall choose its own officers and judge of the qualifications, elections, and returns of its own members.

9. A majority of each house shall constitute a quorum to do business; but a smaller number may adjourn from day to day, and may compel the attendance of absent members, in such manner and under such penalties as each house may provide.

10. Each house shall determine the rules of its own proceedings, and may, with the concurrence of two-thirds of all the members elected, expel a member.

11. Each house shall keep a journal of its own proceedings, and publish the same, and the yeas and nays of the members of either house, on any question, shall, at the desire of any three members present, be entered on the journal.

12. Members of the legislature shall, in all cases except treason, felony, and breach of the peace, be privileged from arrest, and they shall not be subject to any civil process during the session of the legislature, nor for fifteen days next before the commencement and after the termination of each session.

13. When vacancies occur in either house, the governor, or the person exercising the functions of the governor, shall issue writs of election to fill such vacancies.

14. The doors of each house shall be open, except on such occasions as, in the opinion of the house, may require secrecy.

15. Neither house shall, without the consent of the other, adjourn for more than three days, nor to any other place than that in which they may be sitting.

16 Any bill may originate in either house of the legislature, and all bills passed by one house may be amended in the other.

17. Every bill which may have passed the legislature, shall, before it becomes a law, be presented to the governor. If he approves it, he shall sign it; but if not, he shall return it, with his objections, to the house in which it originated, which shall enter the same upon the journal and proceed to reconsider it. If, after such reconsideration, it again pass both houses, by yeas and nays, by a majority of two-thirds of the members of each house present, it shall become a law, notwithstanding the governor's objections. If any bill shall not be returned within ten days after it shall have been presented to him, (Sunday excepted,) the same shall be a law, in like manner as if he had signed it, unless the legislature by adjournment prevent such return.

18. The assembly shall have the sole power of impeachment; and all impeachments shall be tried by the senate. When sitting for that purpose, the senators shall be upon oath or affirmation; and no person shall be convicted without the concurrence of two-thirds of the members present.

19. The Governor, Lieutenant-Governor, Secretary of State, Comptroller, Treasurer, Attorney-General, Surveyor-General, Justices of the Supreme Court, and Judges of District Courts, shall be liable to impeachment for any misdemeanor in office; but judgment in such cases shall extend only to removal from office, and disqualification to hold any office of honour, trust or profit, under the state: but the party convicted, or acquitted, shall nevertheless be liable to indictment, trial and punishment, according to law. All other civil officers shall be tried, for misdemeanors in office, in such manner as the legislature may provide.

20. No senator, or member of assembly, shall, during the term for which he shall have been elected, be appointed to any civil office of profit, under this state, which shall have been created, or the emoluments of which shall have been increased during such term, except such office as may be filled by elections by the people.

21. No person holding any lucrative office under the United States, or any other power, shall be eligible to any civil office of profit, under this state: Provided, that officers in the militia, to which there is attached no annual salary, or local officers and postmasters, whose compensation does not exceed five hundred dollars per annum, shall not be deemed lucrative.

22. No person who shall be convicted of the embezzlement or defalcation of the public funds of this state, shall ever be eligible to any office of honour, trust or profit, under this state: and the legislature shall, as soon as practicable, pass a law providing for the punishment of such embezzlement, or defalcation, as a felony.

23. No money shall be drawn from the treasury but in consequence of appropriations made by law. An actual statement of the receipts and expenditures of the public moneys, shall be attached to, and published with the laws at every regular session of the legislature.

24. The members of the legislature shall receive for their services, a compensation to be fixed by law, and paid out of the public treasury; but no increase of the compensation shall take effect during the term for which the members of either house shall have been elected.

25. Every law enacted by the legislature shall embrace but one object, and that shall be expressed in the title: and no law shall be revised, or amended, by reference to its title; but in such case, the act revised, or section amended, shall be re-enacted and published at length.

26. No divorce shall be granted by the legislature.

27. No lottery shall be authorized by this state, nor shall the sale of lottery tickets be allowed.

28. The enumeration of the inhabitants of this state shall be taken, under the direction of the legislature, in the year one thousand eight hundred and fifty-two, and one thousand eight hundred and fifty-five, and at the end of

every ten years thereafter; and these enumerations, together with the census that may be taken, under the direction of the Congress of the United States, in the year one thousand eight hundred and fifty, and every subsequent ten years, shall serve as the basis of representation in both houses of the legislature.

29. The number of senators and members of assembly shall, at the first session of the legislature, holden after the enumerations herein provided for are made, be fixed by the legislature, and apportioned among the several counties and districts to be established by law, according to the number of white inhabitants. The number of members of assembly shall not be less than twenty-four, nor more than thirty-six, until the number of inhabitants within this state shall amount to one hundred thousand; and after that period, at such ratio that the whole number of members of assembly shall never be less than thirty, nor more than eighty.

30. When a congressional, senatorial, or assembly district shall be composed of two or more counties, it shall not be separated by any county belonging to another district; and no county shall be divided, in forming a congressional, senatorial, or assembly district.

31. Corporations may be formed under general laws, but shall not be created by special act, except for municipal purposes. All general laws and special acts passed pursuant to this section may be altered from time to time, or repealed.

32. Dues from corporations shall be secured by such individual liability of the corporators, and other means, as may be prescribed by law.

33. The term corporations, as used in this article, shall be construed to include all associations and joint stock companies, having any of the powers or privileges of corporations not possessed by individuals or partnerships. And all corporations shall have the right to sue, and shall be subject to be sued, in all courts, in like cases as natural persons.

34. The legislature shall have no power to pass any act granting any charter for banking purposes; but associations may be formed under general laws, for the deposite of gold and silver; but no such association shall make, issue, or put in circulation, any bill, check, ticket, promissory note, or other paper or the paper of any bank to circulate as money.

35. The legislature of this state shall prohibit, by law, any person or persons, associations, company, or corporation, from exercising the privileges of banking, or creating paper to circulate as money.

36. Each stockholder of a corporation or joint stock association, shall be individually and personally liable for his proportion of all its debts and liabilities.

37. It shall be the duty of the legislature to provide for the organization of cities and incorporated villages, and to restrict their power of taxation, assessment, borrowing money, contracting debts, and loaning their credit, so as to prevent abuses in assessments, and in contracting debts by such municipal corporations.

38. In all elections by the legislature, the members thereof shall vote *viva voce*, and the votes shall be entered on the journal.

ARTICLE V.—EXECUTIVE DEPARTMENT.

SEC. 1. The supreme executive power of this state shall be vested in a chief magistrate, who shall be styled the Governor of the State of California.

2. The governor shall be elected by the qualified electors, at the time and places of voting for members of assembly, and shall hold his office two years from the time of his installation, and until his successor shall be qualified.

3. No person shall be eligible to the office of governor, (except at the first election,) who has not been a citizen of the United States and a resident of

this state two years next preceding the election, and attained the age of twenty-five years at the time of said election.

4. The returns of every election for governor shall be sealed up and transmitted to the seat of government, directed to the speaker of the assembly, who shall, during the first week of the session, open and publish them in presence of both houses of the legislature. The person having the highest number of votes shall be governor: but in case any two or more have an equal and the highest number of votes, the legislature shall, by joint vote of both houses, choose one of said persons, so having an equal and the highest number of votes, for governor.

5. The governor shall be commander-in-chief of the militia, the army, and navy of this state.

6. He shall transact all executive business with the officers of government, civil and military, and may require information in writing from the officers of the executive department, upon any subject relating to the duties of their respective offices.

7. He shall see that the laws are faithfully executed.

8. When any office shall, from any cause, become vacant, and no mode is provided by the constitution and laws for filling such vacancy, the governor shall have power to fill such vacancy by granting a commission, which shall expire at the end of the next session of the legislature, or at the next election by the people.

9. He may, on extraordinary occasions, convene the legislature by proclamation, and shall state to both houses, when assembled, the purpose for which they shall have been convened.

10. He shall communicate, by message, to the legislature at every session, the condition of the state, and recommend such matters as he shall deem expedient.

11. In case of a disagreement between the two houses, with respect to the time of adjournment, the governor shall have power to adjourn the legislature to such time as he may think proper; provided it be not beyond the time fixed for the meeting of the next legislature.

12. No person shall, while holding any office under the United States, or this state, exercise the office of governor, except as hereinafter expressly provided.

13. The governor shall have the power to grant reprieves, and pardons after conviction, for all offences except treason, and cases of impeachment, upon such conditions, and with such restrictions and limitations, as he may think proper, subject to such regulations as may be provided by law relative to the manner of applying for pardons. Upon conviction for treason, he shall have the power to suspend the execution of the sentence until the case shall be reported to the legislature at its next meeting, when the legislature shall either pardon, direct the execution of the sentence, or grant a further reprieve. He shall communicate to the legislature, at the beginning of every session, every case of reprieve, or pardon granted, stating the name of the convict, the crime of which he was convicted, the sentence and its date, and the date of the pardon or reprieve.

14. There shall be a seal of this state, which shall be kept by the governor, and used by him officially, and shall be called "The great Seal of the State of California."

15. All grants and commissions shall be in the name and by the authority of the people of the state of California, sealed with the great seal of the state, signed by the governor, and countersigned by the secretary of state.

16 A lieutenant-governor shall be elected at the same time and place, and in the same manner as the governor; and his term of office, and his qualifications of eligibility shall also be the same. He shall be president of the senate, but shall only have the casting vote therein. If, during a vacancy of

the office of governor, the lieutenant governor shall be impeached, displaced, resign, die, or become incapable of performing the duties of his office, or be absent from the state, the president of the senate shall act as governor, until the vacancy be filled, or the disability shall cease.

17. In case of the impeachment of the governor, or his removal from office, death, inability to discharge the powers and duties of the said office, resignation, or absence from the state, the powers and duties of the office shall devolve upon the lieutenant governor for the residue of the term, or until the disability shall cease. But when the governor shall, with the consent of the legislature, be out of the state in time of war, at the head of any military force thereof, he shall continue commander-in-chief of all the military force of the state.

18. A secretary of state, a comptroller, a treasurer, an attorney-general, and surveyor-general, shall be chosen in the manner provided in this constitution; and the term of office, and eligibility of each, shall be the same as are prescribed for the governor and lieutenant-governor.

19. The secretary of state shall be appointed by the governor, by and with the advice and consent of the senate. He shall keep a fair record of the official acts of the legislative and executive departments of the government; and shall, when required, lay the same, and all matters relative thereto, before either branch of the legislature; and shall perform such other duties as shall be assigned him by law.

20. The comptroller, treasurer, attorney-general, and surveyor-general shall be chosen by joint vote of the two houses of the legislature, at their first session under the constitution, and thereafter shall be elected at the same time and place, and in the same manner as the governor and lieutenant-governor.

21. The governor, lieutenant-governor, secretary of state, comptroller, treasurer, attorney-general, and surveyor-general, shall each, at stated times during their continuance in office, receive for their services a compensation which shall not be increased or diminished during the term for which they shall have been elected; but neither of these officers shall receive for his own use any fees for the performance of his official duties.

ARTICLE VI.—JUDICIAL DEPARTMENT.

1. The judicial power of this State shall be vested in a Supreme Court, District Courts, in County Courts, and in Justices of the Peace. The legislature may also establish such municipal and other inferior courts as may be deemed necessary.

2. The Supreme Court shall consist of a Chief Justice and two Associate Justices, any two of whom shall constitute a quorum.

3. The Justices of the Supreme Court shall be elected at the general election, by the qualified electors of the State, and shall hold their office for the term of six years from the first day of January next after their election; provided that the legislature shall, at its first meeting, elect a Chief Justice and two Associate Justices of the Supreme Court, by joint vote of both houses, and so classify them that one shall go out of office every two years. After the first election the senior justice in commission shall be the chief justice.

4. The supreme court shall have appellate jurisdiction in all the cases when the matter in dispute exceeds two hundred dollars, when the legality of any tax, toll, or impost or municipal fine is in question: and in all criminal cases amounting to felony or questions of law alone. And the said court, and each of the justices thereof, as well as all district and county judges, shall have power to issue writs of habeas corpus at the instance of any person held in actual custody. They shall also have power to issue all other writs and process necessary to the exercise of their appellate jurisdiction, and shall be conservators of peace throughout the state.

5. The state shall be divided by the first legislature into a convenient number of districts subject to such alteration from time to time as the public good may require; for each of which a district judge shall be appointed by the joint vote of the legislature, at its first meeting, who shall hold his office for two years from the first day of January next after his election; after which, said judges shall be elected by the qualified electors of their respective districts, at the general election, and shall hold their office for the term of six years.

6. The district courts shall have original jurisdiction, in law and equity, in all civil cases where the amount in dispute exceeds two hundred dollars, exclusive of interest. In all criminal cases not otherwise provided for, and in all issues of fact joined in the probate courts, their jurisdiction shall be unlimited.

7. The legislature shall provide for the election, by the people, of a clerk of the supreme court, and county clerks, district attorneys, sheriffs, coroners, and other necessary officers; and shall fix by law their duties and compensation. County clerks shall be, *ex officio*, clerks of the district courts in and for their respective counties.

8. There shall be elected in each of the organized counties of this state, one county judge, who shall hold his office for four years. He shall hold the county court, and perform the duties of surrogate, or probate judge. The county judge, with two justices of the peace, to be designated according to law, shall hold courts of sessions, with such criminal jurisdiction as the legislature shall prescribe, and he shall perform such other duties as shall be required by law.

9. The county courts shall have jurisdiction, in cases arising in justices' courts, and in special cases, as the legislature may prescribe, but shall have no original civil jurisdiction, except in such special cases.

10. The times and places of holding the terms of the supreme court, and the general and special terms of the district courts, within the several districts, shall be provided for by law.

11. No judicial officer, except a justice of the peace, shall receive to his own use, any fees or perquisites of office.

12. The legislature shall provide for the speedy publication of all statute laws, and of such judicial decisions as it may deem expedient; and all laws and judicial decisions shall be free for publication by any person.

13. Tribunals for conciliation may be established, with such powers and duties as may be prescribed by law; but such tribunals shall have no power to render judgment to be obligatory on the parties, except they voluntarily submit their matters in difference, and agree to abide the judgment, or assent thereto in the presence of such tribunal, in such cases as shall be prescribed by law.

14. The legislature shall determine the number of justices of the peace, to be elected in each county, city, and town, and incorporated village of the state, and fix by law their powers, duties and responsibilities. It shall also determine in what cases appeals may be made from justices' courts to the county courts.

15. The justices of the supreme court, and judges of the district court, shall severally, at stated times during their continuance in office, receive for their services a compensation, to be paid out of the treasury, which shall not be increased or diminished during the term for which they shall have been elected. The county judges shall also severally, at stated times, receive for their services a compensation to be paid out of the county treasury of their respective counties, which shall not be increased or diminished during the term for which they shall have been elected.

16. The justices of the supreme court and district judges shall be ineli-

gible to any other office, during the term for which they shall have been elected.

17. Judges shall not charge juries with respect to matters of fact, but may state the testimony and declare the law.

18. The style of all process shall be "The People of the State of California;" all the prosecutions shall be conducted in the name and by the authority of the same.

ARTICLE VII.—MILITIA.

SEC. 1. The Legislature shall provide by law, for organizing and disciplining the militia, in such manner as they shall deem expedient, not incompatible with the Constitution and laws of the United States.

2. Officers of the militia shall be elected, or appointed, in such manner as the legislature shall from time to time direct; and shall be commissioned by the governor.

3. The governor shall have power to call forth the militia, to execute the laws of the state, to suppress insurrections, and repel invasions.

ARTICLE VIII.—STATE DEBTS.

The legislature shall not in any manner create any debt or debts, liability or liabilities, which shall singly, or in the aggregate, with any previous debts or liabilities, exceed the sum of three thousand dollars, except in case of war, to repel invasion or suppress insurrection, unless the same shall be authorized by some law for some single object or work, to be distinctly specified therein, which law shall provide ways and means, exclusive of loans, for the payment of the interest of such debt or liability, as it falls due, and also pay and discharge the principal of such debt or liability within twenty years from the time of the contracting thereof, and shall be irrepealable until the principal and interest thereon shall be paid and discharged; but no such law shall take effect until, at a general election, it shall have been submitted to the people, and have received a majority of all the votes cast for and against it at such election; and all money raised by authority of such law, shall be applied only to the specific object therein stated, or to the payment of the debt thereby created; and such law shall be published in at least one newspaper in each judicial district, if one be published therein, throughout the state, for three months next preceding the election at which it is submitted to the people.

ARTICLE IX.—EDUCATION.

SEC. 1. The legislature shall provide for the election, by the people, of a superintendent of public instruction who shall hold his office for three years, and whose duties shall be prescribed by law, and who shall receive such compensation as the legislature may direct.

2. The legislature shall encourage, by all suitable means, the promotion of intellectual, scientific, moral and agricultural improvements. The proceeds of all land that may be granted by the United States to this State for the support of schools, which may be sold or disposed of, and the five hundred thousand acres of land granted to the new states, under an act of congress distributing the proceeds of the public lands among the several states of the Union, approved A. D. 1841; and all estates of deceased persons who may have died without leaving a will or heir, and also such per cent. as may be granted by Congress on the sale of lands in this state, shall be and remain a perpetual fund, the interest of which, together with all the rents of the unsold lands, and such other means as the legislature may provide, shall be inviolably appropriated to the support of common schools throughout the state.

3. The legislature shall provide for a system of common schools, by which a school shall be kept up and supported in each district at least three months

in every year: and any school district neglecting to keep up and support such a school, may be deprived of its proportion of the interest of the public fund during such neglect.

4. The legislature shall take measures for the protection, improvement, or other disposition of such lands as have been, or may hereafter be reserved or granted by the United States, or any person or persons to this state for the use of a university; and the funds accruing from the rents or sale of such lands, or from any other source for the purpose aforesaid, shall be and remain a permanent fund, the interest of which shall be applied to the support of said university, with such branches as the public convenience may demand, for the promotion of literature, the arts and sciences, as may be authorized by the terms of such grant. And it shall be the duty of the legislature as soon as may be, to provide effectual means for the improvement and permanent security of the funds of said university.

ARTICLE X.—MODE OF AMENDING AND REVISING THE CONSTITUTION.

SECTION 1. Any amendment, or amendments to this constitution, may be proposed in the senate or assembly; and if the same shall be agreed to by a majority of the members elected to each of the two houses, such proposed amendment, or amendments, shall be entered on their journals, with the yeas and nays taken thereon, and referred to the legislature then next to be chosen, and shall be published for three months next preceding the time of making such choice. And if, in the legislature next chosen as aforesaid, such proposed amendment or amendments shall be agreed to by a majority of all the members elected to each house, then it shall be the duty of the legislature to submit such proposed amendment or amendments to the people, in such manner, and at such time as the legislature shall prescribe; and if the people shall approve and ratify such amendment or amendments, by a majority of the electors qualified to vote for members of the legislature voting thereon, such amendment or amendments shall become part of the constitution.

2. And if, at any time, two-thirds of the senate and assembly shall think it necessary to revise and change this entire constitution, they shall recommend to the electors, at the next election for members of the legislature, to vote for or against the convention, if it shall appear that a majority of the electors voting at such election have voted in favour of calling a convention, the legislature shall, at its next session, provide by law for calling a convention, to be holden within six months after the passage of such law; and such convention shall consist of a number of members not less than that of both branches of the legislature.

ARTICLE XI.—MISCELLANEOUS PROVISIONS.

SEC. 1. The first session of the legislature shall be held at Pueblo de San Jose; which place shall be the permanent seat of government; until removed by law: Provided, however, that two-thirds of all the members elected to each house of the legislature shall concur in the passage of each law.

2. Any citizen of this state who shall, after the adoption of this constitution, fight a duel with deadly weapons, either within this state or out of it; or who shall act as second, or knowingly aid and assist in any manner those thus offending, shall not be allowed to hold any office of profit, or enjoy the right of suffrage under this constitution.

3. Members of the legislature, and all officers, executive and judicial, except such inferior officers as may be by law exempted, shall before they enter on the duties of their respective offices, take and subscribe the following oath or affirmation;

"I do solemnly swear (or affirm, as the case may be) that I will support the constitution of the United States and the constitution of the state of

California; and that I will faithfully discharge the duties of the office—according to the best of my ability." And no other oath, declaration, or test, shall be required as a qualification for any office or public trust.

4. The legislature shall establish a system of county and town governments, which shall be as nearly uniform as practicable throughout the state.

5. The legislature shall have power to provide for the election of a board of supervisors in each county; and these supervisors shall, jointly and individually, perform such duties as may be prescribed by law.

6. All officers whose election or appointment is not provided for by this constitution, and all officers whose offices may hereafter be created by law, shall be elected by the people or appointed, as the legislature may direct.

7. When the duration of any office is not provided for by this constitution it may be declared by law; and if not so declared, such office shall be held during the pleasure of the authority making the appointment; nor shall the duration of any office, not fixed by this constitution, ever exceed four years.

8. The fiscal year shall commence on the first day of July.

9. Each county, town, city, and incorporated village, shall make provision for the support of its own officers, subject to such restrictions and regulations as the legislature may prescribe.

10. The credit of the state shall not in any manner be given or loaned to, or in aid of any individual, association, or corporation; nor shall the state, directly or indirectly, become a stockholder in any association or corporation.

11. Suits may be brought against the state in such manner, and in such courts, as shall be directed by law.

12. No contract of marriage, if otherwise duly made, shall be invalidated, for want of conformity to the requirements of any religious sect.

13. Taxation shall be equal and uniform throughout the state. All property in this state shall be taxed in proportion to its value, to be ascertained as directed by law; but assessors and collectors of town, county, and state taxes, shall be elected by the qualified electors of the district, county, or town, in which the property taxed for state, county, or town purposes is situated.

14. All property, both real and personal, of the wife, owned or claimed, by her before her marriage, and that acquired afterward by gift, devise, or descent, shall be her separate property; and laws shall be passed more clearly defining the rights of the wife, in relation as well to her separate property, as to that held in common with her husband. Laws shall also be passed providing for the registration of the wife's separate property.

15. The legislature shall protect by law, from forced sale, a certain portion of the homestead and other property of all heads of families.

16. No perpetuities shall be allowed, except for eleemosynary purposes.

17. Every person shall be disqualified from holding any office of profit in this state, who shall have been convicted of having given, or offered a bribe, to procure his election or appointment.

18. Laws shall be made, to exclude from office, serving on juries, and from the right of suffrage, those who shall hereafter be convicted of bribery, perjury, forgery, or other high crimes. The privilege of free suffrage shall be supported by laws regulating elections, and prohibiting, under adequate penalties, all undue influence thereon, from power, bribery, tumult, or other improper practice.

19. Absence from this state on business of this state or of the United States, shall not affect the question of residence of any person.

20. A plurality of the votes given at any election shall constitute a choice, where not otherwise directed in this constitution.

21. All laws, decrees, regulations, and provisions, which from their nature require publication, shall be published in English and Spanish.

ARTICLE XII.—BOUNDARY.

The boundary of the state of California shall be as follows:

Commencing at the point of intersection of the 42d degree of north latitude with the 120th degree of longitude west from Greenwich, and running south on the line of said 120th degree of west longitude, until it intersects the 39th degree of north latitude, thence running in a straight line in a south-easterly direction to the river Colorado, at a point where it intersects the 35th degree of north latitude, thence down the middle of the channel of said river, to the boundary line between the United States and Mexico, as established by the treaty of May 30th, 1848; thence running west and along said boundary line to the Pacific Ocean, and extending therein three English miles; thence running in a north-westerly direction, and following the direction of the Pacific coast to the 42d degree of north latitude, thence on the line of the 42d degree of north latitude to the place of beginning. Also all the islands, harbours and bays, along and adjacent to the Pacific coast.

SCHEDULE.

Sec. 1. All rights, prosecutions, claims and contracts, as well of individuals as of bodies corporate, and all laws in force at the time of the adoption of this constitution, and not inconsistent therewith, until altered or repealed by the legislature, shall continue, as if the same had not been adopted.

2. The legislature shall provide for the removal of all causes which may be pending when this constitution goes into effect, to courts created by the same.

3. In order that no inconvenience may result to the public service, from the taking effect of this constitution, no officer shall be superseded thereby, nor the laws relative to the duties of the several officers be changed until the entering into office of the new officers to be appointed under this constitution.

4. The provisions of this constitution concerning the term of residence necessary to enable persons to hold certain offices therein mentioned, shall not be held to apply to officers chosen by the people at the first election, or by the legislature at its first session.

5. Every citizen of California, declared a legal voter by this constitution, and every citizen of the United States, a resident of this state on the day of election, shall be entitled to vote at the first general election under this constitution, and on the question of the adoption thereof.

6. This constitution shall be submitted to the people, for their ratification or rejection, at the general election to be held on Tuesday, the thirteenth day of November next. The executive of the existing government of California is hereby requested to issue a proclamation to the people, directing the prefects of the several districts, or in case of vacancy, the sub-prefect, or senior judge of first instance, to cause such election to be held, on the day aforesaid, in their respective districts. The election shall be conducted in the manner which was prescribed for the election of delegates to this convention, except that the prefect, sub-prefect, or senior judge of first instance ordering such election in each district, shall have power to designate any additional number of places for opening the polls, and that in every place of holding the election, a regular poll-list shall be kept by the judges and inspectors of election. It shall also be the duty of these judges and inspectors of election, on the day aforesaid, to receive the votes of the electors qualified to vote at such election. Each voter shall express his opinion, by depositing in the ballot-box a ticket, whereon shall be written or printed, "For the constitution," or "Against the constitution," or some such words as

will distinctly convey the intention of the voter. These judges and inspectors shall also receive the votes for the several officers to be voted for at the said election as herein provided. At the close of the election, the judges and inspectors shall carefully count each ballot, and forthwith make duplicate returns thereof to the prefect, sub-prefect, or senior judge of the first instance, as the case may be, of their respective districts; and said prefect, sub-prefect, or senior judge of first instance, shall transmit one of the same, by the most safe and rapid conveyance, to the secretary of state. Upon the receipt of said returns, or on the tenth day of December next, if the returns be not sooner received, it shall be the duty of a board of canvassers, to consist of the secretary of state, one of the judges of the superior court, the prefect, judge of first instance, and an alcalde of the district of Monterey, or any three of the aforementioned officers, in the presence of all who shall choose to attend, to compare the votes given at said election, and to immediately publish an abstract of the same in one or more of the newspapers of California. And the executive will also immediately after ascertaining that the constitution has been ratified by the people, make proclamation of the fact; and thenceforth this constitution shall be ordained and established as the constitution of California.

7. If this constitution shall be ratified by the people of California, the executive of the existing government is hereby requested, immediately after the same shall be ascertained, in the manner herein directed, to cause a fair copy thereof to be forwarded to the president of the United States, in order that he may lay it before the congress of the United States.

8. At the general election aforesaid, viz.: the thirteenth day of November next, there shall be elected a governor, lieutenant-governor, members of the legislature, and also two members of congress.

9. If this constitution shall be ratified by the people of California, the legislature shall assemble at the seat of government, on the fifteenth day of December next, and in order to complete the organization of that body, the senate shall elect a president *pro tempore*, until the lieutenant-governor shall be installed into office.

10. On the organization of the legislature, it shall be the duty of the secretary of state to lay before each house a copy of the abstract made by the board of canvassers, and if called for, the original returns of election; in order that each house may judge of the correctness of the report of said board of canvassers.

11. The legislature, at its first session, shall elect such officers as may be ordered by this constitution to be elected by that body, and within four days after its organization, proceed to elect two senators to the congress of the United States. But no law passed by this legislature shall take effect until signed by the governor after his installation into office.

12. The senators and representatives to the congress of the United States, elected by the legislature and people of California, as herein directed, shall be furnished with certified copies of this constitution, when ratified, which they shall lay before the congress of the United States, requesting in the name of the people of California, the admission of the state of California into the American Union.

13. All officers of this state, other than members of the legislature, shall be installed into office on the fifteenth day of December next, or as soon thereafter as practicable.

14. Until the legislature shall divide the state into counties, and senatorial and assembly districts, as directed by this constitution, the following shall be the apportionment of the two houses of the legislature, viz.: the districts of San Diego and Los Angelos, shall jointly elect two senators; the districts of Santa Barbara and San Luis Obispo, shall jointly elect one senator; the

district of Monterey, one senator; the district of San Jose, one senator; the district of San Francisco, two senators; the district of Sonoma, one senator; the district of Sacramento, four senators; and the district of San Joaquin, four senators: and the district of San Diego shall elect one member of assembly; the district of Los Angelos, two members of assembly; the district of Santa Barbara, two members of assembly; the district of San Luis Obispo, one member of assembly; the district of Monterey, two members of assembly; the district of San Jose, three members of assembly; the district of San Francisco, five members of assembly; the district of Sonoma, two members of assembly; the district of Sacramento, nine members of assembly; and the district of San Joaquin, nine members of assembly.

15. Until the legislature shall otherwise direct, in accordance with the provisions of this constitution, the salary of the governor shall be ten thousand dollars per annum; and the salary of a lieutenant governor shall be double the pay of a state senator; and the pay of members of the legislature shall be sixteen dollars per diem, while in attendance, and sixteen dollars for every twenty miles' travel by the usual route from their residences to the place of holding the session of the legislature, and in returning therefrom. And the legislature shall fix the salaries of all officers, other than those elected by the people, at the first election.

16. The limitation of the powers of the legislature contained in article 8th of this constitution, shall not extend to the first legislature elected under the same, which is hereby authorized to negotiate for such amount as may be necessary to pay the expenses of the state government.

R. SEMPLE.
President of the Convention and Delegate from Benicia.

Wm. G. Marcy, Secretary.

J. Aram,	C. T. Botts,	E. Brown,
J. A. Carrillo,	J. M. Covarrubias,	E. O. Crosby,
P. De La Guerra,	L. Dent,	M. Dominguez,
K. H. Dimmick,	A. J. Ellis,	S. C. Foster,
E. Gilbert,	W. M. Gwinn,	H. W. Halleck,
Julian Hanks,	L. W. Hastings,	Henry Hill,
J. Hobson,	J. M'H. Hollingsworth,	J. D. Hoppe,
J. M. Jones,	T. O. Larkin,	Francis J. Lippitt,
B. S. Lippincott,	M. M. M'Carver,	John M'Dougal,
B. F. Moore,	Myron Norton,	P. Ord,
Miguel Pedrorena,	A. M. Pico,	R. M. Price,
Hugo Reid,	Jacinto Rodriguez,	Pedro Sansevain,
W. E. Shannon,	W. S. Sherwood,	J. R. Snyder,
A. Stearns,	W. M. Steuart,	J. A. Sutter,
Henry A. Tefft,	S. L. Vermule,	M. G. Vallejo,
J. Walker,	O. M. Wozencraft.	

THE CONSTITUTION OF THE NEW STATE OF DESERET.*

Whereas, A large number of citizens of the United States, before and since the treaty of peace with the Republic of Mexico, emigrated to, and settled in, that portion of the territory of the United States, lying west of the Rocky Mountains, and in the Great Interior Basin of Upper California; and,

Whereas, By reason of said treaty, all civil organization originating from the republic of Mexico became abrogated; and

* The State of Deseret is the name given by the Mormons of the Salt Lake Valley to the country in which they live. The title is of Mormon origin, signifying the "Honey Bee," as typical of industry and its kindred virtues.

Whereas, The Congress of the United States has failed to provide a form of civil government for the territory so acquired, or any portion thereof; and

Whereas, Civil government and laws are necessary for the security, peace, and prosperity of society; and

Whereas, It is a fundamental principle in all republican governments, that all political power is inherent in the people; and governments instituted for their protection, security and benefit, should emanate from the same—

Therefore, Your committee beg leave to recommend the adoption of the following Constitution, until the Congress of the United States shall otherwise provide for the government of the territory hereinafter named and described.

We, the people, grateful to the Supreme Being for the blessings hitherto enjoyed, and feeling our dependence on Him for a continuation of those blessings, do ordain and establish a free and independent government, by the name of the state of Deseret; including all the territory of the United States within the following boundaries, to wit: commencing at the 33d degree of north latitude, where it crosses the 108th degree of longitude, west of Greenwich; thence running south and west to the northern boundary of Mexico; thence west to, and down the main channel of the Gila River, on the northern line of Mexico, and on the northern boundary of Lower California to the Pacific Ocean; thence along the coast north-westerly to 118 deg. 30 min. of west longitude; thence north-to where said line intersects the dividing ridge of the Sierra Nevada mountains; thence north along the summit of the Sierra Nevada mountains to the dividing range of mountains that separate the waters flowing into the Columbia river, from the waters flowing into the Great Basin; thence easterly, along the dividing range of mountains that separate said waters flowing into the Columbia River on the north, from the waters flowing into the Great Basin on the south, to the summit of the Wind River chain of mountains; thence south-east and south, by the dividing range of mountains that separate the waters flowing into the Gulf of Mexico from the waters flowing into the Gulf of California; to the place of beginning, as set forth in a map drawn by Charles Preuss, and published by order of the Senate of the United States, in 1848.

ARTICLE I.

The powers of government of the state of Deseret shall be divided into three distinct departments, viz.:—Legislative, Executive and Judiciary.

ARTICLE II.—OF THE LEGISLATIVE.

Sec. 1. The legislative authority of this state shall be vested in a general assembly, consisting of a senate and house of representatives; both to be elected by the people.

Sec. 2. The session of the general assembly shall be annual; and the first session be held on the first Monday of July next; and, thereafter, on the first Monday of December, unless the governor of the state shall convene the assembly, in the interim, by proclamation.

Sec. 3. The members of the house of representatives shall be chosen biennially, by the qualified electors of their respective districts, on the first Monday in August; whose term of office shall continue two years from the day of the general election.

Sec. 4. No person shall be a member of the house of representatives, who has not attained the age of twenty-five years; the same to be a free white male citizen of the United States, and an inhabitant of this State one year preceding the time of his election, and a resident of the district or county thirty days next preceding his election; and have, at his election, an actual residence in the district he may be chosen to represent.

Sec. 5. Senators shall be chosen for the term of four years, at the same time and place of representatives; they shall be thirty years of age, and possess the qualifications of representatives, as to residence and citizenship.

Sec. 6. The number of senators shall not be less than one-third, nor more than one-half of the representatives; and at the first session of the general assembly, after this constitution takes effect, the senate shall be divided by lot, as equal as may be, into two classes; the seats of the senators of the first class shall be vacated at the expiration of two years, so that one-half of the Senate shall be elected biennially.

Sec. 7. Each house shall choose its own officers, and judge of the qualification, election, and return of its own members, and contested elections shall be determined in such a manner as shall hereafter be determined by law.

Sec. 8. A majority in each house shall constitute a quorum to do business; but a smaller number may adjourn from day to day, and compel the attendance of absent members, in such manner and under such penalty as each house may provide.

Sec. 9. Each house shall have all powers necessary for a branch of the General Assembly of a free and independent government.

Sec. 10. Each member of the assembly shall be privileged from civil arrest during any session, and going to and returning from the same.

Sec. 11. Neither house shall, without the consent of the other, adjourn for more than three days; nor to any other place than that in which they may be sitting.

Sec. 12. The assembly shall, at its first session, provide for an enumeration of the white inhabitants, and an apportionment for the senators and representatives.

Sec. 13. Each member of the assembly shall take an oath or affirmation to support the constitution of the United States, and of this state; and members shall, and are hereby empowered to administer said oath or affirmation to each other.

Sec. 14. The veto power of the governor shall be allowed by the assembly, except on bills, which, when re-considered, shall be again passed by a majority of two-thirds of those present; and any bill vetoed by the governor shall be returned within ten days, (Sundays excepted,) with his objections; otherwise it shall become a law, unless the assembly, by adjournment, prevents its return.

Sec. 15. Every law passed by the assembly shall take effect from and after due publication by authority.

Sec. 16. The voters of this state may elect, at the first election, not exceeding seventeen Senators, and thirty-five Representatives.

ARTICLE III.—OF THE EXECUTIVE.

Sec. 1. The executive power shall be vested in a governor, who shall hold his office for four years. A lieutenant governor shall be elected at the same time, and for the same term, who shall be the president of the senate.

Sec. 2. No person shall be eligible to the office of governor or lieutenant governor, who has not been a citizen of the United States, and a resident of this State, two years next preceding his election, and attained the age of thirty-five years at the time of his election.

Sec. 3. The governor shall be commander-in-chief of the militia, navy, and all the armies of this state.

Sec. 4. He shall transact all executive business with the officers of government, civil and military; and may require information in writing from the officers of the executive department, upon any subject relating to the duties of their respective offices.

Sec. 5. He shall see that the laws are faithfully executed.

Sec. 6. When any office shall, from any cause, become vacant, and no mode is prescribed by the constitution and laws for filling such vacancy, the governor shall have power to fill such vacancy, by granting a commission, which shall expire when such vacancy shall be filled by due course of law.

Sec. 7. He shall also have power to convene the general assembly by proclamation, when, in his opinion, the interests of the state require it.

Sec. 8. He shall communicate by message to the general assembly, at every session, the condition of the state, and recommend such matters as he shall deem expedient.

Sec. 9. In case of disagreement in the general assembly, with regard to the time of adjournment, the governor shall have power to dissolve the session by proclamation.

Sec. 10. No person shall, while holding any lucrative office under the United States, or this State, execute the office of governor, except as shall be prescribed by law.

Sec. 11. The governor shall have power to grant reprieves and pardons, and commute punishments after convictions, except in cases of impeachments.

Sec. 12. The governor shall receive for his services such compensation as shall hereafter be provided by law.

Sec. 13. There shall be a seal of this state, which shall be kept by the governor, and used by him officially; and shall be called the great seal of the State of Deseret.

Sec. 14. All grants and commissions shall be in the name and by the authority of the people of the State of Deseret; sealed with the great seal of this State, signed by the governor, and countersigned by the secretary of state.

Sec. 15. A secretary of state, auditor of public accounts, and treasurer, shall be elected by the qualified electors, who shall continue in office for the term of four years. The secretary of state shall keep a fair register of all the official acts of the governor, and shall, when required, lay the same, together with all papers, minutes and vouchers, relative thereto, before either branch of the general assembly, and shall perform such other duties as shall be assigned him by law.

Sec. 16. In case of the impeachment of the governor, his removal from office, death, resignation, or absence from the state, the powers and duties of the office shall devolve upon the lieutenant governor, until such disability shall cease, or the vacancy be filled.

ARTICLE IV.—OF THE JUDICIARY.

Sec. 1. The judicial power shall be vested in a supreme court, and such inferior courts as the general assembly shall from time to time establish.

Sec. 2. The supreme court shall consist of a chief justice, and two associates, either two of whom shall be a quorum to hold courts.

Sec. 3. The judges of the supreme court shall be elected by joint vote of both houses of the general assembly, and shall hold their courts at such time and place as the general assembly shall direct; and hold their office for the term of four years, and until their successors are elected and qualified. The judges of the supreme court shall be conservators of the peace throughout the state, and shall exercise such other jurisdictions and appellate powers as shall be prescribed by law.

Sec. 4. The style of all process shall be the state of Deseret; and all prosecutions shall be in the name and by the authority of the state.

ARTICLE V.—OF ELECTIONS.

Sec. 1. The governor, lieutenant governor, auditor of accounts, treasurer, and secretary of state, shall be elected by the qualified electors, as provided for members of the general assembly, and at the time and place appointed for holding the same.

Sec. 2. The returns of every election for governor, lieutenant governor, auditor, treasurer and secretary of state, shall be sealed up, and transmitted forthwith to the seat of government, directed to the speaker of the house of representatives, who shall, during the first week of the session, open and publish them in the presence of both houses of the general assembly; and the persons receiving a majority of all the legal votes cast for their respective offices, shall be declared duly elected.

Sec. 3. The governor, lieutenant governor, auditor, treasurer and secretary of state, shall, before entering upon the duties of their respective offices, take an oath or affirmation, to support the constitution of the United States, and of this state; which oath, or affirmation, shall be administered by the speaker of the house of representatives.

Sec. 4. The first election for members of the general assembly, and other officers under this constitution, shall be held on the first Monday of May next, at the usual places of holding public meetings, in the different districts and settlements; at which time and place the qualified voters shall vote for or against the adoption of this constitution; and if a majority of all the legal votes shall be in favour of its adoption, the same shall take effect from and after said election.

Sec. 5. At the time and place of holding the elections, the qualified electors shall organize the polls by appointing two judges, who shall be authorized to qualify each other, and appoint two suitable persons as clerks; and said judges shall, at the close of said election, seal up the number of votes so cast, and forthwith transmit them to the president of this convention.

Sec. 6. The returns of the first election herein provided for, shall be made to the chairman of this convention, who, together with the two secretaries, shall proceed immediately to open said returns, and count the votes; upon ascertaining the persons receiving a majority of votes, they shall forthwith notify them of their election.

Sec. 7. The general assembly shall, at its first session, provide by law a general system of election for officers, under this constitution, and such other officers as may be hereafter created by law.

Sec. 8. The manner of voting shall be by ballot.

Sec. 9. The general assembly shall meet at Great Salt Lake city, which place shall be the seat of government until otherwise provided by law.

Sec. 10. All white male residents of this state, over the age of twenty-one years, shall have the privilege of voting at the first election, and at the adoption of this constitution; provided, that no person in the military, naval, or marine service of the United States, shall be considered a resident of this state, by being stationed in any garrison, barrack, military or naval place, or station within this state, unless otherwise provided for by law.

ARTICLE VI.—OF MILITIA.

Sec. 1. The militia of this state shall be composed of all able-bodied white male citizens, between the ages of eighteen and forty-five years, except such as are or may hereafter be exempt, by the laws of the United States, or of this state, and shall be armed, equipped and trained, as the general assembly may provide by law.

Sec. 2. All commissioned officers of the militia (staff officers excepted) shall be elected by the persons liable to perform military duty in their respective divisions; and all commissioned officers shall be commissioned by the governor.

ARTICLE VII.—AMENDMENTS OF THE CONSTITUTION.

Sec. 1. If at any time the general assembly shall deem it necessary, and for the best interest of the state, that this constitution should be revised, altered or amended, the assembly shall cause such revisions, alterations or amendments, to be published in the same manner as shall be provided for the publication of the statutes; and appoint a day, not less than thirty days thereafter, for the electors of the commonwealth to assemble in their several precincts, and vote for, or against, said revisions, alterations or amendments; and if a majority of said electors shall vote in favour of said revisions, alterations or amendments, the same shall thereafter become parts and parcels of this constitution; otherwise, this constitution shall remain unaltered.

ARTICLE VIII.—DECLARATION OF RIGHTS.

Sec. 1. In republican governments, all men should be born equally free and independent, and possess certain natural, essential, and inalienable rights, among which are those of enjoying and defending their life and liberty; acquiring, possessing and protecting property; and of seeking and obtaining their safety and happiness.

Sec. 2. All political power is inherent in the people, and all free governments are founded in their authority, and instituted for their benefit; therefore they have an inalienable and indefeasible right to institute government; and to alter, reform, and totally change the same, when their safety, happiness, and the public good shall require it.

Sec. 3. All men have a natural and inalienable right to worship God according to the dictates of their own consciences; and the general assembly shall make no law respecting an establishment of religion, or prohibiting the free exercise thereof, or disturb any person in his religious worship or sentiments; provided, he does not disturb the public peace, nor obstruct others in their religious worship; and all persons demeaning themselves peaceably, as good members of the state, shall be equally under the protection of the laws; and no subordination or preference of any one sect or denomination to another, shall ever be established by law; nor shall any religious test be ever required for any office of trust under this state.

Sec. 4. Any citizen of this state, who may hereafter be engaged, either directly or indirectly, in a duel, either as principal or accessory before the fact, shall be disqualified from holding any office under the constitution and laws of this state.

Sec. 5. Every person may speak, write, and publish his sentiments, on all subjects, being responsible for the abuse of that right; and no law shall be passed to abridge the liberty of speech or of the press.

Sec. 6. The people shall be secure in their persons, houses, papers and possessions, from unreasonable searches and seizures.

Sec. 7. The right of trial by jury shall remain inviolate; and all criminals shall be heard by self, or counsel, at their own election.

Sec. 8. All penalties and punishments shall be in proportion to the offence; and all offences, before conviction, shall be bailable; except capital offences, where the proof is evident, or the presumption great.

Sec. 9. The writ of *habeas corpus* shall not be suspended, unless in case of rebellion, or invasion, or the public safety shall require it.

Sec. 10. Treason against this state shall consist only in levying war against it, or adhering to its enemies, or giving them aid and comfort.

Sec. 11. The general assembly shall pass no bill of attainder, or *ex post facto* laws, or law impairing the obligation of contracts, to hinder the execution of justice.

Sec. 12. The laws shall not be suspended, but by the legislative or executive authority.

Sec. 13. The right of petition, by the people, shall be preserved inviolate.

Sec. 14. The right of citizens to keep and bear arms for common defence, shall not be questioned.

Sec. 15. Private property shall not be taken for public use, without just compensation.

Sec. 16. No standing army shall be kept up in time of peace, and the military shall, at all times, and in all places, be in strict subordination to the civil power.

Sec. 17. The enumeration of certain rights, shall not be construed to impair, nor deny others, retained by the people.

GREAT SALT LAKE CITY, GREAT BASIN, ⎱
North America, March 8, 1849.   ⎰

MEMORIAL.

To the Honourable Senate and House of Representatives, in Congress assembled:

Your memorialists, members of the general assembly of the state of Deseret, would respectfully lay before your honourable body the wishes and interests of our constituents, together with the reasons and design of our early organization as a civil government, to which the consideration of your honourable body is most earnestly solicited.

Whereas, The history of all ages proves that civil governments, combining in their administration the protection of person, property, character, and religion—encouraging the science of agriculture, manufactures, and literature, are productive of the highest, happiest, and purest state of society; and,

Whereas, All political power is inherent in the people, and governments, to be permanent and satisfactory, should emanate from the same; and,

Whereas, The inhabitants of all newly settled countries and territories, who have become acquainted with their climate, cultivated their soil, tested their mineral productions, and investigated their commercial advantages, are the best judges of the kinds of government and laws necessary for their growth and prosperity; and,

Whereas, Congress have failed to provide, by law, a form of civil government for this or any other portion of territory ceded to the United States by the republic of Mexico, in the late treaty of peace; and

Whereas, Since the expiration of the Mexican civil authority, however weak and imbecile, anarchy to an alarming extent has prevailed—the revolver and bowie knife have been the highest law of the land—the strong have prevailed against the weak—while person, property, character and religion, have been unaided, and virtue unprotected; and,

Whereas, From the discovery of the valuable gold mines west of the Sierra Nevada mountains, many thousands of able bodied men are emigrating to that section, armed with all the implements and munitions of war; and,

Whereas, Strong fears have been, and still are entertained, from the failure of Congress to provide legal civil authorities, that political aspirants may subject the government of the United States to the sacrifice of much blood and treasure in extending jurisdiction over that valuable country; and,

Whereas, The inhabitants of the state of Deseret, in view of their own security, and for the preservation of the constitutional right of the United States to hold jurisdiction there, have organized a provisional state government, under which the civil policy of the nation is duly maintained; and,

Whereas, There are so many natural barriers to prevent communication with any other state or territory belonging to the United States, during a great portion of the year, such as snow-capped mountains, sandy deserts, sedge plains, saleratus lakes and swamps, over which it is very difficult to effect a passage; and,

Whereas, It is important in meting out the boundaries of the states and territories, so to establish them that the heads of departments may be able to communicate with all branches of their government with the least possible delay; and,

Whereas, There are comparatively no navigable rivers, lakes, or other natural channels of commerce; and whereas, no valuable mines of gold, silver, iron, copper, or lead, have as yet been discovered within the boundaries of this state, commerce must necessarily be limited to few branches of trade and manufactures; and whereas, the laws of all states and territories should be adapted to their geographical location, protecting and regulating those branches of trade only which the country is capable of sustaining; thereby relieving the government from the expense of those complicated and voluminous statutes which a more commercial state requires; and whereas, there is now a sufficient number of individuals residing within the state of Deseret to support a state government, thereby relieving the general government from the expense of a territorial government, in that section; and in evidence of which, the inhabitants have already erected a legislative hall, equal to most, and surpassed by few in the older states—

Your memorialists, therefore, ask your honourable body to favourably consider their interests; and, if consistent with the constitution and usages of the federal government, that the constitution accompanying this memorial be ratified, and that the state of Deseret be admitted into the Union on an equal footing with other states, or such other form of civil government as your wisdom and magnanimity may award to the people of Deseret. And, upon the adoption of any form of government here, that their delegate be received, and their interests properly and faithfully represented in the Congress of the United States. And your memorialists, as in duty bound, will ever pray.

On motion, it was voted that the report be accepted, and the committee discharged from further duties.

Parley P. Pratt offered the following resolutions:—

Resolved, 1st. The senate concurring therein, that two thousand copies of this memorial, together with the constitution, and an abstract of all records, journals, and other documents pertaining to the organization of this state, be printed.

Resolved, 2d. That the President of the United States, the senate, and the house of representatives, each be furnished with a copy thereof.

The resolutions were seconded and passed.

House adjourned until Monday, at 10 A. M.

PROVISIONAL STATE OF DESERET; ss.

I hereby certify that the foregoing constitution, memorial, synopsis of journal, &c., are a true copy of public documents on file in my office.

Given under my hand, at my office, in the Great Salt Lake City, this 18th day of July, A. D. 1849.

WILLARD RICHARDS.
Secretary of State.

THE WRONGS OF HUNGARY STATED BY THE LONDON HUNGARIAN COMMITTEE.

The following document has been issued by the London Hungarian Committee:

I. Hungary is an ancient constitutional monarchy, which used to elect its kings. Every new king was solemnly crowned with the crown of St. Stephen, after taking the coronation oath on Hungarian soil, in which he swore to uphold the constitution. In the year 1687, the royalty was made hereditary in the family of Hapsburg; but, so far was Hungary from becoming a province of Austria, to this year not a single Austrian has been allowed to hold office in the Hungarian kingdom. An Austrian is a foreigner in Hungarian law and practice.

II. The kings of the house of Hapsburg have, notwithstanding, made various attempts to overthrow the liberties of Hungary. After repeated attempts to fuse Hungary into Austria, and repeated insurrections, a long struggle, begun by Leopold I., was ended in 1711 by Joseph I., who was constrained to confirm the old constitution. Again, by the efforts of Joseph II. to enforce the German language, and suppress the municipalities, a revolt was kindled, which his successor, Leopold II. finally pacified (in 1790) only by withdrawing all his brother's innovations, and making a peculiarly distinct avowal, that (Art. 10) "Hungary, with her appanages, is a free kingdom, and in regard to her whole legal form of Government (including all the tribunals) independent; that is, entangled with no other kingdom or people; but having her own peculiar consistence and constitution, accordingly to be governed by her legitimately crowned King after her peculiar laws and customs." Nevertheless, Francis I. dared to violate his coronation oath by not assembling the Diet from 1811 to 1825. At last he was compelled to give way by the passive resistance to all government. From that year onward, the Hungarians have struggled successfully for internal reforms by constitutional methods, though perpetually thwarted by the bigotry, ignorance, and perverse ambition of the Austrian cabinet or crown.

III. The internal reforms which they desire were chiefly the following: To remove or lessen the distinctions between the privileged and unprivileged classes; and improve the principles of taxation and of the tenure of land. Next, to extend perfect toleration of religious creed to all. The high Magyar nobility are generally Roman Catholics; yet they have been as willing to concede toleration as the lower nobility and middle classes, who are generally Protestants. Thirdly, to establish free trade with all nations. For the Austrian cabinet choose to confine this great country to Austria for its market, while treating Hungarian produce as foreign. Fourthly, to maintain a free press, and the right especially of publishing the debates and proceedings of the Diet. Fifthly, in general to develop the great resources of Hungary by all sorts of material improvement in agriculture, in roads, in bridges. To this, of late, has been added a struggle for general education.

IV. One mode of resistance applied by Austria, was to extinguish Parliamentary bills by the *veto* of the crown; the fear of which paralyzed the upper house—a body always naturally disposed to lean to Austria. Against this the Hungarians had no adequate constitutional weapon to use, since the Austrian cabinet was not responsible to the Hungarian Diet. The often repeated legal declaration of their independence, and in particular the distinct compact of Leopold II. in 1790–91, justified them in desiring by peaceful and constitutional means to attain an independent ministry directly responsible to their own parliament.

V. Such a Ministry had been long talked of and claimed in the Diet. In fact the Conservative party and the opposition had differed little as to the objects at which they aimed, but chiefly as to the vehemence with which they should press them; the Conservatives pleading to "give time" to the Austrian cabinet. But in March, 1848, the Conservatives, as a separate party, vanished, by the great mass of them acceding to the opposition. Kossuth carried a unanimous vote, that the Constitution of Hungary could never be free from the eternal machinations of the Austrian cabinet, until Constitutional Government was established in the foreign possessions of the crown, so as to restore the legal *status* of the period at which the Diet freely conferred the royalty on the house of Hapsburg. This vote paralyzed the Austrian authorities. Vienna arose against Metternich, and a revolution took place there. A Constitution and a National Guard were enacted. The Hungarian Diet immediately claimed for itself also a responsible Ministry. This was granted without delay, and Count Louis Batthyany was made Premier. But on the same day, March 15, Jellachich was appointed Ban of Croatia. In a letter to Vienna, dated

March 24, 1848, the Archduke Stephen, Viceroy of Hungary, is found to have suggested three modes of destroying the Hungarian Constitution; either to excite the peasants against the nobles, as in Gallicia, and stand by while the parties slaughter each other; or to tamper with Batthyany's honesty; or to invade and overpower Hungary by military force. A transcript of this letter, in the Archduke's handwriting, was afterwards found among his papers when he fled from Pesth, and was officially published with all the necessary verifications. The Austrians have not dared to disown it.

Before March ended, a deputation of all the leading members of both Houses from Hungary appeared in Vienna, carrying to the King their unanimous claim that he would consent to various bills. In these, the greatest constitutional change was the restoration of the old union between the Diets of Hungary and of Transylvania. But socially the most important laws were the equalizing of all classes and creeds, and the noble enactment which converted the peasants into freeholders of the soil, quit of all the old feudal burdens. This bill had passed both the Houses by Feb. 4, 1848, before the French Revolution had broken out; so little had that great event to do with the reforming efforts of the Hungarians. The Austrian cabinet, seeing their overwhelming unanimity, felt that resistance was impossible. Accordingly Ferdinand proceeded with the Court to Presburg, and ratified the laws by oath. This is the reform of April 11, 1848, which all patriotic Hungarians fondly looked upon as their charter of constitutional rights, opening to them the promise of a career in which they should emulate Great Britain, as a pattern of a united, legal, tolerant, free, and loyal country.

VI. Croatia is a province of the Hungarian crown; and there Jellachich, as Governor, openly organized revolt against Hungary, by military terrorism, and by promising Slavonic supremacy. On Batthyany's urgency, King Ferdinand declared Jellachich a rebel, and exhorted the Diet to raise up an army against him; but always avoided finally to sanction their bills. Meanwhile Radetzky defeated Charles Albert. Jellachich dropped the mask of Croatianism, and announced to Batthyany that there should be no peace until a ministry at Vienna ruled over Hungary. In September, as the King would neither allow troops to be raised in Hungary, nor the Hungarian regiments to be recalled from Italy for home defence, a Hungarian deputation was sent to the Austrian Diet; but it was denied admittance by aid of the Slavonic party. To catch stray votes (it seems,) Latour, Austrian Minister at War, in the Diet, Sept. 2, solemnly disavowed any connexion with Jellachich's movement; yet, on Sept. 4, a royal ordinance (officially published in Croatia only,) reinstated Jellachich in all his dignities; who, soon after, crossed the Drave to invade Hungary, with a well-appointed army 65,000 strong. As he openly showed the King's commission, Batthyany resigned, Sept. 9, since he did not know how to act by the King's command against the King's command. No successor was appointed; and the Hungarian Diet had no choice but to form a committee of safety. To embarrass them in this, the King reopened negotiation with Batthyany, Sept. 14, but still eluded any practical result by refusing to put down Jellachich. Meanwhile, Sept. 16, despatches were intercepted, in which Jellachich thanked Latour for supplies of money and material of war. The Hungarian Diet published them officially, and distributed them by thousands. But Hungary was still unarmed, and Jellachich was burning, plundering, slaughtering. Sept. 25, Lamberg was sent to Pesth, in the illegal character of Imperial Commissary of Hungary, but was immediately murdered by the rage of the populace. Masses of volunteers were assembled by the eloquence of Kossuth, which, with the aid of only 3,000 regular troops, met and repulsed Jellachich at Sukoro, Sept. 29, and chased him out of their country. But Latour was far too deep in guilt to recede. A royal rescript of October 3, dissolved the Hungarian Diet, forbade all municipal action, superseded the judicial tribunals, declared Hungary under martial law, and appointed Jella-chich civil and military governor of that country, with discretionary power of life and death, and an expressly unlimited despotism. It likewise distinctly announced the determination of the crown to incorporate Hungary into Austria. Troops from Vienna were publicly ordered by Latour (Oct. 6) to march against the Hungarians. This order, coupled with alarm inspired by the approach of Jellachich (whose defeat was kept secret,) led to the *émeute* in Vienna, in which Latour was murdered, a murder which was made a pretext for bombarding Vienna, and destroying the newly sanctioned constitution. Windischgratz, the agent in this work, joined his forces to those of Auersperg, who, meanwhile, had sheltered Jellachich.

At all this the Hungarians were so infuriated that, after deposing the Generals (who were believed traitorously to have allowed Jellachich to escape,) with inferior artillery, and with forces not half of the Austrians, who were 15,000 strong beside their reserves, they fought and lost the battle of Schwechat, Oct. 30. This was the first and last battle fought by the Hungarians on Austrian soil, fought only against those who were protecting a ruthless enemy, who had desolated Hungary by countless outrages; yet this is trumpeted by the Austrians as Hungarian aggression. Jellachich (Nov. 2) entered Vienna in triumph, and was intrusted with a great army in the course of the whole war that followed. It is, then, impossible to doubt that the Austrians had supplied him with arms, money, and authority from the beginning, and that they began this bloody war by combined violence and treachery, while Hungary was in profound peace.

VII. The cabinet now tried to obtain from Ferdinand a direct permission to carry into detail the rescript of October 3, and seize Hungary by right of conquest. But as Ferdinand began to be troubled with religious scruples, they resolved to depose him, and put his nephew on the throne—a youth of eighteen, educated by the Jesuits, and accustomed to obey his mother, the Archduchess Sophia, who was so identified by the Viennese with the cabinet as to be called the Lady Camarilla.

By intrigue of some sort they induced the half-witted Emperor to sign the act of his own abdication, and at once seated Francis Joseph in his place, who, not having taken the coronation oath, might be assured by his directors that he committed no wrong in invading the laws and constitution of Hungary! An Austrian army marched into the country, and in the course of January and February overran and occupied it as far as the Theiss, eastward, and as high as the Moroscb, northward: the Russians meanwhile penetrated into Transylvania. The usurpation of the archduchess and cabinet seemed to have triumphed.

VIII. On March 4, 1849, Count Stadion published his new constitution for fusing down Hungary into a part of the Austrian empire. If previously Hungary had been under Russian despotism, this constitution would have seemed highly liberal, and from an Austrian point of view such it was; but to the Hungarians it was an intolerable slavery. First, it virtually annihilated their municipalities, and subjected their police to Vienna. Next, it would have enabled the Austrian cabinet to put in Austrian civil and military officers every where in Hungary—an innovation as odious to the Hungarians, as would French police magistrates, excisemen, overseers, colonels and lord-lieutenants, be to the English nation. Thirdly, it swamped their parliament among a host of foreigners, ignorant of Hungary and its wants, and incapable of legislating well for it. Fourthly, it was enacted without the pretence of law, by the mere stroke of Count Stadion's pen. If the Hungarian constitution, fourteen times solemnly sworn to by kings of the house of Hapsburg, was to be thus violated, what possible security could the nation have for this new-fangled constitution of Stadion, if it were ever so good in itself? If they admitted such a right in the Austrian crown, in six months a new ordinance might reduce them under a pure despotism. In the face of wrong so intense, it is not worth while to name secondary grievances; but it was most bitterly felt that such was the reward of the constant loyalty of Hungary to the house of Hapsburg, and such the sequel to that solemn act by which Ferdinand had so happily ratified their recent glorious reforms! '

On reviewing the constitutional question, it was clear to the Hungarians, first, that Ferdinand had no legal power to abdicate without leave of the Diet, which leave it was impossible to grant, since, in the course of nature, Ferdinand might yet have direct heirs; secondly, that if he became incapacitated, it was the right of the Diet to appoint a regent; thirdly, that if Ferdinand had died, Francis Joseph was not the heir to the Hungarian crown, but his father, Ferdinand's brother; fourthly, that allegiance is not fully due to the true heir until he has been crowned; fifthly, that if Francis Joseph had been ever so much the true heir, and had been ever so lawfully crowned, the ordinances would be a breach of his oath, essentially null and void, and equivalent to a renunciation of his compact with the people; sixthly, that even to Austria the ministry of Stadion—or, rather, the Archduchess—was no better than a knot of intriguers, which had practised on the clouded intellect of the sovereign to grasp a despotism for itself, while over Hungary it had no more ostensible right than had that of Prussia or France. All Hungary, therefore, rose to resist—Slovachs and Magyars, Germans and Wallechs, Catholics and Protestants, Greeks and Jews, nobles, traders and peasants, rich and poor, progressionists and conservatives. Ferdinand was still regarded as their legitimate, but unlawfully deposed King.

IX. Between the Theiss and the Marosch, Kossuth organized the means of fabricating arms and money; and in the course of March and April a series of tremendous battles took place in which the Austrians were some fifteen times defeated, and, without a single change of fortune, their armies, 130,000 strong, were swept out of Hungary with immense slaughter. Only certain fortresses remained in their power, and those were sure to fall by mere lapse of time. The Austrian cabinet was desperate at losing a game in which it had risked so much. Its more scrupulous members had retired, including Stadion himself. Bloodier generals were brought forward, and the intervention of Russia (long promised, and granted as early as February in Transylvania) was publicly avowed. This act finally alienated from Austria every patriotic Hungarian.

X. Upon the entrance of the Russians with the consent of Francis Joseph, the Hungarian Parliament, on the 14th April, after reciting the acts of perfidy and atrocity by which the house of Hapsburg had destroyed its compact with the nation, solemnly pronounced that house to have forfeited the crown. During the existing crisis, Kossuth, according to the Constitutional precedent, was made Governor of the country.

XI. We all know how Hungary, deprived of her ports, taken by surprise, isolated and abandoned, has been overwhelmed by the combined hosts of her unscrupulous foes. But has England nothing to say to this?

For three centuries, at least, Hungary has been a prominent member of the European family of nations. Her constitutional union to the house of Hapsburg has been a notorious public fact; and in the Emperor of Austria, as King of Hungary, Europe has long seen a powerful barrier against Russian encroachment. That Hungary is not Austria—that the Emperor of Austria has no right in Hungary except as its Constitutional King—is as public a fact in Europe as that Hanover was never part of England. When Hungary proclaimed to us that the Emperor of Austria was no longer her King—that she had found the house of Hapsburg traitorous, and had legally deposed it; and when the Hungarian nation had, by a unanimous effort, actually expelled her invaders—there was the very same reason for our acknowledging the independence of Hungary, as we ever had for recognising the Emperor of Austria as King of Hungary at all. We have grievously neglected our duty by supineness; but the Emperor of Russia has perpetrated a breach of international law, most cruel and dreadful; only less wicked than the outrage of Austria, because it was not also treacherous and ungrateful. Indignation and pity for the Hungarians is for a moment swallowed up by admiration, when we contrast their humane generosity toward prisoners of war with the ferocious cruelty of the Austrians toward the armed and unarmed of both sexes.

XII. The English crown is peculiarly affected by these events; because they destroy the confidence of nations in the oaths of Princes; especially considering that Hungary was the only great community on the continent, whose ancient liberties had not been violently and treacherously annihilated by its King. No guarantees of right any longer exist, except those which have been wrested out by popular violence, and established on some doctrinaire basis. The aristocracy of England are deeply concerned, when the only remaining continental aristocracy possessed of constitutional rights and taking the lead of a willing nation, is remorselessly trampled under foot. Our commonalty is concerned, when deprived of commercial intercourse with fourteen millions of agriculturists. Our religious feelings are shocked, when Hungarian zeal for universal toleration is overridden by the Romanist bigotry of Austria. Our liberties are endangered by the spectacle of two sovereigns tearing in pieces a noble nation from pure hatred of its constitutionalism which nine centuries have not made sacred in their eyes. The security of all Europe is endangered by the virtual vassalage of Austria to Russia, which this calamitous outrage has entailed; for Austria is now so abhorred in Hungary that she cannot keep her conquest except by Russian aid. Every one foresaw this from the beginning: the Government of Vienna knew it, as well as that of St. Petersburg. Such are the results of the conspiracy of the Austrian cabinet against their Emperor, against his kingdom of Hungary, against the new-born liberties of Vienna, and against the balance of power in Europe.

XIII. What remains for England to do, but firmly to declare to Austria: "Until we see the Constitution as it was before October, 1848, re-established in Hungary, we do not acknowledge your position in Lombardy; for Hungary had a far better right to her national existence and independence than you to your empire over the foreign Lombards?"

A military tyrant may, at any moment, commit an act of rapine with summary speed; sage and moderate by-standers need time to learn and judge of the case. If we extend the doctrine of *faits accomplis* to the high-handed crime under which Hungary still lies bleeding, we proclaim impunity and recognition to every unprincipled marauder.

KOSSUTH'S LETTER TO LORD PALMERSTON.

"WIDDIN, (TURKEY,) Sept. 20.

"Your Excellency is no doubt already informed of the fall of my country— unhappy Hungary, assuredly worthy of a better fate.

"It was not prompted by the spirit of disorder, or the ambitious views of faction; it was not a revolutionary leaning which induced my native country to accept the mortal struggle maintained so gloriously, and brought, by nefarious means, to so unfortunate an end.

"Hungary has deserved from her kings the historical epithet of 'generous nation,' for she never allowed herself to be surpassed in loyalty and faithful adherence to her sovereigns by any nation in the world.

"Nothing but the most revolting treachery, the most tyrannical oppression, and cruelties unheard of in the words of history—nothing but the infernal doom of annihilation to her national existence preserved through a thousand years, through adversities so numerous—were able to rouse her to oppose the fatal stroke aimed at her very life, to enable her to repulse the tyrannical assaults of the ungrateful Hapsburghs, or to accept the struggle for life, honour, and liberty, forced upon her. And she has nobly fought the holy battle, in which, with the aid of Almighty God, she prevailed against Austria, whom we crushed to the earth, standing firm even when attacked by the Russian giant in the consciousness of justice, in our hope in God, and in our hope, my lord, in the generous feelings of your great and glorious nation, the natural supporter of justice and humanity throughout the world. But this is over— what tyranny began, has been by treachery concluded. On all sides abandoned, my poor country has fallen, not through the overwhelming power of two great empires, but by the faults, and I may say treason, of her own sons.

"To these untoward events, I pray God, that my unhappy country may be the only sacrifice; and that the true interests of peace, freedom, and civilization through the world may not be involved in our unhappy fate.

"Mr. Francis Pulasky, our diplomatic agent in London, has received ample information as to the cause of this sudden and unlooked-for change in the affairs of Hungary, and is instructed to communicate it to your excellency, if you are graciously pleased to receive the same. It is not antipathy to Austria, though so well merited at the hands of every Hungarian, but a true conviction which makes me say, that even Austria has lost far more by her victory—gained through Russian aid—than she would have lost in merited defeat through honourable arrangement. Fallen from her position of a first-rate power, she has now forfeited her self-consistency, and has sunk into the obedient instrument of Russian ambition and of Russian commands.

"Russia only has gained at this sanguinary game; she has extended and strengthened her influence in the east of Europe, and threatens already in a fearful manner, with outstretching arms, not only the integrity, but the moral basis of the Turkish empire.

"May it please you, my lord, to allow me to communicate to your excellency a most revolting condition which the Turkish government, at the suggestion of Russia, is about to impose upon us, poor houseless exiles.

"I, the governor of unhappy Hungary, after having, I believe, as a good citizen and honest man, fulfilled to the last my duties to my country, had no choice left me between the repose of the grave and the inexpressible anguish of expatriation.

"Many of my brethren in misfortune had preceded me on the Turkish territory. I followed thither in the hope that I should be permitted to pass to England, and there, under the protection of the English people—a protection never yet denied to persecuted man—allowed to repose for awhile my wearied head on the hospitable shore of your happy island.

"But even with these views, I would rather have surrendered myself to my deadliest enemy, than to cause any difficulty to the Turkish government, whose situation I well knew how to appreciate, and therefore did not intrude on the Turkish territories without previously inquiring whether I and my companions in misfortune would be willingly received, and the protection of the Sultan granted to us.

"We received the assurance that we were welcome guests, and should enjoy the full protection of his majesty, the Padisha, who would rather sacrifice 50,000 men of his own subjects than allow one hair of our heads to be injured.

"It was only on this assurance that we passed into Turkish territory, and according to the generous assurance we were received and tended on our journey, received in Widdin as the Sultan's guests, and treated hospitably

during four weeks, whilst waiting from Constantinople further orders as to the
continuation of our sad journey to some distant shore.

"Even the ambassadors of England and France, to whom I ventured in the
name of humanity to appeal, were so kind as to assure me of their full sympathy.

"His Majesty, the Sultan, was also so gracious as to give a decided negative to the inhuman pretensions of our extradition demanded by Russia and
Austria.

"But a fresh letter from his Majesty, the Czar, arrived at Constantinople,
and its consequence was the suggestion sent to us by an express messenger
of the Turkish government, that the Poles and Hungarians, and particularly
myself, Count Casimer Batthiany, Minister of Foreign Affairs of Hungary under
my government, and the Generals Messaros and Perczel, (all present here,)
would be surrendered, unless we choose to abjure the faith of our forefathers
in the religion of Christ, and become Mussulmans. And thus five thousand
Christians are placed in the terrible alternative, either of facing the scaffold
or of purchasing their lives by abandoning their faith. So low is already
fallen the once mighty Turkey, that she can devise no other means to answer
or evade the demands of Russia.

"Words fail me to qualify these astonishing suggestions, such as never
have been made yet to the fallen chief of a generous nation, and could hardly
have been expected in the nineteenth century.

"My answer does not admit of hesitation. Between death and shame, the
choice can be neither dubious nor difficult. Governor of Hungary, and elected
to that high place by the confidence of fifteen millions of my countrymen, I
know well what I owe to the honour of my country, even in exile. Even as
a private individual, I have an honourable path to pursue. Once the governor
of a generous country—I leave no inheritance to my children—they shall, at
least, bear an unsullied name. God's will be done. I am prepared to die;
but as I think this measure dishonourable and injurious to Turkey, whose interest I sincerely have at heart, and as I feel it a duty to save my companions
in exile, if I can, from a degrading alternative, I have replied to the Grand
Vizier, in a conciliatory manner, and took also the liberty to apply to Sir Stratford Canning and General Aupich, for their generous aid against this tyrannic
act. In full reliance on the noble sentiments and generous principles of your
excellency, by which, as well as through your wisdom, I trust to be excused
in enclosing copies of my two letters to the Grand Vizier and Sir Stratford
Canning.

"I am informed that the whole matter is a cabal against the ministry of
Reschid Pacha, whose enemies would wish to force him to our extradition, in
order to lower it in public estimation, and render impossible its continuance
in office. It is certain, that in the grand council, held on the 9th and 10th of
September, after a tumultuous debate, the majority of the council declared in
favour of our extradition, the majority of the ministry against it. No decision
was come to, in consequence of the altercation which took place; but, notwithstanding, the ministry thought fit to make us the revolting suggestion I
have named.

"This mode of solving the difficulty would not, I am convinced, save the
ministry, because a protection only given, in contradiction of the Sultan's generous feeling, of the price of five thousand Christians abandoning their faith,
would be revolting to the whole Christian world, and prove badly calculated
to win sympathies for Turkey, in the event of a war with Russia, which, in
the opinion of the most experienced Turkish statesmen, is approaching fast.

"As to my native country, Turkey does, I believe, already feel the loss of
the neglected opportunity of having given to Hungary, at least, some moral
help to enable it to check the advance of the common enemy. But, it ap-

pears to me, that it would be a very ill-advised mode of gaining Hungarian sympathy, by sending me to an Austrian scaffold, and forcing my unhappy companions to abjure their religion or accept the same alternative.

"No friends to the Turkish government would spring up from my blood, shed by her broken faith, but many deadly foes. My lord, your heart will, I am sure, excuse my having called your attention to our unhappy faith, since it has now assumed political importance. Abandoned, in this unsocial land, by the whole world, even the first duties of humanity give us no promise of protection, unless, my lord, you and your generous nation come forward to protect us.

"What steps it may be expedient that you should take, what we have a right to expect from the well known generosity of England, it would be hardly fitting for me to enter on. I place my own and my companions' fate in your hands, my lord, and, in the name of humanity, throw myself under the protection of England.

"Time presses—our doom may in a few days be sealed. Allow me to make an humble, personal request. I am a man, my lord, prepared to face the worst; and I can die with a free look at heaven, as I have lived. But I am, also, my lord, a husband, son, and father; my poor, true-hearted wife, my children, and my noble old mother are wandering about Hungary. They will probably soon fall into the hands of those Austrians who delight in torturing even feeble women, and with whom the innocence of childhood is no protection against persecutions. I conjure your excellency, in the name of the Most High, to put a stop to these cruelties by your powerful mediation, and especially to accord to my wife and children an asylum on the soil of the generous English people.

"As to my poor, my loved, and noble country, must she, too, perish for ever? Shall she, unaided, abandoned to her fate, and unavenged, be doomed to annihilation by her tyrants? Will England, once her hope, not become her consolation?

"The political interests of civilized Europe, so many weighty considerations respecting England herself, and chiefly the maintenance of the Ottoman Empire, are too intimately bound up with the existence of Hungary for me to lose all hope. My lord, may God, the Almighty, for many years shield you, that you may long protect the unfortunate, and live to be the guardian of the rights of freedom and humanity. I subscribe myself, with the most perfect respect and esteem,   (Signed)   L. KOSSUTH."

CALIFORNIA.

Secretary of War to the President.

WAR DEPARTMENT,
WASHINGTON, JANUARY 18, 1850.

Sir: I have the honour of laying before you copies of documents embracing the information called for from this department by the resolution of the house of representatives on the 31st ultimo.

I beg leave to remark that the exercise of civil authority by any military officer in California, since the termination of the war with Mexico, was first assumed by Brevet Brigadier General Mason, under his proclamation, which was issued on the 7th of August, 1848, the next day after the intelligence reached him that peace had been restored between the United States and Mexico. This proclamation was communicated to the department on the 22d of November, 1848, and its receipt acknowledged by the proper bureau on the 27th of January, 1849, without any comment.

On the 13th of April, 1849, this officer was relieved of his command in California, and was succeeded by Brevet Brigadier General Riley. At this period it appears to have been the purpose of this latter officer, with the advice of his predecessor, to have secured to the people of that territory a further enjoyment of the laws, customs, and usages applicable to their condition and wants, and at the same time to have provided for the organization of a government, such as is contemplated by the ninth article of the treaty of Guadalupe Hidalgo and the constitution of the United States. The cause of delay in executing the purpose of this officer is fully explained by the following extract from a communication from the commanding general of the Pacific division, dated January 20, 1849, to this department.

"Under the hope that some act of the last congress had provided, or at least defined, the government of California, it was thought prudent to await intelligence of the close of the session, and then, if nothing had been done in Washington, to put in action the machinery of the laws already existing here, and at the same time propose to the people of California to form a state constitution, and present it at the next session of Congress, when their admission into the Union as a State would at once solve so many difficulties; and, while it removed a cause of disagreement at home, would give them an opportunity of legislating for themselves.

"The steamer Edith has been sent to Mazatlan for the necessary intelligence, and, on her arrival with information that no other than a revenue law had been passed, General Riley issued a proclamation for the election of the necessary executive and judicial officers under the existing laws, and recommending, at the same time, the election of delegates to a convention to form a State constitution. Mr. King arrived at the time these proclamations were about being issued, and it was matter of great congratulation that the Government, by anticipation, had approved of the latter measure. Every means will be used to give the people of California an opportunity of expressing their wishes on this point, and of bringing the matter to a happy conclusion."

The necessity of a civil government in California, adequate to protect and control its increased population, composed of persons who had flocked from all quarters of the globe, was daily rendered more apparent. The common employment in which every interest was directly or remotely connected, and of a mass so dissimilar in habits and languages, and probably a part not without a lively sense of an exclusive enjoyment, showed the absolute want of an authority capable of upholding public and private rights. Indeed, this want was so obvious and urgent, that legislative assemblies were established in several districts of California, and by their authority the existing customs and laws, already adverted to, were attempted to be superseded. The whole plan was considered as irregular, and would, in the end, have been dangerous to the public peace and the public interests.

The first duty of the army was to execute the order of March 15, 1848, "to take measures with a view to its (California) permanent occupation;" and the second, in my opinion, was to separate, as far as practicable, the citizens from the control of martial law. The executive powers exercised by the two commanding officers in California were varied only by the emergencies as they arose, which may be seen by their several reports on the civil affairs of that territory. In their respective administrations, each has endeavoured to avoid the application of the principles and practices of military law.

Respectfully submitted,

To the PRESIDENT.   G. W. CRAWFORD.

INDEX TO VOL. III.

THE

AMERICAN REGISTER
And Magazine.

JAMES STRYKER, EDITOR AND PROPRIETOR.

THIS work contains a history of the times after the manner of the British Annual Register, embracing all the important facts as they arise, written out semi-annually; also, a chronicle of independent events; public documents; statistical tables and statements; biographical notices of eminent persons; original contributions to science and literature, with a selected miscellany; notices of books; congressional proceedings; obituary, &c.

It will be published half-yearly, instead of quarterly, as heretofore, in a handsomely bound volume of six hundred pages. The price *per annum*, or for *two* volumes, is five dollars, payable in advance.

RECOMMENDATIONS.

The following summary is made from the numerous commendatory notices of the work:

Extracts from the opinions of distinguished gentlemen.

The Hon. HORACE BINNEY, of Philadelphia, writes,—

"The plan is excellent; and the sections which have already appeared give adequate proof of the ability, candour, research, and taste which are applied to all its parts—it must become, in time, a treasury of valuable facts, which, unless exhibited and preserved in this connexion, will hardly be recalled and put together again by any degree of labour."

Professor JOSEPH HENRY, of the Smithsonian Institution :—

"Before the publication of the American Register, Judge Stryker explained to me the plan and the object of the work, and I then expressed a very favourable opinion of its importance, as supplying a deficiency constantly felt. I have since seen the first number of the journal, and am confirmed in the opinion previously expressed, of its being a work of great value to the public."

The Hon. JOHN C. SPENCER, late Secretary of the Treasury of the United States :—

"I repeat what I said in June, the original matter is able and interesting; and the selected articles are precisely such as should be found in such a work. It has already become a reservoir of various and important contributions to the history, constitutional jurisprudence, and commercial and social progress of our country, and my prediction will soon be verified, 'that it will be indispensable in every library.'"

The Hon. MILLARD FILLMORE, Vice President of the United States :—

"I unite most cordially with Mr. Spencer in recommending the work."

Gen. JOHN A. DIX, late U. S. senator :—"I take pleasure in expressing my concurrence with Hon. J. C. Spencer in the favourable opinion he entertains. I consider the statistical information of great value."

Similar testimonials have been received from President Wayland, Dr. T. Romeyn Beck, Hon. J. K. Kane, J. R. Tyson. Esq., Dr. Mutter, Professor Tucker, Dr. J. Bartlett, Dr. R. M. Patterson, Hon. John M. Scott, Gen. Dearborn, Chas. G. Loring, Esq., Hon. Abbott Lawrence, and Hon. Jos. Quincy, jr.

The Hon. C. MORGAN, the present Secretary of State of New York, writes:— "I am well satisfied with the plan and execution of the work. It has taken possession of a field hitherto unoccupied by any periodical—the day-book of the world's history is posted up."

Rev. Dr. R. BAIRD, the well-known lecturer on the nations and courts of Europe:— "It is superior, in my opinion, to the celebrated British Annual Register, because it gives, in addition to a well digested record of the most important events, a vast amount of statistical matter of great importance to all well-informed men."

The Hon. THEODORE FRELINGHUYSEN, Chancellor of the University of New York:—"It is a work of great excellence, and deserving of large patronage."

Written approvals of the work, and complimentary notices of the editor, have also been received from the following gentlemen:—

Hon. LEWIS CASS,	Hon. A. H. TRACY,	DANIEL GARDNER, Esq.
Dr. JOHN W. FRANCIS,	J. T. HATCH, Esq.	Hon. F. A. TALLMADGE,
Hon. WM. H. SEWARD,	H. K. SMITH, Esq.	Gen. H. B. POTTER,
ROBT. H. MORRIS, Esq.	Dr. J. P. WHITE.	G. W. CLINTON, Esq.
Hon. J. W. EDMONDS,	Hon. B. F. BUTLER,	Hon. S. E. SILL,
OGDEN HOFFMAN, Esq.	Hon. LUTHER BRADISH,	H. W. ROGERS, Esq.
JAMES W. GERARD, Esq.	H. R. SCHOOLCRAFT, LL.D.	Hon. E. SPAULDING,
R. EMOET, Esq.	Hon. R. H. GILLET,	JAMES ERNOTT, jr., Esq.

From the notices by the press we make the following extracts.

"No body of historic materials has ever proved more useful in its day than the famous 'Annual Register,' founded by Edmund Burke, and subsequently conducted by Sir Walter Scott, a great repository of all important facts of the times, and of such public documents as were either necessary for their elucidation, or offered of themselves useful information of the progress of things throughout the world. Such a continuous publication for this continent had become an urgent want; and the work of Judge Stryker, so far as we can judge, seems about to supply it."—*National Intelligencer.*

"We cannot but congratulate the statesmen, political economists, and lovers of historical record, and sound information of every class, that we have at length among our periodicals one which is eminently suited to its design, and worthy of being preserved in their libraries. Such a work has long been deemed a *desideratum.*"—*Washington Union.*

"It is a work of very great permanent value,—one which supplies a lack long felt, and which ought, therefore, to be well sustained. It is the only work in the country which preserves, in a convenient form and accessible shape, official documents—the true material of history, and every man in any way connected with public life, finds it indispensable to have them constantly within reach. This is the only work on which reliance for that purpose can be placed.

"It is edited with great industry and intelligence, and contains an immense amount of valuable information upon the greatest variety of subjects. It is a most excellent and useful work, and we commend it very warmly to the attention and favour of the whole community."—*N. Y. Courier and Enquirer.*

"The American Register has just been issued by its enterprising editor, Judge Stryker. It is the most widely useful and valuable periodical published in this country—is unique in its design, and fully realizes the purpose of its editor. It is conducted with singular industry, vigilance and correctness, and can be earnestly recommended to those who wish for accurate and copious information on the various subjects which come within its range, as without a rival in our periodical literature."—*New York Tribune.*

"It creates a feeling of regret, almost of complaint, on looking over such a work, to think that it had not been commenced before. We know not whether to value it more as a book of immediate reference, which one wants every day by him, or as a safe and convenient repository for the future, to which he may safely refer for facts in coming years, when the newspapers and loose pamphlets in which they are ordinarily seen shall be torn, mislaid, or forgotten. In either view of the work, it is one of high value and public importance."—*American Courier.*

"Stryker's American Register is just published, forming the first portion of the third volume. It shows increased skill in collecting and digesting the multifarious information which gives such a work its value. It is issued under the superintendence of Judge Stryker, well known as a former resident of this State, and who gives evidence of his ability to perform his task to the public acceptance. An annual Register like this, is an indispensable work in the library of all who desire to keep themselves well acquainted with the history of the times. It is of great value both as a work of instruction and reference."—*New York Evening Post.*

"The Register is issued by Judge Stryker, and is, in our view, invaluable to every statesman, politician, merchant, financier and statistician in the country. It abounds with facts, always reliable, and gleaned from the most authentic sources.

A work like this has long been needed. Some of the most distinguished men in the country have commended it in the warmest manner. The editor is at once able, discriminating and indefatigable. Such a treasury of valuable facts cannot be too liberally patronized."—*Pennsylvania Inquirer.*

"The last number of this excellent work, The American Register, has just reached us. The labour of its editor must have been great and untiring, to bring together, in so condensed a form, a collection of intelligence so complete and valuable. The only work of its kind in the United States, it deserves a general circulation.

"Judge Stryker enjoyed, for many years in this state, a reputation for ability and learning, and we know of no one more competent to the task of compiling the history of the passing period in a form at once compendious and comprehensive, with impartiality and judgment."—*N. Y. Journal of Commerce.*

"Each successive number of Judge Stryker's valuable journal, illustrates the necessity of such a work. It contains a most accurate digest of the recent historical events of the Old and New World, and valuable statistical tables; and is conducted with great ability and tact."—*Pennsylvanian.*

"The American Register and Magazine is a most excellent specimen of what we consider as altogether the most valuable quarterly published in America ; with more absolutely useful matter that is really worth preservation, than all the other put together."—*Evening Bulletin.*

"This work is on a new plan, and is designed to embody, quarterly, a history of the times, together with valuable literary, scientific and statistical information. The editor is Judge Stryker, a gentleman of conceded ability. The Register is likely to become one of the most valuable of our periodicals, and necessary to every statesman, politician, agriculturist and merchant in the country."—*Bicknell's Reporter.*

"The Register is one of the best conducted and most valuable periodicals issued from the American press, and we wish it, as it deserves, signal success."—*New York Express.*

"A compendium like 'The American Register' is an invaluable acquisition; for it is, to a very considerable extent, an encyclopedia of instruction, annually revised."—*Boston Courier.*

"Judge Stryker's American Register is a work of value, of which we have always had occasion to speak with favour, and which has received the commendations of the press generally, as well as those of Vice President Fillmore, Governor Seward, Lewis Cass, Abbot Lawrence, Horace Binney, and many others of the most distinguished men in the country. The useful character of such a publication is, in fact, evident at a glance, forming, as it does, a methodized and authentic book of reference, as convenient as it is necessary."—*North American.*

"Having just seen a bound volume of the American Register, published by Judge Stryker, of Philadelphia, we cannot refrain from again expressing our sense of the value of this publication, especially in the semi-annual form in which it is now presented, handsomely and durably bound. This work is eminently worthy of support."—*Boston Evening Traveller.*

"It is not like the ephemeral magazines which have fulfilled their whole mission when once read, but in all future time is likely to be referred to as a reliable historical record of great value."—*Presbyterian.*

"For varied information, and for the amount of its interesting and instructive reading, we know of no publication of the kind more desirable."—*Banner of the Cross.*

"This efficient editor displays great tact and industry in condensing a vast amount of information on subjects interesting to every class of intelligent readers."—*Episcopal Recorder.*

"It fills a chasm in the world of letters, the existence of which we have long deplored. The amount of information contained in the Register is astonishing. The editor, Judge Stryker, a gentleman of varied learning, and accomplished taste, seems to have a thorough acquaintance with every department of human knowledge, and to give his readers the key by which they may enter into the temple."—*Christian Chronicle.*

"Its pages are admirably filled with contemporaneous history, public documents, interesting items of intelligence, and statistical information on many subjects."—*Christian Observer.*

"As a register of events, and record of documentary and statistical information, this work has no superior.

"The ability with which Judge Stryker has thus far conducted this publication, and the favour with which it has been received by the public, are ample guarantees for its future popularity and success."—*Buffalo Courier.*

"As a book of reference, we know of none so happy in its design. The number before us bears every indication of being ably conducted."—*Savannah Georgian.*

"It is a rich library of itself, and fully meets the highest expectation of a magazine, combining interest and usefulness in such proportion as to make it a treasury of knowledge for the present and future, being alike valuable to this and the coming generations."—*New York School Journal.*

"We have before spoken of the merits of this highly valuable publication. It contains a large mass of important matter; it is the history of the times—of the world as it is."—*Hartford Times.*

"We every where perceive the influence of a determination, neither to falsify, nor to extenuate, and we have been unable to detect a single instance where prejudice or passion have distorted fact. Politicians on every side will be ready to do justice to the decorous manliness and moderation which signalize this work."—*Fredonian.*

"We take great pleasure in noticing this capital periodical, for we know of no magazine or review that can begin to compare with it in interest or value."—*Lady's Book.*

Lightning Source UK Ltd.
Milton Keynes UK
UKHW020610120219
337137UK00005B/691/P